D1614989

Law after Auschwitz

Law after Auschwitz

Towards a Jurisprudence of the Holocaust

David Fraser

Professor of Law and Social Theory
University of Nottingham
School of Law

CAROLINA ACADEMIC PRESS

Durham, North Carolina

Library of Congress Cataloging-in-Publication Data

Fraser, David, 1953-
  Law after Auschwitz : towards a jurisprudence of the Holocaust / by David
Fraser.
    p. cm.
  Includes bibliographical references and index.
  ISBN 0-89089-243-1 (alk. paper)
  1. Genocide--Europe--History. 2. Holocaust, Jewish (1939-1945). I. Title.

K5302.F73 2004
340'.115'094309043--dc22

2004018078

Carolina Academic Press
700 Kent Street
Durham, North Carolina 27701
Telephone (919) 489-7486
Fax (919) 493-5668
www.cap-press.com

Printed in the United States of America

Par conséquent, je dis qu'il y a les fléaux et les victimes, et rien de plus.
Si, disant cela, je deviens fléau moi-même, du moins, je n'y suis pas consentant.
J'essaie d'être un meurtrier innocent. Vous voyez que c'est n'est pas une grande
ambition.

(Consequently, I say that there are pestilences and victims, and nothing more. If
in saying this I become a pestilence myself, at least I am not a consenting one. I
am trying to be an innocent murderer. You see, it's not a high ambition.)

Albert Camus
La Peste (The Plague)

CONTENTS

Acknowledgments

Parts of this book were written while I was on sabbatical at the University of Texas, Austin and then again at the European University Institute, Florence. Special thanks are due to Professor Roy Mersky at Texas for his welcome and his ongoing encouragement. Professor Christian Joerges at the EUI gave me the unprecedented opportunity to participate in his project on the "Dark Legacy of European Law", for which I am grateful.

In addition, I have been able to present parts of the book at the University of Southampton, Department of Law, the Centre for Social Theory, University of Warwick, and the Conference of Europeanists, Chicago. Thanks here are owed to Laurence Lustgarten, Ralf Rumkowski, and once more, Christian Joerges.

Jock Morrow provided early and invaluable research assistance for much of Chapter 4.

Some aspects of this book have appeared in different form elsewhere. Chapter 4 appears in a shortened version in the collection compiled by Christian Joerges and Navraj Galheigh, *Darker Legacies of European Law* (Oxford: Hart, 2003) and is published here with the kind permission of Richard Hart of Hart Publishing. Chapter 3 was published in its original form in 1999 in Volume 12 (4) of the *International Journal of the Semiotics of Law,* (pp. 397-417) and appears here with the kind permission of Kluwer Law International. Chapter 6 also had an early life in 1998, Volume 12 of *Holocaust and Genocide Studies* (pp. 139-58) and is published with thanks to Oxford University Press and by permission of The United States Holocaust Memorial Museum.

As always, special thanks to Kathryn.

Law after Auschwitz

CHAPTER 1

LAW AFTER AUSCHWITZ

1. Introduction

For several years, I occasionally taught a course in the Faculty of Law, University of Sydney, entitled *The Holocaust, Moral Responsibility and the Rule of Law*. Both as a cause and effect of teaching this course, and of conducting the research which has led to this book, I remain troubled by the idea that I might, by dint of my profession, be more deeply implicated in the theory and practice of genocide than my colleagues in law would have us believe. The purpose of this project is perhaps the self-serving one of trying to remain or to become, as Camus would have it, an "innocent murderer", to seek solace and self-justification in a careful examination of the existential and historical realities of law and its role in the Holocaust. A central theme, and dilemma, which informs my teaching and research is the question of systemic and semiotic continuity within my chosen professional discourse of law.

I want to examine whether the Nazi regime and its legal system constituted a radical and revolutionary point of rupture with the juridical structure which had preceded it. Was there a shift from "law" to "not law" in Germany in 1933? Did the defeat of Hitler in 1945 re-institute a new, democratic legal order which constituted a radical *caesura* with Nazi law and a return to legality? This is the predominant jurisprudential and legal historical reality which informed my legal education and which is the basis for our professional self-understanding today. We are not Nazis, we are lawyers and democrats. We have law, the Nazis had something else, something "not law".

Informing my inquiries is the uncomfortable idea that there is fact little which distinguishes our fundamental understandings and practices of law today from what German lawyers and judges between 1933 and 1945 understood and did. If this idea is correct, very basic questions about what lawyers and judges profess and practice today, or about what, how and why we teach in law schools begin to bubble to the surface. If law, in its discursive practices,

3

its ideological frames and its practical impact, offers evidence of continuity with Nazi law, are we all implicated in the killing machine? This troubling, yet I believe inevitable, conclusion about the direct relationship between the Holocaust and the law informs what follows.

In his fascinating and controversial book about the Holocaust and American society and politics, Peter Novick makes two basic arguments which surface, in part in a different form and from a different perspective than the one I shall pursue here.[1] First, he asserts that our memory and understanding of the Holocaust, under the rubric of "collective memory",[2] is in fact a historical, culturally determined and tells us more about the collectivity which remembers than it does about historical events themselves. In the rest of this book, I attempt to demonstrate the basic soundness of this idea, especially when applied to legal constructions of the Holocaust and of the Nazi juridical regime. I will argue throughout that the historicity of the Holocaust, in legal discourse and practices concerning the killing of European Jewry, particularly in perpetrator trials, has almost always played a secondary role to other ideological, political, cultural and legal goals and concerns. Ideas and ideologies about the rule of law, justice, the fate and place of ethnic immigrant communities, Jewish and non-Jewish, citizenship and identity, the Cold War struggle against capitalism or communism etc., have all been present in legal attempts to construct a collective memory of the Holocaust. In all of this contextualization and positing of the Holocaust within other frameworks yet within the overarching context of the legislative and judicial processes, the key and essential elements of the legality of the Holocaust have been deliberately elided. It is my small aim in this book to go some way in attempting to demonstrate the error of our legal ways. I try to refocus our jurisprudential efforts in such a manner as to confront our collective and institutional and professional participation and complicity in the murder, or at least the killing, of millions.

This brings me to the second of Novick's assertions and the point at which I diverge from the traditional understandings and characterizations of the Holocaust. For Novick, the Holocaust was and is such an extraordinary phenomenon, an extreme set of events, that we can and should draw few, if any, pedagogical and ethical lessons from it. He argues, for example, that

> If there are, in fact, lessons to be drawn from history, the Holocaust would seem an unlikely source, not because of its alleged uniqueness,

---

1. *The Holocaust in American Life*, (Boston and New York: Houghton Mifflin, 1999).

2. For critical discussions of the concept in historical discourse see e.g., Noa Gedi and Yigal Elam, "Collective memory—What Is It?", 8 *History & Memory* 30 (1996).

but because of its extremity. Lessons for dealing with the sorts of issues that confront us in ordinary life, public or private, are not likely to be found in this most extraordinary of events. There are, in my view, more important lessons about how easily we become victimizers to be drawn from the behavior of normal Americans in normal times than from the behavior of the SS in wartime.[3]

Here I believe, Novick comes close to falling into the all-too-common trap of viewing and constructing the Holocaust as a simple process of brutal and barbaric mass murder of European Jews and other racial and biological enemies of the German *Volk* by the lunatic fringe of the Nazi SS. If instead, we examine the social, political and legal framework in which the identification, exclusion, concentration and finally the extermination of these enemies occurred, we might, and I argue throughout, should, reach different conclusions. If we think of the ways in which lawyers, police and judges, the entire legal apparatus of Germany and of other (particularly Western) European nations mustered and applied themselves to the processes of identifying and defining, of excluding and then killing the Jewish and other "vermin" who endangered the health and survival of the body politic, we might begin to conceive of the Holocaust as the culmination of the acts of ordinary people in the ordinary course of events within ordinary governmental and legal structures. We can see the Shoah not as extraordinary and special in the sense in which Novick and others deploy the arguments, albeit for often different and opposed purposes, but as ordinary, as unexceptional, and in the context which concerns me particularly, as perfectly lawful and legal.

This is the lesson I believe we can and should learn from the Holocaust. Lawyers, judges and police, acting as lawyers, judges and police acted and act, then and now, were responsible for the exclusion, enslavement, spoliation and death of millions of their fellow human beings. Whether this recovery of the Holocaust for and within law will in fact ever lead to any collective, professional re-thinking of lawyers' or judges' roles and functions as ethical and morally responsible human beings, whether we as a group allegedly dedicated to truth or at least to justice, can ever hope to play a part

> ... to establish those bonds of common humanity that were so lacking during the Holocaust ...[4]

---

3. Op. cit. at 13.
4. Tony Kushner, *The Holocaust and the Liberal Imagination* (Oxford: Blackwell, 1994), at 278.

is, of course, another and more complex question, and one about which I am not, as shall become apparent in the pages which follow, optimistic. What is clear, however, is that we collectively have not truly begun in any meaningful fashion to confront these questions. The Holocaust is absent from law schools, from legal education and from legal consciousness, precisely because it has been declared "not law". Nor can we begin to make the Holocaust legally relevant, unless and until we are willing to construct a collective memory of the Holocaust as a lawful phenomenon.

Central to this possible understanding of the Holocaust as a lawful enterprise is the study of the processes of the construction of the "Jew" as a new legal category. Under pre-existing republican legal ideology, all citizens were simply citizens. Emancipation had eliminated the Jew as a separate legal subject. Nazi law recreated the Jew as a separate and distinct legal category in order then to destroy the category itself. This foundational violence of Nazi law is vital not just to the thesis of the legality of the Holocaust but to the post-Holocaust traumas and amnesia of judicial and legislative attempts to deal with that centrality of law. How can the victims, in this case "Jews," seek justice and attempt to establish the Holocaust as an element of legal memory and collective, societal self-understanding, while avoiding the fatal legal pitfall of creating the "Jew" once again as a separate and particular legal category? In other words, through law, is it possible to, at one and the same time, instill and systematize the specificity of Jewish suffering and crimes against the Jewish people between 1933 and 1945, and yet reaffirm the republican, legal ideal of an undifferentiated and universal citizenship? Are assertions of Jewish or Roma specificity as victims of the Nazis essentialized categories which recreate in the current context the phenomenon of a new ethnically defined category of citizen? Are such assertions simply tactically necessary invocations of a contextualized and temporary political strategy in the name of an idea of justice?[5] What is clear is that all of these questions must remain unanswered until we can redefine the parameter of our understanding of Nazi law.

From the earliest days of the war against Germany, particularly after the entry of America, efforts were made to construct a legal edifice upon which it might be possible to condemn the Nazi regime as criminal. The Nuremberg Trials of Major War Criminals and other prosecutions of "Nazi war criminals" today are all premised on the foundation of a jurisprudence which pronounces the Nazi period of one in which Germany became a "criminal state". I believe,

---

5. Jacques Derrida and Elisabeth Roudinesco, "Politiques de la Différence", in *De quoi demain…Dialogue* (Paris: Fayard/Galilée, 2001), at 41–45.

and argue throughout what follows, that this is and was in fact and in law a mistaken and dangerous juridical course of action.

There can be no doubt that Nazism was and is evil, and that evil was done in its name. What I am asserting here is simply that evil can be and was perpetrated in, by, through and under law. Attempts to paint Nazi law as "not law" have resulted, I believe, in a fatal misunderstanding and misrepresentation of the true legal character of Nazi law. These distortions of history and jurisprudence have meant that we have ignored, or paid insufficient attention to what Michael Stolleis has characterized as the "more important things"

> ...namely, a more thorough historical examination of Nazi law, an answer to the basic problem of legal theory, as well as the creation of a certain minimum standard of political awareness and political ethics in the culture at large.[6]

The focus within the various legal systems which are examined later in this book has instead turned first to issues and debates surrounding the construction of "the rule of law" or "justice" in the specific context of the position of alleged Holocaust perpetrators. The passage of time, the frailty and age of many of the accused, limitation periods, vengeance, forgiveness, the reliability or not of eyewitness testimony etc., these are the technical and jurisprudential issues which have dominated the debates surrounding the place of the Holocaust within functioning legal systems.[7]

In essence, the problem raised by this jurisprudence of the Holocaust is the same as the original problem concerning the portrayal of Nazi law as a perversion of law. Debates about the Holocaust and the rule of law have remained constant and remarkably consistent because there is no agreement about what we mean by "law", or more broadly by "the rule of law." There have been, are, and will be persuasive arguments about whether the Nuremberg Trials imposed *ex post facto* liability or conversely that the Allied Powers simply enunciated already existing "universal" principles. Many argue that it is perfectly within the normal function of trial by jury to assert that people can weigh the reliability of eyewitness testimony fifty or more years after the fact. Others assert that such testimony is so unreliable as to challenge the integrity of the legal proceedings in which it is presented. The function of the jury, carefully

---

6. *The Law Under the Swastika* (Chicago: University of Chicago Press, 1998).

7. For a study of many of these issues from a variety of perspectives and in other contexts, see Daniel W. Shuman and Alexander McCall Smith, *Justice and the Prosecution of Old Crimes: Balancing Legal, Psychological and Moral Concerns* (Washington, D.C.: American Psychological Association, 2000).

and adroitly instructed by a judge, allows the system to work and to weed out unreliable evidence, fifty years or fifty minutes after a crime was allegedly committed, for some, while for their opponents, such testimony should, as a matter of law and justice, never reach a jury in the first place. Similarly, vengeance and retribution, as well as forgiveness and rehabilitation, are equal and contemporaneous parts of our criminal justice systems. The arguments are endless because law is in reality little more than the persuasive deployment of rhetorical devices and signifiers. Natural law and positivism, except for the most ardent proponents of one or the other jurisprudential school, or the many variants of each, hardly stand up to practical scrutiny, nor do they advance the real issues of the debate here.

Yet all of the elements of these and similar debates ignore the basic and fundamental problem or at least the jurisprudential danger, that law may be incapable of judging the Holocaust. This incapacity comes not from systemic weaknesses of the jury, or from difficulties within the law of evidence and procedure, but from law's own part in the crime. Law cannot judge the Holocaust if the Holocaust was, in part, lawful. This is the irony and tragedy of the Holocaust and the rule of law in western democracies.

We live in a world of law and politics in which the issues of justice, apology, compensation and retribution are once again on the discursive agenda. African Americans seek compensation for the horrors of slavery; Aboriginal Australians demand apology and redress for historic governmental practices of "cultural genocide"; American and Canadian citizens of Japanese descent want the true history of their lives in concentration camps to be told; post-Apartheid South Africa seeks "truth and reconciliation"; former slave laborers seek damages from German companies; families and heirs engage in the search for lost property and bank accounts, "Aryanized" by the Germans and their allies; citizens in eastern Europe seek redress for the injustices of Soviet-era laws.[8] We live in a world of confession, forgiveness, reconciliation, compensation, retribution, justice as the tropes of a legalized search for truth and justice.

Arguments again emerge about "victims" and about the Holocaust, and necessarily about the law. Can the concept of "crime against humanity" be said to include, for example, the theft of works of art owned by those identified as "Jews" Is a crime against property a crime against humanity? Is the family who lost its art works or its apartment a "victim", a "victim of the Holocaust"? Is

---

8. For a discussion of some of these issues, see, Istvan Deak, Jan Gross and Tony Judt, *The Politics of Retribution in Europe* (Princeton: Princeton University Press, 2000).

there, can there be any intellectual or legal integrity to a category "victim" which includes those who are killed and those who lost property? Can we argue that the latter are "victims of National Socialism" to repeat the formula of post-war West German law? If so, must we not interrogate that category, investigate why Roma or male homosexual "victims" were often considered ineligible for compensation, excluded from the "taxonomy", because they were arrested and imprisoned under ordinary criminal law provisions? But the problem does not stop, nor even begin here.

Instead, the problem lies in the very existence of an idea that confession, forgiveness, compensation etc. can ever adequately be found within or given by the law, even though they are all concepts and practices essential to law's function.[9] Demands for retribution and for apology are essentially linked within the theological origins of the law and laws of confession and pardon.[10] Here, a confession becomes the condition precedent for forgiveness, for the pardon. The problem which appears to face the law here when dealing with the Holocaust and with the issue of Holocaust perpetrators in particular is multiplicitous. For many, as we shall see later, the "victim", who can offer for-giveness, is dead, the pardon is a thanatological impossibility. For others, like Vladimir Jankélévitch, some sins, some crimes are complexly unforgivable. Expiation is impossible.[11] Conversely, as Derrida argues, it may be possible to assert that it is precisely for the unforgivable that the pardon is required.[12] But at this point, as Derrida would recognize, we would have left the domain of the law.

All of these current issues and discourses about pardon and reconciliation, confession and retribution, are also intimately entwined with the juridical con-cept of amnesty, which is precisely not a pardon or forgiveness, but a forget-ting, an amnesia. This then must bring to the surface longstanding arguments and assertions about the failure of Western governments and legal systems to deal adequately with the question of Holocaust perpetrators. The law in ef-fect, for many, forgot about the Holocaust and offered if not a pardon, then an amnesty, a forgetting of the Holocaust and of the victims. Much debate

---

9. See e.g. Jacques Derrida, *L'Université sans condition* (Paris: Galilée, 2001), at 17.

10. For general introductions see Renaud Dulong (ed.), *L'aveu* (Paris: Presses Univer-sitaires de France, 2001); Olivier Abel (ed.), *Le pardon: Briser la dette et l'oubli* (Paris: Edi-tions Autrement, 1998).

11. See "L'impardonnable: plus malheureux que méchants, plus méchants que mal-heureux", in *Philosophie morale* (Paris: Flammarion, 1998), at 1141.

12. "Le Siècle et le Pardon: Entretien avec Michel Wieviorka", in *Foi et Savoir* (Paris: Seuil, 2000).

has circulated around the trials of various alleged Holocaust perpetrators concerning issues of collective memory, the duty not to forget, and the inherent conflict between these cultural, political and legal imperatives and ideas of amnesty and pardon. In the Federal Republic of Germany on several occasions and in France in 1964, these issues surfaced when it appeared that statutory limitation periods would allow many "Nazis" to escape "justice". Two pieces of ideological and legal conflation characterized such debates, as they do in related areas today. The first is the most obvious, the apparent unquestioned symmetry between law and justice, a theme to which I shall return throughout. The second is more intriguing. Here we find the idea that the abolition of limitation periods for crimes against humanity is somehow the same as placing these crimes and their perpetrators beyond forgiveness. What the French call *l'imprescriptible* (*la prescription* is the statutory limitation period for any action in justice. *L'imprescriptible* is a legal proceeding for which there is no limitation period.) is not the same as *l'impardonnable (the unforgivable)*. Putting a crime beyond the purview and applicability of normal limitation periods does not prevent the operation of an extra-legal forgiving of the offence and of the offender. Similarly, the forgiveness offered for example by a victim, survivor of the Shoah does not limit the ability, capacity or even one might argue, the duty of the law to prosecute the perpetrator or of the society to remember the crime.[13] Law and memory, forgiveness and justice may or may not coexist depending upon a variety of contingent social, political, theological and jurisprudential factors and considerations.

I set out in the chapters which follow many of the ways and contexts in which these notions of forgetting, amnesty/amnesia etc have manifested themselves in law. Here, I want to make a more basic point. Law was, is, and must be, engaged in a more vital and more basic amnesty/amnesia in relation to the Holocaust. What is forgotten here, what is wiped from today's legal consciousness, from the consideration of my colleagues in law schools, like the trauma it appears to be, is the lawfulness of the Shoah.[14] Law forgets and forgives itself. If I am correct about this operating thesis, then pardon and confession are, if not impossible, at the very least beyond the capacity of law itself. Law cannot offer itself a pardon, it cannot confess to itself. It can merely try to forget itself. More importantly, perhaps, law has nothing to forgive. It was and is, simply being itself. Where can the victims turn for remembrance and for compensation if it was the law which victimized. They can turn, as I

---

13. Ibid., at 109–10.

14. See generally, Dominic LaCapra, *Representing the Holocaust: History Theory Trauma* (Ithaca and London: Cornell University Press, 1994).

shall demonstrate in what follows, to a law which deludes itself, which calls Nazi law "not law," and which always emerges victorious in the game in which it sets its own rules.

I believe that the law sits uncomfortably with and within the Holocaust, not because the Holocaust is somehow beyond law or beyond forgiveness, but rather because it can never extricate itself from that which it helped produce. The self-understanding of lawyers today, the profession and confession of democratic values, of the protection of us all from "crimes against humanity", is not, nor can it ever be, grounded in "learning the lessons" of the Holocaust. The law is part of the lesson because it was part of the Holocaust. Perhaps we must, if we seek a better understanding of "evil" or more precisely of law, pass here into the realm of justice, into that Derridean point at which the impossible demand for justice requires the forgiving of that which is beyond pardon, where the law is beyond law.

In any event, what I want to explore is a notion based in understandings of continuity, in my case of legal continuity, between law before the Nazis came to power, law under the Nazis and law today. It is my belief that what has rendered ineffective or unconvincing much of the discussion and analysis of the issues surrounding trials of alleged Holocaust perpetrators, and perhaps of others now being pursued for crimes against humanity, is that our true existential and institutional understandings of law operate under the shadow of Auschwitz. By this I mean that we try to understand Auschwitz, because this is the understanding of our culture, our history and our law, as a unique and defining "moment", an event at the limit as Paul Ricoeur has recently put it.[15] This perceptual and analytical framework raises issues which are both practically important and philosophically challenging. How can a legal system structured to deal with crimes committed by individuals, comprehend and deal with crimes against humanity, an entire Nazi system bent on the implementation of a plan and policy aimed at the extermination of Jews? What lessons can we learn from, how can we understand "Auschwitz"? How was law "perverted" by the Nazis? Here I attempt to show how it might be possible to offer a different interpretation of the law of the Holocaust, of the Holocaust as law. First, instead of positing Nazi law as an aberration, instead of placing 1933–1945 in an airtight legal quarantine, I want to begin to imagine what happens when and if we can present Nazi law as law, plain and simple. If law which preceded Nazi law can be recognized after 1933 in Ger-

---

15. "Devant l'inacceptable: le juge, l'historien, l'écrivain", 67 *Philosophie* 3 (2000). See also his *La Mémoire, L'Histoire, L'Oubli* (Paris: Seuil, 2000).

many, if law outside of Germany after 1933 recognized Nazi law as law, if law from 1933–1945 continued after that date, then we might begin to imagine a new jurisprudence of the Holocaust. The Holocaust, "Auschwitz", becomes not limit and therefore limiting experience, but instead it becomes part of the normal continuities of history and law in the traditions of Western culture. The Holocaust is therefore no longer an extreme from which nothing can be learned but instead an example of the ordinary from which we refuse to draw any useful lessons in the pursuit of jurisprudential self-assurance and a guilt-less juridical conscience.

This is, I believe, the real source of unease about so-called Holocaust trials. If we cannot mark 1933–1945 as a period of radical disjuncture, if we must admit its place in our history and within our legal system, if the Holocaust was to some extent at least lawful, then law after Auschwitz takes on a completely new complexion. It is not because the Holocaust was unique that it poses challenges to our legal system or to our conceptions of law and justice. It is the very normality of the Holocaust and of the legal basis of the Holocaust which challenges us. Law must face itself. Law Before and After Auschwitz

2. Law before Auschwitz

"Auschwitz"—a crime. *The* crime. The death of the subject and, so it would seem, the death of the Other, an Other, "the Jew" who was first inscribed in the law. "Auschwitz"—the place and time where, in the haze of the Zyklon B, in the shower rooms and in the smoke of the crematoria, the Law seemed to die. "Auschwitz"—a place, a time, a metaphor, a crime, after which we stand, seeking, in vain, perhaps, an ethical and legal point of view which does not sink into the mire and shit of "after Auschwitz". This was and is the goal of the Nuremberg War Crimes trials, of debates about positivism, of other legal events in the "theater of ideas", to reinscribe a body of law "after Auschwitz". [16] To write in the *corpus juris*, the prohibition of crimes against humanity, to place "Auschwitz" outside the Law. To save the Law through the spectacular of the trial, at Nuremberg, where the non-German "Jew" was written in the Law, and later with Eichmann, Barbie, Papon, Sawoniuk, Finta, Polyukovich, and others, to place the Law "after Auschwitz", which was law-

---

16. See Mark Osiel, *Mass Atrocity, Collective Memory, and The Law* (New Brunswick and London: Transaction, 1997). See also Lawrence Douglas, *The Memory of Judgment: Making Law and History in the Trials of the Holocaust* (New Haven and London: Yale University Press, 2001).

less, after Nuremberg, which was lawful. But the Law was in fact not absent from Auschwitz. It was not a lawless time or place. Auschwitz was lawful, it was full of law—lawful prescriptions of "Aryan" and "Jew", lawful sterilizations and euthanasia to protect the blood, lawful orders, from lawyers and doctors, for the removal, isolation, and then extermination of those enemies of the State, those parasites who would infect the *Volksgemeinschaft*. The "selection" on the ramp offers us the moment and place of medico-legal judgment *par excellence*. To seek an ethical/legal standpoint after Auschwitz, to stand after Auschwitz (or again to ignore it as do my colleagues in the legal academy in general), the Law (or perhaps justice) must now be the principal accused and the accused in principle. Law must, but cannot, judge itself.

For Law, however, to be judged by Auschwitz, another fundamental and insurmountable difficulty presents itself—the *différend*.[17] The victim demands justice, the tribunal, even a tribunal as powerful as Auschwitz can offer at best law, but never Law.

> …the "perfect crime" does not consist in killing the victim or the witnesses (that adds new crimes to the first one and aggravates the difficulty of effacing everything), but rather in obtaining the silence of the witnesses, the deafness of the judges, and the inconsistency (insanity) of the testimony.[18]

What can be more insane for us, for whom Auschwitz must remain the ultimate rupture, than testimony about Auschwitz? What can be greater than the silence of forgetting the forgotten? Who could be deafer than judges of Law after Auschwitz? But that is, I hope, to pre-judge the case. What if we begin by placing Auschwitz at the center of a lawful project, of Nazi law as the legal killing of the Jew?

The case, then, comes before Auschwitz, when Nazi law created the Jew. Auschwitz stands awaiting judgment and justice because Auschwitz was legal. For Auschwitz is both a time and place we can grasp and locate and a metaphor which seeks to escape this very capacity for location and for judgment. It is the metaphor of Auschwitz which presents itself to us as beyond comprehension, as a radical rupture, as a point beyond law. To understand the reality of Auschwitz is to understand its legality, and to understand its legality is to understand its reality.

---

17. Jean-François Lyotard, *The Différend* (Minneapolis: University of Minnesota Press, 1988).

18. Ibid., at 8.

As Lyotard reminds us, if we need reminding, the evidence was destroyed.

> The SS did everything possible to remove all traces of the extermina-
> tion. Its orders were to make sure nothing was recorded...It had to
> be a perfect crime, one would plead not guilty, certain of the lack of
> proof.[19]

Of course, there is some evidence, some evidence even of and after the
complete destruction of Treblinka, Sobibor and Belzec. The desire for efficiency required the keeping of some records, so there is the beginning of
proof. There are witnesses, survivors, legal subjects, subjected to the law before and after Auschwitz. The most damning and irrefutable evidence which
can be placed before "Auschwitz" is "before Auschwitz". After 1933, before the
mass killings, an entire history of removal, isolation, criminalization, transportation. An entire jurisprudence of how and why being a Jew was an offence
against public order. It is found in Jean Améry's realization that the Nuremberg Laws were the legalization of the extermination of the Jews remembered
every day after the camps, as he looked at his tattooed arm, a persistent legal
text.[20] The body of evidence presented here is evidence of the bodies—bodies of/in Law. Out of the gas and fire comes the body of evidence, evidence of
bodies. *Corpus juris, corpus delicti*. But this is only half the story. A story of
law which law refuses to hear today.

The evidence of the law before Auschwitz requires and commands a re-or-
dering of jurisprudential time. The evidence of the law of Aryan/Jew, in
essence the law of identification and differentiation carried to its logical, mech-
anized, biologized modern extreme is available for all to see. *The Law for the
Restoration of the Professional Civil Service, the Editors' Law, the Reich Entailed
Farm Law, the Law for the Protection of German Blood and Honor, the Reich
Citizenship Law*—the non-Aryan becomes the Jew, who becomes the non-
German, who becomes the subject who can be killed. The causal chain exists,
inscribed in legal text and practice, from the *Blood Law* to the crematoria.
Building a case for Auschwitz before Auschwitz. The tribunal and the crema-
toria are both *loci legi*. This corporeality of law and the Holocaust is the prime
example of the continuity of embodied racial difference central to Western
culture.

The acts and actors which stand before Auschwitz and which are inscribed
before Auschwitz are acts of law and acts of lawyers. The case to answer I pres-

---

19. Jean-François Lyotard, *Heidegger and "the jews"* (Minneapolis, University Press,
1990), at 25.

20. *At the Mind's Limit* (New York: Schocken Books, 1990), at 82–101.

LAW AFTER AUSCHWITZ   15

ent in the rest of this book proceeds on the view that Auschwitz was legal, that that status of legality can be traced in a body of law which circles back upon itself to reveal the bodies hidden in the smoke and ashes. In the politics (and law) of forgetting after Auschwitz this case presents the first fact to be remembered and the one always already forgotten—the law which led to the doors of the gas chambers.

The Nazi social state was also a *Rechtsstaat*. The Holocaust, the Shoah, Auschwitz, these are all, beyond the horrific factual reality, legal metaphors, lawful descriptors of what we can call modernity. And Auschwitz is nothing if not modern and, therefore, law-ful.

> Like everything else in our modern society, the Holocaust was an accomplishment in every respect superior, if measured by the standard that this society has preached and institutionalized.[21]

Before Auschwitz, there was law. A legally constituted state and a people which defined itself, legally, almost purely in terms of its Other, the Jew. A *Volksgemeinschaft*, a lawfully constituted and constitutional *corpus juris* in which membership was determined by the absence of contaminated blood. The body of the *Volk*—kept legally free from contamination, yet defined in terms which could not help but include "the Jew". Throughout the Nazi state was *Recht* and through the law—the *Volk*. No-where, but in the Nazi myth, was there a positive, even if "only" imaginary, constitution of the *Volk*—the Aryan.[22] The constitution of the Aryan can be found only in one site—in the body of the Law, in the law of the body and ultimately, in the body of "the Jew". What is truly constituted, what authentically and in the only real sense "constitutes" the Nazi *Rechtsstaat* and *Volk*, is "the Jew". This then is the constitutional and jurisprudential key to Nazi law as law. Aryan blood must be freed from contamination, the land purged of the vermin, but the Jew is the worm at the heart of the Aryan dream of Nazi law. This is the legally constituted truth of law within modernity, before and after Auschwitz.

---

21. Zygmunt Bauman, *Modernity and the Holocaust* (Ithaca: Cornell University Press, 1991), at 89. For a more recent, specific and important contribution on the intimate connections between modernity and racism, see Paul Gilroy, *Between Camps* (London: Penguin, 2000). Gilroy's book, in its American edition is entitled *Against Race* (Cambridge, MA: Belkap: Harvard, 2000), a comparison/distinction which raises important political and ethical questions. Enzo Traverso also attempts to situate the Holocaust within the broader and central tropes of modern European history. See *La violence nazi: une généalogie européene* (Paris: La fabrique, 2002).

22. Phillipe Lacoue-Larbarthe and Jean-Luc Nancy, "The Nazi Myth", 16 *Critical Inquiry* 291 (1990).

This is the truth of law before Auschwitz. The *Volksgemeinschaft* is that community based on blood and written in the body of the law. The law writes and delimits the subject and citizen not just in terms of merit and obligation, but finally, ultimately and primarily in the foundation of the blood and the body. The Jew cannot be citizen because the citizen must be the non-Jew. This is the constitutive force of law under Nazi rule, a constitutional first principle.[23]

In law, for Derrida, we must doubt, question, the possibility of separating

> ...all the shared portions and all the partitions that organize such a configuration, of the vertiginous proximities, the radical reversals of pro into con on the basis of sometimes common premises.[24]

Yet for the Nazis, and for law under the Nazis, the Jew and the Aryan, the destroyed and the destroyer are linked, inextricably bound, in the body of the law before Auschwitz. In the mystical foundation of the authority of the force of Law which precedes law, are the Jew and the Aryan, the Other whose call cannot be heard in justice before or after Auschwitz. The Other who must be heard, who will testify, called before the tribunal of Auschwitz which judges not the Other, not the ineffable, the *différend* between law and Law, between Law and Justice, but which can only judge itself, but which must refuse to do so. This is why we need Auschwitz as we now have it—to escape the legality of the killing-machine, the judicial mechanisms which sought out, identified and imprisoned those to be killed because they were non-Aryans, unlawful subjects of the law.

It is not, therefore, accidental that Derrida focuses on "the phantom body of the police"[25] when turning his discussion of the Force of Law towards the question of spirit (*Geist*).[26] The phantom body of the police marks the law and the body of the Jew, the policed, surveilled, subjected, disciplined body *par excellence*. The Jew, arrested, sterilized, deported, ghettoized, marked, enslaved, exterminated, but not murdered. But in the end, Derrida appears to elide the juridical, to avoid being caught in the trap of law before Auschwitz:

> In other words, one cannot think the uniqueness of an event like the final solution, as extreme point of mythic and representational vio-

---

23. Lyotard, *Heidegger and "the jews"*, op. cit., at 70.

24. Jacques Derrida, 'Force of law: the mystical foundation of authority', 11 *Cardozo Law Review* 919 (1990), at 1040.

25. Ibid., at 1011.

26. Jacques Derrida, *Of Spirit: Heidegger and the Question* (Chicago: University of Chicago Press, 1991).

lence within its own system.........it kept the archive of its destruction, produced simulacra of justificatory arguments, with a terrifying legal, bureaucratic, statist objectivity and paradoxically produced a system in which its logic, the logic of objectivity made possible the invalidation and therefore the effacement of testimony and of responsibilities; the neutralization of the singularity of the final solution.[27]

Before Auschwitz, there was a complex body of law, the law of the body of the Aryan and "the Jew". An entire body of legal texts and practices aimed at the constitution and destruction of the legal subject capable of being killed, but not murdered. This is the body of evidence which presents itself to us, now, after Auschwitz. The law before Auschwitz may not, it is true, be able to offer justice, for justice is no doubt withheld, even, or especially after Auschwitz. But the law does offer a body of evidence to be judged before Auschwitz. The Holocaust, Auschwitz, I believe and argue in what follows, judges itself. It must, but cannot, judge, for to judge rationally, law must find itself guilty. The legalized death of the "Jew" was the legal consequence of law. Law before Auschwitz, Nazi law was nonetheless law. And after Auschwitz, what of law? This is, again, what frightens and traumatizes law and lawyers today. When Slobodan Milosevic stands in the Hague and refutes the court as "a false tribunal", he gives voice to our worst nightmares of law after Auschwitz. Perhaps we must face a state of law in which Auschwitz, the limit, is the rule. Auschwitz as the normal jurisprudential state.[28]

---

27. "Force of Law", op. cit., at 1042.
28. See Giorgio Agamben, "The Messiah and the Sovereign: The Problem of Law in Walter Benjamin", in *Potentialities* (Stanford: Stanford University Press, 1999) at 160 et. seq.

CHAPTER 2

LAW BEFORE AUSCHWITZ—
THE BODY OF THE LAW

A singular construction of the role, place and function of the legal and police apparatus under Hitler has dominated popular and jurisprudential understandings of Nazi law. We are all familiar with the Hollywood renderings of the leather trench-coated Gestapo thugs breaking down the doors of terrified and cowed German citizens in the middle of the night. This is the popular imagining of the Nazi state as a criminal state, ruled by madmen in a brutal hierarchical regime of top-down terror.[1]

An almost identical jurisprudential imaginary of Nazi law exists. From the earliest days of the post-war era, in which the daily horrors and unimaginable devastation of the Hitler period emerged, the idea of the Nazi regime as a "criminal state" has dominated legal discourse.[2] Nazi jurists were singled out for their own Nuremberg trial, and the entire period was portrayed as one characterized by arbitrary arrest, Gestapo terror from above, unlawful procedures before kangaroo courts, exemplified and embodied in Freisler's People's Court system.[3] In the immediate post-war period, Leo Alexander, for example, argued that Nazi ideology created and celebrated a worldview of delight in death, or *thanatolatry*.[4] For Alexander, the entire structure of German so-

---

1. For recent, sophisticated and nuanced work embodying this view of Germany as a criminal state, see Eric A. Johnson, *Nazi Terror: The Gestapo, Jews and Ordinary Germans* (New York: Basic Books, 1999).

2. See Eugen Kogon, *The Theory and Practice of Hell* (New York: Farrar Straus and Cudahy, 1950). This somewhat more theatrical English-language title of Kogon's work, is a translation of the more prosaic, but clearly defined, *Der SS Staat*.

3. See generally, H.W. Koch, *In the Name of the Volk: Political Justice in Hitler's Germany* (London: I.B.Tauris, 1989).

4. Leo Alexander, "Destructive and Self-Destructive Trends in Criminalized Society", 39 *Journal of Criminal Law and Criminology* 553 (1949). The same Leo Alexander served as a Research Associate for the Carnegie Foundation funded study by the American Neurological Association on sterilization. The Committee concluded, *inter alia*, that eugenic

ciety was dominated by this ideology as embodied in the terror state inflicted from above by the murderous and mentally ill SS.

> The complete destruction of all moral principles had, as inevitably it must, gotten out of hand. The complete destruction of all moral principles by the SS itself, the complete destructive demoralization of the Third Reich is exemplified by nothing more striking than by the men who composed the WVHA of the SS; and the cunning trickery and cheating which they practiced on their victims they ultimately also practiced in dealing with the German State and the German people themselves.[5]

Alexander's work is a classic example of the criminalization within legal discourse of an entire juridical epoch, and indeed of an entire nation. The Nazi state, and therefore Nazi law, is here pathologized, excluded from the normative universe of modernity, civilization and the common understanding of concepts of the rule of law. Morality is completely destroyed. Law is replaced by "not law". An additional effect of this criminalization of Nazi law is of course, the concomitant de-pathologizing of the German people. They are, after a dose of deNazification and other forms of democratic social, political and legal therapy, cured of this psychotic episode inflicted upon them by the SS. Germany is returned to democratic normality under the rule of law.

The idea of Nazi law as "criminal law," i.e. as not law, also carries with it an important, indeed vital, element of periodization. If the Nazi state was a criminal state and Nazi law was not law, then the Nazi epoch must stand outside the normal course of progress towards and under democratic norms which characterize and are essential to, the modern state in western Europe. In other words, Nazi law must be understood as a form of rupture both with that which preceded it, the modern, democratic, if deeply flawed, Weimar Republic, and that which follows it, the modern democracy of the then Federal

---

sterilization should be permitted if it took place under an administrative machinery of boards composed of experts and that Huntington's chorea, feeblemindedness "of the family type", schizophrenia, manic-depressive psychosis and some forms of epilepsy would be medical grounds for such procedures. A comparison with the Nazi Hereditary Health Courts and legislation provides intriguing insights into the "criminal state" hypothesis pronounced with such certainty by Doctor Alexander here. See The Committee of the American Neurological Association for the Investigation of Eugenical Sterilization, *Eugenical Sterilization: A Reorientation of the Problem* (New York: Macmillan, 1936), especially at 177–83.

5. Alexander, "Destructive and Self-Destructive Trends", op. cit., at 563.

Republic. Nazi law, like the Nazi state, must be radically discontinuous with the practically tainted but ideologically acceptable, liberal legality of Weimar and of the new Federal Republic.[6] A type of jurisprudential quarantine needed to be established around Nazi law, in order not just to allow the fledging German democracy to take root and to flourish, but to permit the theory of rupture and discontinuity to establish itself. If the Nazi state arose from thuggery and the fraudulent takeover of power in 1933, then its entire foundations, including especially its legal framework, can only be, and must only be, understood as "not law", as operating within and reinforcing an illegitimate and illegal regime.

I shall attempt to demonstrate in subsequent sections of this book the deep and fatal flaws which characterize the construction of Nazi law as "not law". In doing so, it is not my intention to revisit the debates around natural law and positivism which have dominated legal scholars' concerns about Nazi law. Instead I shall try to set up a framework of analysis which allows us first to see the ways in which contemporary actors understood law and Nazi law and secondly permits us to perceive some of the basic practical and jurisprudential continuities which preceded and followed the 1933–1945 period. By adopting this approach which simply sets up law and lawyers on their own professional terrain and self-understanding, I hope to raise some basic and troubling questions about law and what we now understand about the Nazi legal regime. In the second section of the book, I begin to trace the ways in which law, history and memory have to a greater or lesser extent all been prejudiced by the ongoing legacy of the "criminal state" theory of the radical discontinuity construction of Nazi law. In doing so, I am not attempting to argue that that Nazism was inevitable within modernity, or that law is inherently evil, or that we are all Nazis etc. I want to stake out a simpler and I believe more important jurisprudential terrain. If, as I believe, it is impossible to characterize Nazi law as "not law" in any coherent fashion, what, if anything, does that do to our ability to understand, to face and to combat evil? Is the historical and legal construction of Germany 1933–1945 as radically discontinuous a necessary falsehood, a collective lie we tell ourselves in order to make the line between good and evil, justice and injustice, a brighter one? Or is it, as I believe, a way of ignoring our own responsibilities when faced with basic questions of right and wrong? The answer lies first of all in an attempt to characterize both Nazism and law in their appropriate contexts. The ways in which law, or "law",

---

6. See Panikos Panayi (ed.), *Weimar and Nazi Germany: Continuities and Discontinuities* (Harlow, Essex: Longman, 2001).

for the proponents of the "criminal state" thesis, was invoked and deployed at the heart of the Nazi worldview and political practice is as good a place to start as any.

In 1945, Professor Friedrich Roetter wrote that:

> Although Nazi doctrines may have been conceived in cool calculation as a means to power and nurtured through emotion, the point of interest to the lawyer is that the acts of the Nazi regime were committed under law. The Nazis recognized the necessity of law. But their law had little in common with what lawyers had theretofore called law.[7]

Here Roetter clearly signals the jurisprudential difficulty which continues to haunt us and which inspired me to write this book. There was something called Nazi law but Nazi law, if it informed and underpinned the atrocities of the regime, must not be considered law. Others had already signaled this "perversion" of legality. This Nazi law as "perversion" thesis would be central to subsequent prosecutions of German legal officials.[8] It is hardly surprising that the discontinuity thesis should be prominently displayed in these contexts. If we are to construct an historical memory of the rule of law and the Holocaust, within an ideological and political tradition which cherishes and values law, that memory must rely on the radical historical discontinuity of the period 1933–1945. The Nazi State must be characterized as a "criminal state" in which "law" existed in form only. Like the Nazis themselves[9], Nazi law must be turned into "a most egregious case of legal pathology".[10] In the post-war era, this characterization of the Nazi legal system has been adopted by those propounding natural law theories and rejected by those who, to some extent, interrogate the idea that law has an underlying moral, substantive content, the legal positivists.[11] This debate has raged in Western jurisprudential circles since the days of the opposing articles in the pages of the *Harvard Law Review* by H.L.A. Hart representing positivism and Lon Fuller proposing a natural law

---

7. "The Impact of Nazi Law", *Wisconsin Law Review* (1945), 516.

8. See infra discussion of the *Justice Trial*, chapter 5.

9. See e.g. Leo Alexander, op. cit.

10. Martin P. Golding, "Transitional Regimes and the Rule of Law", 9 *Ratio Juris* 387 (1996).

11. For a more subtle and politically astute jurisprudential analysis of the issues of morality and legal positivism, see Allan H. Hutchinson, *It's All In The Game* (Duke: Duke University Press, 2000).

theory.[12] Some continue to revisit the debate today, albeit in a theoretically more sophisticated and skeptical fashion.[13] Still others have rejected the claim that Nazi law can accurately be described as falling under the banner of positivism in any event.[14] Recent debates and interventions concerning the political and legal philosophy of Carl Schmitt[15], the so-called "jurist of the Third Reich", also indicate that many today are not at all comfortable with any attempt to define the period 1933–1945 generally and the idea of law in Germany 1933–1945 particularly, in any way but as a pathological deformation of the great and continuing traditions of western legality and the rule of law. At the same time, however, all who reject the "legality" of Nazi Germany are still faced with the existential reality of a legal system which continued to function much as it had before. This is not to suggest that the period of 1933–1945 was completely and unambiguously continuous in every facet and aspect with the legal system under Weimar. Soon after the Nazis came to government, the *Law for the Restoration of the Professional Civil Service* provided the juridical

---

12. H.L. A. Hart, "Positivism and the Separation of Law and Morals", 71 *Harvard Law Review* 593 (1958); Lon Fuller, "Positivism and Fidelity to Law—A Reply to Professor Hart", ibid., 630. See also H.O. Pappe, "On the Validity of Judicial Decisions in the Nazi Era", 23 *Modern Law Review* 264 (1960).

13. See especially David Dyzenhaus, "The Legitimacy of Law: A Response to Critics", 7 *Ratio Juris* 80 (1994); "The Legitimacy of Legality", 46 *University of Toronto Law Journal* 129 (1996); *contra* Matthew Kramer, "Scrupulousness Without Scruple: A Critique of Lon Fuller and His Defenders", 18 *Oxford Journal of Legal Studies* 235 (1998). On law under the Nazis see more specifically, Matthew Lippman, "They Shoot Lawyers Don't They?: Law in the Third Reich and the Global Threat to Independence of the Judiciary", 23 *California Western International Law Journal* 257 (1993); "Law, Lawyers and Legality in the Third Reich: The Perversion of Principle and Professionalism", 11 *Temple International and Comparative Law Journal* 199 (1997); compare Peter C. Caldwell, *Popular Sovereignty and the Crisis of German Constitutional Law: The Theory and Practice of Weimar Constitutionalism* (Duke: Duke University Press, 1997).

14. See e.g. Walter Ott and Franziska Buob, "Did Legal Positivism Render German Jurists Defenceless During the Third Reich?", 2 *Social & Legal Studies* 91 (1993); Markus Dirk Dubber, "Judicial Positivism and Hitler's Justice", 93 *Columbia Law Review* 1807 (1993).

15. See generally, Joseph W. Bendersky, *Carl Schmitt: Theorist for the Reich* (Princeton: Princeton University Press, 1983); Special Issue on Carl Schmitt, 72 *Telos* 1987; William E. Scheuerman, *Between the Norm and the Exception* (Cambridge and London: MIT Press 1994); *The Rule of Law Under Siege: Selected Essays of Franz L. Neumann and Otto Kirchheimer* (William E. Scheuerman ed.) (Berkeley: University of California Press, 1996); Jacques Derrida, *Politiques de l' amitié* (Paris: Galilée, 1994); David Dyzenhaus, "Now the Machine Runs Itself": Carl Schmitt on Hobbes and Kelsen", 16 *Cardozo Law Review* 1 (1994); "Holmes and Carl Schmitt: An Unlikely Pair", 63 *Brooklyn Law Review* 165 (1997).

framework for the purge of Jews and Socialists from the legal profession and many were forced into exile.[16] The content of legal rules changed as anti-Jewish and other Nazi measures were put into effect. Nazi law offered and operated substantive changes to pre-existing legal norms. Nonetheless, other aspects of the legal and jurisprudential context also remain uncontestably true. Article 48 of the Weimar Constitution, permitting executive, emergency government, the provision under which Hitler assumed power, had been invoked numerous times previously under Weimar's democracy.[17] At the level of constitutional law, events in 1933 and the Hitler regime were to a great extent unremarkable under the normative substantive and procedural structures of Weimar legality. It is equally true that, for example, liberal advocacy and professional independence were not historically defining characteristics of the legal world in Germany before 1933. Social conservatism and economic deprivation were predominant among the profession.[18] Judges and lawyers under Weimar legality were often openly hostile to the Republic and the constitutional and juristic norms of a liberal ideal of the rule of law.[19] The profession in Germany, like its counterpart in France a few years later, voluntarily and without objection rid itself of its Jewish members.[20] It entered into the process of consolidation and reorganization which characterized Nazi social structures without hesitation.[21] Judges and lawyers operated as they always had, if not with more vigor and enthusiasm, as the legal system adopted "Nazi legality" as its normative basis. All areas of the profession, from the daily practice of law to judicial decision-making to jurisprudential studies of various fields of

---

16. See Kenneth C. H. Willig, "The Bar in the Third Reich", 20 *American Journal of Legal History* 1 (1976); Udo Reifner, "The Bar in the Third Reich: Anti-semitism and the Decline of Liberal Advocacy", 32 *McGill Law Journal* 96 (1986); Martin Bennhold, "Lawyers in Exile", 17 *International Journal of the Sociology of Law* 63 (1989).

17. For a contemporary discussion of the normality of this extraordinary state of law, see René Brunet, *The German Constitution* (London: T. Fisher Unwin Ltd., 1923).

18. See generally, Geoffrey Cocks and Konrad H. Jarausch, *German Professions, 1800–1950* (New York and Oxford: Oxford University Press, 1990); Konrad H. Jarausch, *The Unfree Professions: German Lawyers, Teachers, and Engineers, 1900–1950* (New York and Oxford: Oxford University Press, 1990); Kenneth F. Ledford, "German Lawyers and the State in the Weimar Republic", 13 *Law and History Review* 317 (1995).

19. See Ingo Müller, "The Judges of the Weimar Republic", in *Hitler's Justice: The Courts of the Third Reich* (Cambridge: Harvard University Press, 1991), at 3 et. seq.; Michael Stolleis, "The Judicial System and the Courts in the Weimar Republic", in *The Law Under the Swastika* (Chicago: University of Chicago Press, 1998), at 1–2.

20. Robert Badinter, *Un antisémitisme ordinaire: Vichy et les avocats juifs (1940–1944)* (Paris: Fayard, 1997).

21. Müller, op. cit., 'Jurists "Coordinate Themselves"', at 36–45.

law by legal academics, occurred either as if "nothing" had changed or as if any change had been for the better. This, then, is the problem for us today. How do we understand and defend law "after Auschwitz" if law "before Auschwitz" was perceived by those who participated in its application and development on a daily basis as one which allowed them to act as they had under Weimar legality?

It would indeed be comforting to be able to accept that events in Germany between 1933 and 1945 constituted a radical break with the history, traditions and practices of European and German history. Of course, even this radical discontinuity would still need be understood as belonging at some level to history, if only to make it more readily capable of this characterization. Accordingly, the Nazi period could be understood and analyzed as having causal connections with the great events which preceded it. An historical understanding of German nationalism, of the aftermath of Versailles, the occupation of the Ruhr, reparations, hyperinflation, Weimar with its fragile and strained democratic institutions, would all be necessary to fully comprehend and characterize Nazi Germany. But this understanding would always be informed by the *grundnorm* of discontinuity. In other words, while it is necessary to engage in causal analysis for greater historical knowledge and understanding, the final point must always be that 1933 to 1945 is to be marked as an aberration. Under this construction, this period constitutes a radical break with Western thought and history. Memory of law is then created and comforted by the great period of "not law", as we write out Nazi legality from Western juridical history.

The second part of this historical epistemological equation then covers the post-1945 period. If 1933 to 1945, the Hitler regime, marked a time of disjunction, the post-Hitler era in Germany and the West more generally must also be marked as another type of disjunction. Thus, Occupation, war crimes trials, deNazification and the democratization of Germany, must all be seen and understood as essential steps in marking this period as radically discontinuous with the twelve-year space which immediately preceded it. In other words, 1933 to 1945 must be understood and characterized as a period of history which is still in some way out of history. It is an aberration through which normality is to be better understood. The pathological nature of Nazi law allows us to take comfort in our own healthy legal normality. The trauma of disjuncture is cured as the healing effects of a return to law and legality are felt. This temporally bipartite thesis of discontinuity/continuity describes the fundamental, dominant, popular historical understanding we have of the Nazi period. In order for us not just to understand the Nazi period and the horrors of the Holocaust, but for us to "manage" these issues, intellectually and ideologically, it has been necessary to portray history in such a way as to relieve us of any real responsibility for the evil associated with the Nazi regime. If 1933 to 1945 can be understood and portrayed as a time out of time, it becomes possible for us to then construct our world and belief system as distinct from and completely unimplicated with, the ideas and practices of Nazism and more particularly of "so-called" Nazi legality. We must naturally understand and learn from the lessons of history, just as we must be ever vigilant in preventing any re-occurrence. But it remains understood, both implicitly and explicitly, that our historical knowledge of this time and our duty to be vigilant are informed by our even more essential knowledge that this period marks an epoch which is estranged from our epistemological and moral jurisprudential universe. Our frame of reference must be one which re-enforces the discontinuity thesis, for without it, how can we mark ourselves as "not Nazi", as "never Nazi"? Otherwise, how could we inscribe our historical and social self-understanding as "post-Holocaust", as "after Auschwitz", in anything but an essentially meaningless temporal sense? "After Auschwitz" can only have real ethical import if we can somehow delimit 1933–1945 as discontinuous. Law after Auschwitz can only carry some deontological weight if we can inscribe Nazi law as somehow fundamentally, "not law".

Others have noted as a matter of sociological[22], historical[23] and philosophical[24] "fact", that there is more than sufficient evidence to indicate that the discontinuity thesis must now be considered inadequate to ground our understanding of what it means to live after Auschwitz. As I hope to demonstrate in this and succeeding chapters, law too can offer us more than adequate proof that we do not, in any meaningful sense, live after Auschwitz. For lawyers, and for law, and therefore for all citizens of those Western countries who define themselves as living in democracies characterized by the rule of law, this is a vital point.

One way in which the discontinuity thesis has managed to inculcate itself in our historical, social and ideological understanding of 1933 to 1945, is through the characterization of Nazi Germany as the antithesis of a system of government informed by the rule of law. For proponents of this position, Nazi Germany was a "criminal state", one operating merely under "the color of law", rather than a true and authentic legal regime. If that is true, then a clear distinction can be drawn between our system of legality and legitimacy and that

---

22. Zygmunt Bauman, *Modernity and the Holocaust*, op. cit.
23. Omer Bartov, *Murder in Our Midst: The Holocaust, Industrial Killing, and Representation* (New York and Oxford: Oxford University Press, 1996).
24. Jean-François Lyotard, *Heidegger and "the Jews"*, op. cit.

"other" system which is completely separate from our understanding of these principles and concepts. The trials of major war criminals at Nuremberg can, and should be, seen to have operated under this ideological schema. The trials are key events in which the Nazi regime was given this official "criminal" status by the "new" system of the rule of law which, by necessity and by definition, was discontinuous with the regime which ruled between 1933 and 1945.[25] To a greater or lesser extent, subsequent legal proceedings against accused Nazi war criminals can also be said to have served this same purpose of marking the current legal system with this discontinuity. Of course, as we shall see in subsequent chapters, this attempt to mark legal systems after Auschwitz as distinct from Nazi legality has been fraught with difficulties both at the practical level and as a matter of ideology. Nonetheless, it is clear that the legitimacy of post-war prosecutions of Nazi criminals is dependent upon the existence of the continuity/discontinuity thesis. Our historical and institutional memories and practices of law and legality are also grounded in this thesis of Nazi law as not law.

Things, however, are not as simple as proponents of the ideal of Nazi Germany as a criminal state would have us believe. As in other disciplines, more recent work in law has demonstrated that we can, in fact, find certain strong links between the legal system which preceded the Hitler regime and the system which operated under the Nazis. Studies by Ingo Müller and Michael Stolleis underline the fact that not only did most German lawyers continue to function under the Nazis as they had under Weimar, but that the legal profession as a whole welcomed the transition to Nazi justice. Richard Weisberg's more recent investigation of law and lawyers in Vichy France clearly demonstrates the ways in which a legal community, grounded in traditions of Republican liberty and equality under law, adapted to an antisemitic juristic worldview with little or no protest or difficulty.[26]

This is an issue of vital importance. If there was something called Nazi law which participants in the system recognized as "law", this would mean that the thesis of the discontinuity of the Hitler period would have be called into question.[27] If this were to become our understanding of the nature, function and

---

25. See below, chapter 5.

26. *Vichy Law and the Holocaust in France* (New York: New York University Press, 1997). See also Dominique Gros, (ed.), *Le Droit Antisémite de Vichy* (Paris: Seuil, 1995); David Fraser, "Law, Lawyers and the Holocaust: The Case Against Vichy France", 11 *Holocaust and Genocide Studies* 139 (1998).

27. Indeed, even those like Müller and Stolleis who are less prone to accept the "legitimacy" of Nazi legality, clearly focus much of their concern on the failure of a reestablished

role of law before, during, and after the 1933–1945 period, it would then require us to radically re-examine our self-image of living in a world of post-
Auschwitz legality. A more interesting and I believe useful perspective than the
ultimately sterile debates between, around and about natural law and legal
positivism, is offered by employing the concept of the "interpretive community" developed by Stanley Fish.[28] Using this concept, one engages not in an
abstract or even contextualized investigation of jurisprudential concepts and
understandings of legal systems, but instead one looks at the self-understanding of defined professional groups. In other words, in this context, one
looks at the ways in which lawyers, judges and other participants in the "interpretive community", law, understood what they were doing between 1933
and 1945. Did they act as if they were still lawyers and judges, within a "legal"
system, albeit a new or revolutionary Nazi legal system? On this question,
there can be little debate.

While there can be little doubt that Nazi ideology placed law in a different
context and gave it a different role to play than it had under Weimar, it is also
true that in its earliest stages at least, Nazi ideology and practice played under
the legal rules then extant under Weimar's legal, constitutional regime. The Nazi
plan in the early 1930s included the concept of coming "legally to power". The
suspension of the civil rights protections and invocation of emergency powers
which allowed for the consolidation of political power in the hands of Hitler,
all occurred under the provisions of Article 48 of the Weimar Constitution
which permitted executive government. Equally, lawyers continued to play a
key role in the development and implementation of laws and decrees after 1933.

It is important to note, again, that this type of analysis is not one which
requires us to accept the justice or morality of what was happening within the
system, nor is it one which requires us to offer moral or ethical approbation
of the acts and actors therein. Rather, what is required is to grasp simply that
the understanding at the time of the participants themselves was that they
were in fact still acting as lawyers, magistrates, police officers and judges. For
them, the law and the legal system continued to operate. In some circumstances, the system may have operated in a different way, a way which was

system of legitimate legality in the Federal Republic to properly account for the responsibility of legal actors under Nazism. For each of them there is a clear and troubling element
of continuity between the personnel of Nazi legality and those operating under the Constitutional rule of law in the Federal Republic.

28. See *Is There A Text in This Class?* (Cambridge: Harvard University Press, 1980);
There Is No Such Thing As Free Speech (New York and Oxford: Oxford University Press,
1994).

more "morally" or "politically" acceptable because it now operated within an overarching "Aryan" or *volkisch* worldview and politics. That we do not understand or accept the morality or ethical validity of this perception or the legalization of this worldview is not, at this point, relevant or analytically useful. Conceived of in this way, from the perspective of the participants in the system, by the members of the "interpretive community", the questions raised by the continuity/discontinuity debate take on a radically different complexion. If the judges and lawyers who had worked under the Weimar Constitution, which can easily be characterized as offering the theoretical framework for a liberal, democratic, rule of law based system, could continue to function under the Nazi legal system, as they always had i.e. as judges and lawyers, then the issue of continuity/discontinuity becomes much more complex.

In such circumstances, it might be possible to object that the complete Nazification of German society meant that lawyers and judges could not function as lawyers and judges, nor could they have objected to the perversion of the rule of law. It is for others to address the underlying question of whether the period 1933 to 1945 was indeed a revolutionary rupture with all that preceded it in German society and history.[29] Insofar as the legal regime is concerned, however, the voluntary nature of the "Nazification" of the legal profession should again be underlined. Lawyers and judges were not compelled at gunpoint, in the middle of the night by the leather-clad Gestapo of Hollywood legend, to convert to the Nazi worldview. Rather, they readily adopted this ideology and adapted to its legal premises. It seems clear that German legal professionals, like their colleagues later in Vichy France, never doubted the legality or legitimacy of a legal system which systematically eliminated their Jewish co-citizens (and others) from state and civil society.[30]

Before turning to an overview of the ways in which Nazi law operated and was perceived, both in Germany and abroad, I begin my analysis with a brief view of the centrality of law as a mechanism for constructing and embodying central and core elements of the Nazi worldview. More particularly, I shall, in a necessarily abbreviated fashion, introduce the argument that the very core

---

29. Although it is important to note that as a matter of international law theory and practice, revolutionary governments and their legal systems are not by definition illegitimate or illegal. As a practical matter, it is equally important to remember that the Hitler regime was recognized internationally by other actors as the legitimate government of Germany.

30. In this, German lawyers were no different from their colleagues in the Anglo-American world who continued to accept the basic legality of the Nazi regime and its substantive measures. See chapter 4 below.

ideas of the Nazi state, the protection of the German *Volksgemeinschaft* and the elimination of its racial enemies, could only be embodied and achieved in and through law.

1. Nazi Law: Embodying and Destroying the Other

Others have written the history of Western antisemitism and I will not repeat their efforts here. Instead I want to emphasize the legality of Western antisemitism. The entire history of the exclusion of the Jews from Christian communities and from Christian states, is written largely in the body of legal regulation. We find rules and limitations in relation to dress, occupational restrictions, residential limitations, *etc.* Vestementary regulations marked the body of the Jew for all to see, from the Yellow Star to the pointed hat, who was and who was not, one of "us". The ghetto and later the Pale of Settlement marked, by lawful decree, the physical boundaries of the body politic and served as a firm border between "them" and "us". The Jew was allowed to do the "dirty work", to lend money, as a legal exception to the legal restriction imposed on ordinary members of the sovereign body of the nation. All of these types of prohibition and regulation resurface in Nazi legality, accompanied both by a firm and well-established history of legal precedent and by a body of myths which bear most importantly on the Jew's body and the body politic. The physical attributes of "the Jew" become inscribed in myth, legend and eventually science and law as the paradigmatic traits of the Other. Antisemitism becomes over time the inscription of the body of the Jew in the body of the law.

The rise of modernity does not completely replace the myths of Christian and *volkisch* antisemitism but simply displaces their metaphoric applications. With industrialization, growing urbanization, the rise of the nation-state and the triumph of a rationalized scientific worldview, in short with modernity and the Enlightenment, the Jew's body is simply re-inscribed, over-determined, in the body of medical and biological theory, and ultimately in racial hygiene and eugenics and thence in codified legal prescriptions. This time the body under Jewish attack becomes the nation—the body politic. Thus,

> The regime's 'national community' was based upon the exclusion and extermination of all those deemed to be 'alien', 'hereditarily ill', or 'asocial'. These 'elements' were subject to constant and escalating forms of selection. The 'national community' itself was categorised in

accordance with racial criteria. The criteria included not merely 'racial purity' but also biological health and socio-economic performance. Members of the 'national community' were also compelled to reproduce through a series of measures ranging from financial inducements to criminal sanctions. The inducements contained in the regime's social legislation were also conditional upon an individual's racial 'value', health, and performance.[31]

The Nazi worldview was a eugenic one, informed by what was for them a scientific ideal of racial purity. The health of the body politic would be promoted through "positive" eugenic measures, while at the same time a set of prophylactic measures, "negative" eugenics, would serve as protection of the *Volksgemeinschaft*. Not surprisingly, the chief enemy of the German body politic was "the Jew".

This re-orientation of the discursive political attachment to antisemitism, to a re-positioning of "the Jew", under the Nazis takes place at the level of several instances of the historical discourses of modernity. At the first stage, we witness the rise of medico-biological discourse which describes "races" in terms of hierarchically ordered attributes and which sees the inferior almost purely in terms of this new internalized self-referential language of racial "science" within modernity.[32] The body politic comes under threat from "parasites", "vermin", "bacillus", even the more "modern" cancer becomes Judeified, as Nazi scientists portray the Jew as a cancer and cancer as a Jewish disease attacking the nation's germ plasm.[33] The Aryan body politic must be immunized against these foreign and dangerous bodies. The chief means for self-preservation come to be found in the newly emergent medico-legal discursive matrix. Public health law becomes the precursor of the Holocaust.

The growth of political antisemitism in Germany, coinciding with the arrival of the new racial science, sees the creation of the most important concept in terms of Aryan-Jewish relations, the *Volksgemeinschaft*. "The Jew" is the unwritten and necessary Other of the *Volk*. The law, coming under Nazi jurisprudence from the inherent wisdom of the *Volk*, must then also come to embody the exclusion of "the Jew".[34]

---

31. Michael Burleigh and Wolfgang Wippermann, *The Racial State: Germany 1933–1945* (Cambridge: Cambridge University Press, 1991) at 305–6.

32. On the central place of the discourses and imagery of science within modernity, see generally, Zygmunt Bauman, *Modernity and the Holocaust*, op. cit.

33. See Robert N. Proctor, *The Nazi War on Cancer* (Princeton and Oxford: Princeton University Press, 2000), at 45–57.

34. See Michael Stolleis, The *Law Under the Swastika*, op. cit.

"*Mein Volk is alles, ich bin nichts*", said Hitler. My nation is everything, I am nothing. Jews are a threat to the *Volk*. Aryan/Germanic blood and soil are under a constant and imminent danger of contamination from this foreign body. Such a threat, against the present and future *Volksgemeinschaft*, can be dealt with by bringing together other bodies, bodies of Aryan knowledge and power, medicine and law.[35] The Nazi *Rechtsstaat* is the protection of the racial state, *Volk, Staat und Rechts*. The merger of medical and legal science in Nazi Germany becomes a logical and natural focus for protective measures against the enemies of the body politic.

The transformation in German law after Hitler came to power in 1933 depended on one fundamental re-writing of the content of the legal system. This re-inscription required the writing in of "the Jew" as a legal subject. The universal, universalized, emancipated "citizen" of Enlightenment philosophy and law had to be replaced by a new hierarchical ordering which would legally create "the Jew" as a new category of juridical import. Once "the Jew" was written into law, s/he could then be written out, legally eliminated as a precursor to the physical elimination which we now call the Holocaust. "The Jew" needed to be created in order to be legally destroyed. This power both of creation and of destruction of a legally embodied subject is, of course, at the very heart and core of sovereignty, itself a concept at the very heart and core of our construction of law.[36] The process of creation and destruction in the name of the sovereign *Volk*, here as legalized antisemitism, began early in the Nazi period, with the adoption of the *Law for the Restoration of the Professional Civil Service* on April 7, 1933.§3 provided that:

> Civil servants who are not of Aryan descent are to be retired; if they are honorary officials, they are to be dismissed from their official status.[37]

The *Law* itself did not, however, actually write the Jew into the new German legal system. It refers only to those members of the civil service who are

---

35. These ideas of embodiment, blood, soil etc. are at the very heart of Nazi philosophy and for Lévinas serve to mark the continuity of Nazism within elements of modernity and the rupture with an ethical ideal of humanity. See Emmanuel Lévinas, "Reflections on the Philosophy of Hitlerism", 17 *Critical Inquiry* 62 (1990), especially at 69.

36. See Michel Foucault, *Discipline and Punish* (New York: Vintage, 1995). More recently, the work of Jean-Luc Nancy has opened up important possibilities for re-imagining the body as the *corpus* for/of justice and conversely then for seeing the destruction of the body, here through law, as the ultimate injustice. See *Corpus* (Paris: Métaillé, 2000), especially at 43 et. seq.

37. The *Law* allowed exceptions to be made for World War I veterans and for survivors of the war dead.

"not of Aryan descent". The First Regulation under the *Law*, passed four days later on April 11, 1933, is the first legal instrument which inscribes the Jews of Germany as members of a new juridical category. It stated:

> A person is to be considered non-Aryan if he is descended from non-Aryan, and especially from Jewish parents or grandparents. It is sufficient if one parent or grandparent is non-Aryan. This is to be assumed in particular where one parent or grandparent was of the Jewish religion.

The legal definition of a non-Aryan or Jew is here, in the early days of the Nazi legal system, much more inclusive than would be the definition adopted two years later under the provisions of the First Regulation to the *Reich Citizenship Law* of November 14, 1935. *The Law for the Protection of German Blood and Honor* then declared:

> Entirely convinced that the purity of German blood is essential to the further existence of the German people, and inspired by the uncompromising determination to safeguard the future of the German nation, the Reichstag has unanimously adopted the following law, which is promulgated herewith:
>
> I.   Marriages between Jews and citizens of German or kindred blood are forbidden.
>
> ...
>
> II.   Sexual relations outside marriage between Jews and nationals of German blood or kindred blood are forbidden.

The *Reich Citizenship Law* provided further clarification:

> I.1. A subject of the state is a person who belongs to the protective union of the German Reich and who therefore has particular obligations towards the Reich.
> II.1. A citizen of the Reich is that subject only who is of German or kindred blood and who, through his conduct, shows that he is both desirous and fit to serve the German people and Reich faithfully.

The *First Regulation* of November 14 defines, in case there was any doubt, Jews as non-citizen (§4). A Jew is further defined as someone who is descended from at least three grandparents who are racially full Jews (§5), or as someone who has two Jewish grandparents if he is a practicing Jew, or if he is married to a Jew, or is the offspring of a Jewish marriage or an extramarital relationship with a Jew (§5(2)) or, finally, if he is of mixed Jewish blood with one or two Jewish grandparents.

The importance of these provisions is clear—Jews are not citizens, nor are they German. German blood must be protected. German blood is to be protected from contamination primarily, at first, at last, through the prohibition of sexual contact between Aryans and Jews. This inscription of the Jew's body in the corpus of German law goes beyond the purely contraceptive and therapeutic protection of the *Volksgemeinschaft* through the proscriptions of various legal provisions. The inscriptions of the Jew's body in juxtaposition to German blood replicates in the biological discourse of the Nazis the same contradiction/dependence of relationship we find in traditional *volkisch* antisemitism. Nowhere do we discover a legal definition of the German or the Aryan. The definitional thrust of the *Law* is all in one direction—the delimiting of the Jew—the not-German. Like the term *Volksgemeinschaft* itself, the legal body of texts giving life to the Aryan body politic does so through a process of definitional exclusion—the Jew is not-German, but the German is even more, the not-Jew. Throughout the history of Nazi Germany, the search for racial purity was undertaken almost entirely in terms of defining the Aryan not positively (although there was a failed biological/eugenic attempt to delimit and propagate Aryan traits) but by demonstrating the absence of Jewish blood/contamination.

The Aryan was always the non-Jew, even as "the Jew" was a non-Aryan. The thousand-year Reich, the policy of *Lebensraum*, the Shoah—all Nazi racial policies were pursued with the goal of achieving a Europe which would be *Judenrein*—free from, purified of, Jews. Yet again, the Reich exists purely in relational terms, "the Jew", even in, or especially by, his/her absence, will be the ultimate defining characteristic of the Nazi *Rechtsstaat*. But, again, this absence of the Jew for the body of the law and from the body of the law could not occur unless and until the Jew was in fact constructed as a legal subject. The Jew of the Nazi State was literally and figuratively, a creation of the law, a juridical fact and fiction. S/he could not be destroyed unless and until s/he existed and s/he could exist only through the operation of the law. More importantly, the immunity for eliminating the newly created legal subject could only operate through and by these very same legal processes and taxonomies.

2. Law and Legitimacy in the Nazi *Rechtsstaat*

This, then, is the difficulty we now face in any attempt to understand law both "before" and "after" Auschwitz. The Nazi state, with its racial/scientific vision of the *Volksgemeinschaft*, at its very core was grounded in an ideal which could be achieved only through the exclusion and elimination of the Jew. This process of excluding and eliminating the foreign cancer from the body politic was from its very inception itself embodied in a series of legal prohibitions and permissions. Both positive and negative eugenics were grounded in law.

> These anti-Semitic laws, and the subsequent decrees on their imple-
> mentation, continue to preoccupy historians. This interest is war-
> ranted, for in addition to shedding light on the *ad hoc* way in which
> the regime legislated, these measures ultimately created a pseudo-legal
> basis for later policies, including mass murder. However, while Hitler
> may have regarded these laws as being the most significant creation
> of his regime, they were not unique. Anti-Semitic legislation was ac-
> companied by other laws and decrees, whose object was the 'racial-
> hygienic improvement' of the 'body of the German nation'.[38]

Thus, as Burleigh and Wippermann, who it should be noted continue to refer unconvincingly to these measures as "pseudo-legal", point out, the entire systems of public hygiene and public health were progressively grounded in a series of measures which included sterilization, castration, internment in concentration camps, euthanasia etc., all embodied in law. The medical professions, public health officials, the judiciary, lawyers, the prison system and the police, all played essential roles in implementing governmental legal policy aimed at protecting and improving the health and safety of the German body politic.

The policies and practices which would lead to the destruction of European Jewry were all made possible through the operation of law. The Shoah was en-abled as the Jew was written in, only to be written out, by and through legal instruments, from the *Law for the Restoration of the Professional Civil Service* to the Nuremberg Laws. The Holocaust was built in and around the bricks and mortar of legal categories and legal arguments. Most importantly here, and for any effort grounded in an attempt to bring into question the bases of the radical discontinuity "criminal state" theory, almost all of the relevant legal actors concerned, i.e. those people who participated in the system as its pro-fessional members, considered that they were in fact, still acting as they al-ways had as judges and lawyers. A brief examination of some of the elements of the Nazi legal system will help to demonstrate this point.

No area of Nazi juridical norms better displays and manifests the continu-ing tensions over the issues of legitimacy and legality than the series of meas-

---

38. Burleigh and Wippermann, op. cit., at pp. 46–47.

ures specifically targeting German Jews. Nazi legality was centrally characterized by the creation of the Jew as legal category, a category whose very existence demanded its members' removal and legalized destruction.[39] But for all
its careful legislative drafting and scientific, eugenic research, the Nazi state
apparatus could still not quite define this legal Other. The problem of *Mischlinge*, the offspring of "mixed" marriages, became one of vital importance
to the bureaucrats of extermination.[40]

The story of Bernhard Loesener, the lawyer who was the Jewish expert (*Ju-
denreferent*) in the Ministry of the Interior, is instructive.[41] Eminent historians have called into question the truthfulness of Loesener's recollections. For
my purposes, however, the "factual" accuracy of his statements is of little relevance. What is essential is the ideological framework in which Loesener seeks
to justify his work as a lawyer with expertise in the "Jewish" question. He presents detailed arguments about the ways in which he opposed the so-called
"Aryan" paragraph of the *Law for the Restoration of the Professional Civil Service* and other measures relating to Jews. For Loesener, the prohibitions imposed on those with one Jewish grandparent were simply too extensive and
covered too many potentially valuable members of society. He fought, using
his legal skills and his position in the Ministry, to limit and draw back on, the
application of these provisions. For him, it was important to act, or to be seen
or believed to have been acting, as a lawyer. He was someone who put his technical skills as a drafter of legal provisions, as an interpreter of laws and regulations, to limit the extent of the application of a prohibition he thought to
be over-extensive. He never questioned, as a matter of principle or law, the
fact that prohibitions on "Jews" were a necessary or good policy idea. He was,
after all, a Nazi. But he was still and always a lawyer. For him there was no
contradiction in this. Instead, he put his legal training and skills to work to
achieve the optimum policy result within the framework of a valid set of legal
measures targeting Jews for exclusion. In other words, he is engaging in what

---

39. As a matter relating to the issue of continuity, it is important to note that the introduction of Nazi anti-Jewish legislation operated as a rupture with existing Weimar legal
norms. It is equally important to note, however, that anti-Jewish measures were part of
pre-existing Weimar political discourse. See Shaul Esh, "Designs for Anti-Jewish Policy in
Germany up to the Nazi Rule", 6 *Yad Vashem Studies* 83 (1967).

40. U. Büttner, "The Persecution of Christian Jewish Families in the Third Reich", 34
Leo Baeck Institute Year Book 267, 1989; J. Noakes, "The Development of Nazi Policy Towards the German Jewish 'Mischlinge' 1933–1945", 34 *Leo Baeck Institute Year Book* 291
(1989).

41. See Karl. A. Schleunes, (ed.), *Legislating the Holocaust* (Boulder, CO and Oxford:
Westview Press, 2001).

Richard Weisberg has described as "the hermeneutic of acceptance".[42] He brings his technical professional skills to bear within a morally repugnant legal context from which morality is expunged. Law is always and only about argument within the context. The context must remain unchallenged. The question is not about the exclusion of "Jews" as an ethical or even as a higher-order constitutional discussion, but about who is or is not a "Jew". Loesener was, or wished to be seen to be, a good lawyer. That he could be one within a legal universe in which "Jews" were excluded and later killed was of little, if any, relevance to his status and continuing professional self-understanding.

Even a cursory examination of the Nazi *Rechtsstaat* on other related matters of law relating to German Jews underlines the fact that lawyers and judges continued to operate largely as they had before. Loesener was the legal rule, not the legal exception.

So-called "Nazi" courts, for example, applied standard legal techniques, rules and worldviews to achieve what Justice Minister Frank called the "encouragement of the racial volkisch community". Their goals may have been aberrant and abhorrent (although the existence of racial and eugenicist worldviews in the legal system of other nations might well belie this point). Their techniques and substantive formulations of legal rules on the other hand were perfectly consistent with much more widely accepted views of the nature and function of law. Some brief examples from the plethora of "Nazi" cases will suffice to properly situate the body of law and the law of the body within a broader juristic context and continuous tradition.

Again, the first and most important antisemitic legislative measure targeting "the Jew" by the Nazi State was the *Law for the Restoration of the Professional Civil Service* in April 1933. While this statute dealt only with racial qualifications for government service, it came to be seen as grounding a much broader notion of the racial ideal of the Nazi *Rechtsstaat*, an ideal which was to be given subsequent formal status in the Nuremberg Laws. In a series of decisions, for example, German courts began to find that divorces or annulments could now be granted on the grounds that one's spouse was "Jewish". The logic of the judicial argument in such cases is quite simple. For the German lawyers making the argument and the members of the judiciary who enshrined the position as a legal rule in their judgments, the *Law for the Restoration of the Professional Civil Service* evidenced, as a principle of public policy, that one's Jewishness was not only a fundamental personal characteristic, but

---

42. "The Hermeneutic of Acceptance and the Discourse of the Grotesque With a Classroom Exercise on Vichy Law", 17 *Cardozo L. R.*1875 (1996).

that it was a characteristic that carried with it quite clear civil impediments. That the *Reichstag* as the ruling body had deemed it necessary to single out "Jewishness" as a negative personal characteristic could then mean that the principle should be carried into other realms, not specifically the subject of legislative edict. A German or more precisely an Aryan, married to a Jew would and indeed should now realize that this characteristic of his/her spouse was such as to go to the very validity of the marriage bond. Divorce or annulment would necessarily become, for a loyal member of the *Volksgemeinschaft*, a necessary step to ensure that all contaminating forces were to be excluded. However, Article 1333 of the *Civil Code* permitted dissolution of a marriage only

> …by a spouse who at the time of its contraction was unaware of personal qualities in the other spouse, qualities that would have prevented a person from entering into the marriage had he had knowledge of the true circumstances and a proper understanding of the nature of marriage.

Legally, then, in all those cases where the spouse's Jewishness was known to his/her partner at the time of marriage, Article 1333 would appear to pose an insurmountable barrier. The Courts were not to be stopped, however. The argument which developed was a simple one. It was only in light of current and evolving scientific and legal standards and knowledge that one could know the true meaning of the personal quality of Jewishness. Accordingly, the passage of the *Law for the Restoration of the Professional Civil Service* marked an important stage in the growth of both legal and general public knowledge about Jewishness and its debilitating attributes. Consequently, the Court could and should give effect to this new degree of awareness by finding as a matter of law that had the true nature, rather than the simple fact, of the spouse's Jewishness been known at the time, the complaining partner would never have entered into the marriage. In other words, knowledge that the spouse was Jewish at the time of marriage did not, as a matter of law, include knowledge of what the true impact of that Jewishness really was. Such knowledge could only be said to have arisen once the true character of the *Volksgemeinschaft* emerged in legislation following the Nazi rise to power.

Some have called such decisions "perversions of justice". For them, German judges simply engaged in a Nazified *post hoc propter hoc* appearance of legal reasoning. It seems clear, however, that while the underlying epistemological, ontological and deontological assumptions behind these decisions are offensive and immoral, the techniques and reasoning which the courts employed here are perfectly consistent with legal thinking in the civil law tradition. To find in legislative enactments general principles of public policy, to argue that literal interpretations of the *Civil Code* are to be replaced with a method of teleological reasoning in the light of general scientific or specific legislative public policy propositions, these are not perversions. Instead they are techniques of judicial law-making which, in other contexts, are considered to be highly desirable and progressive.[43] In the context of Nazi Germany, it was not, in fact the law which was "perverted" but the underlying social and political assumptions informing the legal process.[44] There can be little doubt that as Saul Friedländer wrote:

> The Civil Service Law was the only one of these to be implemented at this early stage, but the symbolic statements they expressed and the ideological message they carried were unmistakable.[45]

It can hardly be surprising, then, that German judges and lawyers, who saw it as their duty to protect, defend and promote the new vision of the nation, to defend the body politic against foreign germ plasm, should, in considering the appropriateness and legality of a marriage involving Aryan and Jewish blood stock, have adopted recognizable interpretive techniques and adapted them to their new teleology.

The example of the judicial re-writing of the epistemological and hence legal character of Jewishness in marital annulment cases is but one of many. The legal history of Germany from 1933–1945 is full of legal decisions, regulations, memoranda, all of which operate in a lifeworld in which the participants continued to consider themselves to be acting as lawyers. Another issue which later vexed the legal world was that of the proper judicial construction of the concept of "sexual intercourse". The *Law for the Protection of German Blood and Honor* provided in §2 that:

> Extramarital intercourse between Jews and subjects of the state of German or related blood is forbidden.

---

43. See e.g. François Gény, *Methode d' Interprétation et Sources en Droit Privé Positif* (Baton Rouge: Louisiana Law Institute, 1963).

44. For a nuanced and careful jurisprudential analysis of the broader consequences of such a view, see Allan H. Hutchinson, *It's All in the Game*, op. cit.

45. *Nazi Germany and the Jews, Vol. 1* (New York: HarperCollins, 1997), at 33. See also Raul Hilberg, "Physicians and Lawyers", in *Perpetrators, Victims, Bystanders* (New York: Harper, 1993), at 65–74.

The problem which arose was how far to extend the meaning of "intercourse" to acts which did not include coition. The Supreme Court held that:

> The term "sexual intercourse" as meant by the Law for the Protection of German Blood does not include every obscene act, but it is also not limited to coition. It includes all forms of natural and unnatural sexual intercourse—that is, coition as well as those sexual activities with the person of the opposite sex which are designed, in the manner in which they are performed, to serve in place of coition to satisfy the sex drive of at least one of the partners.[46]

The definition was extended to include such "unnatural acts" as kisses by an impotent man and therapeutic massage. Again, while some might see these decisions as "perversions" of the rule of law, two points must be considered. First, as already pointed out, the interpretive technique employed here is not perverse in the very real sense that it was and still is employed in other contexts to perfectly acceptable effect. The idea that literal meaning is or can be attributed to legislative intent is but one view of judicial interpretation, and perhaps today a minority one. Second, the idea of judicial interpretation of such concepts as "intercourse" by relying on vague and unspecific concepts as the "public interest", or in this case "German Blood and Honor" is not, by definition, completely foreign to the judicial enterprise today. Anyone who, for example, has read judicial decisions defining the "circumstances of indecency" which must accompany an assault to transform it into an "indecent assault", will recognize the interpretive technique at work here. Those familiar judicial machinations in various jurisdictions concerning the meaning of a "public" place in relation to so-called public morals offences, will find that the judicial techniques employed by the "Nazi judges" in these cases fit quite easily into the world of judicial decision-making in rule of law democracies.

The reliance on such vague, ill-defined, general provisions such as "in the public interest" and the delegation of responsibility to specialized tribunals have been criticized by some as an affront to the rule of law which is seen to require certainty and a full judicial process. This is the basis of William Scheuerman's critique of Carl Schmitt and of the Frankfurt School's reliance on his work for their critique of bourgeois law.[47] For Scheuerman, the danger for progressive forces lies precisely in this "soft" law and dispersed form of authority which he finds at the heart of the Schmittian, and therefore the Nazi,

---

46. Ibid., at 159, footnote omitted. See also Müller, op. cit., at 98–111.
47. *The Rule of Law Under Siege*, op. cit.

judicial imperative. Yet vague concepts such as the public interest and the delegation of decision-making authority to non- or quasi-judicial bodies characterize much of the post-War western welfare state. For proponents of "informal justice" and the flexible delivery of necessary public services, such mechanisms are seen to be more just to the extent that reliance on the rigid formalism of judicial proceedings is replaced by a more flexible, informal, socially aware process. Scheuerman recognizes this but is in the end unmoved from his critique which he attempts to complexify by introducing a combination of a Dworkinian distinction between policy and principle[48] and a Habermasian fealty to a process-based constitutional communicative *grundnorm*.[49] In the end, such critiques founder in theory, in history and in present day reality. Ultimately, the fact that adjudication is politicized and indeterminate has no real impact on the underlying strength or otherwise of democracy and the rule of law.[50] Scheuerman's argument that the absence of a particular set of rigid definitions in a legal instrument leads to the absence of the rule of law places a naïve and unsupportable faith in the literalness of language and of truth. He asserts an ideal of the rule of law which is untenable.

In the end, whatever one makes of such jurisprudential debates, the existential and phenomenological point remains unchanged.[51] The self-referential understanding of those involved in the system and decision-making processes of Nazi law did not, in essence, undergo a revolutionary change in 1933. German lawyers and judges continued to see themselves as operating as lawyers and judges. As important as this is the fact that we today can still see that the interpretive techniques applied in these "Jewish" cases are the same techniques which in other circumstances we would also wish to see applied. The debate here then must be refocused from a simple rejection of Nazi

---

48. For a critique of this see, David Fraser, "Truth and Hierarchy: Will the Circle be Unbroken?", 33 *Buffalo Law Review* 729 (1984).

49. For a critique, see David Fraser, "The Day the Music Died: The Civil Law Tradition from a Critical Legal Studies Perspective", 34 *Loyola Law Review* 861 (1987).

50. For a much more nuanced and persuasive analysis of these points see, Duncan Kennedy, *A Critique of Adjudication (fin de siècle)* (Cambridge: Harvard University Press, 1997).

51. Historically, it is also important to note that ideas of the very flexibility of some Nazi legal bodies was an element which was praised by American legal scholars See e.g., Nathan Albert Pelcovits, "The Social Honor Courts of Nazi Germany", 53 *Political Science Quarterly* 350 (1938). Compare Harlow J. Heneman, "German Social Honor Courts", 37 *Michigan Law Review* 725 (1939). For the reception of Nazi law in the United States more generally, see below, chapter 4.

law as "not law" to a different set of questions about law and justice, good and evil. The real focus, one with which lawyers seem to be extremely uncomfortable, should be on the "politics of law" i.e. on the substantive normative content of laws and on the preferred outcome of judicial interpretation. The question of Nazi law is not, I believe a question of "not law" versus law but rather what we should, can and must do when confronted with legalized evil.

Other examples from the world of Nazi law could be analyzed in detail here to give more evidence of the continuity between Nazi law and law under Weimar as well as between Nazi law and law after Auschwitz. I will mention only three. The most important of these is the practice of compulsory sterilization of those suffering from "hereditary disease." On July 14, 1933, the Nazis brought into force the *Law for the Prevention of Hereditarily Diseased Offspring*. Two aspects of this legislation and its enforcement are important. First, similar statutes existed and continued to exist in many countries which were not governed by "Nazi law" and which we consider exemplars of the system of the "rule of law".[52] In other words, the legislation which many see as the first, almost inevitable and inexorable step to the euthanasia program and then to the mass extermination of the Shoah, was not in any really significant way different from the regime in other countries.[53] Secondly, it is important to note that the system of compulsory eugenic sterilization was in fact "lawful". The process was filled with formal, technical requirements, rights to representation, rights to appeal etc. The scheme was designed by lawyers who appeared before the special courts and lodged (sometimes successful) appeals to the special appellate jurisdiction established under the regime. There is little if anything to distinguish the quasi-judicial system established under Nazi law from any number of schemes extant and functioning today in Western democracies.

In a similar fashion, the system of policing which is now portrayed as the most perfect embodiment of the Nazi state as "criminal state" can, in fact, be constructed and understood as continuous with the system of policing under

---

52. See below, chapters 4 and 11.

53. A full discussion of the complexities of these issues is beyond the scope of this presentation. For more detailed discussion of the ideology and legality of the system, see Michael Burleigh and Wolfgang Wippermann, *The Racial State: Germany 1933–1945*, op. cit. Michael Burleigh, *Death and Deliverance: 'Euthanasia' in Germany 1900–1945* (New York and Cambridge: Cambridge University Press, 1994); Henry Friedlander, *The Origins of Nazi Genocide: From Euthanasia to the Final Solution* (Chapel Hill: University of North Carolina Press, 1995); James M. Glass, *"Life Unworthy of Life": Racial Phobia and Mass Murder in Hitler's Germany* (New York: Basic Books, 1997).

Weimar.[54] The idea of a specially created criminal police, the Gestapo, leather-clad thugs knocking down the doors of a completely terrorized civilian populace, is again one which resonates with our popularly constructed notion of the basic criminality of the Nazi state. However, more careful study of the history of German policing demonstrates that the Gestapo is clearly part of the historical continuity not just with German police practices but also with the police practices in other European countries. Political police units, acting as counter-subversive forces, were an essential part of European[55] and German police forces long before their function was centralized under the Gestapo in Germany.[56] As in the cases of the legal profession and the judiciary, the discontinuity which some see as central to our understanding of Nazi law, did not manifest itself in such terms to the individuals actually involved in the operation of the system.

> The transformation from the old decentralized political police forces across the individual German states did not require a widespread cleansing of the ranks or purge of the old political police. In a word, the police became Nazis or at least adjusted to Nazi conceptions of the police; there was no wholesale expulsion of the old custodians in favour of Nazi party members....[57]

Studies of other specialized police forces, for example individuals responsible for Weimar- and Nazi-era actions relating to Gypsy (Roma and Sinti) questions, confirm the continuity of these repressive structures which would become central to the enforcement of racial laws and decrees. In other words,

54. See George C. Browder, *Foundations of the Nazi Police State: The Formation of SIPO and SD* (Lexington: University Press of Kentucky, 1990); Robert Gellately, *The Gestapo and German Society: Enforcing Racial Policy 1933–1945* (New York and Oxford: Clarendon, 1990); Ted Harrison, "Political Police and Lawyers in Hitler's Germany", 10 *German History* 226 (1992). *Cf.* Eric A. Johnson, *Nazi Terror: The Gestapo, Jews and Ordinary Germans*, op. cit.

55. See e.g. Maurice Rajfus, *La Police de Vichy: Les forces de l'ordre françaises au service de la Gestapo, 1940/1944*, (Paris: le cherche midi, 1995); see also Jean-Marc Berlière and Laurent Chabrun, *Les Policiers français sous l'Occupation, d'après les archives inédits de l'épuration*, (Paris: Perrin, 2001); Bob Moore, *Victims & Survivors: The Nazi Persecution of the Jews in the Netherlands 1940–1945* (New York and London: Arnold, 1997). See generally Mark Mazower (ed.), *Policing of Politics in the Twentieth Century*, (Pittsburgh: Duquesne University Press, 1996).

56. Likewise, the creation of specialized courts to deal with political offences was also part of the European and Weimar legacy. See H.W. Koch, *In the Name of the Volk: Political Justice in Hitler's Germany* (London: I. B. Tauris, 1989), at ix–18.

57. Gellateley, *The Gestapo and German Society*, op. cit., at 253.

the idea of the Nazi terror regime, of the "criminal state" operating as a radical caesura with Republican and democratic legality, is simply not true.[58] The policing structure of the Nazi state finds its precursors in a long history of European and German practice, the personnel remain unchanged, and the police, like judges and lawyers, still see themselves as police. For those charged with surveillance of Roma in Germany, there was little remarkable difference between Weimar and Nazi policing and in many parts of Europe today, one would be hard pressed to find a discernable difference in police practice in this area. While the Nazis re-organized most aspects of the structure of police forces in Germany through a practice and policy of centralization, the daily activities of the vast majority of police forces remained remarkably unchanged.

Other aspects of the repressive apparatus of criminal state policing after 1933 also indicate elements of continuity both before Auschwitz and after Auschwitz. The two groups which were singled out for specific attention for crimes against the blood purity of the *Volksgemeinschaft* under the Nazis were the Sinti and Roma (the Gypsies)[59] and gay men.[60] In each case, Nazi policing and persecution of these groups built on already established police units and bureaucratic filing and record systems from the Weimar period. Vice squads targeted homosexuals under Article 175 of the *Criminal Code* and Gypsies were subjected to surveillance and imprisonment as vagabonds and "asocials". In each case, the Nazis simply continued and deepened existing police structures and practices. In each case, the fact of continuity with Weimar criminalization of each group meant that in the time after Auschwitz, gay men and Gypsies encountered and continue to encounter numerous difficulties in gaining compensation for their suffering under the "criminal state". Because the Nazis simply supplemented Article 175, homosexuals could be and were

---

58. See the recent work of Michael Zimmermann, 'The National Socialist "Solution of the Gypsy Question": Central Decisions, Local Initiatives, and Their Interrelation', 15 *Holocaust & Genocide Studies* 412 (2001).

59. See Burleigh and Wippermann, op. cit., at 113–35.

60. See Richard Plant. *The Pink Triangle: The Nazi War Against Homosexuals* (New York: Henry Holt, 1986); Günter Grau (ed.), *Hidden Holocaust?* (New York and London: Cassell, 1995); Ruediger Lautmann, "Gay Prisoners in Concentration Camps as Compared with Jehovah's Witnesses and Political Prisoners", in Michael Berenbaum (ed.), *A Mosaic of Victims: Non-Jews Persecuted and Murdered by the Nazis* (New York and London: I. B. Tauris, 1990); "The Pink Triangle: The Persecution of Homosexual Males in Concentration Camps in Nazi Germany", 6 *Journal of Homosexuality* 141 (1981). For more recent studies of the continuities between Nazi police practice and ideology and the historical construction of outsiders in Germany, see Robert Gellately and Nathan Stoltzfus (eds.), *Social Outsiders in Nazi Germany* (Princeton: Princeton University Press, 2001).

constructed not as "victims of National Socialism" but as common criminals, imprisoned for committing pre-existing criminal offences.[61] Similarly, because to a greater or lesser extent, Gypsies fell under the criminalized category of "asocials", they too could be and were constructed as common criminals, rather than as victims of Nazi racial persecution.

It should not come as a great surprise that law after Auschwitz should validate Nazi criminalization of gay men and Gypsies. Homosexual intercourse remained a criminal offence in Germany until well after the end of the Second World War. It was until very recently an offence in several states in the United States. The continuing criminalization[62] and persecution of Gypsy populations is common throughout Europe.[63] This does not mean that the United States and western Europe today are just like Nazi Germany in the 1930s. Claims that Nazi law was not law because it singled out specific groups and members of those groups for criminalization and exclusion on the basis of a theory of racial inferiority and/or in order to protect the physical and social well-being of the body politic from outsiders, however, simply can not stand up to critical examination.

Other aspects of criminal law and policing under the Nazis strengthen the continuity thesis. The compilation of police files and systems of citizen registration, while perhaps foreign to American or British sensibilities, were an ordinary part of police life in Europe and in Germany.[64] Similarly, careful study of Gestapo files does not indicate that the populace were hostile to or terrified of a foreign police force imposed on them. Rather the documentary evidence tends to show that large elements of the population in Germany actively participated in the "criminal state" by informing on their fellow citizens. They did so sometimes out of ideological loyalty but more often as a utilitarian tool for the settling of private grudges or obtaining personal advantage or revenge for some slight.

I have already argued that the disculpation of the mass of German citizens was a central goal and aspect of the "criminal state" position. The majority of

61. On the legal issue of what to do with Article 175 and its application and interpretation 1933–1945, see Stolleis, op. cit., at 181.

62. See e.g. Helen O'Nions, The Marginalisation of Gypsies, 3 *Web Journal of Current Legal Issues* (1995) and Gilad Margalit, *Antigypsyism in the Political Culture of the Federal Republic of Germany: A Parallel with Antisemitism* (Jerusalem: Vidal Sassoon International Center for the Study of Antisemitism, 1996).

63. See David Fraser, "To Belong or Not to Belong: The Roma, State Violence and the New Europe in the House of Lords", 21 *Legal Studies* 569 (2001).

64. See René Rémond (ed.), Le "Fichier Juif" (Paris: Plon, 1996); Robert M. W. Kempner, "The German National Registration System as Means of Police Control of Population", 36 *Journal of Criminal Law and Criminology* 362 (1945–1946).

Germans were not Nazis, they did not share the regime's goals and if they participated in objectionable practices from 1933–1945, they did so only because of the omnipresent threat of the Gestapo and the concentration camp system. As Gellately puts it:

> The question of motives aside, denunciations from the population were the key link in the three-way interaction between the police, people, and policy in Nazi Germany. Popular participation by provision of information was one of the most important factors in making the terror system work. That conclusion suggests rethinking the notion of the Gestapo as an 'instrument of domination': if it was an instrument it was one which was constructed within German society and whose functioning was structurally dependent on the continuing cooperation of German citizens.[65]

He later added

> The conclusion is inescapable—without the active collaboration of the general population it would have been next to impossible for the Gestapo to enforce these kinds of racial policies.[66]

What is important here is the idea that the Gestapo was to a great extent dependent on information received from ordinary Germans for its success in implementing Nazi policy. This quite clearly undermines the terror from above thesis upon which the "criminal state" and radical rupture theories of Nazi law are based. Like the police in today's democracy, crime prevention and detection in Germany between 1933–1945 were based largely on "information received" from the general German public. Gellately also demonstrates that this information was not passed on and received because of a widespread fear of the terror apparatus, but for a complex variety of motives and reasons. Most importantly, he establishes that in so far as anti-Jewish measures were concerned, the majority of Germans seem to have given their consent and approval to police actions in this domain. Writing about the evidence in Gestapo files of reactions against anti-Jewish measures he says:

> …given the vigilance of the volunteer denouncers and attentiveness of the Gestapo, it would seem fair to conclude that the relative paucity of negative remarks aimed at the regime's antisemitism is an indication of the extent to which citizens accommodated themselves to the

---

65. *The Gestapo and German Society*, op. cit., at 136 (footnote omitted).
66. *Backing Hitler* (Oxford and New York: Oxford University Press, 2001, at 135.

official line, and to all intents and purposes, did not stand in the way of the persecution of the Jews.[67]

The French Republican government set up concentration camps to hold Spaniards and others fleeing fascism under Franco.[68] Americans had established similar systems of control in Cuba at the turn of the 20th century, as had the British in South Africa. Mass imprisonment of political enemies was not without precedent when the Nazis came to power. Other studies indicate that while the concentration camp system in Germany eventually became an instrument of unrelenting terror, the criminal confinement system in Germany was not, in the early days at least, homogenous or hegemonic.[69] The centralization of police power and the prime authority of the SS in the implementation of the Nazi legal worldview of bio-politics would have consequences which are tragically well-known to us now. At the same time, we must always bear in mind the even more frightening fact that the power of the police state was a power which emerged from law, and from lawful precedent in other jurisdictions.

A contextualized understanding of the instrumental and jurisprudential origins of the legal regime of Nazi Germany, allows us to see that it was always as "German" as it was "Nazi". It was also always legal, grounded in preexisting practices and structures. It can then come as no surprise that the Wannsee Conference at which the plans for the "Final Solution" were discussed and the bureaucracy of death was first put into place should in fact have been scheduled at the Interpol headquarters. The security police apparatus was given primary responsibility. The Holocaust was the legalized killing, by the police, of a criminalized outlaw group of public enemies. At every stage along the way, this exclusion of "the Jew" was confirmed by and established within, a legal and lawful framework and bureaucratic edifice.

Again the point here is not to offer a detailed examination of Nazi racial policies. Nor is it to enter into studies of comparative victimhood. Nor finally is it to offer an apologia for the horrors of the Nazi regime. Rather it is to make what I think is a simple point but also a point which has been obscured in our collective rush to save ourselves from a careful examination of law after Auschwitz. That point is that Nazi law was, whether we like it or not, law. No

---

67. At 206.

68. Not to mention the forced removal of Americans and Canadians of Japanese heritage in those countries.

69. See Wolfgang Sofsky, *The Order of Terror: The Concentration Camp* (Princeton: Princeton University Press, 1996).

amount of debating natural law and positivism or legality and legitimacy will relieve us of the awful ethical responsibility which flows from this fact.

Law and lawyers under the Nazis continued to operate on the assumption of the vital importance of "the Jew" and the Jew's body to the *Volksgemeinschaft*. This legalized antisemitism continued as the Nazi regime began its seemingly inexorable path to the medico-legal extermination of the Jewish people. It must always be borne in mind, and underlined at this point, that the Holocaust was not, as many would have it, a law-less barbarism. It was, on the contrary, a law-ful barbarism. In other words, the Holocaust occurred not as a mindless series of actions without rules or limiting bounds but rather within a framework of legal, scientific, rule-making. The problem which faces us when we confront the horror and terror of 1933–1945 is this fact of historical, philosophical and legal continuity of this period both with its predecessors and with its successors. Legal memory after Auschwitz is always inscribed with law before Auschwitz.

The primary legal-ideological function of post-Auschwitz juristic events involving the prosecution of Nazi war criminals has been, I believe, to convince us instead of the discontinuity, the radical break of 1933–1945. Once that epistemological step has been accomplished, law can then assure us of a return to the safety of modernity, of the primacy of the rule of law. But the epistemological certainty of such legal spectaculars is undermined not just by internal critiques of the legality and justice of such events, but by a more fundamental unveiling and unrobing of the rule of law by the legal actors themselves. "Nazi lawyers" and "Nazi judges" were always "lawyers" and "judges". Some were more "Nazi" than others but like Bernhard Loesener, they continued to operate within a world of professional self-understanding which confirmed their professional status and function. They were the "desk killers", the bureaucrats who signed the orders, drafted the regulations, read and circulated the memoranda about "the Jewish question". Aryan landlords should be permitted to breach their contracts with Jewish tenants within the law. Should Jews be allowed to testify in criminal proceedings? What weight if any could be given to their testimony? Jewish property was transferred according to the due form of law. The "hermeneutic of acceptance" was the daily reality of German judges and lawyers. Nazi law was for them, always law.

As lawyers today, however, we should also remember, by way of example only, Einsatzgruppe A which worked its way through the northeastern areas of the former Soviet Union in the course of Operation Barbarossa, killing hundreds of thousands of people. Of the 17 group leaders of Einsatzgruppe A, 11 were lawyers. Nine of the eleven had doctorates in law. Let us also remember the members of Reserve Police Battalion 101, ordinary men[70] or ordinary Germans[71], but always ordinary policemen, who found the mass execution of Jews to be an ordinary part of ordinary police work. The mythology of law after Auschwitz, and of our collective legal memory of the Holocaust, is grounded in the ideal of the period of Nazi rule, 1933–1945, as a lawless time of the barbarians. The Nuremberg Trials and their offspring, debates about natural law and legitimacy, about constitutional citizenship, are meant to legitimize the modern, civilized, rule of law by defining the Nazi period as not—not modern, not civilized, not the rule of law. Here we come to the crux of the issue of law before Auschwitz and of the law after Auschwitz. As I shall try to demonstrate, the problem of law after Auschwitz is grounded in a philosophical, ideological and legal misunderstanding of this nature and function of law before Auschwitz.

---

70. Christopher Browning, *Ordinary Men: Reserve Police Battalion 101 and the Final Solution in Poland* (New York: HarperCollins, 1992).

71. Daniel J. Goldhagen, *Hitler's Willing Executioners: Ordinary Germans and the Holocaust* (New York: Knopf, 1996).

CHAPTER 3

DEAD MAN WALKING: LAW AND ETHICS AFTER AUSCHWITZ

1. Introduction

God, or more precisely G-d, is in some religious traditions the unrepresentable and the unspeakable. The unrepresentable absolute can only ever be incompletely written or spoken by way of a name which can never fully name. In what some might prefer to call more secular fields of collective memory, Auschwitz has become the unspeakable, *l'indicible*. The semiotic, political irony and tragedy of this juxtaposition in the writing of the unspeakable is, in addition to the always irreparable gap between signifier and signified, the place of death and absence which arises out of the smoke and ashes of Auschwitz and our attempts to come to grips with the past and present of the horror. For some, God died at Auschwitz, or in another variant of the thanato-theological consequentialism of Nazism, Auschwitz is proof that there is no God. At the same time, a horrible legal logic might conclude that if G-d is the unspeakable name, and Auschwitz is *l' indicible*, then Auschwitz may be G-d, and God is Auschwitz.[1]

Such semiotico-theological concerns are at a basic level beyond the scope of my work here, although the significance of the interrogation of the signifying chain Auschwitz/G-d clearly underlies much of what follows. Instead,

---

1. See Dan Cohn-Sherbok, *Holocaust Theology* (London: Lamp Press, 1989) and Richard L. Rubenstein and John K. Roth, *Approaches to Auschwitz: The Holocaust and its Legacy* (Atlanta: John Knox Press, 1987) for the presentation of various theological perspectives. On law, God and Auschwitz, see, Alexander Garcia Düttmann, *The Gift of Language* (London: Athlone, 2000) and *The Memory of Thought* (London: Athlone, 2001).

my concern is with the more human element of the semiotics of Auschwitz, and more specifically with the issues of law and ethics of and after Auschwitz.

In a series of recent interventions, the Italian philosopher Giorgio Agamben has constructed a particular and important set of ethical assertions concerning the place and role of Nazism and "the camp" in our modern ethical understanding of politics.[2] More particularly, he offers an intriguing reading of the idea of the ethical status of the witness and of testimony in relation to Auschwitz. It is no accident, I believe, that Agamben started out his intellectual career as a law student or that he abandoned law for philosophy. In the sections which follow, I shall briefly sketch the most important and unnerving aspects of Agamben's writings on the subject of ethics after Auschwitz and offer a sympathetic critique of his apparent undervaluing of the necessary place of law, in some of his work, in the project of constructing ethics at and after Auschwitz. Agamben offers here, by repositioning our understanding of the body and bodies of the law, a new way of witnessing the lawfulness of Auschwitz.

One of the dangers inherent in writing about Auschwitz and the Holocaust is precisely that which underlies the claim that Auschwitz is in fact the unspeakable and unrepresentable culmination of hatred, horror and death. In such circumstances, any attempt to write Auschwitz dishonors the victims and the indescribable suffering which was Auschwitz. One should then, speak and write, if one is able to do so at all, only of "Auschwitz", a sign written under an ethically imposed erasure, the very construction of which represents its own self-conscious inability to represent. At some point here, where Auschwitz becomes "Auschwitz", philosophy and history (and law) confront the postmodern dilemma of the loss of faith in metanarratives, of the absence of a basis of truth. What can be remembered and memorialized, if there is no foundation for truth? The foundation of Agamben's project, I believe, lies precisely in this gap, this *trace*, the remainder (*reste*), of Auschwitz. It is an ethically compelling, if not entirely convincing, attempt to construct an ethical project of memory in which memory is constructed as a forgetting of itself. It is a complex effort to write and remember a time and place which is at once Auschwitz and "Auschwitz."[3]

But Agamben, if he is to succeed, must also confront another idea, seemingly opposed to the unspeakable nature of Auschwitz. Here, Auschwitz was and is a lawful place, a space full of law. This might seem logically and ethi-

---

2. For another important discussion of the political and ethical importance of the camp within modernity, especially concerning issues of race, nation and identity, see Paul Gilroy, *Between Camps*, op. cit., at 81–96.

3. See Giorgio Agamben, "Tradition of the Immemorial", in *Potentialities: Collected Essays in Philosophy* (Stanford, Stanford University Press, 1999), at pp. 104–15.

cally to offend the idea of the unarticuable remainder. Law is a masterful discourse, one which dominates, colonizes, and commits countless acts of violence in the very act and fact of its presence.[4] Thus, a discussion of the legal ethics of Auschwitz might be seen to start from a position which is structurally and inevitably unethical. Nonetheless, I shall argue in what follows that it is this unspeakable, the *l'indicible*, which serves to indict both law and Auschwitz in any ethical project today. It is also this lawfulness of Auschwitz which must be read to underlie and inform Agamben's attempt to construct a vision of justice before and after Auschwitz.

The semiotic barriers to a legal construction of "Auschwitz", or Auschwitz or of the Holocaust stop either at the point of '*l'indicible*' or at the trace of justice which might be found within the lawfulness of the camp. There is of course the already well-known problem of the periodization of "after Auschwitz".[5] Law "after Auschwitz" draws a line of demarcation through a horror, it inscribes the time 1933–1945 as outside law, both before and after "Auschwitz". To speak and write of post-Holocaust law and/or ethics marks us as separate, as legally empowered subjects for whom the Holocaust is history and more importantly, it inscribes the destruction which is Auschwitz as not legal history. This is, of course, the philosophical variant of the broader phenomenon and strategy which seeks to construct a memory of Nazi law as not law with which I attempt to deal throughout this work. This periodization of law before and after Auschwitz is the temporal barrier which seeks to prevent what I believe is the essential character of the Holocaust more generally from emerging from the myths of post-war jurisprudence

The very presence of a signifier which fails to signify, of a time which is not appropriately temporalized, of an obligation to speak of the unspeakable, all present semiological barriers to the presentation of a philosophy or ethics of Auschwitz. To further complicate our attempts to account, the very assertion that Auschwitz is in fact and must remain "Auschwitz", itself inscribes a legal and ethical prohibition within and outside the law. If "Auschwitz" is unrepresentable, unspeakable, *l'indicible*, the very embodiment of that which can never be understood or embodied, it imposes a silence which conflicts with the obligation to memory and testimony which compels and informs any ethical project. If the extermination is, in Lacanian terms, a rupture in the signifying chain, the *non lieu* of memory,[6] then there is, legally, a *non-lieu*, no

---

4. Jacques Derrida, 'Force of law', op. cit.

5. Jean-François Lyotard, *Heidegger and "the jews"*, op. cit.

6. Jacques Hassoun, Mireille Nathan-Murat and Annie Radzynski, *Non Lieu de la Mémoire: La cassure d'Auschwitz* (Paris: Bibliophane, 1990).

grounds on which to prosecute, no true bill, no legal or lawful positioning for the place of Auschwitz, or more certainly of "Auschwitz". Finally, of course, there must always remain the possibility that "Auschwitz" and certainly Auschwitz itself operates a legally prohibitive, historical semiotic function, as "industrialized" killing replaces starvation, horror, suicide, killing squads etc., as the only memorial site and signifier for the many ways and places of dying in Hitler's Europe.

In fact, this is a major dilemma which confronts Agamben in one of his recent interventions in what appears to be a broader project of coming to terms with the ethical *aporia* of Auschwitz.[7] This scheme, in which he specifically rejects the applicability of legal norms and understandings in relation to the function and role of the witness and of testimony, is one which is nonetheless self-consciously juridical in scope and nature. In fact, one of Agamben's self-proclaimed goals for his inquiry is to engage in a kind of legal semiotic policing exercise. He wants to see to it that the very words we use to describe and understand the political and ethical significance of the Nazi process of extermination are re-inscribed, banned, their meaning changed. He writes that his aim as the author will be satisfied if

> ...the book succeeds only in correcting some of the terms with which we register the decisive lesson of the century and if this book makes it possible for certain words to be left behind and others to be understood in a different sense.[8]

The authorial project is one of linguistic ordering, of authority, of a significant and signifying change commanded by ethical obligation and by Auschwitz, but not by "Auschwitz". Agamben refuses the strategy of writing the time and place of the horror and terror he wishes to confront and to understand as if it were unrepresentable. Instead he opts for another linguistic control strategy, under which he refuses the terms Holocaust and Shoah because they tend for him to confer mystical prestige on the brutal reality of the process of extermination.[9] Thus, for Agamben, Auschwitz is not a place of mystery or of theology. The question of God or G-d, is not one with which

---

7. *Ce qui reste d'Auschwitz* (Paris: Rivages, 1999); *Remnants of Auschwitz* (New York: Zone Books, 1999). But cf., Phillipe Mesnard, Claudine Kahan, *Giorgio Agamben à l'épreuve d'Auschwitz* (Paris, Editions Kimé, 2002).

8. *Remnants of Auschwitz*, at 14.

9. Id., at 34–39. There is however no discussion of the theologically charged, but less common, Hebrew, *churban*.

he is concerned because for him, the camp is the place and time where biology and politics come together in the apotheosis of Foucauldian bio-power,[10] the place where the sacred man, *homo sacer*, may, must, be killed but cannot be sacrificed. Auschwitz is the paradigm camp, it is a political space from which God is absent, and where the sacred, *homo sacer*, is re-inscribed in and through the mass of corpses. This must be the ethical and political project for Agamben, to construct a language capable of capturing the horror of extermination without sanctifying the process. To re-humanize the dehumanization of the Nazi camp regime, and to rewrite the sacred nature of destruction, without G-d, and perhaps even without Law.

Yet it also important to note that despite his protestations about the politics of language in so far as the Holocaust is concerned, Agamben is acutely aware of the juridico-theological nature of the time and space which he studies. Auschwitz is and was a camp, and the camp is for Agamben a space opened up and made possible only by the very nature of the law.[11] I believe that Agamben's ethics is always informed by the dilemma which must underlie all our efforts to construct a jurisprudence of the Holocaust. If Auschwitz is a lawful place, then where and how can we begin to articulate an ethico-political project where justice can be found "after Auschwitz"?

Again, the endeavor upon which Agamben sets out comes across significant and signifying hurdles. In addition to the problem of language and the gap left in language by the experience of terror, Agamben also must face, as must I in writing here, about Agamben's writing about Auschwitz and the law, the gap left in translation. Agamben writes in Italian, about the polyglot experience of the inmates of Auschwitz, drawn from all parts of Europe by the Nazi killing machine. He writes in Italian about the testimony of the survivors of Auschwitz and about the ethical status of the witness, a witness who speaks of the unspeakable in several languages because s/he is not a witness, but several witnesses. Here translation and identification may well play a role of betrayal, of ethical over-inclusiveness in the way in which the witness is constructed as bearer of truth. Since Agamben's project is a self-proclaimed exercise in linguistic re-ordering, this ethical betrayal in translation may result in the imposition of a judgment, a juridical maneuver, which is itself unjust. The laws of translation and the translation of the lawful experience of Auschwitz may lead Agamben to an *aporia* of justice.

---

10. *Homo Sacer: Sovereign Power and Bare Life* (Stanford: Stanford University Press, 1998).

11. See Giorgio Agamben, *Le temps qui reste*, op. cit., especially at 168.

The eminent French historian Annette Wieviorka carefully outlines the problem of language and the concept of testimony in relation to the events which Agamben refuses to name the Holocaust.[12] If a witness is to be believed, let alone understood, language is the only medium through which the testimony can be transmitted. Witnesses, survivors, in the multi-lingual world of Auschwitz, nonetheless experienced this universe in their own languages, Yiddish, Polish, German, Czech, Italian etc. As Wieviorka points out, the relation of factual details is only part of the role and function of the witness and of testimony, legal or historical. While factual detail may be the same, for example in the Yiddish original and the German translation, it is almost inevitable that something will be lost, some trace, some nuance, some link in the chain of meaning where the process of trying to make us understand the reality of quotidian horror will be disappear in and through language. Agamben's interrogation of the witnesses on which he bases his ethical semiotics of Auschwitz must always be read again with the faults of language, and the embodiment of suffering though and within language, as our historical and ethical hermeneutic compass.

This problem is simply exacerbated in my own reading and rendering of Agamben. I read his work in translation, from Italian to French or English. He himself reads testimony from Yiddish and Polish in German and translates that into Italian, where it is passed on to me etc. In the end, I believe language and testimony can, as Agamben argues, offer invaluable ethical lessons about what he has called "the camp as *nomos*"[13] but only if we bear in mind Robert Cover's admonition that *nomos* and narrative in law and ethics are always inextricably linked.[14]

2. Nomos and Narrative: Agamben Witnessing Auschwitz

The ethical problem of and after Auschwitz is the *aporia* of testimony, of the impossibility of an eyewitness account of the process of industrialized, mass killing and death. How, in other words, is it possible to re-tell and recount the extermination when the truth is literally smoke and ashes? Of course, at some obvious level, we are here revisiting the well-known set of inquiries established by Lyotard in his interrogation of the ways in which a vic-

12. *L' Ère du témoin* (Paris: Plon, 1998), at 52–62.
13. *Homo Sacer*, at 166–80.
14. Robert Cover, "Forward: Nomos and Narrative", 97 *Harvard Law Review* 4 (1983).

tim can never become a plaintiff as law proves inadequate to bridge the gap of horror and ethical memory.[15]

For Agamben, the concern of ethics after Auschwitz arises at an earlier, preliminary stage. For him, as for Derrida, Lévinas and Lyotard, the real dilemma comes from the necessary engagement with the philosophy of being and death articulated by Heidegger. If, in Heideggerian philosophy, the knowledge and recognition of the inevitability of death is the ultimate moment of freedom for the individual, then those arriving by train and presenting themselves for selection by the doctors and lawyers of the SS at Auschwitz, those who see the smoke from the chimneys, who hear the cries of their loved ones, of their children, those about to die in the Nazi killing machine, are the most free.[16] Agamben must revisit his earlier engagements with Heidegger in an attempt to find a way in which it is possible to give voice to the victims, through speaking and testifying about the horror of unfreedom. Testimony, the role of the witness, to give a voice to the victim, is inextricably intertwined with this Heideggerian experience of death, yet in its original and powerful philosophical manifestation, its function can only remain basically and inextricably unethical.

> Here the theme of the Voice demonstrates its inextricable connection to that of death. Only inasmuch as Dasein finds a Voice and lets itself be called by this Voice, can it accede to that Insuperable that is the possibility to not be *Da*, to not be the place of language.[17]

The ethical question and the legal question, before and after Auschwitz, the question of a legal semiotics of extermination, is a simple one. What is the role of the witness, of testimony in this testament to humanity which is the embodied destruction of humanity and of the human? How can this knowledge of death in its ultimate, but never final, manifestation of modernity's bio-politics, be translated into ethical discourse? For Agamben, law fails because it requires a declaration of responsibility, a judgment which exceeds justice and ethics.

> The concept of responsibility is also irremediably contaminated by law.[18]

---

15. Jean-François Lyotard, *The Differend*, op. cit.

16. This is of course my own reading of Agamben's rendering of Heidegger and Nazism. For Agamben, the primacy of facticity in Heidegger's philosophy lays the groundwork for the creation of the "bare life" of the biologized *homo sacer* of Nazism, the life unworthy of life. *Homo sacer*, at 150–53.

17. Giorgio Agamben, *Language and Death: The Place of Negativity* (Minneapolis: University of Minnesota Press, 1991), at 59. See also, Agamben, *Infancy and History: Essays on the Destruction of Experience* (London and New York: Verso, 1993).

18. *Remnants of Auschwitz*, at 20.

Ethics, politics, even religion, in other words the possibilities of a moral existence in the shadows of Auschwitz, can only ever be found and articulated in the *aporia* of the place and time, in the field of testimony, of the witness who is the survivor of the horror. At the same time, however, Agamben comes face to face with the problem of the witness/survivor, and the impossibility of testimony, outside the law, not by the existence of the *différend*, but by the existence of the witness who cannot testify. This is the seemingly irresolvable dilemma of the gray zone of Auschwitz for Agamben; there is neither *différend* nor litigation; there are no ties that bind the witness and that to which s/he might, but cannot testify. For Agamben, there is an ethical, but not a legal, solution to this problem. The solution is to found in the very *aporia* of the gray area itself, in the impossible possibility of the witness to the Auschwitz experience. For him, the key to a new ethics of and after Auschwitz comes from the insight of Primo Levi, the very literate and literary, but never literal, embodiment of the witness who cannot but must testify to that which he has not experienced. For Levi, the problem of the witness and the survivor comes to this very point of impossibility.

> I must repeat: we, the survivors, are not the true witnesses. This is
> the uncomfortable notion of which I have become conscious little by
> little, reading the memoirs of others and reading mine at a distance
> of years. We survivors are not only an exiguous but also an anom-
> alous minority; we are those who by their prevarications or abilities
> or good luck did not touch bottom. Those who did so, those who saw
> the Gorgon, have not returned to tell about it or have returned mute,
> but they are the "Muslims", the submerged, the complete witnesses,
> the ones whose deposition would have a general significance. They
> are the rule, we are the exception.[19]

The real victims for Levi and now for Agamben, are not those who died, nor those who survived, but those for whom the experience of the camps was the embodiment, literally and figuratively, of the goal of Nazi bio-power. Those who were reduced to the walking dead, stripped of their humanity, for whom resistance, existence and survival were equally unimaginable, these are the witnesses, for they are the only ones to have experienced the ultimate non-life of the camp, they are for Agamben, the *homo sacer*, who can be killed but not sacrificed. They are the "Muslims", the *Musulmänner*.

For Agamben, as for Levi, the entire project of an ethics of/after Auschwitz must be situated in this figure, the *Musulmann*. The *aporia*, the lacuna of lan-

---

19. Primo Levi, *The Drowned and the Saved* (New York: Vintage, 1989), at 83–84.

guage and testimony, can be situated at the point of the impossible possibility of a language of the complete witness, s/he who by definition cannot testify.[20] The *Musulmann* is precisely this witness for s/he has seen the Gorgon, s/he has reached the bottom, or in the Nazi world, the top, of the Auschwitz experience. The *Musulmann* is the figure of Auschwitz, the bio-political space where inmates and bodies became in the Nazi lexicon, *Figuren*, a mere physical presence without a remaining speck of humanity.

> The *Muselmänner* are persons destroyed, devastated, shattered wrecks strung between life and death. They are the victims of a stepwise annihilation of human beings. Before absolute power kills using immediate physical violence, it pursues a policy of deliberate misery, the transmogrification of the *condito humana*.
>
> …
>
> Their skulls seemed elongated; their noses dripped constantly, mucus running down their chins. Their eyeballs had sunk deep into their sockets; their gaze was glazed. Their limbs moved slowly, hesitantly, almost mechanically.…
> Their increasing emaciation eradicated the dividing line between life and death.[21]

This being, this being as *Musulmann*, becomes for Agamben the paradigm for a new ethical understanding of the camp as nomos, of Auschwitz as a site not of extermination, but as the site for the production of material to be destroyed, the ultimate logic of modernity, capitalism and bio-power in the service of the racial vision of the Nazi State. The productive capacity of the destroyer state, of Auschwitz, is literally embodied in the inhuman *Musulmänner*, the *homo sacer*, who may be created to be destroyed. The Jew becomes the *Musulmann*, the about-to-die becomes the undead, and the human becomes the inhuman. According to Agamben, we can never begin to understand Auschwitz, and thence an ethics after and of Auschwitz, unless and until we can understand what it was and is to be a *Musulmann*.[22]

Here, we must yet again confront the impossibility of testimony and of the semiotically insignificant, or un-signifying, witness. The state of the *Musulmann* is a state of muteness, a state of non-humanity, of the loss of language and in a Heideggarian turn, then, not a loss of life but of the loss of death.

---

20. *Remnants of Auschwitz*, at 39.
21. Wolfgang Sofsky, *The Order of Terror: The Concentration Camp*, op. cit., at 199.
22. *Remnants of Auschwitz*, at 51–52.

The ethical (and legal) project of a re-interpretation of Auschwitz as a camp for the production of the un-dead *Musulmänner*, is, in the end, once more dependent upon finding a way to speak of the unspeakable.

Since the *Musulmann* is incapable of speech, someone must testify for, on behalf of the *Musulmann*. Here Agamben returns to the law, to a notion of the fiduciary relationship which grounds for him the first step in the construction of a new ethics of/after Auschwitz. The survivor here offers a testimony "by delegation", on behalf of the silent and silenced *Musulmann*. Under the legal principle that the acts of a delegatee are attributable to the delegator, this means that in a legal and ethical sense the *Musulmann* is bearing witness, s/he is testifying. And if the un-dead can testify about their "undeadness", about bio-power, about Auschwitz, this must come to mean that all testimony embodies the un-human, that it is the un-human who testifies.[23] For Agamben, the *Musulmann* and the testimony of the survivor for and on behalf of the un-dead, offer an example of the embodiment of the ethical moment in the remainder, the remnant, (*le reste*), the trace and *aporia* of a relationship with the Other. This is the paradox of all theo-philosophical interventions concerning testimony, law and ethics, before and after Auschwitz.

> The paradox here is that if the only one bearing witness to the human is the one whose humanity has been wholly destroyed, this means that the identity between human and inhuman is never perfect and that it is not truly possible to destroy the human, that something always *remains. The witness is this remnant.*[24]

3. Witnessing Law after Auschwitz

Agamben identifies what is for him the fundamental problem of law and ethics after Auschwitz. Once we have re-configured Auschwitz as a place the function of which was not extermination, but the production of the *Musulmänner*, the fundamental source of our possible understanding of that place becomes the impossible possibility of eyewitness testimony. The survivor cannot be a reliable witness for s/he was not a *Musulmann*. Only through a complex legal and ethical reconstruction of the signifying chain of the witness at Auschwitz can we come face to face with the true meaning of that time and place. Of course, this epistemological and semiotic policing of Auschwitz re-

23. At 120–21.
24. At 133–34.

quires not just the primacy of significance accorded to the *Musulmänner* but is also dependent upon an acceptance of the assertion that the meaning of Auschwitz must be re-articulated to accommodate this primacy. From this lexical surveillance of ethics at Auschwitz, we must then accept the ethical reconstruction of the witness and the fate of testimony. Here again, Agamben returns to a consideration of the intimate connections between language and death. To reconfigure the legal and ethical status of the only possible witnesses to Auschwitz, those about to be *Figuren*, law, language and death must all be rethought. The delegation of responsibility to the survivor requires a radical, extra-legal testimony.

> Whoever assumes the charge of bearing witness in their name knows that he or she must bear witness in the name of the impossibility of bearing witness. But this alters the value of testimony in a definitive way: it makes it necessary to look for its meaning in an unexpected area.[25]

There are possibilities and complexities inherent in Agamben's approach which might allow us to come to a more complete understanding of law and ethics before and after Auschwitz. This particular reading of law and Auschwitz, I believe, permits us not just to better understand the ethical and legal implications of the culmination of bio-power which concerns and informs Agamben's approach to these questions, but also gives us the ability to replace Agamben's apparent rejection of law with a more legally nuanced understanding of Auschwitz as a lawful place, as a place full of law. We must, as Agamben argues, reconsider our construction of testimony and the witness, but we must do so within a slightly different or modified ethical framework in which law must re-emerge at Auschwitz. In the end this framework is, I believe, more faithful to Agamben's approach than he himself may be willing to admit. In the end, Agamben is a witness both for and against himself.

First, the fate of the witness and of testimony at/about and after Auschwitz must inevitably confront the possibility of perjury, of untruth. I am not speaking here of the lies of the Deniers, but of the remainder which must always haunt testimony, the idea that testimony must always be informed by an untruth. Testimony can never not be untrue, just as it must always be true. This is the trace of all representation, the unrepresented political remainder.[26] Like Agamben's construction of the *Musulmann* as the ultimate witness because

---

25. At 34.
26. Jacques Derrida, *Of Grammatology* (Baltimore: Johns Hopkins University Press, 1976), at 295–302.

s/he can only testify to the untruth of humanity, and of language and death, for Derrida, testimony must always bear with it another trace, an Agambenian *reste*.

> Si cette possibilité qu'il semble interdire était effectivement exclue, si le témoignage, dès lors, devenait preuve, information, certitude ou archive, il perdrait sa fonction de témoignage. Pour rester témoignage, il doit se laisser hanter.[27]

> "If this possibility, which it appears to forbid, were effectively excluded, if testimony, from that point onwards, became proof, information, certainty, an archive, it would lose its function as testimony. To remain testimony, it must let itself be haunted." (my translation)

What Derrida offers here, for law and ethics, is a reading of testimony and the function and role of the witness which supplements and augments Agamben's repositioning of the survivor as the legally and ethically bound fiduciary of the *Musulmann*. For Agamben, the difficulty of an ethical understanding of Auschwitz is that we must confront, outside the law, the incommensurabilty between the witness, the survivor, and the victim, the *Musulmann*, who is reduced to silence. For Derrida, this is the very nature of all testimony, for the witness, who is by definition a survivor,[28] by asserting, by offering up evidence, is making an impossible claim to the universality of that claim.[29] A singular and impossible embodiment of the universal, and of substitutability, a truth claim bound and determined by perjury, this is the legal and ethical notice, the *mise en demeure*, which Derrida issues to the law. The fiduciary relationship through which Agamben constructs the ethical status and function of the witness/survivor is to be found, in other words, at the heart of any onto-theological structure of legal testimony.

> In testimony, truth is promised beyond all proof, all perception, all intuitive demonstration. Even if I lie or perjure myself (and always and especially when I do), I promise truth and ask the other to believe the other that I am, there where I am the only one able to bear witness and where the order of proof or of intuition will never be re-

---

27. Jacques Derrida, *Demeure* (Paris: Galilée, 1998), at 31. See Maurice Blanchot, *L'instant de ma mort* (Paris: Fata Morgana, 1994).
28. At 54.
29. At 48.

ducible to or homogeneous with the elementary trust [fiduciarité], the "good faith" that is promised and demanded.[30]

This fiduciary relationship, then, is at the basis of all testimony and depends on and is created by the very process of voice and language, the ineffaceable promise of the witness, of the impossibly perfect substitution of language and experience within the law, the perfect or perfectible presence of the Other. In the circumstances of Auschwitz and the testimony of the survivor/witness, the problem of language and testimony is complicated not by the fact that the survivor must communicate with and to an Other, but rather by the fact of the survivor's relationship with the Other for whom the testimony is offered. There must be in this offertory, the *credo* of the witness at and to Auschwitz, I believe, an element of sacrifice, a potential legal conflation of the sacred and of the *homo sacer* who may be killed but not sacrificed. The sacred and the profane, the two sources of testimony of the Derridean witness, simply find themselves embodied in the survivor/witness, speaking of, for and through the silence of the *Musulmann*, as the law of the *Musulmann*. The problem here, again, is the Derridean *trace*, the Agambenian *reste*, the remainder which is the impossible possibility of the speaking of silence, in the first case of the immortal mortality of the witness,[31] and in the second, of the inhuman humanity of the one who testifies.[32] The ethical and legal dilemma of testimony of and about Auschwitz then comes down again to the question of the possibility of constructing a language of death which is neither a dead language, nor a language of the dead. For Derrida in his discussion of Blanchot, the fiduciary relationship which informs all testimony begins in the declarative

Je suis mort. I am dead.[33]

For Agamben, the language of death and of the impossible but absolutely necessary witness must be embodied in the equally inconceivable declaration.

Je suis un Musulmann. Ich bin ein Musulmann. I am a Musulmann.

The two conceptions of an ethical, fiduciary definition of testimony, and one which must always therefore be a legal conception, come together, if we take

30. Jacques Derrida, "…and pomegranates", in Hent de Vries and Samuel Weber, eds., *Violence, Identity, and Self-Determination* (Stanford: Stanford University Press, 1997), 326–44, at 341. A fuller version can be found in, "Foi et savoir", in Jacques Derrida and Gianni Vattimo, *La religion* (Paris: Seuil, 1996), at 9–86.
31. *Demeure*, at 86.
32. *Remnants of Auschwitz*, at 120–21.
33. *Demeure*, at 54–61.

Agamben's semiotic paradigm Auschwitz/*Musulmänner*, as our guide for the moment, at the moment before, or in the continuing industrial process which constitutes, the living death of the *Musulmann*. The fictionalized testimony of the survivor can not, in legal or moral language, capture the experience of this presence/absence of humanity and of mortality, because of the unsubstitute-ablity of death, and of language in the very present moment of death. The necessary legal statement under oath here, the only testimony which can be given, *Je suis mort/Ich bin ein Musulmann*, can never be given because the rule of law which haunts this testimony[34] is its status as unspeakable, *l'indicible* can never be indicted through the statement of the witness because the witness is the unspeakable. Law, like G-d, becomes at Auschwitz, the name which cannot be spoken.

4. Witnessing Law as the Death of the Other at Auschwitz

This problem of language and death which haunted Agamben's earlier interventions, now comes face to face with Auschwitz and the impossibility of law. For him, this means that law and legal testimony must be replaced by an extra-legal conception and re-articulation of the witness and of testimony. Yet he can only manage this ethical rebirth of the witness/survivor through the legal maneuver of constructing an ethical duty to speak the unspeakable by way of the fiduciary relationship. In invoking this legal semiotic strategy, Agamben hopes to avoid the possible, if not inevitable, immoral Heideggerian instant of facticity, of the "bare life" of the about to be victim.[35] This is the consequence of the facticity which Agamben recognizes as being at the core of the relationship between Heidegger's philosophy and Auschwitz. I would argue, again, that this leads us to the lawful constitution of language and death at Auschwitz as an ultimate moment of freedom for the victim.

What seems to be missing from Agamben's construction of this new ethical language of death and the inhuman is a consideration of the way in which death, or the living dead, the sunken faced, glazed and discarded, might have become this ethically and legally binding fiduciary moment for the survivor.

---

34. Derrida, *Demeure*, at 123.

35. See also here, Giorgio Agamben, "The Passion of Facticity", in *Potentialities*, op. cit., at 185–204, for a sophisticated attempt by Agamben to again ethically confront Heidegger.

The important issue throughout Agamben's moral reconstruction of testimony and the witness at/of and after Auschwitz is the ethical relationship between the survivor, the saved in Levi's formulation, and the *Musulmann*, the drowned. However, he never truly constructs a convincing existential or de-ontological basis for the creation of this relationship. We know, for example, from countless survivor accounts of life in the Nazi camps, that the psychological phenomenon of survivor guilt plays a particularly strong role in the lives and memories of the saved.

The causes and sources of this particular manifestation of guilt are myriad and complex and beyond the scope of this book. What is important for the moment is the role which dealing with this issue of survivor guilt played in the work of Primo Levi, the source and inspiration of Agamben's insights into the ethical status of testimony in relation to Auschwitz. Without offering here an analysis of Levi as witness, it is beyond doubt that Levi's apparent suicide in April 1987 served both to reinforce and problematize the role of guilt in Holocaust accounts. The circumstances of his death underline the legal hermeneutic force of his assertions that the survivor was not and could not be the true witness. Levi's death confirmed and reinforced his language claim, by force of law. In order to offer a reading of the *Musulmann* which might allow us to fill in this legal and ethical *aporia* in Agamben's philosophy after Auschwitz, it is important to return to the unseen and unarticulated status of the *Musulmann*.[36] It is in this existential and juridical position of the drowned where I believe we can find a possible source for the responsibility and guilt, in the legal and ethical sense, of the saved, a guilt which must haunt and create all survivor testimony. This is the law, the law of guilt, and the guilt of the law which haunts Agamben's Auschwitz.

The most important aspect of the fate of this group of prisoners is the way in which their relationship was constructed with other inmates. From this relationship, between the saved and the drowned, between those who testify and those who are the true witnesses, we might then be able to elucidate the status of Agamben's reconstruction of Auschwitz and ethics. Sofsky offers the following description:

> The fate of the *Muselmänner* was a social concern. They were subject to a process of dissociation in which their fellow prisoners also played a part. As they increasingly withdrew from the world, the others

---

36. Benny Lévy, *Visage continu: La pensée du Retour chez Emmanuel Lévinas* (Paris: Verdier, 1998).

turned away from them, withdrew their interest in them, persecuted and isolated them.

...

In the barracks, they dirtied the halls, bunks, and blankets. At meal distribution, they tried to push their way to the front, were shoved aside, and had to look on as the others ate. They relieved themselves in soup bowls; they begged and stole. They did not care about punishments. Thus, many prisoner-functionaries declared war on them. They chased the *Muselmänner* into the latrine or washroom and made them sleep there.[37]

The reality of the relationship between the drowned and the saved, in the contemporaneous circumstances of life in the camp, was never one of an ethical or fiduciary nature. It was rather one of antagonism, fear and hostility. Their ever more ragged and resigned appearance, their sunken faces, their mucus stained visages, instilled loathing, fear and repugnance. The prisoners turned away from the *Musulmann*; they did not wish to see the future of their own (non)existence. For them, the saved, there was no fiduciary relationship at the time when ethics mattered.[38] Levi, at least, was honest about this. His realization of the ethical dimension of testimony, of the fiduciary relationship between the drowned and the saved was not immediate but gradual. It is this temporal element which must now be seen to trouble and problematize Agamben's construction of Auschwitz and testimony.

What is manifested in the reality of the relationship between the prisoners and the *Muselmänner* is the failure of Agamben's conception of the witness to address the connection with time, in the equation language and death,[39] which is central to his project. Given the crucial rapport between being and time in the Heideggerian worldview which he is attempting to defuse, this is an extraordinary lacuna in Agamben's Auschwitz project. Yet a simple reading and application of some of the insights of Emmanuel Lévinas may well bring us to a point at which the rupture inherent in Agamben's failure to construct a contextualized and properly historicized ethics of Auschwitz will be repaired, although perhaps not redeemed. From there, an ethically and legally binding reading of the significance of Auschwitz may emerge. In Lévinas, this comes

---

37. *The Order of Terror*, at 202–3.

38. Tzetvan Todorov, *Facing the Extreme: Moral Life in the Concentration Camps* (New York: Metropolitan Books, 1996).

39. See e.g., Emmanuel Lévinas, *Dieu, La Mort et Le Temps* (Paris: Grasset, 1993).

down to an anti-Heideggerian semiotic maneuver through which the central-ity of death as the moment of potential freedom to be realized is replaced by the contemplation of the death of the Other as the first and infinite moment of ethical responsibility.[40]

In this way, our ethical accountability through alterity and identity, the im-possible possibility of justice, comes at the moment we realize that the death of the Other imposes a moral responsibility and limit on our freedom. Death, language and freedom, speaking the unspeakable, become the possible and nec-essary testimony only and always when the death in question is the death of the Other. The unspeakable must be articulated. This is the moment at which an ethical obligation and a fiduciary relationship can be found and founded be-tween the drowned and the saved, between the survivors and the *Musulmän-ner*, in the face to face as they walk across the camp to their work detail, as they line up for food, as they sleep in the barracks. The problem here for Agamben's ethical project is that the prisoners were almost by definition prevented from assuming their fiduciary relationships and duties. They could not look into the sunken and abandoned face of the *Musulmann* because to do so would be to recognize the inevitability of their fate and bring them face to face with the law of Auschwitz. The face to face, the ethical responsibility born of the relation-ship with the about-to-die Other, was made impossible by the death machine of Nazi law. This is perhaps the true nature of Auschwitz, not Auschwitz as death factory, not Auschwitz as manufacturer of *Musulmänner*, but Auschwitz as the place where law attempts to inscribe bodies which cannot be confronted and addressed ethically, where responsibility is rendered impossible. The role of testimony, philosophy, and ethics after/in Auschwitz within the modern state is not only, as Alain Finkielkraut claims of Lévinas, to speak in the name of the tears which the bureaucrat can no longer see.[41] Ethics must also command us to look into the face of the *Musulmänner*, to assume our responsibility, to look into the glazed eyes and sunken face and to recognize a fleeting glimpse of the human in the inhuman, the mortal in the immortal, and finally to examine the forces of law which have constructed both the face into which it is impossible to look and those who cannot bring themselves to an encounter with the *homo sacer* of law. In the absence of such an ethical project, Auschwitz then becomes not just *l'indicible* but the invisible.

---

40. Ibid.
41. "Une philosophie affectée par l'histoire du xxe siècle", in Nathalie Frogeux and Françoise Mies, eds., *Emmanuel Lévinas et l'histoire* (Paris-Namur: Éditions du Cerf, Presses Universitaires de Namur, 1998), 81–95, at 93.

5. Law and Blindness in
Agamben's Auschwitz

The ethical dilemma established by and through Agamben's construction of Auschwitz as a place for the creation of *Musulmänner* is, at some problematic level, a direct product of the lexical prohibition which denies significance to the terms "Holocaust" and "Shoah". He asserts that he wishes to deal with the political and ethical implications of "extermination". Then by treating the extermination as not Holocaust and not Shoah, he arrives at the inevitable position whereby the status of witness who cannot testify afforded to the *Musulmann* makes her/him into the product of Auschwitz. In other words, Agamben here comes perilously close to creating Auschwitz as a product of ethical discourse about Auschwitz.

One of the reasons Agamben arrives at this potentially unethical, declaratory, sovereign law-giving state is precisely because he forgets, or at least elides, his own interventions on law and sovereignty. Instead he creates a conception of the witness and of testimony which rejects the law as an element which "contaminates" ethics and which must be forgotten in the world of testimony and Auschwitz.

In the work leading up to his contemplations on extermination, that is to say on his own road to Auschwitz, Agamben however clearly establishes a critique and understanding of law and sovereign power which should have led him to a somewhat more complex reading of Auschwitz ethics.

For him, modern law, law within modernity, is characterized by a fundamental Schmittian shift in which sovereignty becomes manifest in law as a state of exception. In other words, that moment of divine violence which grounds sovereignty and law in the ability to give death, is the true moment of modern law.[42] Nazi law, which institutionalized this normal and lawful state of exception in which death became the rule of legal life, for Agamben, is the moment and place, *par excellence*, in which language, death and law come together as bio-power. Writing about the combination of a eugenic legal normativity of "life unworthy of life" and a racial vision in the Nazi *Rechtsstaat*, Agamben said:

> And yet the laws concerning the Jews can only be fully understood if they are brought back to the general context of National Socialism's legislation and biopolitical praxis. This legislation and this praxis are not simply reducible to the Nuremberg Laws, to the deportations to

---

42. *Homo Sacer*, at 65.

the camps, or even to the "Final Solution"; these decisive events of our century have their foundation in the unconditional assumption of a biopolitical task in which life and politics become one.[43]

Life unworthy of life is and must always be life worthy of law. In other words, the Nazi state can only be grasped in its legal form if we understand that its legal form is that in which the role of the state is not one of protecting the safety and rights of its citizens, but one in which the death of some legal subjects becomes necessary to the survival of the body politic. Here the killing of the *homo sacer*, the destruction of the Jews, becomes a condition precedent to the existence of the rule of law. What Agamben leaves out of his analysis of the ethical and political evaluation of Auschwitz is precisely a study of the mechanisms, especially the legal and lawful mechanisms by and through which Auschwitz and the *Musulmänner* could be and were created. These mechanisms, as I have mentioned, include the medico-legal discursive patterns, the semiotics of law under Nazism, which not only had to destroy "life unworthy of life", but which first and foremost had to create that life. The Jew, in other words, is the paradigmatic creation of Nazi law and bio-power. The body politic over which sovereign power exercises its death giving authority, by which *homo sacer*, the Jew, may be killed, is one in which the Jew must first be created.

The circumcised and perversely sexualized body of the Jew is created in medical discourse just as legal discourse circumscribes the Jewish body as a virus in the body politic.[44] The object, the only possible goal of this creative force of law, is the destruction of the enemy of the law, the extermination of the Jew. Auschwitz is the place, or rather a place, where the law may be carried out. It is a site of memory, but it is more than anything, a site of remembering the force of law.

This then, is the ethical dilemma of law at Auschwitz, the legal dilemma of ethics at Auschwitz. How can the witness, whose very function was to be destroyed, i.e. to be a lawful subject, come to testify about that destruction, about the law? Can the witness become a witness to the law before the law? This is the ethical interrogation which I believe must be seen to underlie the intervention of Agamben at Auschwitz. This is also why Agamben appears to run from the law in his reconceptualization of the witness at Auschwitz, because the law must not be allowed to testify on its own behalf. That would be the Heideggerian moment, the bare facticity of law, of language and death and

---

43. Ibid., at 147.
44. See David Fraser, "Law Before Auschwitz: Aryan and Jew in the Nazi Rechtsstaat", op. cit.

law as empowerment and freedom. That is the instant, the legal instance, and the juridical facticity, from which Agamben must inevitably resile.

His task he then defines as locating the impossible possibility of speaking the unspeakable. This is the search for a possibility of conceiving death and law and sovereignty, of constructing a legally ethical language, which informs his attempts to find in the fiduciary relationship of the survivor witness and the *Musulmann*, a way around the haunting of language by the death embodied in Nazi law.

This is also the possible impossibility embodied for example in the writing and testimony of Kazetnick 135633, the inmate known also both as Yehiel Dinour and Dinenberg. Kazetnick 135633 was a *Musulmann*, saved from the death pit by a Nazi guard who saw him as *ein braver Kerl* ("a good guy"). He is a saved *Musulmann*, the embodied impossible witness to the unspeakable; he was and is the un-human who was recognized and granted life by the SS, the lawgiver and master of death. This legal and ethical paradox determined his fate; he was compelled to be a witness, *sub poena vitae*, under penalty of life.

> He remains alive, but he has become, in the full paradoxical sense, one of the living dead who no longer knows what to do with himself, with death, with life. From then on, he has a nameless name, he writes for others, but really the others write in and through him. He is fully aware of this, after the war too; so one can maintain that the madness that prevents him from living and from dying has also been desired, he desired it, and at the same time he suffered under it.[45]

In fact, even Agamben must come to recognize this. The *Musulmänner* speak and write. Their bodies, tattooed, legally inscribed, name them as legal subjects. Their minds and memories, again legally inscribed in and by Auschwitz, require them to testify. They are their own fiduciaries. The last section of *The Remnants of Auschwitz* contains a short series of excerpts from Ryn and Klodzinski's study of the *Musulmänner*.[46] Here the witnesses speak the legal language of the impossibility of survival as testimony to the legal success and failure of Auschwitz. At this point, two sets of interrogations remain for future study, in order to allow Agamben and us to return to the ethics of

---

45. Sem Dresden, *Persecution, Extermination, Literature* (Toronto and Buffalo: University of Toronto Press, 1995), at 175. See also Annette Wierviorka, *L'Ère du Témoin*, at 109. He died for the second time in Tel Aviv in July 2001. See Michael Illouz and Antoine De Baecque, "Katzetnik 135633", *Libération*, 11–12 August 2001.

46. *An der Grenze zwischen Leben und Tod-Eine Studie die Erscheinung des "Muselmans" im Konzentrationslager* (Weinheim and Basel, 1987).

Auschwitz. First, to what, in what forum, do the witnesses speak and testify? We know that Kazetnick 135633 wrote literature and testified at the trial of Eichmann. In other words, he confronted truth and literature, testimony and perjury wherever the opportunity to bear witness presented itself.

The real, insurmountable problem here is that to which, legally, the *Musul-mann* can and does testify. The law must tremble in Auschwitz because it cannot or will not deal with itself as Auschwitz, with extermination as lawful. The dilemma for the law is how to name itself in that lawful place Auschwitz. This is the cause of the collective professional amnesia which seems to haunt our understanding of law after Auschwitz. "Murder" is true, "murder" is real.[47] At the same time, murder is the possible impossibility for the subject of law, the *homo sacer* and/or the Jew.

> It is significant from this perspective that the extermination of the Jews was not conceived as homicide, neither by the executioners nor by the judges; rather the judges presented it as a crime against humanity.[48]

Second, do or can the *Musulmänner* speak in and for the present and the future or are they condemned by Auschwitz to speak of and in the past? Murder, of which they may not speak by law, is also limited in time, its very temporality requires a new legal category, the *imprescriptible* for the indescribable.[49] We confront a newer, more ethically complex question about the periodization of Auschwitz. Is testimony by definition limited to what was and bound to ignore what may or will be? In other words, we seem to return to the possible impossibility of testimony yet again—the impossible *Je suis mort*, the inconceivable *Ich bin ein Musulmann*. Are they to be forever replaced by the past tense, as evidence fades, as witnesses die, as law after Auschwitz becomes only more possible in the camp as *nomos*? *Ich war ein Musulmann, J'étais un musulmann, I was a Musulmann.* Can one be a *Musulmann* now and in the future? Can we find any way to testify, to witness justice and ethics if Auschwitz is legal history? Who would/will believe the *Musulmänner* when they come to testify before the law about the law, about Auschwitz? Again, can we place Auschwitz and law in such a way as to avoid asserting a point of rupture, a discontinuity which would deny the legality of the Holocaust? This is the ethical question of law for which Agamben does

---

47. But murder is also unacceptable to the law. See Dick de Mildt, *In the Name of the People: Perpetrators of Genocide in the Reflection of their Post-War Prosecution in West Germany* (The Hague: Martinus Nijhoff, 1996).

48. *The Coming Community*, at 87.

49. See Vladimir Jankélévitch, *L'imprescriptible* (Paris: Seuil, 1986).

not offer a direct answer in his specific writings on Auschwitz. If his project is to be successful, we must take the next step and realize that Auschwitz and law must always be spoken of, testified to, in the same place, time and language. Murder at Auschwitz was normal and lawful, it was the legal norm and normal legality. What can we hope for in such circumstances? In attempting what might be read here as a possible response to the dilemma posed by the legality of the murder of the *homo sacer*, Lévinas argued for example that

> For in reality, murder is possible, but it is possible only when one has not looked the Other in the face. The impossibility of killing is not real, but moral.[50]

The *Musulmänner* can only be raised to the status of witness, as the embodiment of ethical understanding today, because they were not the ethical subjects in Auschwitz. Faces were turned; their fate was sealed. No one saw, and no one would listen to the unspeakable silence of the un-dead. No one would or could confront the humanity of the un-human. The law could do its work because the words of the witnesses and the judges, the *Musulmänner*, were unspoken.

In more recent interventions, Agamben perhaps begins to offer an intriguing way in which to understand both his ethical project and the problematics of constructing law and Auschwitz as contemporaneous. In his study of Saint Paul's vision of the messianic, Agamben traces the beginnings of a theo-juridical understanding of the lawfulness of Auschwitz. For my purposes, Agamben's most important, yet still unperfected, insight begins with his discussion of the distinction between an apostle, like Paul, and a prophet. For him, the key differentiating characteristic is that the apostle serves as what I would construct, given his earlier interventions on the functions of the *Musulmänner* witnesses, as fiduciary for the messianic. S/He speaks not of the future, *contra* the prophet, but of the "past" i.e. of the fact that the messiah has come. S/He offers a testimony about the truth of the messianic time. Thus,

> ...l'apôtre qui, comme mandataire chargé d'une tâche déterminée, doit au contraire exécuter ce qu'il a à faire avec lucidité et trouver tout seul les mots du message....[51]

---

50. "Ethics and Spirit", in *Difficult Freedom: Essays on Judaism* (Baltimore: The Johns Hopkins University Press, 1990), 3–10, at 10.

51. Agamben, *Le temps qui reste*, op. cit., at 101. For an exploration of Walter Benjamin's ideas upon which much of Agamben's work is based, see also, Michael Löwy, *Walter Benjamin: Avertissement d'incendie* (Paris: Presses Universitaires de France, 2001).

"…the apostle who, as a agent charged with a specific task, must on the other hand do what he has to do with lucidity and must find by himself the words of the message…."

The apostle then is a fiduciary (*mandataire*) who must find the words, testify, about a truth which has occurred. Here, the possibility of the Derridean untruth of testimony is elided, (but not eliminated, I believe) by the direct relationship between and among, the apostle's faith, his oath and the law.[52] Here, Agamben returns to Carl Schmitt's construction of the law as a state of exception in which clearly the enunciated norms of liberal legality are submerged in the unarticulated and unarticuable ideals of the *Volk* (for Schmitt) or the messianic (for Benjamin and thence for Agamben).[53] The strength and appeal of Agamben's analysis here is twofold. First, it allows him to articulate a notion of the apostle, whom I assimilate here to the *Musulmann*/witness, who can assert the "facticity" of Auschwitz and secondly that facticity of Auschwitz is grounded in legality.

> Les camps de concentration, dans lesquels tout est possible, naissent dans l'espace ouvert par cette informulabilité de la loi. Cela veut dire que, dans l'état d'exception, la loi ne se présente pas comme une nouvelle normation qui énoncerait de nouveaux interdits et de nouvelles obligations, elle n'agit qu'à travers son informulabilité.[54]

> "Concentration camps, in which anything is possible, are born in the space opened up by the unarticulable nature of law. This means that, in the state of exception, law is not present as a new set of norms which set out new prohibitions or new obligations, law only acts through its very unarticualablity."

The problem which remains for Agamben, and for those who wish to articulate a vision of justice after Auschwitz and "after Auschwitz", resides in the lawfulness of Auschwitz. This is the function of the witness, the apostle who testifies about that which has occurred, who presents law to itself through a process, testimony, which is part of law itself. This is Agamben's project, as he attempts to elucidate law to itself, as I would reformulate his position, as Auschwitz. The remainder of time (*Le temps qui reste*) and the remainder of Auschwitz, are precisely the faith which we must place, to be just, according

---

52. Ibid., especially at 181–86.
53. See "The Messiah and the Sovereign: The Problem of Law in Walter Benjamin", in *Potentialities*, op. cit., at 160–74.
54. *Le temps qui reste* at 168.

to his argument, in the veracity of the *Musulmann* witness. Again, we must return, in a non-temporal sense, to Heidegger and time, to the freedom of unfree, law bound inmate, the about to die.

For Agamben, we find a positive rewriting of time and freedom in messianic time, the time which remains between time and its end.[55] Here we find the remainder, the excess, the *trace* of law, the Derridean ideal that deconstruction is justice. By understanding and rearticulating law in Schmittian terms as an unarticulated and unarticuable exception, we find the transgressive idea of justice which exceeds law but is part of law.

> ...une loi de la foi: l'antithèse ne concerne pas deux principes séparés et hétérogènes, car il s'agit au contraire d'une opposition interne au *nomos* lui-même—l'opposition entre un élément normatif et un élément promissif. Il y a dans la loi quelque chose qui excède constitutivement la norme et qui lui est irréductible— [56]

> "a law of faith: the antithesis does not deal with two separate and heterogeneous principles, since it refers rather to an opposition which is internal to the *nomos* itself—the opposition between a normative element and a promissory element. There is something within the law which by its very constitution exceeds the norm and is irreducible thereto-...."

For Agamben, the *Musulmann*/witness/apostle testifies that at Auschwitz, in the state of exception which characterizes law within modernity, the transcendence of law opens up the possibility of justice.

> Une justice sans loi n'est pas la négation, mais la réalisation et l'accomplissement—le plérôme—de la loi.[57]

> "A justice without law is not the negation, but the realization and the accomplishment—the completion—of law".

Here Agamben wants us to listen, to heed and to understand the fate of law within modernity. He demands an act of faith within and beyond law. He wants to raise the victim from the dead, Lazarus and law of Auschwitz. More

---

55. "...le temps qui reste enter le temps et sa fin". Ibid., at 104.

56. Ibid., at 151. See also, "The Messiah and the Sovereign", op. cit. at 174. "This paradigm is the only way in which one can conceive something which like an *eskhaton*—that is something that belongs to historical time and its law and, at the same time, puts an end to it."

57. At 169.

precisely, Agamben wishes to send back someone to testify, to bear and be witness, to be the apostle of the messianic time of Auschwitz, here the *Musulmann*. But can we ethically and as a matter of justice understand and posit Auschwitz as lawful, and still be faithful to law?

The tale of the second biblical Lazarus may serve as a binding precedent and as rebuttal.

In the parable, the rich man asks that the leper Lazarus be returned to life so that his brothers might learn the truth and avoid the place of torment. During his lifetime, the rich man would not look upon Lazarus, and "even the dogs would come and lick his sores". Like the *Musulmann*, in life he was ignored, he was not even Other, he was inhuman. In death, for Agamben, Lazarus of Auschwitz, like the law at Auschwitz, is to be revived in order to serve our ethical desires. Agamben asks us to listen to the voice of the law against the law, the *Musulmann* who comes back from the dead to save us from the law and from lawful extermination, through an excess of law itself, through justice without and within law. Are we beyond redemption because we cannot accept the lawfulness of Auschwitz?

> Abraham replied, "They have Moses and the prophets; they should listen to them". He said, "No Father Abraham; but if someone goes to them from the dead they will repent". He said to him, "If they do not listen to Moses and the prophets, neither will they be convinced if someone rises from the dead."[58]

---

58. Luke 19–31, at 29–31 (NRSV).

CHAPTER 4

"THE OUTSIDER DOES NOT SEE ALL THE GAME...": PERCEPTIONS OF GERMAN LAW IN THE ANGLO-AMERICAN WORLD, 1933–1940

1. Nazi Law, Continuity and the Stakes of the Debate

One popular and perhaps intellectually dominant jurisprudential view in the English-speaking world, after 1945, is of course, that Nazi law is "not law". According to this position, Nazi ideology so perverted our normal and accepted notions of right and wrong, of law and justice, that Nazi law was law in form only. Of course, this view can be refuted as a jurisprudential matter either by arguing at length, as have others, that it is based in a foundational normative view of natural law which is epistemologically unsound and historically untenable or perhaps even more basically that it confuses concepts of law and justice.

Nonetheless, this traditional post-war view remains a powerful and often necessary one.[1] Again, if we cannot distinguish law before and after Auschwitz, what does that say about our ability as a theoretical or principled matter, to characterize the rule of law as "good" and desirable? If we do not

---

1. See e.g. Richard Primus, "A Brooding Omnipresence: Totalitarianism in Postwar Constitutional Thought", 106 *Yale L. J.* 423 (1996) for the argument that anti-totalitarianism informs most important recent American jurisprudence.

live in a time and under principles and norms which are radically discontinuous with "Auschwitz", what does that say about our own ethical universe and about our relationship with good and evil, with justice, or at the very least with law?

This is, I believe, the vital role played by the discontinuity thesis and the key function served by the apparently widely accepted characterization of Nazi law as not law. The "perversion" idea, based as it is in our belief that Nazi law was not law, would of course be central to the prosecutions of German legal officials at Nuremberg. It is perhaps interesting and important to note however, that the "new" international criminal offence created at Nuremberg, "crimes against humanity", and unlike the other offences in the Nuremberg Charter, nonetheless required a specific dispensation from the norms of domestic legality. Article 6 (c) of the Charter specifically states that acts governed by the concept of "crimes against humanity" would be unlawful:

> ...whether or not in violation of the domestic law of the country
> where perpetrated.

The drafters of the Charter were conscious therefore that "offences" or actions including "murder", "extermination", "enslavement", "deportation" etc. could have been, (or I would argue perhaps often were) "lawful" under domestic law. This is the trauma which continues to trouble law and lawyers in relation to the Holocaust or at the very least in relation to Nazi law. The very idea that Nazi law was law, that Nazi lawyers and judges were lawyers and judges, or even that a Nazi judge could be a "good" judge[2], is one which we viscerally reject but which many might find intellectually intriguing or even simply obvious.

The dilemma, which I believe is both jurisprudential and psychological, still haunts us. Key questions remain unanswered. Is natural law a tenable position? Is there some other way of defining the jurisprudential point of no return at which an otherwise apparently legal system, or more precisely a legitimate system of law, crosses over into criminality? Did German "law" become "not law" simply by the operation of historical circumstances i.e. because once America and Britain were at war with Germany, Nazi law was now a tool of the "enemy"? If so, the discontinuity thesis becomes nothing more

---

2. See David Fraser, "South African Cricketers, Nazi Judges and Other Thoughts on (Not) Playing the Game", 38 *Osgoode Hall Law Journal* 563 (2000).

than another element in a propaganda campaign during wartime and loses any claim to jurisprudential meaning or standing. Or, on the other hand, did some fundamental change operate in the German legal system after 1940 so that the last vestiges of "law" or "legality" were destroyed? If this is the case, then the discontinuity thesis can retain its jurisprudential standing, if a review of the historical facts reveals that such a dramatic change did occur in the German legal system at the time in question. Of course, such a reading and analysis would still demand a particular periodization of Nazi law which would require even proponents of the discontinuity thesis to acknowledge that German or Nazi law was both procedurally and substantively "law" prior to that time. This would mean that as a matter of accepted and acceptable jurisprudential principles, the content of Nazi law, including the racial, biological exclusion of the unacceptable enemies of the *Volk*, was nonetheless recognizable as law.

We know that German lawyers did not perceive themselves to be "not lawyers" while they proceeded to construct the jurisprudential edifice which lead ultimately to lethal injections for "lives unworthy of life" and to the doors of the gas chambers for the Jews and Gypsies, legally constructed as Other.[3] While one might wish to dismiss the members of this particular interpretive community as offering a clearly self-interested understanding of their positions within the Western legal tradition, the same cannot as easily be said of others, who did not live and work in a Nazified society. As we shall see in what follows, Anglo-American lawyers, in their discussions of Nazi legality, did not universally reject the German legal system after 1933 as being "not law". A careful examination of the legal discourse in English language countries, particularly the United States and Great Britain, indicates that the idea of a basic and continuing law and legality operating within German society after 1933, was always present.[4] The idea of the Nazi state as an unlawful, illegitimate, criminal enterprise, operating outside Western understandings of law was not, I believe, one which was dominant in the period between the Nazis' coming to power in 1933 and the time of entry of the United States into the war. If coeval external understandings and constructions of the Nazi legal apparatus did not portray German law as "not law", as completely lacking in legitimacy, as "beyond the pale", if the irony of the phrase can be for-

---

3. "Law Before Auschwitz: Aryan and Jew in the Nazi Rechtsstaat", op. cit.

4. Lawyers and legal scholars were not alone. Scholars in many fields offered similar responses to the Nazi regime. See Magda Lauwers-Rech, *Nazi Germany and the American Germanists* (New York: Peter Lang 1995).

given, then again basic questions about the jurisprudential nature of the Nazi state must be re-opened.

2. Critiques of Nazi Legality: The International Law Exception

The temporal element of many well-known Anglo-American works dealing with various aspects of Nazi law explains why the discontinuity thesis was prominently displayed.[5] America was either just about to enter the war or was at war with Germany. The "legal" system of the totalitarian enemy had to be portrayed as completely at odds with the rule of law under democracy. This discontinuity, which again marked Nazi law as not law, could be and was addressed as a matter of jurisprudential and legal definition, most commonly by relying on some normative underpinning based in natural law theories. However, it is also important to note here that principled legal opposition to the Nazi regime and to Nazi jurisprudential practices was not limited to this period of imminent or actual hostilities.

American international lawyers were at the forefront of academic and jurisprudential critiques of Nazi legality from the very early stages of the Hitler regime. Criticism from international law scholars ranged from discussions of the "Reichstag fire" trial,[6] to analyses of Nazi legal theory[7], and included attacks on the undemocratic nature of the referenda used to legitimate Nazi

---

5. See e.g., Arno A. Herzberg, "The Situation of the Lawyer in Germany", 27 *American Bar Association Journal* 294 (1941); Friedrich Pollock, "Is National Socialism a New Order?", 9 *Studies in Philosophy and Social Sciences* 440 (1941); E. C. Helmreich, "The Return of the Baltic Germans", 36 *American Political Science Review* 711 (1942); Alexander F. Kiefer, "Government Control of Publishing in Germany", 57 *Political Science Quarterly* 73 (1942); William J. Dickman, "An Outline of Nazi Civil Law", 15 *Mississippi Law Journal* 127 (1943); Burke Shartel and Hans Julius Wolf, "Civil Justice in Germany", 42 *Michigan Law Review* 863 (1944); John Brown Mason, "The Judicial System of the Nazi Party", 38 *Am. Pol. Sci. Rev.* 96 (1944).

6. See Van Hamel, "The "Van Der Lubbe" Case and Diplomatic Protection of Citizens Abroad", 19 *Iowa Law Review* 237 (1933–1934).

7. Lawrence Preuss, "Germanic Law Versus Roman Law in National Socialist Legal Theory", 16 *Journal of Comparative Legislation* 269 (1934); Virginia L. Gott, "The National Socialist Theory of International Law", 32 *American Journal of International Law* 704 (1938); John H. Herz, "The National Socialist Doctrine of International Law and the Problems of International Organization", 54 *Pol. Sci. Q.*, 536 (1939).

power[8], racial legislation, and its impact[9] on the annexation of Austria[10] and on the international refugee crisis.[11]

There are, I believe, two main explanatory factors which would help us understand why American international law scholars were at the forefront of legal opposition to Nazi law in the English-speaking world. First, the very nature of their field means that the level of knowledge and interest in the affairs of a foreign country would have been higher than that in the legal community as a whole. Second, international law, then as now, operates largely and by necessity, on the basis of underlying legal and moral norms. While international legal morality today may be said to find its embodiment in various formal legal instruments, at the time, the existence of something called "international law" was not necessarily universally accepted nor was there a broadly recognized and actualized normative content of the discipline. Of all the legal academics and practitioners who had to base their understanding of the fundamental norms of "law" in unwritten and unarticulated underlying epistemological and moral categories, international lawyers were at the forefront. It would only be natural then, that it would be they who were most aware of what was happening in Germany and who were also able to bring to their analyses of the situation, a basic moral and ethical framework for their legal critique. At some level, then, international lawyers, it could be argued, constituted an "interpretive community" apart, a group of legal scholars and practitioners whose worldview distinguished them from their municipal and inward-looking colleagues. This in no way should be read to obviate the moral correctness of their position and of their opposition to what was happening in Germany and in the German legal system. Instead their attitude more simply underlines internal epistemological and political distinctions within the broader Anglo-American legal community.

It should also be noted here, however, that international law discourse of the period continued, in some instances, to draw a distinction, vital to the is-

---

8. Arnold J. Zurcher, "The Hitler Referenda", 29 *Am. Pol. Sci. Rev.* 91 (1935).

9. Lawrence Preuss, "The Position of Aliens in National Socialist Penal Law Reform", 29 *Am. J. Intl. L.* 206 (1935); James Wilford Garner, "Recent German Nationality Legislation", 30 *Am. J. Intl. L.* 96 (1936); James Wilford Garner, "The Nazi Proscription of German Professors of International Law", 33 *Am. J. Intl. L.* 112 (1939).

10. C. G. Fenwick, "Editorial Comment: Fuit Austria", 32 *Am. J. Intl. L.* 312 (1938); James Wilford Garner, "Questions of State Succession Raised by the German Annexation of Austria", *ibid.*, p. 421.

11. Ellery C. Stowell, "Intercession Against the Persecution of Jews", 30 *Am J. Intl. L.* 102 (1936); Louise W. Holborn, "The Legal Status of Political Refugees, 1920–1938", 32 *Am. J. Intl. L.* 680 (1938).

sues under discussion here, between "law" and "morality". Thus, in his critique of the Nuremberg Laws, Garner makes it clear that even a violation of "the conscience of mankind" did not *per se* render Nazi law invalid under then existing international law norms. He wrote:

> As international law now stands, it probably cannot be successfully argued that the German Citizenship law of 1935 violates any positive prescription of the law of nations. It is a municipal statute—a piece of domestic legislation—which falls within the legislative competence of any independent State, unless that competence has been limited by treaty engagements with other States. Nevertheless, it is believed that such legislation as this will meet with general disapproval, because it is an outstanding example of race discrimination, if it is not in violation of one of the fundamental rights of man as they are generally recognized today and generally approved by the conscience of mankind.[12]

Here we find, in the leading journal of American international legal scholarship, the clear, and I believe correct and obvious, assertion that racial discrimination within the context of domestic legislation was not at this time considered to be a violation of international "law". It may however have been contrary to the norms of international morality. This is important for our understanding of the construction of Nazi law in the Anglo-American literature not just because it may be used to bring into question basic assertions about the nature and content of the substantive legal norms of international law post Nuremberg, but equally because it establishes that international legal discourse at the time did not exclude the Nazi legal regime from the category "law". Indeed, it may be argued, at least tentatively here, that the Nazi "criminal state" was in fact partially "invented" through the epistemological and ontological maneuvers of the International Military Tribunal at Nuremberg. At the time Garner wrote his commentary, the Nazi system was functioning under the operative legal normativity of the epoch. Indeed, we know that whatever the op-

---

12. "Recent German Nationality Legislation", op. cit., at 99. It might also be noted here that as far as Garner is concerned certain restrictions on citizens' rights may be perfectly acceptable if they are based on other criteria which would disqualify the individual on the grounds of a real incapacity. He states: "…under the law of the latter States, the first category of persons usually embraces only those who for reasons of age, sex, lack of education or moral character are not deemed qualified to exercise political privileges for the best interests of the State, whereas the basis of the German distinction is primarily racial." (at 98). Discrimination against women clearly was part of acceptable legality and did not shock the conscience of "mankind".

erative norms of international law and morality concerning racial discrimination may have been, domestic legislation at least as obnoxious as that found in 1930s Germany continued to be in force in the United States and in other Western democracies. Nazi legality was perfectly legal, at the same time as it was perfectly, or at least partly, immoral.

Thus while many American and other international law scholars expressed the view that the Nazi regime may have been "illegal", or at least that some of its policies and practices, may have been contrary to international law, this position was far from universal. In other words, there was divided opinion even among the most knowledgeable English-language legal scholars about the correct way to characterize the German legal system after 1933.

This uncertainty, or lack of unanimity, can be seen at different levels of academic legal discourse. The key issue raised here is the definitional one. Not only must we decide what it is we mean by "law", "legality" and the "rule of law", but we must also engage in careful analyses about various concepts, ideas and positions which are put forward by the different claimants in the rhetorical and ideological debate, both then and now. The issue becomes, to put it simply, at what point, if ever, does something which looks like law from the procedural or formal perspective, because of its substantive content, become "not law"? Where is the point of rupture between "law" and "Nazi law"? More broadly, is it accurate, fair or even useful, to understand the period between 1933 and 1945 in German law and politics, as an aberrant time, in which all normative and institutional characteristics of that nation, must be quarantined? I shall return to this issue in more detail in parts of my discussion of eugenics and rule of law discourse. It is important to note at this stage, however, that the questions of rupture, continuity and discontinuity, are vital from both the practical and theoretical perspective. The very idea of definitional stability, of a *grundnorm*, of something which is clearly "law" and something which is clearly "not law", is absolutely essential to determining the philosophical soundness of the discontinuity thesis. At the practical level, for some at least, it is crucial to be able to point to the time at which German judges and lawyers stopped acting as legal personalities and when they began to take actions which could and should be seen to impose criminal liability on them.

A brief survey of the attitudes expressed by legal academics and lawyers outside Germany, writing in mainstream professional and learned periodicals can prove invaluable in testing the discontinuity thesis.[13] If, as many international

---

13. The survey is in fact brief, not because of some methodological weakness inherent in the project, but rather because, by and large, Anglo-American legal scholarship was, at this time at least, insular and myopic in focus and interest.

lawyers of the time seem to have claimed, Nazi law was in violation of international legal norms, then a strong argument for discontinuity can be established. That argument would be further strengthened if other members of the
legal interpretive community shared this opinion about the correct characterization of Nazi law as not law. Unfortunately for the proponents of the discontinuity thesis, the proof of a unanimous or even majority condemnation
of Nazi law in the interpretive community of lawyers themselves is clearly lacking. Indeed, the thesis which argues that there were and still are many points
of continuity between Nazi law and the legal traditions and practices both of
preceding German conceptions of law and of the Western democracies operating under the principles of the rule of law, seems to find support in the writings of legal scholars at the time of Nazi rule in Germany. This does not mean,
nor does it suggest, that Western democracies could not or can not be, distinguished from Nazi Germany. Nor does it mean that the Holocaust happened or could have happened in the United States or Great Britain. Clearly,
there are, at these levels, points of radical discontinuity between the two cases.
It does suggest, however, that there are equally strong points of communality
and continuity between the normative rules and discourses of German law
after 1933 and those rules and discourses in the Western English-speaking
world of that period. I would suggest that we may indeed learn more useful
legal, moral and ethical lessons from an examination of these points of continuity between legal systems than we ever will from the more comforting view
that we share nothing in common with Nazi law.

3. Understanding Nazi Law: Contemporary Anglo-American Accounts

An article written in 1940 by Richard Flournoy, after the invasion of
Poland and the start of World War II, and long after the exclusion of Jews
from an Aryan German State and civil society, demonstrates at a general level
the continuity thesis.[14] Published in a professional journal which was at the
forefront of condemning Nazi policies, this article deals with the history of
the various attempts to legislate with regards to American citizenship.
Flournoy writes:

---

14. Richard W. Flournoy, "Revision of Nationality Laws of the United States", 34 *Am.
J. Intl. L.* 36 (1940); see also "Development of German Law on Nationality", 186 *Law Times*
122 (1938).

Thus the nationality laws of any state necessarily reflect its political history and character.

An outstanding example of the fact last mentioned may be found in the nationality laws adopted in Germany in recent years.[15]

He then goes on to analyze German nationality law from 1914, with extensive references to the deprivation of citizenship rights of Jewish Germans contained in the *Reich Citizenship Law*. He follows this discussion with an examination of British and American nationality legislation. For this author, and for the editors of the most prestigious international law journal in the United States, the Nuremberg Laws fit comfortably not just within the historical evolution of German law under the *Kaiserreich*, but they also serve as a useful point of comparison for developments in the two great English-speaking democracies. There is no idea here, after the Nuremberg Laws, after the refugee crises of the previous years, and after the beginning of the war in Europe, that German nationality legislation, the legalized exclusion of German Jews, what we now "know" was the legal first step on the road to Auschwitz, was anything other than the perfectly valid expression of that state's "political history and character".

But there is more. The author goes beyond a simple approbation by silence of legalized antisemitism as a valid legislative goal. Instead he apparently wishes to issue a call for the adoption of a worldview which is not particularly distinguishable from the ideological and jurisprudential underpinnings of Nazi racial legislation. Flournoy writes:

Laws, in their nature, require some sacrifices on the part of individuals or groups, and this is especially true with regard to nationality laws, which relate to the very substance and texture of the state itself. In the shaping of such laws, affecting profoundly, as they do, the character of the country, it is especially important to consider first and last, not only claims of special groups and individuals, who are likely to be represented by special advocates, but the welfare of the people as a whole, whose only advocates are to be found in the membership of the Congress itself.[16]

While it is possible to read this part of the text as a call for a Burkean idealization of the functions of representative government, it must also be noted that the rhetorical deployment invoked by the author here clearly echoes many

15. Ibid.
16. Ibid., at 46.

of the themes of Nazi ideology and legal practice surrounding citizenship. The invocation of notions of sacrifice for the collective good, the idea of the nation as a whole (the *volk*) would not have been out of place in Nazi rhetoric about the duties of the *Reich* citizen. In the context of an article on nationality law which at the very least is indifferent to the Nuremberg Laws and at the most extreme reading is sympathetic thereto, the invocation of the duty of sacrifice for the greater good of the nation as a whole might be seen as something other than purely accidental.

Again, this does not mean that Flournoy was a Nazi, nor that the United States was planning to deprive its Jewish citizens of their rights.[17] What it does mean is that even in 1940, it was not considered inappropriate to compare the goals of US nationality and citizenship law to those of Germany. It goes without saying that one can also find many of these same themes, the threat from unchecked immigration and naturalization to the national fabric and fiber, in many of today's interventions on the subjects of immigration and national identity. Arguments that Nazi Germany was a criminal state, cast out from the community of nations because of its perversion of the democratic principles of the rule of law generally, are belied, I believe, by the discursive reality of Anglo-American jurisprudence, of which the Flournoy article is but one example. Such arguments about the ways in which we have learned from the Nazi experience may also be seen to be at least less persuasive when one begins to examine and notice the rhetorical continuities with today's legal and political discourses in certain fields.[18]

Concern among American scholars, many of them German-born, about events in Germany, is clearly evidenced in the scholarly literature of the period. The country and its political system were carefully and knowledgeably studied. Even before Hitler's formal rise to power, American scholars were examining the political situation in that country. Importantly for the issues to be examined here, however, there is little evidence of unanimity among Germanists or comparative lawyers on events in that country. In 1930, three years before the beginning of what would come to be characterized by some as the "criminal" Hitler State, Carl Friedrich published an important article "Dictatorship in Germany?"[19] Discussing the uncertain domestic political situation

---

17. Although the history of US immigration law and practice would lend support to the idea that antisemitism was rife among those in charge of immigration and that American Jews in particular were aware of the dangers of legalized taxonomies based on race. See Joel Perlmann, "'Race or People": Federal race Classifications for Europeans in America, 1898–1913', SSRN Working Paper No. 320, January, 2001.
    18. See below discussion on criminal law and eugenics.
    19. *Foreign Affairs*, vol. 9, at 118.

in Germany following the end of the occupation of the Rhineland pursuant
to the Treaty of Versailles, Friedrich carefully analyzed all the political factors
leading to the possible establishment of an authoritarian regime in Germany,
including the invocation of emergency powers under Article 48 of the Constitution.[20] Rather than interpreting this constitutional maneuver as leading
inevitably in the direction of a dictatorship, Friedrich saw the invocation of
emergency powers as actually promoting stability and democracy. He wrote:

> In such conditions, Germany might well be congratulated for the
> wisdom of its constitution-makers, who included in their funda-
> mental charter provisions which enable a responsible minority to tide
> the country over a temporary impasse, if it has the backing of a con-
> stitutionally elected President and a permanent civil service of high
> excellence and proven loyalty to the state. The advantage of such an
> arrangement to Germany is shared by those who deal with her inter-
> nationally. For the obligations of the country are safeguarded by such
> a flexible constitution. Truly benevolent despotism of this sort fore-
> stalls internal chaos and a complete breakdown of the government,
> particularly when it is placed in the hands of a man who has grown
> old in unswerving loyalty and service to his country.[21]

Of course, the benefit of hindsight allows us to see now how wrong
Friedrich was in his prognostications.[22] But this is not the most important
point. The situation in Germany in the early 1930s, while confused, was not
seen to be a legal system in a position of radical rupture or of revolutionary
change. More importantly, however, it is vital to the issue of continuity/dis-
continuity to underline that for Friedrich, the use of the emergency provisions
of Article 48 of the Weimar Constitution was not *per se* contrary to a general
understanding of the paradigm and parameter of constitutional governance.
The history of the economic and social dislocations caused by the Great De-

---

20. At 123 et. seq.

21. At p.132. The French constitutional scholar René Brunet made similar points in his
discussion of Article 48. See *The German Constitution*, Joseph Gollomb (trans.) (London:
T. Fisher Unwin Ltd, 1923), pp. 162–70.

22. Friedrich persisted even later in insisting that Article 48 posed no threat to democracy and constitutionalism. He wrote in April 1933 that "...Germany will remain a constitutional, democratic state with strong socializing tendencies whose backbone will continue to be its professional civil service." "The Development of the Executive Power in
Germany", 27 *Am. Pol. Sci.* Rev. 185. In that same month, the *Law for the Restoration of the
Professional Civil Service* was passed. This statute imposed the first legal prohibitions on
German Jews since their emancipation in 1871.

pression in the United States, at the same time, also gave rise to many instances of government by emergency decree, often of a problematic constitutional nature, both at the state and national levels. Indeed, at least one American scholar urged courts to adopt interpretive mechanisms and strategies which would confirm the constitutional normality of such decrees.

> If we are entering upon an era of social and economic planning, legislation upheld on emergency grounds with the corollary that it would be unconstitutional in "normal" times can only shackle real adjustments of the social framework to new economic situations and conditions. It is better openly to make such adjustment without any doctrine of emergency....
>
> The Constitution and the police power provide ample scope for the allowance of reasonable experimentation not only to meet the needs of the present depression but to prevent the ever-recurring cataclysmic disturbances to which our economic system has been periodically subject.[23]

It cannot be argued, then, that the invocation of a similar constitutional mechanism in 1933 by Hitler and the Nazi party, marks *per se* the beginning of the extralegality of the Nazi legal system. While hindsight might allow us to see this constitutional maneuver as one committed in bad faith and as part of a broader plan to gain control of the state apparatus, through the subsequent unification of the executive, party and *Volk*, such an analysis misses what is vital about the "interpretive community" viewpoint. How did the participants in the legal system, the creators of legal discourse at the time, experience the system itself and their role therein?

Friedrich, a professor at Harvard, and Clark, from Columbia, clearly did not see strong executive government, which characterized the early days of Nazi legality, as anything other than in keeping with the political, economic, social and constitutional requirements of the time.

Other interventions in related fields after the Hitler regime came to power reveal a similar belief that while the Nazis were operating fundamental changes to the German state apparatus, these changes did not qualify for immediate and definitional exclusion from the concept "law". Thus, Fritz Marx, writing about the revolutionary reconstruction wrought upon the Civil Service, largely as a result of its politicization under the Nazis and the removal of "non-Aryans" under the provisions of the *Law for the Restoration of the Professional*

---

23. Jane Perry Clark, "Emergency Powers", 49 *Pol. Sci. Q.* 268 (1934), at 283.

Civil Service, could see and explain the "logic" and even necessity of the Nazi policies.

> In a spiritually homogeneous people, he can enforce the will of the leader without the formal safeguards of "independence" through life tenure. Such logic could readily legitimize a thoroughgoing transformation of the legal status of civil servants...[24]

Not only did Marx assert that the changes to the basic structure of the administrative branch of government did not by definition violate democratic or rule of law norms, he further asserted that the changes brought about in Germany could be seen to be similar to, or continuous with, certain changes brought about during recent events in the United States, He wrote:

> A permanence of the one-party state will certainly ease transitional difficulties for the German civil service; for there is no more essential condition for the smooth functioning of the public service as the instrument of government than stability. And the ethical foundation of civil service ideology has much in common with the emotional pattern of the New Deal, with its emphasis on allegiance, devotion, and sacrifice and its middle-class appeals.[25]

While others did not draw such clear parallels between the politics and policies of governmental reform in the United States and Germany, or between the New Deal and Hitler, neither did they assert that what was happening at the time in Germany was completely unacceptable. While they continued to be bothered by certain aspects of Nazi reform, they also saw much of what was happening as being consistent with the previous history of government reform in Germany.[26] Nazi agricultural and land-holding policy, based in the ideology of blood and soil, was described as consistent in intent and practice with the "Internal Colonization" policy of the pre-World War I era and with concepts of land redistribution and social justice.[27] The exclusion of

---

24. "German Bureaucracy in Transition", 28 *Am. Pol. Sci. Rev.* 467 (1934), at 480.

25. Ibid., at 479.

26. See e.g. Fritz Marx, "Germany's New Civil Service Act", 31 *Am. Pol. Sci. Rev.* 878 (1937), Gerhard Krebs, "A Step Toward *Reichsreform* in Germany", 32 *Am. Pol. Sci. Rev.* 536 (1938); Alfred V. Boerner, "The Position of the NSDAP in the German Constitutional Order", 32 *Am. Pol. Sci. Rev.* 1059 (1938); "Toward Reichsreform: The Reichsgaue", 33 *Am. Pol. Sci. Rev.* 853 (1939); cf. Jane Caplan, *Government Without Administration: State and Civil Service in Weimar and Nazi Germany* (Oxford: Clarendon, 1988).

27. Marie Philippi Jasny, "Some Aspects of German Agricultural Settlement", 52 *Pol. Sci. Q.* 208 (1937).

German Jews from the *volkisch* peasantry was not deemed worthy of mention. Similarly, a detailed study of the German railway system from the perspective of what we might now call public governance, conspicuously situated the Nazi model as one which was in practice consistent with the entire history of public enterprise in modern Germany.[28] Once again, for Macmahon and Dittmar, "German" and "Nazi" policy were not only continuous, but Nazi practice was in some ways a marked improvement in the governance model.

The clearest example of their analysis of Nazi practice and its connections with previous policies can be seen in their discussion of personnel issues in state enterprises. As we now know in the post-Thatcher and post-Reaganomics era, rigid civil service protections afforded to state employees lead to inefficiencies and poor performance. Thus,

> Rigidity in the personnel of a large public undertaking is apt to be lessened by keeping down the proportion of full civil servants. In the decade before 1933, the managements of autonomous public enterprise in Germany were pushing in that direction. It is interesting to note how far the tendency has been carried since the advent of National Socialism.[29]

In addition,

> Most of this, of course, is the mere continuation of the practices of an old and progressive state industry which had been developed in the context of German social legislation. The National Socialist régime, while contracting the proportion of railway workers who have civil service status, has conserved and extended certain elements of security.[30]

Macmahon and Dittmar are here underlining two elements of contemporary political and legal analysis of the Nazi reforms to employment and civil service structures. First, the changes are seen to be, and are portrayed to the audience as being, consistent with long standing trends and practices in Germany. Second, the changes are interpreted as being for the good. Progress demands more efficient and responsive structures. They introduce greater flexibility in corporate governance and service provision while at the same time

---

28. Arthur W. Macmahon and W.R. Dittmar, "Autonomous Public Enterprise — The German Railways", 54 *Political Science Quarterly* 481 (1939), and Part II, 55 *Pol. Sci. Q.* 25 (1940).

29. At 506.

30. At 509.

maintaining protections and benefits for the workers. At a certain level, the analysis of the German railway system offered here would not necessarily be out of place in literature about today's administrative and corporatized state.

More importantly however, for the debate about continuity and discontinuity, the authors expressly address the legislative and legal framework for the changes brought about by the Nazis in the corporate governance of the railway and the employment status of railroad employees. Here, the law in question is the statute which dealt with "*the Restoration of the Professional Civil Service*".[31] In other words, as far as the first broad-based legislative instrument which began the slow and inexorable process of the legalized exclusion of German Jews from state and civil society is concerned, Macmahon and Dittmar simply describe

> The law of April 7, 1933, which declared its purpose to be the "restoration of the professional civil service" and the supplementary decrees applied to Reichsbahn employees as regards the paragraphs relating to Aryans and to communists.[32]

At some level at least, for these American scholars, the exclusion of Jewish Germans and others from employment in civil service jobs was noteworthy only in so far as it could be seen to be part of the continuous improvements being made to the governance structure of the railways. Again, the relatively late date of publication of the two part articles by Macmahon and Dittmar, (1939 and 1940), gives a stark illustration of the way in which American scholars continued, at a point in time at which Nazi policy and practice could no longer be said to give rise to any illusion about its true character, to construct Nazi legal mechanisms as perfectly continuous, acceptable and ordinary in the minds of members of the academic community. The changes and improvements to the German railway system and its corporate structure fit easily into a long line of structural readjustments dating back to the period of the *Kaiser-*

---

31. Article I (4) of the law stated that "The Reich Bank and the German State Railway are empowered to make corresponding regulations." The 11 April 1933 regulation under the *Law* defined those to be excluded as anyone with one grandparent who was a non-Aryan, a broader definition than would later be operative under the *Law for the Protection of German Blood and Honor*, which required three Jewish grandparents. None of this was particularly relevant or of any concern for the authors of this study.

32. At 507. The Reichsbahn had further experience with "the new managerialism" of Nazi racial policy. See e.g. Alfred C. Mierzejewski, "A Public Enterprise in the Service of Mass Murder: The Deutsche Reichsbahn and the Holocaust", 15 *Holocaust and Genocide Studies* 33 (2001).

reich. The exclusion through legislation of German Jews from state employ-ment is for these authors barely worthy of comment and hardly indicative of any radical break with the legal and administrative past.

In a similar vein, other reputable journals simply published descriptive ar-ticles by German lawyers about the situation in their country, including as a matter of fact and of law, the legal exclusion of German Jews from the Civil Service, without further elaboration or comment.[33] It seems clear even from this rather cursory examination of the leading literature in the English lan-guage dealing with the reform of the constitutional order in Germany brought about by Hitler, including the exclusion of German Jews from the State and increasingly from civil society, that such measures, which included the aban-donment of Parliamentary democracy, the creation of a one-party state, the abolition of civil service neutrality and the implementation of legalized anti-semitism, were not considered by experts in various legal fields at the time as constituting an affront to acceptable governmental or legal norms.

Throughout the 1930s, articles continued to appear in the leading period-icals of the English-speaking legal profession and academy supporting the Nazi legal regime. Writing in the *Scottish Law Review*, on the Reichstag Fire Trial, C. de B. Murray urged his readers to place themselves in the position of im-aging that a similar process were occurring in Britain. In such a case, he ar-gued, no one would dare pretend that the accused would not receive a fair trial. It would be unjust to reach the opposite conclusion where Nazi justice was concerned. After all, he wrote:

> For example, to the foreigner the feeling against the Jews appears very ugly but it must be remembered that the outsider does not see all the game, whatever the proverb may say. A strong conviction (supposing it exists in Germany) that too much power is at present in the hands of financiers is not *per se* an unreasonable conviction, though it may produce a very bitter feeling against the Jews.[34]

He goes on to add:

> We are in the presence of a new civilisation, and, one hopes, a new cul-ture. And for that reason one ought to look at the picture as a whole, not extenuating the blemishes, but to not obscuring the merits either.[35]

---

33. H. Tasse, "Civil Service Law in Germany", 19 *Journal of Comparative Legislation and International Law* 260 (1937).

34. "The Reichstag Trial", 49 *Scottish Law Review* 307 (1933), at 308.

35. Ibid., at 309.

In other words, if one adopts the proper perspective and puts developments in their real context, then one must really attempt to understand events from the perspective of the Germans. The Jews, who are here universally and without question assimilated to "financiers", and by definition of course excluded from the status of Germans by Murray's analysis, are probably to some extent to blame for their own situation. After all, one must expect a few rough spots in the creation of a new civilization. In at least part of the English-speaking world of law, Nazi law, like the Nazi system as a whole, was considered by some to be a wholly acceptable manifestation of a desirable change in Western civilization and culture. From its open endorsement of Nazism's underlying legalized antisemitism to its call for a strict analogy between the Reichstag Fire trial and an arson trial in Britain, Murray's article is a clear example of the idea that Nazi law was not, in its early stages at least, so outside the norms of Western legal culture that the discontinuity thesis can look to contemporary British legal discourse for complete and unqualified support.

American legal academia was likewise not totally inimical to Nazi law. Two years after Murray's article, a reputable American law review published a symposium on comparative property law. Among the articles included in the collection was one by a Germanophone Swiss law professor on the new Nazi regime of farmland holding.[36] The *Reich Farm Law* was a key, if somewhat controversial and ultimately unsuccessful, component of the Nazi legal revolution as part of a broader "blood and soil" ideology. The preamble to the law stated that

> By upholding the old German custom of entailment, the Reich Government wishes to retain the peasantry as the blood spring of the German nation.

This particular legal reform sought to integrate notions of "duty" and "citizenship" into the legal relations of the *volk* by abolishing "liberal" ideas of property and replacing them with *volkisch* and therefore more racially pure, principles. Liberal, non-German, notions of the free transfer of land, in the words of Professor Kaden are pernicious because

> They threaten the peasantry as such and thereby endanger the existence of the nation and the State to which that peasantry belongs.[37]

---

36. Eric Hans Kaden, "The Peasant Inheritance Law in Germany—On the Basis of the Reich's Hereditary Peasant Farm Law of 1933", 20 *Iowa Law Review* 350 (1934–1935). See also, Jasny, "Some Aspects of German Agricultural Settlement", op. cit., supra.

37. Ibid., at 352. The law declared that "Only German citizens of German blood or of that of a similar race and who are respectable are eligible to be peasants." See generally,

It can simply be said without further elaboration here that proper and clear legal principles need to be established to create appropriate and acceptable qualifications for land holding. Professor Kaden elaborates:

> First of all, it is necessary, according to these (paragraphs), that the owner hold German citizenship. This is paramount, because the peasantry is to constitute the basic stock of the German people. Secondly, it is necessary that the owner of the farm be of Germanic blood. Whoever is of non-Germanic blood cannot fulfill the mission which the law imposes upon and instrusts (sic) to the owner of an hereditary peasant farm—to be the "life fountain of the German people".[38]

As the Professor goes on to explain, this means that Jews are by legal definition disqualified, although this does leave open for him the intriguing legal question as to whether English blood, as non-German, would disqualify a putative owner. In any event, all of these issues simply come down to the fact that while some technical legal difficulties may remain, the statute

> ...shows to what extent the law giver was concerned to master these problems and to solve them in an intelligible and just manner.[39]

This article is not the only one which allows us to see the ease with which Nazi antisemitic legislation fit into existing legal discourse, not just within Germany, but more importantly within the legal practice and understanding of "law" within the Western English-speaking democracies.

The *Tulane Law Review*, noted for its strength in comparative law and a leading journal in communicating knowledge of European legal systems among US lawyers, published a series of reports from a leading German lawyer on developments in that country during the 1930s. These articles all deal with Nazi antisemitic legislation as if this type of enactment were to be expected and as if there could be nothing extraordinary about the content of German law.[40] Describing the Nuremberg Laws, the German attorney simply states that the laws:

Gustavo Corni, *Hitler and the Peasants: Agrarian Policy of the Third Reich* (New York: Berg, 1990); Shelley Baranowski, *The Sanctity of Rural Life: Nobility, Protestantism and Nazism in Weimar Prussia* (New York and Oxford: Oxford University Press, 1995).

38. Ibid., at 370.

39. Ibid., at 388.

40. See Robert R. Kuhlewein, "German Legislation Since 1933", 10 *Tulane Law Review* 425 (1936); "Recent German Legislation", 11 *Tulane L.R.* 601 (1937); "German Legislation From 1937 to 1939", 14 *Tulane L. R.* 593 (1939–1940).

…inflict various legal incapacities upon the Jews affecting their civil and political status and establish special criminal offences. Thus, marriages of Jews or members of racially undesirable people, such as gypsies and negroes, with nationals of German or kindred blood are prohibited.[41]

For the editors of the *Law Review* of the segregated Tulane University, in the Deep South state of Louisiana, any discussion of "racially undesirable people" and of legal restrictions imposed upon them, would not have struck a chord of disharmony or existential, professional self-doubt. Such ideas were part and parcel of the legal systems of many states of the United States where legalized racial discrimination was the norm, and where anti-miscegenation statutes were at the time on the books and where they remained until well after the time Nazi law had been declared "not law" after the triumph of the forces of democracy in Europe.[42] Again, what is important here is not so much the substantive content of German or American law, but the discursive climate in which these articles appeared. Antisemitism and race-based discriminations were not foreign to legal discourse in the Anglo-American world. Developments in Germany, which codified and legalized the Nazi racialist worldview, were not universally or even in a majority sense, seen to be outside the bounds of what lawyers saw to be part of a procedurally and normatively recognizable and acceptable legal system. For them Nazi law was still clearly recognizable as "law". Indeed, even the anti-Jewish purge of the legal profession itself and the Aryanization of legal education in Germany were not enough to convince Anglo-American lawyers that their German counterparts were stepping outside the boundaries of the interpretive community of law and lawyers.

Several articles published during this period dealt with changes to the legal education system in Germany, changes which it must be remembered would include the expulsion of Jewish German law professors and students as well as lawyers and judges. Yet, one can detect little, if any, overt criticism of the Nazification of the German legal academy.[43] I could find no mention of the

---

41. Op. cit., 1936. at 431–32.

42. For historical examples of the legal lengths to which American courts would go to uphold the validity of legislative prohibitions on inter-racial marriage, see e.g. *Dupre v. Executor of Boulard*, 10 La.411 (1855); *State v. Tutty*, 41 F. 753 (1890); *Baker v. Carter* 68 P. 2d 85 (1937); *In re Shun T. Takahashi's Estate*, 129 P. 2d 217 (1942).

43. See L. Loewensohn, "Legal Education in Austria and Germany", 55 *Scottish Law Journal* 166 (1939); M. Schmittoff, "Recent Reform of Legal Education in Germany", 1936 *Society of Public Teachers of Law Journal* 34; H. Weniger, "The Profession of the Bar in Germany", 34 *Illinois Law Review* 85 (1939); Max Rheinstein, "Law Faculties and Law Schools:

"Aryanization" of legal education and of the profession in the literature on German law published between 1933–1938 in the standard periodical literature of the legal profession and academy in the Anglo-American world. Instead, what one can find is work that would easily, in hindsight, be classified as Nazi propaganda. For example, the article by German lawyer Weniger in the *Illinois Law Review* contains the following history of the legal profession in his country:

> After National-Socialism had come to power in 1933, and new men had taken the lead in government as well as in the professional organizations, it was urgently pointed out that the profession could not be left to drift into decay.[44]

This drift into decay was dealt with in several ways but the result was a desirable one, despite some minor inconvenience.

> Whilst entry into the profession is thus restricted in many respects, its exercise is entirely free, being subject only to the law, to the rules of professional ethics, and to supervision by the professional organization.[45]

Weniger's contribution is interesting for several reasons. It can be read in hindsight, if it could not be so read at the time, as little more than an apologia for the Nazification of German law and the legal profession. But its interest is much deeper for present purposes. Here we have a member of the "interpretive community" offering his view that practicing law in Germany in 1939 is just like practicing law in the United States. This view is expressed in an academic journal from a reputable law school, and is nowhere contradicted. Of course, he recognizes that there are some restrictions placed upon entry into the profession but "Jews" are not mentioned, just as the restrictions on their entry into certain institutions of higher learning were also not mentioned in America at the time. Again, I am not making the point that America and Nazi Germany in 1939 were the same, or that German antisemitism under the Nazis was the same as American antisemitism. Rather, I am simply pointing out that articles in the academic mainstream of American legal education easily convey the impression that Nazi law in the 1930s, with its antisemitism and policy of racial biology, was not considered to be completely excludable from that mainstream of American legal thought.

A Comparison of Legal Education in the United States and Germany", 1938 *Wisconsin Law Review* 5.

44. "The Profession of the Bar in Germany", op. cit., at 85–86.

45. At 87.

For some, the parallels were clear. Thus, Professor Max Rheinstein could write (and the *Wisconsin Law Review* could publish) as late as 1938 that as far as the academy was concerned:

> If a man who has been a member of a German law faculty has, like the writer of this article, the thrilling experience of being appointed to the staff of an American law school, he is struck by the similarity of his new and his old surroundings. He finds an impressive illustration of the essential unity of Western civilization and its institutions. He moves in a familiar atmosphere; he has little difficulty in feeling himself at home. There are differences, of course, and they will be emphasized in the following, as in any comparison. We should not forget, however, that they are less important than the essential unity of common traditions, common aims, common social functions, and a common spirit.[46]

The existential accuracy of Rheinstein's observations is not of vital interest here. What is important is the fact that once more we find a leading law journal publishing an article which proposes a clear parallel between the systems of legal education in the United States and in Nazi Germany, a parallel strengthened by the points of commonality and continuity in Western civilization. Law, German and/or American, is a foundation stone in the bulwark of the common traditions which unite the two nations as members of Western civilization. This article, which reproduces in an appendix the translated statutes dealing with legal education under Hitler, makes and is able to make, these claims of commonality and continuity at such a late date without any sense of self-doubt.[47] Not a word is written about purges or expulsions from the academy or the profession. No mention of the Aryanization of University faculties in Germany is made. These are apparently only minor concerns, unworthy of note as compared to the continuity of the great traditions of American and German culture and law.

4. Criminal Law and the Criminal State in Anglo-American Legal Scholarship

It is perhaps appropriate here to examine western portrayals of Nazi criminal law. Criminal law best embodies the practical experience and ideology of

---

46. "Law Faculties and Law Schools", op. cit., at 5.
47. At 29 et. seq.

legal Nazism with its centralization of the State/Criminal Law/Police bureaucracy functions under a racial state ideology. At the same time, the characterization of this key governmental arrangement of Nazism as itself "criminal" is central to the idea that Nazi law was not law and that the Hitler state was in fact a "criminal state". An examination of the discourse circulating in the interpretative community of Anglo-American legal thought and practice will perhaps offer us invaluable clues as to the status of Nazi criminal law within Western legal tradition and culture.

The general field of criminal law offers perhaps the clearest example of Nazi ideology in its legal form. This area of law, characterized in all jurisdictions by the manifestation and implementation of the repressive power of the State, under the Nazis, incorporated two of the most important elements of the Nazi *Weltanschauung*, the identity and identification of the Nazi party, the State and the *volk*, on the one hand, and the centrality of racial bio-ideology on the other hand. These two elements, while perhaps analytically separable, are, in fact, part and parcel of an overriding legal vision of the racial state. Law is seen as the embodiment of the will and wisdom of the *Volk*, who are represented by the Party and above all by the Führer. In such circumstances, values and legal norms which must reflect the will of the people replace traditional values of the liberal democratic state, with its particular identification with the individual. At the same time, the will of the people and its destiny, are threatened by the parasites which attack the body politic and the body of the law. The "Jew", under Nazi criminal theory and practice, along with the Gypsy, and the more ill-defined "asocial", is criminalized. "Biological" categories are criminalized as criminal law categories are biologized. In other words, the Nazi state is a police state, not because of the suppression of "civil liberties" (which in its original form was perfectly legal under Art. 48 of the Weimar Constitution), but because the policing of the body politic against the enemies of the Volk is the very *raison d'être* of the Nazi State itself.

That such an ideological vision is in clear conflict with the ideals of individual freedom and autonomy which apparently characterize traditional Western versions of the rule of law is clear. In the field of criminal law, for example, a basic principle is that of *nulla poenem sine lege*, i.e. that no one may be found guilty of a criminal offence unless that offence is previously clearly defined and known. In other words, criminal law must always be non-retroactive, strictly defined and limited in application, so that citizens may act, or refrain from acting, in full knowledge of their duties and of the limitations placed on their freedom.

Because the National Socialist view of the nature and place of criminal law was so contrary to the predominant historical tradition of the West, it is hardly surprising that one can find examples of legal discourse outside Germany criticizing Nazi legality and placing it outside the normative universe of the "interpretive community". Lawrence Preuss is one author who consistently criticized Nazi law in the strongest terms. Preuss offers this summary of the Nazi position which for him abandoned the principle of *nulla poena sine lege.*

> The principle of the non-retroactivity of the criminal law stands at the beginning of the *Reichsstrafgesestzbuch,* and is among the fundamental rights guaranteed by the Weimar Constitution. That it is the product of the liberal, humanitarian thought of the *Aufklärungzeit* apparently suffices to condemn it, however, in nationalist eyes.

He adds:

> Law, in the National Socialist conception, is not created by statute, but in the expression of the German legal conscience. The state cannot create it arbitrarily, but can only give it the sanction of its coercive authority.[48]

However, at this stage, even a critic of the Nazi regime like Preuss was not willing or able to dismiss the system of Nazi legality in the criminal law arena with its vast array of repressive mechanisms as outside "law". At this most vital and definitional point of Nazi legality, the criminal justice system and the repressive state apparatus, even critics were forced to recognize that a high degree of continuity existed with numerous aspects of previous embodiments of German criminal law. Preuss himself states that:

> When the National Socialists came to power, they found at their disposal a well-stocked armory of legal weapons with which to combat their enemies. There remained only the tasks of filling certain gaps, of increasing the severity of penalties, and of applying the law in the spirit of the authoritarian state.[49]

Even such well-known critics of Nazi legality as Otto Kirchheimer were compelled to construct their attacks in terms which to a reader today might seem conceptually problematic. For him, the ideological underpinnings of Nazi criminal law could be found in the complete shift

---

48. "The Position of Aliens in National Socialist Penal Law Reform", 29 *Am. J. Intl.* 206 (1935) at 216, 217. Footnotes omitted.
49. Ibid., at 209. Footnote omitted.

...from the objective characteristics of the criminal act to its subjective elements. It is suggested that the state is justified in demanding greater self-control from the individual as the main object of the offensive action of the authorities.[50]

Current debates in the Western democracies about penal and criminal justice policies, from Tony Blair and New Labour's rediscovery of law and order, to more traditional conservative ideas about crime control, also place a renewed emphasis on the individual responsibility of those engaging in anti-social behavior. Concerns about the appropriate balance between the objective and subjective elements of liability, *mens rea* and *actus reus* etc. are and have been current in common law jurisdictions in recent years. Of course, this does not mean that we are seeing a resurgence of Nazi-inspired criminology. It does mean, on the other hand, that simplistic assertions about the criminality of Nazi law as epitomized in Hitler's criminal justice system need to be more carefully and explicitly articulated in light of even contemporary understandings about what was happening in Germany.

A brief survey of English-language legal literature also indicates that as far as many members of the legal interpretive community were concerned, Nazi theory and practice fit clearly and identifiably into the mainstream of criminal law and criminological discourse. As in the case of law more generally, some legal scholars seem to have been content to offer uncritical exegeses of Nazi criminal law theory and practice. A Canadian scholar, for example, wrote,

> The significant figure in the new criminal law is not the unworthy member of society, but society itself. The criminal law is to be built up on broad lines of defence of the strong and proved and capable element of the German people as against the morally ill and unworthy element of social decadence. The identity of law and morals must be restored, that is, it must replace the un-German contrast between morality on the one hand and the feeling for law on the other. The wrongdoer in a criminal sense must be the wrongdoer in a social sense. In particular, factors of social security must be built up; society must not any longer wait to act until an unworthy member of its group has begun a wrongful act; the dangerous element in society

---

50. "Criminal Law in National-Socialist Germany", 8 *Studies in Philosophy and Social Sciences* 444 (1939). See more generally, Karl Lowenstein, "Law in the Third Reich", 45 *Yale Law Journal* 779 (1938).

must, as early as possible, be forestalled by preventive measures. The ideal of racial security must be made operative.[51]

A close reading of this text describing German criminal law reveals quickly why English-language scholars by and large could not and did not exclude Nazi criminal law from the category "law". All of the goals of Nazi legality, prevention of criminality, the creation of a nexus between law and morality etc. can be identified within the jurisprudential traditions of Western democracies. Debates about the law/morality nexus, the struggle to balance the rights of individuals and the rights of society as a whole to be protected from dangerous individuals and actions, social responsibility of offenders, these are all elements of historic and current criminological study and discourses about the appropriate function of repressive state power.

Similarly, it is important to note at this stage that Nazi legality was not homogenous and uniform. What we know of the horrors of the concentration camps[52] must not be permitted to mask the reality both of Nazi policy and practices on the one hand and of the discourse about Nazi policies and practices on the other. For example, it is possible to easily trace a continuous, if twisted, path, from the category "asocial" to the concentration camps, to sterilization policies, to the organized attacks on male homosexuals, to the mass killing of the Sinti and Roma. We also know that the "asocial" category itself was not only mutable within Nazi penology but also that the idea of "rehabilitation" of asocials was to some extent at least part of Nazi criminology. Again, I make these points simply to underline the fact that what is under examination here is the "reality" of Nazi legality as it was experienced at the time, both inside and outside Germany, not the historically constructed post-Nuremberg "criminal state".

A brief examination of the contemporary English-language literature in the field of criminology and criminal justice indicates the same uncertainties and debates about German law as was found in other learned discussions of different aspects of post-1933 legality. For each example of critique of German and Nazi penal policy and practice, we can find one lauding or at the very least refusing to condemn Nazi law as outside the accepted definitions of the "rule of law". As already noted, Lawrence Preuss was willing to condemn the elimination of the protection afforded to the accused by the maxim *nulla poena sine lege.* He wrote in the following terms:

---

51. F. C. Auld, "Law Reform in Germany", *Canadian Bar Review*, 1934, p. 26.
52. See e.g., Wolfgang Sofsky, *The Order of Terror: The Concentration Camp,* op. cit.

In a country in which judicial independence, as understood in western states, has utterly disappeared, the right of the courts to punish without a written law destroys the last defense of the individual against the totalitarian National Socialist state.[53]

On the other hand, E.A.M. Wedderburn dismissed such criticisms by arguing:

The Nationalist Socialist view is that *all* behaviour worthy of punishment shall meet with its just reward and that there shall be no evasion of the meshes of the law. Henceforward in Germany the ruling maxim is *nullum crimen sine poena,* and it is the arduous duty of the judge to realise true justice. Revolutionary as this may sound, anyone familiar with the fictions, distinctions, and interpretations resorted to in the development of the Criminal Law of many other nations will agree that the principle at least is not new.[54]

He then goes on to argue that Nazi legality is indeed at least partly consistent with some idea of the "rule of law":

With these new duties it is clear that judges will in future have to create as well as administer law. This is contrary to the democratic doctrine of the division of authority in the sphere of judiciary and legislature, but it is not a complete negation of the idea.[55]

Anyone familiar with current debates in various countries governed by the "rule of law" will indeed recognize the familiar jurisprudential tension between those who argue that judges should simply apply the law and those who argue that the very principle of judicial decision-making requires that judges "make" law within certain boundaries. But the important point here is not so much that one can recognize recurrent themes in present day debates over jurisprudential basics and judicial politics, but rather that at the time, these debates took place within a context which did not automatically, at least for some of the participants, eliminate Nazi legality from consideration. What is clear is that while some contemporaries were extremely critical of developments within the criminal justice system in Germany from 1933 onwards, others were nonetheless willing to consider that these changes were not totally unac-

---

53. "Punishment by Analogy in National Socialist Penal Law", 26 *Journal of Criminal Law and Criminology* 847 at 856 (footnote omitted).

54. "Criminal Law in the Third Reich", 48 *Juridical Review* 373, at 378–79.

55. Ibid., at 380.

ceptable or that they fell completely outside the realm of what was then recognized as "law". As the war progressed, the characterization of Nazi legality
took on a different complexion and we begin to see the emergence of the construction of the "criminal state" in Western legal discourse about Nazi criminal law. Such a shift in the discursive boundaries might be attributable to several factors alone or in combination. It might be the case that the shifting
characterization is due to a greater knowledge of the "facts" of what was really
happening in Germany and in Europe. It may also be true that Nazi policy
and practice shifted at some time in the period between the mid-1930s and
the mid-1940s. Finally, it may be argued that the shifting discourse reflected
the time in another way i.e. now Germany was the enemy and everything German, or at least everything Nazi, had to be characterized as evil.

None of these arguments can be truly dispositive. Learned discourse at the
earlier time was at least as well informed as to what was happening in Germany as were authorities during the war. If Nazi policy and practice did in
fact shift, the debate must then itself turn to a careful analysis of just when
the shift occurred and just what it involved. Only after a very careful consideration of these factors can we truly address the basic issues of continuity and
discontinuity raised here. Finally, it is important to note that here we are in
fact dealing with a rather more specific and narrow timeframe. In the pre-war
period, from the Nazi seizure of power onwards, it is clear that Western legal
discourse considered the changes operating in Germany under Nazi legality to
be changes occurring within a continuous context of Western, or at least rec-
ognizably German, legality and the rule of law. While there was disagreement
about the nature of the changes and the dangers they posed to some basic
principles of the "rule of law", there was never a dominant discourse within
the Western legal and academic community which completely rejected Nazi
legality and placed it outside the realm of "law".

Furthermore, it is clear from many of the analyses of the Nazi penal system that the continuity existed not just at this broader level of discourse about
"law" in the West, but that developments under the Nazis could find their
roots and sources within the historical evolution of German legality.

A discussion in a leading English-language learned journal of the first major
reforms to the penal law under the Nazis highlights this aspect of the continuity issue.[56] As Professor Mannheim makes clear, reform and debate within
the German criminal law system were influenced by earlier and non-Nazi de-

---

56. Hermann Mannheim, "The German Prevention of Crime Act, 1933", 26 *J. Crim. L.
and Crim.* 517 (1935–36).

velopments in the field of criminology. He outlines the different approaches to the issue of penalties in criminal law in each of the historically dominant schools of criminology. In conclusion, Professor Mannheim argues that while the system may operate as a threat to the liberty of the individual, the reforms have a positive aspect as well.

> The advantages of the new Act are that it has introduced for the first time into German Criminal Law important measures of protection of society and has strengthened the power of the Criminal Courts instead of that of the Administrative Authorities.[57]

One of the key themes developed by Mannheim is the historical, ideological and jurisprudential bases of the various conflicts between different schools of thought within criminology.[58] These conflicts, then as now, centered on two primary themes, causation of crime and treatment of criminals. In Nazi criminology, with its bio-racial roots, biological explanations of causation clearly predominated, although, as the literature also makes clear, such views had not yet achieved hegemonic status in the German legal system.

For Mannheim, the introduction of legislation within the German penal law system dealing with the problems of habitual and mentally ill criminals, was by and large a good and potentially progressive step. He placed German debates and legislative provisions dealing with preventive detention within the broader criminological context of public safety and order, and argued that much of the German system could be said to have been based in English law reform proposals.[59] Further he argued that one of the problems with the German i.e. Nazi, preventive detention system, in 1938–1939, after *Kristallnacht* and subsequent steps in the institutional development of the concentration camp system, was its failure to adequately distinguish between ordinary prison establishments and regimes and preventive detention facilities and practices.

> It is, however, questionable whether these differences, will in the whole, be practically important enough to be appreciated by the inmates, all the more since the Preventive Detention Establishment, as mentioned before, can be connected with the ordinary prison. If the

---

57. Ibid., at 537.
58. See also, Werner S. Landecker, "Criminology in Germany", 31 *J. Crim. L and Crim.* 551 (1940–1941). For a case specific study see, Otto Kirchheimer, "Recent Trends in German Treatment of Juvenile Delinquency", 29 *J. Crim. L. and Crim.* 362 (1938–1939).
59. At 523–24.

differentiation is imperceptible, then the transfer of the prisoners from prison to the Preventive Detention Establishments would mean only a change of name, not of aim, and the whole double-track system becomes useless.[60]

For him, a key issue was not the existence of preventive detention establishments, concentration camps, but the failure to physically and institutionally separate them from ordinary prisons. Punishment, in order to be effective, had to be recognizable as such, by the prisoners themselves.

Hindsight permits us to see the tragic underestimation of the efficiency of the German criminal law apparatus which characterizes Mannheim's analysis. Again, more importantly, Mannheim's article offers clear evidence that contemporary scholars did not, even when they had grave doubts about the racial biological worldview which informed Nazi law, seek to understand German law after 1933 as discontinuous in a radical sense with what had gone before or with the legal systems of other "civilized" countries.[61]

Thus, in so far as the introduction of measures aimed at "dangerous sexual offenders" was concerned, Mannheim wrote that

The provisions dealing with the *castration of dangerous sexual offenders*, may, perhaps, be interesting especially for the American reader, since just in the whole of this sphere the example of the United States has been suggestive for Germany. For many decades the German criminal and biological science has devoted its deepest attention to the United States legislation and practice.[62]

For Mannheim, as for others, a central element of Nazi criminal policy, a bio-racial worldview which informed a eugenic crime prevention practice, a practice which would lead ultimately to the extermination of millions of asocial and anti-social "elements", found its inspiration in the United States. Clearly, any idea that the body of Nazi law, even in its most vital conceptual elements, informed by the bio-politics of the *Volksgemeinschaft*, was (or can

---

60. At 526.

61. Mannheim himself simply asserted that the criminal justice system was ill-suited to implement racial and biologically informed notions of national improvement. He wrote that "Personally, I should think that criminal justice should rather content itself with the protection of the public against crime and should leave the racial improvement of the people to other institutions which are better fitted for this work." At 536.

62. At 530.

be) understood as inimical to other ideals or practices inherent in democratic rule of law notions or in rule of law nations, is refuted here.

Indeed, other writers saw the emergence of biological explanations of the origins of crime and criminals as a corrective antidote to what they perceived as an unhealthy American obsession with psychological or psychiatric constructions of criminal behavior.[63] It is at the juncture of the issues of causation and treatment that the discourses of the English-speaking West and of Nazi legality come together in the clearest example of the continuity between Western legal practice and Nazi legality. In the eugenic worldview according to which criminals and asocials are born, not made, and in which society can only protect itself by taking what we now call proactive measures, Nazi legality and other versions and understandings of law as we know it live in almost total harmony.

In the legalization of the eugenic sterilization of the "defective", our law and the law of the so-called "criminal state" operated almost as one. At the point at which the coercive power of the state can be and is brought to bear on the most intimate aspects of its citizens and subjects, in a concrete manifestation of a eugenic aspiration for a perfectible society, Nazi law and our law most clearly resembled one another. Here the body of the law and the law of the body inscribe, create and destroy the embodied *homo sacer*.[64] If it is true that the Nazi state was at its epitome a racial state, characterized by a bio-racial view of the world and the social order, then the program whereby the state ordered and organized the compulsory sterilization of those who did not conform to the accepted and decreed standard, must surely be the most clear legal embodiment of that Nazi ideology, an ideology which we now believe, according to the discontinuity thesis, distorted and destroyed the rule of law.[65] At the same time, however, if we can find evidence that our own legal system permitted and compelled similar practices for similar reasons, then we must begin once more to question the idea and ideology of discontinuity which has been so popular until recently. Indeed, we must also begin to question even more fundamental and cherished notions of law, legality, the rule of law etc. Exactly where, if at all, can we situate and locate the point at which Nazi law

---

63. See Nathaniel Cantor, "Recent Tendencies in Criminological Research in Germany", 27 *J. Crim. L. and Crim.* 782 (1936–1937). But cf., Cantor, "Prison Reform in Germany-1933", 25 *J. Crim. L. and Crim.* 84 (1934–1935) and Cantor, "Untermassfeld-An Experiment in Prison Education", ibid., at 721.

64. See Giorgio Agamben, *Homo Sacer*, op. cit., supra chapter 3.

65. See e.g. Michael Burleigh and Wolfgang Wipperman, *The Racial State*: Germany *1933–1945*, op. cit.

diverges so radically from our own legal system that we may once more comfortably assert our difference? When the camp, which segregates and excludes the Other, and the physical mutilation and later elimination of that Other, come to epitomize and embody the law in its sovereign function, where can we even begin to imagine an epistemological circumstance separating our law from Nazi law?[66]

5. Sterilization, Anglo-American Legal Discourse and the Rule of Law: Continuity

It is important yet again to underline and emphasize exactly what is at stake in this examination of discursive practices surrounding the contemporary construction of Nazi law. I am, for example, not asserting that eugenics leads inevitably to the Holocaust. It is clear that support for eugenic legislation and the implementation of such legislation in the United States and Canada did not lead to the Holocaust in those countries. I am not asserting a universal causality within eugenic discourse as it relates to the Shoah. Nor am I asserting a universal and homogenous discourse and legal practice among proponents of eugenics and compulsory sterilization. For all its support among the intellectual, legal and political elite in Great Britain, for example, eugenic sterilization was never embodied there in legislative enactment nor was it an accepted or widespread medical legal practice.[67] In the United Kingdom, despite the best efforts of its supporters, compulsory (and even voluntary) sterilization was always considered beyond medical and legal acceptability.[68] The closest proponents of eugenic legislation in Britain managed to come was the pas-

---

66. See David Fraser, "To Belong or Nor To Belong", op. cit., supra chapter 3.

67. See generally, Daniel J. Kevles, *In the Name of Eugenics* (Cambridge: Harvard University Press, 1995), at 59 et. seq. and Wendy Kline, *Building a Better Race: Gender, Sexuality, and Eugenics from the Turn of the Century to the Baby Boom* (Berkeley and Los Angeles: University of California Press, 2001).

68. See "The Right of Sterilisation", 73 *Solicitors' Journal* 258 (1929); "Birth Control by Order", 74 *Solicitors' Journal* 37 (1930); "Legislation-Sterilisation", 172 *Law Times* 99 (1931); "Sterilization", 15 *J. of Comp. Leg. and Intl. Law* 126 (1933); "Conference on Mental Health", 176 *Law Times* 433 (1933); "Legalisation of Sterilisation", 177 *Law Times* 52 (1934); see also, Harvey G. Simmons, "Explaining Social Policy: The English Mental Deficiency Act of 1913", *Journal of Social History*, Winter 1977, p. 38.

sage of *An Act to make further and better provision for the care of Feeble-minded and other Mentally Defective Persons and to amend the Lunacy Acts* in 1913. The *Act* contained no provision for the sterilization of the "mentally defective".

In France, despite support for eugenic legislation and compulsory sterilization among certain elements of the medical and scientific communities, the only legislation enacted in the field related to compulsory pre-nuptial examinations.[69] At the same time, tens of thousands of Jews were deported from France to their deaths by the forces of French law and order. The experiences of both Britain and France indicate without doubt that historically there was no homogenous practice in relation to compulsory sterilization regimes, as well as demonstrating, in the French case, that such legislation was not a *sine qua non* of the Holocaust.

Three other key points remain, however. First, eugenic discourse and legislative practice around the issue of compulsory sterilization of "asocials" and of the "mentally defective" were clearly on the agenda of Western industrialized countries in the early part of this century. Second, the fact that such discourses and practices of sterilization were on the "legal" agenda of the Western democracies must cause us to question the "illegality" of a central component of Nazi law. Third, as many others have pointed out, we must not allow the *ex post facto* existence of the Holocaust to blind us to the moral and ethical issues raised by debates and practices of compulsory sterilization in the early part of this century. In Germany, compulsory sterilization might now be said to have lead inextricably to euthanasia, which in turn lead to the Holocaust. While this did not occur in other Western countries such as Canada and the United States, which did adopt legalized, compulsory sterilization, the commonality and continuity between and among legal, political and medical discourses at the time can not be ignored simply by invoking the Holocaust both as some kind of historical trump card or conversely, as a mark of radical disjuncture.

Instead, I believe that an examination of the self-understanding of participants in the policies and practices of eugenic sterilization at the time demonstrates once again that any critique of Nazi law as radically discontinuous with law as we understand (or at least understood) it in Anglo-American democracies, must be brought into question. If lawyers in the United States, for example, considered "eugenics", or "racial hygiene" to be an acceptable normative underpinning for operative and operating legal measures within and upon the body politic, then it simply cannot be asserted, *tout court*, that Nazi law,

---

69. See generally, Anne Carol, *Histoire de l'Eugénisme en France* (Paris: Seuil, 1995).

with its *grundnorm* insuring the health and survival of the *Volksgemeinschaft*, was a criminal aberration, unworthy of the name "law".

A brief examination of the law and legal literature of the time in question will provide useful points of departure for our continuing investigation into the discursive practices of the legal communities in various countries. I have, of course, already discussed Hermann Mannheim's construction of the close relationship between Nazi sterilization practices within the criminal justice system and the example set by American law.

Others, dealing with the scientific aspects of Nazi ideology and practice, have pointed out and examined the individual and institutional relationships between those in the United States and those in Germany working in the field of eugenic legislation.[70] What is useful for our purposes here is to note the fact both that lawyers in the English-speaking world were also aware of the similarities with and developments in German criminal law and that such similarities and developments were treated in such a manner as to indicate that they were considered to be, to a certain degree at least, unproblematic and acceptably normal. In other words, the compulsory sterilization of those deemed to be "defective" was well within the bounds of the legally recognizable role and function of the state, as understood within contemporary Anglo-American legal discursive practices.

While ideas of racial purity, biological hygiene and compulsory steriliza-tion are now most commonly (but not universally) associated with a rigid, rightwing authoritarianism (like Nazism), eugenic discourse was in fact pop-ular with elements from all parts of the political spectrum. The idea and ideals of progress, improvement, the conquest of nature, of science as the way to a better future, are all perfectly in tune with many liberal and leftwing visions of modernity.[71] The rhetorical devices deployed by proponents and opponents of eugenics and compulsory sterilization were not, in the period which inter-ests us here, homogeneously identified or identifiable with easy categories of left and right or conservative and liberal.[72] Indeed, perhaps the best known

---

70. See Robert Proctor, *Nazi Doctors*, op. cit.; Götz Aly, Peter Chroust and Christian Pross, *Cleanisng The Fatherland* (Baltimore: Johns Hopkins University Press, 1994); Stefan Kühl, *The Nazi Connection* (New York and Oxford: Oxford University Press, 1994).

71. Kevles, *In the Name of Eugenics*, op. cit., at 63 et. seq.

72. See Elof Axel Carlson, *The Unfit: A History of a Bad Idea* (New York: Cold Stream Harbor Laboratory Press, 2001); Marouf Arif Hasian, *The Rhetoric of Eugenics in Anglo-American Thought* (Athens, Georgia: University of Georgia Press, 1996). In a related fash-ion, Robert Proctor's recent work on various aspects of Nazi science points out ways in which "progressive" concerns about tobacco, diet, environmental factors in disease etc. were also part of the complex focus of Nazi ideals of the protection of the body politic. *The Nazi War on Cancer*, op cit.

example of eugenic discourse in Western law comes not from a traditional conservative source but from a legal scholar and thinker most commonly (and accurately) associated with "progressive" social and legal reform in the United States in the first decades of the 20th century, Oliver Wendell Holmes.[73]

In the now infamous case of Carrie Buck, a young woman sterilized by the state of Virginia, Holmes wrote the opinion of the Supreme Court of the United States upholding the validity of the statute under which Buck would be made infertile. Therein, he wrote the words which continue (or should continue) to haunt US constitutional jurisprudence.

> We have seen more than once that the public welfare may call upon the best citizens for their lives. It would be strange if it could not call upon those who already sap the strength of the State for these lesser sacrifices, often not felt to be such by those concerned, in order to prevent our being swamped with incompetence. It is better for all the world, if instead of waiting to execute degenerate offspring for crime, or to let them starve for their imbecility, society can prevent those who are manifestly unfit from continuing their kind. The principle that sustains compulsory vaccination is broad enough to cover cutting the Fallopian tubes. Three generations of imbeciles are enough.[74]

Others have documented the sad and tragic history both of Carrie Buck[75] and of the eugenics movement in the United States[76] and it is not my purpose

---

73. For a detailed study of Holmes' legal and political philosophy and its relationship with eugenics see, Mary L. Dudziak, "Oliver Wendell Holmes as a Eugenic Reformer: Rhetoric in the Writing of Constitutional Law", 71 *Iowa L.* R. 833 (1986).

74. *Buck v Bell*, 274 U.S. 200 (1927) at p. 207 (reference omitted). Virginia apologized for its forced sterilization policy in 2002. See Matthew Engel, "State says sorry for forced sterilizations", *Guardian*, 4 May 2002.

75. See Stephen Jay Gould, *The Mismeasure of Man* (New York and London: Penguin, 1992) and Stephen Trombley, *The Right to Reproduce: A History of Coercive Sterilization* (London: Weidenfeld and Nicolson, 1988) at 88 et. seq.

76. See Kevles, *In the Name of Eugenics*, op. cit.; Nicole Hahn Rafter, *White Trash: The Eugenic Family Studies, 1877–1919* (Boston: Northeastern University Press, 1998); James W. Trent Jr., *Inventing the Feeble Mind: A History of Mental Retardation in the United States* (Berkeley: University of California Press, 1994); William H. Tucker, *The Science and Politics of Racial Research* (Urbana and Chicago: University of Illinois Press, 1994); Edward J. Larson, *Sex, Race, and Science: Eugenics in the Deep South* (Baltimore: Johns Hopkins University Press, 1995); Ellen Brantlinger, *Sterilization of People with Mental Disabilities* (Westport and London: Auburn House, 1995); John P. Radford, "Sterilization Versus Segregation: Control of the 'Feebleminded'", 33 *Soc. Sci. Med* 449 (1991). See also, Joseph P.

or intention here to repeat their efforts. At this point, I wish simply to briefly examine some of the dominant themes of the Court's judgment as expressed by Holmes. It is clear that one can find in Holmes' opinion many of the common themes from eugenics debates generally, and more specifically one can easily discover elements of the discussions about eugenics and "useless eaters" which were taking place in Germany at the same time. The devastation wrecked by World War I on the young men of the nation combined with the offsetting effect of the increasing numbers of "defectives" is one such motif. Fear of the rising tide of "incompetence" threatening the very welfare and existence of the healthy body politic is also evident, as is the clear connection between and among degeneracy, "feeblemindedness" and criminality. The very survival of the "public welfare", "the State" and even of "all the world", for Holmes is dependent upon the removal of Carrie Buck's capacity to reproduce. It does not require a leap of imagination beyond the capacity of any lawyer, to see and read here echoes of concerns for the body politic, the nation's germ plasm, the continuation of a healthy *Volksgemeinschaft*, which would come to dominate German medico-legal ideology and practice just a few years after Holmes' intervention from the Bench of the United States Supreme Court.

In other words, Holmes' opinion in *Buck v. Bell* simply reflects and repeats many of the dominant medical, political, social and legal themes from contemporary debates about eugenics, debates which again are not completely foreign to today's political scene. As far as Holmes and many of his contemporaries were concerned, the idea of applying "scientific" eugenic principles in the legal and medical context of compulsory sterilization of the "feebleminded" or "mentally defective" was perfectly normal and acceptable as part of everyday political and legal practice and discourse. Indeed, for them it was seen as a more humane and scientific method for dealing with various social problems. Better to sterilize to prevent a criminal or "defective" from being born than to execute the criminal or watch the "defective" starve to death some years later. Science, medicine and law here united under the aegis of "progress", just as they would unite in Germany under the banner of a new order. Ideas such as these were not, as many might now believe, or desperately want to believe, a legal nightmare, part of the racial biological vision of the Master Race under Nazism, achievable in a concrete "legalized" form only within the context of a criminal state. Rather, they were here part of a "progressive" social vision in the world's greatest democracy.

Chamberlain, "Eugenics in Legislatures and Courts", 15 *American Bar Association Journal* 165 (1929).

In Holmes' decision and in the legal instruments mandating sterilization, we find a clear legislative and judicial policy decision, accepted and legitimized within the democratic context, to give preeminence to notions of the protection of the public welfare, of the "strength of the state" through the invasive and coercive regulation of reproduction on "scientific" grounds. All of this is not, again, taking place in a totalitarian *volksgemeinschaft*, ruled by the *führerprinzip*, but in the land of the Constitution and the Bill of Rights. Dangerous individuals, who posed a threat to the social welfare, either because they threatened to reproduce further generations of "imbeciles" or because of their inherent criminal tendencies, were to be singled out in a medical-legal process governed by scientific principle, for sterilization.

Of course, a decision, such as *Buck v. Bell*, informed as it was within a context of the broader discourses of science and law, did not arise in isolation. Legal discourse among the profession had long been concerned with such issues and lawyers had practical experience in dealing with the legislation which had been in place in the United States since the earliest part of the century.[77] Writing in the leading journal of America's legal practitioners, J.P. Chamberlain explained that:

> Recent legislation limiting the right to marry is based not on historic rules or race feeling but on scientific facts. It is directed against two evils, the bringing into the world of children with hereditary taints and the protection of the public health by preventing the spread of disease through marriage.[78]

The battle against the evil of degeneracy and the threat it posed to the very fabric of society and to the health of the body politic, had not always been an easy one. American legal discourse on the issue of compulsory sterilization of the period can be characterized as falling into two primary categories. On the one hand, on the side of proponents and opponents of compulsory sterilization legislation, the tone was often moral i.e. each side argued its position from first principles.[79] At the same time, and particularly as legislation was adopted in various jurisdictions, the discourse shifted from the moral and ethical to the more "purely" legal. Arguments based on principles of equal protection, the police power, due process and cruel and unusual punishment,

---

77. See "Sterilization of Criminals: Report of Committee "H" of the Institute", 2 *ABA J.* 128 (1916). See also, Kevles, op. cit., at 96 et. seq.

78. "Eugenics and Limitations of Marriage", 9 *ABA J.* 429 (1923). See also "Eugenics in the Modern State: The Saltiel Law", 32 *Ill. L.* 327 (1937–1938).

79. See Hasian, *The Rhetoric of Eugenics*, op. cit. supra.

were raised and met concerning the constitutional validity of various statutes.[80] Particularly after *Buck v. Bell* confirmed the general power of the States to legislate in the domain, the debates within the legal community take on a more technical aspect, seeking to find the appropriate legal and constitutional limits of the practice.[81] The history of American legal discourse in this area is of interest because it can be seen to embody, at the same point in history, many if not all of the tropes and rhetorical devices which were current in Nazi legal discourse on the subject at the time and later. "Race feeling", crude ungrounded prejudice, is replaced with objective scientific normativity. The welfare of the individual "degenerate" is invoked to reinforce the social desirability of compulsory sterilization. Opponents of the compulsory sterilization measures do not question the idea of reproductive coercion by the state in principle but simply examine the "science" of mental defects. The debate which takes place within the legal hermeneutic community is not one as to whether compulsory sterilization of "defectives" is acceptable but rather it is one as to when science allows one to determine with precision the exact extent of the category "defective". Finally, the real menace to society and the body politic is again invoked. Mental defectives, asocials, feebleminded individuals are criminals or breeders of criminals. They must be stopped, by limiting them from immigrating or from reproducing. It is with the invocation of the mentally handicapped as criminals posing a direct physical, biological threat to the body politic that American legal discourse and practice comes closest to the rhetoric and practice of Nazi criminal racial biology. Indeed, any and all of the preceding arguments about concern for the poor individual, the im-

---

80. See e.g. Aubrey E. Strode, "Sterilization of Defectives", 11 *Va. L. R.* 296 (1925); Burke Shartel, "Sterilization of Mental Defectives", 16 *Journal of the American Institute of Criminal Law and Criminology* 537 (1925–1926); "Note, Constitutional Law—Eugenical Sterilization Statutes", 12 *Va. L. R.* 419, (1925–1926); "Constitutionality of the Iowa Sterilization Statute", 11 *Iowa L. R.* 262 (1925–1926); Jacob B. Aronoff, "The Constitutionality of Asexualization Legislation in the United States", 1 *St. John's L. R.* 146 (1926); "News of State and Local Bar Associations", 13 *ABA J.* 296 (1927); Clarence J. Ruddy, "Compulsory Sterilization: An Unwarranted Extension of the Powers of Government", 3 *Notre Dame Lawyer* 1 (1927).
81. See e.g., "Comment", 1 *S. Cal. L. R.* 73 (1927–1928); "The New Iowa Statute on Sterilization of Defectives", 15 *Iowa L. R.* 238 (1929–1930); Joseph P. Chamberlain, "Eugenics in Legislatures and Courts", 15 *ABA J.* 165 (1929); Lester B. Orfield, "Notes—Constitutional Law—Sterilization", 10 *Neb. L. R.* 164 (1931); J.H. Landman, "The History of Human Sterilization in the United States—Theory, Statute, and Adjudication", 63 *American Law Review* 48 (1929); Leonard V. Finder, "Note", 26 *Ill. L. R.* 819 (1932); Alvin E. Bielefeld, "Note", 28 *Ill. L. R.* 120 (1934); Frank C. Richmond, "Sterilization in Wisconsin", 25 *J. Am* Inst. *Crim L. and Crim.* 586 (1934–1935).

pact of feeblemindedness on the family and the community, fears of criminality and anti-social behavior, could just as easily have been (and were) made
in Germany of the 1920s and 1930s. Few, if any, who made such arguments,
in Germany, the United States, and Canada, at the time believed that by engaging in these discursive practices one was being unfaithful to democracy or
the rule of law. Indeed, for proponents of eugenic laws, the very fabric of the
nation and of constitutional government, however understood, was dependent upon the adoption and implementation of such measures.

An important example taken from legal literature of an even later and more
important period, demonstrates the normalcy and acceptability of legalized eugenic discourse even more starkly. Here, a leading expert on the world of law and
politics under the new Nazi regime in Germany brought his insights to an elite
American legal audience. Karl Lowenstein, in his article describing the Nazi legal
system in otherwise less than laudatory terms, said about one aspect of Nazi law:

> Other legislation from the race myth attempts to weed out the phys-
> ically unfit and to provide for a healthy progeny in the future. Despite
> the vagueness and uncertainty of underlying biological and anthro-
> pological theories, they constitute, on the whole, a commendable ef-
> fort to promote eugenics and national hygiene.[82]

He adds in a footnote:

> The public health offices take care of many questions of biological hy-
> giene. Stripped of its racial exaggerations the public health legislation
> seems soundly conceived.[83]

Lowenstein's comments are important for several reasons. The article itself
is, in all other respects, highly critical of Nazi legal theory and practice, and
indeed of the underlying racial norms central to all Nazi law. It is dismissive
and contemptuous of what Lowenstein refers to as the basic "race myth",
which informs Nazism. Lowenstein, a former Professor at Munich, was no
sympathizer. He would, after the Allied victory, become a key player in the
legal program set up by the United States to reestablish the administration of
justice in Occupied Germany. Nonetheless, at this time, Lowenstein clearly

---

82. "Law in the Third Reich", op. cit., at 797 (footnote omitted). For his later work on
Nazi and German legality see, "Reconstruction of the Administration of Justice in Ameri-
can-Occupied Germany", 61 *Harvard L.R.* 419 (1948) and "Law and the Legislative Process
in Occupied Germany", 57 *Yale L. J.* 724 (1948).
83. Ibid., footnote 61.

believed not just that compulsory sterilization formed a valuable part of any public health legislation, but also that readers of the *Yale Law Journal* will not be shocked to their moral or legal core by reading these assertions. In other words, an opponent of the Nazi regime, who would spend much of his career trying to (re)establish the rule of law after years of Nazi (il)legality, found, in 1936, parts of a legal system based on racial hygiene to be perfectly sound and quite worthy functions of a law-bound state.

Of course, Lowenstein rejected many of the racial "exaggerations" of Nazi racial theory and legal practice, but the basic idea of "eugenic" principles being applied in a coercive legal setting was for him, and for many of his fellow members of the American legal interpretive community, not outside the realm of the acceptable or normal. Such a scheme, in which the government bureaucracy and legal machinery of the state takes charge of the "biological hygiene" of the people was an entirely permissible and even laudatory goal. While these positions may seem problematic to many of us in hindsight, it is important to remember that part of that hindsight is informed by the historical facticity of the Holocaust and I believe, by the ideological juridical construction of the Nazi state as a "criminal state".

Even a cursory examination of the discourses and arguments deployed at the relevant time in non-German jurisdictions and legal systems indicates that the dominant conceptions and understandings of these issues are themselves historically and contextually constructed. We need, for a variety of reasons, to believe that Nazi law was not law. Lowenstein's analysis of the state of German law underlines the fact of the continuity between what lawyers then understood as being acceptable within the broader construct of "the rule of law" and some key aspects of Nazi legality.

While Lowenstein's comments on the acceptability of Nazi marriage and public health regulations find support, as I have noted, in a much earlier examples of legal discourse on the subject of eugenic controls, it is important to note that Anglophone discourse on the subject was not homogenous. English writers for example clearly recognized the politically and socially unacceptable nature of cries for sterilization and for the most part argued for the more "humane" treatment of "born criminals" by segregation from society. Americans were divided on the issue on whether migrant criminality could be explained by biology or by sociological and environmental factors.[85]

---

85. See Grace Abbott, "Immigration and Crime — Report of Committee "G" of the Institute", 2 *ABA* J 116 (1916); Ervin Hacker, "Criminality and Immigration", 20 *J. Am. Inst. of Crim. L. and Crim.* 429 (1929).

Similar divisions existed with regards to "native" criminality. Some doubted biological explanations while others believed hereditary played an important role.[86] What is still the issue here is not, however, whether an homogenous or even hegemonic discourse and practice existed, but rather whether the issue of a biologically driven and informed criminal justice system was conceivable. There can be little doubt that for a time at least, in some parts of the American legal system, such notions were not just acceptable but were in fact put into practice. Criminals and mental defectives as they were known were involuntarily sterilized by a legally sanctioned mental health system.

While the numbers of those sterilized may not have reached the total of those subjected to the same procedures in Germany after 1933, it is nonetheless true that at the time one might have been hard pressed, in engaging in discourse about the compulsory sterilization of the mentally handicapped, to distinguish between its American and its German practitioners. Indeed, in some instances, as much of the American legal literature of the time makes clear, it may well have been the case that the provisions of the German legal system and its mechanisms of Hereditary Health Courts and appellate bodies, offered more formal legal protections to the mentally and physically handicapped than did American law. Other historical examples can be found to buttress my basic assertion here that Nazi law was by no means outside the parameter of what was considered to be normal and lawful by Anglo-American legal standards, practices and discourses of the period. Here, the experience of the Canadian province of Alberta is perhaps instructive.[87]

Along with British Columbia, Alberta was the only Canadian jurisdiction to adopt a fully-fledged eugenic sterilization statutory mechanism. Fears raised by the existence of a large indigenous population, the influx of "inferior" stock from Europe and the existence of a sometimes-idiosyncratic Prairie conservatism all helped influence the Alberta experience. While some attempts to introduce similar legislation were made in Canada's most populous province,

---

86. Compare e.g. Johannes Lange, *Crime as Destiny: A Study of Criminal Twins* (1931) and Aaron J. Rosanoff, Leva M. Handy and Isabel Avis Rosanoff, "Criminality and Delinquency in Twins", 24 *J. Crim. L. and Crim.* 923 (1933).

87. At the same time, various European jurisdictions were adopting and implementing similar measures as part of their legislative and legal systems. In Sweden and Switzerland, compulsory sterilization was put into effect and other countries considered such measures See Stephanie Hyatt, "A Shared History of Shame: Sweden's Four-Decade Policy of Forced Sterilization and the Eugenics Movement in the United States", 8 *Ind. Int'l. & Comp. L. R.* 475 (1998).

Ontario, and were met with favorable commentary from parts of the legal community, the Alberta experience remains Canada's sole long-term experiment with eugenic sterilization.[88] The Alberta statute, in addition to being Canada's most extensive legalized eugenic instrument, is interesting for several other reasons.[89] First, it demonstrates the widespread nature of eugenics and the law in the English-speaking world. Second, as a statutory instrument, it offered a detailed example of the intersections between and among the legislature, the legal profession and the medical community. Third, the *Act* is important because it was amended by the Alberta legislature first in 1937 to include some more "mentally defective persons" as well as "psychotics"[90] and again in 1942 to permit the sterilization of certain categories of epileptics not previously covered by the statute.[91] The latter amendments also extended the framework of the legislation to cover those suffering from Huntington's Chorea. These legislative changes clarify not just the extent to which eugenic sterilization was permitted but also once more serve to underline the idea that eugenically informed, compulsory, coercive sterilizations were accepted practice in Western democracies. Indeed, the extension of the Alberta statute to cover epilepsy and Huntington's Chorea offers striking parallels to the *Hereditary Health Act* in Germany which also allowed for the sterilization of persons suffering from these conditions.

Moreover, it must be underlined here that the amendments to the Alberta statute occurred in the first instance after the Nazi regime had been in power for some time and after the passage of both compulsory sterilization measures and the racist Nuremberg Laws. In the second instance, Huntington's Chorea was added to the list in the middle of the war against the "criminal state", whose doctors and lawyers would be prosecuted for their participation in the Nazi racial legal/medical enterprise. In 1942, while Canadians were fighting to protect and preserve freedom and democracy from Axis criminals, Canadians were being subjected to precisely the same coercive bio-medical and racial procedures which were central to Nazi conceptions of the body of the law. Again, if this element of racial hygiene, the legalized imposition of the sanction of compulsory sterilization of various types of "defectives" was being implemented and expanded in Canada in the middle of World War II, any assertion that Nazi law, based and grounded as it was, was somehow "not law", must be radically rethought.

---

88. "Sterilization of the Unfit", 48 *Canada Law Journal* 207 (1912).
89. *The Sexual Sterilization Act*, 1928.
90. C.47, 1937. See also 2 *University of Toronto Law Journal* 381 (1937–1938).
91. *An Act to Amend The Sexual Sterilization Act*, c. 48, 1942; 5 *U.T.L.J.* (1943–1944).

6. Conclusion

It appears that there was, on this key, characteristic issue of compulsory eugenic sterilization of those individuals whose ability to procreate was deemed to pose a threat to the well-being of society, little, if anything, which would have permitted one to distinguish between American and Canadian law and legal practice and German, or more precisely Nazi, law and legal practice. Indeed, very few at the time sought to make the distinction and any who did, did not go so far as to characterize what was happening in Germany as not recognizable as law. When Canadian and American legislators, doctors and lawyers were actively pursuing the eugenic sterilization of their own citizens within the context of democracy and the rule of law, German doctors and lawyers were pursuing the same policies and practices within the context of a "criminal state". At this level, it was difficult then, as it appears to be now, to know where one began and the other ended.

Eugenic sterilization was, as I have argued, not the only element of Nazi law to have found a counterpart in Anglo-American jurisdictions. Nor was it the only key principle of Nazi legal ideology and practice to have been contemplated and accepted by English-speaking jurists or by Anglophone learned journals. Jews were excluded from the civil service and German civil service reforms were seen by some as being beneficial to the country. Jews were forbidden from owning agricultural property and Nazi "blood and soil" ideology was portrayed as essential to national survival. German Jewish professors were removed from their positions, students were expelled because they were Jews and American readers of leading law publications were told that German and American culture, civilization and law sprang from and preserved common values. For many, if not most, lawyers in the English-speaking world at the time, the question of whether German law had crossed over the line into the territory of "not law", much less the realm of the morally unacceptable, did not seem to arise. Legal memory has, I believe, been distorted by the passage of time and more crucially by the post-1945 construction of Hitler's Germany as a "criminal state". It seems clear, however, that the English-speaking interpretive community, whether dealing with Nazi land law, penal law, legal education or the compulsory sterilization of "defectives" never conceived of Nazi law as "not law".

Contemporary lawyers and legal academics understood and constructed law under the Hitler regime as more or less normal. For them, German law was often interesting, developments were sometimes innovative, sometimes merely the continuation in different circumstances of long-standing German practices, but never particularly problematic because of some utterly unacceptable breach of normative standards. For non-Germans, and especially for those of us from the Anglo-American legal tradition, our own legal history relating to Nazi law has much to teach us. Whether the interpretive community is willing or able to learn the lessons and face the demons of our own past is a vital existential question for us all.

CHAPTER 5

NUREMBERG — CONSTRUCTING NAZI CRIMINALITY AND THE RULE OF LAW

1. Introduction

Nazi law was law. Nazi law created, in order to destroy, the Jew, the *homo sacer*. Auschwitz places law at the center of the Nazi killing machine. How can we in good conscience, ethically, as a matter of justice, forget the Professors of Law at German Universities as their Jewish colleagues and students were removed? Can we really fail to remember the thousands of lawyers and judges who drafted, implemented and applied anti-Jewish laws, laws for the compulsory sterilization of so-called "mental defectives", laws for the protection of the *Volk*. Finally, can we not recall the Doctors in Law who led Einsatzgruppe A? Instead of law and ethical remembrance, we have law and legal amnesia. The mythology of law after Auschwitz, and of our collective legal memory of the Holocaust, is still grounded in the ideal of the period of Nazi rule, 1933–1945, as a lawless time of the barbarians.

All of this is, or has been, too much to bear. We are not Nazis. We have constructed a complex set of legal discourses in order to avoid the fundamental truth of law after Auschwitz. The primary legal-ideological function of post-Auschwitz juristic events involving the prosecution of Nazi and other war criminals is, I argue, to attempt to convince us again and again, with each case against each perpetrator, of the discontinuity, the radical break of 1933–1945. Once that epistemological step has been accomplished, law assures us of a return to the safety of modernity, of the primacy of the rule of law. The epistemological certainty of such legal spectaculars is undermined, or at least challenged, by internal critiques of the "legality" and "justice" of such events, the ongoing arguments about "victors' justice," which have emerged again in relation to the trial of Slobodan Milosevic, or the pursuit of Osama Bin Laden. A more fundamental unveiling and disrobing of the rule of law by the legal actors themselves took place at Nuremberg.

The Nuremberg Trials and their offspring, debates about natural law and legitimacy, assertions about German or European identity and constitutional citizenship, are meant to legitimize the modern, civilized, rule of law by defining the Nazi period as not—not modern, not civilized, not the rule of law. Here we come to the crux of the issue of law "before Auschwitz" and of the law "after Auschwitz".

The "Trial of Major War Criminals" at Nuremberg marks the point in our collective construction of Nazi law at which the criminality of the 1933–1945 period is inscribed in our official legal memory. From this point on, our understanding of the "rule of law", legality, *Rechtsstaat*, is one which is underscored with the essential truth of the illegality of the Nazi regime. Indeed, "illegality" is perhaps too mild a descriptor. The Nuremberg Trial created and confirmed not just the illegal, or extra-legal nature of the Nazi period but marked and inscribed that time period as "Criminal". The Nazi state was a Criminal State and its leadership nothing more or less than a bunch of criminal thugs. This criminalization of Nazi law, the effective erasure of the "law" from the trope "Nazi law" was, and remains the main goal and contribution of the Nuremberg Trial of Major War Criminals.[1]

I am not asserting here that this ideological goal was *per se* unacceptable or unworthy in the context of the immediate post-war period. Both sides of the emergent Cold War, the Soviets and the West, at this moment shared some common understanding of the evils of Nazism and a desire to punish the guilty. The ideological construction of Nazi illegality at Nuremberg was therefore a part of an ideology shared by ideological enemies. Nor am I asserting that the trial and subsequent judicial proceedings against Nazi perpetrators were not justified, or at least justifiable, in a practical, moral or ethical sense. My position is simply that, as we have already seen from the treatment of Nazi law in the West in the pre-war period, Nazi law was never "not law". It was "bad law" but it was law. From this perspective, then, the ideological and teleological jurisprudential goals and functions of the

---

1. For a recent study of Nuremberg and its inscription in legal memory, see Donald Bloxham, *Genocide on Trial: War Crimes Trials and the Formation of History and Memory* (Oxford: Oxford University Press, 2001).

Nuremberg Trials, or to put it another way, the rule of law and the search for justice, could only be served through a basic and fundamental distortion both of the historical facts and of the legal philosophical premises which informed and continue to inform our basic understandings of the principles of the rule of law. At Nuremberg, in order to save itself, law had to betray itself.

The internal conflicts and contradictions of the rule of law discourses and historical distortions which informed Nuremberg arose at some level between the legal functions of the process and the broader political, representational or metaphoric roles assigned to the Trials. In other words, subjecting the accused to a juridical process of a criminal trial, with the consequent finding of guilt or innocence came into a conflict with the pedagogical function of a "show trial" meant to demonstrate not just the technical legal guilt of the accused but to teach the population of the victorious allied countries about the evil against which they had been struggling and to teach the defeated German populace of the evils perpetrated in their name.

Others have written, from a variety of perspectives, of the history of the Trials, of the care with which the defendants were chosen not just for their personal responsibility, but also for their representative character, and of the machinations which informed the process of trial and judgment. It is not my purpose to repeat these historical facts and descriptions here.[2] Rather I wish to briefly outline some of those points of disjunction between the "law" of Nuremberg and the "politics" of Nuremberg. It is in the interstices of these competing and sometimes contradictory discursive constructions where we can find the traumatic schisms which continue to trouble legal memory after Auschwitz. Here we find the first staging of a set of legal events aimed primarily at constructing the legal systems of various Western countries as operating in disjuncture with Nazi law.

---

2. See *inter alia*, G. M. Gilbert, *Nuremberg Diary* (New York: Da Capo Press, 1995); J.J. Heydecker and J. Leeb, *The Nuremberg Trials* (London: William Heinemann, 1962); Eugene Davidson, *The Trial of the Germans* (New York: Macmillan, 1966); Bradley F. Smith, *Reaching Judgment at Nuremberg* (New York: Basic Books, 1977); Joseph E. Persico, *Nuremberg: Infamy on Trial* (New York: Viking, 1994); Michael M. Marrus, *The Nuremberg War Crimes Trial, 1945–1946* (New York and Boston: Bedford Books, 1997); George Ginsbergs, *Moscow's Road to Nuremberg* (The Hague and Boston: Kluwer Law International, 1996); Airey Neave, *Nuremberg* (London: Grafton Books, 1989); Whitney R. Harris, *Tyranny on Trial* (New York: Barnes and Noble Books, 1995); Telford Taylor, *The Anatomy of the Nuremberg Trials* (New York: Knopf, 1992); Ann Tusa and John Tusa, *The Nuremberg Trial* (London: BBC Books, 1991). There is also a massive periodical literature on the subject.

2. Law and Politics: Trying the Nazis

As an Allied triumph over the Nazis became the most likely outcome of the Second World War, the soon-to-be victors began to consider the mechanisms by which the defeated enemy would be brought to justice.[3] Various plans were hatched, discussed, rejected, modified and implemented. Stalin's idea of a simple moral and legal equation of 50,000 Germans = 50,000 bullets offended Churchill who nonetheless continued to propose a series of drumhead Courts-Martial, which would identify leading Nazis and execute them. As Professor Lauterpacht wrote at the time the various proposals were being mooted, many of the basic questions fell more properly into the domain of political decision-making while lawyers awaited the outcome.

> The question whether the punishment of war crimes committed by the enemy is desirable, expedient and practicable is a problem of politics rather than of law. It includes such questions as the relative merits and disadvantages of providing a deterrent against criminal violations of the law of war; the prospective effectiveness of such deterrent; the taking into account of a widespread and not inherently reprehensible desire for retribution, the consequences of impunity upon national and international law and morality; the desirability, partly in the interest of the culprits, of containing a hitherto ruthlessly suppressed craving for revenge within the channels of a regularized legal procedure, and the effects of a policy of punishing war crimes upon the prospects of reconciliation or, at least, of a return to a minimum degree of normalcy in international relations.[4]

Once these political considerations were addressed, several legal dilemmas remained. The basis for a prosecution of war criminals in existing international law was problematic. Issues of *noella poena sine lege*, retroactivity of the legal rules invoked by the prosecution, the responsibility of individuals as opposed to states under international law norms and the general problem of the political nature of the prosecution of Nazis, "victors' justice", vexed not just discussions about the suitability of the trial at Nuremberg but also the trial itself once the decision to prosecute had been taken. Again, these diffi-

---

3. See op. cit. supra and George Creel, *War Criminals and Their Punishment* (New York: Robert M. McBride, 1944) and an extensive periodical literature.

4. "The Law of Nations and the Punishment of War Crimes", 21 *British Yearbook of International Law* 58 (1944).

culties and problems are well-documented and discussed in sometimes ago-nizing detail by others. For present purposes, two main points must be un-derlined.

First, Lauterpacht's distinction between legal and political considerations is revealed in the trial process to be more than just problematic. It is impossible. Each of the possible "political" objections or problems associated with taking the decision to proceed by way of prosecution instead of by summary execution for example, manifested itself during the trial in a "legal" guise. Indeed, the basic ob-jection which was raised at the trial and which has been invoked since, that the trial was illegitimate because it was nothing more than "victors' justice" is both a political and a legal issue. Before the prosecution authorities could proceed to the pedagogical stage of the trial, they had to establish that the trial itself was legiti-mate and that international law, existing at the times of the alleged offences, al-lowed violators to be prosecuted. Therefore, much of the Nuremberg Trial, both in the prosecutions' arguments and in the judgment of the International Military Tribunal itself, was spent establishing not the illegitimacy of Nazi legality but the legitimacy of international legality. In other words, the Allies were to some ex-tent at least hoist on their own jurisprudential petard. The illegitimacy of Nazi legality depended on the legitimacy of the norms they were alleged to have vio-lated. The political decision to proceed by law had to be legally justifiable and justified. The Nuremberg Trial became to a certain extent and at the insistence of the defendants' legal representatives, the trial of the Nuremberg Trial. If, for example, Nazi law was not law because it had abolished the *nulla poena* princi-ple in criminal proceedings, Nuremberg could not proceed, a judgment could not be reached unless and until the continuing validity of *nulla poena* was con-firmed and the proceedings were seen to be fully consistent with that principle.

The second point which it is important to emphasize is the relatively minor role played by the Holocaust at Nuremberg. This political, historical and legal fact is in large part a necessary consequence of the difficulties as-sociated with the legitimacy of international law itself and of the strategy adopted by the prosecution. As a result of the particular and peculiar views of the Americans and Justice Robert Jackson, the chief American prosecutor, the Nuremberg case against the Nazi leadership proceeded on the basis that Nazism and the Nazis constituted a criminal conspiracy against peace, the main purpose of which, from the rise to power in 1933, was to wage an ag-gressive war in violation of the basic principle of the international order which established the illegality of wars of aggression. Therefore, the Holo-caust was legally constructed from the outset of the Nuremberg Trial as a minor set of events which was to be largely subsumed by the main thrust of the Allied case against the Nazis, that they were part of an illegal conspiracy against peace.

This does not mean that the Nuremberg Trial did not and does not continue to play a major role in the construction of the Holocaust and Nazi legality in our collective juridical memories. The massive documentary evidence of Nazi atrocities against the Jews uncovered by Allied war crimes investigators continues to serve to this day as the basis of our understanding of the legalized horror of the Holocaust.[5] In popular memory and understanding, I would suggest, the Nazis convicted at Nuremberg, were convicted for their role in the Holocaust. That this is not in fact reflective of the evidentiary and legal reality of the Trial is perhaps unimportant at some level. That the public at large continue to see the Holocaust as central to Nazism and to Nazi guilt is not necessarily a bad thing. At other levels, however, it is important to remember that our memory of the Holocaust at Nuremberg is a counter-factual and counter-legal memory. The Trial did construct Nazi rule as criminal and Nazi law as not law, but this construction, contrary to our current popular and I would argue legal, memory and jurisprudential conventions, had little to do with the Holocaust and the role of Nazi law and lawyers in the Shoah.

3. Nuremberg and the Holocaust— Constructing the Shoah in Legal Memory

As I have noted, both as an evidentiary question and as a matter of legal principle, the Holocaust was, in fact, a minor element of the prosecution case against the Major War Criminals at the Nuremberg Trial. Again, it is not my intention here to repeat and rehash the well-worn ground of the historical narratives of the Trial. Instead, I wish to briefly examine some points which will serve to underscore the ways in which legal memory of the Holocaust was constructed at, by and through the Trial at Nuremberg.

The first point at which Nuremberg constructs our continuing imagery of the Holocaust and the rule of law is in the very choice of venue for the Trial of Major War Criminals. Of course, Nuremberg was chosen as a result of several factors, not the least of which was the fact that the Court House was one

---

5. See Marrus, op. cit. For another aspect of the Nuremberg Trial which has had an important impact on our understanding of the Holocaust, see Lawrence Douglas, "Film as Witness: Screening *Nazi Concentration Camps* Before the Nuremberg Tribunal", 105 *Yale L. J.* 449 (1995), and Douglas, *The Memory of Judgment*, op. cit.

of the few intact after massive Allied bombing raids. However, Nuremberg was also chosen as the venue for the Trial because of its symbolic and metaphorical value. Telford Taylor summarizes the situation

> Symbolically the city was quite appropriate for a trial of the Nazi leaders, as it was here that the Nazi party had staged its annual mass demonstrations and where the anti-Semitic "Nuremberg Laws" had been decreed in 1935.[6]

In other words, Nuremberg was chosen as the place to stage the Trial of Major War Criminals in part at least because it was symbolically the physical geographical manifestation of all that was wrong with Nazi law. Taylor is careful to construct Nazi law as unlawful by the rhetorical deployment of scare quotes around "Nuremberg Laws". Legalized antisemitism goes to the heart of Nazi law and it is at this metaphorical point that the incisive incursion of the rule of law must, for Taylor and the prosecution, take place. This is more than simple "victors' justice". Instead it is the literal and symbolic reconstruction of the law, a reconfiguring of real law as opposed to Nazi law, "criminal law", an illegal edifice constructed as the result of a criminal conspiracy under the mere superficial guise of law. As we shall see, however, the symbolism of Nuremberg and the rule of law falls short of its goal in the way in which the nature and extent of Nazi legalized antisemitism and destruction was legally constructed at the Trial itself.

The most important point at which the destruction of European Jewry was constructed as a legal phenomenon, or more precisely as part of the broader scheme of Nazi state and individual criminality, can be found in the actual textual provisions of Article 6 of the Charter of the International Military Tribunal. Under these provisions, the Tribunal was given jurisdiction over crimes committed by persons

> …who, acting in the interests of the European Axis countries, whether as individuals or as members of organisations, committed any of the following crimes…

Paragraphs *a* and *b* deal with crimes against peace and war crimes. These, of course, constituted the primary focus and thrust of Justice Jackson's grand prosecution plan to portray the Nazi regime as a giant criminal conspiracy against the existing international political and legal order. What is of more im-

---

6. Op. cit., at 61.

portance here is the criminal scope of Paragraph *c* which for the first time codified the concept of crimes against humanity. Both as a practical embodiment of a positive international legal norm and as a symbolic invocation of aspirational justice in the forum of international law and politics, this constituted a major step forward. However, the actual drafting of Paragraph *c* and the way in which it was applied must also be brought to bear in any analysis of exactly happened at Nuremberg and what "Nuremberg" means for law after Auschwitz. Paragraph *c* reads as follows:

> Crimes against humanity: namely, murder, extermination, enslavement, deportation, and other inhumane acts committed against any civilian population, before or during the war, or persecutions on political, racial, or religious grounds in execution of or in connection with any crime within the jurisdiction of the Tribunal, whether or not in violation of the domestic law of the country where perpetrated.

Paragraph *c* without doubt creates two interconnected and important legal principles. First, crimes against humanity are crimes against international law. Second, domestic or municipal law is subsumed if it is contrary to international law. In the context of legalized antisemitism, for example, it is no defense to a charge of crimes against humanity that domestic law provisions such as the Nuremberg Laws or the *Law for the Protection of Hereditarily Diseased Offspring* permitted the actions in question. However, the "legislative history" of Paragraph *c* reveals the fatal flaw in the construction of the Holocaust and the rule of law at Nuremberg.[7]

In fact and as a matter of law and legal history, the fate of the Holocaust in legal memory at Nuremberg comes down to a difference between a comma and a semi-colon, between , and ; . In the drafting process, French, English and Russian, the languages of the Allied powers were used. In drafting Paragraph *c*, one version read

> ...namely, murder...against any civilian population, before or during the war; or persecutions etc.....

while another read

> ...namely, murder...against any civilian population, before or during the war, or persecutions, etc....

---

7. See Egon Schwelb, "Crimes Against Humanity", 23 *British Yearbook of International Law* 178 (1946).

The technical and legal difference between the two versions is crucial. In the semi-colon version, it is arguable that the punctuation separates the two lists of types of acts which constitute crimes against humanity. This would mean that the limiting and qualifying provision that the acts occur

> …in execution of or in connection with any crime within the juris-
> diction of the Tribunal…

would in law apply only to those acts which follow the semi-colon. On the other hand, if the comma is the correct punctuation, all of the named acts are subjected to the limiting qualifier. After some discussion, it was decided that the comma would constitute the official version.

Thus, from the difference between the comma and the semi-colon, the fate of law, legal history and memory of the Holocaust at Nuremberg was decided. The distinction here is not one of minor or mere semantic, technical and obscure legal interpretation. The effect of the drafting change was to make "crimes against humanity" as a legal category at Nuremberg, secondary and subsidiary. In other words, "crimes against humanity" could only occur if they were part of "crimes against peace" or "war crimes" or the conspiracy to commit either of these categories of offence.

This reduction of "crimes against humanity" to subsidiary and dependent status had and continues to have important consequences. First, at the level of symbolism and metaphor, so important to the prosecuting authorities, the message is sent that only those acts which were part of the great Nazi plan for aggressive war are of sufficient import to the international legal community to be worthy of consideration. Second, the defense of national law could in fact apply to many acts which occurred under the Nazis because those acts did not constitute "crimes against humanity." In other words, the Tribunal was forced to find, as a result of the wording of the provisions of Article 6 and of the thrust of the prosecution case against the Nazi state as a vast conspiracy against peace, that many atrocities and acts of persecution which were committed as a direct result of Nazi ideology and under Nazi law, did not in fact or in law, constitute crimes against humanity.

Acts of persecution against Sinti and Roma were not *per se* violations of Article 6 because the Nazi legal construction of Gypsies as asocials and common criminals was not part of the Nazi plan to commit crimes against peace or war crimes. Indeed, it was a legal and lawful construction of criminality which had a perfectly legal historical pedigree within the traditions of German law. In a similar fashion, Nazi persecution of homosexual men, even if grounded in Nazi racial ideology, could not be considered *per se* violations of Article 6, again because Nazi amendments to Paragraph 175 of the Penal Code simply continued the already existing criminalization of a category of asocials. Nazi racial hygiene policies were equally sheltered from the status of *per se* violations of the prohibition against crimes against humanity because they could not be linked to the plan to carry out aggressive war which was the overriding ideological and legal construction of the Nazi state as developed by the prosecution authorities. Finally, measures against Jews, especially against German Jews, were not crimes against humanity because they did not necessarily fit this legal construction of Nazi law as a criminal conspiracy to wage war. They were simple provisions of domestic law, unconnected to the vast conspiracy and therefore perfectly legal.

This narrow construction of crimes against humanity as subsidiary to crimes against peace or war crimes continued to have important legal and political consequences after Nuremberg. Victims of Nazi racial and political persecution could not rely on the Nuremberg Tribunal findings to support their claims. Prosecutions under post-Nuremberg occupation legislation continued to be hampered by the narrow legal definitions of Nazi atrocities.[8] Attempts to pursue perpetrators under German law met with mixed success in part at least as a result of the conflicts surrounding issues of the legality of Nazi laws relating to racial hygiene and racial separation.[9]

At a broader level, the Nuremberg proceedings which reduced the Holocaust and Nazism's racialized legality to this secondary status grossly mischaracterized the nature of Nazi rule and the rule of law under Hitler. Nazism was not just or primarily a conspiracy against the established peace of the international legal order. Racial doctrine, informed by a scientific and legal worldview of Aryan superiority and a Jewish threat to the *Volksgemeinschaft*, was vital to the German state and to German law after 1933. Not only did this mischaracterization of Nazi law mean that the Shoah was constructed as a phenomenon which was a secondary consequence of Nazi aggression, and that victims of Nazi racial policy could only be included if the acts of which they complained could be fitted into this artificial and ahistorical legal construction of the criminal Nazi state, but it also meant that central elements of the Nazi legal system after 1933 were never adequately subjected to careful political and legal analysis.

Of course, as I have argued already, such an analysis would have revealed some basis for the defense claim and the claim of many elements in German

---

8. See, Frank M. Buscher, *The U.S. War Crimes Trial Program in Germany, 1946–1955* (New York: Greenwood Press, 1989); Henri Meyrowitz, *La Répression par les Tribunaux Allemands des Crimes contre l'Humanité et de l'Appartenance à une Organasation Criminelle* (Paris: Librarie Générale de Droit et de Jurisprudence, 1960).

9. See Dick de Mildt, *In the Name of the People*, op. cit.

society that Nazi law was not, in some key elements, distinguishable from Allied law. Racial hygiene informed the laws of many Allied countries, both before and after Auschwitz and Nuremberg. Compulsory sterilization of the racially defective was part of the rule of law in the United States, Canada, and Scandinavia.[10] By constructing Nazism's "criminal legality" only in the context of war crimes or crimes against peace, the prosecution, in addition to creating a false historical record of Nazi law, also managed to avoid the really difficult but nonetheless fundamental jurisprudential question after Auschwitz, what is the difference between Nazi law and law?

4. Julius Streicher and the Rule of Law: Legality and Antisemitism at/after Nuremberg

The answer to this question, or at least a more complex way of posing the query, may be found in the brief study of the case of one accused Major War Criminal at Nuremberg and of other proceedings at Nuremberg. I turn first to the case of Julius Streicher.

One of the most intriguing, not to say puzzling, legal precedents established at Nuremberg arises from the conviction and execution of Julius Streicher. Indicted in relation to count one (crimes against peace) and count four (crimes against humanity), Streicher was convicted only of the latter offence. This raises several difficult legal and ethical issues. First, given the ancillary character of the crimes against humanity offence in the Nuremberg Charter, one might well ask how Streicher could have legally been convicted of such an offence if he did not participate in the primary and condition precedent crime. It may well be possible to argue that the ancillary character of the crimes against humanity offence in the Charter merely requires that one of the three principal offences be committed by *someone* and that Streicher's actions be enough to indicate his participation or complicity therein and this will then be enough to justify a conviction.

But the more difficult and important issue raised by Streicher's conviction goes the very heart of the substantive content of the offence "crime against humanity". The basis of Streicher's conviction by the Nuremberg Tribunal rests almost exclusively in his "speech". The Tribunal wrote of the Defendant:

> For his 25 years of speaking, writing, and preaching hatred of the Jews, Streicher was widely known as "Jew-Baiter Number One". In his speeches and articles, week after week, month after month, he in-

---

10. See discussion chapters 4 supra and 11 infra.

fected the German mind with the virus of anti-Semitism, and incited the German people to active persecution. Each issue of "Der Sturmer", which reached a circulation of 600,000 in 1935, was filled with such articles, often lewd and disgusting.[11]

The Tribunal then concluded:

Streicher's incitement to murder and extermination at the time when Jews in the east were being killed under the most horrible conditions most clearly constitutes persecution on political and racial grounds in connection with war crimes, as defined by the Charter, and constitutes a crime against humanity.[12]

This part of the Tribunal's decision is important for several reasons. First, the Court slips from acts of propaganda and moral and political support to the recognized crime of "incitement". Many of the discussions of the Nuremberg Trial point to the problematic nature of this basis for Streicher's conviction. The proof that his comments, speeches and writings were a) made with knowledge of the extermination practices of the Holocaust and b) substantive causes of the acts in question, is quite obviously not established beyond a reasonable doubt. It seems clear now, as it was to some contemporary observers, that Streicher was convicted and executed because of who he was and not because of what he did. The lessons and symbolic impact for the rule of law at Nuremberg and for our memory and legal construction of the Holocaust are here ironically contradictory. The conviction of an individual, no matter how reprehensible and obnoxious, on the basis of these characteristics quite clearly violates basic principles of our Western criminal justice traditions. The distortions of the law of incitement which led to such a conviction can only be seen to undermine general public faith in the rule of law. In addition, of course, the idea that someone should be convicted and executed on the basis of some general and generalizable offence rather than on the basis of subjective, personal liability, comes dangerously close to the practices and principles of Nazi criminal law which stands condemned by the vary process which replicates them in Streicher's case. At the same time, the fact that a virulent antisemite, in the immediate aftermath of the Holocaust would be and was executed as a "major war criminal" cannot be said to be without its symbolic

---

11. *Nazi Conspiracy and Aggression: Opinion and Judgment*, 1947, at 129.
12. Ibid., at 131.

importance. The real question is whether the legality of the execution was or is more important than the fact of the execution.

This brings us to another important consideration raised in the context of the Streicher case. While much of the focus in the reasons of the Tribunal is on Streicher's involvement with the party and with *Der Stürmer* in the early days of the regime, the Tribunal only convicted him for inciting atrocities during the murderous assault on Eastern Jewry after 1941.Thus, the Court seems to be operating at a level which clearly confuses ideology and criminality. The legal basis for Streicher's liability seems to have been his active encouragement of persecution i.e. killing of Jews after Operation Barbarossa or at the earliest after the invasion of Poland. If this is the case, he cannot be guilty of crimes against humanity for his writings before September 1939, since the Tribunal found that he was not a party to the conspiracy against peace which characterized its findings of criminality against other defendants. Indeed, the Tribunal specifically found that crimes committed prior to the beginning of the War, could not legally be classified as "crimes against humanity". It held:

> To constitute crimes against humanity, the acts relied on before the outbreak of war must have been in execution of, or in connection with, any such crime within the jurisdiction of the Tribunal. The Tribunal is of the opinion that revolting and horrible as many of these crimes were, it has not been satisfactorily proved that that they were done in execution of, or in connection with, any such crime. The Tribunal therefore cannot make a general declaration that the acts before 1939 were crimes against humanity within the meaning of the Charter, but from the beginning of the War in 1939 war crimes were committed on a vast scale, which were also crimes against humanity; and insofar as the inhumane acts charged in the indictment, and committed after the beginning of the war, did not constitute war crimes, they were all committed in execution of, or in connection with, the aggressive war, and therefore constituted crimes against humanity.[13]

Much of the evidence at the trial indicated that Streicher was never truly part of the Nazi inner circle, indeed this is the basis on which the Tribunal acquits him on Count One. Other parts of the evidence indicate as clearly that both he personally and *Der Stürmer* as a newspaper, lost much of their influence as he was increasingly marginalized within the Party and within German society. This must therefore raise serious legal questions as to whether he could

---

13. *Nazi Conspiracy and Aggression*, at 84.

be said to have been an operating influence on the practices of extermination which he is found to have incited. Indeed, one might raise serious questions as to the relevance and admissibility of much of the evidence reiterated by the Tribunal in its judgment against Streicher. Surely, evidence of his pre-1939 writings and activities can be said to be relevant to the charge of crimes against humanity only if one considers them to part of a "pattern of activity", or "similar fact evidence" or even as going to "character". Yet, criminal courts were and are reluctant to engage in such "fact finding" exercises for the very reason that such evidence tends to establish an aura of culpability around the accused without actually establishing his guilt for the specific offence for which he has been charged.

As already discussed, the subsidiary character of crimes against humanity as a matter of law in the Charter of the International Military Tribunal, created both ideological and practical legal difficulties which continue to operate today. These difficulties are made manifest in the case of Julius Streicher. His virulent antisemitism no doubt reflected a certain element of German society and the Nazi Party. His support for the Nuremberg Laws and his calls for their vigorous enforcement were hateful and disgusting. But they were not part of a conspiracy or plan to wage aggressive war or commit war crimes. Streicher did not need to wage war to hate Jews or to call for their extermination. In this he was perhaps a radical embodiment of Nazi racial and legal ideology. He was guilty of inciting actions against Jews and their property and encouraged their physical elimination from German society. This was, however, not sufficient as a matter of law to convict him of crimes against humanity. This is the flaw of the case against Streicher and it is the flaw of a major part of the construction of Nazi law and the Holocaust at Nuremberg. The Nazis did not need war to hate Jews or to take steps against them. What they needed, or at least what they used, was law. The Nuremberg Tribunal, as a legal forum which constructed Nazi law as criminal only in so far as it participated in the plans of the broader Nazi conspiracy, and which constructed the Holocaust as illegal only in so far as it was part of crimes against peace or war crimes, could never, if it wished to preserve its own legitimacy as a legal forum, come to terms with this legal and historical reality.

What really seems to have happened to the Tribunal during the case against Streicher is that they were offended at a basic level by his bilious hatreds and antisemitic utterances. Indeed, Streicher's culpability is a necessary part not just of the legal condemnation of Nazi antisemitism by the Tribunal, but it also plays a key and almost irony-filled part in the jurisprudential rejection of some of the strongest notions of "collective" guilt or of the culpability of the German people. Streicher the criminal convinced otherwise innocent Germans to commit and to condone atrocities through his implication in a criminally motivated practice of propaganda and persuasion. The conviction of the chief "Jew hater" serves to reinforce the corollary juridical notion established by the Nuremberg Tribunal i.e. that Nazi criminality exculpates the German people. Thus, the Tribunal's emphasis on the early Streicher propaganda, and on his impact where he "infected the German mind".[14]

The decision of the Tribunal here fits into the matrix of discursive practices and legal propaganda motifs which informed and continue to inform much of the collective, historical understanding of Nazi Germany and Nazi law. "Nazis" are the real criminals, "Germans" the innocent victims. More recent sociological, historical and legal studies now refute the clear distinction between "Nazi" culpability and "German" innocence, and deconstruct the neat ethical and legal difference between those who belong in the perpetrator category and those who might fit into some other "victim" or "bystander" taxonomy. Earlier efforts, of which the Nuremberg Trial is the jurisprudential embodiment, were clearly aimed at doing what the Streicher decision, if not the actual facts on which the conviction was based, did i.e. to portray the majority of Germans as the victims of a complex police system of physical and psychological constraint and conversion to Nazi antisemitic hatred.

A clear example of the way in which this interpretive strategy was used and employed in socio-legal discourse in the United States in the early post-war years can be found in the series of studies and articles published by Dr. Leo Alexander.[15] It is not important here to engage in a detailed examination of Alexander's work or in a critique of the underlying theories of German society and of the role of the Nuremberg Trials. Rather, it might simply be useful to point out again that in 1936 Leo Alexander participated in the study by the American Neurological Association of the practice of eugenically based sterilization. While the Committee was critical of many of the "scientific" claims put forward by the proponents of wide-ranging eugenic sterilization, it nonetheless gave its expert support to limited sterilization programs practiced in cases of *inter alia*, Huntington's chorea, feeblemindedness of the familial type, dementia praecox (schizophrenia), manic-depressive psychosis and

---

14. At 129.

15. See "War Crimes and Their Motivations—The Socio-Psychological Structure and the Criminalization of a Society", 39 *J.Crim.L and Crim.* 298 (1948); "Destructive and Self-Destructive Trends in Criminalized Society—A Study of Totalitarianism", ibid., 553 (1949); "The Molding of Personality Under Dictatorship—The Importance of The Destructive Drives in the Socio-Psychological Structure of Nazism", ibid., vol. 40, at 3 (1949).

epilepsy.[16] Again, I must emphasize that I am not suggesting that Alexander was a Nazi or that the American Neurological Association presaged the Holocaust. Rather, I am suggesting that even in the immediate post-war period and as a result of the Nuremberg Trials, there is still clear evidence of a lack of critical self-evaluation among the "victors" on the issues of commonality and continuity. In this instance, Alexander and the legal and medical communities are more than willing to engage in complex scientific studies of "the German mind" in order to come to a better understanding of the Nazi regime, a regime which they have characterized as criminal and punished accordingly. At the same time, they seem to be specifically blind to the fact that many of the central ideals and policies of Nazism and the German "criminal state" were not particularly distinguishable in many details from those still operating in the governmental structures and discourses of the Allies. This level of ideological and jurisprudential disingenuousness continues to trouble us and our understanding and construction of Nazi law today. Again, the sources of this disingenuousness are multiple but the practical legal and metaphorical impact of the creation of the Holocaust as at one and the same time legally secondary and conceptually primary cannot be underestimated.

On this front, the conviction of Streicher serves several connected ideological and legal purposes essential to the Tribunal's *raison d'être* and to our certainty today that Nazi law was not law. The Nazi Party and leaders are established as the real and only culprits, while the German people are the innocent victims not just of a criminally repressive and totalitarian police state but of the propaganda arm of that state apparatus. At the same time, with its emphasis on Streicher's long-term activities, the Court establishes in a slightly round about way, the intentionalist thesis which informs the entire prosecution theory of "Nazi Conspiracy and Aggression". Arguably, Streicher's early writings are at some basic level, legally irrelevant to the charges that he "incited" the Holocaust. That "incitement" only encouraged crimes which could have taken place, as part of the racial and political persecution which resulted from the principal conspiracy and aggression in violation of international law, after September 1, 1939. Surely, there is some legal necessity to establish a clear *nexus* between the "incitement" and the substantive criminal offence and surely the lapse of time is a relevant evidentiary factor in establishing or defeating the *nexus* in question. At some level of logic and perhaps of justice then, Streicher's conviction flies in the face both of that same logic and legal principle and exposes the contradictions inherent in the jurisprudential approach to

---

16. *Eugenical Sterilization: A Reorientation of the Problem*, op. cit.

crimes against humanity by the Nuremberg prosecutors. In other words, Streicher's conviction and execution were ideologically and jurisprudentially required within the self-justifying logic of Nuremberg and yet impossible according to other equally valid aspects of the Tribunal's status as the embodiment of the new, post-Auschwitz international legal order. Streicher could only be lawfully executed by distorting the basic legal principles which allegedly separate law from Nazi law. Streicher by the force of that law becomes again the *homo sacer*, who can be killed but not murdered.

There is one final issue surrounding the conviction of Julius Streicher at Nuremberg which deserves out attention. While it is true as a technical matter that he was convicted for "incitement", it might well be argued that his crime never really went beyond the realm of hate mongering. I do not wish to suggest here that Streicher merits our sympathy or that he did not "deserve" to be hanged. Indeed, it may well be argued that any discussion of the rule of law in such circumstances obscures the valid concerns for vengeance or what Professor Lauterpacht referred to as the "not inherently reprehensible desire for retribution".[17] Rather, I want to suggest that the legal basis for his conviction, in addition to being problematic on the facts as set out by the Tribunal, is one which has been ignored by legal scholars in the mainstream and in their discussions of law and jurisprudence after Auschwitz. In effect, Streicher's conviction establishes that hate speech can and does incite others to commit hate crimes.[18] It further establishes that hate speech is and can be sufficient to constitute a crime against humanity. This is an element of the Nuremberg Trial which has escaped the attention of most legal scholars, particularly those in the United States. They almost automatically invoke the Constitutional protections afforded to all forms of speech by the First Amendment and then follow up this position by taking the "slippery slope" position. Accordingly, we must necessarily construe criminal offences like "incitement" in a particularly narrow fashion in order to avoid infringing upon basic Constitutional norms. Because of this normative legal position, hate speech and its sub-species, Holocaust Denial, flourish and grow in the United States, despite the conviction of Julius Streicher at Nuremberg.

At the same time, the INS and American legislators and courts recognize that those who participated in Nazi propaganda activities in Occupied Europe

---

17. "The Law of Nations and the Punishment of War Crimes", op cit., at 58.

18. Indeed, current international law seems to have evolved to the point of having recognized just such a position. The case against Ferdinand Nahimana concerning his involvement in the Rwandan genocide relies on his role as a radio propagandist. See Yair Reiner, "Hate Radio", *Lingua Franca*, February 1999, at 9. See also, Jon Silverman, "Poison pens", *Guardian*, 24 June 2002.

are as excludable as undesirable aliens as are those who pulled the triggers against European Jewry.[19] Thus, we have the post-Nuremberg, post-Streicher paradox that hate speech and propaganda for Americans are acceptable, that limitations on speech by other countries are to be condemned when compared to the American constitutional litmus test, while the Government takes action against those whose only crime was to write or speak and treats them as criminals. In relation to the tragedies in Burundi and Rwanda, to allegations against Osama Bin Laden as a terrorist mastermind, and to a lesser extent the former Yugoslavia, the role of propaganda and incitement to atrocity is again surfacing as an area of concern, indictment and conviction.[20] Fortunately for those of us who live in "civilized" countries, we are able to ignore the possible impact of vicious hate-filled propaganda and live in the marketplace of ideas. Again, in the context of the Holocaust, the failings of liberal legalism, the very basis of the International Military Tribunal at Nuremberg, manifest themselves in the inherent contradictions and hypocrisies of jurisprudence in the shadows of the death camps. Perhaps these contradictions are no more manifest than in those instances in which the victorious Allies specifically targeted Nazi legality for jurisprudential opprobrium.

5. The Justice Trial and the Trial of Justice

A central purpose and function of the Trial of Major War Criminals at Nuremberg was the construction in jurisprudence and legal ideology of the Nazi state as a criminal state. While the major focus of the Trial itself was the notion of a common plan and conspiracy against the international legal order, and while this focus reduced the Holocaust to a secondary status, it is nonetheless true that after Nuremberg the metaphoric and symbolic construction of Nazi law as not law became a dominant trait of Western jurisprudential thought. As we have seen, however, these political and cultural lessons of the Nuremberg Trial were not universally accepted. Indeed, the Hart/Fuller debate, the conflict between legal positivism and natural law jurisprudence was, if anything, exacerbated in the post-Nuremberg era.

---

19. See the discussion below, chapter 7.
20. See e.g., Joshua Wallenstein, "Punishing Words: An Analysis of the Necessity of the Element of Causation in Prosecutions for Incitement to Genocide", 54 *Stanford L. R.* 351 (2001); Marlise Simons, "Trial Centers on Role of Press During Rwanda Massacre", *New York Times*, 3 March 2001.

Nonetheless, the legalized criminalization of Nazi law, lawyers and justice was a thematic constant of the Allied trial process in post-war Germany. Again, it is important to underline here the possible conflict between Allied policy and its ideological impact and the actual and practical effect of post-war criminal trials in Germany. Frank Buscher concludes his study of the U.S. war crimes program as follows:

> It is questionable if the occupation as a whole convinced the Germans that their society needed to undergo significant change, or if later events such as the economic miracle actually achieved what the occupation tried to accomplish—a Federal Republic which shared the values of the West. The war crimes program, criticized because of its procedural rules and lack of legal precedent, was hardly suited for another controversial undertaking, the reform of post-war German society.[21]

The post-Nuremberg trials, like the Major War Criminals proceeding itself, clearly fit into a broader ideological and political frame. The trial and punishment of war criminals was meant to re-establish the rule of law in Germany, just as the occupation was meant to re-establish democratic self-rule in the West as a bulwark against the Soviet East.[22] In addition to the penal proceedings against perpetrators, an administrative program of deNazification was implemented. Recent studies by Müller, Stolleis and others demonstrate the difference between the rhetoric and practice of deNazification in the legal and judicial professions. Indeed, one of the ironies of the post war criminalization of Nazi law through the ideological practices of the West is that more recent studies actually demonstrate the validity of many claims made by those in the then German Democratic Republic that West Germany's legal system was populated with former Nazis and war criminals.[23] Thus, the issue of continuity between Weimar and Nazi legality is further complicated by the issue of continuity between Nazi and Federal Republic legality and legal personnel.

---

21. *The U.S. War Crimes Trial Program in Germany*, op. cit., at 164.

22. See, Richard L. Merritt, *Democracy Imposed: U.S. Occupation Policy and the German Public, 1945–1949* (New Haven: Yale University Press, 1995); Jeffrey Herf, *Divided Memory: The Nazi Past in the Two Germanys* (Cambridge: Harvard University Press, 1997); Jeffrey S. Gaab, *Justice Delayed: The Restoration of Justice in Bavaria Under American Occupation* (New York: Peter Lang, 1999); Bill Niven, *Facing the Nazi Past: United Germany and the Legacy of the Third Reich* (London and New York: Routledge, 2001).

23. See, *The Brown Book: War and Nazi Criminals in West Germany* (Berlin: Verlag Zeit Im Bild, National Council of the National Front of Democratic Germany, Documentation Centre of the State Archives Administration of the German Democratic Republic, n.d.).

While these issues are fascinating and in need of further exploration, they are beyond the scope of this study. What is important here is that this legal historical, factual record, conflicts with the legal historical, ideological record with which we continue to live. For us today, Nazi law is not law. It is the powerful way in which the judicial process was deployed to create and perpetuate this construction of the post-Nuremberg, post-Auschwitz rule of law to which we must turn our attention now.

After the trial of Major War Criminals before the International Military Tribunal concluded, the Allied powers, largely under American auspices, mounted a series of secondary trials of war criminals. Like the Nuremberg Trial, these proceedings targeted not just individual guilt but also symbolic culpability. Thus, the trials took place against a number of defendants who represented various aspects of the Nazi regime, from members of the High Command to the Krupp and Flick industrial concerns, to the *Einsatzgruppen*. Of concern to us here, is the "Justice Case", which involved representatives of various parts of the Nazi juridico-legal system.[24]

Once again, it is important to underline the distinction between the legal facts and historical record of the "Justice Case", and the rhetorical deployment which characterized the prosecutions' pleadings and evidence. I shall not deal here with the cases against the accused which concerned the "Night and Fog" decree, nor with the participation of the accused in acts of extermination during the Holocaust. The characterization of such acts as "criminal" or as simply "evil" does not seem to be problematic. Instead, I wish to focus briefly on the ways in which the prosecution, led by Telford Taylor, characterized Nazi law generally and then on the issue of the race and racial hygiene laws which I believe not only characterized much of Nazi law but which also served as the juridico-ideological basis for the Holocaust.

The first point which must be made in relation to the "Justice Case" is that the prosecution again proceeded against the accused on the basis that they were part of "a common design" to "conspire...to commit war crimes and crimes against humanity".[25] In other words, the Nazi legal system was from its origins, a criminal legal system. The common plan was further described in

---

24. See Matthew Lippman, "They Shoot Lawyers Don't They? Law in the Third Reich and the Global Threat to the Independence of the Judiciary"; "Law, Lawyers, and Legality in the Third Reich: The Perversion of Principle and Professionalism", op. cit., for a more traditional jurisprudential approach to the question of the rule of law.

25. *Trials of War Criminals Before the Nuernberg Military Tribunals under Control Council Law No. 10, Volume III, "The Justice Case"* (Washington: United States Government Printing Office, 1951), at 17.

Paragraph 4 of Count One as involving plans to "enact, issue, enforce, and give effect to certain purported statutes, decrees, and orders, which were criminal both in inception and execution".[26] The indictment further alleged in paragraph 7 that "Judges were removed from the bench for political and "racial" reasons."[27]

The next Counts in relation to War Crimes and Crimes Against Humanity offered further details of the illegal nature of Nazi law. Most important for our purposes here is Paragraph 15 relating to the charge of War Crimes which reads:

> The Ministry of Justice participated in the Nazi program of racial purity pursuant to which sterilization and castration were perverted for the extermination of Jews, "asocials", and certain nationals of the occupied territories. In the course of the program, thousands of Jews were sterilized. Insane, aged and sick nationals of occupied territories, the so-called "useless eaters", were systematically murdered. In the course of the above described proceedings, thousands of persons were murdered and ill-treated. The defendants Lautz, Schlegelberger, and Westphal are charged with special responsibility for and participation in these crimes.[28]

Several issues need to be highlighted here. First, while the indictment in Count One alleges a criminal conspiracy beginning in January 1933, the allegations in relation to the sterilization and euthanasia programs in the War Crimes Count refer only to actions in the Occupied Countries. It seems clear from this fact alone that the contradictions and problems associated with the Allied conceptions of Nazi law are manifest and multiple. At the most basic level, it is evident from this Count that the same acts committed in Germany against Germans were not considered to be part of the war crimes committed in the pursuit of the sterilization program for instance. This is the case despite the fact that the criminal plan and conspiracy dated from January 1933 and that the Tribunal specifically rejected the defense claim that their acts were legal and justified by domestic German legislation. On the one hand, then, the Tribunal rejected the idea that domestic Nazi legislation was a shield against prosecution, thereby enforcing the broader ideological claim that Nazi law was not law, while at the same time deciding, by implication at least, that the compulsory sterilization of German Jews, the insane, ill or the aged did

---

26. Ibid.
27. Id., at 19.
28. Id., at 21–22.

not constitute part of the war crimes offence. Indeed, euthanasia fell into the same category. Therefore, some acts of barbarity were punishable while others were not, even though, to use the prosecution's same logic, acts in each category took place under the same illegal "legal" regime.

Again, part of this contradiction is explicable by reference to the problems inherent in the "common plan or conspiracy" conception of the Nazi regime and of Nazi legality. Part of the contradiction and tension is also explicable, I believe, by reference to the historical and judicial record of the prosecuting authorities. As we have already seen, the United States, Canada and several other countries practiced and would continue to practice compulsory sterilization against the racially and socially impure. Nazi legislation, modeled on American precedent, could not be condemned *per se* as criminal without calling into question the legitimacy of the rule of law in those countries which were attempting to use this trial to impose the very ideals of the rule of law in Germany.

This reading of the contradictions of the prosecution's case on this point is confirmed by the invocation in paragraph 15 of the qualifier "perverted" to describe "sterilization and castration laws". In other words, such statutory provisions are nor part of a *per se* criminality or illegality which is invoked in the wording of Paragraph 5 i.e. "certain purported statutes etc.," but rather they are valid provisions recognizable under the rule of law until they are perverted by the accused for their own means, at which point law becomes not law. Of course, we know that in the case of similar statutory instruments in Virginia, the case against Carrie Buck was constructed as a legal sham to justify the validity of the legal regime in force there. Whether such machinations were or are consistent with Telford Taylor's understanding of the rule of law must at this point remain unknown. Moreover, we can recognize in the "perversion" thesis the position soon thereafter adopted by Radbruch in his renunciation of legal positivism. As with Radbruch's jurisprudential touchstone, the problem of the way in which we might identify the point at which law is in fact "perverted", when, in other words, law becomes not law, remains unknown and unknowable.

What we do know is that the prosecution continued to construct the criminal nature of Nazi legality throughout the indictment. In relation to Crimes Against Humanity, Paragraph 27 read

> Special health courts (Erbgesundsheitgerichte) perverted eugenic and sterilization laws or policies regarding German civilians and nationals of other countries which resulted in the systematic murder and ill-treatment of thousands of persons.[29]

29. Id., at 24.

We can note here that German nationals are this time included in the concept of "crimes against humanity". This demonstrates the innovative jurisprudence of Nuremberg, whereby crimes against nationals, excluded by traditional understandings of the category "war crimes" are included in the broader "crimes against humanity". Again, however, we must note that it is only in those cases where sterilization laws are "perverted" that an offence is committed and a legal state becomes a criminal state. This idea of perversion is of course the key to understanding the ways in which the Trial of Major War Criminals at Nuremberg, cases such as the "Justice Case" and other legal constructions of Nazi law have operated to create our understanding of Nazi law as not law. The basic conflict must be portrayed as one between the rule of law and those who would use the ineffable justice embodied in that term as a mere mask for evil ends. In his opening statement in the "Justice Case", Telford Taylor invokes a number of metaphors and other rhetorical devices to convince his audience and the audience of history of the fundamental distinction between law and not law, between the rule of law and Nazi law.

Thus,

> …those men, leaders of the German judicial system, consciously and deliberately suppressed the law, engaged in an unholy masquerade of brutish tyranny disguised as justice, and converted the German judicial system to an engine of despotism, conquest, pillage, and slaughter.…The defendants and their colleagues distorted, perverted, and finally accomplished the complete overthrow of justice and law in Germany.[30]

Taylor offers a further set of rhetorical flourishes in which he clearly admits that the reestablishment of the rule of law is a vital part of the judicial process of the "Justice Case" and that such a task is a sacred one. He declared

> Great as was their crime against those who died or suffered at their hands, their crime against Germany was even more shameful. They defiled the German temple of justice…
>
> …
>
> The temple must be reconsecrated. This cannot be done in the twinkling of an eye or by any mere ritual. It cannot be done in any single proceeding or at any one place. It certainly cannot be done at Nuernberg alone. But we have here, I think, a special opportunity and grave responsibility to help achieve this goal. We have here the men who

---

30. Id., at 31.

played a leading part in the destruction of law in Germany. They are about to be judged in accordance with the law. It is more than fitting that these men be judged under that which they, as jurists, denied to others. Judgment under law is the only just fate for the defendants; the prosecution asks no other.[31]

No one could deny the rhetorical brilliance of Taylor's presentation. Nor would I wish to be seen to be asserting that the defendants here, or the defendants at other similar proceedings, including at the Trial of Major War Criminals were somehow "innocent". What I do argue is that for all Taylor's bravura and for all the mass of evidence against the accused here and elsewhere, there is a lie at the base of these attempts to reestablish the rule of law through these proceedings. That lie is the lie that Nazi law was not law.

It seems clear that, as I have discussed already, the invocation of Article 48 of the Weimar Constitution under which Hitler can be said to have come to power, was an ordinary and lawful event. It seems clear, as I have also already discussed, that some central tenets and practices of Nazi law, for example sterilization on "racial hygiene" grounds, were perfectly consistent with the rule of law in many other countries. It seems clear that the characterization of Nazi law as not law and the Nazi state as a criminal state was not one shared either by the legal and judicial professions in Germany or by those in the same professions outside Germany at the time. Finally, it seems clear that the characterization of Nazi law as not law, of Nazi lawyers as criminals etc., is in light of these other facts disingenuous and misleading.

Again, it worth underlining here that the entire basis of the Allied prosecution in the Justice Case was and remains grounded in the idea of Nazi law as a "perversion". At some point in time, the Nazis took the legal form and transformed it into a substantive system of injustice.

In the "Justice Trial" the defense mounted expert evidence, over vigorous cross-examination by the prosecution, to the effect that both in form and substance, the formation of the Hitler government in 1933 was in perfect accordance with the Weimar Constitution.[32]

Indeed, the argument that Nazi law was, from the very beginning, in a state of rupture with pre-existing German law, or even with law in non-German jurisdictions, becomes more problematic if we return here to the question of "racial hygiene" and the law. I have already argued that practices of steriliza-

---

31. Id., at 33.
32. Id., at 252 etc seq., "Expert Opinion by Defense Witness Professor Jahrreiss concerning the Development of German Law".

tion grounded in eugenic theory were constitutionally valid in the United States, practiced in Canada throughout the period in question and that non-German lawyers found the basis of Nazi practices to be well-founded.[33] Even the terms of the indictment itself are at pains to establish that Nazi lawyers and legal officials are being charged not with participation in eugenic sterilization as a crime *per se*, but rather that the special jurisdictions "perverted eugenic and sterilization laws or policies". In the end, none of the accused to whom specific liability for these "perversions" has been attributed was in fact convicted on that ground. The indictments alleged the "perversion" of law in the field of "hereditary health", the prosecution deployed natural law rhetoric about the evils of named individuals accused of having perverted the law in these areas, and in the end there was no possible justification or proof that established the defendants' guilt for perverting law in this context.

That Nazi law at some point slipped over some line to mass extermination is beyond doubt. Where that point occurred, or whether the entire system slipped over the line and never crossed back is a more problematic assertion. Indeed, I believe that the principle that the extermination of Jews and Roma, as the death-giving function of the state against the *homo sacer* was ever "murder" i.e. unlawful, is much more doubtful.

Sterilization of the racially unfit was carried out in Augsberg and in Alberta in the 1940s. People suffering from "congenital defects" in Edmonton and Erfurt, in Charlottesville and Cologne, Stockholm and Stuttgart, individuals, "defectives", suffered for the benefit of the health of the body politic and after a medical and legal practice not dissimilar to the one which continues to authorize the sterilization of the "intellectually handicapped" today.

Throughout the Nazi period, German lawyers continued to act as lawyers in any number of instances even after the mass killings in the East were under way. Judges judged, even while Auschwitz spewed forth its smoke and ash. The rhetoric and ideology of the rule of law and the criminal Nazi state do not allow for such complications, This is the lie of law after Nuremberg, just as it is the lie of law after Auschwitz. Law continued while six million died.

Only if we can begin to come to grips with this idea, that Auschwitz and the rule of law do not sit on opposite sides of a huge jurisprudential and historical abyss, can we begin to understand the ideological function of rule of law discourse at Nuremberg and in the "Justice Case". We must remember that for all Telford Taylor's invocations of the sacred nature of the courts' task, the three named defendants charged with special responsibility for the perversion

---

33. See above, chapter 4.

of the rule of law in relation to the sterilization program, Lantz, Schlegelberger and Westphal, were not convicted of these offences. We must also remember Julius Streicher, mad and bad, an evil antisemite executed for crimes he probably did not commit. We must not remember Streicher because he was an innocent victim, but because his case demonstrates most clearly that the rule of law had very little to do with what happened at Nuremberg. The "rule of law" was present at Nuremberg just as it was present at Auschwitz. Exactly what needs to be reconsecrated in Taylor's words is perhaps not law and the rule of law, but some understanding of justice which transcends a law which can be omnipresent as cause and effect in the *nomos* of the Holocaust.

CHAPTER 6

The Case against Vichy: Law, History and Memory in France

1. Introduction: Constructing Vichy

France appears to be obsessed with collective memory. Every village, neighborhood and city has its historic sites, memorials and monuments. These *lieux de mémoire* seem to dominate not just the physical space they occupy but also the psyche of the country.[1] For example, battles have raged in recent years over the fate of the "mutineers" of the Great War. Should those who were made examples of and executed for desertion be remembered on November 11?[2] More controversially, the nature of French colonialism and the use of "illegal" means during the Algerian War of Independence continues to haunt French public memory and to bring into stark contrast the theory and practice of French Republican law and justice.[3] Can France deal with the history of torture and murder committed in the name of an *Algérie française,* of Algeria as a part of France? At some level, this struggle over memory and the politics of public remembrance can appear to follow a traditional and distinctly un-postmodern left/right political divide. The issue of the fate of the *poilus* (literally, the hairy ones, the term used to describe ordinary French soldiers during the First

---

1. Pierre Nora (ed.), *Les Lieux de Mémoire* (Paris: Gallimard, 1984–1986).
2. See "La guerre des deux mémoires, *Libération*, 11 November 1998.
3. For example, a recent French legal decision granted extended pension rights to a child born after the rape of his mother by French soldiers during the Algerian conflict. While the decision is a technical one, marked by psychiatric expertise and not by a detailed analysis of the "illegality" of French intervention, it does mark a possible first tentative recognition of French Republican complicity in war crimes. See Jacqueline Coignard, "Toute une vie reconnue victime de guerre", *Libération*, 23 November 2001.

World War) resurfaced during the co-habitation between the Socialist Prime Minister Lionel Jospin and the conservative President, Jacques Chirac.[4] However, as is often the case with issues of collective memory, the contest here carries with it much more complex and nuanced historical precedents, not the least of which is the ongoing debate over a hero of World War I France, Maréchal Phillipe Pétain, the leader of the government under the Vichy regime. In many subtle ways, the battle over World War I memories and memorials is also a battle over World War II memories and memorials. In a similar fashion, debates over the Algerian question also raise stark questions about the continuity of a Vichy regime and French practices in North Africa.

Similarly, French self-understanding is confused and contested when Islamic schoolgirls wear the traditional *hijab* or head scarf to school. Can a lay Republic allow the expression of religious identity in the very institution whose function is the inculcation of Republican values among the young? What of the assertion of identity among religious minorities and respect for the rights of others, equally Republican values? How can these *affaires des foulards* (scarf affairs) arise on a regular basis in the same country in which the national team which emerged victorious in the 1998 World Cup was celebrated as giving a concrete face to the new France, one in which Zidane, the son of Algerian immigrants, could be the team leader and national hero? Why does Islam haunt the government?[5] Of course, the very presence of citizens of the Islamic faith in France is largely attributable to the historical and economic dynamics of the French colonial presence in Africa, a history which continues to haunt the land of Republican equality and justice. These *affaires des foulards* must also be constructed by and within a public political context which defines France and the Other in very particular and one-dimensional terms. There is, for example, no reason to think that the Republic and Islam are inexorably opposed.[6] Nor is there any reason to believe that such obvious com-

---

4. See e.g. Nicolas Offenstadt, *Les Fusillés de la grande guerre et la mémoire collective (1914–1919)* (Paris: Odile Jacob, 1999).

5. See Chouki El Hamel, "Muslim Diaspora in Western Europe: The Islamic Headscarf (Hijab), the Media and Muslims' Integration in France", 6 *Citizenship Studies* 293 (2002); Gabrielle Serraz, "Une lycéenne exclue sans foulard", *Libération*, 9 January 1997; Daniel Licht, "L'islam, le fantôme qui hante l'Elysée," *Libération*, 7 January 1999; Phillipe Lemoine, "Grève au collège de Flers (Orne) contre le port du foulard islamique", *Le Monde*, 9 January 1999; Daniel Licht, "Foulard: la preuve par la médiatrice", *Libération*, 9–10 January 1999; "Foulard à l'école: la médiatrice déplore le "durcissement des attitudes"", *Le Monde*, 10 January 1999; Olivier Bertrand, "Flers refoule les foulards", *Libération*, 11 February 1999.

6. Daniel Licht, "A Lyon, un Islam musclé mais républicain", *Libération*, 18 January 1999. The government has recently taken steps to legislate against all ostentatious religious

plexities and political and ideological realities will serve to eliminate the struggles over the public self-imagination of France and of public history and memory in that country.

Why does the fate of the long dead *poilus* feature on the front pages of national newspapers? Why does the political and fashion taste of a few schoolgirls seem to be constructed as a threat to the survival of the nation? Why is torture practiced over forty years ago still on the surface of the traumatized French collective psyche? In fact, each of these phenomena of current French politics finds itself placed as a kind of bookend in the contest over public memory about the Holocaust in France today. What links them is the troubled history and collective memory of the Vichy regime which governed France from 1940–1944. The fate of France during and after the First World War and the continuing issues of the history of French colonialism have each played themselves out not just in public memory generally but more particularly in the battles which have been waged in the legal domain over the appropriate meaning to be afforded to Vichy and to Vichy's role in the Holocaust in France. The *poilus* and the *foulards* are joined by the spectre of Vichy. The question which must be addressed if not resolved is why, finally, more than fifty years after the end of the Second World War, does Vichy haunt France? France offers an excellent case study of the ways in which the post-war legal system of a Western democracy has failed to come to grips with its own intimate involvement in the mass extermination of its Jewish population while maintaining the myth of an uninterrupted Republican and democratic legality.

In the various struggles which have come to define the French past, present and future, the Vichy regime has served as a focal point in the various attempts to come to terms with the country's history.[7] In his seminal study of the vagaries of public memory and the reality of the Vichy regime, French historian Henry Rousso demonstrates how law has played a particular role in the creation of the environment in which debates about the appropriate meaning(s) to be attributed to that era of the country's past have circulated in public discourse. One of the crucial problems identified by Rousso in such public debates about the past and the construction of public memories and myths

---

symbols in schools in the name of Republican identity. See, Béatrice Gurrey, "M. Chirac prône le "sursuat républicain" et interdit le voile à l'école", *Le Monde*, 19 December 2003; Phillippe Bernard, "Les "sages" de la commission Stasi se félicitent du travail accompli",; Jean-Luc Nancy, "Laïcité monothéiste", *Le Monde*, 2 January 2004; Régis Debray, *Ce que nous voile le voile* (Paris: Gallimard, 2004).

7. See Jon Cowans, "Visions of the Postwar: The Politics of Memory and Expectation in 1940s France", 10 *History &Memory* 68 (1998).

is what appears to be a fundamental contradiction between the subjects of the discourse, here, Vichy, antisemitism, and the Holocaust in France, on the one hand, and the instance or forum in which the debate takes place, the judicial system and the various celebrated "*affairs*" which have troubled the collective French psyche since the 1980s. Each of these "*affairs*" has stirred emotion, controversy and heated public debate, not just on the facts of the individual cases, but more importantly on the broader issue of how "France" and French "memory" are to be constructed and reconstructed in light of the broader issues of historical truth and collective/national self-imaginings.

For Rousso, there is an irresolvable conflict between the vital issues to be debated and the limited legal context in which the issues were in fact to be resolved.

> Memories, which now enjoyed the symbolic support of the law, began to crystallize; the involvement of the courts gave such memories a legitimate reason for existing in the present. The suspension of the statute of limitations, like the operation of memory itself, abolished time. There was, however, one crucial difference: memory is by definition selective, unfaithful, and changeable. Justice is not....
> Writing history is one thing; judging an individual according to the rules of law is another. The courts in many cases were forced to rely on shaky interpretations of events, and thus the trials unintentionally exacerbated the existing tension between memory, history, and truth.[8]

This conflict, which for Rousso is symptomatic of an incomplete national mourning, is sometimes more broadly characterized as reflecting a reluctance to come to terms with Vichy.[9] More particularly, the claim is raised that France has failed to accept French responsibility for the role of local government and police officials in implementing anti-Jewish measures. As Rousso and others point out, however, this position oversimplifies the complexities of various debates in France concerning Vichy.[10] French historians and historians of France have written extensive studies detailing Vichy's role in creating and implementing anti-Jewish legal measures and in cooperating with German actions against Jews. Jacques Chirac, President of France, has offered an official statement of responsibility and regret. This does not mean that there is no de-

---

8. *The Vichy Syndrome: History and Memory in France since 1944* (Arthur Goldhammer trans.) (Cambridge: Harvard University Press, 1991), at 160–61.

9. Eric Conan and Henry Rousso, *Vichy: Un passé qui ne passe pas* (Paris: Fayard, 1994), at 9.

10. See particularly Michael R. Marrus, "Coming to Terms with Vichy", 9 *Holocaust and Genocide Studies* 23 (1995).

bate on these and other issues. It does mean, however, that official, public and collective memory is not now totally surrounded by silence or obfuscation. As Rousso points out however, a continuing conflict appears in the very specific context of law and memory. What role, if any, does or can law and the judicial process play in the construction of collective memory of the Holocaust in France?

Can perpetrator trials serve a useful political or historical function which goes beyond the limited issues of the guilt or innocence of an individual accused? In France, the public and overt construction of such trials as "pedagogical" events, along the Nuremberg model, specifically designed to provide public history lessons, has led to a problematic opposition and juxtaposition between understandings of the trial as the embodiment of the rule of law and the trial as the embodiment of publicly constructed historical truth.

This debate has come to the surface of heated public polemics about law, justice and memory most recently during the trial in Bordeaux of Maurice Papon, the sub-prefect there under Vichy. After Klaus Barbie and Paul Touvier, Papon became the third, and probably last, person tried for crimes against humanity in France in relation to the Shoah. Again, Rousso puts forward the position that while the trial may have been able to determine the guilt or innocence of Papon in relation to the charges, it was not a proper instance for the construction of historical fact.

> Ces tribunaux sont dans l'illusion que le verdict prononcé, réel ou virtuel, va se substituer au tribunal de l'Histoire, alors qu'il n'a au bout du compte qu'un goût de provisoire, d'inachevé, dans l'attente d'une relance du dossier ou de la polémique.[11]

> (These courts operate under the illusion that the verdict they give, be it real or virtual, can be substituted for the tribunal of history. In the end, the court's verdict will leave only a taste of the provisional, the incomplete while we await the reopening of the case or of polemics surrounding it.)

This vital problem of memory and law identified by Rousso and others as the difficult, if not impossible, nexus between law and justice in the form

---

11. *La hantise du passé* (Paris: Textuel, 1998), at 89. More recently, Rousso has argued that the culture of memory surrounding the Algerian question raises similar complex issues about the demand for memory and the institutional limitations of law. See Henry Rousso, "La guerre d'Algérie et la culture de la mémoire", *Le Monde*, 5 April 2002; Cf. Jean-Noël Jeanney, *Le Passé dans le Prétoire* (Paris: Seuil, 1998).

of a collectively elaborated memory is, however, preceded in the history of the Holocaust in France by another, perhaps more fundamental, issue, as to the nature and function of law and legal forms. One construction of the Holocaust, perhaps the historically and ideologically dominant one, posits an interpretation of events and perpetrators as criminal and lawless. Indeed, the very basis for the trials of major war criminals at Nuremberg and those prosecutions which have followed, including those of Barbie, Touvier and Papon in France, was and is still the idea that fundamental norms of international and national law could not permit the deeds of the perpetrators to go unpunished. But in order for a national or international legal system to intervene, there must be a basic legal norm which existed at the time the acts in question occurred and there must have been a breach of that norm. Otherwise, the rule of law will simply become a rhetorical mask for raw political power or "victors' justice". Law would not be distinguishable from Nazi law.

A competing interpretation of the Holocaust in France (and elsewhere) has revealed that many of the events surrounding the policy and practice of the extermination of European Jewry were in fact "lawful". Again I mean simply that the system of law and legal norms and the principal legal actors, lawyers, magistrates, police and judges, were intimately involved in those policies and practices. The history of the Holocaust in France, as elsewhere, can, in part at least, be reconstructed through the legal history of the Holocaust; laws, statutes, police regulations, judicial decisions, all served as the legal basis for the exclusionary policies and practices which set the legal stage for the extermination of many of the Jews who had the misfortune to believe that the land of *liberté, égalité, et fraternité* (liberty, equality, and fraternity), would offer them a safe haven from persecution and extermination.

Any historical or legal understanding of the Holocaust in France and of the role played by Vichy officials must come to grips with the important fact that the vast majority of lawyers, judges and other legal officials in France at that time continued to operate on a daily basis as if they were in fact living under a system of law which was continuous with the system of law under which they had always worked. The issues of law, justice and memory in France must first and foremost come to a more complete understanding of law under Vichy. If that legal system is understood as lawful and legitimate, then the fundamental problem which must be confronted by French lawyers and citizens today is how one lawful regime such as today's Fifth Republic might face up to and judge, in legal, historical and ethical terms, the acts and actors of a previous legal regime, in this case the *Révolution Nationale* (National Revolution) of Maréchal Pétain. How then could Vichy law be tried by a Republican system of justice which is historically and factually continuous? How can public memory and the rule of law be constructed in such a way as to pay homage both to historical reality and justice? In other words, the French example is perhaps paradigmatic of the issues of continuity/discontinuity and the rule and role of law which are of major interest here.

Unique in Western Europe, France, for a significant period following the German conquest and Occupation, maintained an autonomous, independent government, seated in the "Unoccupied Zone", but with powers extending largely to most of the country. As Michael Marrus and Robert Paxton demonstrated in their path-breaking study, the Vichy government instituted almost all of the antisemitic measures which led the way to the Holocaust in France, not, as had been the "official" and public memory of post-war France, under the direct orders and armed threats of the occupying Germans, but rather freely and of their own accord and for their own domestic reasons.[12]

Marrus and Paxton, a Canadian and an American, caused much consternation in France with the publication of their work. A vital element in the construction of post-war collective memory and mythology in that country had been the portrayal of the Vichy regime as subject to a very specific legal characterization. Under this dominant, but by no means universal, myth, France was legally defined as a nation conquered by the Nazi enemy, yet resisting the conqueror at every turn. Thus, the Free French government-in-exile, situated in London and then Algiers, under the leadership of General de Gaulle, was legally constituted according to its own claims to legitimacy. France was, under this view, always resistant, always Republican. As far as Vichy was concerned, then, that government was by definition, illegitimate and illegal, a band of collaborators who had signed an illegal and unconstitutional armistice with the enemy. The legal or legalistic consequence of this view of French constitutional history or mythology can be found in the law of 9 August 1944 which states that the form of French government was and always had been the Republic and that all legal measures taken on French soil after 16 June 1940 "under the color of law" were null and void.

Thus, from the date of the appointment of Maréchal Phillipe Pétain as head of government, all acts of the "so-called" French government are illegal and un-

---

12. Michael R. Marrus and Robert O. Paxton, *Vichy France and the Jews* (New York: Basic Books, 1981).

constitutional. In this Gaullist recreation of French political and legal history, the Vichy regime under Pétain can claim only the status of a "*de facto*" but not a "*de jure*" government. It is important not to underestimate the importance of this particular jurisprudential point. With the living myth of the continuity of French Republicanism and the aberrant, extra-legal nature of Vichy, "law" and legitimacy under Vichy ceased to a large extent to exist since the regime itself was illegal.

This view is one which continues and which exercises a strong influence on French legal thinking and self-understanding today. For example, a published compilation of the laws passed in France, by the French government between 1940–1944, carries the title '*Les lois de Vichy: Actes dits "lois" de l'autorité de fait se prétendant "gouvernement de l'État français*" (*The Laws of Vichy: Acts called "laws" of the de facto authority calling itself "government of the French State"*).[13]

As a result of international scandals and revelations concerning "Swiss gold" and broader issues of the fate of expropriated or "Aryanized" Jewish property, the French government appointed a special commission under Jean Mattéoli to investigate the gamut of issues surrounding these questions in that country. The Mattéoli Commission came after the official apology issued by President Jacques Chirac for the crimes against Jews committed by the French state under the Vichy regime. In other words, in terms of law and public constructions of collective memory, the Mattéoli Commission could be configured under a rubric in which the question of collective responsibility and some form of historical continuity had at last been recognized by the highest representative of the body politic. Yet despite the important work done by the Commission on the subject of Aryanization, it continued to construct Vichy and crimes against Jews in France as fundamentally foreign to French legality. Like the unofficial compilation of Vichy statutes which semiotically figured Vichy as a *de facto* regime, the Mattéoli Commission continued to portray Vichy legality as somehow not French, and certainly as not law. Thus, in 2000, it issued a set of documents including all relevant laws and regulations containing anti-Jewish measures under the title, *La Persécution des Juifs de France 1940–1944 et le Rétablissement de la Légalité Républicaine* (The Persecution of Jews in France 1940-1944 and the Re-establishment of Republican Legality).[14] Vichy law and its anti-Jewish provisions are again positioned here as having operated as a point of rupture with Republican i.e. true French legality which

---

13. Dominique Rémy, ed. (Paris: romillat, 1992).
14. *Mission d'étude sur la spoliation des Juifs de France, République Française.*

pre-existed Vichy and was re-instituted, in fact, after Liberation. Like the period of 1933–1945 in Germany, the Pétain period is a (il)legal moment of aberration, a rupture within the great traditions of French law and justice, a tradition maintained by the government-in-exile in London. Vichy law is again and still, not law.

More recent developments, however, provide some tentative evidence that the construction of Vichy as a subject of law may be undergoing a transformation. After his conviction as a accessory to crimes against humanity and his condemnation to pay damages of 4.7 million francs ($719,000), Maurice Papon argued that the financial penalty should be assumed by the French government, under the orders of which he was acting at the time of the offence. The French *Conseil d'Etat* (Council of State, the Supreme Administrative Court) gave a partial victory to Papon and in doing so partially rewrote several decades of French constitutional self-delusion. The *Conseil d'Etat* found in effect that the arrest of Jews in the Gironde, between 1942 and 1944, where Papon worked, was the work of the German occupiers. But it also found that the creation of the Merignac internment camp, and the authority given in 1940 to the prefect to hold foreign Jews there, and the order given to the French police to arrest and intern Jews, as well as the very existence of a bureaucracy within the local prefecture charged with "Jewish affairs", were all facts and acts attributable to the French government and not attributable directly to compulsion by the occupying authority. Thus, anti-Jewish measures, the responsibilities of the French government and its agents and the "reestablishment of republican legality" can not be considered to have relieved the government of liability for the faults of its agents.[15] What remains unclear and contentious after the decision of the *Conseil d'Etat* is exactly what "fault" the government and its agents committed in the Gironde and elsewhere. At some level, the *Statuts des Juifs* (Statutes concerning the Jews), and other legislation passed under Vichy were valid, legitimate and lawful measures. While the decision here at some level does establish the responsibility of the current Fifth Republic for the acts of the Vichy regime, it does so only by continuing to (mis)characterize the Vichy regime as illegal, unlawful, unconstitutional and contrary to Republican legality, the only recognizable form of French legality. What the *Conseil d'Etat* decides is that the simple fact that the law reestablishing Republican legality does not relieve the state of responsibility for the "fault" of Vichy bureaucrats. Their fault here, was, as it always was, to follow the law.

---

15. *Conseil d'Etat*, No 238689, 12 April 2002. See also, Dominique Simonnot, "L'Etat devra partager la condamnation de Papon", *Libération*, 13 April 2002.

Without entering into sometimes arcane jurisprudential debates or detailed discussions of French constitutional law and issues of government succession in international law, it was always quite clear that simply characterizing the Vichy regime as "unconstitutional" or "illegal" from either a positivist or anti-positivist perspective does little to add to our historical understanding of that period of French history. More importantly, this characterization of Vichy shared by Gaullist and Socialist Republicans such as the late French President François Mitterand, does not enhance our understanding of an equally key and irrefutable historical fact under Vichy i.e., that life continued in a state of normalcy for the vast majority of French legal officials. Lawyers, notaries, magistrates, police officers, and judges all continued to act as if little, if anything, had changed in their daily routine. In other words, as far as the lawyers and judges in France between 1940–1944 were concerned, the change of government and the change of governmental form from Republic to "*l'État français*" under Pétain's "National Revolution", mattered little. It operated no fundamental change in the daily mundane and routine practice of law, or in the self-understanding of legal professionals. Thus, the decision by the *Conseil d'Etat*, which appears to establish the legal continuity of Vichy and post-war French governments, in fact and in law, continues the jurisprudential practice of characterizing Vichy as unlawful.

Of course, stories of the adaptability of the legal profession to new circumstances or even of the profession's ability to define new circumstances as if they were not in fact new, are hardly interesting or even surprising. What is interesting and important about the story of law and lawyers under Vichy is that the new circumstances which they so ably assimilated into their daily routine with so little trauma included a complex system of laws and regulations which saw their Jewish colleagues arrested, imprisoned and deported[16], which saw "Jew" become a legally-defined category of pariah, which saw "Jewish" property expropriated and "Aryanized" etc.[17] For the vast majority of French lawyers and judges these issues simply became one more set of legal problems to which they turned their professional attention and expertise.

From October 1940 to December of the next year, the Vichy legal regime adopted and implemented 109 laws and administrative decrees dealing with "the

---

16. See Robert Badinter, *Un Antisémitisme Ordinaire: Vichy et Les Avocats Juifs (1940–1944)* (Paris: Fayard, 1997).

17. See *Juger Sous Vichy* (Paris: Seuil, 1994) and Dominique Gros (ed.), *Le Droit Antisémite de Vichy* (Paris: Seuil, 1995); Richard Weisberg, *Vichy Law and the Holocaust in France* (New York: New York University Press, 1996).

Jewish Question". These legal instruments did not spring out of the air. Legal exceptions always existed in France from the early days of emancipation.[18] Anti-immigrant agitation, often infected with antisemitism, was periodically important in legislative action.[19] Indeed, as Catherine Kessedjian, in her essay on the law of nationality,[20] underlines, the legal and political basis of the modern nation state, which allowed Vichy to engage in attempts to strip "Jews" of their citizenship, remains unchanged today.[21] Indeed such legal principles legitimize recent changes to France's immigration laws, another area of national identity which continues to be hotly contested as debates rage in France, as in other parts of Europe, over the issue of illegal immigration and the fate of the *sans papiers* (the undocumented aliens).

Such continuities, both factual and juridical, underline the basic need not just to understand Vichy law on its own terms but also to understand legal continuities between French law then and today's legal system. These continuities, I argue, haunt legal memory generally and legal memory of the Holocaust more particularly within France today.

Vichy's legalized antisemitism operated a fundamental conceptual change in the way in which it created and constructed "the Jew" and "Jewishness" as legal categories. "Jewish law" became an essential part of the legal system under Pétain's National Revolution. Indeed, "antisemitic law" operated under Vichy as a universalizing norm. It was not a separate field but rather an overriding set of ideological principles given concrete legal form in various areas of legal practice.

The "Aryanization" program offers a useful example of the overriding nature of antisemitism as a legal norm under Vichy. The compulsory "Aryanization" of "Jewish" property was a vital part of the entire legalized process through which Jews were deprived of their assets, reduced to a state of impoverishment and excluded from the realms of civil society.

Industries and business had to be defined as "Jewish" by reference to the "race" of the legal owners or others exercising substantial control over the business. Once the "Jewish" character of the business was identified, a legal and bureaucratic structure had to be put into place to remove the "Jewish" influence,

---

18. Jean-Jacques Clère, "Une émancipation tardivement contestée", in *Le Droit Antisémite de Vichy*, at 58.

19. Marie-Claire Laval-Reviglio, "Parlementaires xénophobes et antisémites sous la IIIe République", ibid., at 85. See also, P.-J. Deschodt and F. Huguemin, *La République Xenophobe* (Paris: Jean-Claude Lattès, 2001).

20. "Le Juif déchu de la nationalité française", *Le Droit Antisémite*, op. cit. 231 at 240.

21. See discussion infra.

to run the business and to place the business in "Aryan" hands. The legal mechanisms were complex. First, the individual in question had to be identified as legally "Jewish". This involved the application of legal tests as determined by the appropriate statutory instrument.[22] Once identified, "the Jew" had then to be legally characterized as incapable of administering his or her property and a trustee (*administrateur provisoire*) appointed to manage and then dispose of the property.[23] In addition, various governmental departments, charged with administrative jurisdiction over various economic issues had to apply and implement the legal principles of "Aryanization."[24] Then, a centralized administrative structure, in the form of the *Commissariat Général aux Questions Juives* (General Commission for Jewish Questions), had to be established, organized, staffed and charged with the twin tasks of determining who was or was not "a Jew" and with overseeing the "Aryanization" of French society in general and the economy in particular.[25]

Of course, all of this meant the continuing and important involvement of the various actors in the Vichy legal system. Lawyers advised and appeared for clients who were concerned with the legal definition of "Jew", who sought to obtain property from the trustees, or who wished to contest the administrator's actions. The courts had to determine which court, if any, had jurisdiction over these matters and others, as well as determining the legal rules to be applied in each case.[26] The "Aryanization" program, then, involved the lawyers, bureaucrats and judges of Vichy on a daily basis in issues of "Jewish law". "Aryanization" became a legal question involving an analysis of the law of personal status, property law, administrative law, the law of fiduciaries and jurisdictional issues. While the traditional forms and categories of the civil law remained intact, the content of "republication legality" was erased through the creation of the new legal category of "the Jew". But this new legal category did not, as far as the actors within the system of French law, serve to operate a Radbruchian point or moment of rupture with "law" itself. "Jewish law" became nothing more or less than daily routine in the Vichy legal system. Lawyers, notaries, administrators and judges, simply adapted their profes-

---

22. Jean Marcou, 'La "qualité de Juif"', in *Le Droit Antisémite de Vichy*, op. cit., at 153.

23. Éric Loquin, 'Le Juif "incapable"', ibid., at 173.

24. Claire Andrieu, "L' "aryanisation" et les Finances extérieurs", id., at 267.

25. Marguerite Blocaille-Boutelet, "L' "aryanisation" des biens", id., at 243. See also Emmanuelle Triol, "L'aryanisation des biens: L'application judiciare du statut des juifs", in *Juger Sous Vichy*, op. cit., at 61.

26. Gérald Simon, "L'administration de l'antisémitisme", *Le Droit Antisémite de Vichy*, op. cit., at 307; Jean-Pierre Dubois, "La jurisprudence administrative", ibid., at 327.

sional worldview to reflect this new area of legal practice. The new world of the French lawyer was much like the old world, the only difference being the daily involvement of the legal and judicial system in the interpretation and application of a system of legal rules aimed at the lawful exclusion of "the Jew" from French civil society. For French lawyers and judges, "Jew" became another legal category like "sale" or "lease" to be defined, delimited and applied in traditional fashion.

A key question which must be raised as result of the recent publication of books dealing specifically with law, lawyers and judges under Vichy is why it has taken over fifty years since the end of the Vichy regime for legal works examining Vichy law to appear. Marrus and Paxton clearly demonstrated in the early 1980s that an autonomous French governmental legal system was at work in the adoption and application of the *Statut des Juifs* and other anti-semitic legal norms in France. Unlike historians who have experienced and continue to experience some clear difficulties in gaining access to primary materials through the maze of French archival regulations, lawyers and legal academics have always had access to the primary materials on which the analyses of Vichy law could be based. Decisions of French courts under Vichy are reported in the several traditional collections which have always published French judicial decisions and professional commentaries. The key word "*Juif*" appears helpfully in indices of judgments and in doctrinal reviews of the period. These are not secret sources hidden and jealously guarded by mischievous or obstreperous archivists. These files did not disappear but can be found in any legal library or law office in the country. They constitute the daily and mundane material with which French lawyers, judges and academics deal on a regular basis.

Why has it taken so long for French legal professionals to begin to come to terms with Vichy and with the role of lawyers and law in that period of French history? Why did we have to wait until 1994, fifty years after the restoration of the "Republic" for the publication of the first volume of real self-examination by the French legal community?[27] One might well ask why it has only been since late 1996 that the French government has at last been asked to account for the property expropriated from French Jews under Vichy's legal system.[28] While commissions of inquiry are now studying the origins of residential properties owned by the city of Paris or Bordeaux and of art works found in French government museums, one might usefully pause to ask where have all the lawyers been?

---

27. *Juger Sous Vichy*, op. cit.
28. See Mattéoli, *Commission d'Etude*, op. cit.

One possible working hypothesis for future examinations of the willful amnesia of the French legal profession will surely involve a careful study of the
importance of the structures of collective memory in the French legal community and more particularly of the prophylactic function of a constitutional
mythology which has simply defined "Vichy" out of legal existence by characterizing it as unconstitutional, *de facto* and therefore of no vital importance
within a continuous tradition of Republican legality. Concerns about continuity and connection between Vichy law and French law, and about French
lawyers' implication in these continuities, have been avoided by hiding behind
the legalistic curtain of a constitutional history which defines Vichy as non-
law. By decree, Vichy law was "disappeared". Like the airbrushed photos of
Stalinist Russia, Vichy law was erased from constitutional and legal history.
This constitutionally created mode of legal amnesia cannot however eliminate
the reality of historical facts, or the recorded judgments and commentaries
dealing with questions of "Jewish law" from 1940. Those on the inside of Vichy
law functioned much as they always had, dealing with antisemitic legislation
and legal issues first and foremost as "legal" issues. For them, Vichy law was
in fact and in practice, law.

2. Constructing Vichy bis.

Others have demonstrated the ways in which law continued as "normal"
under Vichy. It is also important to note that outside France, as was the case
for Nazi law, perceptions of Vichy and law under Pétain constructed the
regime as legitimate. The idea of Vichy as a *de facto* but not a *de jure* government, while put forward by the exiles under General de Gaulle for obvious reasons of both domestic and international politics, did not accurately
reflect either domestic or international political and legal reality. The situation was summarized in the immediate post-war period by Dr. Benjamin R.
Payn in his legislative summary of the French government-in-exile. He wrote:

> Among the governments-in-exile which carried on the fight of their
> enemy-occupied countries during World War II, the Free French au-
> thorities are in a category *sui generis*. Whereas no problems at all, or
> comparatively simple ones, surrounded the recognition and function-
> ing of the other governments-in-exile the position of the Free French
> was complicated by the continued recognition of the Vichy régime. It
> is therefore not surprising that an important part of the legislative ef-
> forts of the Free French should have centered around the problem of

defining their own powers and obtaining full recognition—a status which in the case of other governments-in-exile was a starting point not a goal.[29]

The situation of Vichy law, then, is intimately linked to the validity of the assertion of the representative nature of the government-in-exile and to the subsequent mythology of *la France résistante* (France the resister). Vichy law was and is defined out of existence by the lawyers whose very authenticity in both the existential and institutional sense is contingent upon just such a declaration. The legitimacy of the government-in-exile was contingent on the complex rules of international law relating to changes of government and recognition as well as on the vagaries of French domestic constitutional law. Were the delegations of power from the legislature to the executive under Pétain and the subsequent exercise of these powers constitutionally valid?[30] For supporters of the dominant historical and constitutional position, the answer here is clearly negative. From this conclusion of the illegality and illegitimacy of the Pétain regime flow the legality and legitimacy of the de Gaulle rump in London. Rupture, discontinuity and illegality characterize and define Vichy law. The idea of any possible continuity between law under Vichy and the Republican rule of law restored after the Liberation is rendered a juridical nullity and impossibility by the Republican self-definition of the rule of law.

It is not my intention here to offer to resolve the complicated debates of international law or of French constitutional history. Rather I wish once more to offer a brief overview of contemporary legal discourse on the subject in order to demonstrate the contestability and contested nature of the claims asserted by those who wished to delegitimize the government in Vichy.

Otto Kirchheimer, no supporter of fascism or of trends to executive government, each of which can be said to a greater or lesser extent to characterize the Pétain regime, described the situation shortly after the French defeat of 1940.[31] In this important and neglected article, Kirchheimer describes the political processes adopted in France before the Occupation whereby a general enabling law permitted the executive branch to adopt emergency legislative measures. Quite naturally, he draws parallels with the situation in Weimar Germany under the provisions of Article 48 of the Constitution.[32] What is of

---

29. "French Legislation in Exile", 28 *Journal of Comparative Legislation and International Law* 44 (1946). Footnote omitted.

30. See Pierre Miquel, *Les Quatre-Vingts* (Paris: Fayard, 1995).

31. "Decree Powers and Constitutional Law in France Under the Third Republic", 34 *American Political Science Review* 1104 (1940).

32. See chapter 2 above.

importance here is not the critique offered by the Frankfurt School theorist of fascist tendencies in modern executive government, but rather the fact that for Kirchheimer the delegation of powers from the legislative branch to Pétain had a clear precedent under the Constitution of the Third Republic, where such a strategy did not *ipso facto* delegitimize in the constitutional sense the "democratic" government. Here a leading opponent of executive government constructs and analyzes the elements of continuity between the rule of law under the Third Republic and the Pétain regime.

An even more persuasive and important article appeared at around the same time, this one under the imprimatur of Karl Lowenstein, another legal academic hardly sympathetic to fascist regimes.[33] In this extended treatment of the July 1940 delegation of power to Pétain, Lowenstein surveys the history of French constitutional law and politics under revolutionary conditions. More on point he describes the events surrounding the delegation of powers to Pétain as legal.

> It was a *coup d'état* from above, a deliberate act of the defeated military leaders and their political advisors—in short, a skillfully engineered political stratagem. The politicians among the group must have been well aware of the character of the Constitution as the supreme law of the land, capable of being abrogated only by a legislative act of equal rank. The men who carried France into fascism are lawyers and soldiers of the old régime inured to democratic legality and remote from the supine disregard for constitutional forms inherent in genuine revolutionaries. To most of the parliamentary representatives, observance of legal forms was congenital.[34]

Lowenstein then adds this crucial statement:

> These observations—and they could be multiplied—help to explain why the transformation of democratic France into an authoritarian state followed the traditional procedure of constitutional revision prescribed by the constitution of 1875.[35]

At the time at which General de Gaulle was in London proclaiming the illegal nature of the Vichy government, eminent constitutional and political opponents of executive government and fascism were explaining in articles in a leading American academic journal how and why that same "illegal"

---

33. "The Demise of the French Constitution of 1875", 34 *Am. Pol. Sci. Rev.* 867 (1940). See the discussion of Lowenstein's position on Nazi legality in chapter 4 supra.

34. At 867–68. Footnote omitted.

35. At 868.

Vichy government had come to power using mechanisms which had been lawfully deployed under the Third Republic and following pre-established constitutional means. In other words, no matter how objectionable the Vichy regime may have been, it was seen, even by contemporary opponents, as legally constituted. Like subsequent appreciations of the Nazi regime, analysis of Vichy gradually shifted as its illegality was proclaimed in the pages of the same journal in which the opposite view had appeared a few years earlier.[36] Nonetheless, even during the war, academic experts, including some exiled French citizens, refused to categorically reject the political and legal validity of some of the most important reforms which the Vichy government tried to introduce into French society, from changes in the country's administrative structures to modifications in economic ordering, including those of a corporatist nature.[37]

Again, I am not suggesting here that such opinions were unanimous, nor do I argue that acceptance of the legitimacy and legality of the Vichy government leads to an acceptance of the ethical or moral correctness of the substantive content of the regime's laws. Rather, I wish again to point out that both among the vast majority of French lawyers who stayed in the country from 1940 to 1944 and continued to practice law there and among many overseas observers, the view of Vichy's illegitimacy was by no means the majority position.

The uncomfortable conclusions which might be drawn from this analysis of daily legal reality in Vichy France are two-fold. First, as a general analytic principle for future study, we must conclude that the regime which laid the legislative groundwork for the Holocaust in France, and that framework itself, were "lawful". Second, we must also conclude that there appears to be nothing inherent in the system of law which allows us to assume that "crimes against humanity" and "genocide" are by definition to be situated "outside" the law. The discomfort engendered by a careful analysis of Vichy law is summarized by Dominique Gros. Gros points out that any attempt to characterize Vichy's legal system as "monstrous" must first come to recognize the essential characteristics of the "monster". The first defining characteristic of the "monster", Vichy law, is the anomalous practice of defining "citizens" according to "ethno-religious" criteria and discriminating on the basis of those criteria. The second characteristic of the "monster" is its "normality". Under

---

36. See Maximilian Koessler, "Vichy's Sham Constitutionality", 39 *Am. Pol. Sci. Rev.* 86 (1945).

37. See e.g. Paul Vaucher, "The "National Revolution"in France", 57 *Political Science Quarterly* 7 (1942); Shepard B. Clough, "The House That Pétain Built", 59 *Pol. Sci. Q.* 30 (1944).

Vichy, the legal system continued to function in a normal way.[38] No special court structure was established to interpret and apply Vichy's antisemitic legislation. University law faculties incorporated "Jewish law" and other legal aspects of the National Revolution into their curricula. Judges, magistrates and lawyers simply dealt with "Jewish law" in the daily tasks which they set about fulfilling as part of their professional lives. As Jews were being rounded up by French police and deported "to the East" from Drancy and other French concentration camps, French lawyers continued to produce learned legal arguments about who was or was not "a Jew". Legal business continued as usual.

Lawyers under Vichy jealously guarded their autonomy and insisted on the Republican tradition of the independence of legal practitioners. Litigation expanded in France between 1940–1944 to such an extent that many in the profession feared that there simply would not be enough judges and lawyers to deal with the weight and number of cases which presented themselves within the system, largely as a result of the new field of "Jewish law".

Vichy lawyers took this apparently "revolutionary" change in the legal system much in their stride. While some clearly adopted the discourse and ideology of the "National Revolution" as part of their new personal and professional *weltanschauung*, it would appear that most French lawyers simply treated fundamental ethical and moral issues as involving little more than technical legal expertise and professional competence. Complex arguments were developed around questions such as who should bear the burden of proof in cases where a person was alleged to fit the legal definition of "Jew". Must the person prove s/he is not a "Jew", thus carrying the burden of proof, or must the state agency or the police prove that the person is a "Jew" as defined by the statute? Traditional norms of French justice would impose the burden on the state but there was under Vichy's legal system a serious question of law as to whether such an important issue, as a matter of overriding public interest, as one's status as "Jew", should be subject to normal legal rules governing the burden of proof. After, or even before, the burden of proof question was resolved, another question arose. How could one prove that she or he was not a "Jew" or conversely, how could the state prove that they were?[39]

These examples and numerous others demonstrate again the two key and related points for understanding Vichy law. First, French lawyers and judges saw questions raised under the *Statut des Juifs* and related instruments as real, legal issues, to be dealt with as any other legal issue arising from a contract, a

---

38. "Un droit monstrueux?", in *Le Droit Antisémite de Vichy*, 561 at 563.

39. For a detailed analysis of these and other questions, see Richard Weisberg, *Vichy Law and the Holocaust*, op. cit.

will, a partnership agreement etc. They all operated under the daily assumption that they were lawyers, doing law as they had always done.

The second valuable insight which can be extracted from the reality of Vichy law is one which appears to be in contradiction with the first. French lawyers persisted not only in their self-understanding as lawyers in the face of the immoral exclusion of their "Jewish" co-citizens and colleagues, but they also persisted to a great extent in their self-understanding as lawyers in the tradition of liberal Republicanism, resisting government interference and dictates in their professional lives by invoking the very principles of independence and autonomy central to professional life in modernity and democracy. At the same time, they quite willingly excluded their Jewish colleagues from government, courts and the profession and stood by as those few Jewish lawyers who were permitted to continue to exercise their profession appeared in the corridors of the *Palais de Justice* (Court House) with a Yellow Star attached to their robes.[40]

In virtually every instance, appeals to and belief in the great traditions of French law stopped short of invoking those same principles to protest against legalized antisemitism or to contest the constitutional legality of those measures. It appears to be the case that the very notion of Republican legality, the equality of every citizen, was subverted by a legal reading and practice among the legal community, of the constitutional norm of equality as applying to every French citizen. "Citizen", the basis of Republican democracy, became under Vichy, a category from which "the Jew" was excluded, by a series of legislative efforts, some bearing fruit, others not, to formally strip naturalized "Jews" of French citizenship.

Why and how could Vichy lawyers, French lawyers, brought up in the traditions of the Republic, in the country of the *Declaration of the Rights of Man*, of *liberté, égalité, fraternité*, as members of the educated, liberal elite, not protest against the evil contained in the *Statut des Juifs*? How could they accommodate themselves to a professional existence which involved them in the daily, minute examination of these iniquitous provisions without raising a visceral, basic protest against them? Why did they choose, instead of arguing from first principles of Constitutional Law, to simply revert to treating "Jewish law" as another area of legal practice to which they would only apply basic arguments based on technical, precise, issues of legal grammar?

A recent explanatory system elaborated by Danièle Lochack argues that the French jurisprudential and professional tradition and practice of legal positivism can help us understand Vichy lawyers' compliance in the evils of an an-

---

40. See Robert Badinter, *Un Droit Antisémite*, op. cit.

tisemitic legal system.[41] Others have offered or debated a similar explanation for the failure of law in Germany.[42] For Lochack, French judges and lawyers saw themselves primarily as detached, expert, scientific, technical appliers of rules. This attitude and the practices associated with it led to the situation where lawyers became distanced, amoral readers and appliers of texts, for whom moral or ethical norms were completely foreign and irrelevant in their tasks. For them, a law was a law, was a law. Thus, as professionals, the lawyers' function was to represent his/her client's interest, whether, under Vichy law, that client wished to be defined as a "non-Jew" or whether the client wanted the other party defined as a "Jew". To the professional, expert, scientific lawyer, the application of the law in a particular case was simply a matter of the technical interpretation of a text to define and suit the client's interest. Whether the text in question defines the legal category "Jew" or the legal category "domicile", would have been a matter of strict indifference for the true professional.

When one combines all of the legal techniques of professional expertise, one arrives at a situation not just where "Jewish law" is voided of its immoral content but more perniciously where "Jewish law", through a complex process of routinization, of employing euphemisms and other traditional legal techniques, is legitimated by its very ordinariness. This for Lochack, is the true "banality of evil" inherent in Vichy law. Of course, Lochack's analysis is much more subtle and complex than this, but the basic idea of the lawyer as a detached technocrat both does justice to her position and resonates with certain notions not just of what lawyers should do[43] and what they actually do even today, but also with certain explanatory models of bureaucratic and professional participation in the Holocaust.

Instead of relying on the "positivism" explanation, Richard Weisberg offers a much more subtle, nuanced and controversial interpretation of why Vichy lawyers acted as they did, excluding "Jews" from all calculations in high level

41. Danièle Lochack, "La doctrine sous Vichy ou les mésaventures du positivisme", in *Les Usages sociaux du droit* (Paris: PUF, 1989), at 252. Also "Ecrire, se taire…Réflexions sur l'attitude de la doctrine française", in *Le Droit Antisémite de Vichy*, op. cit., at 433

42. See generally, Walter Ott and Franziska Buob, "Did Legal Positivism Render German Jurists Defenceless During the Third Reich?", 2 *Social & Legal Studies* 91 (1993); Peter Caldwell, "Legal Positivism and Weimar Democracy", 39 *American Journal of Jurisprudence* 273 (1994).

43. Although such ideas were not completely uncontested in French legal theory immediately before the start of the war. See e.g. Henri Dupeyroux, "Les Grands Problèmes Du Droit", 2 *Archives de Philosophie du droit et de Sociologie Juridique* 7 (1938). Cf. Marcel Waline, "Défense Du Positivisme Juridique", id., vol 1–2, 1939, 83.

or principled constitutional discourse, while at the same time, applying all of their technical, low level professional competence and skills in creating arguments about who carried the burden of proof etc. For Weisberg, the great moral failure of Vichy lawyers lies here. They did not raise basic objections to the creation of a new field of "Jewish law". Instead, they accommodated themselves to the reality of its existence and simply limited themselves to the production of daily, routine, skilled and professional analyses of the *Statut des Juifs* as they did for every other legal text.

What Weisberg offers as a model for understanding the actions of lawyers within the Vichy legal system is itself a legal explanation but is one which engages legal and factual arguments against the position which attributes liability to legal positivism. Once again, he tries to offer an understanding or to provide an explanation of lawyers in Vichy France "from the inside", from the lawyers' own self-understanding. For Weisberg, Vichy lawyers' willingness to create a legal practice which "read Jews out" at the upper level, while "reading them in" at the lower level of the constitutional/legal textual hierarchy is based in a particular legal reading of "the Jew" and the law practiced by the lawyers of Vichy themselves.

According to his interpretation of Vichy legal thought and practice, a certain French Roman Catholic view of "the Jew", portrayed him as "Talmudic" i.e. as having a fundamentally different relationship with the "law" than the real Frenchman. For Weisberg, the French Catholic worldview always constructed "the Jew" as loyal to other traditions, other practices, other law—the Talmud. It therefore becomes possible, if not inevitable, to "read out", to legally exclude, "the Jew" from the polity of France and from the French Constitution because "the Jew" was never, and could never be, truly "French". He was always the Talmudic Other whose loyalty lay elsewhere. Thus the French legal interpretation of "the Jew" as "Talmudic", as overly legalistic, itself permits a legalistic reading of French law and constitutional tradition which eliminates "the Jew" as an equal, recognized legal subject, as a French citizen deserving by that fact alone the protection of the basic principles of the Constitution. Like the Christianizing reading of the foundational or constitutional text of the Old Testament as a Christian text which removes "the Jew" from any real role in the foundational structure, the Catholic and Christianizing reading of the French constitutional text, which Weisberg argues informed the jurisprudential ideology and daily legal practice of Vichy, removes "the Jew" from the body politic and the body of the law.

This reading of legal practice offered as a text constructed by an interpretative community has much to commend it. It does fill in the lacunae which have troubled the positivism thesis on Vichy law and avoids the arcane jurisprudential debates about the legitimacy of legal positivism. It is powerfully self-refer-

ential, allowing us to come to grips with lawyers acting as lawyers in a fundamentally evil system, adopting immoral norms as their daily basis for the practice of law. In addition it engages with the construction of a French self-identity as a Catholic nation, an element in ongoing debates about the role of
Christianity in the construction of a lay Republic or of the very legitimacy of
that lay Republic as reflective of the real France. Yet, as with all explanatory
models, this one is not without its own lacunae or problematic and troubling
aspects.

It would be possible to argue that Weisberg paints a somewhat one-dimensional portrait of lawyers and life generally under Vichy. For example, much
of the debate about the ways in which proof of an individual's "Jewishness"
might be established, a debate which led to a certain degree of conflict between
Vichy legal officials and the Germans, was in fact concern among French officials about the issuing of false documents like birth certificates, especially by
parish priests. In addition to the clergy who attempted to subvert the system
of legalized antisemitism and exclusion, it is clear that many French legal officials, in prefects' offices or local town halls especially, also participated in protecting Jews by issuing false documents. In addition, as Claire Andrieu points
out, some elements of the French governmental bureaucracy, including
lawyers, to a greater or lesser extent, refused to co-operate in implementing
the "Aryanization" program.[44] Finally, one might mention those jurists who
played a key role in the French government-in-exile or who joined the internal Resistance movements, and who were involved in the "re-establishment"
of Republican democracy after the Liberation. Weisberg makes little or no
mention of these resisting lawyers and some might accuse him of universalizing his criticism in an inappropriate fashion and of ignoring the "good" lawyers.

At the same time, Weisberg might also be subjected to some degree of criticism for the somewhat ahistorical nature of his criticism of the moral failure of French lawyers. Professor Weisberg highlights throughout his work the
fact that Vichy lawyers' reactions to legalized antisemitism is marked by the
absence of principled "jugular" arguments based on the unconstitutionality
or illegality of Vichy's *Statut de Juifs*. Yet, as he and others point out a more
principled stance of opposition was attempted by Belgian lawyers and failed
utterly to have any effect on the practices and policies of discrimination and
deportation in that country.[45] Here, we come face to face not just with issues
of comparative legal history, as they might relate to differences between a

---

44. "L' ayranisation et les Finances extérieures", Le Droit Antisémite de Vichy, op. cit.
45. Didier Boden, "Le droit belge sous l'Occupation", ibid., at 543.

fully occupied Belgium and a relatively autonomous France, but also with possible basic distinctions between ethical imperatives and efficacy. Would French lawyers have been successful if they had attempted such principled legal opposition to Vichy's antisemitic legislation? Unfortunately, as Weisberg points out all too tragically, we will never know because they simply did not act in this way, although he does seem to believe that such principled opposition by the legal community would have had certain positive effects. The next issue of ethical duty and utility is more complex. Would it have been better if French lawyers had appealed to high jurisprudential principles to oppose Vichy law, even if, analogizing from the Belgian experience, with such arguments, it could be presumed that such appeals would have been unsuccessful? Weisberg clearly believes that to do the right thing even in the face of impossibility is always better than to become complicit in a legalized evil. It is difficult if not impossible to disagree with this ethical position although it is also open to assert that Weisberg's faith in law in general and in lawyers in particular is sadly misplaced given the clear historical record. While he wants to condemn Vichy law and lawyers, Weisberg also wants desperately to save law and lawyers by offering a way to law which could have redeemed the French.

More generally, however, it might well be argued in Professor Weisberg's defense against charges of various ahistorical failings, that his concern is with the daily practice of the vast majority of lawyers, notaries, magistrates and judges, the majority who did not "resist", just as it is with the fact that principled legal practice was apparently distinctly absent from law in Vichy France.

Here again we come not just to a point of what one chooses to emphasize but also to the issue of history, memory and justice and to the history and mythology of resistance, rescue and ethical choice. Jews in France were deprived of their rights and their property and many were sent to their deaths as the end and natural result of Vichy's legalized antisemitism. The property of some was saved by friends and lawyers who set up "straw man" operations to preserve the property for the true owners. Bureaucrats who issued false documents saved some Jews. Which side of the opposing legal coins tells the "real" story of Vichy law?

Weisberg may not be fair to those who resisted, and he may, in some cases, be imposing an extremely severe, after the fact, moral judgment on Vichy lawyers, but the justice of his analysis of those who did not resist, of the lawyers who dealt with "Jewish law" as if nothing had really changed is perhaps a different type of issue. Of course, this does not necessarily mean that Professor Weisberg is beyond criticism in this regard either.

The problem seems to me to be with the interpretation of legalized anti-semitism which Weisberg offers as his explanatory model for understanding Vichy law. I would argue that the possible interpretations at play might be somewhat more complex than Weisberg wishes to acknowledge. There can be little doubt that animosity to the French Revolution and to Republicanism has formed a constant, if evolving, discourse in French politics from the days of the Revolution to the present. Nor can it be doubted that antisemitism has clearly played a role, again evolving over time, in the so-called internal French war (*la guerre franco-française*). Moreover, the ideal identification of true "Frenchness" with Catholicism has always been central to this battle, with its proponents identifying a series of outsiders, those who can never be truly French, from Free Masons, to Protestants, to Communists, to Jews.[46] It follows, then, that something more might be needed to explain Vichy law than Weisberg's reliance upon the existence of a Catholic view of Jewish otherness, given the long history of such an interpretation in French political, legal and social life. In other words, why Vichy? Why Vichy law? Was it simply a matter of opportunity or opportunism or was something else at work? Can a reference to a single causal factor, to a simple explanatory model truly explain the complex reality of those who participated in Vichy's legal system? This level of objection to Weisberg's thesis or case for the prosecution against Vichy law is perhaps a legal objection, as seeking further and better particulars of the indictment, but not as one which goes to the foundation of the case itself. Moreover, such an objection does not effect the basic and primary truth that for whatever reason, Vichy law remained in the eyes of the legal professions, always law.

The basis of Weisberg's legal argument is that a legal way of reading legal texts allowed Vichy lawyers, or compelled Vichy lawyers, in a stronger form of the argument which Weisberg does not himself specifically make, to "read out" "the Jew" as always/already excluded from the constitutional juridical framework. This is contrasted with the other available discursive and legal strategy which would have permitted or compelled lawyers under Vichy to engage in what Weisberg refers to as the "jugular" argument of full frontal attack on the legitimacy of the norms of antisemitic law themselves by invoking pre-existing constitutional, Republican norms of liberty and equality. In other words, lawyers could or should have attacked the very "legality" of Vichy and legalized antisemitism by invoking constitutional arguments about fundamental

---

46. Pierre Birnbaum, *"La France aux Français": Histoire des haines nationalistes* (Paris: Fayard, 1993).

Republican values. That they failed to do so informs much of Weisberg's distaste for Vichy lawyers and lies at the heart of the unease which many lawyers feel when confronted with the law's complicity in the Holocaust in France.

The problem I want to raise here is not with the practicality of Weisberg's position or with the validity of his assertion that such "jugular" attacks are justified and necessary. Rather, I want to briefly raise an issue of Republican legal interpretation and doctrine under French law. If it is true that the Catholic anti-Talmudist interpretative strategy which Weisberg argues dominated and informed legal theory and practice under Vichy by making "the Jew" always/already "other", or absent from the general Constitutional norm or more specifically constructed the Jew as not French, it is also the case that "the Jew" was always/already ironically absent from the norms and practices of Republican constitutionalism. Under the basic and fundamental principle of equality and the secularization of the state and of citizenship, "the Jew" simply ceased to exist as a subject of constitutional concern. Any "religious" or "racial" characterization of the citizen of France was inimical to the norms and ideals of the Republic and of constitutionalism. As I noted in the introduction to this chapter, this Republican ideal also wishes to erase from the body politic both the image and reality of young Muslim women wearing traditional modest headwear from public educational institutions. There is no place in classic French Republican law for Jews or for Muslims.

Thus, it was not that under Vichy the Catholic theological and legal worldview "read the Jew out", but rather that the Catholic belief when concretized in law "read the Jew in" where before there had been no "Jew", simply citizen and non-citizen. The legal strategy invoked as his explanatory model by Richard Weisberg is one which he claims was aimed at eliminating "the Jew" as legal subject and citizen. No doubt this phenomenon existed and continues to exist, but it did not and could not function as he claims. It could only "read in the Jew" in order to "read out the Jew"; like Nazi antisemitic legislation before it, Vichy law was hoist on its own hermeneutic and epistemological petard—it had to create "the Jew" in order to destroy "the Jew".[47] The *homo sacer* must be definitionally situated inside the law before s/he can be out-lawed. Ironically, it is the jugular Republican constitutional position of equality and secularization which excludes "the Jew" and which eliminated "the Jew" in any constitutional normative debate. The emancipatory vision and ideal of the Republic ignores "the Jew" as legal subject while Vichy creates "the Jew" as legal pariah.[48] Weisberg's

47. See chapter 3.

reading of the Catholic theological, legal view of the "Talmudic Jew" as fundamentally disloyal and "unFrench" may be correct in one sense, but it may also be the case that as a legal argument, his position must be given a more nuanced and complex reading in order to deal with the norms of Republicanism which he himself argues were available to the interpretive community of Vichy judges and lawyers. At this level, again, law cannot necessarily be saved from itself.

Indeed, the very strength of this Republican ideal of the "citizen" has played a key role in post-war constructions of the Shoah in French collective and legal memory. When survivors returned from the camps, many were reluctant to declare their suffering in the public forum precisely because they wished to be identified not as "Jews" but as French. After all, public identity as a "Jew" was the first step in their confrontation with the horrors of legalized evil. For most of the returnees, the reestablishment of normality meant a return to universal Republican norms. Subsequent debates in France surrounding the precise "identity" of victims of the legal category "crimes against humanity" have also focussed around the complex ways in which it is possible to assert one's status as "Jew" in a Republican prosecution of alleged perpetrators as well as how it is possible to create a category of victim of Nazi crimes against humanity such as members of the Resistance, without ignoring the specificity of Jewish suffering.[49] The politics of identity within a Republic based on notions and ideals of universal equality surfaced and troubled France in its self-understanding during the Barbie, Touvier and Papon trials just as it surfaces and troubles Republican self-comprehension when French schoolgirls show up wearing the *hijab*.

The fact that the interpretative community chose not to invoke these higher constitutional norms or to have recourse to them might also serve to problematize Weisberg's proposed interpretation and explanation. If the participants themselves chose to rely on one set of textual practices over another, in this case, the Catholic "Talmudist" text, rather than the text of Republican idealism, this may indicate one of several possible alternative, legal understandings.

First, it might be the case that under Vichy law, the battle for the appropriate legal, constitutional norm was a heated and uncertain one within the community. Weisberg himself dedicates much of his work to debunking this

48. Pierre Birnbaum, *Destins Juifs: De la Révolution française à Carpentras* (Paris: Calmann-Lévy, 1995), at 253–59.

49. See discussion below and compare Guyora Binder, "Representing Nazism: Advocacy and Identity at the Trial of Klaus Barbie", 98 *Yale Law Journal* 1321 (1989) and Vivian Grosswald Curran, "Deconstruction, structuralism, antisemitism and the law", 36 *Boston College Law Review* 1 (1994).

possibility. Weisberg might have benefited by a more detailed examination of legal "resistance". Furthermore, he might usefully have engaged the idea put forward by Gérald Simon[50] that a basic understanding among the French citizenry in general and French lawyers in particular, including Republicans, of the vital role of a confused idea of sovereignty and of respect for the legitimacy of the law, may well help to further our understanding of the complex ways in which French lawyers were unquestioning or complicit in Vichy's legalized antisemitism. Indeed, this idea of the rule of law is at the very core of conflicts and debates which problematize any legal understanding of the Holocaust as a legal phenomenon.

Finally, Weisberg's characterization of the role played by the particular version of Catholic legal antisemitism which he invokes might also be made more complex by pointing out the statutory, legal fact that the *Statut des Juifs* on its face appears at some level to read in "the Jew" under the National Revolution. Thus, unlike the Nuremberg Laws, the French statute created a set of exceptions and exemptions for "Jews". Unlike the overriding German legal concern with the issue of the status of the *Mischlinge* (which also obsessed parts of the French bureaucratic, legal machinery) and therefore with the actual extent of the legal category "Jew", under the Nuremberg Laws, the French created categories of "Jews" who were exempted from the application of some statutory prohibitions which applied to "Jews" generally. Lawyers for example were not subjected to a total ban, but were regulated by a *numerus clausus*. Outstanding service to the country, an exceptional military record, a long-standing family connection with French soil (*vielle souche*), all these elements created a legal category of acceptable, legally differentiated "Jew" as "French". I am not suggesting that these exceptions and exemptions somehow make the *Statut des Juifs* less evil, nor that these categories actually made a great difference in practice for many French Jews, although they did operate in fact and in law.

Rather I would argue that as a matter of defining and describing the legal and constitutional context in which Vichy lawyers operated, it is important to note that "the Jew" was not absolutely and totally not French, "read out" or eliminated, but rather that it was *legally* possible for individuals to some extent to be both "Jews" and "French". In the end this means that antisemitic legal provisions were perhaps more deeply embedded in French law and practice than they were, at the formal textual level at least, in Germany. Legal professionals applied anti-Jewish laws without the slightest hesitation or self-doubt. The head

---

50. "L'administration de l'antisémitisme", *Le Droit Antisémite de Vichy*, op. cit., at 318–19.

of the Paris Bar, Charpentier, came to Drancy to announce to his former friends and colleagues, imprisoned Jewish lawyers, that they were no longer permitted to practice their profession. Yves Jouffa, the late French lawyer and human rights activist, who was in Drancy and witnessed Charpentier's actions reported that:

> Lorsque le bâtonnier est arrivé à Drancy (j'y étais) pour annoncer aux avocats qui étaient là (et dont certains étaient abondamment décorés sur le plan militaire) qu'ils étaient radiés du barreau de Paris, il n'a pas eu un mot, même pour dire qu'il accomplissait une démarche qui lui était difficile d'accomplir.[51]

> (When the President of the Bar arrived in Drancy (I was there) to announce to the lawyers there (among whom several had many military honors) that they were struck off the Roll of the Paris Bar, he did not say even a single word about how difficult it was for him to do what he was doing.)

Vichy law was essentially antisemitic but it was always essentially law, and French lawyers were still always French lawyers. At some level, these historical realities seem to be beyond the existential capacities of French lawyers today. For them, Vichy is a subject to be studied and elucidated but it is not one on which they wish to pass judgment. As Dominique Gros has written, French lawyers and legal scholars seem content to present the facts but they are strangely reluctant to proceed by a *mise en cause* of Vichy law. Modern French lawyers

> ...n'ont pas qualité pour instruire un procès contre les juristes de Vichy, ni pour émettre après coup un jugement éthique à l'aune duquel, cinquante ans après, ils ne risquent ni la censure, ni la persécution. Les rapporteurs ont fait l'effort scientifique—à la suite des historiens—de rassembler les données relatives à l'implication des métiers du droit dans la persécution des Juifs en France de 1940 à 1944. (note omitted)[52]

> (...are nor qualified to put Vichy jurists on trial, nor are they in a position to pass any ethical judgment fifty years after the facts, by a standard under which they themselves would risk neither censure nor per-

---

51. *Il y a 50 Ans: Le Statut des Juifs de Vichy* (Paris: Centre de Documentation Juive Contemporaine, 1991), at 45.

52. "Peut-on parler d'un droit antisémite?", op. cit., at 14.

secution. The authors have carried out the objective task—following on the work of historians—of gathering the facts relating to the involvement of the various legal professions in the persecution of Jews in France from 1940 to 1944.)

Many will feel more comfortable with the French lawyers' approach—the facts and nothing but the facts. However, one senses as a non-French outsider how many of the legal authors who have dealt with the history of Vichy's legalized antisemitism, are ill at ease in their task. For some, this was their first confrontation with the ugly legal history of Vichy. For others, this was the opportunity to discover the little-known works of their former mentors from University, the *Professeurs* who sit atop the French system of higher education, and to come face to face with the former public engagement by these same professors in Vichy's legalized antisemitism.

Finally, one senses that the malaise which seems to infect many stems from the reality which they have discovered and in which they find themselves now implicated. The "scientific task" of describing in neutral terms their various discoveries comes uncomfortably close to the professional detachment with which Vichy lawyers proceeded to interpret and implement "Jewish law". Most try to come to terms with the conflict by expressing, in unscientific terms, their discomfort and disagreement at the "distortion" of law under Vichy. We come to the most basic issues of memory and justice and law. Whether one should proceed from the largely uncontested and uncontestable facts to a finding of guilt is another question which raises issues of law, justice and memory. The French appear to have avoided issues of moral responsibility because of some fear of having to deal with troubling issues of continuity in French law between Vichy and the present. This is the area of avoidance and the central issue for law and legal memory of the Holocaust in France.

3. Judging Vichy

There is one part of French legal history which unites, as a point of transfer between Vichy and its apparent or presumed illegality on the one hand and the restoration of Republican legality on the other, all of the stories told about law and lawyers and collective memory of the war years. What unites these two periods and provides some trace of a possible resolution of the issues of law, memory and justice for the legalized French Holocaust, as well as for the vexed debate about continuity, is that set of proceedings after the war in

France known as *l'épuration*, the purge trials of collaborators. The purge trials, from the prosecutions and convictions of Pétain and his Prime Minister
Pierre Laval at the top, to the purges in the judiciary, the police, the civil service etc. offered at the time and offer in one present-day mythological rendering, an example of the restoration of legality to France and punishment of
Vichy and the practice of collaboration.[53] There are, of course, competing
mythologies; from the continuing belief in the martyrdom of Pétain on the
Right and, on the Left, to the interpretation of the purges as too soft on collaborators, culminating in the failure of revenge or punishment or justice as
symbolized by the amnesty decisions of the 1950s. There are, in addition,
problems with the process of *l'épuration* as a truly cleansing, cathartic event
in collective memory and justice, many of which will remain unresolved until
a more definitive history of the purge process as a legal phenomenon can be
written. It is not my goal to do so here. Rather I wish merely to touch upon
some of the important themes and issues which arose at the time of the purge
trials and which have recurred since. These are the issues which raise, directly
and indirectly, the issues of continuity and discontinuity within the French
legal system and within debates about the construction of national, collective
memory through legal debates and proceedings about the legalized French
Holocaust.

As a legal phenomenon, the purge participates clearly in the myths of Vichy
illegality and in the concomitant myth of Republican continuity. Without
these mutually complementary myth structures and jurisprudential practices,
the trials of the purges could be characterized as having been no more than
"victors' justice" in *la guerre franco-française*.

Indeed, the first stage of the purges, known as the period of *épuration sauvage*
or the wild purges, most easily carries this characterization. Occurring just before and just after the Allied landings on D-Day, this set of acts most clearly re-
sembles the political expedient mentioned in discussions among the Americans,
Soviets and British, in which the hypothesis of "50,000 Germans = 50,000 bul-

---

53. See *inter alia*, Peter Novick, *The Resistance versus Vichy: The Purge of Collaborators
in Liberated France* (London: Chatto & Windus, 1968); Herbert R. Lottman, *The People's
Anger: Justice and Revenge in Post-Liberation France* (London: Hutchinson, 1986); Phillipe
Bourdrel, *L'Épuration Sauvage, 1944–1945* (Paris: Perrin, 1991); François Rouquet, *L'Épu-
ration dans l'administration Française* (Paris: CNRS Éditions, 1993); Marcel Baudot, "La
Résistance française face aux problèmes de répression et d' épuration", 81 *Revue d'Histoire
de la Deuxième Guerre Mondiale* 23 (1971); J. Larrieu, "L'épuration judiciare dans les
Pyrénées-Orientales, ibid., 112, at 29 (1978). Cf., Henri Amouroux, *Les Règlements de
Comptes, Septembre 1944–Janvier 1945* (Paris: Robert Laffont, 1991).

lets" was mooted. While the experience of various regions of the country dif-
fered depending upon the rapidity with which some semblance of control
through local or departmental liberation committees was established, generally
speaking this was a time for revenge against those defined according to loose and
variable local standards as collaborators.[54] Punishment ranged from the infamous public humiliation of the shaved heads of those women guilty of hori-
zontal collaboration to execution. Of the approximately 10,000 persons executed
for collaboration and associated crimes, only one-half were killed in this period.
In other words, the ratio of judicial to extra-judicial killings during the *épuration* process was 1:1.[55] Indeed, one American lawyer observer commented at the
time that

> Though the methods employed were not always in conformity with
> ideal patterns of legal procedure there is no doubt that they were effec-
> tive and that very few hostile civilians went undetected. The abuses that
> existed could hardly have been prevented under the existing circum-
> stances. They were immediately recognized as such by all competent of-
> ficials and the speed with which they were corrected is a tribute to the
> efficiency of the American, British, and French military governments.[56]

For participants and observers, the wild purge process, while perhaps lacking in the best of procedural safeguards, was at worst a necessary evil. The situation obtaining during this period of *épuration sauvage*, while in need of further analysis and study, was in its implementation and consequences hardly
more severe than the subsequent period of judicial purges. One might therefore raise serious analytical questions about any attempt to brand these
processes as "extra legal" given the remarkable similarity in results and consequences between these actions against collaborators and the subsequent period of reestablished Republican legality. There the situation, with its formal
legal setting, clearly sought to judge the crimes committed under the Occupation within the context of the re-establishment of Republican justice. As
Rousso writes, the failures of the legal purge had important consequences.

> The purge thus made everybody unhappy, because it had proved
> impossible to strike a satisfactory compromise between traditional

---

54. See generally, André Kaspi, *La Libération de la France* (Paris: Perrin, 1995).
55. See Rousso, *The Vichy Syndrome*, op. cit., at 249.
56. Benjamin B. Ferencz, "Hostile French Civilians", 35 *Journal of Criminal Law and
Criminology* 228 (1944–1945), at 232.

justice, which was what most moderates (as well as those with the most to lose politically) were calling for, and the need to root out fascism.[57]

For opponents of the purge, the judicial phase offered no improvement, in form or substance, over the wild purge stage. The trials of Pétain and his Prime Minister Pierre Laval struck many, including those who were not outright opponents of purges, as political show trials and as the worst examples of victors' justice.[58] The tribunal which judged Pétain and Laval and many others, the High Court (*la Haute Cour de Justice*), was a specially and specifically constituted court meant to deal with cases involving political offences and offenders.[59]

The creation of special "political" courts to judge "political" offences committed by politicians was not outside the rules of French constitutional law and history.[60] Indeed, when French cabinet ministers were indicted for criminal negligence in relation to the circulation of HIV contaminated blood, the High Court was again reconstituted, albeit under the new nomenclature of the *Cour de justice de la République* (the Court of Justice of the Republic) and a "political" trial took place in 1999.[61] The trial was condemned by many and from different parts of the French political spectrum, yet no one seriously argued that Republican justice and the rule of law were under real threat by the existence of one "political" court.[62] While some asserted that the functions of

---

57. Rousso, *The Vichy Syndrome*, op. cit., at 21.

58. See generally, Fred Kupferman, *Le Procès de Vichy: Pucheu, Pétain, Laval* (Brussels: Complexe, 1980); Yves-Frédéric Jaffé, *Pierre Laval: le Procès qui n'a pas eu lieu* (Paris: Albin Michel, 1995); Jules Roy, *Le Grand Naufrage: Chronique du Procès Pétain* (Paris: Albin Michel, 1995); Jean-Marc Varaut, *Le Procès Pétain 1945–1995* (Paris: Perrin, 1995); Leon Werth, *Impressions d'Audience: le Procès Pétain* (Paris: Viviane Hamy, 1995).

59. For an early analysis of the place of the Court within French law, see Jean Brouchot, "La Haute Cour de Justice (Constitution de 1946)", 8 *Revue de Science Criminelle et de Droit Pénal Comparé* 317, (1947).

60. See Raymond Lindon and Daniel Amson, *La Haute Cour 1789–1987* (Paris: Presses Universitaires de France, 1987) and Jean Brouchot, "La Haute Cour de Justice".

61. See Olivier Duhamel and Georges Vedel, "Du bon usage de la Haute Cour", *Le Monde*, 25 November 1992; Judith Perrignon and Armelle Thoraval, "La Cour chosit le noir pour le procès du sang contaminé", *Libération*, 26 November 1998; Christophe Forcari, "Aux origines de la Cour de Justice", 25 *Libération*, February 1999; Gerard Dupuy, "Inconvénients d'une justice d'exception", *Libération*, 25 February 1999; Dominique Simonnot, "Sang contaminé: une juridiction en doute", *Libération*, 1 March 1999.

62. See e.g., Eric Favereau, "Sang contaminé: l'histore d'une affaire d' État", *Libération*, 8 February 1999; Marie-France Etchegoin, "Sang contaminé: pas condemnables", *Le Nouvel Observateur*, 25 February 1999.

control over executive branch actions were better placed in the hands of a properly constituted and democratic legislative branch no real claims that French democracy ceased to exist were or could be made.[63] Indeed, in late 1998 and early 1999, Americans and everyone with access to TV witnessed the debates over the proper procedures to be followed by the Senate in an impeachment trial of a sitting President. In the United States judicial and political system, a peculiar legislative/judicial hybrid called "impeachment" exists for the precise purpose of avoiding, rather than creating, a crisis of democracy. Clearly, such proceedings are unusual. This does not make them illegal or unjust. It is evident, however, as Jean-Marc Theolleyre wrote, that the trial of Pierre Laval was riddled with substantive and procedural problems which marked it as perhaps the most political of all the purge trials.

> Alors, au "non-droit" de ces quatre années, on pensa que pouvaient être apposés des accommodements avec le droit, il en résulta un scandale. Il marque encore la justice de ce temps. Il faut l'assumer. Et parce qu'il fut tel, certains propos de Laval devant ses juges font apparaître celui-ci dans le meilleur rôle. Car c'est vrai qu'il pouvait dire au procureur général Mornet qui énumérait les charges: "Mais vous étiez aux ordres du gouvernement à cette époque! Vous tous qui me jugez, magistrats et vous monsieur le procureur général."[64]
> (It was believed that it was possible to deal with the "not law" of these four years with legal compromises. The result was a scandal. We must accept that the legal system of this period still suffers the effects of this. And because this was the case, some of Laval's words before his judges place him in a superior position. Because he could truthfully say to the Attorney-General Mornet who read the list of charges against him: "But all of you who judge me, you the judges and you Mr. Attorney-General, you all followed the orders of the government at the time!")

The Laval trial, then, posed the most vital question facing the purge and French justice at this time, the issue of continuity and rupture. French judges and magistrates stayed in France during the Vichy years and most maintained their positions. All but one sitting magistrate swore an oath of personal allegiance to Pétain. How then, without purging itself, could French justice judge? The answer carried two aspects. First, there was a purge of sorts and the most egregious of-

---

63. See Olivier Beaud, "Abandonnons la Cour de justice à son triste sort", *Libération*, 6–7 March 1999.
64. *Procès d'après-guerre* (Paris: La Découverte, 1985), at 17.

fenders, for example some but not all of those who sat on special "anti-terror-ist" courts and ordered the deaths of members of the Resistance,[65] lost their po-sitions. However, the more important part of the law's response to its own ille-gality or illegitimacy was the construction of the legal and political historical myth of Vichy as a regime of "not law". With that, all else became secondary and most importantly, the regime which convened the High Court and sought to try the leaders of Vichy established through an act of legal self-definition, both the basis for its own legitimacy and the grounds on which Laval could be found guilty of treason and executed. Despite various cries for the rehabilitation of Maréchal Pétain which surface from time to time[66] and which in part inform the more recent debates over the rehabilitation of the *poilus*, or scandals such as revelations of François Mitterand's past allegiance to the Maréchal,[67] the fate of Pierre Laval and the legitimacy of the post-war purges seem to be of little im-portance. Indeed, the most recent manifestations of interest around the purge phenomenon revolve not around its excesses, alleged or real, but rather around its failures to deal adequately with the case of Maurice Papon. How did Papon, with his close connections with the Pétain regime and his actions while sub-pre-fect in Bordeaux, manage to escape the purge of the administration and go on to a successful career in government? His trial addressed all of these questions and more. Whether any clarification was achieved is another question.

Many of the problems surrounding the purges stem not from their "ille-gality" or their continuity with Vichy, but with their Republican heritage. Thus, one major issue facing those who sought judicial sanctions or perhaps even justice against those guilty of collaboration was that such offences were in fact quite narrowly circumscribed under the provisions of French criminal law. While clear and high level acts of aiding and abetting the Germans were covered by traditional offences of treason or *intelligence avec l'ennemi* (illegal dealing and contact with the enemy), other more common and pernicious low level activities such as informing and denouncing (*la délation*) were not nec-essarily pre-existing criminal offences.[68] While these activities were criminal-ized by the adoption of regulations, such measures smacked of *ex post facto* penal law. At the same time, they did prove to be more or less effective in deal-ing with the realities of quotidian collaboration within a process which at least

65. See Hervé Lamarre, *L' affaire de la Section Spéciale* (2 vols.) (Paris: Fayard, 1973).
66. See Rousso, *The Vichy Syndrome*, op. cit, at 283 et. seq.
67. See Conan and Rousso, *Vichy, Un Passé Qui Ne Passe Pas*, op. cit., at 173 et. seq., and Pierre Péan, *Une jeunesse française: François Mitterand 1934–1947* (Paris: Fayard, 1994).
68. See André Halimi, *La Délation sous l'Occuaption* (Paris: Edition°1, 1998).

offered the semblance of legal protections to the accused and which allowed for the appearance of the re-establishment of Republican normality and the rule of law. Like Nazi law before it, efficiency and justice were achieved simply by removing the principle of *nulla poena* from the operative normative legal universe. Law did not, for all that, in either case, stop being law; judges continued to act as judges and lawyers suffered no existential traumas.

Interestingly, Republican legality reasserted itself most clearly in the highly controversial decision to grant amnesty for many offenders.[69] This was seen by many as the legal victory of the vanquished who now benefited from this form of legal amnesia. They were forgiven and forgotten as the process of the return to legal, political and social normality required that the law, which had imposed severe sanctions for acts undertaken in and under a state of not law, literally and figuratively forget itself.

There was a second and more important act of legal amnesia surrounding the legal and collective history and memory of the purge trials. These legal proceedings dealt very rarely and only in a secondary fashion with crimes committed under Vichy against the Jews who had the misfortune to be on French soil at the time. The purges were about collaboration and treason, about *délation* and *intelligence avec l'ennemi*, they were not about "the Jews" or complicity in the Holocaust.

This failure to deal with crimes against the Jews through the legalized structures of the purge was not, however, necessarily based on an ignorance about the Holocaust. France participated as a prosecuting party at the Nuremberg trial. Academics offered detailed studies of war crimes and crimes against humanity committed against Jews in France.[70] In fact, in one of the most famous trials of the post-war period, the role played by Vichy in the persecution of the Jews was given prominent mention. Karl Oberg and Helmut Knochen were two high-ranking German police officials in occupied France. The agreement under which French police were given ultimate responsibility for the arrest and imprisonment of Jews became infamous as the Oberg-Bousquet accord. The Germans' French lawyers, in their final pleas, clearly invoked the role played by indigenous French antisemitism and underlined the autonomous nature of Vichy's *Statut des Juifs*.[71] Oberg and Knochen were naturally con-

---

69. See generally Rousso, *The Vichy Syndrome*, op. cit., at 49 et. seq.

70. See Francis Rey, "Violations du Droit International Commises Par Les Allemands en France dans La Guerre de 1939", *Revue Générale de Droit International Public* 1 (1946) at 11 et. seq.

71. See, Jean-Marc Theolleyre, "1954: Oberg et Knochen: police et crimes de guerre", in *Procès d'après guerre*, op. cit., 174 at 217–18.

victed and subsequently pardoned.[72] Nonetheless, the fact remains that while Vichy's own role in the legalized persecution of the Jews in France was proclaimed in public judicial proceedings less than ten years after the end of the war, the official and public legal memory of the fate of the Jews continued to be obscured under the dominant mythologies of Vichy's extra-legal character. Facts and law played a secondary role to the social and political myth structure. The reestablishment of Republican justice meant the Shoah had to be placed in the ahistorical and incomplete context of German responsibility. This strange and ultimately untrue combination of Vichy illegality and sole German responsibility for the Holocaust in France is for some the most pernicious consequence of the Gaullist constitutional mythological structure of *la France résistante.*

The problem here was that of the taxonomical and epistemological structures of collective memory caused by the characterization of the crimes as "German" rather than as crimes committed by the French and more particularly as crimes committed by the French state against, in many cases, its own citizens. This was in part due to the fact that the particular offence of "crimes against humanity" did not become part of French law until 1964. Combined with the construction of the purge as a legal process dealing with crimes of treason etc., the juridical environment in which the purge trials operated created and was created by a cultural understanding of the horrors of the Occupation as the result of actions by the Germans and by an illegal clique of collaborators. The indigenous French antisemitism which served to allow the adoption and implementation of Vichy's various legal measures against Jews was masked, obfuscated and obscured. The mythology of Vichy as a *de facto* but not *de jure* regime was compounded and complimented by a concurrent mythology which attributed the fate of the Jews solely to the actions of the German occupiers. The combination of the desire of many returning Jews to define themselves not as "Jews" in their public identity but as citizens of the re-established Republican society, the technical hurdles raised by the legal structure of the purge, and the mythology of a criminal Vichy government and a France populated by resisters, resulted in the willful and legalized forgetting of the role played by Vichy in the Shoah. The law of genocide and crimes against humanity in France came to play a key role in the perpetuation of an historically inaccurate and pernicious myth of the French Holocaust as not French but as German. As Henry Rousso put it,

---

72. The issue of a pardon, and of the connection between official forgiveness and forgetting would again arise in the case of Maurice Papon, see below.

Il a fallu longtemps pour que la spécificité de la politique antijuive de Vichy émerge dans la conscience collective. Marginale au lendemain de la guerre, occultée dans les années 1950–1960, cette dimension de l'histoire a constitué au contraire un élément essentiel dans la remise en mémoire de l'épisode de Vichy à partir de 1967, et surtout dans les années 1970–1980. Depuis quelques années enfin, elle en est devenue l'élément central, voire exclusif. En vingt ans, le souvenir de l'antisémitisme français des années noires nourrit un débat récurrent d'envergure nationale.[73]

(It took a long time for the specific nature of Vichy's anti-Jewish policies to become part of the collective consciousness. Marginalized just after the war, hidden from view between 1950-1960, this part of history became an essential element in the remembering of Vichy beginning in 1967 and especially between 1970-1980. Finally, for the past several years, they have become the key, if not the only, factor. In twenty years, the memory of French antisemitism during these dark years has informed a recurring nationwide debate.)

While Rousso is not uncritical of this turn of events in the construction of collective memory in France, he does note that the purge was incapable of properly constructing and understanding the nature and impact of Vichy's native antisemitic policies and practices.[74] What is important for present purposes is that the changes which have occurred in French public memory about the Vichy regime and its role in implementing laws and practices aimed at the country's Jews have taken place largely in and around the legal forum. The legal amnesia which can be said to have characterized the purge era has been "cured" by a series of cases or "*affaires*", Klaus Barbie, Paul Touvier and Maurice Papon. The sections which follow briefly examine some of the more important aspects of the legalized battle over the construction and control of collective memory in France.

---

73. "Une Justice Impossible: L'épuration et la politique antijuive de Vichy", *Annales ESC* (1993), 745.

74. See Eric Conan and Henry Rousso, *Vichy, Un Passé Qui Ne Passe Pas*, op. cit., at 16.

4. Prosecuting Klaus Barbie and the Politics of Law in France

For some, the cases against Klaus Barbie, Paul Touvier, and now Maurice Papon are the last of the purge trials. In another sense they are the first of the "real" purge trials, because they are for the first time trials which make possible a purification of French "legal" history and its attempts to deal with the Holocaust. Here, in each case and in each case's particular legal phenomenology, the connections between Vichy law and the Holocaust and between Vichy law and French law today, have been elucidated, obscured, and struggled over. These are legal events which might also permit the French system to address its own post-war failures in dealing with crimes against humanity committed against the Jews of France. Why did the *Statut des Juifs*, or the participation of the Parisian or Bordeaux police in the round up and deportations of the Jews of those cities not figure primarily or prominently in the indictments of the Vichy regime at the end of the war? The problem here is not that the purge trials were unjust, unfair or even illegal, as they still are for many. Rather the problem here is that the purge trials were as legal as the regime they put on trial. The legitimacy, if not the legality, of the *épuration* depended on the illegitimacy, if not the illegality, of the Vichy regime. If the Vichy regime is now constructed as legitimate and/or as legal, it becomes possible to construct not just the purge trials of the immediate post-war period but more recent trials of perpetrators as somehow illegitimate on their own self-referential terms. How can the law judge itself when law was central to the exclusion and subsequent extermination practiced against the Jews of France?

Somewhat ironically, the first trial in which many of these issues resurfaced in French public consciousness was not really a purge trial at all. Klaus Barbie was a German, a Gestapo official responsible for the death and torture of French men and women during his sojourn in Lyon, the center of the Resistance movement. Thus, Barbie's trial could be seen not as dealing with the issues of the purge and collaboration, but rather as the last major trial of a German war criminal in France. However, as is often the case with highly publicized legal proceedings, things are not as simple as they seem.

First, while Barbie's trial took place in the 1980s, it was clearly marked by important elements of continuity with the purge era and the political and legal decisions which had marked the creation of a mythology of the rule of law under Vichy and the restored Republic. In fact, Barbie was no stranger to French justice. He had been sentenced to death *in absentia* shortly after the war. Another important element of Barbie's trial is marked by the history of the immediate post-war period. As a Nazi police intelligence official, Barbie possessed information about Communist organizations in Europe. In the Cold War period which followed Allied victory, anti-communism replaced anti-nazism as the dominant political trope. Barbie became an important "asset" for United States intelligence agencies and the story of his escape to South America, his discovery there and the struggle to deport him to stand trial for his crimes in France has been well-documented. What is perhaps less well-documented is that the protection afforded to Barbie by US intelligence agencies was part of the contemporary French purge era judicial discourse.

During the trial of René Hardy, accused of betraying his Resistance comrades, including Jean Moulin, to the Germans, Klaus Barbie was listed as an important prosecution witness, since as a Gestapo chief in Lyon, he was intimately involved in the arrest and subsequent death under torture of Moulin. Indeed, at his trial in the 1980s, this Jean Moulin affair would play a vital and controversial role.[75] The Americans refused to hand over Barbie:

> Il reste aussi que les principaux témoins à charge sont d'anciens agents de la Gestapo, et que l'extradition du principal, l'infâme Barbier (c'est un Allemand, et le greffier prononce Barbire), a été refusée par les Américains. Il paraît que ceux-ci l'utilisent actuellement. A quelle besogne, grand Dieu?[76]

> (It still remains the case that the main witnesses for the prosecution are former Gestapo agents, and that the Americans have refused the extradition of the main one, the infamous Barbier (He is a German and the clerk pronounces his name Barbire). It appears that the Americans are still making use of him. Good God, at what dirty task?)

When he finally faced a French court in Lyon, the case of Jean Moulin and the fate of the Resistance would again confront Klaus Barbie. This was

---

75. See generally, "L'affaire Jean Moulin", *Le Monde*, November 1998; Annette Lévy-Willard and Béatrice Vallaeys, "Pierre Péan et Jacques Baynac, deux antagonistes pour un sujet unique", *Libération*, 24 November 1998; Antoine De Gaudemar, "Jean Moulin, un mythe en question", id.; Olivier Wieviorka, "La romance ne nuit pas à l'Histoire," id.

76. Jean-Marc Theolleyre, "1950. René Hardy pour la seconde fois en accusation", in *Procès d'après-guerre*, op. cit., 57 at 64. The confusion over Barbie's name here appears to be attributable to the existence of a French fascist, Jean Barbier, who was in charge of many Gestapo actions in the Grenoble region against the Resistance. Barbier was finally arrested in 1963, tried and sentenced to death in 1965, and reprieved from execution the next year.

the result both of the twists and turns of history and international politics as well as the vagaries of memory and law in France. The fate of the Jews and the Holocaust had in the meantime become much more central to debates about history and memory. At the same time, the complexities and rivalries of the real history of the Resistance had also begun to come to light as the myths of France and the Occupation began to come under public scrutiny.

On the legal front, Barbie could no longer be tried or convicted for the same offences under which he had originally be found guilty *in absentia* because those offences had now been erased by the limitation period or as the French legal system has it, *la prescription*. However, the 1964 law which had made crimes against humanity a part of French law had also declared such crimes to be beyond the application of limitation periods. Crimes against humanity are *imprescriptible*.

Vladimir Jankélévich succinctly summarizes the moral and ethical imperative which for him commands this legislative decision to circumvent the legal norm in the name of justice.

> Lorsqu'un acte nie l'essence de l'homme en tant qu'homme, la prescription qui tendrait à l'absoudre au nom de la morale contredit elle-même la morale. N'est-il pas contradictoire et même absurde d'invoquer ici le pardon? Oublier ce crime gigantesque contre l'humanité serait un nouveau crime contre le genre humain.[77]

> (When an act denies the essence of humanity as such, a limitation period which would absolve that act in the name of morality itself comes into conflict with morality. Is it not contradictory and even absurd to invoke a pardon here? To forget this enormous crime against humanity would be a new crime against human kind.)

Thus, by charging Barbie with crimes against humanity, the French justice system was at one and the same time able to avoid the problem of time limits and impose on Barbie's actions what many had come to see as the correct and appropriate legal label. The crimes committed here were not "common law" crimes but exceptional acts, violations of international law norms protecting basic human dignity. Philosophically of course, this view fits within the jurisprudential norm of post-war legality, defining the Holocaust as a case

---

77. "Pardonner?", in *L'imprescriptible* (Paris: Seuil, 1986), 17 at 25.

of exception, as beyond the realm of ordinary law. The problem, politically and legally, for the Barbie trial, was that the 1964 French legislation did not offer a clear definition of what constituted a "crime against humanity". Instead the *Code Pénal* (Criminal Code) simply stated that

> Crimes against humanity, as defined by the United Nations Resolution of 13 February 1946, which refers to the definition of crimes against humanity contained in the Charter of the International Military Tribunal of 8 August 945, are by their nature not subject to statutory limitations of prosecution.

As we have already seen the Nuremberg definition of crimes against humanity is problematic for several reasons not the least of which is its legislatively mandated subsidiary character. Crimes against humanity must be committed in the context of "war crimes" or of an "aggressive war" as defined in Article 8. While this debate about the legal content of the particular offence played itself out in several ways in the context of the Barbie prosecution, the most important aspect of the debate from the perspective of the conflicts over law and memory in the judicial construction of the Holocaust, was the role to be played by Resistance victims of Barbie.

In other words, the debate about legal memory in the Barbie trial largely evolved around whether crimes of torture, murder and deportation of members of the Resistance could fall under the definition of "crimes against humanity".[78] If they could, then the Barbie trial could serve not just to prosecute the offender for these acts but also to serve through the presence of various individuals and organizations of former members of the Resistance, as *parties civiles* (civil parties. French criminal procedure permits those who are the victims of a crime to be present with legal representation and to participate in criminal proceedings) the pedagogical role of educating a younger generation of French men and women about the sacrifices of that generation which fought Nazism.

In addition to raising complex issues about the Resistance and the history of French opposition to the Occupier, the trial also risked opening old wounds about the betrayal of Jean Moulin and of intra-Resistance rivalries. More importantly, however, the conflict which characterized this aspect of the Barbie trial concerned the struggle over legal and cultural claims to the status of "vic-

---

78. It is important to note here that the taxonomical opposition Resistance/Jews is historically false if universalized. Many Jews participated in Resistance movements.

tim".[79] If the concept of crimes against humanity was found to include and embrace crimes committed against members of the Resistance, two consequences would flow. First, for many, from the technical legal perspective, the distinction between "war crimes" and "crimes against humanity" would lose whatever epistemological status it had in international and French domestic law. Second, the specificity and uniqueness of the Holocaust, an issue of ongoing philosophical, historical, moral and legal complexity, would be rendered legally insignificant. In other words, if the Resistance were granted "victim" status in the Barbie trial, the policies and practices of Nazism's murderous antisemitism would become nothing more than the same as all other crimes committed by the Germans between 1933–1945. Jews throughout the world, and French Jews in this particular context, had struggled for the collective and legal remembering of the Holocaust through the prosecution of perpetrators of the Shoah under the rubric of crimes against humanity. For them, Jews were and should remain the first, if not the sole, victims of the Holocaust. The legal forgetting of the Jewish victims of French and German actions in France from 1940–1945, now risked being reinscribed in French legal and collective memory if the crimes of Barbie against non-Jewish members of the Resistance were part of the jurisprudential pedagogy of this trial.[80]

Of course, it is important to note that in this controversy, as in almost all of the struggles over issues of identity and memory which occur in the legal domain of a trial, many of the historical and political complexities of the debate might tend to be lost. The very dichotomy Resistance/Jew ignores the role played by many Jews in Resistance organizations. The idea that there was a single Resistance is itself equally problematic. Indeed, much of the debate over the Jean Moulin question, in the Barbie trial and elsewhere, flows in part from the complex histories and rivalries which characterized much of the Resistance movement.[81] Even today, years after the end of the war, years after the decision in the Barbie case, the view of the Resistance in public memory and culture in France remains a complex and confused one. One can purchase a CD

---

79. For more detailed debates on this issue, see Guyora Binder and Vivian G. Curran's conflicting constructions of these issues, op. cit., above. On the Barbie trial in general, see Erna Paris, *Unhealed Wounds: France and the Klaus Barbie Affair* (New York: Grove, 1985).

80. See particularly, Alain Finkielkraut, *Remembering in Vain: The Klaus Barbie Trial and Crimes Against Humanit,* (New York: Columbia University Press, 1992).

81. See generally Jean-Marie Guillon and Pierre Laborie, (eds.), *Mémoire et Histoire, la Résistance* (Toulouse: Privat, 1995). See also Anny Latour, *The Jewish Resistance in France, 1940–1945* (New York: Holocaust Library, 1981); Olivier Wieviorka, *Une Certaine Idée de la Résistance* (Paris: Seuil, 1996).

ROM which offers a multimedia presentation of the Resistance as a moment of the movement as another instance in the long French history of liberty or one can view a film like *Un Héro Très Discret*, which portrays the Resistance and the purge era in a vision informed by postmodern irony.[82] The law, however, has proved itself distinctly incapable of articulating these and other complexities. Instead it has consistently opted for an ahistorical construction of collective memory which persists in maintaining the essential, primary and central myth structures of resistance and Vichy's illegality.

The *Cour de Cassation* (France's Supreme Court) rendered its verdict on the question which would again play a vital role in the subsequent trials of Paul Touvier and Maurice Papon and decided that crimes against humanity included

> …inhumane acts and persecution committed in a systematic manner in the name of a state practising a policy of ideology supremacy, not only against persons by reason of their membership of a racial or religious community, but also against the opponents of that policy, whatever the form of their opposition.[83]

Thus, the official judicial recognition of the imprescriptible crime against humanity as a part of French law by the highest court was at once an act of remembering and publicly constituting Nazi crimes and at the same time yet another instance in which the French system of law and justice, for reasons of the propagation of a myth of resistance, forgot the Shoah and in these circumstances laid the definitional groundwork for the legalized forgetting of the specificity and normality of Vichy's antisemitic juridical structures.[84]

But issues of remembrance and forgetting were not to finish with the definitional pronouncements of the *Cour de Cassation*. Barbie's French lawyer, Jacques Vergès, had other pedagogical goals in mind.[85] In Vergès and Barbie we find the symbiosis of the extreme left and the extreme right, united in their contempt for the mythologies of the Resistance, Republican justice and the hypocrisy of colonial powers. For Vergès, representing Barbie was the opportunity to engage yet again in attacks on the French legal and political system

---

82. "La Résistance en France: Une épopée de la liberté", Montparnasse Multimédia, 1997.

83. *Barbie*, 78 *International Law Reports* 124 at 137 (1988).

84. See discussion, infra.

85. On Vergès, see Binder and Paris op. cit. See also Jacques Vergès, *Le salaud lumineux*, (Paris: Édition°1/Michel Lafont,(1990); Jacques Vergès, *La Justice est un jeu* (Paris: Albin Michel, 1992). On Vergès' view of legal strategy, see Jacques Vergès, *De la stratégie judiciare*, (Paris: Minuit, 1968); Jacques Vergès et. al., *Le droit et la colère* (Paris: Minuit, 1960).

in order to point out what were for him the fatal flaws of any prosecution mounted by the Republic for "political crimes".

For him, the trial, with its self-avowed goals of educating current French generations to the crimes of Nazis would be turned into an opportunity to educate current generations about the crimes of their forebears, in Indochina, Africa and Algeria.[86]

Vergès launched an unremitting publicity campaign aimed *inter alia* at shifting blame for the death of Jean Moulin from the shoulders of his accused client, to the members of the Resistance who must have betrayed him. Here he simply turned the historical legal tables by using the same arguments which the French government had invoked against René Hardy into arguments aimed at discrediting many of the civil plaintiffs and the mythologies of the Resistance. At the same time Vergès attempted to attack at the very core of the prosecution's case by asserting that the French government could not claim that what Barbie had done, torture, beatings, concentration camps etc., constituted crimes against humanity without itself admitting that it had committed exactly the same crimes in its colonies. What happened in Algeria was, for Vergès, no different than what had happened in Lyon under Barbie.

Vergès' strategy of "rupture" explicitly attacked the other civil parties, the Jewish victims, in antisemitic terms. During one exchange, he invoked his interracial heritage in order to disparage claims of Jewish suffering.

> Ma mère, elle, n'avait pas besoin de porter l'étoile jaune, elle était jaune de la tête aux pieds...[87]

> (My mother did not need to wear a yellow star, she was yellow from head to toe...)

---

86. Somewhat ironically perhaps, in the autumn of 2001, a group representing the *harkis*, Algerian Muslims who fought for France during the War of Independence, filed a suit charging the French government with crimes against humanity for their mistreatment in France after fleeing and settling there. See, Charles Tamazount, "Les harkis en appellent à la justice", *Libération*, 29 August 2001; "Guerre d'Algérie: neuf harkis portent plainte pour "crimes contre l'humanité", *Le Monde*, 30 August 2001; Jean-Dominique Merchet, "Le sacrifice des harkis sur la place publique", *Libération*, 25 September 2001; Natalie Castetz, "Les harkis contre Barre, par exemple", *Libération*, 4 October 2001. At the same time, the accusations of systemic torture and abuse by the French army in Algeria continue to be demonstrated. See, Raphaëlle Branche, *La Torture et l'armée pendant la guerre d'Algérie* (Paris: Gallimard, 2001).

87. *Le salaud lumineux*, op. cit., 14.

For Vergès, any claim of specifically Jewish suffering was simply typical of a Eurocentrism which was invoked not to proclaim the reality of that suffering but to deny the real suffering of the victims of colonial violence and criminality in the Third World. The trial of France, and of French culpability which many had proclaimed since the end of the war, was here turned into the trial of France by a lawyer representing a Nazi police official who had beaten, tortured, and killed. Indeed, Vergès' statements about his strategy outside of court had often provoked prosecution witnesses and lawyers to raise the issues of French atrocities in Algeria of their own accord in order to preempt his position. As would be the case in the trial of Maurice Papon in Bordeaux in 1998, the trial of Klaus Barbie in Lyon often appeared to be the trial of everyone and everything but the accused.

The problem with Vergès' position, beside his execrable antisemitism, is that his arguments about continuity and mythologies of Resistance proved to be logically and ideologically misplaced. The undoubted crimes committed by the French in Algeria had nothing to do with the guilt or innocence of Klaus Barbie in Lyon. That a member of the Resistance may have betrayed Jean Moulin had nothing to do with the fact that Barbie probably killed Moulin by torturing him. Indeed, the idea of Moulin having been betrayed by a fellow *résistant* already figured in official French legal history with the proceedings against René Hardy. The specificity of Jewish suffering had already been officially and legally undermined by the decision of the *Cour de Cassation*. Of course, the guilt or innocence of the defendant, or the finding of the court on this question is largely irrelevant to the trial of rupture prepared and orchestrated by Vergès. To a certain extent, his position is understandable. There was little doubt about the outcome of the trial. The fact that it was promoted by some and has come to be understood by others, as a pedagogical exercise rests not on its role in educating the French public about criminal procedure or the presumption of innocence, but in its function as a theatrical staging of history for younger generations. In an ironic but perhaps inevitable twist, the continuities proclaimed by Vergès between the crimes of the French Republic and the Nazi occupier of France had little to do with the guilt or innocence of his client. Rather, what Vergès contested was the pedagogical lesson proclaimed by Barbie's victims and the French state. The lesson was illegitimate and falsifiable because of the elements of continuity established by Vergès. The crimes of colonialism are abhorrent. If the trial of Klaus Barbie was political and politicized, Jacques Vergès was not the first to seek to extract political and historical lessons from the judicial proceedings in Lyon. Again, the problem here is not one of guilt or innocence, the traditional concern of a criminal trial.

The issue is whether or how it is possible to add to this function a more general epistemological role in the construction of public memory and understanding. There is no doubt that this is a role assigned in the public and political imagination to such trials. The Barbie case and subsequent French proceedings starkly raise not just the question as to the ultimate desirability of such trials, but more fundamentally they bring into question the ability of law to judge itself when it comes to the Holocaust and other crimes against humanity. If Auschwitz was fundamentally a legal phenomenon, if almost all modern atrocities are committed in the name of a nation state, or of a people, with a claim to legality, legitimacy and sovereignty, what business has law in any of this?

Klaus Barbie was guilty. The real stakes for legal and public memory in his trial related to the history of the Resistance and the evils of the Gestapo as constructed by some of the civil parties and the prosecution after the decision of the *Cour de Cassation* offered the first domestic French legal definition of "crimes against humanity". Jewish suffering was diminished, if not forgotten, through the construction of that legal definition of "crimes against humanity". Perhaps Klaus Barbie understood this better than most. He simply refused to be part of the trial and stayed in his jail cell for most of the proceedings. His absence, or unnecessary presence, in a bizarre and tragically ironic reflection of the absence of many of his victims, is perhaps the most remarkable and important element of his trial for the construction of memory and justice, if not of law.

The subsequent trials of Paul Touvier and Maurice Papon illustrate in their own unique ways, the manner in which reality can be and is replaced by law in the construction of legal memory and forgetting of the Holocaust.

5. Vichy on Trial: Paul Touvier, Crimes against Humanity and French Legal Memory

The tale of Paul Touvier is familiar to many readers through the critical and popular success of novelist Brian Moore's book, *The Statement*.[88] Moore's novel offers a fictionalized account of the story of Touvier's travels among right wing and sometimes naive elements in the French Roman Catholic Church as he sought refuge from the French government's various attempts to arrest

---

88. New York: Dutton, 1996.

him.[89] As is often the case in the annals of the law, and particularly in the annals of the French legal system's attempts to deal with the trials of perpetrators for crimes against humanity, truth can stranger than fiction.

Touvier grew up in a family dedicated to a right wing, Catholic political worldview and politics. Under Vichy, he almost automatically migrated to the *Milice*, a quasi-military, police organization which worked hand in hand with the Gestapo in France in actions against the Resistance and against "the Jews". While it worked with the Gestapo, the *Milice* was established at the behest of Maréchal Pétain and was an integral part of the French policing structure as instituted under the National Revolution. As head of the Second Section of the *Milice* in Lyon, Touvier was able to combine low-level nasty criminality and corruption with his official actions against the "enemies of France". Following the assassination of Phillipe Henriot, head of Vichy's "Information Ministry" and patron and member of the *Milice*, Touvier commanded and participated in the massacre of Jewish prisoners taken from the cells under his orders and executed on the outskirts of Lyon at Rillieux-la-Pape. After the war, Touvier was twice sentenced to death *in absentia* for treason and collaboration with the enemy, and stripped of his civil rights as a consequence. He escaped capture, "worked" as a petty criminal and police informer and then began his life on the run.

The particularly fascinating aspect of the Touvier case and "*affair*" is that such an insignificant and minor minion should become, as he did, the focus of so much attention, agony, controversy and legal wrangling. At the same time as he was, in fact, a minor figure in the *collaboration d'état* (state-based collaboration) which characterized Vichy France, Touvier and his case raise all the issues of law, memory and justice which continue to haunt any possibility of France "coming to terms" with Vichy. Again, Paul Touvier became a symbol and a trope for all sides, as history, memory and politics informed the hermeneutics of his legal fate. Law itself, if it has a separate existence, again became a part of the discursive matrix informing the wider issues. First, there is the obvious and always troubling question of the Church and the Holocaust. That Touvier found refuge with certain elements of the Catholic Church in France after the war up to our own time, raises questions not just about the Church in Vichy, but also about continuing connections between Catholicism, or one version of Catholicism, and ideals of French identity which operate continuously from pre-Vichy. Throughout the Vichy and post-war periods, up to controversies surrounding Pope John Paul II's 1996 visit and connections with the debate around the conversion of Clovis to Chris-

89. René Rémond et.al., *Paul Touvier et l'Église* (Paris: Fayard, 1992).

tianity as the founding moment of *la vraie France* (true France), parts of French Catholicism have been associated with anti-Republican, antisemitic agitation and political movements. Here, Touvier's case raises profound questions which echo in the legal context with Richard Weisberg's troubling thesis about a latent and vital Catholic antisemitism at the heart of French national identity and legal politics.

But the truly vexing issues surrounding Touvier find their most profound resonances in the legal domain and in debates surrounding various aspects of the juridical questions raised by attempts to bring Paul Touvier before French justice. First, there is the political and legal controversy surrounding President Georges Pompidou's decision, after much lobbying on Touvier's behalf from elements in the Church and despite strong advice to the contrary, to grant a pardon to Touvier. This *grâce*, this legal forgetting, (*l'oubli légal*), accompanied by the President's express wish that it was finally time to forget that time in French history when the French were so divided and "did not like each other", struck a cord among those in French society who saw the issues not in terms of forgetting, but in terms of trying to remember Vichy and Vichy law. The issue of a pardon for Touvier raised two starkly contrasting views of memory and identity, those who wished to forgive and forget and those who felt that it was impossible to forget what the vast majority of French citizens, including the political leadership and the legal system, had not yet properly remembered and acknowledged. Justice is impossible if there has not been what criminal lawyers call an allocution in which the guilty party repeats in public the basic facts of responsibility. The troubling and troubled history of the amnesties for collaborators in the 1950s, the amnesia which surrounded much of France's public memory of Vichy, and especially of the role played by the French bureaucratic, legal and police structures in the French Shoah, all came bubbling to the surface of political and legal debates surrounding the pardon granted to Paul Touvier.

Connected with this battle for memory and justice was the key legal event of a series of legislative interventions in the 1950s which had already amnestied Touvier and others found guilty of collaboration offences during the war. These measures were hotly and bitterly contested at the time but were adopted as a way of "putting the past behind" and uniting the populace under a new Republic looking forward to the future. The only penalties which still effected Touvier were the so-called civil rights sanctions which limited his rights as a citizen, to vote or to hold office for example and which prevented him from living in certain proscribed areas of the country. Thus, at this level, the symbolic power of the pardon in terms of justice and memory far outweighed the actual very limited legal impact of the President's decision. But the pardon, with its symbolism, raised another key political and legal battle which would become central to later developments in the "*affair*". By the time Touvier's case became a central element in legal and political discourse about justice and memory, the legal system seemed to have little hold over Touvier. With the earlier amnesties and the pardon, he could not be tried again for those crimes. At the same time, the passage of the years had meant that the limitation period for other possible crimes committed by Touvier under Vichy had expired. Paul Touvier seemed to have escaped French justice, or at least French law.

But there was one more possibility. In 1964, the French Parliament had incorporated the Nuremberg trials' notion of crimes against humanity into the Criminal Code. In addition to this substantive legal change, the French had also decided that, unlike all other criminal acts known to French law, crimes against humanity would remain *imprescriptible*. It is at this point that all the issues of law, justice and memory come to a head in the Touvier "*affair*". There are well-known justice-based arguments against the concept of unlimited temporal criminal liability. Many argue that it is unfair to the accused to place him/her on trial after so many years when the evidence against them may have deteriorated or when possibly exculpatory proof has disappeared. Many also argue that certainty, an essential element in any system grounded in the rule of law, must be served by bringing legal proceedings to an end after the passage of a period of time. There are on the other hand well-known arguments in favor of classifying crimes against humanity as somehow different from other crimes, as involving so great a violation of the standards of the rule of law, of justice and of human dignity, that special rules are not only acceptable but necessary. Many of these latter arguments are based on the idea that there must be, that there is, an intimate jurisprudential connection between an obligation to remember and an obligation to do justice. Law owes a duty to the victims, a duty which is not erased by the "mere" passage of time. This is the jurisprudential basis for all prosecutions of perpetrators of the Holocaust and this was the jurisprudential basis for the prosecution of Paul Touvier for the massacre at Rillieux.

The Nuremberg definition of crimes against humanity, incorporated into the French *Code*, is general and somewhat vague. As was the case in the prosecution of Klaus Barbie, the definitional contours of the concept of "crimes against humanity" also came into play in attempts to prosecute Touvier. The actual limits of the charge are ill-defined, and lawyers everywhere, and French lawyers in particular, abhor ill-definition on principle. The problem raised by the Touvier case in particular is that it offers clear and convincing proof, if it is necessary, that arcane judicial debates about the technical legal definition of a particular crime are not necessarily the best forum for working out historical facts or issues of collective memory. Unfortunately, events and history in France combined to make the legal forum of the Touvier case the very place and context in which such questions were to some extent decided.

But because Touvier was first and foremost a legal case, it also took place in a more constrained legal interpretive circle, one of the key elements of which is precedent, decided cases which precede the case in question and which define and limit the interpretive possibilities open in all cases which follow. The precedent which governed Touvier was the case of Klaus Barbie.

A state exercising a "policy of ideological supremacy" (or hegemony in some translations) became a central definitional element in determining whether circumstances warranted a charge of "crimes against humanity". Demonstrating that the accused was acting in the name of a state "practising a policy of ideological supremacy" was not a legal or factual issue in Barbie's case since he was a German Gestapo officer. The case of Paul Touvier was problematic. He acted as a member of the *Milice*, a branch and organism of the Vichy government. Could Vichy be said to be a "state practicing a policy of ideological hegemony"? Here again, a technical legal question of defining the limits and extent of a criminal indictment becomes an inquiry into the historical and political memories and mythologies of France. Under one possible strict Gaullist interpretation, Touvier could not be guilty of crimes against humanity because Vichy was never a state. The Republic was the French State. If Vichy is defined under this and other possible Gaullist or Republican historical imaginings of Vichy as a *de facto* state collaborating with the German occupier, then Touvier could be found guilty as an accomplice of the Germans, either directly or because the Vichy "state" and the *Milice* were accomplices of the German occupier.

The problem with this definition is of course that while it may well accord with the wide-spread mythology of France as resistant and Vichy as non-State, it does not accord with the historically accurate understanding of Vichy, especially in the early period of the Occupation, as widely independent and autonomous, particularly in its antisemitic laws, policies and practices. The dilemma facing the French legal system and the French collectivity in the Touvier case came down finally to a fundamental conflict between definitions of historical truth and justice, a conflict played out in the arcane language and procedures of the legal system, about a legal system with which it by definition had to deny any relationship. To convict the obviously guilty Touvier, Vichy's historical reality had to be ignored and distorted. If the legal system were to acknowledge Vichy's independent, homegrown French legality and "guilt", Touvier could not be convicted since he acted as an agent of Vichy, and would fall outside the technical definition of "crimes against humanity."

In this case, the French courts and the lawyers for the civil parties, representing the victims, who, under the French system, are participants in the criminal trial, blinked. The Court of Appeal defined Vichy as a regime without a dominant ideology and therefore as one not covered by the *Cour de Cassation's* definition of crimes against humanity. On a further appeal, the *Cour de Cassation* allowed Touvier's trial to proceed on the basis that the *Milice* acted at the instigation of the Gestapo and therefore Touvier could be found to be an accomplice of an organism of a state practising political hegemony.[90] Touvier was convicted of crimes against humanity, sentenced to life in prison and died there in 1996. Vichy escaped judgment but according to the decision of the Court of Appeal, which remains uncontroverted, it could not legally be found to have committed crimes against humanity of its own accord. Conan and Rousso decried the French Court's narrow legalism by saying:

> Surtout elles ont failli évacuer des débats un problème crucial, à savoir la part d'autonomie, voire d'initiative, d'un milicien français aux ordres de Vichy. Elles faisaient montre d'un juridisme étroit, sans doute inattaquable sur le plan formel, mais qui limitait singulièrement la "leçon" qu'était supposée délivrer le procès Touvier.[91]

> (Above all, these decisions almost entirely removed a crucial problem from the debates, the question of the autonomy, even the initiative of a French member of the *Milice*, under the command of Vichy. They demonstrate a narrow legalism, doubtless beyond reproach on the technical level, but which has the effect of severally limiting the "lesson" which the Touvier trial was supposed to teach.)

---

90. *Touvier, International Law Reports*, 100 (1994) at 337; Arno Klarsfeld, *Touvier, un crime français* (Paris: Fayard, 1994); Alain Jakubowicz and René Raffin, *Touvier, Histoire du procès* (Paris: Éditions Julliard, 1995); Laurent Greilsamer and Daniel Schneidermann, *Un certain Monsieur Paul* (Paris: Fayard, 1989 and 1994); François Bédarida, *Touvier: Le Dossier d' Accusation* (Paris: Seuil, 1996). See also Claire Finkelstein, "Changing Notions of State Agency in International Law: The Case of Paul Touvier", 30 *Texas International Law Journal* 261 (1995); Michael Tigar et. al., "Paul Touvier and the Crime Against Humanity", id., at 285; Leila Sadat Wexler, "The Interpretation of the Nuremberg Principles by the French Court of Cassation: From Touvier to Barbie and Back Again", 32 *Columbia Journal of Transnational Law* 289 (1994); "Reflections on the Trial of Vichy Collaborator Paul Touvier for Crimes against Humanity in France", 20 *Law & Social Inquiry* 191 (1995). On January 23 1997, the same Court found, in the case of Maurice Papon, that an accomplice need not have shared in the policy of political or ideological hegemony of the principal offender in order to be found guilty.

91. *Vichy, Un Passée Qui Ne Passe Pas*, op. cit., at 134.

Once again, the strict techniques of the law and of legal reasoning come into conflict with the pedagogical role which many saw as appropriate for the Touvier trial, not to mention serving as a means of avoiding a confrontation with law's own complicity. The legal definition of "crimes against humanity" conflicted with the historical truth of Vichy's legalized antisemitism. Again, what Touvier did seemed unimportant except in so far as it fit within one or another vision of the educational role of the trial. Here Conan and Rousso criticize the law for being too legal. As in the case of Klaus Barbie, this may perhaps miss the point since the law is simply here one part of the discursive matrix at play in the construction of public memory. While the decision of the Court in refining the definition of "crimes against humanity" may have established the parameter in which the Touvier trial was technically played out, the rhetorical interventions of the parties clearly demonstrate the ultimate flexibility of legal discourse in constructing and redefining facts and rules to serve other purposes or to ignore other uncomfortable realities.

6. Vichy on Trial?: The Prosecution of Maurice Papon

All that remained, for French law, justice and memory and the interplay among them, was the trial of Maurice Papon for his role in the deportation of Jews from Bordeaux.[92] How could the French successfully prosecute a Vichy bureaucrat for crimes against humanity under the restrictive definition of the offence and at the same time hope to do justice to the obligations of memory? Specifically, in Papon's case, can a prosecution for crimes against humanity completely air the issues of the autonomy and independence of Vichy's policies and practices of exclusion and extermination without by a necessity imposed by the rules of French law, relying upon the distortion of the historical

---

92. Gérard Boulanger, *Maurice Papon, un technocrate français dans la collaboration* (Paris: Éditions du Seuil, 1994). See also Michel Slitinsky, *L'Affaire Papon* (Paris: Alain Moreau, 1983); *Le pouvoir préfectoral lavaliste à Bordeaux* (Bordeaux: Walladon, 1988); Phillippe Cohen-Grillet, *Maurice Papon: De la Collaboration aux Assises*, (Bordeaux: le Bord de l' Eau, 1997); Bernard Violet, *Le Dossier Papon* (Paris: Flammarion, 1997); Compare, Jean Bruno and Frédéric de Monicault, *L'affaire Papon: Bordeaux 1942–1944* (Paris: Tallandier,1997). A good collection of documents which discuss the various aspects of the Papon case is now available in English. See, Richard J. Golsan (ed.), *The Papon Affair: Memory and Justice on Trial* (New York and London: Routledge, 2000).

facts? Can justice be served by a legal system which creates facts unrecogniz-able to the historian? Can it properly and completely address and redress the mythology and legal construction of Vichy's fundamental "illegality" which have been of such central importance in the reconstruction of the Republic?

In Papon's case, this is a particularly vital and sensitive issue of continuity, rupture and justice. Papon successfully made the transition from his position as a Vichy civil servant to become a Republican public servant. He became Po-lice Chief of Paris and later served as a member of the French cabinet. Any prosecution of Papon would have to raise these issues of continuity and dis-continuity, of legitimacy and illegitimacy, if it were to be seen to do justice to the memory of France's legalized Holocaust.

Thus when Maurice Papon finally stood trial in the autumn of 1997 and the winter of 1998, the proceedings were portrayed alternatively as the first and last trial of Vichy.[93] For the first time, it was said, a high-ranking Vichy official would be tried for his role in the implementation of measures against the Jews. Maurice Papon, a sub-prefect under the Occupation, stood trial as the first and last representative of Vichy's anti-Jewish legal and governmental system.

The ersatz nature of Papon's representative status played itself out here at two sometimes complimentary levels. On the one hand, an issue which more often than not appears to have been submerged in the various trials for crimes against humanity in France, the actual guilt or innocence of the individual accused, often took a back seat to the representative and pedagogical role of the trial. Like the proceedings against Barbie and Touvier, the trial of Maurice Papon in Bor-deaux often appeared to take on the patina of a show trial. Vichy and Vichy's role in the persecution, arrest and deportation of Jews quite often seemed to be in the dock, while the idea that an individual accused was present before the court slipped into the background. This does not mean that Papon was inno-cent or that he did not receive a fair trial. It does however reflect the ever-pres-ent conflict between the norms of the rule of law insofar as they are reflected in the legal system's concern for the rights of an individual accused and the needs of justice and memory which attribute to an individual the role of historical rep-resentative. As in the trial of Major War Criminals at Nuremberg, the symbolic function of the accused superseded questions of practical guilt or innocence.

The second level at which Papon's representative status played itself out dur-ing the trial was more directly relevant to his status as the accused. Because he

---

93. On the trial, see Éric Conan, *Le Procès Papon: Un Journal d'Audience* (Paris: Galli-mard, 1998); Daniel Schneidermann, *L'Étrange Procès* (Paris: Fayard, 1998); Compare Arno Klarsfeld, *Papon: Un Verdict Français* (Paris: Ramsey, 1998) and Jean-Marc Varaut, *Plaidoirie* (Paris: Plon, 1998).

was the sub-prefect, and responsible to the prefect Sabatier, Papon invoked a classic defense often found in trials such as these. He was "just following orders" or more precisely, just because his signature appeared on several documents related to measures against the Jews, this did not mean that he was actually personally responsible. In other words, he had a delegated power to sign, but the key legal characteristics of this power were that all he did was sign and he signed on behalf of the prefect. He was an administrative rubber stamp whose signature, as far as proving his personal legal responsibility was concerned, was irrelevant.

Throughout the history of proceedings against perpetrators there has been a legal and historical conflict and debate over the weight to be given to documentary *versus* eyewitness evidence. While the testimony of the victims themselves is emotionally compelling and morally devastating, the law has always been leery of the fallibility of human recall. Legal memory, as constructed in these trials, much prefers documentary evidence, because documents, once authenticated, speak for themselves and are not subject to human fallibility or the passage of time. Here, Papon was making a legal argument against the reliability of the documents invoked against him.[94] He signed but he did not decide, therefore he did not commit the crimes for which he was charged. Unfortunately for Papon, this technical argument about responsibility in administrative law terms could not carry the day either by itself or in light of the other, often overwhelming evidence, of his daily involvement in the process of implementing various measures against the Jews who fell under his jurisdiction. For them, he did "speak the law" (*juris + dire*).

And the law spoke of Maurice Papon throughout his trial. For France, or for the French media at least, this became the trial of Vichy. Major daily newspapers such as *Le Monde* and *Libération* on a national level and *Sud Ouest* in Bordeaux placed their coverage of the trial on the WWW, as did the French television stations. Some of the groups representing the victims, the civil plaintiffs, also set up their own Web pages to present their views on the various events which occurred during the trial. The Papon trial was ubiquitous, as Vichy was "finally" to be judged.

The educational usefulness of the case was not however unanimously recognized. Prominent French historian, Henry Rousso, who had offered evidence as an expert during the proceedings against Paul Touvier refused to testify in Bordeaux. Rousso claimed that history and law had reached an impasse in the construction of memory about Vichy in present day France. For him,

---

94. See *Le Procès de Maurice Papon*, t.1, at 415 et. seq.

as an historian, Vichy was well known and had been sufficiently documented and characterized by members of his profession. Rousso denounced the trial as a "spectacle" which had little if anything to do with his role as an historian. This does not mean that Rousso was unaware of the historical nature of the Papon trial. Rather his claim is that the legal process, by its very nature, is unaware of its own role in the construction of history and memory. For Rousso,

> Cette judiciarisation du passé appartient bien au temps de la mémoire, elle en est même un élément constitutif qui participe de la mise au présent du passé.[95]

> (This legalization of the past clearly belongs to the period of remembering, and is even a constitutive element in bringing the past to the present.)

However, the unreflective nature of the law means that:

> Ces tribunaux sont dans l'illusion que le verdict prononcé, réel ou virtuel, va se substituer au tribunal de l'Histoire, alors qu'il n'a au bout du compte qu'un goût de provisoire, d'inachevé, dans l'attente d'une relance du dossier ou de la polémique.[96]

> (These courts are under the illusion that the real or virtual verdict which they render, can take the place of the tribunal of history. In reality, this judicial verdict can only carry with it a hint of the provisional or incomplete, while we await the reopening of the file or the argument.)

Here, Rousso touches upon a central dilemma which has troubled French society, and I believe Western law more generally, since the period of the purges. How is the relationship between law and memory to be understood? Can, do or should courts play a role in the construction of collective memory particularly when this most often involves a deliberate distortion or obfuscation of law's own role in events? As Rousso himself points out, there can be little doubt that courts and legal proceedings do in fact play a role in the construction of public memories about events. Whether they play a role which is limited and proper depends both upon one's construction and understanding of the rule of law and the role of law on the one hand, and of one's construction of the role of "history" as a discipline on the other.

---

95. *La hantise du passé*, op. cit., at 88. See also, Laurent Greilsamer and Nicolas Weill, "Le tribunal de l'Histoire a jugé Vichy depuis longtemps", *Le Monde*, 7 April 1998.
96. Id., at 89. Compare, Jeanney, op. cit., and Nadine Fresco, "Le prétoire et l'histoire", *Le Monde*, 19 March 1998.

However, this is more than a mere boundary dispute between intellectual areas of expertise. What is at stake in the construction of Maurice Papon's guilt or innocence is the continuing construction of public memory and understanding of Vichy and the fate of the French Jewry under a French government and legal system. We already know that law at the time of the purges played a key role in constructing a collective memory which remained dominant for several decades. First, Vichy was not a government of law but of fact. Second, France was a nation of resisters. Third, the persecution of Jews was a German affair. Finally, the fate of the Jews was largely ignored and irrelevant. Each of these elements of collective memory has since been reimagined and reconfigured, both inside and outside the legal system. The trial of Maurice Papon offered another opportunity for the French legal system and the French populace to once more establish its understanding of Vichy law and the fate of the Jews.

The trial was marked by extensive examinations *inter alia* of the role of Vichy in constructing its own legalized antisemitic edifice, of the Resistance and of Papon's alleged role therein, and of the ways in which Papon was able to escape the rigors of the purge despite his well-known role in the administration under Vichy. Daily headlines, op. ed. pieces and editorial comments dealt extensively with all of these issues as the French public was exposed to this legalized history lesson. It is impossible to know empirically if this had a positive, negative or neutral impact, either in opinions about Papon's guilt or innocence or in the public's understanding or memory of Vichy. What we do know is that the mass of daily information and opinion circulated in France and was absorbed (or ignored) by the population. We know that the many opinion polls published during the trial indicated that the majority of the French public thought the proceedings were worthwhile. We also know that the trial, in part at least, led to the public recognition of fault in support for, silence about or implementation of measures against the Jews by bodies representing the French police, medical profession and the Church.

Debates continue over and about the trial of Maurice Papon. Again and always, the principal issue is the suitability of the legal forum as a *lieu de mémoire*. More specifically, can the law serve as a means through which public and collective memory in relation to Vichy and the fate of French Jewry are constructed? The question is of course complex and can lead to different conclusions, both of degree and kind.[97] Debates circulate here at two basic levels. First, a set of questions is asked concerning the appropriateness of such spec-

---

97. For detailed explorations see, Nancy Wood, "Memory on Trial in Contemporary France", 11 *History & Memory* 41 (1999); Robert O. Paxton, "The Trial of Maurice Papon", *New York Review of Books*, December 16, 1999, 27.

tacles. Second, a further group of inquiries is made about the "accuracy" of such spectacles. Again, each fails to comprehend the role and function of law in defining and limiting itself. When Papon failed to turn himself in to French police before his appeal was to be heard by the *Cour de Cassation* and instead fled to Switzerland, the affair was once again turned into a spectacular event in which law, criminality and history intersected in newspaper headlines and televised images of the police helicopter returning the fugitive to custody. *Libération* featured Papon's photo on the front page under the caption "Wanted".[98] To resort in the face of this story to arguments about the proper role of historians and lawyers, to discussions of appropriate taxonomies of knowledge quite simply ignores the ideological, political and legal realities informing the whole situation. For Papon's opponents, his flight proved his criminality and cowardice. For his supporters, his decision to leave France served as an indictment of the judicial system which had unjustly convicted him, and an attack on the illegality of the system of *mise en état* in French criminal procedure.[99] For the Swiss, the idea that their country could serve as a refuge for someone convicted of crimes against Jews, in light of the Swiss Gold and other related affairs, was politically, emotionally and ideologically unacceptable. Collective memory, legality, and history are not neat categories into which we can fit our notions of justice and identity without difficulty or distortion.

Subsequent proceedings, including Papon's 2001 appeal to the European Court of Human Rights in Strasbourg, continued to raise vexing issues for French law, justice and memory. The echoes reverberated with more vigor when the Court ruled that part of the French criminal procedures used in the Papon case deprived him of basic human rights under the operative provisions of European law.[100] Some on the left, including Robert Badinter and Mrap (Le Mouvement contre le racisme et pour l'amité entre les peuples) issued calls for Papon's release from prison. Others, like Gilles Bernheim, an

---

98. 21 October 1999.

99. Under this system, a convicted person freed pending appeal was required to surrender to authorities before the Court would hear their appeal. The European Court of Human Rights declared this practice a violation of the right to a fair trial. See Jean-Michel Dumay, "La Cour de cassation renonce à la procédure de mise en état la veille de l' examen des pourvois", *Le Monde*, 6 January 2000.

100. See Cour Européenne des Droits de l'Homme, *Affaire Papon c. France (54210/00)*, 25 July 2002; European Court of Human Rights, Press Release, "Chamber Judgment in the Case of Papon v. France," 25 July 2002; Jon Henley, "France denied Papon fair trial, court rules", *Guardian*, 26 July 2002; Adam Sage, "Court rules that Papon Nazi trial was unfair", *Times*, 26 July 2002.

important Parisian rabbi, joined in the call for Papon's liberation on humanitarian grounds.[101] For them the continued incarceration of a ninety-year-old
man, suffering from a variety of ailments, had no place in the justice system
of a liberal democracy. The trial and conviction had served their concrete and
symbolic purposes. His release would serve them as well by demonstrating the
strength of the rule law. For Badinter, the "humanity" of "crimes against humanity" must triumph. For others, however, the proper emphasis must be
placed on the crime, and on the absolute evil of the crime. The impre-
scriptibility of the offence itself was the essence of the law of the land, and any
pleas based on a notion of humanity failed to understand and appreciate the
basic nature of Papon's fault.[102] His failure to apologize for his offence, his
stubborn refusal to recognize and to define himself as a perpetrator, his continued self-understanding as a victim, all served to condemn him in the eyes
of those opposed to his release.[103] As Alain Jakubowicz, a lawyer representing
some of Papon's victims put it

> Le procès de Maurice Papon appartient désormais à l'histoire de notre
> pays, au même titre que ceux de Klaus Barbie et de Paul Touvier. L'un
> et l'autre sont morts en détention, vieux et malades, sans que quiconque
> s'en émeuve. L'humanité ferait-elle une différence entre le nazi, le mili-
> cien, et le collaborateur? Les uns comme les autres ont appartenu à la
> même chaîne de l'horreur qui menait inexorablement de l'arrestation à
> la chambre à gaz. La "qualité" de Maurice Papon ne le rend pas digne
> d'une compassion plus grande que ceux dont il a été le complice.[104]

> ('The trial of Maurice Papon from now on belongs to the history of
> our country, just like those of Klaus Barbie and Paul Touvier. Each
> of the latter two died in prison, old and sick, and no one got upset
> about it. Will "humanity" now differentiate among the Nazi, the
> member of the *Milice* and the collaborator? Each of them in his own
> way belonged to the same chain of horror which led inexorably from
> arrest to the gas chamber. The "status" of Maurice Papon does not

---

101. "Des voix pour Papon," *Libération*, 22 January 2001; "Controverse autour de la
grâce de Maurice Papon", *Le Monde*, 28 July 2001; Jon Henley, "Fury over call to free collaborator Papon", *Guardian*, 31 July 2001.

102. Germain Latour, "La valeur des années", *Libération*, 15 January 2001. "Le Mrap
pour la libération de Papon, *Libération*, 17 January 2001.

103. "La bête rôde toujours", *Libération*, 24 January 2001.

104. "Qui expliquera aux familles bafouées?", *Libération*, 24 January 2001. See also,
Daniel Sibony, "Papon et les âmes en peine", *Libération*, 1 February 2001.

make him more worthy of compassion than those for whom he was the accomplice".)

Here Jakubowicz touches upon at least two points which are of vital jurisprudential import in any discussion of the place of trials for crimes against humanity and the construction of collective memory and notions of justice. First, there is the complicated set of debates and concerns which surround the traditional "perpetrator" category in Holocaust legal taxonomy. There is, as far as law is concerned, a distinction between and among different levels and degrees of participation in any criminal offence, a distinction which can be reflected either in the type of charge which an accused must face or in the sentence imposed after a finding of guilt. Not every accomplice is as guilty as every principal, just as distinctions are made between and among principals.

Naturally enough, when we are faced, as in the Papon case, with charges of crimes against humanity, conceptual and practical difficulties seem to emerge. The offence itself is almost by definition so absolute, so horrible, a crime "against humanity", that any notion of relativity seems almost impossible to comprehend. Perhaps this is the first level of controversy and difficulty which is a direct consequence of the differences which emerged between various representatives of the *parties civiles* in this case. The very idea of a lesser role for Papon, embodied in the "complicity" conviction and thence in a ten-year prison sentence, becomes, for those like Maître Jakubowicz, evidence of an unacceptable diminution of the guilt of Vichy.

This is the second important issue and controversy for collective memory and justice which continues to emerge in French debates. The very idea that there could be, morally and legally, valid arguments about different levels of responsibility between and among perpetrators, leads, in the eyes of many, to a continuing distortion of the historical and legal records, and a distinct and persistent failure to face up to and admit the reality of the past. To distinguish among Barbie, the Nazi torturer, Touvier, the *Milice* thug, and Maurice Papon, who signed the papers and stood by as Jews were selected, arrested and deported, does more than allow Papon to escape responsibility and punishment. The argument here is about the signifying function of each of the accused. Papon represents the history and truth of Vichy complicity and initiative in the Shoah in France. To allow him to be released, to treat him as different and distinguishable from Touvier and Barbie, is simply to re-create, to perpetuate the mythology of French governmental and legal innocence in the tragedy of the Jews of that country after 1940. The release of Papon would diminish, if not eliminate, the lesson of history which was thought to have been embodied in his trial.[105]

In September 2002, all of these issue of legality, justice, and memory came to the fore yet again as Papon was released from prison under a new provision of French law relating to the early release from custody of seriously ill prisoners. The outrage was instant and all of the questions and debates which had already been canvassed again reemerged. The argument that Papon's victims were not spared from deportation and death on the grounds of ill-health was invoked. The exceptional nature of crimes against humanity was urged as grounds for requiring that Papon remain in prison. The cases of Klaus Barbie and Paul Touvier, who died in jail, were raised to again call into question the special treatment Papon had received from the elite circles of French law and government. On the other hand, discourses of equity, humanity and justice were invoked, by Papon's friends and enemies alike, to assert the supremacy of legality in the face of barbarity.[106]

The spectacular elements of law are in fact again and again haunted here not so much by competing taxonomies which seek to maintain a professional control over historical truth, but rather by the specters of law itself. The failure of the Papon trial, and other elements of the "affair", like the failure of all other French trials in relation to the fate of the Jews of that country, as well as the success of the Papon trial for those who support the sometimes problematic balance between truth and justice, is the failure and success of law itself. Truth, law, memory and history are complicated and interrelated ideas.

In fact, it was in relation to one element which was not directly relevant to Papon's guilt or innocence concerning the charges against him that we can find perhaps some measure of the impact which the trial and his subsequent flight may have had. In relation to this question, both the issue of the lay pub-

---

105. Pierre Marcelle "Utilité de Papon," *Libération*, 15 January 2001. For still others, Badinter's intervention in the name of justice and humanity might have been seen to invoke questions and controversies raging at the time about the heritage of François Mitterand, under whom Badinter served as Attorney-General. Mitterand's son was being investigated for illegal arms trading with various African dictators and the shadow of Mitterand's close relationship with former senior Vichy police official René Bousquet still hung over collective memory.

106. See Jacqueline Coignard, "Papon cherche la sortie de la Santé", *Libération*, 5 September 2002; "Doutes et protestations à la libération de Papon", *Le Monde*, 18 September 2002. The editions of French daily newspapers were full of the Papon case and reactions to his release in the days which followed. See also, "Vichy war criminal too ill to stay in jail, court rules", *Guardian*, 19 September 2002; "Fight to put Papon back in jail begins", *Guardian*, 20 September 2002.

lic and the professional stature of the legal and historical professions come into play.

As I have mentioned, the one issue which seems to dominate the complex interplay of forces at work in the French public consciousness is that of continuity and discontinuity. In this, of course, as I have also argued, France is not alone. The unique characteristics of French history do however raise interesting and intriguing questions. The continuity/discontinuity debate here plays itself out at two distinct historical junctures. The first is the relationship between the regime of the Third Republic and Vichy. The second level is between Vichy and the Fourth and Fifth Republics. I have argued that the forces of continuity are perhaps stronger than those of discontinuity in the first instance and that this fact is what has been the subject of legal and historical occultation of the mythologies of Vichy's illegality and the purge's success or failure. I would also argue that the forces of continuity between the Vichy period and subsequent Republican regimes are stronger than official legal, collective memory would have us believe.

I am referring here not to the all too apparent failures of the purge as a revolutionary expurgative for the legal and governmental systems of France after 1944, but rather to the way in which crimes against humanity were also perpetrated under subsequent Republican regimes and the ways in which those state crimes have also been swept under the same carpet as many of the crimes of Vichy. All of this surfaced in two particularly bizarre, French ways during and after the trial of Maurice Papon.

After Papon was found guilty, one of the civil parties, the *Fédération nationale des déportés et internés résistants et patriotes* (National Federation of Deported and Imprisoned Resistance Fighters and Patriots) filed an action against the French government for symbolic damages of one franc. The basis and purpose of the suit was to establish the legal and more importantly, the moral and ethical responsibility of the French state for the Papon's actions. In other words, the suit is an attempt to employ the judicial system of the French state to condemn the French state for its role as a perpetrator of the Holocaust.

The political, legal and ideological questions raised by this case are complex. There are important legal issues of the possible co-existence of state liability for the illegal activities of its agents. But more vital for the construction of French memory and identity is the fundamental assertion of the plaintiff that there is in fact and in law, a legal and moral continuity between Vichy and the current government of the French Republic. The then French Minister of the Interior, Jean-Jacques Chevènement, totally rejected this assertion as being a complete contradiction of the real political, moral and juridical identity of the modern French state. He declared that

Il ne saurait être question de confondre l'État républicain avec l'État français de Vichy qui en fut la négation.[107]

(There can never be any question of confusing the Republic with the French State of Vichy, which was its very negation.)

The battle lines drawn in the course of another legal dispute are familiar. Does the assumption of some sort of moral responsibility for Vichy by President Chirac render the Republican government legally liable for the faults of Vichy bureaucrats? Can the questions of moral and ethical responsibility of the French state and its representatives in the Holocaust be determined before courts of law? Can an award of symbolic damages truly be symbolic of a legal, historical and ideological construction of continuity within French governmental structures, personnel and collective memory? Once again, the case of Maurice Papon serves as the lynchpin around which law and memory do battle in the configuration of justice in modern French consciousness. And this is not the only way in which these struggles have played themselves out around the life and career of Maurice Papon.

Before being sent Bordeaux, Papon spent some time in that part of the French government responsible for the department of Algeria. After the war, Papon returned to serve in Constantine. Still later, as Prefect of Police in Paris, Papon was in charge of local antiterrorist police measures against the strong Algerian independence movement in the metropolitan capital.

At a basic level, of course, this is and was largely irrelevant to the charges against the accused in Bordeaux. Nonetheless, the "Algerian question" figured prominently in the public and media construction of the Papon case. Each criminal accused is required in the course of his or her trial to provide a *curriculum vitae* to the court so that the triers of fact can gain an idea of the context of the offence and of the character of the accused. Papon's resume included his Algerian connections. Ironically perhaps, given the pedagogical and spectacular nature of the proceedings, the presiding judge referred to this part of the trial in a Baudrillardian moment as the "film" of the accused's life.[108]

---

107. Jean-Michel Dumay, "La responsabilité de L'Etat dans la déportation des juifs soumise au tribunal administratif", *Le Monde*, 7 March 2000; Dominique Simonnot, "Affaire Papon: les déportés contre l'Etat", *Libération*, 7 March 2000.

108. The presence of the media and their function in representing the pedagogical functions of law and perpetrator trials in France has had a more recent manifestation with the screening of extracts of the Touvier trial on French television. See Annick Peigné-Giuly, "Le procès Touvier à l'écran", *Libération*, 5 December 2001.

We have already seen a previous attempt to bring the crimes of French colonialism before the bar of French justice. In the trial of Klaus Barbie, Jacques Vergès made much of his assertions of the hypocrisy and incompetence of the prosecution to try his client for crimes against humanity in the face of the massive criminal offence of colonialism. In that case, French self-understanding and memory were challenged in the legal context by the accused, a Nazi who sought to draw direct comparisons between torture and murder in Algiers and torture and murder in Lyon. Such claims were met with outrage and offence by the justice system and by the public, as well as by many representatives of the plaintiffs.

In Papon's case, however, the Algerian question was raised by the prosecution and by the plaintiffs. Here, there was in fact an attempt to draw a direct line of parallels between the crimes of Vichy and the crimes of the colonial Republic. However, the line drawn was in fact brought out almost as an example of *post hoc, propter hoc*. Papon, it was argued, was aware of torture in Algeria and did nothing to prevent it. Papon, as Prefect of Police, was aware of, if not responsible for, the massacres of innocent Algerian protestors by Paris police in October 1961.[109] He was equally aware of torture and deportation of Jews in Bordeaux and did nothing about that either. The Papon leopard did not, so the argument went, ever change its spots. In his testimony about the Paris events, Papon denied that hundreds of Algerians had been killed and placed responsibility for those who were killed on a settling of accounts between opposing Algerian independence groups, just as he tried to place responsibility for the deportations from Bordeaux either on the Germans or on the Jews themselves.[110] As he himself put it, he always remained a faithful servant of the government. He had no regrets and

Si c'était à refaire, je le referais.[111]

(If I had it to do over again, I would do the same thing.)

---

109. See Jean-Luc Einaudi, *La Bataille de Paris: 17 octobre 1961* (Paris: Seuil, 1991). In November 2000, French Prime Minister, Lionel Jospin, spoke in Parliament of the need for an exhaustive and objective study of the events. The controversy continues. See e.g. Olivier Le Cour Grandmaison (ed.), *Le 17 octobre 1961. Un Crime d'Etat à Paris* (Paris: La Dispute, 2001); Jim House, "Antiracist memories: the case of 17 October 1961 in historical perspective", 9 *Modern & Contemporary France* 355 (2001).

110. Papon carried the battle into another judicial forum when he sued Einaudi for defamation. He lost. See *inter alia*, David Dufresne, "Papon-Einaudi, face-à-face sur un massacre", *Libération*, 4 February 1999; "Procès Einaudi: Papon débouté", 27–28 March 1999.

111. *Le Procès de Maurice Papon*, op. cit., at 210.

Again, Henry Rousso publicly attacked this turn of legal events.

De surcroît, l'exemplarité du cas, déjà discutable en soi, recelait des risques dus à la conjoncture même du procès. Pouvait-on sérieusement soutenir que les crimes commis sous l'autorité de Maurice Papon, durant la guerre d'Algérie constituaient une forme de récidive de ceux qui furent commis sous l'Occupation, comme le sentiment en a été donné aux audiences de Bordeaux, prises dans la logique des assises ? Certes, Maurice Papon représente une forme de continuité administrative assez exceptionnelle bien que non isolée. Mais ses supérieurs, ceux qui ont donné les ordres ou les ont couverts ? Peut-on faire ainsi l'équation entre les rafles antijuives de 1942–1944 et les massacres d'Algériens de 1961, et donc entre Pétain et de Gaulle ? Absurde![112]

(Moreover, the exemplary nature of the case, already highly questionable, hid some dangers due to the circumstances surrounding the case itself. Could anyone seriously argue that the crimes committed under the authority of Maurice Papon during the Algerian War, were a repetition of those committed under the Occupation? This was the impression given to the spectators in Bordeaux, according to the logic of the trial. Without doubt, Maurice Papon represents an exceptional, albeit not isolated, form of administrative continuity. But his bosses, the ones who gave the orders or were responsible for them? Is it possible to make an equivalency between the round up of Jews between 1942–1944 and the massacre of Algerians in 1961, and thus between Pétain and de Gaulle! Absurd!)

Here, of course, lies the major problem with law and memory in France today. Even a respected historian like Rousso cannot imagine, or allow himself to publicly imagine, parallels between Vichy and Algeria, or between Pétain and de Gaulle. This does not mean that one must bring into question some idea of the uniqueness of the Holocaust, nor again, that the analogy, parallel and continuity are direct, or unidimensional. However, one must be willing and able to see those moments of institutional and individual continuity which exist between the period of the Shoah and those which characterize more recent experience.

I have already noted the institutional and collective reluctance of French lawyers to come to terms with the nature and role of law under Vichy and

---

112. *La hantise du passé*, op. cit., at 121.

with the basic normality of that experience. Reluctance about law in Algeria is perhaps even more deeply embedded partly because of the more recent nature of the Algerian experience and the ongoing political and cultural ties with tragic events in that country.[113] More generally, there is an absence of a Vichy-like reckoning with "Algeria" in French history and public memory.[114] While novelist Didier Daeninckx can use a fictionalized Papon-like character to make the deeply resonant point about continuity between Vichy and Algeria in French popular culture, attempts to raise similar concerns in the context of the actual trial of Papon for crimes against humanity are dismissed as absurd.[115]

Again, I am not asserting that Vichy and Algeria are the same, or that the fate of the Jews was the same as the fate of the Algerians.[116] Rather, I am arguing that the idea of a complete disjuncture between the two troubling periods of French history, law and memory is as absurd as an argument for an absolute symmetry. As far as the law is concerned, in fact, it would be quite possible to argue that Vichy law, in which lawyers continued to operate in a legal system characterized by "normality", is and was closer to legal continuity than the military and religious laws of exception which can be said to have defined law and legality in Algeria in the post-Vichy era. What unites the two, in the person and personality of Maurice Papon, is the idea that the French state is the representative of the French nation and obedience to that state is required at all times. Whether that state defines its enemies as "Jews" or as "Arabs", French police and government officials have shown themselves ready, willing and able to commit acts of torture and killing in the defense of the nation. At the existential and quotidian level, Parisians had twice witnessed public transport buses of the RATP (*Régie Autonome des Transports Parisiens*/The Paris Public Transport Authority) being used by police to transport racial enemies of the French nation, once during the *rafles* (round-ups) against the Jews and again in the cold October night against the Algerians. This idea and ideal of the civil servant's duty to and identification with the French state and nation is what unites the Papon of Bordeaux and the Papon of Paris, just as it unites the lawyers of Vichy with

---

113. See *Juger en Algérie, 1944–1962* (Paris: Seuil, 1997) and Sylvie Theynaud, *Une Drôle de Justice: Les Magistrats dans la Guerre d'Algérie* (Paris: La Découverte, 2001).

114. See Benjamin Stora, *La gangrène et l'oubli: La mémoire de la guerre d' Algérie* (Paris: La Découverte, 1998).

115. See *Meurtres pour mémoire* (*Murder In Memoriam*) (Paris: Gallimard, 1984).

116. See Jacques Derrida, *Le monolinguisme de l'autre* (Paris: Galilée, 1996) for an example of how the category "Jew" and "Algerian" are not necessarily mutually exclusive in the history of French colonialism.

the lawyers who stood by while torture became the rule of law in Algeria and France. It is this continuity which unites the case of the Jews of Bordeaux with the Algerians of Paris, which also unites Pétain and de Gaulle as the embodiment of a tyrannical "nation" or "Republic" and which finally unites the life of Papon. And it is this continuity which unites the various elements of recent French history under the rule of law which Rousso and others refuse to recognize. If the trial of Maurice Papon was the last trial of Vichy perhaps it might also be the first trial of Algeria. The connection is not as Rousso claims "absurd". It is real, it is historical and it is legal. This is the tragedy of Vichy and its legacy.

There are at least two elements of French collective memory which unite the events of Bordeaux and those of Paris under Papon. The first is the idea of official forgetting which informed French collective memory about Vichy and which still surrounds the massacres in Paris in October 1961. Only because of the publicity surrounding the Papon trial did the French government agree to open the official files to historical scrutiny.[117] The second element of historical continuity is that the rule of law is omnipresent and virtually powerless to offer us guidance, from Bordeaux to Constantine to Paris and back to Bordeaux. Judges, lawyers and law were always there. And the deportations and massacres continued. Choosing law is never the same as choosing justice.

7. Conclusion

The issues which lawyers above all are unwilling to face and confront are starkly raised by the history of the law and the Holocaust in France. Firstly, the historical record of the Holocaust, particularly in France but generally as well, demonstrates clearly that when faced with a fundamental choice between right and wrong, lawyers generally failed to make the right moral choice. Instead they chose law. Secondly, there appears to be nothing available to lawyers

---

117. See Laurent Chabrun, "Les ratonnades d'octobre 1961-La confession d'un policier", *L'Express*, 16 October 1997; "M. Chevènement prêt à "faire la vérité" sur la répression des Algériens", *Le Monde*, 17 October 1997; Phillippe Bernard, "17 octobre 1961, la police parsienne jette des Algériens à la Seine", id., Phillippe Bernard, "Catherine Trautmann va ouvrir les archives sur les événements du 17 octobre 1961", *Le Monde*, 18 October 1997; "Exception française", Editorial, id.; Annette Levy-Willard, "Le procès Papon rouvre les blessures d'octobre 1961", *Libération*, 18 October 1997. In 2001 further controversies surrounding the history of the Algerian War of Independence also had their echoes in earlier battles over access to French government archives. Jean-Pierre Thibaudat, "Deux gardiens de la mémoire au placard", *Libération*, 1 June 2001.

or to law to allow them in practice when faced with such decisions, to characterize the evils of antisemitism, of persecution and exclusion, as "not law" within their own interpretive community. Thirdly and finally, the French experience demonstrates, as I believe do the experiences and failures surrounding the prosecution, or non-prosecution of perpetrators in other countries where issues of national memory and identity are posed somewhat differently, that memory and justice can be and have been ill-served by law and jurisprudence. In all these cases, the gap between law on one hand and justice on the other, is so great that memory can not be served within the legal system. Ideas of compensation, reconciliation and apology must always in such circumstances attempt to escape from the shadow imposed by the law.[118] At the very least, the contestable nature of memory comes into clear conflict with legal norms which must by definition strive for certainty of one particular sort. Whether this conflict between legal memory and other forms of public memory is a tragedy or a boon for our collective understandings of law and justice in relation to the Holocaust is another question. In the end, law will always emerge triumphant. The contestability of evidence, the frailty of memories and of memory, the gap between law and justice, between legal proof and truth, these are all elements which are central to law's understanding of itself. The jurisprudence of the Holocaust in France is, like the jurisprudence of the Holocaust elsewhere, an often-futile examination of law's self-delusion.

---

118. Charles Bremner, "France accepts guilt for wartime anti-Semitism", *Times*, 17 July 2000.

CHAPTER 7

"The Civil Equivalent of Excommunication": Constructing the Holocaust and the Rule of Law in the United States

1. Introduction

As we have already seen, the United States was the prime architect of the Nuremberg trials and more particularly of the political, popular and legal construction of the mythology and pathology of Nazi law at Nuremberg. In this chapter, it is not my intention to offer a complete legal history of the Holocaust and American law, nor to closely examine the many legal issues which have arisen in the course of America's pursuit of perpetrators.[1] It is also be-

---

1. Many authors have dealt with various aspects of these questions for both a general and professional audience. See *inter alia*, Howard Blum, *Wanted! The Search for Nazis in America* (New York: Quadrangle, 1977); Allan A. Ryan, Jr., *Quiet Neighbors: Prosecuting Nazi War Criminals in America* (New York and London: Harcourt Brace Jovanovich, 1984); Michael J. Bazyler, "Litigating the Holocaust", 33 *U. Rich. L. R.* 601 (1999); James W. Moeller, "United States Treatment of Alleged Nazi War Criminals: International Law, Immigration Law, and the Need for International Cooperation", 25 *Vir. J. of Intl. L.* 793 (1985); Elizabeth Holtzman, "United States Involvement with Nazi War Crimes", 11 *N.Y. L. Sch. J. Int'l & Comp. L.* 337 (1990); Elliott M. Abramson, "Reflections on the Unthinkable: Standards Relating to the Denaturalization and Deportation of Nazis and Those Who Collaborated with the Nazis During World War II", 57 *Cincinnati L. R.* 1311 (1989); Stephen J.

yond the scope of the present work to closely engage with the controversies surrounding the place of the Holocaust and of Holocaust memory more broadly in the American context. Instead, I shall offer what I hope are useful insights into the ways in which the Holocaust and the rule of law have served as mutually reinforcing tropes in the construction through both popular and judicial discourses, of a particular American version of law after Auschwitz.

In his study of the creation of the United States Holocaust Museum in Washington, Edward Linenthal focuses on the vagaries of memory in the post-war construction of the Shoah. He writes that

> Forgetfulness, however,—the treachery of memory—became a strategic ally in the postwar holy crusade against the Soviet Union, as West Germany quickly became a symbol of miraculous transformation to democracy and a bulwark against Soviet aggression. Russians became "Nazis"; Germans became freedom-loving allies. Active memory of the Nazi past was considered a needless complication in the struggle to win the Cold War. Even legal memory was short.[2]

Linenthal here identifies what would become in the post-war years a dominant theme of American (and other Western) attempts to come to terms with the Holocaust i.e. the hegemony of the anti-Communist worldview which would inform politics and law. In effect, this would mean that the centrality of the Holocaust as the defining historical and legal moment within legal modernity was quickly displaced by more important political and ideological constructions of what Ronald Reagan would call the Evil Empire. I have already argued that at some level of political discourse and certainly at the level of legal discourse, the Holocaust was in fact even more quickly and effectively removed from and distorted within our understandings of modernity. The key political, ideological and legal themes of Nuremberg—the construction of "wars of aggression" as the central criminal enterprise of the Nazi state, the conceptualization of Nazi law as not law, and the pathologization of Nazism and Nazis, all served to place the Holocaust and the legality of the Holocaust outside mainstream understandings of both Nazism and the rule of law. When this already secondary status of the Holocaust within the ideology of law in the United States was combined with the omnipresent threat of a new, nuclear Holocaust initiated by the new, old enemy, it was hardly surprising that the effects described by Linenthal predominated American constructions of these questions.

Massey, "Individual Responsibility for Assisting the Nazis in Persecuting Civilians", 71 *Minn. L. R.* 97 (1986).

   2. *Preserving Memory* (New York and London, Penguin Books, 1995) at 7.

At the same time, broader social semiotic and political phenomena served to reinforce this secondary status of the Holocaust, particularly in so far as the law and legal discourse were concerned. Lawrence Langer for example controversially asserts that the Holocaust is in fact an essentially anti-American phenomenon. By this, he means that American constructions of the Shoah have tended to distort its facticity and its factual realities by their desire to offer an Americanized "understanding" of the Holocaust according to culturally specific signifying practices. Thus,

> The Holocaust—alas!—provides us with only something to die with—something from those who died with nothing left to give. There is no final solace, no redeeming truth, no hope that so many millions may not have died in vain. They have. But the American vision of the Holocaust…continues to insist that they have not, trying to parlay hope, sacrifice, justice and the future into a victory that will mitigate despair.[3]

Turning to the film, *Judgment at Nuremberg*, Langer underlines and highlights the closing of the movie and the statement that by July 1949, all those convicted and imprisoned at the second Nuremberg Trials had been freed. He writes

> I suppose that for those who still see the Holocaust as a situation of violated justice, this announcement is as exasperating and offensive as the news in 1980 that 200 alleged Nazi war criminals are still living safely in the United States. But both truths are accompanied by an overwhelming sense of futility, especially to those who have already understood that the logic of the law can never make sense of the illogic of extermination.[4]

He then makes a more specific claim not about American memory but specifically about the state of law and the Holocaust. First he asks

> What system of justice can render homage to the mounds of corpses being shoved into the mass grave by a giant British bulldozer?[5]

Then he asserts that

---

3. *Admitting the Holocaust* (New York and Oxford: Oxford University Press, 1996) at 158.
4. Ibid., at 171.
5. Id., at 172.

Judgment at Nuremberg, with its concluding irony that by July 1949 none of the ninety-nine sentenced to prison at the last of the second series of trials was still behind bars, renders a judgment *of* Nuremberg, of Nazism, and of the contemporary world that it probably never wished to impose: that uncorrupted justice, the highest expression of law, order, morality and civilization, is only a charade in the presence of atrocities literally embodied by the mounds of twisted corpses in mass graves at Belsen.[6]

I have already argued and will continue to do so here that such statements are in fact wide of the mark and informed by a fundamental epistemological, ontological and jurisprudential error. I do not intend to interrogate all of the assumptions inherent in Langer's work, many of which are extremely useful and insightful. Instead, I want to point out here and then elaborate in subsequent parts of this and other chapters of the book, how he misses the basic point about the Holocaust and justice or at least about the Holocaust and law. The key point here is not that the horror and reality of the Holocaust are irredeemable as Langer asserts. Instead, what we must remember is that Nuremberg, law and yes even justice (at least as understood and deployed by Langer) fail in relation to the Holocaust, become a mere "charade" when faced with the embodied reality of the victims. They fail because the embodiment which is central to the Holocaust is the body of the law. When and if we begin to apprehend the Holocaust as a set of historical events informed by and based upon the legal inscription of the body politic and of its biological, racial enemies in a concomitant set of juridical prescriptions, the creation of the *homo sacer*, the legal subject beyond lawful redemption, the possibility and systemization of legalized killing which is not murder, we can begin to see all "jurisprudential" efforts such as those considered by Langer, not as failures brought about by the incapacity of law but as failures caused by the very success of the lawful process of extermination itself. "The highest expression of law, order, morality and civilization" is not a charade, but a juridical self-reflection in the legal world of Auschwitz and Belsen. The literal embodiment of the victims at Belsen is the legal embodiment of the victims at Belsen.

The apparently idiosyncratic study of the American legal system and its positioning of the Holocaust and collective memory within the confines of legal discourse and discourse about law which follows will, I hope, serve to illustrate in the post-war context, the impossibility of a law after Auschwitz which is not a law of Auschwitz.

---

6. Id., at 173.

2. America and the Construction of Nazi Criminality

I have already discussed the ways in which Nuremberg served to construct a particular version of the triumphant return and reinstitution of the rule of law in and over Germany. I have also demonstrated the ways in which contemporary legal discourse in the United States in fact treated Nazi law as law. At Nuremberg, Nazi law was demonized, criminalized and defeated by the vigorous enforcement and application of "real" law. In American eyes, this meant quite naturally American law. In other words, Nazi law was to be seen in clear and stark contrast to the correct understanding of the rule of law as embodied in democratic systems such as those of the United States. Thus, Nazi law was to a great extent defined by what it was not—it was not law, it was not American law. From the earliest stages of the post-war era, the idea of Nazism and Nazi law as not American would inform the construction of an ideological understanding of these phenomena in negative comparative terms. Here, of course, American law and American legal understandings of Nazism in general and of the Holocaust in particular were faced with an apparent epistemological and existential dilemma. In order to construct Nazi law and the Holocaust as foreign to correct historical and jurisprudential renderings of the rule of law, in other words as un-American, the legal system had to confront Nazi law and the Holocaust in such a way as to avoid confronting the competing reality of the Holocaust as a legal phenomenon. Therefore, United States courts and law-makers had to devise ways in which to internalize legal issues related to Nazism and the Holocaust in order to define these issues as foreign. Thus, as in the process of criminalization more generally, law had to define Nazism, Nazis and the Holocaust as something which came within the jurisdiction of American courts so that law could then define these issues and individuals as not worthy of inclusion in the body politic and *corpus juris* of America. The primary function of American law in relation to the Holocaust and to Holocaust perpetrators has always been to serve as the legitimate and legitimating progeny of the jurisprudence of Nuremberg, to serve and to protect the American polity and American law by effectively and constantly reasserting and reaffirming the rule of law and contrasting Nazism, Nazis and the Holocaust as antithetical to that same rule of law.[7] The Holocaust is de-

---

7. In his complex and controversial study of the Holocaust and its place in American cultural and politics more generally, Peter Novick presents the much stronger argument that the very process of Americanizing the Holocaust is so fraught with historical, cultural,

fined as relevant to American law only in so far as it can then be defined out of and rendered discontinuous with, American law.

In the early days after the end of the Second World War, of course, the imposition of the rule of law through the Occupation of Germany and the pursuit of war criminals was the most obvious and perhaps necessary way in which these goals could be achieved. It is clear from the legal historical record that both the deNazification and the war crimes programs were abysmal practical failures.[8] However, the question of the practical impact of such legal systems is to a large extent of little significance. What is important is the hegemonic success at home in the construction and reinforcement of an ideological system of popular belief that the rule of law had triumphed over evil and that evil could and can never be part of the rule of law. The American judicial system was even prepared to some extent to take cognizance of claims based in fundamental rule of law notions like *habeas corpus* writs filed by convicted war criminals.[9] While these claims to American law were rejected on the basis that American law and legal procedure were not applicable, the simple juridical act of considering and rejecting such claims allowed the law to establish and confirm itself in both its prophylactic and ideological gatekeeping functions. Jurisdiction was accepted in order to deny the existence of jurisdiction and to again mark the point of discontinuity.

Indeed, in some instances the law itself could recognize its evil cousin Nazi law as law without ever endangering its own self-understanding. Thus, in a typical conflicts of law fashion, when the Court of Appeals was faced with a case involving the forced sale of Jewish property under a contract imposed by Nazi law for the Aryanization of the economy, it could recognize the validity of the contract by relying on traditional principles of conflict of laws and the proper law of contract, while at the same time condemning the law itself as objectionable.[10] What must be borne in mind here is that the actual solution

---

political and even logical difficulties, that it founders on its assumptions. See *The Holocaust in American Life* (Boston and New York: Houghton Mifflin, 1999). I would argue that the very process of Americanizing the Holocaust is no more fraught than is any other attempt to create any form of collective memory. My focus here is rather on the ways in which a legal system which has always attempted to define the Holocaust as "not American" creates its own difficulties of cultural memory and professional self-understanding.

8. See Frank M. Buscher, *The U.S. War Crimes Trial Program in Germany, 1945–1955* (Westport: Greenwood, 1989).

9. See e.g., *Milch v. U.S.*, 332 U.S. 789; *Brandt et al v. U.S.*, 333 U.S. 836; *Hirota v. Mac Arthur* 338 U.S. 197.

10. *Bernstein v. Van Heyghen Frères*, 163 F. 2d 246. See David Fraser, "'This is Not Like Any Other Question": A Brief History of Nazi Law Before U.K. and U.S. Courts', 19 *Connecticut Journal of International Law* 59 (2003).

or substantive outcome of the case is irrelevant in terms of the ideological survival and control function of the rule of law as embodied by the court and its
ruling. The actual decision can clearly be justified simply in terms of a crude
positivism i.e. the court has decided therefore it is correct and must be accepted. It can be justified through a careful exercise of applying private international law norms, standards and tests concerning the proper law of contract
and at some level an understanding of the technical legal situation which obtained in Germany at the relevant time. Conversely, of course, an entirely different result could be obtained and welcomed by invoking the competing conflict of law principle of public order analysis which would reject Nazi law as
not law. In either case, the rule of law wins, Nazi law is characterized as not
law acceptable to American jurisprudence or as an operative and operating
legal system ruling the contract in question. The actual outcome of the case
is of no importance in a debate which is simply a concrete rehashing of natural law and legal positivism with which we are all familiar.

This triumph of the rule of law and the centrality of the contraceptive function of the legal process can be found at another level in a series of cases dealing with government attempts to denaturalize and deport various members
of the German American *Bund* and similar organizations.[11] Here, the domestic legal system was faced with individuals who were *prima facie* American citizens. These American citizens had nonetheless apparently expressed their
preference for and fealty to a foreign power, i.e. Hitler's Germany. Given the
fact that America had been at war with this foreign power and given the ideological construction of Nazi Germany as antithetical to the very core of
America's legal self-understanding, the apparent dilemma facing the legal system in the immediate post-war period was how to afford American citizens
the protections of the rule of law while simultaneously protecting the rule of
law itself. In a series of decisions, the Federal judiciary acquitted themselves
of the task with little difficulty. General principles of law in relation to citizenship and naturalization, due process, evidence etc. were simply applied in
order to determine whether the individual accused had not taken the oath of
citizenship in good faith by harboring allegiances to a foreign power.[12] Douglas J of the Supreme Court wrote that

---

11. For a history of the *Bund* and the issues and individuals involved, see Susan Canedy,
America's Nazis: A Democratic Dilemma (Menlo Park: Markgraf Publications, 1990).

12. See *United States v. Borchers et al*, 163 F. 2d 347; *U.S. v. Kunz*, 163 F. 2d 344; *U.S.
v. Holtz et al*, 54 F. Supp. 63; *Knauer v. U.S.*, 328 U.S. 654; *U.S. v. Knauer*, 149 F. 2d 519;
U.S. v. Hauck et al, 155 F. 2d 141; *Sanders v. Clark*, 85 F. Supp. 253; *Bechtel v. U.S.*, 176 F.
2d 741; *Fix v. U.S.*, 176 F. 2d 746.

> But it is plain that citizenship obtained through naturalization carries with it the privilege of full participation in the affairs of our society, including the right to speak freely, to criticize officials and administrators, and to promote changes in our laws including the very Charter of our Government.
>
> Great tolerance and caution are necessary, lest good faith exercise of the rights of citizenship be turned against the naturalized citizen and be used to deprive him of the cherished status.[13]

Here Douglas articulates the strength of the rule of law in the United States. Even opponents of the rule of law itself must be given the right to speak against the rule of law without by this fact alone running the risk of losing the precious right of citizenship. It is again not my intention here to offer a further or careful examination of the *Bund* cases or of the law relating to the loss of citizenship. Instead I wish only to underline the way in which the rule of law protects itself and the body politic at one and the same time through the invocation of such judicial rhetoric and the application of its own apparently coherent rules of both substance and procedure. It does not matter which of the individuals lost their citizenship and which of them remained Americans in good standing. Instead it matters that the question was posed within a legal framework in which the rule of law could be upheld and strengthened at the same time as the body politic could expel those who are found to be its enemies. Nazism could be and was defined as foreign and dangerous to America and the rule of law as law defined itself as immune to Nazism within the body politic.

It is important to note here that the Court invokes and applies its understanding of the centrality of the rule of law and the concomitant rejection of Nazism in a context which deals with citizenship, denaturalization and more centrally the idea of Nazis as anti-American and therefore as anti-law. In those few cases of alleged perpetrators and the American judicial system, this invocation of these particular ideological signifiers would come into contact with the other dominant tropes of post-war American memory of the Holocaust, anti-Communism and Cold War realities. One case in particular offers invaluable insights into the ways in which these apparently competing discourses were deployed in a judicial construction of the Holocaust and the rule of law, which again has proved to be content neutral yet self-enforcing.

Andrija Artukovic was the Minister of Internal Affairs in the fascist Ustashe government of wartime Croatia, established under the leadership of Ante

---

13. *Knauer v. US*, op. cit., at 656.

Pavelic. In his capacity as a Minister in the Pavelic government he was responsible for a system of police and paramilitary forces which imprisoned, tortured and killed thousands upon thousands of Jews, Gypsies and Serbs. His travels though the American legal system offer us important insights into the ways in which the Holocaust was and can be constructed in competing and apparently mutually exclusive ways within American legal discourse without any adverse impact upon the overarching ideological and political hegemony of the rule of law, or on popular understandings of law and not law. His story is one of history, politics, ideology and law and the ways in which the malleability of these discursive practices belies and distorts collective memory of and about the Holocaust and the rule of law.

Artukovic's travails and travels in the American legal system began with an extradition request from the government of what was then Yugoslavia in 1952. Students of history and politics then and now will quickly realize that the first legal hurdle in the case against the Ustashe Minister can be found in the complexities of the region we refer to either for the sake of simplicity or to refute the need for a careful and nuanced study and understanding, as the Balkans. Extradition is a legal mechanism under which nations, usually by way of bilateral treaty, hand over to the legal processes of one country an individual physically present in the second. Here, the then Kingdom of Serbia had entered into an extradition treaty with the United States. Yugoslavia, the socialist federation under Tito, sought Artukovic's extradition in virtue of its status as the successor nation under international law to the Kingdom of Serbia. Artukovic's lawyers sought a writ of *habeas corpus* to free their client on the grounds that Tito's Yugoslavia was a completely new and distinct political entity from the former Kingdom of Serbia and that therefore there was no treaty upon which the Yugoslavs could rely to seek his extradition.[14] In addition to the technical legal, political and historical debates which arose surrounding Serbia, wartime Balkan allegiances and government succession in international law, it must of course be remembered that at this time the Iron Curtain had descended upon Europe and the Yugoslav version of non-alignment, meant to separate that state from the Soviet Bloc and Warsaw Pact alliance had not yet emerged. In the heart of the Cold War, the legal system of the greatest democracy on earth was asked to send back an individual who was staunchly anti-Communist to the heart of the evil beast. It was hardly surprising then when the District Court in Los Angles held that there was no convincing evidence under existing international law standards that Yu-

---

14. *Artukovic v. Boyle*, 107 F. Supp. 11.

goslavia was the legitimate and accepted successor to the Kingdom of Serbia. Therefore there was no extant treaty under which Artukovic's extradition could be requested.[15]

Nor, if we understand the way in which the rule of law can and does manifest itself in liberal democracies, would we be surprised to learn that the Court of Appeals, in 1954, rejected this finding by the lower court and held that Yugoslavia was indeed the legal successor to the Kingdom of Serbia and that there did exist an extradition treaty under which the request could be made.[16]

Of course, nowhere here is either court concerned with the Holocaust, or crimes against humanity or with Artukovic's possible guilt. The focus is purely and simply on arcane areas of state succession under international law, a subject of continuing relevance to the area even today. The result of these two years of law and legal mechanism was simply to require the District Court to proceed to hear the request under the Treaty. The next set of legal proceedings in 1956 are however more instructive in any attempt to understand the ways in which the American legal system has actually constructed historical renderings of the Holocaust. As already noted, Artukovic was being sought for crimes committed during the period of Ustashe reign in Croatia. Under a general and longstanding principle of international law, extradition is not to be granted in cases where the defendant is being sought for "political" offences. This principle is meant to protect both the individual and the integrity of the governmental system of the party to whom the extradition request is being made from being manipulated for the purpose of persecuting political enemies of the current regime under the guise of law. In this instance, Artukovic argued that because he was being charged with offences which directly related to his time as a government Minister, the crimes were by definition "political" crimes and therefore outside the purview of the extradition treaty.[17]

Here of course we find a legal argument which is redolent of claims made by the Defendants at Nuremberg and soundly rejected as inimical to the re-established rule of law by the Charter and the judgment of the International Military Tribunal. Six years after Nuremberg and the triumph of the rule of law over Nazi law, an American court is faced with the assertion that the mass killing of Jews, Gypsies and other enemies of the state, under the guise of a lawfully constituted governmental authority, was "political" and not "criminal" in nature. In the District Court, Hall J had no difficulty in dealing with such an argument. He held

---

15. Ibid.
16. *Ivancevic v. Artukovic*, 211 F. 2d 565, cert. denied, 348 U.S. 818.
17. *Artukovic v. Boyle*, 140 F. Supp. 245.

…the plain reading of the Indictment here makes it immediately apparent that the offenses for which the surrender of the petitioner is sought were offenses of a political character.[18]

The next year, in 1957, the Court of Appeals confirmed this extraordinary conclusion. In doing so, the Court presaged the now well-known category in Holocaust historiographical taxonomy of the desk killer, but they did so to facilitate an analysis which allowed them to classify mass killing as a political and therefore a non-extraditable offence. They wrote

Appellant Artukovic is not charged with personally murdering anyone, rather it is charged that the murders were carried out on his "orders".[19]

The Court not only confirmed the finding of the District Judge that the offences in question were "political" but it also specifically found that the characterization of the offences as war crimes under international law was of no moment because U.S. law did not recognize that category of offence. The Supreme Court vacated this judgment in 1958 without giving reasons and the case was sent back down the judicial hierarchical chain for a hearing.[20]

Seven years after the first legal proceedings against him, Andrija Artukovic finally stood before an American judicial commissioner to learn his fate.[21] He had nothing to fear but law itself and law did not fail him here. Commissioner Hocke adopted many of the arguments accepted by his judicial brethren in earlier proceedings. After finding that murder *per se* was a crime under both Yugoslav and United States law, a requirement of reciprocity essential to extradition law, he found

Absolutely no evidence was presented that the defendant himself committed murder. The complainant relies entirely upon their evidence that members of the "ustasha" committed murders upon orders from the defendant.[22]

The basic decision to deny the extradition request was not motivated by this but by the Commissioner's finding that the affidavit evidence presented was likely to be unreliable and the passage of time made eyewitness testimony doubtful, two common themes in almost all subsequent debates surrounding

18. At 247.
19. *Karadzole v. Artukovic*, 247 F. 2d 198 at 204.
20. *Karadzole v. Artukovic* 355 U.S. 393.
21. *U.S. v. Artukovic*, 170 F. Supp. 383.
22. At 389.

perpetrator trials. Nonetheless, he did address the "political" crime question and found that the two previous judges who had considered the issue had indeed reached the correct decision on this point. The construction of the Holocaust by three different United States judicial bodies in the 13 years following Nuremberg is at one level quite extraordinary. In essence these findings construct the Holocaust not as a crime, not as the acts of criminal state apparatuses as was the case at Nuremberg. Instead under U.S. law they hold that the arrest, internment and murder of Jews, Gypsies and others was a part of politics. In their own bizarre and perhaps unintentional way, the United States courts in *Artukovic* struck upon a basic and fundamental reality of law after and before Auschwitz, a reality which flies in the face of the mythology constructed by and at Nuremberg. The acts of mass killing and other "crimes" committed against Jews and others by the Nazi state and by, in this case the Croatian state, were in effect acts of ordinary politics. They were not acts of pathological insanity, of state criminality. They were acts of law. Indeed, the words of Commissioner Hocke go to the very heart of the thesis of this book. In his analysis of the actions of the Pavelic government against racial enemies of the Croatian people and state he writes

> The evidence is conflicting as to the orders made with reference to the Serbs, Jews and Gypsies. Some of the orders were for internment and deportation. Some of the evidence shows alleged verbal orders for the killing of the enemies of the Independent State of Croatia.
> It was common practice during World War II to intern anyone who was even suspected to be an enemy of the government in power. Our own government saw fit to intern all Japanese on the west coast, men, women and children of all ages, immediately following Pearl Harbor.[23]

And of course the Supreme Court of the United States, like the Supreme Court of Canada, confirmed the constitutionality and legality of such measures. Again it is not necessary to suggest that there is an exact equivalence between the United States and Japanese Americans and Germany or Croatia and Jews. The simpler yet vital point is that the legality of these atrocities was unquestioned in any basic sense within the rule of law at the time. Again, I am not speaking here of humanity, decency, or even of justice in any meaningful sense. I am merely referring to law and legality. The judicial officers of the greatest democracy in the world have the ironic good sense in the cases of Andrija Artukovic of having inadvertently arrived at a jurisprudentially

---

23. At 390.

sound and historical accurate rendering of the Holocaust and the rule of law.[24] Artukovic was a desk killer who did not dirty his hands. He was a cold-hearted homicidal bastard who must bear responsibility for the deaths of hundreds of thousands. He was also a homicidal bastard who at some basic level committed no crime, no violation of the law. He killed thousands, but he murdered no one. This is the lesson of this stage of the case of Andrija Artukovic and the rule of law, but it is a lesson which we are reluctant to learn and one which the rule of law does not permit today's Americans to contemplate.

3. American Law, Citizenship and the Pursuit of Perpetrators

Of course, this is not the only legal imagining of the Holocaust. The Nuremberg ideal, of a Holocaust totally foreign to law, the Other of the dominant conception of the rule of law and of legality, is now the apparently dominant norm. Indeed, it is the existence of this norm, against which cases such as those of Artukovic are judged, which leads to a sense of outrage and injustice, and finally which has led to the current legal situation. Again it is not my intention here to trace the technical legal history of the American pursuit of alleged Nazi war criminals. Others have done so and the project is not one which impinges greatly on my aim here. Simply put, a combination of a number of disparate elements, political, historical, social and legal led to the adoption of what has become known as the Holtzman Amendment to America's immigration laws. Under these new provisions, those who had entered the country and/or obtained citizenship by hiding or lying about their Nazi past could be stripped of their citizenship and expelled from the United States. This is the process of denaturalization and deportation.

The political and legal symbolism of the process is clear. Those who perpetrated the horrors of the Holocaust are not to be tolerated in the United States. The body politic is not to be subjected to this invasion of the foreign epitome of the not law which was the Holocaust and the legal system of the world's greatest democracy is to be deployed as a prophylactic against these foreign invaders. The former head of the Justice Departments' Special Investigation Unit, established to deal with "Nazi cases", Allan A. Ryan, explains the significance and signifying function of the law as follows

---

24. See infra chapter 9.

The true significance of bringing Nazi persecutors to account for their crimes in American courts lies not in the number of actual deportees, but in their expulsion from the body of citizens. By revoking citizenship, the polity—the American people joined together in a society and a government—takes the most solemn and drastic step available to it: the civil equivalent of excommunication. Citizenship is the most fundamental right accorded to any member of the polity: its revocation is a highly unusual and difficult procedure, and it represents the judgment of the polity that the individual does not share its commitment to the basic values on which the society is founded.[25]

Echoing the sentiments of Justice Douglas mentioned earlier, Ryan also notes that

We give them law. How much law did they give their victims?
…
But recognize why we give them benefit of law. It is not for their sake but for ours. The repulsive bullies who destroyed millions of families and then ran to America are entitled to nothing from our hearts but contempt. Yet they are entitled to law, not because they have earned it but because we cannot afford to sacrifice it. A civilized society that resorts to barbarism to deal with barbarians begins to let go of its civilization. It is our adherence to law which separates us from them.[26]

Here we find all of the elements necessary for the construction of the rule of law in a post-Auschwitz world. The body politic must be protected from the infection of fascism and extermination. The absence of law is the defining characteristic of the Holocaust. Only by upholding the rule of law can we distinguish ourselves from the evil perpetrators. I have already identified the reasons which cause me to reject the particular, but apparently necessary, jurisprudential conceit, that Auschwitz was a lawless place and I will not belabor them here. Instead I wish to examine more carefully the internal problematics of the American position which constructs the Holocaust and Holocaust perpetrators according to the symbolism described by Ryan.

The first level of difficulty which has faced the American legal system and the political rhetoric which informs the broader polity is the confusion between law's symbolic function in constructing the popular and legal imagery of the Holocaust and law's practical function of determining "guilt and inno-

---

25. *Quiet Neighbors*, op. cit., at 340.
26. Ibid., at 339.

cence" of an individual targeted for denaturalization and deportation. Indeed, some like Ryan are distinctly uncomfortable with the symbolic function of the law in constructing the Holocaust in American collective memory. While recognizing that the trial of perpetrators is perhaps the one remaining concrete step which the government can accomplish he also is

> …uncomfortable at any suggestion that the prosecution of Nazi criminals is one aspect of the government's greater efforts to see that the Holocaust is not forgotten. We are not placing people on trial as a symbolic gesture, or to serve some larger purpose of conscience. We are putting them on trial because they broke the law. That is the only reason people should be put on trial.[27]

The question of whether law is the proper forum and medium through which to fulfill broader collective purposes concerning national memory is not one which, as the case of France amply demonstrates and as we shall see in subsequent chapters, is limited to the United States. There must always be a conflict, and an essential conflict, between notions of individual responsibility and individual justice within Western liberal conceptions of the rule of law and the trial process as a component thereof, and the collective symbolism which must also necessarily be embodied in every trial. Ryan himself notes that "we give them law", but not for the accused. Law is given, but for the purposes of democratic survival and the self-justification required for the continuance of the rule of law.

At this point, other conflicts between the individual and the collectivity must also arise. If the function of the legal system here is to remove the perpetrator from the body politic, then the definition of the body politic itself must be brought into a contested position. From the very earliest days of the renewed interest in the place of the Holocaust in the United States' collective memory and therefore within the body politic, various "immigrant" groups have engaged in debates and discourses surrounding their place within the American polity. Naturally, the role and place of American Jewry was and is central to the imagining and positioning of the Holocaust within this particular context. In addition, German Americans, Polish Americans, Ukrainian Americans, Americans from the Baltic States and from the former Yugoslavia have all engaged in legal and political discourses about and around the Holocaust and the place and function of ethnic identity in America.[28] Peter Novick, for example,

---

27. Id., at. 335.
28. See e.g., Douglas E. Kneeland, "German-Americans Grow Uneasy", *New York Times*, 24 June 1978; Diane Henry, " 'Holocaust' on TV Stirs Poles' Anger", *New York Times*, 23

argues that debates surrounding the legal processes of American democracy and the Holocaust were in fact relevant only to these limited sections of the polity and did not have a large impact on American society as a whole.

> But most early cases didn't get much publicity, except in the communities where the target resided and within the ethnic community from which he came. (Although in some, though not all, Eastern European ethnic organizations there was angry talk of persecution, often with an anti-Semitic subtext, but their complaints didn't attract the attention of the wider public.[29]

Again the issues here are many and complex and beyond the scope of this work. Nonetheless it is necessary to highlight two connected concerns. The first is the obvious issue of the sheeting home of collective blame to immigrant groups because of the historical realities of the Holocaust. Not every Pole, Ukrainian, Latvian etc. was a perpetrator, but some were. The complexities of history can be and often are lost within a court case in which the ethnic or national identity of the individual accused is essential to the "successful" outcome of the case, understood either in individualized terms relating to the accused or in broader terms of legal pedagogy. The second element is one which is intimately connected with the first. Many of the ethnic groups in question fled the Soviet conquest of their countries. An almost innate anti-Communism informed collective identity and group politics within those groups in the United States. This placed them squarely within the orbit of U.S. Cold War politics and made them invaluable to the government of the day. At the same time, many of the crimes and horrors of the Holocaust were perpetrated as the result of this same anti-Communism, which melded with centuries old antisemitism and opportunity, as Lithuanians, Latvians, Estonians, Poles, Ukrainians etc. used the presence of Nazi invaders to battle for the national homeland against Jewish Bolshevism. In other words, the politics of anti-Communism which made these groups and individuals welcome into the United States polity were precisely the politics which caused them to kill millions of Jews in the Holocaust. American national memory here must always come into stark conflict with competing constructions of life and history in the Old Country.

All the complexities of these historical conflicts played (and continue to play) themselves out in the course of the American pursuit of alleged Nazi and collaborationist war criminals. What is the Holocaust for the Jewish victims

---

September 1979; Mark Hosenball, "Emigrés slam US Nazi Hunters", *New York Times*, 21 April 1986.

29. *The Holocaust in American Life*, op. cit., at 228 (footnote omitted).

of Nazism is constructed as a war of national liberation from Soviet domination by those who stand accused of atrocities. Those who were killed were not murdered, but executed in the war of national liberation. They were not Jews, they were Communists. The balance to be struck between and among these competing histories is the cost of battling over collective memory within the context of denaturalization and deportation hearings.

Finally, it is important to note that each of these and other connected issues is but a necessary consequence of the chosen course of legal action and its associated symbolism. The use of denaturalization and deportation proceedings and the symbolism of civil excommunication also carry another semiotics. The Holocaust and Holocaust perpetrators are here by definition and necessarily constructed as being un-American. On the one hand this does provide the opportunity to construct the events and individuals in question as not worthy of inclusion in the body politic. At the same time however, another reading of the un-American character of the Holocaust and of perpetrators can provide a more negative and less salutary meaning. Here the Holocaust becomes someone else's problem, an issue of Ukrainian or Lithuanian responsibility say, an issue to be litigated somewhere else as part of some foreign, non-American history and collective memory. The body politic washes its hands of the whole mess and cleanses itself through an expulsion of foreign matter. The prophylactic function of the law here rejects the Holocaust and the Holocaust perpetrator both as foreign to America. Again, the Holocaust is only American in a tangential and temporary fashion. It can then never be central to any issues of collective memory or political identity. The law incorporates the Holocaust only in order to render it irrelevant as not law and not American.

All of these elements can be seen in the case of Andrija Artukovic, who when last seen was a political refugee in the United States. The Holtzman Amendment had effectively removed the "political crime" defence in deportation cases of alleged perpetrators. Again, this served to create and reinforce a particular construction of the Holocaust and of law which was in essence in stark contrast to the image made by the earlier decisions in Artukovic's case. Thus in 1979, 27 years after the first Yugoslav attempts to extradite him, renewed efforts were made to remove the former Ustashe Minister from the country.[30] Once again Artukovic, as Allan Ryan would say, was given law. Efforts to deport him were met with lengthy legal maneuvers[31] and with claims

---

30. Ivor Davis, "Legal battle in US to deport Nazi collaborator", *Times*, 4 December 1979.

31. *Artukovic v. INS*, 693 F. 2d 894; *Artukovic v. Rison*, 628 F. Supp. 1370; *Artukovic v. Rison* 784 F. 2d 1354.

that the defendant was too old, frail, and mentally unfit to undergo legal proceedings.[32] Finally Artukovic was deported to Yugoslavia in February 1986, some 34 years after the first case against him was heard. He was sentenced to death by a Yugoslav court[33] and died in jail two years later.[34]

At some level then, Artukovic was judged and punished for his crimes. Yet at another level his case reveals the many difficult and troubling issues which surround United States' efforts to deal with alleged Holocaust perpetrators through denaturalization and deportation. First, as I have already argued, there must always be some doubt which hangs over the symbolic effect of such proceedings. The crimes of Artukovic are here necessarily and consistently constructed as a Yugoslav affair.[35] From the earlier hearings relating to the request for his extradition to his ultimate demise in a Zagreb jail cell, the case was always constructed as a Yugoslav concern and not as one dealing with events which were directly relevant to the United States. The idea established at Nuremberg that there are crimes so heinous that they offend the basic morality of humanity, that they are legally relevant to all members of the community of nations, is quickly, effectively and legally rejected by the American practice of de-Americanizing the Holocaust through denaturalization and deportation proceedings.

This position within American legal constructions of the Holocaust and of alleged perpetrators is reinforced by the very nature of offences created under the Holtzman Amendment and of the processes of denaturalization and deportation themselves. Thus, the offence in question, the breach of the law for which the individual is called to account and which is, as Allan Ryan has articulated, the core of the case against him or her under the rule of American law, is that they lied about or concealed their past in order to gain entry or citizenship. In other words, the technical legal violation of the basic principles of the American body politic is dissimulation or fabrication about one's role in the Holocaust, not one's role *per se*.

In some cases, almost inevitably, the government has been hoist on its own symbolic and legal petard. Thus, Tsherin Soobzokov was accused of having been a member of the Waffen SS and of having lied about it before gaining

32. "Croatian unfit to face court", *Times*, 31 January 1985.

33. Dessa Trevisan, "Artukovic sentenced to death for role in Croatian war crimes, *The Times*, 15 May 1986.

34. "Balkans Butcher dies", *Times*, 19 January 1988.

35. This also ignores, as far as American law is concerned, the problematic law and politics of ethnic or national identity in what was then Yugoslavia, the consequences of which have posed clear and stark questions about law and humanity in more recent times.

entry to the United States. However he was able to supply evidence that he had in fact declared his membership in the Nazi organization and that the CIA for whom he worked was well aware of his past. He was therefore permitted to stay in the United States because he had not in fact breached the relevant immigration provisions.[36] His crimes in the SS as a Nazi collaborator in the former Soviet Union were and are completely irrelevant to the United States justice system.

Again the way in which the law and the Holocaust are mutually constructed in the American popular and collective imaginary excludes the Holocaust from the possibility of being defined as an American legal phenomenon. The function of the law here is to protect the boundaries of America, the sanctity of the body politic, from foreign invasion. Its function is to serve literally and figuratively as a gatekeeper. The Holocaust is not American and is to be expelled from the American political and legal system through the mechanisms of the law itself. Not only does this mean that the focus as a matter of law must be not on what the perpetrator did but on the process through which s/he gained entry to the United States, but it must mean that the Holocaust must always be constructed as not American.

Such a construction of law, memory and history must have necessary political, legal and historical consequences. Thus, since the Holocaust and its perpetrators are constructed and created as un-American and the process deployed is that of denaturalization and deportation, the existence of a third country prepared to take the perpetrator is a necessary condition to the semiotics of law and the Holocaust (not) in the United States. In the absence of a request for extradition, a person deported from the U.S., and from any other country for that matter, has the right, within certain limits, to chose the country to which s/he is to be sent.

In some instances, defendants have opted to leave the country voluntarily for their former residence[37]; while others fled to countries more friendly to former Nazis.[38] Perhaps the most interesting and significant case here is that

---

36. "U.S. Dropping Suit Against Ex-SS Man", *New York Times*, 10 July 1980.

37. Thomas O'Toole, "Alleged Nazi Ex-Mayor Leaves U.S. in Justice War Probe: New Jersey Draftsman is 5th to Depart in 20 Months", *Washington Post*, 20 October 1984; "Former Nazi SS guard leaves U.S.", *St. Petersburg Times*, 22 January 1994; Michael Grunwald, "Ex-Nazi Guard, 73, Agrees to Forfeit U.S. Citizenship", *Washington Post*, 17 September 1998; Paul Zielbauer, "Accused Nazi Guard Leaves the Country", *New York Times*, 11 June 1999.

38. *UPI*, 2 March 1989, George Theodorovich fled to Paraguay. "Lisbon check on expelled bishop", *Times*, 18 August 1989, Valerian Trifa fled to Portugal.

of Konrad Kalejs. Kalejs stood accused of having been a member of the notorious Arjas Commando, a local paramilitary group responsible for the mass
killings of Jews and other atrocities committed in Latvia.[39] After the war Kalejs
fled to Australia where he obtained citizenship and shortly thereafter left to
take up residence in the United States. His story was summarized by Cunm-
mings J in the 7th Circuit Court of Appeals.

> ...Kalejs has been a financial success in the United States: he owns
> four homes, had assets in excess of a million dollars in the mid-
> 1980's and was able to post a $750,000 bond to secure his freedom
> while this case was pending. The Justice Department first set its
> sights on Kalejs in late 1984. But when he was about to be nabbed,
> he took $350,000 and fled to Canada and Australia. When Kalejs re-
> turned to the United States, he tried to assume a new identity and
> managed to elude capture for six months. He was finally arrested in
> Florida on April 19, 1985; government agents expended 1,500 hours
> in the search. In the more than eight years since his arrest, Kalejs has
> bitterly disputed the charges that he was an officer in a pro-Nazi unit
> that killed tens of thousands of people, and that he assisted in other
> persecutions as an army officer, policeman and concentration camp
> guard.[40]

Judge Cummings went on to say that

> The immigration judge and the BIA did not believe Kalejs' denials
> and neither do we....
> We hold, therefore, that the BIA was amply justified in concluding
> that Kalejs assisted in the persecution of people because of their race,
> religion, national origin or political beliefs within the meaning of the
> Holtzman Act.[41]

After losing an appeal to the Supreme Court, Kalejs was removed from the
United States.[42] However, as the holder of Australian citizenship and of an
Australian passport, Kalejs was allowed to choose to return to his country of
citizenship. Here again we see one of the fundamental weaknesses of the

---

39. See generally, Andrew Ezergailis, *The Holocaust in Latvia, 1941–1944* (Riga and
Washington: The Historical Institute of Latvia and The United States Holocaust Memorial
Museum, 1996). On Kalejs, see below chapters 8, 9 and 10.
40. *Kalejs v. I.N.S.* 10 F. 3d 441 at 442.
41. Ibid., at 445.
42. "US Deports Nazi Officer", *Press Association Newsfile*, 9 April 1994.

United States system of denaturalization and/or deportation. The aim, both ideological and legal, of such a process is simply to expel the evil foreign element from the body politic. There is no possibility and no willingness within such a set of mechanisms of reaching a legal conclusion on the substantive issue of perpetrator responsibility or culpability. That is quite clearly and intentionally not part of the symbolic significance of the American approach. That is to say, in American law, the illegality of the Holocaust, the not law of the Holocaust, is someone else's problem. Here, because Kalejs could choose to return to Australia where he would not be prosecuted the American purpose of civil excommunication can be served while any symbolic or legal construction of the substance of the Holocaust is left to others.[43] The Holocaust is not an American legal problem. Lying about it to come to the United States is an American problem. This border control function, the role and rule of law in defining in and defining out of the body politic is of course the basis of citizenship and of law within modern nation states and as I have already argued, was equally central to Nazi legal constructions of the Jew. The question here is whether the United States legal system is capable in current circumstances of defining the function of its legal system in controlling entry into the body politic in any way which would satisfactorily eliminate a jurisprudential parallel with the nature and function of the Nuremberg Laws.

Next, of course, even in those cases where the alleged perpetrators are returned to their countries of origin, that is to say to those places where the Holocaust occurred and where it must therefore be a matter of local legal concern, there can be no guarantee under the American system of denaturalization and deportation that a substantive legal proceeding will actually take place. Ironically, it is the death of the evil empire which has further complicated this problem. Historically, anti-Communism was central to United States foreign policy and domestic politics in so far as many immigrant communities were concerned. For them, attempts to denaturalize, deport or extradite fellow members were always caught up within the matrix of anti-Soviet politics. Extradition to any Soviet Bloc country would result in nothing more than a show trial without any real application of the rule of law. Such requests by the Soviets and others were based not in the real guilt of the accused but in attempts by the Communists to subvert émigré communities in their anti-Bolshevist efforts by discrediting them in American eyes. All evidence of the events of the Holocaust which had their source in Soviet documents or in eyewitness testimony from the East were inevitably

---

43. See infra, chapter 10.

and invariably tainted by the same falsehoods and political motivations. In sum, émigré objections to prosecutions of alleged perpetrators were firmly rooted in the basic and unswerving belief that the forces of evil were attempting to use and subvert American law and the system of justice for their own goals.[44]

Such claims met with some success in the U.S. courts. We have already seen that the perceived lack of reliability of Yugoslav evidence played a key role in early refusals to deport Andrija Artukovic. The dissenting appeals judge in the case of Konrad Kalejs clearly based his opinion in the belief that Soviet evidence was inherently unreliable.[45] Nonetheless, Artukovic was in fact deported to Yugoslavia and other defendants were later sent to stand trial in the Soviet Union. Here we encounter one of the dramatic and intriguing ironies of the Holocaust and the rule of law. The Soviet Union under Communism offered a particular and ideological construction of the Holocaust which served its own purposes. Crimes which were committed were the acts of "fascist criminals" and were inflicted upon the Soviet citizenry. The targeting of Jews and their singular status as victims of Nazism did not coincide with Soviet constructions of Nazism as the epitome of the final stages of capitalism. The crimes of the Nazis and their collaborators were crimes against the Soviet state, the Revolution, and the working class and peasantry, and had to be characterized as such. Further there can be no doubt that the Soviets did target particular national groups in exile for very specific political reasons.

Nonetheless, none of this refutes, negatives or denies the other historical reality of the Holocaust in the Soviet Union and of the role played by national groups in the Baltic States and elsewhere in perpetrating crime against Jews, Gypsies and others. Yet the result of the new freedom of the Baltic States for example has been to further problematize this part of history in that part of the world. While the Soviets were willing, often for their own political and ideological purposes, to place perpetrators like Karl Linnas on trial, the so-called newly democratic states of Latvia, Lithuania and Estonia have been more than reluctant to follow a similar course of action. Resurgent nationalism, revived right-wing political movements, the apparent need to construct a post-Soviet collective national identity which is overly reliant on a reconstructed history in which the Holocaust is a minor footnote to the glorious

---

44. See Walter Reich, "Deporting Our Nazis: We can't put them on trial but the Soviets could", *Washington Post Magazine*, 28 April 1985.

45. *Kalejs v. I.N.S.*, op. cit. at 448 et. seq. See the discussion below of the Demanjanjuk case.

struggle for freedom from Soviet domination,[46] have all led to the current situation in which the collaborationist past and the mass crimes against racial
and political enemies are placed contentiously in the legal framework of potential prosecutions of deported perpetrators.[47] Despite ongoing official government declarations that perpetrators will be punished to the full extent of
the new democratic legal system, many accused seem more likely to enjoy a
relatively peaceful retirement in the lands of their childhood.[48] The problem
here is that while the United States legal system has constructed the Holocaust
as un-American and therefore as someone else's legal and historical concern,
that someone else is often reluctant to invoke legal and political discourses to
construct a collective memory in which the Holocaust plays a role. The combined effect of the American decision to select collective legal amnesia and the
failure of perpetrator countries to come to terms with the past is that law now
serves no other role than to act as a barrier to entry of the Holocaust into the
public political and historical consciousness. In Lithuania for example,

> What is worrying to the country's Jews is the majority of Lithuanians
> who passively supported the murder of their neighbours 50 years ago
> and remain unconcerned by it still.[49]

The role of nationalism, anti-Soviet and now anti-Russian popular sentiment, antisemitism now mean that Jews again were never victims of atrocities committed by locals. Bolsheviks were executed in the struggle for national
liberation. A newly instituted democratic legal system cannot punish those
whose sacrifices and actions allowed its creation in the national framework.

Law has served to construct a symbiotic and prophylactic vision of the
Holocaust which means that it resides not in the collective memory of the
United States but always outside that memory. It is distinctly and always un-
American. At the same time of course, this legalized construction of Holo-
caust perpetrators as un-American is carried out in a particularly American
fashion. Indeed, the centrality of the legal process to this construction of the

---

46. See e.g. Alexander Cockburn, "Beasts of the Baltic: nous sommes tous…", Lithuanian war criminals", *The Nation*, 30 September 1991.

47. See also the discussion below, chapter 10.

48. See, Linda Bock, "Delay in Lileikis trial is termed 'an outrage'", *Sunday Telegraph*
(Worcester MA), 31 January 1999; Neela Banerjee, "Nazi war crimes trial ends a century
of martyrdom", *Sydney Morning Herald*, 30 January 1999; "Lithuania reopens Nazi case,
requests medical exam", *CNN.com*, 27 April 2000. Lileikis died in September 2000 without
having been judged for his actions.

49. Banerjee, op. cit.

Holocaust perpetrator as un-American operates again to illustrate in a particular legal context an intriguing and puzzling imagery of the rule of law and the Holocaust in American jurisprudence.

4. John Demjanjuk, the Holocaust and the Rule of Law

If any one set of legal and political circumstances can be said to embody and exemplify all of the disparate and conflicting tropes of the struggle for collective memory and the rule of law in America, it must be the case of John Demjanjuk. Ironically, those elements which made Demjanjuk's case a circumstance of singular focus, also made this instance into the epitome of the battle for the proper place of the Holocaust and the rule of law in American popular and legal consciousness. Again, it is not my intention here to relate in great or complete detail the entire history of John Demjanjuk and the American and Israeli justice systems. Others have done so and the ideological, political and legal lines have been clearly enunciated in the vast literature which surrounds the case.[50] The story here is one of a retired Ukrainian American auto worker from Cleveland who found himself accused by the United States Department of Justice of having lied about his wartime activities and having hidden the fact that he was a notorious concentration and extermination camp guard. In effect, Demjanjuk would stand accused of being Ivan the Terrible, the Ukrainian guard at the Treblinka extermination facility in charge of the gas chamber there. In other words, Demjanjuk, if the allegations against him were true, was the very epitome of the stereotypical sadistic hands-on Holocaust perpetrator, the beastly and sadistic killer who took pleasure in exterminating hundreds of thousands of Jews. Moreover, Demjanjuk was of Ukrainian origin. He came to embody the tens of thousands of non-German

---

50. See e.g., Yoram Sheftel, *The Demjanjuk Affair: The Rise and Fall of a Show-Trial* (London: Victor Gollancz, 1994); William Wagaaner, *Identifying Ivan: A Case Study in Legal Psychology* (Cambridge: Harvard University Press, 1988); Tom Techoltz, *The Trial of Ivan the Terrible: The State of Israel v. John Demjanjuk* (New York: St. Martin's, 1990); Henry Friedlander and Earlean M. McCarrick, "The Extradition of Nazi Criminals: *Ryan, Artukovic, and Demjanjuk*", 4 *Simon Wiesenthal Center Annual* 65 (1987); Jay L. Chavkin, "The Man Without a Country: The Just Deserts of John Demjanjuk", 28 *Loyola of L.A. L. R.* 769 (1995); Michael Gaugh, "The Strange Case of John Demjanjuk: An Argument for a Higher Ethical Standard n Immigration Proceedings Based on Criminal Conduct", 7 *Georgetown J. of Legal Ethics* 783 (1994); John Francis Stephens, "The Denaturalization and Extradition of Ivan the Terrible", 26 *Rutgers L. J.* 821 (1995).

perpetrators, the local populations in Occupied Europe who willingly assisted their German conquerors/liberators in the persecution and execution of Jewish populations. For the United States government in all of this, of course, Demjanjuk was yet another immigrant who had sullied the body politic by lying about and concealing his past. He did not belong in America.[51]

Of course there is another story, or another version of the same story. Demjanjuk was the victim of mistaken identity compounded by the machinations of the KGB and the complicity of the Department of Justice. He was not Ivan the Terrible, he had not served as a concentration camp guard at Treblinka or anywhere else. The testimony of the eyewitnesses who identified him as Ivan was flawed by the passage of time, by the incompetence of the Justice Department procedures and by the pressure and involvement of Soviet intelligence officials. The entire system of American justice was being manipulated and distorted not just against this one individual accused but against the entire community of Ukrainian Americans and by extension all immigrant groups from the Soviet Union and the Eastern Bloc.

> The record being established by the OSI in United States courts will not be remembered as a model for the United States judiciary. The selected prosecution of septuagenarians and octogenarians, on the basis of evidence selected and produced by the KGB, will not only irreparably damage the targeted victims and their nationality groups, but will permanently blemish our legal system.[52]

Here we find all of the themes which have characterized American and other attempts to deal with alleged Holocaust perpetrators according to domestic legal principles and processes. The accused are old men, who have lived quiet and productive lives in the freedom of the West. They are being selected for prosecution i.e. persecution based on a misunderstanding of history and on the manipulations of the evil empire. American justice must resist these Communist attempts to exploit and use the rule of law for its own ends.

The Demjanjuk case came to epitomize and embody these basic conflicts and discourses about law and the Holocaust not just in the United States but elsewhere as well. In part, the reason for this is simply temporal. While pro-

---

51. See e.g., *U.S. v. John Demjanjuk*, 518 F. Supp. 1362; *U.S. v. John Demjanjuk a.k.a. Grozy Ivan (Ivan the Terrible)*, 680 F. 2d 32; *cert. denied*, 459 U. S. 1036; *In the Matter of the Extradition of John Demjanjuk* 612 F. Supp. 544; *Demjanjuk v. Petrovsky*, 612 F. Supp. 571; *Demjanjuk v. Petrovsky*, 776 F. 2d 571.

52. S. Paul Zumbakis, *Soviet Evidence in North American Courts* (Chicago: Americans for Due Process, 1986).

ceedings against him were underway and the various competing discourses were being deployed about the Holocaust and collective memory, the decision about whether to adopt domestic legal actions against alleged perpetrators was being debated in Canada, Australia and Great Britain. In each of these jurisdictions, as we shall see in the chapters which follow, the same tropes and ideological positions were being trotted out by all sides—the passage of time, justice versus vengeance, the distortion of the history of heroic anti-Soviet resistance by the Captive Nations, the need to remember the victims of the Holocaust by bringing their killers to justice etc.—all of these positions were circulating in the West at the time John Demjanjuk was involved in his journey through the American and then the Israeli legal systems.

At the same time, the Demjanjuk case took on even more important international and historic dimensions when he was extradited to Israel. Demjanjuk became the second person after Adolph Eichmann to be brought to Israel to stand trial under the Israeli *Nazi and Nazi Collaborators Act* for his role in the Holocaust. The idea informing United States law and legal practice as well as American popular memory, that the Holocaust was a problem for someone else, here came home to roost. Instead of the Shoah being identified through the operation of American legal processes as an issue of Latvian, Lithuanian, Ukrainian or German responsibility, here it is clearly identified as an Israeli issue. The Israeli position, both legally and ideologically, that it has a special position in relation to the Holocaust, has always been problematic and highly contested.[53] Its right, as the national embodiment of the Jewish people and of the Jewish victims of the Holocaust, to try alleged perpetrators had been asserted in the Eichmann trial but had not again been tested. In international law terms, Israeli jurisdiction as the national representative of the Jewish victims of the Holocaust is problematic to say the least and would feature prominently in defence arguments challenging the legitimacy and legality of the trial.[54] Again, however, it is not my intention here to survey the technical legal arguments surrounding Demjanjuk's trial in Israel. Instead, I want to focus on some of the elements of the proceedings and discourses which

---

53. See Tom Segev, *The Seventh Million: The Israelis and the Holocaust*, (New York: Hill & Wang, 1994).

54. See the discussion of this and related issues of technical international law rules in, Annie Fung, "The Extradition of John Demjanjuk as 'Ivan the Terrible' ", 14 *N.Y.L.Sch. J. Int'l. & Comp. L.* 471 (1993); Rena Hozore Reiss, "The Extradition of John Demjanjuk: War Crimes, Universality Jurisdiction and the Political Offense Doctrine", 20 *Cornell Intl. L. J.* 281 (1987); Stephen Lubet and Jan Stern Reed, "Extradition of Nazis from the United States to Israel: A Survey of Issues in Transnational Criminal Law", 22 *Stanford J. Intl. L.* 1 (1986).

serve to highlight the ways in which the rule of law and the construction of a collective memory of the Holocaust were played out in this particular case. It goes without saying of course, that the collective memory in question is in fact multi-faceted and not hegemonic, as is the rendering of that memory within legal discourse and discourse about law. In this case, we find arguments about the role of the Holocaust and law within Israel itself, in addition to debates within the United States, since Demjanjuk was to some extent still an "American".

The trial and its sequelae in Israel can be broadly divided into two main areas of concern. First there are the technical legal aspects of the case and the way in which discourses about and analyses of these elements played themselves out. Again, these are by now familiar. Eyewitness testimony and its reliability, Soviet machinations and the forging of evidence etc. The second level of interest is the way in which the trial itself served other political, social, historical and legal purposes. Quite clearly from the very beginning, in Israel, where the Holocaust occupies a central but always problematized public space, the trial was intended to serve a variety of extra-legal purposes. It was again meant to place the Shoah at the center of political and historical identity. New generations of Israelis, particularly Sephardi Israelis, were to be taught the lessons of the Holocaust and the centrality of the Israeli state. The older generation was to once again have their day in court, both literally and figuratively.

In the earliest days of the trial it was clear that

> For Israel the educational value of the trial is justification enough for its being held now, 42 years after the end of the war. Demjanjuk is being brought to trial after works published by fringe historians indulged in some dubious historical "revisionism," aimed at demonstrating that the Holocaust never took place. The trial is intended to ensure that the Holocaust does not fade from memory.[55]

The pedagogical function of the trial was accompanied by a spectacular element. The case was heard not in a court building but in a converted theater and was subjected to publicity and media coverage befitting a true public event.[56] Soon after the trial began

---

55. Roy Isacowitz, "Israel split as Nazi guard goes on trial", *Sunday Times*, 15 February 1987.

56. See e.g., Ian Murray, "Theatre for show trial in Israel", *Times*, 16 February 1987; Gitta Sereny, "An irresistible agony", *Times*, 10 March 1987.

The crowds have started to come to the converted theatre in Jerusalem
where the grim story of the Nazi Holocaust is being told on stage. Yesterday there was standing room only.
Parties of schoolchildren were being brought for their real-life lesson,
and old people, whose main memory is of surviving are sitting with
moist eyes as they remember.[57]

The problem and conflict here would become clear as events proceeded.
The story is now well-known. Demjanjuk continued to deny his guilt. He
protested that he was a victim of mistaken identity and that the main piece of
evidence, an identity card with his photograph establishing that he was a concentration camp guard, was a KGB forgery. He was convicted and sentenced
to death. Events unfolded. *Glasnost* and *perestroika* opened up the Soviet
Union. Evidence emerged that the real Ivan the Terrible had either been killed
in an inmate uprising at Treblinka or had been identified and executed after
trial in the Soviet Union. The ID card was probably fake and the eyewitness
testimony was indeed erroneous. After often-complex legal proceedings and
appeals, Demjanjuk was declared innocent of the charges and allowed to return to the United States. The real question raised here is what this tells us
about the Holocaust, collective memory and the rule of law.

It is clear that the evidence in this case was faked, the eyewitnesses were
mistaken and John Demjanjuk was not Ivan the Terrible. For opponents of
war crimes prosecutions and American efforts to denaturalize and deport alleged perpetrators, this case confirmed all of their worst fears. Soviet evidence
is tainted, there is a vast conspiracy to attack and delegitimize immigrant
groups by staining them with the war criminal label. Of course, at the practical legal level this is not a conclusive argument. Evidence in one case was
problematic. Eyewitnesses can always be mistaken. The only practical consequence to be drawn from this is the need for greater care in constructing proceedings in the future. Ironically, the tainted evidence claim now has become
more difficult to make since all parties to similar proceedings will have better
and more complete access to files and witnesses. The Demjanjuk case, in
which exculpatory evidence was discovered in the Soviet Union by the defence,
demonstrates in its own way that the law can now work better. In this and
other ways the acquittal of John Demjanjuk demonstrated that the rule of law
does work even in those circumstances where many strong ideological and political forces and discourses work against it. Indeed, subsequent proceedings

---

57. Ian Murray, "Israelis of all ages are drawn to theatre to hear Holocaust tragedy",
Times, 19 February 1987.

in the United States have involved claims of prosecutorial misconduct in the Department of Justice as well as more recent steps to again remove Demjanjuk from the United States under the Holtzman Amendment.[58]

Indeed, there was certain evidence presented to the Israeli court that while the charges against Demjanjuk for which he stood trial could not be proved, there was in fact some indication that he had in fact been present as a camp guard. If he was not "Ivan the Terrible", he was in fact, "John the Bad Enough".[59] Calls to keep Demjanjuk in Israel for a subsequent trial once sufficient evidence had been gathered were rejected and he was eventually allowed to return to the United States where he continued his legal battles with the government. In all of this, the rule of law emerged triumphant. Israeli Justice Minister David Libai praised the Supreme Court's decision to release Demjanjuk in the following terms

> ...the Supreme Court has proven that Jewish judges in Jerusalem are capable of reaching a fair verdict, even in the case of a defendant who was indicted and convicted of crimes against the Jewish people.[60]

For Israel, the trial and eventual acquittal of John Demjanjuk raised many of the issues common in the various trials of perpetrators discussed above in the chapter concerning France. The basic conflict about law and the Holocaust became one of venue and genre, of choosing the appropriate discursive matrix in which to construct collective memory of the Holocaust. Law proved to be a particularly good and bad choice at the same time. Eyewitness and survivor testimony established again in dramatic, personal and collective terms the history and phenomenology of the Holocaust and its existential reality for the Israeli polity. The public spectacle provided an ideal venue and forum for the telling of the tale. Yet as French experience has shown the juxtaposition of history and legal principle often leads to a diminution of both, or at least to the creation of an insurmountable obstacle between the two. Israeli law was strengthened as a result of the Demjanjuk case, as were collective under-

---

58. See "Clean Up the 'Ivan' Case", *New York Times*, 5 August 1993; Patrice Gilbert, "Was Counsel Guilty of Fraud: Demjanjuk Case Now Haunts Former Prosecutor", *Legal Times*, 4 January 1994; "Internal Probe May Shed Needed Light on OSI Tactics", *Legal Times*, 6 January 1997; M.R. Kropko, "Federal Court Restores Demjanjuk's Citizenship", *Associated Press*, 21 February 1998; "U.S. Tries Again to Deport Demjanjuk", *Associated Press*, 19 May 1999; Mark Gillespie, "Demjanjuk seeking $5 million in damages", *Cleveland Plain Dealer*, 14 March 2000; "Demjanjuk Torture Lawsuit Dismissed", *Associated Press*, 14 July 2000.

59. See Mordechai Kremnitzer, "The Demjanjuk Case", in Y. Dinstein and M. Tabory (eds.), *War Crimes in International Law* (The Hague: Kluwer, 1996) at 321.

60. Press Release, 29 July 1993.

standings and positionings of the Holocaust, but the two were, in the end, established as separate and distinct discursive and ideological practices.

A similar result also obtained in the United States, but as the result of different political and ideological forces. Efforts to denaturalize and deport alleged perpetrators continue to this day. The U.S. legal system continues to deal with the aftermath of the Demjanjuk case as it always has, by drawing and maintaining clear lines between itself and the Holocaust. The only issue here is whether an accused lied to the United States government. Of course, other discourses also circulate around this and related cases, from Pat Buchanan's scarcely veiled anti-semitism to the mobilization of Ukrainian Americans to utilize the political momentum and circumstances of the case to assert and affirm their longheld grievances about their victimization and the distortion of the historical record.[61]

> The Demjanjuk episode brought to the surface tensions that had merely been simmering for a long time. Ukrainians rallied around their brethren not merely because they believed he was innocent, but because they saw his case as another slap as Ukrainian honor.[62]

More intriguing however for the positioning of the Holocaust and American legal memory is the decision of the 6th Circuit Court of Appeals in its decision to restore Demjanjuk's citizenship after his return from Israel,[63] or more recently still in the ongoing attempts by the Department of Justice to prove that Demjanjuk did something, somewhere, to someone at sometime, which would justify his removal from the American body politic.[64] In February 2002, the US District Court in Cleveland determined that Demjanjuk had in fact been a guard at Trawinki, Sobibor, Majdanek, and Flossenbürg and as such had "assisted in the persecution of civilian populations during World War II".[65]

---

61. See Philip Shenon, "The Buchanan Aggravation", *New York Times*, 19 February 1987; Patrick J. Buchanan, "Acquit Demjanjuk: The Case Is Weak", *New York Times*, 31 March 1987; Randell Rothenberg, "Newspaper Faults Columnist for Remarks on Jews", *New York Times*, 20 September 1990; Richard Bernstein, "The Roots of a Populist Who Would Be President", *New York Times*, 24 March 1996.

62. Glenn Sharfman, "The quest for justice: the reaction of the Ukrainian-American community to the John Demjanjuk trials", 2 *Journal of Genocide Research* 65 (2000) at p. 80.

63. See generally *Demjanjuk v. Petrovsky*, 10 F. 3d 338; Deborah Roy, "The Sixth Circuit's Reopening of *Demjanjuk v. Petrovsky*", 42 *Cleveland State L. R.* 737 (1994).

64. See "Demjanjuk: "I was not there", at death camps, Demjanjuk says in deposition", *Cleveland Plain Dealer*, 18 July 2001.

65. *United States v. John Demjanjuk*, USDC, Northern District of Ohio, Case No. 1:99CV1193, at para. 45.

More crucially, he had lied about this in various immigration proceedings which led to his obtaining citizenship. He was subjected to the "civil equivalent of excommunication".

Demjanjuk filed an appeal in April of 2002. Somewhat ironically in war crimes cases, his case is based primarily in an argument that the government's evidence against him is found solely in documents and that the prosecution ignored exculpatory eyewitness testimony.[66] Of course, we know that one of the strongest elements of arguments in favor of Demjanjuk's innocence in the Israeli proceedings was the fallibility of eyewitness testimony. In addition, of course, his lawyers successfully attacked the "forged" Soviet documents in that case. Thus, for Demjanjuk, documents lie, they do not tell the whole truth, eyewitnesses are mistaken unless they testify to his innocence. In this, he takes a position no different to that adopted by lawyers everyday in courts throughout the United States.

Again at some basic level these sets of proceedings and pleadings can only reestablish and reaffirm the primacy of the rule of law as the Court exercises its power to right an apparent injustice. In the first case, the harm inflicted upon Demjanjuk for being wrongly accused and sentenced to death as Ivan the Terrible, and in the second, to the integrity of the United States by Demjanjuk lying about his past to obtain entry to the country. What is remarkable about the former case however is the statement by the Court that

> It is obvious...that the prevailing mindset...was that the office must try to please and maintain very close relationships with various [Jewish] interest groups because their continued existence depended upon it.[67]

Steven Lubet has already analyzed the way in which this judicial narrative constructs and reflects a jurisprudential variant of

> ...the notion that Jews are able, through stealth or pressure, to exert unjustified sway over government bodies.[68]

What is also of importance here is the way in which narratives construct an idea of the Jews and in the circumstances of the Holocaust as somehow es-

---

66. See John Caniglia, "Demjanjuk to argue lack of witnesses", *Cleveland Plain Dealer*, 16 April 2002.

67. *Demjanjuk v. Petrovsky* at 355. See Steven Lubet, "That's Funny, You Don't Look Lke You Control the Government: The Sixth Circuit's Narrative of Jewish Power", 45 *Hastings L.J.* 1527 (1994).

68. At 1528.

sentially foreign to the government and judicial system of the United States. Inherent here is a notion that undue influence has been brought to bear because the interest in question is quite clearly foreign and contrary to the real concerns of the American polity and government. If that were not the case, no influence, undue or otherwise would be required. In other words the narrative of Jewish subterfuge is itself a subterfuge for exposing a basic and informing notion of American jurisprudence that the Holocaust is an entirely un-American affair. Therefore, if Jews seek to invoke the Holocaust as a matter of concern, that must simply serve to demonstrate the fact that their interests are not those of the United States. I am not asserting here that antisemitism of this variety is a dominant or predominant trope of American judicial discourse concerning the place of the Holocaust and of Holocaust perpetrators in American law. Rather I am making again the case that what always informs American legal discussions about the Holocaust is its necessary status as foreign to real and authentic American concern. A brief examination of two other instances when the American court system was faced with important questions about how it would construct the Holocaust and basic understandings of American jurisprudence will serve to illustrate my position in another set of circumstances.

5. Julius Streicher Meets the Holtzman Amendment: Constructing the Rule of Law and the Holocaust in America

I have already outlined the ways in which the Nuremberg construction of Nazi state criminality and of Nazi law as not law was itself subverted by the way in which the antisemite Julius Streicher was himself criminalized by the IMT. Two cases from the more recent past under the rubric of U.S. attempts to expel alleged Holocaust perpetrators reinforce this aspect of my argument that the rule of law constructs itself in ways which are inherently contradictory and often incoherent. Each case under study here reveals ways in which what is perhaps the most basic tenet of American constitutional jurisprudence, at least as an ideology is concerned, free speech has been radically reconstructed within the U.S. legal system in relation to the Holocaust.[69] Again, it is my argument here that these two instances can be read as examples of the

---

69. On this point, the discussion in Allan Hutchinson's *It's All in the Game*, op. cit., is extremely useful.

ways in which the Holocaust has been and continues to be excluded from American law through the processes of American law.

Vladimir Sokolov-Samarin, hereafter Sokolov, was for many years a successful and popular Russian language instructor at Yale University. In 1976, it was revealed that during World War II, he had served as a newspaper columnist for a Nazi sponsored publication and that he had written antisemitic propaganda pieces. He resigned his teaching post and waged a 13-year battle to avoid deportation.[70] Sokolov was not charged with having committed or ordered crimes against Jews. Instead he stood accused of having written antisemitic articles. In other words, he was charged with displaying an antipathy towards the body politic of the United States not by his deeds but by his words. According to the Court of Appeals,

> Under the pseudonym "Samarin," Sokolov wrote anti-Semitic articles urging the Soviet population to support anti-Jewish/Bolshevik actions taken by the Nazis, and articles criticizing the United States and Great Britain and seeking to aid in their military defeat. In addition, as deputy chief editor of *Rech*, Sokolov edited articles with these same themes.[71]

The focus of the appeal was whether there was sufficient evidence that he had made material misrepresentations to U.S. authorities as required by statute to justify his deportation and whether his activities in effect met another statutory ground for expulsion by showing that he had "advocated or assisted" in persecution. The Court found that he had in fact made material misrepresentations about his past.[72] What is of more interest here is the Court's approach to his activities as part of advocating or assisting in persecution.

The Court focuses primarily on two exemplary writings. First an article entitled "The Former Masters of Orel" in which Sokolov pictures "Kikes" as the hidden and evil controlling force behind the Soviet Union. The Court writes

> Altogether, Sokolov names forty-seven Jews in positions of responsibility, and at the end of his article he exhorts his readers to "Thrash them".[73]

The second article was entitled "Protocols of the Elders of Zion" and dealt with the infamous forgery as truth with editorial comments about how the se-

---

70. "Ex-Yale Instructor Faces Deportation", *New York Times*, 28 January 1982.
71. *United States v. Sokolov*, 814 F. 2d 864.
72. Ibid., at 872–73.
73. Id., at 867.

cret plan of Jewish domination had actually been "realized and instituted in the Kikes' state—the USSR".[74] Without a doubt Sokolov's writings are offensive, hateful examples of antisemitism. They are also consistent with the historical construction of a direct link between antisemitism and anti-Communism. The technical question here however is whether this activity constitutes advocacy of persecution or persecution. The Court had no difficulty in answering in the affirmative.

> The Government has shown that Sokolov's work as a German army propagandist involved his "advocating or assisting" in the persecution of Jews in the large area served by *Rech*. Although there was no showing of actual persecution of Jews in the Orel area resulting from these articles, it is plain on the face of DPA § 13 that advocating persecution in itself renders a person ineligible for a visa. In any case, such propaganda does assist persecution by creating an atmosphere of opinion in which such persecution is acceptable.[75]

What is interesting here is not how the Court interpreted the statute or how it reached its decision in a technical sense. Nor is it at this stage and level relevant to consider the moral status of Sokolov's words. Instead I want to underline here the ways in which the Court reflects both the causal assumptions deployed by the prosecution and the IMT in the Streicher case and the form of legal analysis which renders the Holocaust the Other of American law. American courts, particularly in the face of the First Amendment guarantee of free speech, are, to say the least, extremely reluctant to reach any conclusion which draws a direct causal connection between speech and conduct. Even in the field of criminal law and the technical area of incitement, a simple statement that speech creates an atmosphere or "climate of opinion in which such persecution is acceptable" would never sufficiently ground a charge or a conviction. Similarly, the idea that advocacy of persecution is offensive to the American polity applies only to those who are not members of the American polity. Hate speech of a kind more virulent than any engaged in by Sokolov is readily and freely propagated and protected by the First Amendment every day in the United States. *The Protocols of the Elders of Zion* can be easily purchased. Henry Ford was a well-known distributor of the *Protocols* not long before Sokolov wrote the articles in question. Once again, the role and function of the law in relation to the Holocaust here is to place it and all

---

74. Ibid.
75. Id., at 874.

related events and concepts outside the purview of the American legal imagination. Sokolov is responsible for persecution or the advocacy of persecution simply because he advocated that persecution in a time and place which was not America. Had he made similar statements to his students at Yale, First Amendment concerns and the rights of citizens would have been at the forefront of any debate concerning his activities. The Court can and does engage in the analysis of cause and effect and of "advocating persecution" here because the legal framework in which such analysis can and does occur is specifically aimed at the Un-American and at the protection of the body politic from foreign contamination.

A similar process and result obtained in the case of Ferenc Koreh.[76] Koreh served as the editor of the Hungarian newspaper *Szekely Nep* and later worked at the Hungarian Ministry of National Defense and Propaganda in the Information Section. Like Sokolov therefore he was accused of having served as a propagandist. The Court wrote

> For the purposes of summary judgment, the government accepts that Koreh did not write or edit any of these articles. There is no question, however, that the person holding the position of Responsible Editor on the masthead was criminally and civilly liable for all unsigned articles and for those for which the author was unavailable.[77]

During his tenure, the newspaper published fifty-five antisemitic articles of which fifty-one were unsigned. The tone and content of the articles are familiar.

> …*Szekely Nep* frequently coupled its strong anti-Semitic tone with statements supporting or encouraging the Hungarian government's steps to enact or to enforce various anti-Jewish measures.[78]

Koreh argued that such activities did not constitute the advocacy of persecution or persecution itself. The Court rejected his arguments in unequivocal and highly revealing terms.

> In making such a contention, Koreh overlooks that this case is not founded on causation theories of either tort or criminal law. The only issue is whether Koreh had satisfied the congressionally-imposed prerequisite for acquiring citizenship.

---

76. *United States v. Koreh*, 144 FRD 218; 856 F.Supp. 891; 59 F. 3d 431.
77. 59 F. 3d 413 at 434.
78. Ibid., at 435.

In any event, we unequivocally reject Koreh's contention that the propaganda activities of *Szekely Nep* did not "assist in the persecution" of Hungarian Jews. It runs counter to generations of history that attest to the maxim that the pen is at least as mighty, if not mightier, than the sword. That the Nazi powers, and their cohorts, placed great confidence in the power of the word is demonstrated by the emphasis they placed on propaganda.[79]

The Court then proceeds to quote directly from the IMT charges against Julius Streicher to buttress its argument and reaches the inevitable conclusion that

There was ample basis in the undisputed facts for the district court to conclude that Koreh's involvement in the publication of anti-Semitic articles by *Szekely Nep* assisted in the persecution of Hungarian Jews by fostering a climate of anti-Semitism in Northern Transylvania which conditioned the Hungarian public to acquiesce, to encourage, and to carry out the abominable anti-Semitic policies of the Hungarian government in the early 1940's.[80]

The Court here confirms and reinforces the legal and ideological message about the correct positioning of the Holocaust in American law and popular memory. The writings of newspaper journalists are to be condemned as foreign to the interests and policies of the United States. Propaganda, speech, does have a causal effect, when it is speech which is not American speech, in which case it simply is necessary to the blooming of democracy. Indeed, the Court recognizes that under the relevant legislation it need not really concern itself with a legally coherent finding of causation. Antisemitic speech clearly led to the Holocaust, as long as it was anti-Jewish rhetoric outside the United States. Again, as in Sokolov's case, the emphasis here is on the Otherness of the speech in question since if American norms were applied, American law would be powerless to expel and expunge the Holocaust from its own normative universe. Almost as importantly here, the Hungarian people, like the German people, can be exculpated from any responsibility for the Holocaust there since they were the victims of what the American judicial system has characterized as pernicious and effective propaganda.[81]

What is missing by necessity here is any analysis of the ways in which the Hungarian persecution of its Jewish population was itself also an always legal

---

79. Id., at 439.
80. Id., at 440.
81. See the discussion of the case of Imre Finta, *infra*, chapter 9.

and legalized persecution in its origins. Here the emphasis is placed on Koreh's advocacy of better and increased enforcement of the law instead of on the basic norm of legal and legitimate persecution of Jewish Hungarians. As always the dominant American legal theme is as it must be the complete opposition between law and the Holocaust.

The jurisprudential irony of these two cases, like all American legal efforts to deal with the issue of Holocaust perpetrators, is that the legal system must, in the end and in a very real way, abandon the basic ideals, rhetoric and principles of American constitutional identity and practice in order to successfully maintain the dominant mythological structures of the Holocaust as un-American. The great myth of the melting pot, of the Statue of Liberty, of a new life in an America where all are equal, must be delimited through a legislative and judicial construction of a border, a process of entry into the body politic which must be "honest". The ingredients of the melting pot must always remain separate and legally separable in order to avoid contamination.

Similarly, separate rules must apply inside and outside America when the "expression of ideas" is concerned. Inside America, for Americans, it is perfectly acceptable, in the constitutional sense, to call for the destruction of world Jewry, to condemn Jews as conspirators against God's true, white American people. To make similar statements in the former Soviet Union or in Hungary in the 1940s makes one unsuitable for membership in American society and unprotected by the Constitution. Nazis are not wanted unless they are American Nazis. This is the tragedy of the Holocaust in American law. It is built on a belief that the Holocaust has nothing whatsoever to do with American law. I must repeat here that I am not arguing that America today, or America in the early part of the century is or was, Nazi Germany. Instead, I am asserting that attempts to mask the relationships which do exist between law, then and now, and the Holocaust, do us all a disservice.

What American law and its construction of the Holocaust symbolize and embody is, again, the un-American nature of the mass killing of European Jews. "They", the perpetrators come here and "we" give them law. The gift of America is justice or at least law. Auschwitz as law can have no place in this vision of the Holocaust. The Shoah was without law, its perpetrators are outlaws, and they must be placed outside American law. The melting pot of American identity must reject and exclude all attempts to Americanize the Holocaust at any level which would directly and in reality legalize the Holocaust. Popular imagination, Hollywood, and law are all mustered to keep America, democracy and the law free from taint, after Auschwitz.

CHAPTER 8

"To Draw the Sponge across the Crimes and Horrors of the Past": Prosecuting (or Not) the Holocaust in Britain

1. Introduction

The story of the prosecution (or not) of perpetrators in Great Britain in recent years offers us still more intriguing insights into the ways in which rule of law rhetoric has been invoked throughout the construction of our collective legal memory of the Holocaust. Britain, like the United States and France, was one of the four major Allies. It was a signatory to the Moscow agreement on the pursuit of war criminals and was a prosecuting power at Nuremberg. In addition, British courts in Germany tried those accused of war crimes and crimes against humanity in its Zone of Occupation.[1] Thus, at a very real and official level, British legal memory and practice inscribed the Holocaust as an illegal event.

At the same time, however, British legal and memory about the Holocaust is also shrouded by an official and unofficial amnesia. Dunkirk, the "Battle of

---

1. See for example, *The Trial of Joseph Kramer and Forty-Four Others: The Belsen Trial* (London: William Hodge & Co., 1949) and A.P.V. Rogers, "War Crimes Trials Under the Royal Warrant: British Practice 1945–1949", 39 *International and Comparative Law Quarterly* 781 (1990). On related legal difficulties arising out of conflicts between the rule of law and wartime necessity, see G.R. Rubin, "In the Highest Degree Omnious: Hitler's Threatened Invasion and the British War Zone Courts" in Katherine O'Donovan and Gerry R. Rubin (eds.), *Human Rights and Legal History: Essays in Honour of Brian Simpson* (Oxford: Oxford University Press, 2000).

Britain", the British bulldog spirit etc. are all invoked in public commemora-
tion ceremonies and the world of popular culture as part of the historical account which constructs Britain as successfully defending itself from Hitlerism.
Blood, sweat and tears were shed in order to ensure that Britain never suffered
the horrors of occupation, collaboration and extermination. These were the
fate of the others, of "Europe", of the weak-kneed French or of the valiant but
out-numbered Dutch for example. At the same time, the Holocaust, like the
war, is constructed as a German phenomenon. Basil Fawlty stumbles about
trying not to mention the war, while everyone in Britain gets the joke, the
Germans still have a lot to answer for.

Like all official and unofficial constructions of the traumatic events of the
Holocaust, the British account is fatally flawed. The British Channel Islands
were of course occupied and anti-Jewish measures, including transportation
and death, were implemented against Jewish residents.[2] Another flaw which
goes to the heart of British memory and the rule of law after Auschwitz ironically begins in the role played by Britain in Occupied Germany and in the
Nuremberg Trials of Major War Criminals.

As I have already argued, a key element of the construction of the Holocaust played by the proceedings at Nuremberg was the way in which responsibility was placed squarely on the shoulders of the German elite. This had a
major impact on two separate but connected aspects of British post-war rule
of law discourse about the Holocaust. First, it placed primary, if not sole, responsibility on the elite leadership of Hitler's regime, as played out in the representative selection of defendants first at Nuremberg proper and subsequently
at the post-Nuremberg proceedings. This meant that the mass of documentary evidence amassed and introduced at Nuremberg about the actual me-
chanics of the Shoah was distorted and constructed in such a way as to minimize the legal, moral and factual responsibility of first order, but low level,
perpetrators. In fact and in law, these people, both the ones who pulled the
triggers and staffed the bureaucracies, were portrayed as "just following orders" or as the victims of the brutal ideological and police hierarchies which
characterized Germany from 1933–1945. They were another set of victims of
the mass psychology of fascism first inscribed in the legal memory at Nuremberg.

Of course, lower level perpetrators were subjected to legal processes to determine their guilt. Post-1948 jurisprudence in Germany, especially in the Fed-

2. See David Fraser, *"Quite contrary to the principles of British justice": The Jews of the Channel Islands and the Rule of Law, 1940–1945* (Brighton: Sussex Academic Press, 2000).

eral Republic, is filled with cases involving camp guards and others. It remains
nonetheless true that for most, particularly outside Germany not individually
affected by the accused, these trials played little if any role in constructing the
legal reality of the Holocaust. They were simply mopping up exercises which
never truly contested the legal fictions established at Nuremberg.

The second level at which the British legal construction of the Holocaust at
Nuremberg had an adverse and counter-factual effect on juridical and public
memory was the way in which the "war" which is not to be mentioned was and
is a "German" war. Consequently, the Holocaust was and is a German issue. The
role played by other national groups, from the Baltic States to the Ukraine, (not
to mention local authorities in Jersey, Guernsey or Sark), was not simply forgotten, it was never remembered because it was not part of the official legal and
public memory of the Holocaust. Nuremberg was the "Trial of the Germans". If
there was intellectual or legal handwringing about the problematic concept of
collective guilt in British jurisprudence, that conflict manifested itself in debates
about the extent to which the German people, as opposed to the German leadership, or "the Nazis", were to be held accountable. This might have and did raise
issues about the feasibility of "democratization" of West Germany, or in the psychological collective angst in parts of the British public over the question of "Europe" today. What is perfectly clear is that the question of responsibility, as a
legal or philosophical concern, of individuals or groups, never reached beyond
the German borders in any serious aspect of British politics or legal practice.

As in the cases of Australia, Canada and the United States, this is in part at
least attributable to the nature and concerns of the Cold War. As anti-Soviet
ideology became the centerpiece of post-War politics in the West, places such
as the Baltic States of Latvia, Lithuania and Estonia, and to a lesser extent in
Britain perhaps, Poland and the Ukraine, became rhetorical sites of the great
struggle with the Evil Empire. The repression of nationalist sentiment in these
areas and their forcible incorporation into the Union of Soviet Socialist Republics, or in the case of Poland into the Warsaw Pact alliance, became both
in practice and in metaphor, symbols of the evils of the Soviet Union. Baltic
nationalism became anti-Soviet nationalism, which was, by definition, good.
Again, the rise of nationalist cooperation with the German invaders during
the war was constructed as cooperation against Bolshevism and the Soviets.
Lithuanians, Latvians and Estonians who joined the SS were not Nazis, they
were anti-Communists. The enemy of my enemy is my friend became the ideological and political watchword as the West created its primary enemy as Soviet Communism.

Thus, the war and the Holocaust were German phenomena, perpetrated
by a criminally insane Nazi leadership engaged between 1933 and 1945 in a

conspiracy against civilized world order. The new Germany, purged of its Nazi past through the implementation of the rule of law at Nuremberg and the successfully enforced legal, administrative process of deNazification became a Western ally against Communism. The Captive Nations in the Baltic and elsewhere became our friends against Communism. Indeed, they battled Communism while we were busy with the Nazis. As a consequence, it would be unpatriotic to accuse the valiant anti-Communists of the Captive Nations of participating in the Holocaust when they were in fact participating in the war against Communism.

2. The First Stage of Legal Forgetting: The Holocaust and British Law, 1945–1980

At the same time as the West "forgot" Captive Nations' responsibility in the Holocaust, the Soviets continued to insist upon it. For the USSR, the construction of the Great Patriotic War was essential in the ideology of the Stalin and post-Stalin eras. The struggle of the working class led by the Party against the Nazi fascist aggressors was a glorious example of the triumph of the revolutionary spirit. This triumph naturally came at a great cost. The destruction of large parts of the Soviet Union and the death toll in that country were enormous, almost unfathomable to the West and beyond the scale measured in terms of the Blitz. A natural desire for revenge and the punishment of the guilty became key elements in Soviet politics and legal strategy.[3] At the same time, Soviet nationalities policy could be reinforced by characterizing and stigmatizing various groups as Fascist opponents of the Soviet Union and as mass murderers.[4] Overseas agitators could be dismissed as war criminals. Later, the Soviet Union could draw upon its pursuit of Holocaust perpetrators in order to attempt to differentiate its policy in relation to Israel and Jewish immigration (anti-Zionism) from accusations of antisemitism.

At one and the same time then, the constructions of the Captive Nations' record in relation to the Holocaust represented conflicting ideological constructions of the two sides in the global struggle. The Balts were for the British victims of Communism who had fought against the enemy of democracy and the rule of law. For the Soviets, Baltic exile groups were war criminals and en-

---

3. See e.g., Ginsbergs, *The Soviet Path to Nuremberg*, op. cit.
4. See Lucjan Dobroszycki and Jeffrey S. Gurack (eds.), *The Holocaust in the Soviet Union* (Armonk, N.Y.: M.E. Sharpe, 1993).

emies of the state. Lost in all of this, although lost less to "the Russians" than to the British, was the historical record of the Holocaust, a record which proved beyond any real doubt that collaboration in the extermination of Jews in the Baltic states and elsewhere in the German-occupied Soviet Union was rife among Lithuanians, Latvians and Estonians, as it was among Poles, Ukrainians etc. etc.

It was in relation to one other region of post-War Europe where the British legal amnesia about the Holocaust and its perpetrators began. In late 1947 and 1948, British authorities were faced with extradition requests from the government of Yugoslavia in relation to individuals held by them and against whom allegation of serious criminal misconduct had been made. The debates on the matter in the British Parliament reveal all of the concerns which would re-surface forty odd years later there and elsewhere as a result of attempts to revive prosecutions of alleged perpetrators. Issues of the impossibility of fair trials in a Communist country, the confusion over loyalties during the war, with Nazi invasion and internecine battles, the distinction between justice and revenge, and most importantly the relationship between the passage of time and concepts of British justice and the rule of law, all were debated as the government of the day decided to draw a sponge across the past and to adopt a policy of forgetting and forgiving. The position of the majority was expressed by the Member for Birmingham, King's Norton, Mr. Blackburn when he spoke in the House of Commons,

> ...but it is intolerable that, over two years after the end of the war, and sometimes three, four and even five years after the alleged crimes were committed, people should still be brought up on these charges. I feel it is high time that this business of raking up the troubles of the past should come to an end.[5]

The government of the day accepted all of these arguments and the fate of mass killers in British custody in Europe or of those who had managed to immigrate to Britain was to be allowed to live in peace. "The troubles of the past", in the Yugoslav context including the extermination of Jews, Roma, not to mention political, national and religious rivals, were not to be raked over. British justice and the rule of law demanded silence and forgetting. Two years was more than long enough.

Here, the effect of legal amnesia and ideology, as was the case in relation to Australia and Canada, as well as to the United States to a lesser extent, was

---

5. *Hansard*, 4 December 1947, col. 688.

the construction of a system of law which granted safe haven to the killers of European Jewry. It was this image of Britain as a safe haven for perpetrators which would come to be the contested metaphorical terrain of legal memory.

The earliest stages of the construction of legal memory of the Holocaust in Britain, however, fit more precisely into the dominant and broader political and ideological framework. In 1960, within the same strategy which saw the USSR track down Ervin Viks to Australia,[6] the Soviets requested the extradition from Britain of Ain Mere. Mere was an Estonian who, according to the Russians, was in charge of organizing the concentration camp at Jagala and was responsible for the extermination of 125,000 civilians. The Soviet extradition request was made in November 1960 and was rejected by the British government a few months later.[7] He was later tried, convicted and sentenced to death *in absentia*.[8]

The rhetoric which was invoked by the parties concerned with this matter is not just revelatory, but is also a clear precedent for much of the debate which would resurface in Britain years later. Not surprisingly, the Soviet case revealed the details of the atrocities attributed to Mere. Additionally, however, the Soviets resorted to an invocation of the legal historical record of which Britain was a part. Thus, in the original note handed to the British ambassador in Moscow with the extradition request the Russians specifically appealed

> ...to the international agreement of states taking part in the coalition against Nazi Germany, according to which war criminals should be handed over for trial and punishment to countries where they have committed their crimes.[9]

The Soviet appeal to the Moscow agreement, the first real collective declaration by the Allies concerning their policy of pursuing war criminals, is not without political and semiotic merit. Here, the USSR positions itself not as the enemy of Britain but as its wartime ally, following a joint program. Moreover, the Soviet Note by allusion invokes all of the rule of law discourse which surrounded and informed Allied prosecutions of Nazi war criminals. They appeal to ideas of contract and consent and of international law norms govern-

---

6. See infra, chapter 10.

7. See "Soviet Demand to Britain", *Times*, 11 November 1960.

8. See "Former Estonian To Be Tried in Absence", id., 1 March 1961; "Soviet Trial Opens in Estonia", id., 7 March 1961; "Orgies in Estonian Camp", 8 March 1961; "Death Sentence on Estonian in Britain", 13 March 1961.

9. "Soviet Demand To Britain", op. cit. "New Russian Demand for Estonian", *Times*, 1 May 1961; "Soviet Extradition Call Refused", 24 June 1961.

ing the prosecution of perpetrators, in which the idea of Nuremberg style tribunals was replaced with the more practical and traditional international norm and practice of allowing the country most affected by the individual's alleged criminal acts to try that individual.

I am not suggesting here that Soviet motives were chaste and pure. Rather I wish yet again to underline the ease with which rule of law discourse can be invoked in relation to the Holocaust in completely contradictory ways. At the same time, this caveat should not be read as an argument that the Soviets were "wrong" to invoke the Moscow accord or to want to pursue Mere. Whatever the complex mix of their motives, the true nature of local collaboration with the Germans and participation in the Holocaust remains an historical given. Rather, I wish to underline the ease with which rule of law discourse in relation to the Holocaust can be invoked but also the ease with which it can be rejected by counter-arguments which are themselves equally grounded in our understanding of the rule of law and the norms of democratic self-governance.

Mere himself adopted two strategies which appear again in cases involving attempts to prosecute alleged perpetrators. Each of these strategies is grounded in familiar political discourses. More important for present purposes, each strategy also depends on basic jurisprudential understandings. The first of these involves a refutation of the accuser, of characterizing the accusation as motivated by extraneous, extra-legal factors. In the case of Soviet allegations, they are simply placed onto the broader political tropes of the Cold War, anti-communism and Captive Nations ideology. Thus, for Mere

> It is no more than an attempt by the Russians to discredit all Estonians now living in the free world.[10]

Russians and the free world are semiotically and politically opposed. Individual responsibility is obfuscated under the guise of an alleged attack on a collectivity "all Estonians". While Soviet antipathy to émigré groups was well-known, this use of a collective identity as an "excuse" cannot really or convincingly stand by itself under the light of rule of law discourse. While it may be invoked to undermine the credibility and *bona fides* of the accuser, criminal responsibility in the "free world" is a matter of individual guilt or innocence.

This brings us naturally to the second part of the rule of law based attack on Soviet use of rule of law rhetoric against alleged perpetrators. This simply involves the denial of guilt by a refutation of the factual basis of the accusa-

---

10. "Estonian Denies Soviet Charges", *Times*, 12 November 1960.

tion. For Mere, this involved a claim that he was nothing more than a bureaucrat involved in the reorganization of the Estonian police force, where he served as a welfare officer acting for the benefit of the Estonian police who operated solely under the orders of the Germans. According to Mere,

> He hated police work and applied in 1942 for his release, which was granted a year later, when he joined the Estonian Legion fighting with the Germans on the Russian front.[11]

This early public construction of the legal and political situation of émigrés in Britain accused of war crimes and participation in the Holocaust could serve as a template for all subsequent cases. Here we find the prototypical "anti-Bolshevist" position of the collaboration which characterized many Balts. Mere did not like police work but happily and voluntarily joined the SS to fight the Communists. Thus, at a time when the Soviet Union was an ally of Britain, Mere took up arms against that ally. At the same time, Mere perpetuates two of the most commonly invoked defenses or myths which arise in such cases. First, he himself was a simple welfare officer who did not therefore do anything even if there is proof that other Estonian police officers did participate in atrocities. Second, the local police was "commanded by German officers". This of course means that the Estonians, if they did anything, which Mere himself did not, did so under German orders and most likely, since we know from Nuremberg that the German military and police apparatus was a terror machine, acted under compulsion, not to mention the threat of death.

Furthermore, Mere asserted, and this was undoubtedly true, at least to some extent, that

> My record was checked by security officials when I came to England over 10 years ago.[12]

The necessary implication of this, in the Great Britain of the early 1960s, is that no Nazi collaborator, guilty of mass extermination of Estonian Jews and others, would have escaped detection by Britain's elite security services and been allowed to enter the country. The fact of being allowed to enter Britain was almost in and of itself sufficient and incontrovertible evidence of the falsity of Soviet charges. This would be a theme which would be the undoing of legal amnesia about the Holocaust and the rule of law in Britain. At the time of Mere's statement, no one in Britain and certainly no one in the British government was going to dispute either this recitation of facts or the

11. Ibid.
12. "Soviet Trial Opens in Estonia", op. cit.

historical and ideological edifice on which it was based. *A fortiori,* no questions or doubts could be raised in a case involving accusations stemming from the untrustworthy Soviet authorities.

We know, nonetheless, that at the time, 1943, when Mere was transferred from the Estonian police to the SS, Estonia was the one area of occupied Europe declared *Judenrein,* completely free of Jews. The report of June 5, 1942 to the Chief of Security Police concludes

Today, there are no more Jews in Estonia.[13]

The Wannsee conference where the details of the Final Solution were put in to place reported that Estonia was *judenfrei.*[14] Furthermore, we know from the Germans themselves that the extermination of Estonian Jewry was accomplished by the local self-defense force, the *Selbstschutz.*The historical basis for Estonian culpability, or at least for the culpability of many Estonians, is and was clearly established in 1960–1961 when the Soviet authorities were calling upon their former allies to extradite Mere for trial.

Mere's personal culpability was demonstrated at the Soviet trial by the testimony of his co-accused, Ralf Gerrets and Jan Vijk, and by the evidence of the 39 other witnesses against him.[15] Of course, it is important to note that the concept of "truth" and the conduct of criminal trials against alleged war criminals in the Soviet Union in 1961 may not have been in complete accord. Indeed, after Mere's conviction *in absentia* his defense counsel, an assistant professor at Tartu University, was quoted as saying that

It is difficult to return to a country where Mere has committed such brutal crimes, where a severe punishment is awaiting him, but this is the only price by which he can rid himself of the heavy burden of the past, can become a human being again.[16]

If one is concerned with the rule of law, it might be well to interrogate the ease with which defense counsel clearly opted into the prosecution case and verdict against his client. Moreover, one might wonder how and why the two co-accused so readily admitted their guilt. Soviet pre-trial interrogation tech-

13. See, Yitzhak Arad et. al. (eds.), *The Einsatzgruppen Reports* (New York: Holocaust Library, 1989), at 347.
14. See "Protocol of the Wannsee Conference, January 20, 1942" *Documents on the Holocaust* (Tel Aviv: Yad Vashem, 1981) 249 at 255.
15. See "Soviet Trial Opens in Estonia", op. cit. See also "Orgies in Estonian Death Camp", *Times,* 8 March 1961.
16. "Death Sentence On Estonian in Britain", *Times,* 13 March 1961.

niques were not governed by the niceties of the Miranda warning, Judges' Rules, or of PACE. At the same time, of course, it may equally be true that Gerrets and Wijk, as well as Mere, were simply guilty of the offences charged. The errors or terrors of Soviet justice in 1960–1961 do not by definition exclude the possibility that members of the Estonian police were in fact guilty as perpetrators of the Holocaust in their country. Certainly the historical record might at the very least be seen to offer a *prima facie* counter-inference to Mere's claims that as security police chief he was nothing more than a puppet of the Germans and someone who simply looked after the welfare of his men without having any operational role.

However, it was clear from the very beginning of the USSR's attempt to extradite Ain Mere from Britain that historical truth played very little if any part in the decision-making process in the home of Westminster democracy and the rule of law. Mere could not be extradited to the Soviet Union for trial because Britain was bound, by the rule of law itself, to refuse such a request. According to the government

> ...at no time had Britain recognized Estonia's incorporation in the Soviet Union.[17]

In other words, the rules and norms of the international legal community generally and the principles of the Moscow agreement specifically prevented Britain from acceding to the extradition. The Moscow Accord gave to the country in which the crimes had been committed or against whose citizens they had been perpetrated, primary jurisdiction over the alleged war criminal. That country in this case was Estonia. Estonia was not yet able to exercise this jurisdiction because of its illegal incorporation into the Soviet Union. The rule of law prevented Ain Mere, former police chief in the first country to complete the Final Solution, from facing a judicial proceeding to account for his actions. He died in peace in 1969, untroubled by the legal authorities.[18] The rule of law triumphed. Whether the loser was vengeance or justice is another question, raised again in the case of George Chapell.

George Chapell began life as Yuri Yepifanovich Chapodze in the Soviet territory of Georgia. He legally changed his name when he emigrated to England after the war. Ten years after the refusal of the British government to extradite Ain Mere to Estonia to face mass murder charges, the Soviet Union tried its

---

17. "Soviet Trial Opens in Estonia", op. cit.
18. See Philip Jacobson, "Nazi hunter insists that war criminal suspects in Britain be identified", *Times*, 7 March 1987.

luck again and sought the return of George Chapell.[19] The Soviets alleged that Chapell had helped kill 5000 Jews in the Ukraine during the German occupation. Chapell was named as a participant in mass killings by other perpetrators during the course of their trials in the USSR.[20] Again, he proclaimed his innocence and denounced the motives of his attackers. He declared

> This is a Russian demand. They say what they like. I deny everything. These are all lies.[21]

This time however, because Chapell did not come from the Baltic states, the British government was forced to establish other legal reasons for their refusal to extradite him to the country where he was alleged to have committed his crimes against humanity. This they did by invoking other international legal standards which permitted them to reject the extradition request, again on grounds consistent with the rule of law. First, the British government argued correctly that there was no extradition treaty extant between it and the Soviet Union. Therefore, there was no international "contractual" obligation to send Chapell back to face his accusers. This does not end the matter however since extradition may occur under international law in the absence of an express treaty. However, the extraditing country has great, indeed almost unlimited, discretion to accede or not to requests in such circumstances. In cases involving the proposed extradition of a British resident to the Soviet Union to face trial on such charges, the UK government simply had to conclude, as it did in this instance, that Soviet procedural safeguards were not sufficient to guarantee a fair trial. In other words, as with Mere, the rule of law had to be upheld by refusing to allow the trial of a man alleged to have been involved in the killing of 5,000 Jews. No further action was required and Chapell returned to his English wife and their small boarding house in Bournemouth.

3. Further Action is Required: The Anton Gecas Case

The "cases" against Mere and Chapell faded into distant recesses of legal and popular memory. The Holocaust and the fate of the perpetrators did not, however, fade away. As time passed, a new generation of investigators and his-

---

19. "Moscow told man will not be returned", *Times*, 25 April 1970.
20. Garry Lloyd, "Refugee denies role in killing 5,000 Jews", id.
21. Ibid. See also "Chapell to call at Foreign Office", 27 April 1970.

torians began to focus on the Shoah and the role played by the Allied powers in failing to come to terms with the past. The creation of the Office of Special Investigations in the United States meant that the resources of the major Western power were turned to the task of tracking down alleged perpetrators.[22] In turn, the generational passage also meant that historians and journalists in other countries, including Britain, began to re-examine the war and post-war periods. Canada[23] and Australia[24] began their own investigations into the possibility that post-war immigration had served as a mask to grant safe passage and haven to Nazi war criminals. Among the insights gained in these two countries was the confirmation that the former colonial master, Britain, had prevailed upon the dominions to extend migrant status to suspected perpetrators. Suspicion quickly refocused on the United Kingdom as a likely refuge for perpetrators.[25]

In October of 1986, the Simon Wiesenthal Center in Los Angeles delivered a list containing the names of individuals suspected of having participated in the Holocaust, and who were believed to be living in Britain.[26] As we shall see later, the Wiesenthal Center list eventually led to the adoption of the British *War Crimes Act*. Before the issues of memory, the Holocaust and the rule of law would be played out in the House of Commons and the House of Lords, however, legal memory and the Shoah would first appear in the newspapers, on television, and finally in private litigation for defamation. In Britain's "first war crimes" case, the stakes would involve not a public prosecution of an alleged perpetrator meant to establish his criminal liability but rather a private action instigated by the alleged perpetrator to defend his reputation. Ironically perhaps, these proceedings would involve not a search for "justice" or the imposition of retribution. Instead, they would revolve around a concept which sits uncomfortably within the Anglo-American tradition of criminal law, "truth", an idea sometimes relevant to the law of defamation. In its own way, then, British legal history and memory concerning the Holocaust and the rule of law, went more to the heart of the matter in relation to the Shoah than would or could subsequent criminal proceedings. Here, the public/private distinction operated in such a way that the private pursuit of "truth" may be seen to have served the interests of public memory.

---

22. See supra chapter 7.

23. See infra chapter 9.

24. See infra chapter 10.

25. The history of British immigration policy and the influx of alleged perpetrators is documented in David Cesarani, *Justice Delayed* (London: Heinemann, 1992).

26. "Nazi war criminals 'in Britain'", *Times*, 18 October 1986; Nicholas Beetson, "More Nazis 'still living in Britain'", *Times*, 24 October 1986.

The case in question involved Antanas Gecas (formerly Gecevicius).[27] Gecas was named in the Wiesenthal Center list as having participated, as a member of a Lithuanian auxiliary police battalion, in the killings of Jews in German occupied areas of the Soviet Union.[28] Gecas, a retired mining engineer, lived in an Edinburgh suburb. At first blush, the case of Antanas Gecas appeared to bear striking similarities with the early incidents involving Mere and Chapell. The construction of the Baltic States, in this case Lithuania, as Captive Nations, of Lithuanians who fought with the Germans as freedom fighters against the Russian Bolshevik enemy, of accusations as Soviet inspired lies etc., all would emerge during the course of events surrounding Gecas. But in addition to changes, both generational and historical in the West, the Soviet bloc was at this time undergoing the transformations of *glasnost* and *perestroika* which would lead to the eventual break-up of the Soviet Union. At this time, 1986–1987, Prime Minister Margaret Thatcher had adopted the idea that Soviet leader Gorbechov was someone with whom the West could "do business". This did not mean, however, that the traditional elements which has always colored the construction of the Baltic Holocaust and the legal pursuit of perpetrators did not play a significant part in the case of Antanas Gecas.

From the very beginning, Gecas constructed himself as the victim of a Communist plot. He stated that

> The Russians have been hammering and hammering about me since the end of the war.

He then added:

> This is just propaganda. I fought the Russians during the war and would fight them until I drop. They want me for that.[29]

Gecas, however, went further and added to the legal and factual complications which would later cloud his case. He did not deny that he was present

---

27. The story of the Gecas case is related in Roger Hutchinson, *Crimes of War: The Antanas Gecas Affair* (Edinburgh: Mainstream Publishing Projects, 1994).

28. Askold Krushelnycky and Barrie Penrose, "Refugee accused of war crimes by Nazi hunters", *Sunday Times*, 26 October, 1986.

29. "Refugee accused of war crimes by Nazi hunters", op. cit. Gecas' self-portrait as a Lithuanian patriot was echoed by another Baltic refugee to Britain accused of war crimes by the Wiesenthal Center, Paulis Reinhards. See David Shepard, "Latvian exile denounces war claims as 'smears'", *Times*, 9 February 1987. See also Howard Foster, "Prove we are Nazis say two emigrés", *Times*, 28 February 1987.

during "actions" in which Jews were killed. Instead he portrayed the facts in terms which he believed exculpated himself from liability and responsibility.

> Every day when the Germans came, they were collecting the Jews and Lithuanians and doing all the shooting....My unit had to surround an area to protect the Germans from attack while the executions were taking place. I took no part in the shootings, that's abhorrent and I'm a Catholic.

Gecas' statement is fascinating for a number of reasons. Even if we put aside the issue of who actually did the shooting in the incidents in question and ignore all the evidence of Gecas' colleagues in the killing squads who put him in a much more "proactive" position, what Gecas has to say reveals much about him and about the mythologies which surround many issues of moral and legal responsibility in the Holocaust.

First, there is the technical legal issue of the criminal responsibility of accomplices. Like the lookout in a bank robbery who stands watch outside while his colleagues enter the bank, Gecas is liable for the crimes of the principles on his own recounting of events. By standing watch and protecting the Germans from attacks while they killed innocent civilians, Gecas made those practices possible. The idea that the only perpetrators who deserve punishment or who are responsible in a legal or moral sense are those who actually pulled the triggers or issued the orders is one which appears to be as widespread as it is ill-founded in law and in ethical discourse.

At the same time, Gecas' description of himself as a bystander serves another set of discursive constructions of the Holocaust and various levels and degrees of responsibility, again both legal and ethical. This is the all too familiar portrayal of the hierarchy of responsibility and command between the "Germans" and in this case their Lithuanian auxiliaries. Here, for Gecas, it is the Germans who are primarily, if not solely, responsible. It is the Germans who collect those destined for extermination and who pull the triggers while the subordinate Lithuanians simply stand by and obey orders. We know from eyewitness and documentary evidence that this is not a true account of the level of active and often independent action taken by Lithuanian police auxiliaries and other forces in the Holocaust in the Soviet Union. Yet the construction of the Balts as double victims, of the Russians and of the Germans, is a constant and common refrain throughout the construction of the Shoah in the legal arena.

Two other aspects of Gecas' disculpatory statement deserve brief comment here. First it emerges clearly that even forty or more years after the events in question, for him, "Jews" could not be considered to be Lithuanians. The Germans collected "the Jews and Lithuanians". For Gecas, the taxonomy which was at the heart of the juridical extermination machine of the Holocaust is unproblematic and almost natural. This leads to the second part of Gecas' ideological life world, the statement that he could not have committed the "abhorrent" acts of which he stands accused because he is "a Catholic". By definition, then, he is not a Jew, but he is also not someone who could kill Jews because of his religious beliefs or affiliation. There is more than ample evidence, of course, that Protestant and Catholic alike easily participated in the mass killings of Jews in Europe. Religious affiliation was no barrier whatsoever to acts of barbarism. Again, however, Gecas' plea of innocence on this ground is not based on a factual or historically accurate reconstruction of the events of the Holocaust or the profiles and biographies of the killers. Instead it is meant to appeal to the belief that he is just an ordinary man, like the rest of us, and as such he could not possibly have committed the extraordinary acts of which he is accused. This appeal to normality as the trope of the innocent is one which emerges again and again in the metaphoric and ideological constructions of accused perpetrators in the West. It is an appeal both to common sense arguments that ordinary men do not commit such extraordinary acts and it is also an appeal to the incomprehensibility which is often invoked in relation to our collective understanding, or more precisely to our collective inability to understand the Holocaust.

But Gecas' invocation of his defense that he was and is a Catholic also serves, in this context, to underscore a theme which has always been present in debates about the attempts since the 1980s in countries like the United States, Canada, Australia and Britain to establish a legal basis for the prosecution of war criminals and mass killers. That theme, constantly invoked by opponents to construct a legal matrix which would attempt to "domesticate" and "legalize" the Holocaust by allowing for the trials of alleged perpetrators, is the idea that attempts to introduce such themes are part of a Jewish thirst for revenge.[30] Indeed, the writers of the *Times* article in which Gecas' statements are made themselves come dangerously close to such a position when their introductory paragraph reads

> An Edinburgh man accused of war crimes by a Jewish Nazi-hunting organisation said last night that he feared he might be sent to Israel or the Soviet Union and put on trial for his life.[31]

Here the journalists highlight the "Jewish" character of the Center and its accusations. This is then enhanced and exacerbated by their simple repetition

---

30. This would clearly inform many of the more outrageous claims made during the debates about the *War Crimes Act* in Britain. See discussion below.
31. "Refugee accused of war crimes by Nazi hunters", op. cit.

of Gecas' "fears" that he would be deported to "Israel or the Soviet Union and put on trial for his life". Here we find a double invocation of a potentially antisemitic theme in the very earliest days of the war crimes debate in Britain. First, we have a direct comparison between the legal systems of the Soviet Union and Israel. Given the Soviet antipathy to the State of Israel and the fate of Soviet Jews at the time, such a carefully constructed leader in one of Britain's top broadsheets can clearly be read as an unambiguously antisemitic pronouncement. The case against the *Times* and its coverage of the story from this angle is enhanced by the last part of the claim i.e. that Gecas could be put on trial for his life. One might conclude from this that the Jewish Nazi hunters are out for blood, their aim is vengeance and retribution. When the article which broke the Antanas Gecas coverage in the British mainstream press is open to such a possible interpretation, the stage is set for the construction of the Holocaust and the legal pursuit of perpetrators as a legally and ethically tainted process, informed by a blood lust for revenge in which "justice" is a guise for much baser motives.

However, much of the possible strength of any such appeal to antisemitism was taken out of the legal case involving questions of Gecas' responsibility as a perpetrator. The forum and legal basis chosen for the public and legal construction of Gecas' as "war criminal" occurred not in a criminal prosecution involving the strength and resources of the state against an "old man" defendant, but in two defamation actions brought by Gecas, one against the *Times* and the second and more important brought against Scottish Television as the result of the broadcast of the documentary *Crimes of War*.

This does not mean that the public/private distinction operated only in one way or in a one dimensional fashion in the Gecas case. For example, the Hetherington-Chalmers inquiry into war crimes[32] made use of the documentary in the early stages of their investigations.[33] In this way, a privately subsidized research program was used by the state to aid in the compilation of a public report on war criminals in Britain. On the other side of the legal taxonomical coin, the Inquiry later refused to hand over unpublished material which it possessed in order to help the *Times* in its defense of the Gecas defamation suit.[34] In fact, the murky jurisprudential boundaries of the public/private divide played themselves out in the judicial forum as the newspaper unsuccessfully sought an order compelling the Inquiry to hand over relevant material.

---

32. See *War Crimes: Report of the War Crimes Inquiry*, Cm 744, HMSO, London: 1989.

33. See "TV aid in war hunt", *Times*, 16 March 1988.

34. See "Access to war crime report refused", *Times*, 12 May 1990; "Scots war crimes libel trial", 140 *New Law Journal* 771 (1990).

Here, the Home Secretary had decided that it would be contrary to public policy for the Inquiry to reveal the names of individuals who had been investigated or to disclose any evidence. The case of Antanas Gecas became, in legal taxonomical terms, an administrative law case in which the court refused to interfere in the exercise of ministerial discretion. Notions of public interests and private interests played themselves out within the confines of legal principles of the separation of powers and judicial review of executive decisions, cornerstones of the British understanding of the rule of law.

Gecas was also the beneficiary of the triumph of the private over the public interest in another set of judicial proceedings at the periphery of his defamation suits. Here he sought injunctive relief against the distribution of a book by Ephraim Zuroff, former director of the Wiesenthal Center, entitled *Occupation: Nazi Hunter*. Gecas claimed that the distribution of the book would adversely effect his defamation case against the *Times*.[35]

Finally, in relation to his defamation suit against the *Times*, Gecas was also the winner in the battle between the public and private "interests". The newspaper settled the case after being forced to admit that some of its allegation against Gecas, such as that he was a member of the SS and carried the SS blood type tattoo were in fact incorrect.[36] Here Gecas could emerge the "winner" in part because of a "peculiarity" of Scots' defamation. Under the law of Scotland, and unlike the legal system of England and Wales, contingency fee arrangements (no-win, no fee) are allowed in defamation cases. Here the *Times* decided that it was not worth its while defending a suit for which the pursuer (plaintiff) Gecas was not paying.

> Mr Alistair Brett, for Times Newspapers, said after the hearing that lawyers for Mr Gecas had been working on a no-win, no-fee basis. *The Times* was faced with this speculative method had agreed to pay an undisclosed sum of money to meet Mr Gecas's legal expenses.
>
> Mr Brett said *The Times* had been forced to take a commercial view and that, assuming the paper had won the case, it would have been a pyrrhic victory and the newspaper could have run up a bill approaching £ 500,000 with no chance of recouping this money from Mr Gecas.[37]

---

35. See Kerry Gill, "Writ-serving attempt during hearing", *Times*, 13 October 1988; Kerry Gill, "War book is threat to libel witness, QC says", *Times*, 14 October 1988; Kerry Gill, "Court upholds ban on publication", *Times*, 15 October 1988.

36. See Kerry Gill, "Defamation case against The Times is settled", *Times*, 6 June 1990.

37. "Defamation case against The Times is settled", op. cit.

The exact content of the public and/or private interests here is of course subject to debate and disputation. It might be argued that the public interest is served by allowing the disempowered to pursue cases against wealthy corporate interests when they do not otherwise possess the financial means to right the wrongs they may have suffered. At the same time, it might be argued that the public right to know and to be informed may be "chilled" if media outlets are forced to silence themselves because the financial, rather than the factual, stakes are too high.[38] In this particular instance, the real loser was the public interest in the truth about the Holocaust and its perpetrators. Because the *Times* took the "commercial view" about the amount of money it was willing to spend, not only was Gecas not exposed to the facts of his complicity in the mass extermination of the innocent, but the public was also not exposed to the spectacle and spectacular instance of a trial in which truth, law and the Holocaust would be at play before British justice.

Moreover, it might be argued that because the newspaper settled its case, particularly after it admitted that some of its allegation against Gecas were ill-founded, some members of the public may have been left with the impression that Gecas was in fact the innocent victim of a campaign of vilification by powerful forces. Gecas' solicitor seemed to wish to leave readers with this impression when he stated

> Mr Gecas is very pleased that a satisfactory settlement of this case has now been achieved....
> It has been an enormous undertaking for a man of 74, not in the best of health, to take on a national newspaper with all its resources. He now hopes the gentlemen of the press and television will allow him to go home and live his life in peace.[39]

In what the *Times* itself had called "an unofficial war crimes trial", the result which the public were left to contemplate was that the alleged perpetrator of mass atrocities was in fact a sick old man who just wanted to be left in peace after the case against him was proved to be without foundation.

Unfortunately for Mr Gecas, his preferred legal strategy of pursuing his accusers by way of defamation suits proved, in part at least, to be his undoing. Scottish Television and its insurers decided to defend the defamation suit against it by proving to the Court that their accusations were true.[40] *Gecas v.*

---

38. See e.g. Alastair Brett and Derek Currie, "No win, no fee: free speech loses", *Times*, 25 August 1992.

39. "Defamation case against The Times is settled", op. cit.

40. See Roger Hutchinson, *Crimes of War*, op. cit., for a full discussion of events.

Scottish Television went ahead and was trumpeted as the first British war crimes case.[41] In many ways, this metaphorical claim has a symbolic and juridical resonance which was reflected throughout the trial. For the first time in Scottish legal history, a Scottish court sat on foreign soil, in Lithuania, to hear witnesses and conduct a trial.[42] The defamation case against Scottish Television was in this practical way then a trial about and within the context of the Holocaust in Lithuania. The Shoah in the Baltic states was a part, literally and figuratively, of a Scottish trial.

Similarly, the traditional tropes and metaphors associated with the placement of the Holocaust within the context of the Western legal tradition were also invoked and challenged by other counter-narratives within the juridical sphere. Thus Gecas himself admitted that he would have killed Jews if the case had arisen.

What could I do? If not, I would be shot for disobeying military orders.[43]

Here, not surprisingly, Gecas' "admission" is tainted by other considerations. First, it was put forth in a context of what he "would have done" and is strictly speaking not an admission at all. Second, it is framed in such a way as to place primary responsibility on "the Germans" who would have had to issue the orders. And finally, it is put forward as an excuse or a defense rather than as an admission of legal or moral culpability. He was "just obeying orders"; he was acting under extreme duress. The actual legal power of this position is not what is important here. Rather it is the way in which Gecas portrays himself even while appearing to offer an admission which is of vital interest. He is not a perpetrator because he was and still is a victim. He was a victim of the Germans and now he is the victim of the powerful media interests which would besmirch his character and of the witnesses who come to portray him as a perpetrator.[44]

Here we come to the heart of the case against Gecas and to the importance of the trial within the context of establishing the Holocaust as juridical phenomenon in post-war Britain.

---

41. This is not necessarily the case, even at the metaphorical level of a private defamation action. See e.g., Mavis M Hill and L. Norman Williams, *Auschwitz in England* (New York: Stein and Day, 1965).

42. The more recent trial of the defendants in the Lockerbie bombing case is another example. In the Sawoniuk prosecution, the first full British criminal trial of a war criminal, the trial judge and the jury visited Belarus to view the places where the crimes were alleged to have occurred. See below.

43. "Jewish ghetto charge", *Times*, 9 May 1992.

44. See "Slaughter of PoWs 'like conveyor belt'", *Times*, 19 February 1992.

As we have seen, throughout the course of the efforts to prosecute alleged perpetrators of crimes against humanity, a main ideological battle which has been waged is one which in which the Holocaust plays a secondary role to the battle between East and West. In Gecas' case we have also already seen the ways in which anti-Soviet sentiment was deployed from the earliest stages. One of the historically complex elements of the Gecas case is the way in which this anti-Soviet trope would play itself out in the post-Soviet era. Roger Hutchinson narrates the ways in which the collapse of the Soviet Union and the emergence of the newly independent Baltic States manifested themselves at various times in Gecas' case. Soviet "cooperation" was replaced by Lithuanian reluctance to help. The newly independent Baltic states are anxious to establish themselves in the international and Western community of nations. At the same time, they are understandably anxious to pay homage to their own history, in which the struggle against Russian and Soviet domination played a key role. Unfortunately for them, the Holocaust played a key role in the construction of the West's self-image and in the ideological underpinnings of both legal and popular understanding of the rule of law. While this is, as I argue throughout, more a case of appearance than of jurisprudential reality, it is nonetheless true that the ongoing condemnation of the Holocaust and its unlawful nature is vital to Western understandings and constructions of the Shoah. Thus, a willingness to prosecute alleged perpetrators or to assist in their prosecution by others is key to the Baltic states being accepted as part of the community to which they wish to belong. At the same time, this brings local governments and judiciaries into direct conflict with powerful political elements at home and with competing constructions of the Holocaust era as one simply involving freedom struggles against Russian and Soviet imperialism and colonialism.[45]

In the cusp period of the Gecas case, these conflicts became clear and played themselves out in the judicial forum. This was important for the construction of the Holocaust in Scottish and Lithuanian legal historical contexts and it was important as the Baltic/Holocaust connection was constructed in the popular knowledge of the citizens of the two countries involved. Thus, the Lithuanians were keen not just to cooperate in the Scottish proceedings, but to use those proceedings to distinguish Lithuanian justice from Soviet justice.

> Evidence for Scottish Television's program was collated under the old Soviet regime and it is believed that a Lithuanian judge may first wish to verify the statements now that the regime has changed.

---

45. See the discussion below in relation to Konrad Kalejs and the Australian legal system, chapter 10.

Judge Losys, chairman of the Lithuanian supreme court, has said that the original statements were given to Soviet officials and that he wishes to make sure that evidence to be put before the Scottish court is unchanged.[46]

Claims put forward by Gecas to refute the defense position that their allegations about him were truthful attempted to demonstrate that Soviet evidence was by definition tainted evidence.[47] On the other hand, Scottish Television tried to establish that

> ...even when a truth appears from within the belly of a deceitful, despotic state such as the Soviet Union, it is still the truth.[48]

At the level of the semiotics of the Holocaust and the rule of law after Auschwitz, the Gecas case deployed competing signifiers in which the key relationship was to the ultimate sign, truth. While the pursuer put his hopes in the more traditional ideology of anti-communism, the defender put its faith in the ability of a Scottish court to get at the truth amidst the untruths of the ideology invoked by Gecas. Whatever the outcome, one could easily assert that at a basic level, the rule of law would be the winner. If Gecas won, that would mean that a Scottish court could not be fooled by a case concocted with the assistance of those whose very essence was to defeat the rule of law. If Scottish Television emerged triumphant, this would be proof that the rule of law with an independent judiciary bound only by evidence and legality, could win in the search for a judicially recognized truth, despite whatever Soviet machinations might be found. The actual fate of the Jews of Lithuania and other parts of the Soviet Union, was, and could only be, as the case played itself out with the rules of the rule of law, an issue of secondary importance.

The trial judge in fact found that Gecas

> ...participated in many operations involving the killing of innocent Soviet citizens, including Jews, in particular in Belorussia during the last three months of 1941, and in doing so committed war crimes against Soviet citizens, who included old men, women and children.[49]

---

46. Kerry Gill, "UK court sits abroad on war crimes denial", *Times*, 10 February 1992.

47. See Kerry Gill, "Massacre witness says he was forced to exaggerate story", *Times*, 12 February 1992; Kerry Gill, "Priest tells of KGB trial tactics", *Times*, 13 February 1992.

48. Roger Hutchinson, op. cit., 211.

49. Michael Hornsell, "Judge in libel case condemns Gecas as mass murderer", *Times*, 18 July 1992. See also Martin Linton, "Man Loses War Crimes Libel Case", *Guardian*, 18 July 1992.

The legal result of this ruling by the judge was that the defamation case brought by Gecas against Scottish Television was dismissed. As with the *Times* litigation, Gecas was in no position to pay the costs awarded against him as the unsuccessful party to the action. He was branded a war criminal by the trial judge and at some level at least the public was made aware, through the lens of a civil libel suit, that Britain harbored at least one individual who was a Holocaust perpetrator.

However, the case of Antanas Gecas, mass murderer does not end there. After months of investigation and speculation, any idea of pursuing Gecas under the criminal law foundered. Ironically, the case against him failed largely because of considerations which are central both to our understandings of the rule of law within the criminal justice system and to other attempts to construct the pursuit of war criminals as a moral categorical imperative for that same criminal justice system. In so far as the case against Gecas was concerned, the best available witnesses against him were men who were resident in Britain and who had served as his subordinates in the war. Unfortunately for those who would have supported prosecuting Gecas, this meant that a deal of immunity would have had to be granted to these potential witnesses who would themselves have been suspected of war crimes. The idea of "making a deal with the devil" in order to prosecute the devil was simply not an option available within the dominant discursive and practical matrix of the rule of law in the criminal justice system, despite the fact that similar arrangements are made everyday by prosecutors.[50] By constructing the Holocaust not just as criminal, but as a special sort of crime, the worst crime, proponents of prosecution have painted themselves into this particular corner in which the ordinary practices of the criminal justice system are unavailable. Law cannot be law because the crime is not an ordinary crime. Such are the jurisprudential ironies of the Holocaust and the law.

The case against Gecas was dropped[51] and the Scottish War Crimes unit was disbanded.[52] For some time, it looked as if the civil law victory in the Scottish Television case would be the only victory of "truth" in relation to the Holocaust within the British legal system. Criminal law just did not appear capable of dealing with the idea of "war crimes" and "crimes against humanity" without coming into conflict with basic principles of "justice" and the rule of law. Those

50. See Lawrence Donegan, "Lack of Evidence may prevent War Crimes Trial Going Ahead", *Guardian*, 27 April 1993.

51. Kate Alderson, "War crime cases dropped", *Times*, 4 February 1994.

52. Erlend Clouston, "Anger Over Closure of War Crimes Unit", *Guardian*, 4 February 1994.

people who had raised just these objections to the introduction of the *War Crimes Act* appeared after the Gecas case collapsed, to have been right.[53]

4. The War Crimes Act, Parliamentary Democracy and the Rule of Law

As I noted above, a generational shift in Britain, coupled with the evolutionary changes at work in other parts of the international community, meant that the issue of justice, in the form of law, for victims of the Holocaust re-entered the politico-legal agenda of British politics in the late 1980s. Investigations by governmental bodies like the OSI in the United States and official inquiries in Australia and Canada revealed aspects of British post-war migration policy concerning eastern Europe which raised serious questions about the United Kingdom's possible complicity in allowing Nazi and collaborationist war criminals to escape legal processes in the immediate post-war period. In addition to problematizing Britain's international position, these revelations also brought into question certain important elements of Britain's own historical self-understanding.

As a prosecuting power at Nuremberg, as well as an Occupying Power in Germany, the United Kingdom could and did portray itself as a dedicated party in the judicial and political struggle against those who had committed the atrocities of Nazism. Revelations that alleged Nazi war criminals were encouraged to migrate to Britain and had lived there undisturbed for forty years

---

53. The Gecas case continued however. As a result of the multi-party negotiations surrounding the infamous Konrad Kalejs in Latvia, the Lithuanian government was and is also under pressure from the United States and Britain in particular to request the extradition of various alleged perpetrators for trial in their homeland. See Gerard Seenan, "Lithuania demands extradition of Nazi war crime suspect from the UK", *Guardian*, 20 February 2001; "Net closes in on war crimes suspect", ibid., 28 February 2001; "Warrant issued for suspected war killer", *Guardian*, 28 July 2001. In late 2001, Gecas seemed to have received the benefit of a biological amnesty. See "Nazi suspect 'too ill for trial'", *Guardian*, 13 August 2001; Tim Luckhurst, "Why Won't Britain Jail This War Criminal?", *Observer*, 2 September 2001; Kirsty Scott, "'Dying war crimes suspect to escape trial", *Guardian*, 3 September 2001. Despite the calls of others for a trial *in absentia*, Gecas seemed likely to live out whatever remained of his life untroubled by law. Gerard Seenan, "Israelis want 'war criminal' tried in absentia", *Guardian*, 5 September 2001. Less than two weeks after these calls for his trial, he passed in Edinburgh. Gerard Seenan, "'Nazi war criminal' who evaded justice for years dies in Edinburgh", *Guardian*, 13 September 2001.

clearly attacked this myth and self-image.[54] Simon Freeman put the case against the popular social and legal mythology as follows:

> But there is an even more compelling reason why the trials must go on, even if it means wheeling old Nazis into courtrooms. For many years after the war it was assumed that the Allies' governments were determined to catch as many Nazis as possible. Nothing could have been further from the truth. The story of the search for Nazis is also the story of hypocrisy and lies by governments.[55]

The debates which surrounded attempts to create a legal framework under which alleged perpetrators could be prosecuted under British law would manifest themselves within discursive matrices which are at once familiar and unique. These commonalties and points of juridico-political discourse include references to the age of the alleged criminals, to the passage of time since the crimes were committed, the expense involved in potential prosecutions etc. Images of "sick old men" being called before the bar of justice were invoked to dismiss claims that such cases involved anything other than revenge. Once again, "justice" and the "rule of law" were deployed as metaphors and signs by each side of the political debate in order to legitimize its own position while at the same time dismissing claims on the other side as unfounded and in violation of basic British legal principles. At its heart, once again, the debate about the Holocaust and the rule of law became a debate about the rule of law in which the Holocaust played only a secondary role.

These continuities in the discursive environment are exemplified in a column opposing war crimes trials in Britain written by expatriate Canadian Barbara Amiel. Amiel invoked and deployed almost the complete arsenal of war crimes' trials opponents in her attempt to set the ideological tone and framework of the debate. She wrote

> By now the elderly murderers of the Third Reich have lost all capacity to harm us in any way except one—by bending our legal procedures, or creating new, questionable ones to catch them.

She added:

---

54. See Cesarani, op. cit.; see also Howard Foster, "Britain 'gave a safe haven to Nazis'", *Times*, 29 January 1987; "Six 'Nazis' traced to Britain", *Times*, 25 February 1987; Tom Bower, "How the SS Came to Britain", *Times*, 20 August 1987 and "Conspiracy in Whitehall", 21 August 1987.
55. "Shadow of the holocaust", *Sunday Times*, 22 February 1987. See also "And justice for all?", 23 March 1990.

Soviet information could be accurate. It could also have sinister motives: to distract attention from Soviet curbs on Jewish emigration
and to create dissension among émigré and Jewish communities in
the West.

She concluded:

Twisting the law to put these Nazis in jail for a few years would be a
mockery.[56]

Again, all the themes, backed by references to the "bad" experiences in
Canada and the United States, are invoked here. The age of the alleged perpetrators, the unreliability of Soviet evidence, not to mention its pernicious
motivations, and most importantly, the idea that war crimes legislation and
trials are somehow a distortion of the fundamental principles of the British
system of justice and the rule of law. In the final analysis, this is the underlying and basic assertion of all discourse opposing war crimes trials today. The
system, it is argued, must not be distorted in order to achieve a result which
could only be, because the system must by definition be distorted, not justice
or law, but revenge. In the end, we would be no better than the Nazis if we
were to allow base political principles and motives to distort the legal system
of rules and procedures. Political vengeance is not justice and it is not law.

Such rhetoric is not without its political, social and juridical resonance and
reason. Nazi justice was political justice and a system which resorted to such tactics would be self-defeating, both legally and morally. Law must, as I have argued throughout but from a different perspective, betray itself in relation to the
Holocaust. At the same time of course, this is not the only story, nor is it the
only possible interpretation of the pursuit of those responsible for the Shoah.
Justice and revenge are not necessarily always mutually exclusive, nor is revenge
the only or primary motivation of those who seek to invoke current legal mechanisms to try "old Nazis".[57] The system of the rule of law is not by definition distorted by allowing Britain to exercise jurisdiction over residents and citizens who
committed murder in Eastern Europe or the Baltic States forty or fifty years ago.
Murder, if indeed it was murder, was then a "crime". The retroactivity, so dear
to opponents of war crimes legislation and trials, is merely, or at least arguably
as a matter of law and jurisprudence, a jurisdictional retroactivity, not one involving the creation of criminal liability for acts which were not, when com-

56. "War crimes: why the Hurd way is right", *Times*, 11 March 1987.
57. See also Brian James, "Ex-Nazis in fear of the knock on the door", *Times*, 2 March
1987. Bernard Levin, "Evil too old for hounding", 8 June 1989.

mitted, crimes.[58] *Nulla poena*, that juristic touchstone which separates us from Nazi not law, is unaffected here. As the War Crimes Inquiry put it

> In our view, to enact legislation to give the British courts jurisdiction over murder and manslaughter committed as violations of the laws and customs of war would not be to create an offence retrospectively. It would be making an offence triable in British courts to an extent which international law had recognised and permitted at a time before the alleged offences in question had been committed.[59]

The problem here is one of first principles of law and morality, of jurisprudence and ethics, and of political responsibility. Nazi law was law, even as it was unacceptable from a moral or ethical perspective, or in terms of justice. The problem with war crimes legislation and trials is not they are assimilable to Nazi law, but rather that we have no basis, other than politics and ethics, for determining what is acceptable law. Rhetorical invocations which seek to establish moral authority by placing one's position on the same side of the rule of law are morally empty not because the rule of law is without meaning but because any meaning which it may have is determined through the debate and political activity which follows, not before the debate takes place. The rule of law is a political category, not an epistemologically or ontologically certain one with pre-determined content. It is as empty or as full as we can make it, but it does not, at any level beyond the political and rhetorical, determine its own content. It is here that law betrays itself in debates about Holocaust perpetrator trials, not in morally pure and jurisprudentially untainted invocations about justice, retroactivity, temporality etc.

This point is made most clearly I believe if we examine the areas of politics and law where the debate about the *War Crimes Act* in Britain takes on its own character, where the debate becomes particularly British. There are two interconnected levels at which this occurred, as in the late 1980s and early 1990s Britain tried to come to grips with what was to be done with the inescapable "fact" that it had given and was continuing to offer, shelter to those who had committed acts of mass killing against their Jewish fellows. At the first level, we find British Parliamentary government and democracy trying to deal with a conflict between the elected lower House of Commons and the upper House of Lords on this issue. Here, the Commons, in a series of free votes, overwhelmingly approved the introduction of war crimes legislation, while the

---

58. See contra, Graham Zellick, "Bringing war criminals to book", *Times*, 29 August 1989.

59. *War Crimes: Report of the War Crimes Inquiry*, op. cit., at 97.

Lords successively ignored this and voted against the Bills.[60] Whether this was ever a state of affairs which reached the level of "constitutional crisis" is a matter of ongoing debate.[61] What is clear is that at a basic level, parliamentary debate, institutional conflict and basic issues of democracy were all engaged in the issues of war crimes prosecutions in Britain and the predictions of dire consequences on each side turned out to be without foundation. In the end, in other words, the "rule of law" won because it could never lose. There was never a constitutional crisis in which the constitution was threatened, because in good and typical British fashion, the crisis was constructed and resolved purely in terms of the internal political and institutional dynamics of British law and politics themselves.

The second level at which a certain British particularism emerged flowed from this institutional and discursive context of the battle between Commons and Lords. While antisemitism manifested itself in subtle ways in debates about war criminals and war crimes legislation in other jurisdictions such as Canada and Australia, the debate in Britain was clearly and specifically informed by this consideration. As David Cesarani puts it

> Behind the parliamentary fracas of May 1991 stood a mass of preconceptions and prejudices that turned what was to many people a clear-cut moral issue—should Britain be a haven for mass murderers?—into a morass of constitutional niceties and juridical hairsplitting.[62]

In other words, in Britain more than Canada and Australia, opposition to war crimes legislation, in addition to the invocation of traditional arguments like those of Barbara Amiel, and the institutional context of the Lords/Commons split, was seen by those on one side as being largely informed by antisemitism. While a review of the discourse of the time shows that this was not universally true, it is strikingly clear that many who voiced their disagreement with the plan to introduce legislation permitting the pursuit of war criminals before the British courts, did so in terms which are unequivocally antisemitic.

---

60. See Cesarani for an account of these legislative machinations.
61. For the various legal interpretations of these machinations and their consequences see *inter alia*, Andrew J. Cunningham, "To the uttermost ends of the earth'?: The War Crimes Act and international law", 11 *Legal Studies* 281 (1991); Eva Steiner, "Prosecuting War Criminals in England and France", (1991) *Crim. L. R.* 180; Gabriele Ganz, "The War Crimes Act 1991—Why No Constitutional Crisis?", 55 *Modern Law Review* 87 (1992); Sheena N. McMurtrie, "The Constitutionality of the War Crimes Act 1991", 13 *Statute Law Review* 128 (1992); A.T. Richardson, "War Crimes Act 1991", 55 *Mod. L. R.* 73 (1992).
62. *Justice Delayed*, op. cit., at 7.

This has meant that a large part of public debate on the issue and from there, a large section of public perception and public memory of war crimes and of the Holocaust, has been constructed in terms which see the issue as one which is "foreign" to British justice and memory because it is "Jewish". Once again, law and legal discourse, this time in the context of Westminster democracy, construct the "Jew" as Other, as not completely and unproblematically British.

From its earliest stages, public discourse on the issue is characterized by the joint invocation of more traditional, "objective" concerns in conjunction with more overtly antisemitic sentiments. Thus, in an editorial, or "lead article" in the *Times* we find the following two statements in semiotic juxtaposition.

> The claims of Nazi-sympathizers, Soviet sympathizers and resistance fighters form a more delicate equation in the Baltic States than almost anywhere else. In the absence of conclusive evidence that Britain has harboured a serious war criminal it is wise and humane to let matters rest.

This was preceded by

> Britain is a Christian country. Its laws enshrine principles of justice tempered with mercy, not vengeance. Our legal system assumes the accused innocent before proved guilty. It is not a country, like Germany, which has been required to purge the legacy of Nazism. It is not a state like Israel, which is built at least in part on the common memory of the Holocaust. Nor is it a country like France or The Netherlands which experienced the horrors of Nazi occupation. There is no common will to settle old scores.[63]

Here we find, as I have said, many of the more traditional elements of oppositional discourse. The Baltic States were to some extent at least anti-Soviet resisters; Germany has particular problems and Britain was never occupied. Each of these myth structures maintains its strengths in political and jurisprudential debate despite a counter-factual historical debate in each instance which might serve to better inform decision-making. But what is important here is that the *Times*[64] takes pains to distinguish a country's "obligation" "to

---

63. "The Wiesenthal File", 3 March 1987.

64. Throughout the debate, the editorial writers of the paper continued to muster arguments in support of their position that "justice" and war crimes trials were diametrically opposed concepts in the British tradition of the rule of law. See e.g., "A Kind of Wild Justice", 20 March 1990; "Forty Years Too Late", 4 June 1990; "Lords in Action", 6 June 1990; "Pyrrhic Victory" 2 May 1991.

seek justice not vengeance" in a context which it defines as that of a "Christian country".[65] Mercy and justice, the presumption of innocence, these are the values of a Christian country which are, by rhetorical and jurisprudential implication, to be opposed to the non-Christian, i.e. Jewish, Old Testament desire for vengeance. This is a theme which would emerge again and again throughout the war crimes debate in the United Kingdom.

A review of the record of the two Houses of Parliament reveals a striking similarity with the themes and discourses which had emerged elsewhere when similar legislative measures were on the political agenda. All the familiar debates about retrospection and retroactivity and the rule of law can be found in the debates over the *War Crimes Bill*, as can concerns over the fate of the "old men" who would stand accused if the legislation were to become law, and the relationship between the passage of time and the possibility of a fair trial. None of this is or should be surprising. All of these questions are central to our Anglo-American traditions of jurisprudence, especially in so far as out concepts of criminal justice are concerned. What is particularly striking about the British parliamentary debates, however, is the centrality of theology in the construction of discourses about the rule of law and the potential prosecution of war criminals in Britain. More specifically, the debates in the British Parliament revealed the same stark evidence of antisemitism which was evidenced in the press coverage and editorial writing on the subject.

Leading the charge of those who to greater or lesser degrees appear to have adopted the position that the *War Crimes Bill* was the product of a Jewish, and therefore by definition, un-British minority, was the member for Orpington, Mr. Ivor Stanbrook. On November 26, 1987, he asserted that the proposed changes were the work of "the so-called 'war crimes lobby' "[66], and on February 8, 1988, he clarified his position in the following terms

> Therefore is it not very wrong for the Government to attempt to make special arrangements for a special class of people accused of having committed offences a long time ago, which the British people would far rather not pursue? Is my right hon. Friend not surrendering to a lobby whose main motivations are hatred and revenge?[67]

He would later argue that the *Bill* constituted

---

65. Cf. Lord Coggan, "Wiesenthal file and justice", Letter to the Editor, *Times*, 6 March 1987.
66. *Hansard*, col. 391.
67. *Hansard*, col. 29.

...the pursuit of a cruel vendetta...

and that

> The proposition before us, when properly understood, offends all the
> basic instincts of decent British people.[68]

The themes and implications of Stanbrook's various interventions on the
subject of war crimes legislation are clear. A small and non-representative
group is pursuing its own agenda of hatred and vengeance. These feelings and
motivations are in essence non-British and are offensive to the vast majority
of real and authentic citizens of the country. For Stanbrook, it seems clear,
the pursuit of war criminals is little more than a modern incarnation of the
Jewish thirst for blood. Such antisemitic sentiments could be more easily understood and rejected as the ravings of a lone hate-filled lunatic if they were
in fact that. However, in the House of Commons, the Member for Orpington
was far from the lone voice of British antisemitism.

On December 3, 1987, another MP, Mr. Tony Marlow, of Northampton
North, offered the opinion that notice should be taken

> ...of the fact that the supporters of this particular proposal are mo-
> tivated not by justice but by the demands of propaganda...[69]

His feelings became more clearly enunciated when he later claimed that the
war crimes campaign had no other motivation than

> ...smothering the world with a form of moral blackmail as a means
> of covering the present behaviour of the state of Israel.[70]

The consistent and persistent theme of many of those who opposed war
crimes legislation was one which couched the debate in terms of the theo-po-
litical distinction between "justice", an authentic British concern, and
"vengeance", a constant of "Jewish" theology and politics. "Justice", in relation
to war crimes, became a discursive matrix in which a monopoly was afforded
to those who sought to prevent prosecution on the grounds of a complex mix-
ture of the passage of time, anti-Communism, evidentiary difficulties, and
Christian and therefore British ideals of forgiveness. The other side then was
faced with the burden of being un-British, Jewish, vengeful, bent on persecuting tired and probably innocent old men. Again, all of these themes

---

68. *Hansard*, 12 December 1989, col. 890.
69. *Hansard*, col. 1094.
70. *Hansard*, 24 July 1989, col. 743.

emerged in debates in Canada, Australia and the United States, and all are part of a consistent theme of some latent antisemitism which was no doubt present in all those countries. What is singular about the British situation is that this antisemitism was antisemitism given voice in such an unequivocal manner in the Parliament.

Another frequent advocate of an occasionally subtle line of antisemitic argument in the House of Commons was Sir John Stokes, Member for Halesowen and Stourbridge. For him as for others of his ilk and disposition, the only question was about the real division between England and the Jews. On July 24 1989 he rose in the House and stated without any shame or hesitation

> Above all, do the people of England want this? We are not a vengeful nation and I have not heard any demand for it apart from the demand by this small and highly articulate lobby.[71]

He would later characterize himself as the representative of "80,000 good British people"[72], none of whom supported pursuing war criminals and did not hesitate again to characterize those who supported the change to British law as acting out of revenge rather than justice.[73] For him, as for others, the rule of law and justice were British and Christian concepts, largely beyond the ken of those whose inspiration came from non-British and Jewish ideals of vengeance.

Perhaps the most prominent intervention in favor of Christian Britain came from former Prime Minister Edward Heath. Heath described the legislation as the product of

> enormous pressure, and it has all come from California.[74]

Heath would later add that

> The Jewish people will never allow what happened to be forgotten for a moment so that is not a concern of the House either. Our concern is how the people of this country will be affected once this process starts.[75]

Here we find a former Prime Minister of Britain articulating the position, without any apparent self-consciousness, that the question of the pursuit of war criminals or of the memorialization of the Holocaust is the concern of the

---

71. *Hansard*, col. 742.
72. *Hansard*, 12 December 1989, col. 900.
73. *Hansard*, 19 March 1990, col. 956.
74. *Hansard*, 12 December 1989, col. 884.
75. *Hansard*, 19 March 1990, col. 926.

Jews, who by definition are not British. Again the theme common to the Nazis, Lithuanian perpetrators, French lawyers and former British Prime Ministers, is that Jews are never authentically part of the national body politic. For Heath the pursuit of war criminals is nothing but a propaganda exercise cooked up by foreigners, from "California". In other words, the Jews, embodied by the Simon Wiesenthal Center, are at it again, trying to drum up support for a cause which is of no interest or concern for real Britons.

The debate which played itself out in the House of Lords simply exacerbated the problem and painted the theo-legal British concept of justice and the rule of law in even starker antisemitic terms. Lord Jacobovits, then the Chief Rabbi, tried to calm the spirits of his opponents and to strike an ecumenical tone which would remove from the debate the Jew = vengeance, Christian = justice equation. He stated:

> Jews in particular are often charged with feelings of vengeance. This attitude, like many other falsifications which have led to so much persecution and bloodshed over the centuries, is attributed to the Old Testament. Let me once and for all lay the ghost of this vicious canard. My faith abhors vengeance.[76]

This did not placate the most blatant and open antisemites in the House. Lord Houghton intervened to criticize Lord Jacobovits. He said

> I was acutely disappointed with the speech of the noble Lord Chief Rabbi. I thought it was a dreadful speech; dreadful in its literal sense. It was the voice of the Old Testament as I was taught it, and Jehovah was not a kindly God.[77]

He then added that

> I thought that the noble Lord the Chief Rabbi made the kind of speech that one could expect to hear from the steps of the guillotine or the scaffold, except that he did not call for mercy upon their souls.[78]

Even when it comes to executions of the condemned, it would seem, there is an onto-theological distinction to be made between a proper Christian and British killing and a vengeful Jewish one. The Jews, this time according to the Earl of Halsbury, cannot be expected to forget or forgive, but "we" must abhor

---

76. *Hansard*, 4 December 1989, col. 615.
77. Ibid., col. 632.
78. Ibid., col. 633; "Hitler must not have posthumous victory, peers told", *Times* 4 December 1989.

vengeance.[79] Here Jews must abandon their theological identity if they want to be citizens.

Lord Hankey, after referring to his understanding of the "Hebrew Bible" and its "eye for an eye and tooth for tooth philosophy behind such prosecutions", went on to proclaim his opposition to war crimes trials because

It is entirely against our good Christian upbringing and philosophy.

He concluded

I wish to remind noble Lords of a very old, very wise, very British and very Christian motto: The noblest vengeance is to forgive.[80]

Despite interventions against the *Bill* by the two Jewish peers Lords Goodman and Bauer, and despite support for the changes to British law by a majority of the House constituted by non-Jewish Members, opponents of these measures continued to construct the issues as involving fundamental differences between British ideals of the rule of law and of justice which they sought to uphold and a philosophy and practice of vengeance, of Old Testament theology put forward as part of a concerted effort by a group of well-financed foreign Jews. The debate was always couched in terms of an understanding of the rule of law and of justice which was by necessity incapable of including Jews who could not grasp and celebrate all that was British freedom. Opposition to the war crimes legislation was always portrayed in terms and arguments which were informed by a particular understanding of the rule of law. For many in Britain, that understanding was beyond the capacities of Jews. They could not grasp the principles of British justice because they were not properly British.

The media were not averse to passing similar virulent hate-filled commentary to the public. While such comments in Canada and Australia were limited to the more rabid elements of the neo-Nazi and old guard antisemites, in Britain anti-Jewish sentiment became an essential element of mainstream opposition to war crimes legislation. Indeed, it became central to opponents to portray such legislation as "foreign" both in spirit and in inspiration to the values of a Christian England. Here justice and the rule of law became not just "British" but "Christian". Jewish concepts of "law" were simply not British. Like Nazi law, Jewish concepts of law in fact were "not law". Paul Baker had the ear of the opposition to war crimes trials when he wrote

---

79. Ibid., col. 638.
80. Ibid., col. 671–72. See also, Julia Neuberger, "Them and us, with no grey in between", *Sunday Times*, 10 December 1989.

Eye for eye, tooth for tooth....
Time to put the word of Moses back on the shelf, and to take down
the New Testament and the Book of Common Prayer. Even if some
trespasses cannot be forgiven, the day comes to draw a line across the
account book of history, and turn another page.[81]

Jews apparently keep "account books" of history, but then again what
would decent Christians expect of those people. Moses and vengeance, the
New Testament and the Book of Common Prayer and justice. The rule of law
and British justice must be semiotically linked with Christian values and
must, by definition exclude Jews and Jewish values. If debates about the rule
of law and the Holocaust are to be the stage on which the identity of the
British nation is to be played out, let there be no doubt that the Holocaust,
a Jewish concern, plays no part, except by definitional exclusion, in the rule
of law.

Indeed, Lord Shawcross, who was a British prosecutor at Nuremberg, laid
the groundwork for this jurisprudence of exclusion by his constant and consistent opposition to the trial of war criminals in terms of the opposition between "justice" and "retribution". Thus he proclaimed

Retribution...does not cease to be retribution by placing on it a label
called "justice" on top of it.[82]

After the stage had been set, Shawcross was quick to add a further element
to the jurisprudence of antisemitism. He stated

So it was decided in 1948 to cease these prosecutions and I think that
there can be no doubt whatever that public opinion felt that had to
be done. Indeed, the efforts of those like myself, who wanted to do
more to punish those who had slaughtered the Jews, were not helped
by various things that had happened in the meantime, including the
activities of the Stern gang and the bombing of the King David Hotel.
In the atmosphere of those days I am quite sure that it would have
been impossible to continue war crime trials wherever the criminals
happened to be.[83]

81. "Time Moses went back on the shelf", *Sunday Times*, 3 June 1990.
82. *Hansard*, 4 June 1990, col. 1097. See also Matthew Parris, "War debate gets a touch
personal", *Times*, 5 June 1990.
83. Ibid., col. 1098.

The situation now becomes clear. Britain decided not to prosecute war criminals in 1948 not because the Cold War imposed different priorities, or because of concerns over the passage of time, or over a desire to draw a sponge over the past, but because the Jews brought it upon themselves. They were not worthy of the moral intervention of British justice because they were themselves criminals. The moral equivalence between terrorism in Palestine and the Holocaust meant that British justice was no longer interested. The antisemitism inherent in this argument of moral and jurisprudential equivalence is re-enforced by other comments by Lord Shawcross.

Outside the chamber, Shawcross, echoing the position articulated by Edward Heath in the Commons, placed the blame for the legislation he found so repugnant on a powerful and foreign Jewish lobby. He wrote in a letter to the *Times*, that

> The Bill was approved by less than half the membership of the Commons and the only mandate that minority had was from the powerful Wiesenthal Institute.[84]

Not just the rule of law, but democracy itself were under threat in Britain as the result of what Heath, Shawcross and others came to see as yet another "Jewish conspiracy". Again, what is particular about this aspect of the juridico-political debate in Britain is not the presence of antisemitism but rather the overt and blatant presence of antisemitism in the mainstream of that debate. The opposition between the Holocaust and the rule of law here is the opposition between Jews and the rule of law. Nazi law and Jewish law are semiotically identical signs of "not law". Shawcross did however unwittingly make one valuable insight for our understanding of the rhetoric of law in such debates. Just as vengeance is not magically transformed simply by calling it justice, neither is the rule of law mysteriously transmogrified by ritual incantation of assertions as to its content. The debate here, for all its pretense of "justice" on both sides of the question, was always political in nature and content. In the end, the substantive content of "justice" in the context of the Holocaust and the law is determined in a temporary fashion by political debate and judicial decision-making.

For the majority of the House of Commons, and in the end for the positive legal system of law in Britain, the equation between vengeance and justice was not as clear-cut as the antisemites would have it. The *Bill* became

---

84. "Lords ignored on war crimes bill", 4 May 1991. Cf. Letters from Lord Jakobovits and Greville Jenner, 11 May 1991.

law and the Holocaust became a crime recognizable and punishable under the British system of justice. In the end, the rule of law emerged victorious because it could never be otherwise. The debate in the Houses of Parliament demonstrated not just that the content of the rule of law appears to be determined simply by positive law and Parliamentary politics but also that place of the Holocaust within the western tradition of legalism is well-established on all sides of the political divide. It fits and it doesn't fit. It is a Jewish question and it is a question of morality. Nazi law and Jewish law are the same and they are not. Nazi law is law, Nazi law is not law, all of this is possible within the discursive universe of the rule of law in Britain. Subsequent events as English authorities attempted to bring alleged war criminals to trial would prove yet again the strength and weakness of the rule of law in understanding and constructing the issues of the Holocaust and moral responsibility.

5. From Serafimowitz to Sawoniuk to Kalejs: Prosecuting (or Not) War Criminals in Britain

The history of the pursuit of Nazi and collaborationist war criminals after the passage of the *War Crimes Act* is in some ways strikingly similar to the Australian version of the same story. Concern continued to be expressed over the mounting costs of investigations which appeared to lead nowhere.[85] Overt antisemitic interventions in the mainstream of political and legal discourse were replaced by more traditional, respectable and legally recognizable concerns about the extreme age of the potential accused and the inherent unreliability of Soviet evidence. In other words, debate and discourse slipped comfortably into conflicts over the exact meaning and content of "the rule of law" as the Holocaust became legalized in Britain.

This domestication of the Holocaust within British legal discourse resulted in an almost inevitable reduction of historically and morally complex events and categories into the rigid taxonomical structures of the law. Indeed, the very structure of the taxonomy of war crimes within the British legislation confirmed and re-emphasized this basic epistemological and deontological

---

85. See e.g., and compare Owen Bowcott, "War Crimes Trials to Go On", *Guardian*, 18 January 1997 and "Scrap the War Crimes Act", *Daily Telegraph*, 18 January 1997.

flaw within the Western conception(s) of the rule of law as it relates to the Holocaust. Section 1 of the *Act*[86] provides that

> ...proceedings for murder, manslaughter or culpable homicide may be brought against a person in the United Kingdom irrespective of his nationality at the time of the alleged offence of that offence—
>
> (a) was committed during the period beginning with 1st September 1939 and ending with 5th June 1945 in a place which at the time was part of Germany or under German occupation; and
> (b) constituted a violation of the laws and customs of war

The way in which the Legislature chooses to define the criminality of the Holocaust in terms of domestic law is reflective of many of the problematic issues which arise in relation to post-war definitions of the Holocaust as an extra-legal, legal phenomenon. Here the Parliament of Great Britain has chosen, for example, to exclude many offences such as mass deportation of civilian populations, which constitute "crimes against humanity" from its operative legal matrix. The "Holocaust" has instead been limited to acts of "homicide" or unlawful killing. In this way, the Holocaust is defined as a legal phenomenon which occurred only within this limited jurisprudential context. In fact, the War Crimes Inquiry itself, on the basis of which the government of the day decided to proceed, was limited to the consideration of "war crimes" defined in such a narrow fashion.

At the same time, the Parliament has limited the temporal and geographical application of the term "war crimes". The limit is defined as the period of "the war" i.e. after the invasion of Poland and the declaration of hostilities between Britain and Germany. Its physical boundaries are proscribed and limited to areas under German occupation.

The temporal limit imposed also defines the Holocaust and the concept of "war crimes" in a fashion which transforms, as it must almost by jurisprudential definition, the Shoah into a strictly British concern. Thus, acts of atrocity, including killing, committed in Germany, under Nazi law, do not fall under the operative definition. There are a number of complex reasons of international and domestic law and politics which underpin this decision and jurisprudential position. At the same time, however, it is a necessary conclusion of the British decision that Nazi law, which offered an excuse or justification for such killings, is in some way legitimated. Here again, we find a ju-

---

86. *War Crimes Act 1991*, 1991 chapter 13.

risprudential and ethical taxonomical difficulty in relation to the concept of the illegality of the Holocaust arising out of the failure of the Allies before, during and after Nuremberg, to offer a convincing "legal" argument about the point at which Nazi law ceased to operate as law because it violated basic and foundational principles of the "rule of law".

When the British definition of punishable "war crimes" is further limited to those homicides which were not just "unlawful" but were in addition "a violation of the laws and customs of war" we once again confront this jurisprudential dilemma. The judicial or extra-judicial killing of German Jews would probably not be prosecutable under these provisions because such acts against domestic populations would not be considered as violations of the laws of war, even though they might be considered "crimes against humanity" under current international legal norms.

Faced with these and other technical legal difficulties, the British effort to prosecute alleged war criminals stumbled and foundered through its first years as evidence which would meet the burden and standard of proof required in a criminal trial proved difficult to come by. Even when confronted with an individual like Alexander Schweidler, who faced deportation from the United States because of his failure to disclose his service as a concentration camp guard where he admitted killing at least two Jewish prisoners, the British authorities could not muster sufficient evidence to prosecute. Other accused like Harry Svikeris, an officer in the Latvian Arjas Commando, simply died before a case could be mounted against them.[87]

Finally, in 1995, authorities decided that they had enough evidence to proceed against Siemion Serafimowitz, who was charged with committing acts of mass murder as commander of an auxiliary police battalion in the former Soviet Union.[88] Almost immediately, the by now familiar tropes began to appear in the press coverage of the case. His age, 84, featured prominently as did descriptions of his physical and mental infirmities. Almost inevitably, a neighbor was trotted out to make the obligatory statement

> He's a lovely old man. He speaks to the boys when they deliver his paper—he had an awful time looking after his wife at the end. They kept themselves to themselves.

---

87. Stephen Ward, "War crimes suspect dies during inquiry", *Independent*, 8 August 1995.

88. Stewart Tendler, "Britain's first war crimes trial could start next year", *Times*, 23 may 1995.

His son, he is a good man as well. We were all surprised when we heard what they were saying about him. None of the neighbours think he should have to go through all this.
It's time to put the past behind us. We've all done things wrong, she said.[89]

Apparently, according to the good people of Banstead, Surrey, the mass killing of Jews is the moral equivalent of the wrong things we have all done. For the survivors of the massacres, however, Serafimowicz was not an 84 year old retired carpenter but the young man who had served his Nazi masters with diligence and loyalty.[90]

In the eyes of some, Serafimowitz may have betrayed both his past and present feelings and attitudes when he declared

I never killed civilians, not even Jews.[91]

Many in the press continued to portray him sympathetically, most commonly by invoking and deploying descriptions of his age and physical and mental health. Thus,

Frail and white-haired, Mr Serafimowitz approached the dock with faltering steps and was allowed to sit during the hearing.[92]

Or

Clearly in some difficulty, he cupped a hand to his ear and she repeated the question loudly....
Yesterday, Mr Serafimowitz, dressed in a shabby car coat, pullover and thick cotton shirt frequently had difficulty hearing—cupping his hand to his ear and frowning—...[93]

Or

89. Stephen Ward, "War crimes? No, says suburb's 'nice old man'", *Independent*, 24 May 1995.

90. See, Owen Bowcott, " 'Loyal Servant' to Nazi Killers", *Guardian*, 18 January 1997.

91. Anna Blundy, "War criminals set to face trial", *Sunday Times*, 16 October 1994.

92. Tim Jones, "Man of 84 freed on bail in first British war crimes case", *Times*, 14 July 1995.

93. Bill Frost, "Retired carpenter accused of killing three in war atrocities", *Times*, 5 January 1996.

...a tiny, frail man.[94]

In the end, Serafimowicz's mental and physical incapacities reached such a state that a decision was made "in the interests of justice" not to proceed against him.[95] The case against Serafimowicz was a triumph for the rule of law. At his committal, one of the charges against him was dropped for lack of evidence, thereby indicating that the normal procedures and protections offered to any accused in a British criminal trial would and could operate in a "war crimes" trial. In other words, there would be no special justice in such cases. The decision to stay the charges in this case gave further proof that English juries and prosecutors were alive to concerns of "justice" and "fairness", hallmarks of the rule of law and would act according to these general principles in cases involving those accused of having committed "war crimes". These circumstances simply confirmed the statutory framework of the *War Crimes Act* which in effect did nothing more than extend the temporal, personal and geographic jurisdiction of British courts in ordinary homicide cases. The British system specifically modeled its construction of the Holocaust by making it "ordinary." It deals with homicide, not with crimes against humanity. Special treatment, special rules as not required under British law since British courts, judges and juries deal with these offences on a regular and ongoing basis. The idea of some that the Holocaust is unique, that crimes and perpetrators are somehow a case apart in law and in morality is specifically rejected in the British scheme.

Of course, traditional opponents of the very existence of the *War Crimes Act* did not see things in this frame and reiterated their original positions, re-situating the debate once more as one pitting justice and vengeance as competing concepts in the British legal system. Additionally arguments about "waste of public money" and "waste of time" were invoked to buttress first principle arguments.[96]

Others, however, did not hesitate to bring out the more hateful aspects of the original debate surrounding the *War Crimes Act* and stoop to nothing more sophisticated than antisemitic diatribe. Writing in the Glasgow *Herald*, John Macleod offered a sadly typical example of the not so underground antisemitism which contaminates British public political and legal discourse.

---

94. David Pallister, "Man, 85, to Face War Crimes Trial", *Guardian*, 16 April 1996.

95. David Connett, "Uk's First War Crime Trial Set to Collapse", *Guardian*, 3 November 1996; "Fury over £ 5 Million War Crimes Trial Waste", *Mirror*, 18 January 1997; Patricia Wynn Davies, "£ 7m cost as war crimes case fails", *Independent*, 18 January 1997.

96. See the comments of Norman Tebbit, ibid. See also Hugh Muir and Sue Clough, "Nazi suspect freed after £ 4m inquiry", *Daily Telegraph*, 18 January 1997; Auberon Waugh, "The punishment gang", *Daily Telegraph*, 20 January 1997.

After drawing parallels between Serafimowicz and the Nuremberg and Eichmann trials,[97] Macleod offers up the following:

> But I do resent, 50 years on, the vengeful judgment passed on these individuals by Tel Aviv diamond dealers and cosy Liberal MPs, men and women who did not live in that world or that time and know nothing of its terrors.[98]

It is possible to refute Macleod's claims on any one of several fronts. First, of course, the *Act* received the support of members of all political parties in the Parliament, of all ideological stripes on the Left/Right spectrum. Second, many of those who supported the legislation, like many who opposed it, did in fact live through the period in question, several having lost family members in the war and the Shoah. But people like Macleod are not particularly interested in the facts since these only interfere with the larger project of propagating hatred. There can be no other purpose in referring to a piece of legislation passed overwhelmingly in the House of Commons as "The vengeful judgment…by Tel Aviv diamond dealers" than to perpetuate hatred and stereotypes against British Jewry. Macleod and his ilk simply cannot imagine a Britain which harbored mass murderers as part of official policy, nor can they even imagine a Britain in which these policies would be challenged and refuted on the basis of any moral vision of the rule of law or ethical duty which differs from their own. Referring to the current of antisemitism which was exposed in Parliament, David Cesarani wrote:

> What the debate over the War Crimes Bill exposed most painfully was the stubborn refusal in many quarters to acknowledge that Britain is a multi-ethnic society with many strands of history.[99]

Interventions like this after the stay of proceedings against Serafimowitz confirm not just that Cesarani was correct in his assessment of British sentiment, or part thereof, but also that for many reasons, law, and the rule of law, may prove to be an inadequate forum and an inadequate trope for the complex issues of public memory and history which continue to surround the Holocaust. It might be argued that the history of the Parliamentary and political struggle surrounding the *War Crimes Act* demonstrates the absence of a multi-ethnic

---

97. Ignoring the illogic of comparing cases where the accused were convicted (for the most part at Nuremberg) and the case at hand where the accused was set free by the operation of traditional legal norms.

98. "Chilling frenzy of vengeful judgment", 21 January 1997.

99. *Justice Delayed*, op. cit., at p. 263.

Britain. Unlike the situation in Australia, and to a lesser extent that in Canada, the absence of a powerful "ethnic" lobby from the "Captive Nations" meant that there was in fact little counter-weight to the political forces militating outside Parliament for passage of the Bill. The battle which was waged in Britain was one which was fought out between the traditionalist view of Britain and what Cesarani has described as proponents of a multi-ethnic vision of Britain. In Australia, by way of contrast, the battle was one which was waged at a different and more complex level about which of several visions of a multicultural vision of that country would win.[100] In each national instance, however, the point of consistency and unity, which was and continues to be inconsistent and symbolic of political and moral disunity, remains the deployment of the rhetoric and tropes of the rule of law.

In Britain, the subsequent prosecution of Anthony Sawoniuk for war crimes demonstrates the ways in which all of these concepts, law, legality, memory, the Holocaust, are and remain fluid and open to reinterpretation in changing circumstances and contexts. Sawoniuk was charged with the commission of war crimes in Belarus while employed as a police officer under the German occupiers.[101] Again, at a basic level, the tropes deployed in describing his case are the by now familiar ones. He was a "77 (or 78) year old former British Rail employee from Bermondsey, South London", or some variant thereof. He was an old man, he was just obeying orders, he hated Russians and Communists but not Jews etc.[102]

But for some reason, the case against Sawoniuk was different. Following the Gecas precedent in part at least, the judge and jury visited Belarus and saw the sites where Sawoniuk was said to have committed his crimes. The case against him proceeded, as had Serafimowitz's, according to the rules and procedures of ordinary criminal trials. The judge instructed the jury that it would be unsafe to convict on some of the charges against the accused, and in the end, Anthony Sawoniuk became the first person in Britain to be convicted of war crimes. Perhaps he was convicted because the case against him was overwhelming. Perhaps he was convicted because only one of the prosecution's witnesses against him was Jewish and the rest were his former friends and neighbors. Perhaps he was convicted because his defense consisted in large part of accusing Scotland Yard detectives of being in league with the KGB. In

---

100. See discussion infra, chapter 10.

101. See e.g., Cherry Norton, "Second war crimes case", *Sunday Times*, 1 June 1997; Barrie Penrose, "Londoner, 76, in Nazi war trial", *Sunday Times*, 31 August 1997; Christopher Elliott, "Briton Held Over Nazi War Crimes", *Guardian*, 27 September 1997.

102. See e.g., Andrew Collier, "Facing Up To The Past", *Scotsman*, 16 June 1998.

the end, what we do know is that he was convicted by an English jury, in a trial for murder under English law, for crimes committed against Jews and others in Belarus over 50 year ago.

The question raised by the Sawoniuk conviction in the end remains the same as that raised by the Serafimowicz "acquittal". What of the rule of law and the Holocaust in British legal and political memory? In the final analysis, little is or was changed in relation to the substantive law or to the jurisprudential status of the "rule of law". Conviction or acquittal, the rule of law wins out. This immutable jurisprudential strength of this particular vision of the rule of law played itself out in Sawoniuk's appeal against his conviction. Here, his lawyer based his attack on the conviction on the by now well-trodden path of the passage of time, arguing that this alone made the jury's decision unsafe.

> In support of that submission counsel places reliance, in this court as before the judge, on a number of features of this very unusual case; the passage of over 56 years from the date of the alleged crime to the date of the trial; the fact that the sole, unsupported, witness was at the time a boy, who did not mention this incident to the NKVD when interviewed after the war and who made no statement on the subject for over 50 years; the inability of the defence, after this lapse of time, to identify or trace the two other policemen said to have been present at the time of this incident, if indeed it took place; the death of the witness's 16 year old companion, who died in 1986 without communicating his recollection, if any, of the event to anyone, the absence of any other witness able to challenge or dispute the account of Alexander Baglay; and the absence of any scientific support for his evidence.[103]

The Court of Appeal, however, rejected this and similar arguments and instead found that the traditional safeguards of the British system of criminal justice remained in place in war crimes trials, as they did in all other proceedings. After rejecting each of the specific grounds of appeal, Lord Bingham found that

> Given the unique circumstances of this case and the grave consequences of conviction to the appellant, we have considered with care whether there is any more general ground upon which these convictions should be regarded as unsafe. For reasons already given, we conclude that the jury was in a very advantageous position, having seen

---

103. *R. v. Sawoniuk*, [2000] EWCA 19 (10 February 2000) at 6.

the site and heard the evidence, to form a reliable judgment on count three. On count one we remind ourselves that the conviction rested very largely on the evidence of a witness who was, if his evidence was reliable, standing within feet of the appellant when this murder was committed. It was not a case of an identification made 56 years after the event, but one of contemporaneous recognition to which the witness deposed after that lapse of time. It is not easy to imagine any event which, if witnessed, would impress itself more indelibly on the mind of a 13 year old boy. The jury had to consider whether the witness was honest and reliable. They concluded that he was both. We can see no reason to question the soundness of that judgment.[104]

Here we find the classic embodiment of the strength and power of the discourse and method of the rule of law in the British common law tradition. The golden thread of the criminal law, the presumption of innocence, the burden of proof beyond reasonable doubt, respect for the finders of fact, all are embodied in the Court of Appeal's reasoning. Following the will of Parliament, the Court, in the end, treats the fate of Sawoniuk as it would any defendant in any criminal appeal. This is, as it could only ever be, just another murder case.

Perhaps it is also possible to argue that the Sawoniuk trial may nonetheless have played a broader ideological, ethical and pedagogical role in the construction of the Holocaust in British public memory. Indeed David Hirsh has convincingly demonstrated the ways in which witnesses "circumvented" the traditional restrictions of the laws of evidence to turn their testimony into "memoir" of the Holocaust.[105] Hirsh can accurately assert that

> Embedded within the norms and rules of the criminal trial are the mechanisms by which the rules and norms of evidence may be subverted.[106]

While Sawoniuk's trial was being reported daily in the British media, other reports followed the saga of British justice and its attempts to deal with the case of Augusto Pinochet and the rule of law. At the same time, television and newspapers were full of pictures and reports of ethnic cleansing in Kosovo. Trainloads of people removed from their homes at gunpoint and placed en

---

104. Ibid., at p. 17. See also Terri Judd, "Nazi War Criminal Has Appeal Rejected", *Independent*, 11 February 2000. "War Crimes Conviction is Upheld", *Guardian*, 11 February 2000.
105. "The Trial of Andrei Sawoniuk: Holocaust Testimony under Cross-Examination", 10 *Social & Legal Studies* 529 (2001).
106. Ibid, at 544.

masse in trains may well have acted in concert to set public opinion in a certain direction.[107] The *Times* editorial page, so hostile to the *War Crimes Act* just a few years earlier clearly reflected some of this shift in public attitudes.

At the same time of course, it is important to offer some *caveats* here. Kosovo was a horror but it not the Holocaust. Trains to the Macedonian border are not trains to Treblinka. Horror manifests itself in many human forms. Much of the case against Pinochet was lost in the second House of Lords decision based on a technical and legalistic reading of international law in relation to British domestic legislation. The second case was brought because of a technical legalistic reading of the idea of natural justice and procedural fairness. In other words, Pinochet won and lost, as did Serafimowicz and Sawoniuk, because the rule of law worked. The rule of law and the Holocaust are not so much in contradiction as they are occasionally intersecting parallel lines.[108] What war crimes trials can never do, in Britain or elsewhere, is to confront the intimate links between and among discourses and practices of law and the construction of the legal subject who can be killed, but not murdered, the *homo sacer*, the Jew, the Kosovar, the member of MIR.

Again Hirsh puts forward the idea that

> The extraordinariness of the events with which this trial was concerned accentuated the difficulties that the trial process has with abstracting and shaping events in the world so that they can be judged in the court room.[109]

This is at some level the embodiment again in the context of the trial of Holocaust perpetrator of the broader ideological and historical view and construction of the Holocaust as "extraordinary." Events are somehow so enormous in quality and quantity, that they are removed from normal discursive practices and placed therein only with great difficulty and probably only by betraying some rule or another. The real difficulty, I believe, lies at another level altogether. It is the ordinariness, the ordinary lawfulness of the Holo-

---

107. See e.g. Michael Pinto-Duschinsky, "A timely reminder for all tyrants", *Times*, 2 April 1999; Editorial, "Pursuit of Justice", *Times*, 3 April 1999.

108. Following the Sawoniuk conviction, investigations were begun into the case of Avto Pardzhanadze, a former Georgian accused of mass atrocities in the former Soviet Union. In 1968, the USSR had requested his extradition for trial on war crimes. The Crown Prosecution Service decided that there was insufficient evidence to proceed against him. A similar refusal to proceed has also been the result of investigations involving Stanislaw Chrzanowski, alleged to have committed mass murder in Belarus. See "The Nazi behind bars in Britain and the others on whom suspicion fell", *Observer*, 2 January 2000.

109. "The Trial of Andrei Sawoniuk", op. cit. at 544.

caust which poses legal difficulties and difficulties for the law, not the technical conflict between the rules of evidence and the demands of memory.

Hitler, Milosevic and Pinochet all presided over an operative and recognizable legal system, staffed and run on a daily basis by judges and lawyers who never questioned their own positions as legal servants of the people. The law, as the case of Sawoniuk, like so many others, demonstrates, is a flexible instrument, perfectly capable of dealing with all aspects of genocide, enslavement, deportation, torture, etc. except the very lawfulness of these practices.

More recent events in Britain go some way to confirming this analysis of the manner in which the law and rhetoric about the rule of law can be and are manipulated in relation to constructions of the Holocaust and national and legal memory. Late in 1999, the British media reported on investigations being conducted into the fate of Anton Husak, a 78-year-old immigrant from Georgia, then living in Wales. It was alleged that Husak had been a member of an *Einsatzgruppe* unit responsible for the mass killings of Jews. Once again, the information concerning Husak was said to come from the Simon Wiesenthal Center, although it was also shown that his name had appeared on a list of war criminals presented by the then Soviet government to the British authorities in 1988.[110] Once again many of the familiar themes emerged— the passage of time, the age of the alleged perpetrator, the political situation in the former Soviet republic which made the gathering of evidence extremely difficult and finally the triumph of the British system after the Crown Protection Service determined that the results of the police investigation meant that there was no prospect of conviction. In other words, the legal processes of the British system had been deployed and no action on a case of which the authorities had been aware for over eleven years would be taken. The prosecution of alleged war criminals in Britain had apparently come to an end.

That is until the peripatetic Konrad Kalejs made an appearance at a Latvian retirement home in Leicestershire.[111] Kalejs had previously been deported from the United States and Canada and was believed to have been a member of the

---

110. See Julia Hartley-Brewer, "Man, 78, held in Wales war crimes inquiry", *Guardian*, 1 October 1999.

111. Kalejs was first reported to be living in Warwickshire but that proved to be inaccurate. See "Britain Asked to Try Suspected Nazi", *New York Times*, 27 December 1999; Robin Young, "'Nazi war criminal' in Britain", *Times*, 28 December 1999; Stephen Farrell and Helen Johnstone, "Police question man accused of Nazi slaughter", ibid., Roger Boyes and Stephen Farrell, "Fugitive from a restless and murky past", id., Vikram Dodd, "Straw urged to deport 'Nazi war criminal'", *Guardian*, 29 December 1999.

notorious Arjas Commando, responsible for mass killings in the former Soviet Union.

Home Office Minister Jack Straw found himself with a dilemma. The Blair Labour government had recently been involved in the legal process meant to extradite Chilean dictator Augusto Pinochet to Spain to stand trial for crimes of torture and murder. It had been a leader of the "humanitarian" bombing campaign against Serbia and against Iraq. The *War Crimes Act* granted jurisdiction to prosecute Kalejs for his alleged crimes and Kalejs was now under British jurisdiction. However, as we also know, authorities in Australia, Kalejs' adopted home, had on several occasions refused to bring charges against him on the grounds that they lacked sufficient probative evidence. After receiving reports from the competent British authorities, Straw decided to adopt a familiar position and deport Kalejs.[112] In the absence of probative evidence on which to arrest, hold and try Kalejs, and in the absence of an extradition request from Latvia, whose record on wartime atrocities is ambiguous at best,[113] Straw decided in effect that Kalejs was best left as someone else's problem. Before the Minister could order his deportation, Kalejs boarded a Singapore Airlines flight and returned to his not-so-peaceful retirement in Australia.

The decision to deport and then to allow Kalejs to leave Britain was met with mixed reactions. Some urged the government to keep Kalejs pending further inquiries and to seek contact with American, Canadian, Australian and Latvian law enforcement and government agencies to attempt to bring him to trial somewhere. Others like Lord Janner of the Holocaust Education Trust and one of the architects of the *War Crimes Act* praised the government's decision as an example of the superiority of the rule of law. If there was insufficient evidence against Kalejs, Janner argued, it would be contrary to the principles of British justice to seek to bend or change the rules simply because of what he was alleged to have done.[114]

Here we return again to the ever familiar themes and discursive practices which have surrounded the issue of prosecution of alleged war criminals and more particularly the debate over the American and later Canadian decisions

112. Stephen Farrell and Helen Johnstone, "Straw orders inquiry into Nazi suspect", *Times*, 30 December 1999; Linus Gregoriadis, "Straw demands inquiry into how alleged Nazi war criminal entered UK", *Guardian*, 30 December 1999.

113. See also Jon Silverman, "Latvia killers rehabilitated", BBC News, 26 January 1999.

114. John Hibbs and Alan Philps, "Straw attacked for freeing 'war criminal'", *Daily Telegraph*, 4 January 2000; Andrew Buncombe, "Anger as 'nazi war criminal' ordered to leave", *Independent*, 4 January 2000.

to use immigration law to act against individuals.[115] On one side of the debate are those who argue that deportation is a strongly significant declaration, consequent upon the exercise of the due process and other legal protections, whereby a country, in this case Britain, declares that someone like Kalejs is not welcome to enjoy the benefits of membership in the national community. Of course, the message does not carry with it the same rhetorical and ideological weight as those instances, particularly in the United States, where the act of deportation also carries with it the civic degradation of the loss of citizenship.

On the other side of the rhetorical and symbolic legal divide are those who argue that the true effect of the deportation of someone like Kalejs in this instance is the opposite of a national statement recognizing and "nationalizing" the Holocaust. In other words, the semiotic import of deportation here is to declare the fate of Kalejs and the fate of his victims in terms of law, to be of no concern to the government and people of Britain. If he is to be tried, that is someone else's concern.

Other semiotic and legal historical debates also surface in the light of the Kalejs case in Britain.[116] Deportation and recognition of the sovereignty and prosecutorial right of the nation in which the offences were committed were the basic jurisprudential concepts informing the Moscow Accords on the subject of war crimes and crimes against humanity to which Britain was a signatory. Yet we know that Britain decided to cease the practice in 1948 as a result of Cold War politics and some concerns over the justice system in the then Eastern Bloc. Indeed, this decision was invoked on a regular basis throughout the periods of Soviet requests for extradition of various individuals from Britain. It was also the basis of many strong objections to the introduction of the *War Crimes Act*. Finally, deportation was also rejected by many proponents of the same legislation on the basis, *inter alia*, that British justice should deal with perpetrators present on British soil as a British problem. The use to which deportation was put in the Kalejs case would not have satisfied either opponents or proponents of the legislation giving British courts jurisdiction over Kalejs' alleged actions because in effect for them all, justice and the substantive content of law are at loggerheads with their political and moral positions.

At the same time, Britain continues to grapple with the remaining dilemmas posed by the Holocaust and the law in that country. The Kalejs case and

---

115. See discussion below, chapter 9.

116. Not the least of which is the historical resonance of convict transport to Australia and the more recent phenomenon of Britain dumping refugees, including possible war criminals, as part of Commonwealth cooperation after the Second World War.

the publicity surrounding it caused Lord Janner to issue a call for the reopening of the Gecas case with the view of deporting him to stand trial.[117] Lithuanian detectives began reviewing the state of evidence against Gecas for possible trail in that country.[118] Also around this period, news emerged that Alexander Schweidler, who had been deported from the United States was again under investigation by British authorities.[119] Schweidler had obtained British citizenship before going to the United States. When faced with American proceedings to deport him because he had served as a guard at Matthausen, he was therefore legally entitled to return to Great Britain where he lived apparently unmolested for six years.[120] A few days after his case resurfaced as a result of the Kalejs furor, he died of a heart attack.[121] The next week, the Blair government announced the creation of an annual Holocaust Remembrance Day in Britain. Konrad Kalejs was at home in Melbourne Australia.

---

117. "Call to re-open 'Nazi' case", BBC News, 9 January 2000.

118. Severin Carrell, "Alleged Nazi living in Britain faces Lithuanian investigation", *Independent*, 12 January 2000.

119. Helen Johnstone, "Ex-SS guard 'is pensioner in South East'", *Times*, 21 January 2000.

120. See "Former Nazi SS guard leaves U.S.", *St. Petersburg Times*, 22 January 1994.

121. Helen Johnstone, "Suspected war criminal living in Britain dies of heart attack", *Times*, 25 January 2000. Gecas also died before any criminal proceedings were instituted.

CHAPTER 9

"YES, ERRORS WERE MADE IN THE PAST":* PURSUING (OR NOT) HOLOCAUST PERPETRATORS IN CANADA

1. Introduction

The "errors" made in Canada in the pursuit of Holocaust perpetrators are familiar ones. As was the case in the United Kingdom, the Canadian story is one of the failure and/or complicity of its immigration program in the immediate postwar period. It is also a story of a persistent reluctance to address the failures of that program when evidence emerged about the presence on Canadian soil of those who had actively participated in aspects of the mass killings of European Jewry. Finally it is a tale of the victory of the rule of law and of Parliamentary democracy over demands for "justice" for the victims of the Holocaust.

With Australia, Canada shares a history as one of the white settler dominions of the British Empire. With Australia, Canada also shares a history of a postwar immigration policy largely influenced by the political wishes and practices of Whitehall. But the connections with its Commonwealth partners predate postwar migration policy. Just as Britain and Australia turned away Jewish refugees fleeing Nazi rule in Europe in the late 1930s,

---

* Canadian Prime Minister Jean Chrétien at Yad Vashem, April 2000.

Canada's record in that period is marked by a distinctly anti-Jewish immigration policy.[1]

The depth of similarity here is still more profound. In effect, both pre- and post-war migration policies, in Canada, as in Britain and Australia, were informed by an ongoing intense struggle over the meaning and content of national identity. In the various battles over "Canadian-ness", Jews generally and the Holocaust more particularly fit most uncomfortably. Most recent debates over central aspects of national identity are informed by the immediate post-war period as one in which previous population dynamics were radically upset as the result of an influx of migrants from a variety of European nations. Multiculturalism and a multi-ethnic body politic became new focal points in the ongoing debates and political battles over just what it meant and means to be Canadian. A key element in these social conversations about national identity in Canada was the idea that what was and is important and central to the issue is the abandonment of rivalries and animosities from "over there" in favor of a new, shared and harmonious Canadian identity.

At the same time of course, such debates evidenced serious conflicts and contradictions with other aspects of postwar migration policy and Canada's ideological and political situation as a settler dominion and more broadly as a Western nation and member of the NATO alliance. Anti-communism and the associated political and cultural rhetoric of the Cold War became essential to Canada's national identity and as a consequence, central to its migration policies and "ethnic" politics. Large numbers of migrants from the Soviet bloc and from the so-called Captive Nations in particular were welcomed into the Canadian safe haven from Communist oppression. Anti-communism and anti-Soviet agitation, not surprisingly, became part of the political activities of many immigrant communities. At some level at least, this stood in clear contradiction with the policy of harmony and historical and geographical amnesia required under other operative norms of Canadian multiculturalism which demanded that old animosities be left at the border.

Further elements of Canada's ethic national identity politics also complicated the place which the Holocaust was to play in that country's postwar political and legal arenas. Chief among these was and is the presence of an older immigrant community of Ukrainian Canadians. Immigrants from the

---

1. See Irving Abella and Harold Troper, *None Is Too Many* (Toronto: Lester & Orpen Dennys, 1982). Cf., Howard Margolian, *Unauthorized Entry: The Truth About Nazi War Criminals in Canada, 1946–1959* (Toronto: University of Toronto Press, 2000).

Ukraine have a long history in Canada, easily pre-dating the Cold War era. In parts of the country, Ukrainian Canadians constituted the largest ethnic group. Their presence would have a profound influence on Canadian migration policy in the early days after the end of World War 2 and would permit the influx of many more of their "countrymen" in that period. Of course, among those immigrants would be individuals who had participated in the implementation of the Final Solution in the Ukraine and in other parts of eastern Europe. As a long-established and politically powerful "ethnic" group, Ukrainian Canadians would play a key role in the history of Canadian efforts to deal with the issue of Holocaust perpetrators.[2]

Another element which characterizes the Canadian case and the history of the Holocaust and its place within the national culture generally and the legal system more specifically is, of course, the primary "ethnic" division of the country. One can hardly speak of any idea of Canadian identity without confronting the seemingly never-ending struggle for a coherent relationship between French- and English-speaking Canadians. Again, it is not my intention here to revisit the primary definitional struggle for Canadian identity in any detail. Rather I wish to briefly explore and locate the position of the Holocaust and "ethnic" politics specifically within this broader informing matrix of Canadian self-definition in order to point out the problematic and marginal nature of concern about the pursuit of war criminals and Holocaust perpetrators in Canada. More specifically, here we must return to the central taxonomical question of the category "victim" as it relates to the place of the Holocaust within Canadian law. Arguments about the Holocaust as a "crime against humanity" are commonly asserted in order to impose upon government the duty to pursue alleged perpetrators. At the same time the concept of "humanity" as "victim" is easily and often uncritically replaced by assertions of Jewish specificity in relation to the Shoah. This specificity is of course founded in the simple historical and factual truth that "the Jew" was the primary target for extermination under Hitler and his allies. Yet here we face the taxonomical and ethical difficulty of political and legal discourse about the Holocaust in many countries. If Jewish specificity as "victim" is arguably the defining element of the Holocaust, then claims of a general offence against "humanity" are immediately brought into question by many. More particularly, the question of the eth-

2. This story has been well-documented and it is not my intention to rehash the complexities of "ethnic" politics and the war crimes question in Canada. See Harold Troper and Morton Weinfeld, *Old Wounds: Jews, Ukrainians and the Hunt for Nazi War Criminals in Canada* (New York and London: Viking Penguin, 1988).

ical and moral duty of national governments to try alleged perpetrators becomes more problematic. If the law is valid as an expression of national interest, it is valid insofar as the national interest is defined in relation to membership in an international community adhering to the laws of humanity. It must then, almost by self-definition, ignore the Jewish specificity of the Holocaust. The crime before Canadian courts is tried as an affront to the general "peace, order and good government" of Canada, of all of Canada and of no Canadians defined in an ethnically or religiously specific way. The Canadianization of the Holocaust in this context must ignore a central and defining element of historical reality in order to fit comfortably within the legal system of the country.

Within the dominant and primary division and rift in Canadian national identity between Francophone and Anglophone Canadians, and more specifically within the geographic boundaries of the province of Québec, the "Jewish question" plays a role which is at once marginal and central to the broader question. The Jewish presence in the province and particularly in the largest city Montréal has been a long one. The history of antisemitism in Québec is not surprisingly at least as long as the presence of a Jewish minority in the province. Here we find the first element which complicates the related questions of the role of Jews and of the Holocaust in Canadian history and national self-identification i.e. the two-sided nature of antisemitism in Québec. First, anti-Jewish sentiment can be found among the French-speaking majority. In a community which was almost universally Catholic, historical French Canadian antisemitism was itself characterized by two distinct yet oddly related dimensions. There is strong evidence of an almost visceral, yet highly intellectualized, Catholic "theological" antisemitism among certain elements of the ruling élite of French Canadian society. This has been further complicated historically by the dominant tension between the two linguistic camps. French Canadian nationalism in its many variants has managed to combine linguistic (anti-English, pro-French) and religious (Catholic) elements of self-identity.

Thus, Jews were detested both because they were not Catholic and because they were perceived almost as a definitional result of the first factor as being "English" and therefore inimical and hostile to the basic elements of Québécois national identity. At the same time, of course, the dominant English mercantile class in Montréal in particular shared in its own versions of religious and cultural animosity to a Jewish presence. In other words, in Québec, where the most central and important issues of historical Canadian national identity were and are being played out, Jews were the outsiders for each of the competing linguistic and cultural groups. Pre-war anti-Jewish immigration policy at the national level was in part at least influenced by French Canadian sentiment against any further Jewish immigration.[3]

The history of Canadian policy and practice in relation to the pursuit of alleged war criminals and perpetrators of crimes against humanity can only be understood if one begins with the this central element of national identity. Indeed, antisemitism, national identity, the role of Catholic intellectuals and the complex nature of French Canadian nationalism have both direct and indirect connections to the development and unfolding of Canada's sad story of complicity and lethargy in the pursuit of Nazi perpetrators and of the marginalization of the Holocaust in Canadian politics and social life.

2. Fascism, Antisemitism and National Identity in Québec and Canada

The story of the connections between Canadian or more specifically French Canadian identity and elements of a Catholic fascist theocratic vision of a Laurentian nationhood have been documented by others, most particularly controversial historian Esther Delisle.[4] A brief examination of the general issue of antisemitism, French Canadian nationalism and current political debates followed by a more specific discussion of the place of war criminals in these issues will serve to illuminate these aspects of the story of the Canadian struggle to reconcile the Holocaust with that country's version of the rule of law.

The best example of the ways in which the history of a French Canadian theocratic and nationalist antisemitism has been and continues to be constructed in struggles over Canadian identity is the controversy surrounding the resignation of Jean-Louis Roux as Lieutenant-Governor of Québec in 1996. Roux was a greatly respected man of the Québec theatre, film and television stage. He was also a well-known civil libertarian and an avowed federalist i.e. a supporter of Québec and its place in the Canadian confederation. He was appointed to the Canadian Senate and thereafter was named as Lieutenant-Governor of Québec by Liberal Prime Minister Jean Chrétien. Shortly thereafter, Roux resigned from office when it was revealed that as a student in Montréal in 1942, he had participated in an anti-conscription "riot". He admitted

---

3. Abella and Troper at 18.

4. See *The Traitor and the Jew* (Montréal: Robert Davies Publishing, 1993) and *Myths, Memory & Lies* (Montréal: Robert Davies Multimedia, 1998). See also Susan Mann Trofimenkoff, *Action Française: French Canadian Nationalism in the Twenties* (Toronto: University of Toronto Press, 1975).

that he had worn a swastika on his lab coat which he wore to the demonstration and that others had targeted and vandalized Jewish shop fronts during the events. He consistently denied that he himself had engaged in any acts of violence.[5] While the wearing of a swastika in 1942, while Canadian soldiers, French and English-speaking were part of the war against Hitler, whatever may or may not have been known about the Holocaust at that time, was offensive and problematic in the extreme, and while the revelations were enough to make Roux feel that he had to resign his post, the real interest of the Roux affair lies elsewhere. First, there is the debate surrounding his assertions that the regrettable events in which he had participated were in fact in accordance with the *air du temps* (the spirit of the times) and sadly consistent with what was part of the theocratic educational value system of young Québec students at the time. Second, and intimately related to the first, is that way in which Roux's actions were constructed and cynically deployed within the context of contemporary Canadian politics of national identity.

The English-speaking press in Canada had little difficulty in accepting Roux's assertion that a strong element of Catholic crypto-fascism was present in the educational élite in Québec of the 1940s. The editorial writer of Toronto's self-styled "national" newspaper, the *Globe and Mail* easily proclaimed that

> In the cloistered and clerical Quebec of the 1940s, it is not beyond comprehension that a university student eager to win favour with his peers, would wear a swastika and march against conscription in a demonstration with anti-Semitic overtones.[6]

In the French language press, however, things were apparently more complex. *Le Devoir*, the leading intellectual newspaper of French Québec, for example, published two articles by University academics aimed at defusing any attempt to assert that Québec culture was indeed permeated by a tendency towards fascist antisemitism. The first, by Professor Jacques Rouillard of the History Department of l'Université de Montréal set out to establish that while there were elements associated with fascism present in Québec society in the 1930s and 1940s, there had in fact been a deliberate effort by some to distort history (and therefore national identity) by overemphasizing the influence and importance

---

5. See Karen Unland, "Roux admits wearing swastika", *Globe and Mail*, 5 November 1996; "Honesty and hypocrisy and Jean-Louis Roux", Editorial, *Globe and Mail*, 6 November 1996; "Roux quits over swastika admission", *Globe and Mail*, 6 November 1996. Stéphane Baillargeon, "Roux contre les historiens", *Le Devoir*, 6 November 1996.

6. "Honesty and Hypocrisy and Jean-Louis Roux", op. cit.

of these groups.[7] One way in which Professor Rouillard sought to re-balance the historical record was by offering evidence of the presence of fascist and antisemitic political movements in English Canada. Of course, logically this move in no way defeats the argument that French Canadian nationalism was influenced by fascist ideology in general and antisemitism in particular. Instead it simply re-affirms another important point i.e. that antisemitism has always been a element present in aspects of Canadian national identity.

The second way in which antisemitic fascism is marginalized by Professor Rouillard is more interesting and more telling. Here he asserts that Québec's opposition to conscription was based simply in a nationalist (here Rouillard reads "Canadian") aversion to spilling blood in a war being conducted by the imperial master Britain in its own interests. A similar argument was also mounted by Béatrice Richard in her article in the same paper.[8] For her, French Canadian anti-conscription sentiment needs to be understood not in an anti-British Canadian identity, but in a North American isolationist political worldview.

What is important here is not whether these and similar comments which appeared in the Francophone press are more accurate understandings of the events in question or whether they are more in a long line of *apologiae* for the worst and most pernicious elements of Québécois nationalism. Instead what is interesting in this part of the debate of the Roux affair is the way in which each side seeks to present the issue of French Canadian nationalism in a way which either marginalizes or ignores the question of antisemitism. What is of concern here is the way in which Canada and Québec were, are and will be defined in relation to one another. Antisemitism and what that means for the position of Jews, and for present purposes of the Holocaust, in the construction of Canadian history, memory and national identity are removed to a marginal position since that is, in the strangely coincidental yet opposing views of Canadian and Québec identity, exactly where the Jews (and others) belong.

This marginalization of the central issue and its replacement by the struggle over historical memory and collective identity in terms of Canada versus Québec is apparent when one examines the second way in which the Roux affair was played out in the context of Canadian politics. In essence, the Roux affair had very little to do with antisemitism and national identity and everything to do with current political struggles between Ottawa and the forces of federalism on the one hand and Québec and the forces of nationalism and separatism on the other. Roux was an ardent federalist, a Francophone sup-

---

7. "Le Québec était-il fasciste en 1942?", 13 November 1996.
8. "De simples soldats", *Le Devoir*, 18 November 1996.

porter of French Canadian identity within the context of Canada. He had been a vocal opponent of separatists during the preceding referendum campaign on the issue of Québec leaving the federation. He was named by Prime Minister Chrétien as Lieutenant-Governor, officially and constitutionally the representative of Her Majesty, the Queen of Canada, apparently without "consultation" with the provincial government. In Québec City, the provincial government was a Parti Québécois government, dedicated to separation. In Ottawa, the separatist Bloc Québécois was a strong element of the Opposition.

Calls for Roux's resignation came not from the Canadian Jewish community, which was actually quite forgiving and accepting of Roux's contrition in the wake of the revelations.[9] Instead the loudest cries for Roux to step down came from elements of the separatist political parties who saw a political opportunity to score points at the expense of the Liberal federal government.[10] Many commentators, particularly in English Canada were quick to point out that the Québec nationalists' condemnation of antisemitism would be more readily believable if they were willing to authentically engage and come to terms with the past role of antisemitism within their own movement. When questioned in the House of Commons on the matter, Prime Minister Chrétien was quick to point out that those who criticized Roux's actions should have the courage to look at what was written in the pages of *Le Devoir* in the 1930s and 1940s.[11] Here he was referring to the long and clear history of Catholic antisemitism which informed French Canadian intellectual and political debate at that time.[12] Yet even in Chrétien's rhetorical flourishes, it seems clear that the principle debate is not about antisemitism and national identity but about the struggle between federalists and separatists within Québec politics and culture. The debate about Roux's past is little more than a smoke screen for both sides to deal with issues of federalism, of the royal prerogative, of whether Canadian constitutional practice and convention demands "consultation" over vice-regal appointments or whether the Prime Minister may simply "inform" the provincial leaders of his choice.[13] In other words,

9. See "CJC Comments on Resignation of Jean-Louis Roux", Canadian Jewish Congress, Press Release, 5 November 1996.

10. See Robert Sheppard, "The Roux Affair", *Globe and Mail*, 6 November 1996; Rheal Seguin and Hugh Winsor, "Roux quits over swastika admission", ibid.; Karen Unland, "Roux apologizes to Jews, veterans", ibid., 7 November 1996.

11. *Hansard*, 5 November 1996, 6127.

12. See Delisle, *The Traitor and the Jew*, op. cit.

13. *Hansard*, op. cit., at 6129.

even when the history of antisemitism and national identity is at the apparent forefront of political debates in Canada, the real debate almost inevitably returns to the central historical question of Canada's identity as a nation state, the relationship between its two constitutional founding peoples.

This also almost inevitably arises even when the context is that of the pursuit of alleged war criminals on Canadian soil. The more specific question of the relationship between these elements of French Canadian politics of identity and the pursuit of war criminals arose in the public consciousness with recent studies of the Count de Bernonville affair. De Bernonville was an antisemite, a Pétainist who distinguished himself during the period of German occupation of France and the collaborationist regime of the Maréchal for the viciousness of his anti-resistance actions and for his cooperation with Klaus Barbie, the Butcher of Lyon.[14] After the war he fled to Canada, more specifically to Québec where he received aid and succor from a network of Catholic intellectuals and officials in his efforts to remain in the country and to avoid the sentence passed against him by the French justice system. De Bernonville was not the first or only French war criminal to seek and to some extent to find solace among elements of French Canadian nationalist circles.[15] From the very earliest days after the end of the war, Canadian political and legal systems and actors were intimately involved in issues relating to the pursuit of collaborationist war criminals and then, as now, these issues were themselves inextricably wound up with central questions about the nature of Canadian and in this case French Canadian national identity. The story of de Bernonville clearly implicates elements of the government, of the bureaucracy, of the theocracy and finally of the judiciary in an abject failure to deal with those elements of national identity which were, to say the least, sympathetic to fascist and racist ideologies and political programs.

At one level at least, the de Bernonville case and saga are no different from any number of similar stories of post-war immigration and the failures of government and its employees to address the question of the admission and presence of war criminals on Canadian soil. At the same time, however, the way in which the case has again resurfaced indicates the marginalization of what some would argue should be central issues and their replacement on the scene of political rhetoric and discourse with the well-worn saws of traditional issues of Canadian national identity constructed in terms of French Canadian

---

14. See Yves Lavertu, *The Bernonville Affair: A French War Criminal in Québec After World War II* (Montréal: Robert Davies Publishing, 1995). See also Robert Fulford, "An Affair that Quebec would rather forget", *Globe and Mail*, 3 July 1996.

15. See Delisle, "A Strange Sort of Hero: French collaborators exiled in Quebec after World War II" in *Myths, Memory & Lies*, op. cit., at 73.

history. Thus, when asked to address the Roux affair in Parliament, Prime Minister Chrétien replied

> Seulement, s'il faut fouiller dans la vie de tout le monde, est-ce le chef de l'opposition pourrait m'expliquer pourquoi des gens comme Camille Laurin et Denis Lazure ont fait partie du Cabinet de M. Lévesque, eux qui défendait le comte Jacques de Bernonville à l'époque et qui était le bras droit de Klaus Barbie en Europe?[16]

> (Only, if we must go about searching into everyone's life, can the Leader of the Opposition explain to me why people like Camille Lauren and Dennis Lazure, were members of M. Lévesque's cabinet, when at the time they were defenders of Count de Bernonville, Klaus Barbie's right hand man in Europe?)

Once again, this rhetorical flourish of the Prime Minister offers clear and convincing evidence that issues of war crimes, war criminals and the failures of Canadian politics and law to deal with them must almost always take a back seat to what is seen to be the central issue of Canadian identity. Putting aside the historical accuracy or otherwise of Chrétien's assertion that de Bernonville was Barbie's right hand man, the central and vital element of his positioning of war criminals and antisemitism is the attack which his statement carries to the very heart of the separatist enterprise. Lazure and Laurin were key figures in the independence movement. Laurin in particular was the architect of the controversial language policies which are at the heart of all pro- and anti-independence politics and rhetoric. The link between support for fascism and separatist politics is important not for its own sake, and not for the sake of denouncing fascism but rather for the sake of denouncing separatism.

This is the lesson to be drawn from this brief and cursory discussion of national identity in Canada.

3. Antisemitism, the Rule of Law and Canadian Identity

I want to turn here to a brief and not overly detailed introductory summary of the place and function of the Holocaust in another part of the construction of Canadian national identity, themes with which I began this

---

16. *Hansard*, 5 November 1996, 6127.

chapter. I want to assert here, by way of a short discussion of one judicial decision, that Canada, like all the other countries I discuss in this book, must face basic and fundamental contradictions in any attempt to build a national self-image and understanding through the deployment of legal mechanisms which attempt to interpret and "nationalize" the Holocaust. I have argued throughout that most of the problems associated with this and related phenomena necessarily arise from the almost necessary rejection of the idea that the Holocaust was grounded in, informed by and made possible only within the law. In addition, I believe it is clearly the case that each national instance of attempting to build an internal lawful image of the Holocaust and the rule of law must also, again almost by definition, confront the role and rule of law in creating and replicating a form of antisemitism. The Holocaust and its centrality to certain aspects of Jewish cultural, social, and political identity must be at some level rejected as inimical to even a multiethnic national culture. Arguments about the place of the Holocaust in here, Canadian identity, must confront "republican" arguments, however posed, that identity as Canadian must exclude any reference to one's religious or ethnic background. Opposed to this are views that multicultural diversity would permit both "Jewishness" and "Canadian-ness" to coexist or, more perniciously, that arguments from another perspective altogether, that Canada is a Christian country. Antisemitism, or more generally anti-Jewish specificity, does and will always continue to play a role in the legal construction of national identity through a legal confrontation with the Holocaust.

In Canada, we do not have to look far for disparate examples of this. The Department of Justice unit in charge of war crimes and crimes against humanity cases was itself hit by charges of antisemitic bias.[17] More central by way of introduction to my analysis, however, is the intervention of the Mennonite Church during attempts to remove Jacob Luitjens from Canada.[18]

A spokesperson for the Church declared that in addition to the Church's concern for the pain and suffering of the Jewish people it also had to be concerned with "justice". The Church's support for Luitjens in his battle to avoid being sent back to face the Dutch legal system on collaboration charges was based on the fact that he

---

17. David Vienneau, "Anti-semitism allegations reviewed: Jewish group calls for probe", *Toronto Star*, 9 April 1997; "Allegations of anti-semitism dismissed: Probe exonerates head of war crimes unit", *Toronto Star*, 28 March 1998.
18. See below for more detailed discussion.

...had a good record in this country. He had been a faithful church member for the last 35 years and had expressed remorse.[19]

I shall not revisit the traditional good neighbor discourse elements here. Instead I want to use these statements from Christian and Jewish spokespersons to illustrate and introduce again the argument that there is and must almost always be a legal, political, cultural and religious tension and conflict surrounding perpetrator and other cases which invoke the Holocaust as factual background and as a trope about belonging, national identity and legal boundaries. In effect, the fundamental conflict is and will almost inevitably be one between Christianity as the official or unofficial national religion and the presence of a group of persons, the Jews, who claim membership in the national community but who reject Christianity as the embodiment of the sole truth.[20] I have already offered a brief exposé of the ways in which particular constructions of French Canadian identity as essentially and fundamentally Roman Catholic must be always read into the ways in which broader questions of national self-definition are inscribed in political discourse. Antisemitism and questions of perpetrator responsibility have often been articulated in this broader political context. Here I want to address a more Protestant Canadian Christianity as part of the discursive matrix of national identity to identify two further cases in which these basic issues have been articulated within a specifically legal context centering on the Holocaust.

I will not enter into an analysis or discussion of the Holocaust denial activities and legal proceedings involving James Keegstra and Ernst Zundel. These circumstances are sufficiently well-known and have been subjected to other detailed legal and sociological analyses elsewhere. Instead I want to offer a reading of the case and career of Malcolm Ross, schoolteacher and antisemite. Ross was employed by the School Board in the city of Moncton, New Brunswick. Outside his work hours, Ross was the prolific author of works in a variety of genres, ranging from letters to the editor, to pamphlets to monographs, all of which had as a central theme the danger posed to Canada's identity as a Christian country by the presence and activities of perfidious Jews. Following complaints from the parents of a Jewish student, the School Board took a series of measures against Ross which resulted in him losing his job. The Board found that

---

19. "B.C. Mennonites aid man who concealed Nazi ties", *Toronto Star*, 7 December 1991; Michael McAteer, "B'nai Brith concerned by Mennonite support for ex-Nazi Luitjens", ibid., 18 December 1991.

20. More recently, the attempt to extradite Michael Seifert from Vancouver to Italy, where he had already been convicted for war crimes, was characterized by Seifert's parish priest as "persecution". Rod Mickleburgh, "Convicted Nazi war criminal denied bail in Vancouver", *Globe and Mail*, 3 May 2002.

while Ross did not propagate his views in the classroom itself, as had Keegstra, his views were sufficiently known in the broader community that his presence poisoned the pedagogical atmosphere. He complained to the provincial Human Rights Commission claiming that he was the victim of discrimination. He lost before the administrative tribunal but was successful in attacking that decision before the Court of Appeal.[21] The case went before the Supreme Court of Canada. Much of the Supreme Court's analysis is made up of discussion of the appropriate standard of review of the decisions of expert human rights bodies and the level of judicial deference which must be afforded to them under Canadian administrative law principles. While this operates at some level to offer further evidence of the ways in which the Holocaust and questions of the judicial construction of the appropriate body politic of Canadian society can be and are reduced to background noise against important issues of traditional rule of law standards, this is not my reason for choosing to discuss this case.

What is of key importance here is that the Court was specifically asked to address the question of antisemitism "after Auschwitz" and to balance that against Ross' right to his religious beliefs.[22] What is of more relevance is that the Supreme Court of Canada blinked when faced with such a confrontation and failed to address in any adequate fashion what I believe to be the basic and irrefutable "truth" of Ross' writings and of his legal argument and position. There is, and there must be a necessary and continuing conflict between the identity of Canada as a Christian nation and the presence of "Jews" in the body politic. Indeed there is nothing new or radical here either in terms of history or theology. When a Social Credit government was elected in the province of Alberta, the centrality of antisemitism to Christianity in politics became apparent to all concerned.[23] But at the level of Canadian political, social and cultural identity, the pronounced and blatant antisemitism was and is simply a more public and pronounced symptom of the anti-Jewish sentiment which characterizes mainstream political and religious belief. At the level of theology, Social Credit antisemitism simply operates as a manifestation of the fundamental tensions within liberal modern democracies which pay lip service to the separation of Church and State, and to the secular and multi-cultural, -ethnic and -religious nature of Canadian society. None of this lip service can

21. *Re Ross and the Board of School Trustees, District No. 15 et. al.,* 86 D.L.R. (4th), 749 (1991).
22. *Ross v. Board of School Trustees,* [1996] 1 S.C.R. at para. 86.
23. See the recent detailed discussion of this in Janine Stingel, *Social Discredit: Anti-Semitism, Social Credit and the Jewish Response* (Montreal and Kingston: McGll-Queen's University Press, 2000).

remove the historical cultural, political and social hegemony of Christianity in Canadian culture nor, theologically can a liberal democracy ever adequately deal with the central truth of Christianity and Judaism. The former is based on the premise that Jesus Christ was the Messiah, the savior of mankind, sent to wash away our sins and open the gates of heaven. Post-Christian Judaism simply denies this. The two are and must be irreconcilable and this is the truth at the heart of Ross' case. Canada is undeniably a Christian country, just as are France, the United States, the UK and Australia. Canada must then to a degree determined by particular historical and legal contingencies, be an antisemitic country.

This is quite understandably an argument which the Supreme Court of Canada could not countenance. Instead it restated the liberal legal saw that the *Charter* recognizes and imposes reasonable and democratic limits on religious freedom.[24] Indeed, the Court finds that the limits imposed on Ross' religious freedom are justified by a careful legal and factual analysis of the context in which the restrictions were imposed. It carefully analyzes the role of education in a free and democratic society in promoting the values of freedom and tolerance, the role and nature of employee freedoms in a particular employment context and finally and crucially what it calls "the anti-semitism context".[25] Here the Court mixes and matches a series of criteria which leads inevitably to the "desirable" outcome and to the reinforcement of a counterfactual and ahistorical construction of Canadian nationhood. Justice La Forest wrote

> The respondent's expression is expression that undermines democratic values in its condemnation of Jews and the Jewish faith. It impedes meaningful participation in social and political decision-making by Jews, an end wholly antithetical to the democratic process.[26]

He then adds that

> In relation to freedom of religion, any religious belief that denigrates and defames the religions of others erodes the very basis of the guarantees in s. 2(a)—basis that guarantees that every individual is free to hold and to manifest the beliefs dictated by one's conscience. The respondent's religious views serve to deny Jews respect for dignity and equality said to among the fundamental guiding values....[27]

---

24. Ibid., at 72.
25. Para. 85 et. seq.
26. Para. 93.
27. Para. 94.

Here of course, LaForest does little more than reiterate faithful truisms of liberal legality. The problem is that those truisms are not true in any real analysis of legality and context which the Court should have but simply could not have undertaken. Christianity by definition denies respect towards and condemns Jews as apostates who do not accept the word of God and the truth of Jesus, Son of God.[28] The "free exchange of ideas feeding our search for political truth" so cherished by the Supreme Court and so usefully deployed here to uphold an ideologically and legally specific view of Canadian democracy, can only exist in a vacuum which refuses to recognize and condemn the theology which is, for many, at the very heart of the Canadian system of law and national identity.[29] Again, any vision of nationality and citizenship which is grounded in such politics of identity, must almost by definition, come perilously close to revisiting the embodied racialist vision of Nazi law. Similarly, any assertion for the recognition of specifically Jewish suffering and victim status, will equally endanger, in the absence of careful and nuanced debate, a republican ideal of undifferentiated citizenship. Another, competing problematic set of difficulties can also be found in the version of the distortion of political, legal and historical reality evidenced in the triumph of the rule of law in Canadian legal construction of the Holocaust and national identity. It is little wonder then, as I shall illustrate in the following sections of this chapter, that the Holocaust and the pursuit of war criminals and perpetrators has never been central to Canadian national identity or collective memory.

4. War Crimes, War Criminals and Canadian Identity

Canada has historical experience as a prosecutor of war criminals. Crimes of war were committed against Canadian service men in Asian and European theatres. The primary focus of Canadian war crimes prosecutions was in Europe where crimes against Canadian soldiers and airmen were the major con-

---

28. Of course, it also true that there are much more complex questions than can be addressed here about the degree to which theology intervenes in political life within civil society. If Canada is a Christian country, Jews are placed in a dangerous position of definitionally inferior citizenship. If Canada is governed by rules of "republican" equality, then it cannot be a Christian country. If such equality exists, arguments for a legal system which would recognize a Jewish specificity in the Holocaust are rendered extremely problematic.

29. Para. 91.

cern.[30] The Holocaust was the legal remit of the International Military Tribunal and to this day remains a matter of supreme indifference and occasional hostility for Canadian veterans' organizations.[31]

To return to the well-known legal taxonomy for a moment, Canadian legal practice in the immediate post-Liberation European situation was concerned with war crimes rather than with crimes against humanity. Naturally enough, Canadian legal practice was also fraught with typical problems associated with such efforts. As a minor partner in the war in Europe, Canada and its efforts to bring war criminals to justice was often "guided" by the interests and practices of Great Britain and the United States. Investigators and prosecutors also experienced difficulties in gathering evidence in battlefield or post-war conditions. Linguistic and translation problems were constantly present. The ambiguous state of the laws of war and international customary law, which would plague and inform Nuremberg, also had an impact on Canadian efforts to pursue Germans for atrocities committed against Canadians.

Domestic political and legal concerns also dogged Canadian attempts to establish a functioning legal system to deal with war crimes. Attempts to pursue prosecutions based on the indigenous provisions of the *War Measures Act* were replete with technical legal and jurisdictional difficulties and had, as Brode puts it "near disastrous consequences".[32] Eventually a decision was made to base prosecutions on the mechanism of the Royal Warrant. What is of interest here is not the history of Canadian war crimes prosecutions but rather the jurisprudential basis for such prosecutions and what that tells us about subsequent attempts to create a domestic legal framework for dealing with alleged Holocaust perpetrators.

The argument here could be a long and detailed one but I will attempt to be succinct. As I have already argued many of the jurisprudential attacks against Nazi law are intellectually incoherent and historically flawed. A fundamental element in many of the basic criticisms which have been and which continue to be leveled at Nazi law and legality is its basis in executive fiat. For critics of Nazi legality, and more specifically for those who assert that Nazi legality is a jurisprudential oxymoron, the idea that a Hitler order could have the character of supreme law, or that such an order could establish a court and determine the extent of its procedural and substantive jurisdiction forms

---

30. See Patrick Brode, *Casual Slaughter and Accidental Judgments: Canadian War Crimes Prosecutions, 1944–1948* (Toronto: University of Toronto Press, 1997).

31. See Irving Abella, "Why do Canadian veterans belittle their proud actions against the Holocaust?", *Globe and Mail*, 22 November 1997.

32. *Casual Slaughter and Accidental Judgments*, op. cit. at 35.

the basis for their theoretical position condemning Nazi law as not law. Nazi jurists were convicted at Nuremberg for their participation in a legal system which had ceased to be legal because it was grounded in the will of the Party and the Fürher. Yet even a brief examination of the system of justice and law instituted by British and Canadian tribunals under the Royal Warrant system offers some clear indication of the problematic nature of such jurisprudential and ideological denunciations of the Nazi legal system.

Under Royal Warrant, courts are established not by Parliament or by custom, but by the prerogative power of the executive branch. Whether the executive in question is the supreme embodiment of the will of the *Volksgemeinschaft* or the embodiment of centuries of the wisdom of the British nation and the Westminster system and conception of sovereignty is, I would argue, of little persuasive jurisprudential weight. Similarly, it can be noted that many of the procedural safeguards most commonly invoked in theoretical and practical discussions of our conception of the rule of law are clearly absent from the system of justice administered under Royal Warrant. For example, hearsay is admissible and challenges to the composition of the court on the grounds of bias are not recognized. Of course, these and similar provisions characterized the IMT at Nuremberg. Again, this is not a persuasive argument but rather might be seen to go towards establishing the thesis that the Nuremberg Trials were not characterized or epitomized by a careful respect for some universal norms of the rule of law.

Again, I am not arguing here that the Nuremberg trials were unjust in some broader sense or that the system of trial pursuant to Royal Warrant is not somehow "law". Instead, I am making two related points which I have tried to underline throughout this book. First, our understanding of the rule of law at both a practical and theoretical level is so confused and fluid that there is no basis on which it is possible to condemn Nazi law as not law. From this flows the second point, again one which is simply re-emphasized when one looks at trial under Royal Warrant. Our understanding of the rule of law in relation to war crimes and crimes against humanity is so flawed and weak that it is impossible to invoke the concept and principle in any meaningful, independent fashion in any debate in these contexts. The rule of law is a useful and powerful rhetorical tool in political and ideological discussions surrounding the fate of Holocaust perpetrators and it must be understood as such. Thus it is an important element in such debates and is often so powerful that it can become the *sine qua non* of such struggles. But it is not and cannot be epistemologically or ontologically determinative of any of the important issues of justice, collective memory and national identity which circulate in these political contexts.

In the sections which follow I wish to examine some of the ways in which particular understandings of the rule of law have been played out in debates surrounding the pursuit of Holocaust perpetrators in Canada. I will argue and try to demonstrate that in essence the Holocaust has become increasingly marginalized and almost absent in such debates and that this absence of the Holocaust is marked by an ever-stronger presence of the rule of law and legal rhetoric more generally. In Canada, law and the Holocaust have become increasingly strangers to one another in battles over issues of memory and identity.

5. The Pursuit (or Not) of Holocaust Perpetrators in Canada

Again, the Canadian experience in pursuing alleged Holocaust perpetrators has distinct similarities with and parallels to that in Britain, Australia and the United States. Ambivalence at best, overt complicity with escaping Nazis and collaborators at worse, characterized security and immigration practices in each country. Economic booms of the immediate postwar period and a desire to construct harmonious social and political relations in the national body politic combined with the underlying tensions and contradictions of Cold War rhetoric and international relations. Numerous requests to the Canadian government for the extradition of alleged collaborationist war criminals and perpetrators were constructed as part of Soviet agitation against ethnic communities characterized by anticommunist fervor.[33]

Nonetheless the tide gradually shifted in the West. After the United States passed the Holtzman Act and the SIU began its investigations of and actions against accused perpetrators, pressure began to mount in other countries as well, not the least of which was Canada. As almost parallel inquiries began in the UK and Australia, revelations emerged which clearly indicated that there were more than coincidental historical parallels with the Canadian experience. The political environment of the 1980s made it inevitable that Canada would

---

33. On the case of Haralds Puntulis and Latvia, see James E. McKenzie "The Lucky Latvian" in *War Criminals in Canada* (Calgary: Detselig Enterprises, 1995). Also of interest are several Soviet press reports on various individuals. See e.g. "Who Provides Safe Haven for War Criminals?", TASS, 29 July 1987 (Maikovskis, Eichelis and Puntulis, Latvia); "Meeting in Memory of Victims of Fascism", TASS, 27 May 1988 (Panayuk, Artyshuk, Kislyuk, Kupyak, Babenko, Ulitsky and Dik, Ukraine); "Nazi War Criminals Must Not Be Forgiven", TASS 28 August 1987 (Babenko).

join other efforts aimed at seeking out Nazi perpetrators. Others have told the story of the background of these events and of the history of the federal inquiry, known as the Deschênes Commission, which served as the basis and catalyst for the eventual decision to prosecute alleged perpetrators within the Canadian legal system and I shall not duplicate their efforts here.[34] It is important nonetheless to reemphasize here the important role played by conceptions of Canadian identity and the multiethnic character of the Canadian polity. As Troper and Weinfeld put it

> As strands within the Canadian multicultural fabric, Ukrainians and Jews are older, well-organized, white, middle-class communities. No other ethnic groups demonstrate more sophistication in the ins and outs of ethnic politics.[35]

Again the dilemma facing the Canadian body politic in the debates over the presence of alleged Nazi war criminals is familiar. The issues and debates always circulate around and are informed by concerns over the role of ethnic identity and national identity, of the place of different migrant groups in the category "Canadian" etc. More particularly, the issue here was how and why the Holocaust, the extermination of European Jews by the Nazis and their allies, could and should be incorporated into Canadian national identity, politics and law. The events in question occurred many years ago in places far distant from Canada's boundaries. How, if at all, are these events to be constructed as relevant to that nation's identity today in the 21st century?

In effect, I believe that the history of Canadian efforts to come to grips with these questions epitomizes the failures within modernity generally and within modern legal systems more particularly to come to grips with the centrality of the Holocaust to modernity and law themselves. It is only by successfully constructing the Shoah as foreign and strange that legal systems can in fact attempt to construct themselves as law and not as Nazi law. The Canadian story

---

34. See *Commission of Inquiry on War Criminals*, 30 December 1986 (Ottawa); see also Troper and Weinfeld, *Old Wounds*, op. cit., and David Matas with Susan Charendoff, *Justice Delayed: Nazi War Criminals in Canada* (Toronto: Summerhill Press, 1987). For a more favorable view of Canadian policies in the immediate post-war era see, Howard Margolian, *Unauthorized Entry: The Truth about Nazi War Criminals in Canada, 1946–1956*, op. cit. For more legal analyses, see L. C. Green, "Canadian Law, War Crimes and Crimes Against Humanity", 59 *British Yearbook of International Law* 217 (1988); W.J. Fenrick, "The Prosecution of War Criminals in Canada", 12 *Dalhousie Law Journal* 256 (1989); Sharon A. Williams, "Laudable Principles Lacking Application", in Timothy L.H. McCormack and Gerry J. Simpson, *The Law of War Crimes*, op. cit. at 151.

35. Op. cit., at. 28.

is characterized by this tension within modern legal discourse with its need to incorporate in order to expel the Holocaust for the sake of its own apparent intellectual and moral survival. Thus, the Holocaust needed to be Canadian-ized in order for it to be expelled from Canada. This is the first central lesson about present Canadian legal practice which has adopted the American sys-tem of extradition, denaturalization and deportation. Here the legal con-struction of the Holocaust takes second place to the definition of the border and identity control functions of national legal systems.

Ironically, or at least apparently so, the decision of the Canadian govern-ment to abandon the prosecution of alleged perpetrators under domestic criminal law and to instead follow the American example is informed by the triumph of the rule of law. As I shall demonstrate in what follows, Canadian prosecution efforts failed because the Canadian Supreme Court, influenced in part by the adoption of a constitutional *Charter of Rights and Freedoms*, al-most despite itself and to the chagrin of many on the losing side of this par-ticular struggle for rhetorical supremacy about the rule of law, recognized the intimate relationship between and among our understandings of law, re-sponsibility and the Holocaust.

6. Imre Finta and the Legality of the Holocaust

After the Deschênes Commission report and the surprisingly brief discus-sion of the Government's chosen strategy, Canada chose to follow the example of Australia and to prosecute alleged war criminals and perpetrators under Canadian law. In Canada where criminal law falls within the constitutional powers of the federal government, this was accomplished by the simple act of amending the provisions of the general law, the *Criminal Code*. A new section (7 (3.71)) was introduced into the ordinary criminal law of the country. It reads

> Notwithstanding anything in this Act or any other Act, every person who, either before or after the coming into force of this subsection, commits an act or omission outside Canada that constitutes a war crime or a crime against humanity and that, if committed in Canada, would constitute an offence against the laws of Canada in force at the time of the act or omission shall be deemed to commit that act or omission in Canada....

The rhetorical and ideological function and basis of the Canadian provi-sion appears to be relatively straightforward. In essence the Parliament has declared that the Holocaust is at one and the same time relevant to Canadian law and justice and reprehensible to it. In other words, the provisions of the *Criminal Code* here perform a traditional criminal law function, they delimit the boundaries of what is to be excluded as acceptable behavior by the standards of Canadian society. The Holocaust is made relevant to Canadian society by the simple expedient of removing the temporal and spatial barriers which separate the "acts or omissions" from the Canadian context. Then the "acts or omissions" are treated as "ordinary" crimes as the *sine qua non* of applicability of the section is that they "would constitute an offence against the laws of Canada". This is of course the traditional dilemma which faces law and lawyers as they and we attempt to come to grips with the specific and unique horrors of the Shoah. Those specific and unique horrors can only ever become relevant for us and for our conceptions and practices of the rule of law if and when they are in fact normalized. In other words, if we are to be faithful to a certain concept of the rule of law, the Holocaust must be seen as being constituted by ordinary criminality. Only then can any attempt to try alleged perpetrators be said to be consistent with the application of general principles of criminal culpability and responsibility as demanded by this requirement of the rule of law. The uniqueness of the Holocaust, the very fact which militates in favor of the pursuit of perpetrators throughout the world, must in essence be made absent from the law in order for the law to function as ordinary criminal law under the rule of law. Thus, crimes of war and crimes against humanity are made legislative informing concepts but only in so far as they relate to ordinary criminal law principles. Of course, this is an approach which is in fact consistent not just with the rule of law, or at least one conception of the rule of law, but also with the ideological juridical positioning of the Holocaust in the West as a series of events informed by the underlying criminality of the Nazi regime. However, as we shall see in what follows, the case of Imre Finta and his prosecution under the provisions of the *Criminal Code of Canada*, starkly calls into question the very capacity of the rule of law as commonly understood to deal with the Shoah in any intellectually and morally coherent fashion.

Imre Finta, was at the time of his arrest, an elderly Hungarian immigrant who had become a successful restaurateur in Toronto.[36] At the time relevant to the charges against him, he was a legally educated officer in the Hungarian

36. Discussions of the various legal elements and circumstances of the Finta prosecution can be found in David Matas, "The Case of Imre Finta", 43 *University of New Brunswick Law Journal* 281 (1994); Randoml L. Braham, "Canada and the Perpetrators of the Holocaust: The Case of *Regina v. Finta*", 9 *Holocaust and Genocide Studies* 293 (1995); Irwin

police force, the *Gendarmerie*. The prosecution alleged that Finta had been the officer in charge of rounding up and confining the Jewish population of Szeged before they were deported to Nazi death camps. The defence put forth a two-pronged case arguing that Finta was a mere underling and was not in charge of the concentration facility and that in any event his actions were consistent with obedience to a lawful order and he could not therefore be found to posses the requisite mental element or *mens rea* for any of the alleged offences.

The *Finta* case is important for a number of reasons, each of which operates in conjunction with the others to make this the paradigmatic perpetrator trial for our understanding of the Holocaust and the rule of law. In the Canadian context, *Finta* marks the end stage of the first part of the Canadian government's attempts to try alleged perpetrators for offences under the ordinary criminal law. In the broader context of Western perpetrator proceedings, it can and should serve as a classic example of the ways in which out understanding of the Shoah can only ever be distorted as the rule of law serves its own purposes and functions which as the *Finta* case exemplifies, has both nothing and everything to do with the Holocaust. In Imre Finta we have a shining exemplar of the rule and role of law in the perpetration of the Holocaust. Finta was not a Nazi. There is little if any evidence to demonstrate that he was a fanatic or a raving antisemite. Instead he was a police officer doing his job and his job simply included rounding up and incarcerating Jews for transport by the Germans and perhaps stealing valuables from those he had imprisoned. Imre Finta did not shoot anyone. He arrested them and saw to it that the Jews were kept for the Germans. Imre Finta embodied the role and rule of law as a police officer and he continued to embody the role and rule of law as he loaded the Jews onto the death trains. The basic and troubling question posed by the prosecution of Imre Finta was whether and how the law could judge itself and its role in the Holocaust. Once again, this time in Canada the rule of law after Auschwitz came face to face with the rule of law before Auschwitz.

The dilemma for law in the case of Imre Finta came down to two apparently simple arguments about legal principles. The first issue to be decided by the Courts in this case was whether the Parliament of Canada in introducing the war crimes and crimes against humanity provisions of section 7 of the *Criminal Code* has introduced an additional mental element of the of-

---

Cotler, "War Crimes Law and the Finta Case", 6 *Supreme Court Law Review* 577 (1995); Irwin Cotler, "Regina v. Finta", 90 *American Journal of International Law* 460 (1996).

fence. In other words, should judges read these provisions in such a way that proof of the underlying offence i. e. an act or omission "if committed in Canada, would constitute an offence against the laws of Canada in force at the time" would suffice to prove the crime or did the inclusion of "crimes against humanity" and "war crimes" insert an additional element which would form part of the Crown's burden of proof and upon which the jury would decide? In the *Finta* context, the question could be put in the following way. If the Crown proves that the arrest and confinement of the Jews met the definition of the physical and mental elements (*actus reus* and *mens rea*) of the crime of kidnapping, an offence against the laws of Canada at the time, is that sufficient to establish Finta's guilt of crimes against humanity or must the Crown also prove that a crime against humanity in addition to a simple kidnapping was committed?

The first interpretation would appear to be consistent with the argument that the Parliament has in essence wished to "Canadianize" the Holocaust and to ensure by doing this that no one would be subjected to punishment for a crime defined retroactively. In other words, by making liability contingent upon the proof of the commission of an offence which at the time was a crime in Canadian law, Parliament wished to insure that the criminal process against alleged perpetrators would be neither no more nor no less than any other criminal proceeding before the Canadian courts. This was the view which persuaded the Chief Justice of Ontario, Charles Dubin, in his dissent in the Ontario Court of Appeal, but it did not convince the majority of his colleagues there nor did it persuade the majority of the Supreme Court of Canada.[37]

The "correct" position was explained by Cory J. as follows:

> What distinguishes a crime against humanity from any other criminal offence under the Canadian *Criminal Code* is that the cruel and terrible actions which are essential elements of the offence were undertaken in pursuance of a policy of discrimination or persecution of an identifiable group or race.

He added:

> Therefore, while the underlying offences may constitute a base level of moral culpability, Parliament has added a further measure of blameworthiness by requiring that the act or omission constitute a crime against humanity or a war crime.[38]

37. *Regina v. Finta*, 73 C.C.C. (3d) 65 (1992); 112 D.L.R. (4th) 513 (1994).
38. 112 D.L.R. (4th) at 595.

For Cory J context and liability are everything

> The essential quality of a war crime or crime against humanity is that the accused must be aware of or willfully blind to the fact that he is inflicting untold misery on his victims.
>
> The requisite mental element of a war crime or a crime against humanity should be based on a subjective test. I reach this conclusion for a number of reasons. First, the crime itself must be considered in context. Such crimes are usually committed during a time of war. Wars are concerned with death and destruction. Sweet reason is often among its first victims. The manipulation of emotions, often by the dissemination of false information and propaganda, is part and parcel of the terrible tapestry of war. False information and slanted reporting is so predominant that it cannot be automatically assumed that persons in units such as the gendarmerie would really know that they were part of a plot to exterminate an entire race of people.
>
> It cannot be forgotten that the Hungarian people were loyal to the axis cause. There was strong pro-German sentiment throughout the country.[39]

What we find here is an interesting twist in this particular legal context on the historical construction of the Holocaust and notions of personal liability. If Finta is to be personally liable for "crimes against humanity" he must have had some knowledge of the plan to exterminate the Jewish people. His ability to possess such knowledge is adversely effected by the omnipresence of propaganda. The "Hungarian people were loyal to the axis cause". This is perhaps the most troubling and at least partly inconsistent part of the judgment of the majority in *Finta*. Surely knowledge of the Final Solution is not the same as knowingly participating in the infliction of cruelty as part of a plan grounded in "discrimination or persecution". Here Cory seems to be raising the bar of personal liability in a manner which is internally inconsistent, and which defines "discrimination or persecution" in an *ex post facto* construction of the concepts in light of what we now know of the Holocaust. Here law before Auschwitz, in the strict temporal sense, is to be defined by law after Auschwitz.

At the same time, his statement describing the solidarity of the "Hungarian people" must by definition be read to exclude those Hungarian people of Jewish origin. In his attempt to act as an historically sensitive contextual player

---

39. Op. cit. at 596.

of the jurisprudential game, Cory J simply reasserts the epistemologically pernicious basis of European antisemitism i.e. that there are in this case Hungarians and there are Jews who are not and can never be real Hungarians.
Nonetheless, these objections, logical, moral and historical, do not in the end
necessarily undermine the soundness of the majority's legal position as a legal
position.

What is of importance here is not whether I agree or disagree with the
conclusions of Cory J. Instead his argument needs to be placed in a both a
general jurisprudential context and the within the more specific theoretical
context of law after Auschwitz. Generally speaking, Cory's decision is perfectly consistent with a line of case law set down by the Supreme Court for
determining the mental element for various types of offences. He deployed
these precedents, engaged in competent legal argument and convinced the
majority of his colleagues of the correctness of his decision. In other words,
he played the game of adjudication and he won a close victory.[40] There is
nothing about the Cory decision here which is in any way not law, not adjudication in accordance with our general understandings of the rule of law.
That there were strong dissenting judgments in the Court of Appeal and in
the Supreme Court itself negatives this assertion. Instead, what we have here
is evidence of the vibrancy of the rule of law and proof positive that alleged
perpetrators of the Holocaust can and do receive treatment which upholds
and confirms the centrality of the rule of law to our political and judicial
systems.

At the same time, Cory J's decision to add an "extra" element to war crimes
and crimes against humanity is oddly consistent with an understanding of the
Shoah as specific and unique. By asserting a jurisprudential position that the
Holocaust (or "crimes against humanity") involved the "pursuance of a policy of discrimination or persecution of an identifiable group or race" and that
these policies were "cruel and terrible actions", the majority of the Supreme
Court ideologically and graphically here inscribes the Holocaust as unique, a
position which has a wide currency in academic historical debate and which
is consistent with the views of many who advocate the pursuit of alleged perpetrators. However, as I have argued, this also means that the legal system in
some way appears to be engaged in a self-defeating process by creating a "special" category of crime and criminal to which ordinary rules do not apply, in
apparent conflict with basic principles of the rule of law. However, the rest of

---

40. For a brilliant jurisprudential analysis of this and related judicial phenomena, see
Allan Hutchinson, *It's All in the Game*, op. cit.

Cory. J.'s decision in *Finta* demonstrates the inherent flexibility in rule of law reasoning and rhetoric and the system's ability to escape its own internal contradictions.

The position adopted by the Supreme Court here is not only in accordance with the position adopted by many scholars of the Shoah but it is at least in part in keeping with jurisprudential developments from other jurisdictions which have created legal principles and frameworks for prosecuting alleged perpetrators. For example, the key distinction in German law which separates liability for murder from the lesser culpability for manslaughter is grounded in the presence or absence of the elements of "cruelty" identified by Cory J.[41] Of course, the German law still imposes the lesser liability for manslaughter while Canadian law imposes this factor as an element of all offences under the general rubrics of "war crimes" or "crimes against humanity" but such a distinction is not, I believe, jurisprudentially fatal to the analogy based in the rule of law here.

Another example can be found in the much criticized French legal definition of crimes against humanity upon which the prosecutions of Barbie, Touvier and Papon were based and which imposes an element similar to that of a "policy of discrimination or persecution" adopted by the Canadian Court. In France, as we have seen, this test was part of a judicial strategy which had as its goal the exculpation of Vichy and the inscription of a particular historical jurisprudence of collaboration. In Canada, the imposition of this additional mental element to the offences in question serves a completely different purpose and has a different ideological content. In fact, the existence of similar legal tests in these different contexts illustrates once again the fluid and epistemological vacuity of any attempt to ascribe meaning and content to the rule of law.

The political and ideological nature of the rule of law after Auschwitz is even more forcefully inscribed in Canadian law in the reasoning adopted by the majority of the Supreme Court in relation to the question of "superior orders". Finta's defence rested in large part on the assertion that as a regular member of the *Gendarmerie* he was simply doing his job and following orders when he rounded up and confined the local Jewish population and as such he could not be found to have committed a criminal offence. At the same time of course, we are also faced not just with the general post-Nuremberg jurisprudential construction of Nazism and the Holocaust as a large criminal conspiracy but also with the specific finding of the International Military Tri-

---

41. See Dick de Mildt, *In the Name of the People*, op. cit.

bunal, consistent with the provisions of its Charter, that the defence of superior orders is not available to those accused of war crimes and crimes against humanity.

Of course, at some level, the success of the assertion "I was just following orders" is legally dependent upon the preceding position. If one is following lawful orders, then the elements of "cruelty" and a plan of persecution are to some extent absent. The judgment of Cory J is quite extensive in its careful discussion of the nature and extent of the defence of superior orders and its correlative defence of obedience to military orders and more particularly to the question of the test of "manifest illegality" and the related issue of the degree of moral choice available to particular subordinates. I shall not belabor these technical legal arguments here. Instead I want to focus briefly on the ideological and legal consequences of the majority decision.

Again, I should emphasize here that I am not offering a reading of the "law" in *Finta* in a technical and traditional sense. In addition, I wish to reiterate that it is in essence irrelevant whether I agree with Cory J and the majority or whether they are "correct" in their position. The judge in his decision on the "superior orders" question is very careful indeed to point out that he is not supporting a claim for the legality of the orders or the broader assertion that the legitimacy and narrow legality of national systems of law at the time make the actions of Holocaust perpetrators "lawful". Instead, the position of the majority is that what is relevant is the defendant's belief in the legality of the orders and system of which they formed a part. In other words, in classic criminal law speak, the test for liability is a subjective rather than an objective one. What I am arguing here is that this distinction is ideologically and politically meaningless.

Thus,

> The evidence of the state of war, that the country was occupied by German forces, the existence of state-sanctioned conduct by police officers in a state of emergency, and the imminent invasion by the Soviet army which was but 100 km. from Szeged was sufficient, in my view, to give an air of reality to the defence of obedience to superior orders. The evidence from the newspapers of public approval for the deportation, and the open manner in which the confiscations took place could have supported the defence of mistaken belief that the orders to undertake the actions which gave rise to the charges against the respondent were lawful.[42]

---

42. At 619.

Here we find both the narrow and broad elements of criminal justice and the rule of law which render law after Auschwitz problematic if not impossible. The focus in trials within the criminal justice system must be on the elements of the offence. As a result, what is important here is the state of mind of the accused. The victim is always necessarily absent from these efforts to impose criminal liability. More generally, the victims must be absent from any criminal law rendering of the Holocaust and the responsibility of alleged perpetrators. What is vital is the motivation of the accused. Again, an atmosphere of public approval for the deportation of the Jews must be an atmosphere constructed by Cory J as having no Jews. There are Hungarians and there are Jews. The victims, the Jews, are rendered irrelevant in the construction of the Hungarian Holocaust because the definition of the offence focuses on the accused. Thus, a criminal trial will always simply revisit the debate in scholarship about the primacy of focus in Holocaust studies. Does one seek to understand and explore the motivations and actions of those who killed or should one expend one's efforts on the lives and struggles of those who were singled out for extermination? The criminal law can only ever accept the first possibility and the majority of the Supreme Court is here being consistent with the basic thrust of the rule of law and the criminal trial process.

But the real importance of *Finta* lies in its ideological consequences. By focusing on the motivations and state of mind of the alleged perpetrators, the Supreme Court of Canada has given voice, if only indirectly, to a fundamental political and jurisprudential "truth" of the Holocaust. The perpetrators, from those who pulled the triggers, to those like Finta who acted earlier in the chain of events on the road to extermination, to those who drafted the laws criminalizing Jews for being Jews, all believed that what they were doing was right and lawful. The rarity of instances of refusal to kill hospitalized patients, or to shoot congregated Jews, or to make legal arguments about who was or was not a Jew, all offer clear and convincing evidence of a state of existential reality and positive legality in which it was normal to exclude and exterminate individuals for no other reason than that they were "Jews". Whether additional factors from eliminationist antisemitism[43] to peer group pressure[44] or propaganda or brutalization were also present can not remove the historical reality of a widespread, if not almost universal, belief in the legality of measures aimed at the Final Solution of the Jewish problem in Europe. This is the great, if probably unintended, insight of the majority opinion in the case of Imre Finta.

---

43. See Daniel Jonah Goldhagen, *Hitler's Willing Executioners*, op. cit.
44. See Christopher Browning, *Ordinary Men*, op. cit.

In other words, Finta epitomizes the legality and normality of the Holocaust. He was a police officer who arrested Jews, expropriated their property and saw that they were handed over to the Germans for special handling, all under an operative and operating legal system. It is of no real legal or practical consequence that experts can and did testify that the Baky order may have been unconstitutional under some particular construction of Hungarian law. Finta, like most perpetrators operated under law, as a lawfully constituted legal official and his persecution of the Jews under his power was as legal as the mass shooting carried out by Reserve Police Battalion 101 or of the mercy deaths of mental patients at Hadamar. The Supreme Court of Canada decision in *Finta* recommends itself to us for the very reasons for which it was so vociferously condemned by some and applauded by others.

Conservative columnist and critic of Holocaust trials Barbara Amiel got it right when she wrote

> Imre Finta was charged as a criminal for performing his legal duties as a policeman in Hungary during the war.[45]

She also pointed out elsewhere that

> During the same period in Canada, Canadian citizens of Japanese origin were rounded up by the Royal Canadian Mounted Police and forcibly deported to internment camps.[46]

One might also point to the similar situation which obtained in the United States and to the fact that the US Supreme Court found such actions to be perfectly lawful in time of war. Further examples of Dutch and French police rounding up Jews in Amsterdam and Paris could be raised. The spectacle of the British Bobbies on Guernsey escorting Jewish residents for deportation might round off our understanding of the fundamental legality of the Holocaust and of the basic continuities between our understanding and application of principles of law in Canada and the United States, and the very same actions for which Finta was tried and German law was and is condemned as nothing more than a large criminal conspiracy.

But Amiel cannot face the fundamental consequences of her arguments. Instead she turns her vitriol against those like Helen Smolack of the Canadian Holocaust Remembrance Association who said of the original acquittal

---

45. "The trouble of war-crimes trials", *Maclean's*, 11 June 1990.
46. "When obeying orders makes the law an ass", *Times*, 18 May 1990.

It makes us lose faith in the justice system of Canada.[47]

Amiel wrote that

> The only way to prevent another Holocaust or Third Reich is to jealously guard and maintain the rule of law and never ever depart from certain fundamentals in exercising it, no matter how good the cause. Once society departs from these fundamentals—as it has with the war-crimes legislation—and introduces such things as retroactive legislation or tries to judge one situation by the standards of another, then we create precisely the sort of environment that permits the actions that lead to the world of deportations and death camps. Throughout the centuries the rule of law has kept mankind from slipping into total barbarity, and no single group has understood that more soundly than we Jews. It is a terrible irony that some Jews should be the leaders in eliminating our single most important protection.[48]

Amiel here rehashes many of the well-known anti-war crimes legislation arguments and they are no more or less accurate or persuasive here than they are elsewhere. What is interesting is that she fails to see and carry through on the logic of her own arguments. RCMP officers deported Japanese Canadians pursuant to the rule of law. Imre Finta imprisoned Jews and robbed them pursuant to the rule of law. The rule of law does not protect us from a descent into barbarity, it is and was a condition precedent to the camp system, in Germany and in Canada. At the same time, the rule of law does not by definition compel Auschwitz. It is rhetoric, powerful and ideological rhetoric, which can at one and the same time create Auschwitz as a site of law and Imre Finta as an agent of law while allowing us to condemn Nazi Germany as a criminal state and to denounce the pursuit of perpetrators as contrary to its basic principles. I do not pretend to know what keeps us from Auschwitz, nor am I necessarily convinced that we are always all that far away from its shadows, but I do know that the rule of law has nothing and everything to do with it.

The problem here for Helen Smolack and those who so vociferously condemn the original acquittal and subsequent appellate victories of Imre Finta is the almost universal one among Holocaust survivors and those who seek to pursue alleged perpetrators through the legal system. They believe in law and

---

47. Patricia Chisolm, "A war-crimes trial ends with an acquittal", *Maclean's*, 4 June 1990.

48. "The trouble with war-crimes trials", op. cit.

worse still, they believe in the synonymous relationship between law and justice. The legal system in the *Finta* case worked. A trial was held, laws of evidence were applied. The jury rendered its verdict. Appeals were lodged, judges adjudicated. All of the technical requirements for law and for the rule of law were fulfilled. More importantly, the Supreme Court offers us a clear case in support of the argument that the Holocaust was for those who killed and those who helped them kill a lawful and legal experience. What Ms Smolack experienced is not the failure of law but the failure of justice.

Indeed, the three other cases in which the Canadian government attempted to prosecute alleged Holocaust perpetrators under the provisions of the *Criminal Code* can also be read as epitomizing the strength and character of the rule of law in that country. Michael Pawlowski, "a retired carpenter from Renfrew, near Ottawa", was accused of murdering 410 Jews near Minsk in Byelorussia in 1942.[49] While admitting that he had joined a local police unit under duress, Pawlowski always denied any participation in actions which would have constituted war crimes or crimes against humanity. The role of such local units in anti-Jewish and anti-partisan atrocities is now well-known.[50] However, because criminal prosecutions must focus on the culpability of the individual accused, the rule of law required that the Crown prove beyond a reasonable doubt that Pawlowski was in fact a Holocaust perpetrator.

The issue of individual criminal liability under normal standards of proof is extremely complex in such cases. Time has passed, witnesses have died or their memories have faded, evidence is to be found in distant parts of the world, ideological conflict based in the Cold War and nationalist infighting persist, language barriers persist. All of these arguments are of course familiar and in effect constitute the litany of arguments of those who oppose the very thought of present day prosecutions of alleged perpetrators. Each element for these opponents of modern trials militates against the possibility of the principles of the rule of law being applied in any case. On the contrary however, Polyukovich,[51] Sawoniuk[52] and in Canada Pawlowski each offers clear and convincing evidence that the rule of law is alive and well in those jurisdictions.

As the case against Pawlowski developed, the strength and vivacity of the principles of the rule of law manifested themselves. In 1991, half of the

---

49. "Canada probing several people suspected of war crimes", *Reuters*, 21 December 1989.

50. See Martin Dean, *Collaboration in the Holocaust: Crimes of the Local Police in Belorussia and Ukraine, 1941–1944* (New York: St. Martins' Press, 2000).

51. See below, chapter 10.

52. See above, chapter 8.

charges against him were dropped by Canadian prosecutors as a key witness
died.[53] Finally all charges against Pawlowski were stayed after the courts refused to allow the introduction of videotaped evidence in any trial against him
in Canada.[54] Here again we find incontrovertible evidence of the existence and
power of the rule of law. Basic principles of procedural and substantive justice operated here to demonstrate the ways in which the fears of those opponents of prosecutions were not just unfounded but were in effect ideologically
misplaced. The criminal justice system in Westminster political culture is perfectly capable of undertaking such proceedings and ensuring that all the interests of the accused upon which the semiotics of the rule of law are based
are protected. The ultimate outcome of these cases is in essence irrelevant to
any determination of the characteristic power of rule of law rhetoric and its
centrality in war crimes and perpetrator trials. Just as many would argue that
for all its flaws, the Nuremberg trials of major war criminals can be demonstrated to be internally consistent with a basic understanding of the rule of law
by reference to the fact that some of the accused were acquitted, a similar argument can be made here. The rule of law exists because its rules protect a
person accused of the mass killing of Jews through the simple expedient of the
normal application of general rules of procedural and evidentiary fairness.
The charges against Pawlowski were stayed and he was awarded extensive costs
against the Crown.[55] Sawoniuk in the UK was convicted after a trial. The only
distinction between these cases is the outcome, a distinction which within our
understanding of the rule of law is essentially irrelevant.

A similar analysis applies and the same result obtains in the case of Stephen
Reistetter. Reistetter, who was described as someone who "wears hearing aids
and takes drugs for a heart ailment" was accused of having been a member of
the fascist Hlinka Guard in Slovakia where he led the arrest and deportation
of 3000 Jews.[56] Again, he denied the charges and again all the familiar tropes
of recent attempts to prosecute alleged perpetrators are deployed. Reistetter is
an old man, beset by physical infirmities. He led a peaceful and fruitful existence since immigrating to Canada. He was a good employee and a solid family man. Prosecution was rendered difficult if not impossible by the exigencies of travel to then Czechoslovakia and the fragility and age of potential

53. "Canada drops four charges in war crimes trial", *Reuters*, 10 June 1991.
54. Anthony Boadle, "Canada's attempt to try war criminals runs aground", *Reuters*, 13
March 1992.
55. *Re Regina and Pawlowski*, 101 D.L.R. (4th) 267 (1993) (Ont. C.A.).
56. Robert Kozak, "Bail granted to third man accused by Canada of war crimes",
Reuters, 19 January 1990.

witnesses.[57] Finally charges were dropped against Reistetter because the passage of time had made it impossible to gather sufficient, reliable evidence.[58]

" I am happy that everything is over," were his first words to a reporter, "that the Canadian justice system is just".[59]

Here we again find a basic jurisprudential confusion, this time not by spokespersons for those who seek to pursue and convict alleged perpetrators, but by the accused. The important point in cases such as this is not, as far as the jurisprudence of the rule of law after Auschwitz is concerned, that the system is "just", or that the system produces a particular result, but rather that the result it produces is completely irrelevant to the system itself. What matters here is that the normal processes of the Canadian criminal justice system produced a result which is recognizable and recognized as a lawful outcome, that the game of law was played according to the rules of that game.[60] For law after Auschwitz, the Holocaust, the guilt or innocence of the accused, the fate of the 3,000 Slovakian Jews, are all simple parts of the greater game. They are not, nor can they ever be central to the game, because the game is not, can not be, dependent on any of these elements for its continuing legitimacy. Indeed, as I have argued, it is existentially and phenomenologically necessary for the continuing validity of the rule of law, in this instance the Canadian rule of law, that the Holocaust not trouble its existence. By making these assertions I am not claiming that Finta, Reistetter and Pawlowski are not "guilty" or responsible for the acts for which they stood accused. Instead I make the "weaker" claim that the power of the rule of law as a practical ideology is that the actual facts and circumstances of the Holocaust in general or the actual "guilt" of any individual involved in the legal process of constructing the Holocaust is irrelevant to the law.

The final attempt by Canadian authorities to prosecute alleged perpetrators under domestic criminal law is the case of Radislav Grujicic, an 81 year-old Yugoslav immigrant from Windsor, who was charged with participating in the murder of Communists and Communist sympathizers while a policeman. Again, the rule of law triumphed.

---

57. Robert Kozak, "Canada war crimes lawyers travel to Europe to hear witness", *Reuters*, 13 February 1990.
58. Robert Kozak, "Fading memories hamper Canada's war crimes prosecutions", *Reuters*, 6 March 1991.
59. Bob Brent, "War crimes charges dismissed Crown can't produce evidence that man kidnapped 3,000 Jews", *Toronto Star*, 5 March 1991.
60. See Hutchinson, *It's All in the Game*, op. cit.

"He is a diabetic, he had cancer, which is in remission, he had a heart attack and, most recently, his leg was amputated—basically, he's out of it," prosecutor Ivan Whitehall said of Radislav Grujicic.... [61]

Charges were stayed and Canada's program of pursuing war criminals and perpetrators of crimes against humanity under the provisions of the *Criminal Code* came to an end. Two elements are worth noting briefly here. First, it is not jurisprudentially accurate or even helpful here to characterize the cases of Finta, Pawlowski, Reistetter and Grujicic as "failures". Again it is worth repeating that the outcome of these cases is not fundamentally relevant to our understanding of the rule of law and the appropriate functioning of a criminal justice system under those general principles. The system worked, it justifies itself as it inevitably will. This does not mean that justice triumphed, since justice has little if anything to do with the construction of the ideological rule of law.

At the same time, of course, I also underline the more controversial or at least less orthodox jurisprudential point which informs my work and argument here. In essence, the Canadian legal system has paid proper respect and homage to the Holocaust in its handling of the four cases under discussion, most especially in the *Finta* case. By this I do not mean to suggest that the system has afforded justice to the victims of Nazi mass killings. Rather I argue that the system has paid proper respect to itself. Law after the Holocaust can only ever be self-regarding but self-regarding in a process of systematic and systemic bad faith. The Holocaust was an essentially lawful process. The fate of the victims, the *homo sacer*, to return to Agamben's characterization, was and is an essential condition for the correct and complete functioning of law within modernity. But while the victim remains central to the system's existence, s/he must always already be placed outside the system, written under erasure in order to be inscribed as a body within but without law. This reached its apex in *Finta* and we must have the courage to recognize this fundamental rupture between law and justice which is essential to law before and after Auschwitz.

Finally, *Grujicic* begins to reinscribe an essential part of post-*Finta* Canadian legal practice to which I now turn. Here the former Belgrade policeman was accused of crimes against Communists, not, as in the three other prosecutions, of crimes against Jews. Of course, the intimate semiotic link in the coding of "Communist" and "Jew" in Nazi and collaborationist rhetorical and

---

61. "Grujicic war charges stayed for health reasons", *Globe and Mail*, 14 September 1994.

policing practice is well-known. But here, we are addressing the substantive and ideological shift in Canadian government policy. "War crimes" and "crimes against humanity" are each carefully inscribed in the *Criminal Code*. This in part at least distinguishes the graphic and lexical position of the Canadian legal system and those of Australia and Britain which adopt different signifiers.[62] At this level at least, Canada appears to have been more open at the level of legislative drafting to incorporate the Holocaust and its uniqueness within the partial coding of "crimes against humanity". Of course, this is only partly accurate and is not for example, related to the Israeli provision in the *Nazi and Nazi Collaborators Law* which specifies "crimes against the Jewish people" as a separate and distinct criminal offence. The move in the case of Grujicic at some preliminary level signals and signifies a further erasure of the Holocaust as primary ideological and jurisprudential focus of Canadian legal practice.

7. The Americanization of Canadian Law: Extradition, Denaturalization and Deportation

The perceived "failure" of the four prosecutions led to ongoing pressure on the Canadian government to "do something" about the continued and largely untroubled presence of alleged Holocaust perpetrators. Critics of the government's actions argued for greater alacrity in pursuing cases,[63] more serious public and judicial education about the Holocaust and the issue of perpetrator presence in Canada,[64] and finally acceptance of the need to shift from prosecution to deportation and denaturalization proceedings.[65] In essence, Canada adopted the position here that it would mark a rhetorical return to the basic informing concept of all agitation on the perpetrator issue in the post-war era

---

62. See supra chapter 8 and infra chapter 10.

63. Bob Brent, "Jewish Groups Urge Speedier Pursuit of War Criminals", *Toronto Star*, 5 March 1991.

64. David Vienneau, "Crackdown Urged on War Crimes Cases", *Toronto Star*, 28 November 1992.

65. E. Kay Fulton with Scott Steele, "Running Out of Time for Justice", *Maclean's*, 13 February 1995; Robert Sarner and Steve Leibowitz, "Canada Tries to Speed Up Action against Nazis", *Jerusalem Post*, 24 November 1996; Erin Anderssen "Ottawa steps up drive to expel war criminals", *Globe and Mail*, 22 July 1998. Don Lajoie, "Ontario man, 78, lied about Nazi past, judge rules: Faces deportation", *National Post*, 1 September 2001.

and would re-inscribe the Holocaust as an issue which was foreign to Canada and its national self-identity. The prosecution option was and is, as I have argued, underwritten by this notion of exclusion from the body politic of perpetrators of the Holocaust. The denaturalization, deportation and extradition processes are more obviously part of a legal signifying chain which clearly inscribes the Holocaust as a foreign element, an invasion of the body politic and legal system accomplished by subterfuge and lies and one which therefore is better dealt with by other countries with a more direct interest in the substance of the issue. In other words, the deportation and exclusion option is one which in essence marks the Holocaust and therefore by definition its victims as Other.

Of course, this is not the way in which the process is inscribed and described by its proponents. Then Citizenship Minister Sergio Marchi offered the typical position in support of excluding alleged perpetrators as follows:

> Canadian citizenship is something to be looked up to. Canadian citizenship espouses certain values and one of them is certainly not war criminal activity.[66]

Certainly, on the surface at least, this offers some evidence of a willingness to define perpetrators as unworthy of Canadian citizenship and therefore can be seen to provide at least some solace for example to Holocaust survivors by informing them that they do have to share their political and personal space with their persecutors. The implicit construction of the polity then describes perpetrators as Other and allows victims at least some belief that they have been defined into the fabric of national identity. This is not, ideologically or semiotically, however, the same as declaring that the Holocaust is essential to an understanding and construction of Canadian identity. Instead, its ideological and real impact, as I hope to demonstrate in what follows, is in fact to construct a particular version of identity based on the rule of law from which the Holocaust must be and is absent and irrelevant.

Early experience involving the removal of alleged perpetrators from Canada I believe makes my point. Helmut Rauca, was accused of assisting in the mass killing of Jews in Kaunas Lithuania in 1941. Upon the request of the government of the Federal Republic of Germany, Rauca was deported to that country where he died in a prison hospital before standing trial.[67] At this stage

---

66. David Vienneau, "Liberals ready to pursue Nazi war criminals Justice minister seeks more funds for special unit", *Toronto Star*, 18 December 1993.

67. See generally, Sol Littman, *War Criminal on Trial: Rauca of Kaunas* (Toronto: Key Porter Books, 1998).

then, Rauca's guilt was never fixed in legal terms and the ideological and historical functions urged by supporters of war crimes trials could not be fulfilled. As far as the Canadian legal system was concerned, the case of Helmut
Rauca has been constructed as just another instance in which general legal
principles need to be explicated and applied to a particular set of facts. The
Holocaust, the mass extermination of Lithuanian Jewry is rendered irrelevant as the litigation issue is whether the Federal Republic has jurisdiction to
request the extradition and what burden of proof needed to be met by the
government in such a case. Thus, the gravity of the allegations and the existence of the Canadian *Charter of Rights and Freedoms* compelled the Court
to hold that

> In the present case, I am prepared to hold that the onus is upon the
> Federal Republic of Germany to establish that the "limits" i. e. extra-
> dition laws, are reasonable, are prescribed by law and are demon-
> strably justifiable in a free and democratic society. I consider the ex-
> tent of that burden to be the usual civil onus based on the balance of
> probabilities. Because the liberty of the subject is in issue, I am of the
> view that the evidence in support must be clear and unequivocal. Any
> lesser standard would emasculate the individual's rights now en-
> shrined in the Constitution.[68]

Here then we find clear evidence that the primary focus in extradition cases,
as would occur in later criminal prosecutions, had to be on the rights of the
individual accused. The rule of law as embodied in the *Charter* required the
imposition of a burden of proof on the extraditing authority. Evidence of the
"guilt" of the accused in the mass killing of Lithuanian Jewry is not here relevant in and of itself but is simply a necessary precondition to the correct procedural operation of extradition law. The Holocaust is just one more factual
element relevant to the only operative legal issues of whether the extraditing
authority has met its burden.[69] Chief Justice Evans puts the real legal question
surrounding Canadian law and the massacre at Kaunas as follows:

---

68. *Re Federal Republic of Germany and Rauca*, 70 C.C.C. (2d) 416 (1982) (Ont. High
Ct.), at 428. See also *Fed. Republic of Germany v. Rauca*, 41 O.R. (2d) 225 (1984) (Ont.
C.A.).
69. For traditional legal analyses of this and other technical issues raised in the *Rauca*
case, see Neil Finkelstein, "A Question of Emphasis", 30 Criminal Reports (3d) 112, (1982)
and Kenneth M. Narvey, "Trial in Canada of Nazi War Criminals", 34 C.R. (3d) 126
(1984).

I am satisfied that such statutory restriction which has as its objective, the protection and preservation of society from serious criminal activity, is one which members of a free and democratic society such as Canada would accept and embrace. To hold otherwise would be to declare that a procedure which has been accepted in our country for over a century and in most other democratic societies is no longer a reasonable and proper method of protecting our society from serious criminal activities.[70]

What is at issue here is nothing more complicated than whether extradition is an acceptable legal proceeding in a free and democratic society. The Holocaust is quite simply rendered irrelevant.

The secondary role which the Holocaust has come to play in the "new" system of denaturalization and deportation proceedings in Canada is highlighted by the first "successful" such case. Jacob Luitjens was a retired botany instructor at the University of British Columbia when the government targeted him as the first possible subject for deportation based on his war time activities in the Netherlands. Two interesting aspects of the *Luitjens* case deserve brief mention here. Luitjens is unique in the annals of Canadian efforts to pursue World War Two perpetrators because his crimes were alleged to have occurred in Western Europe, in this instance the Netherlands, rather than in the Baltic or Central and Eastern Europe. More importantly however, Luitjens was not targeted for deportation or eventually sent to serve his prison term in Holland for crimes against Jews in that country. Instead the charges against him were that he had been a local collaborator with the German occupier in raids against the Dutch resistance. Again I am not arguing here that crimes against the Dutch resistance are not important nor that they should not be punished, nor that the history and experience of collaboration in Western Europe is not an important historical phenomenon.[71] I simply wish to underline, yet again, the simple legal fact that the first Canadian "success" in its program of deporting World War 2 collaborators took place against an accused who had nothing to do with the Holocaust. From the very beginning of its second phase, the Canadian process of targeting individuals for exclusion was aimed not at the Holocaust but at the process whereby individuals gained admission to the country. In the *Luitjens* case, the absence of the Holocaust from consideration was based in the facts of his collaboration with the Nazi occu-

70. *Re Federal Republic of Germany*, op. cit., at 429.
71. I leave aside intriguing issue as to the legality of such activities under domestic and international law at the time.

piers.[72] The legal focus on the circumstances of his admission to Canada and his failure to disclose his collaborationist activities to authorities at the time was the necessary consequence of the switch from criminal proceedings to deportation hearings. As later cases will indicate, this change in focus, brought about by a perceived "failure" in the prosecution strategy would inevitably lead to a further marginalization of the reality of the Holocaust within the Canadian legal system. Throughout this shift in focus, however, the rule of law retained its hegemonic ideological and practical grasp on legal proceedings.

The epitome of these associated phenomena, the marginalization of the Holocaust and the continuing triumphant self-congratulation of the rule of law can be found in the combined cases of three individuals chosen for deportation on the basis that they had lied about their wartime activities during the immigration process. The decision of the Supreme Court of Canada in the case of Erichs Tobiass, Johann Dueck and Helmut Oberlander and their subsequent peregrinations through the legal system marks the triumph of the rule of law and the virtual exclusion of the Holocaust from the Canadian legal consciousness.

During the course of deportation proceedings against the three men, a high-ranking Department of Justice official had a meeting with the Chief Justice of the Federal Court to express the Department's concern about the apparent lethargy of the judge charged with the cases, Associate Chief Justice James Jerome, in coming to grips with the cases. In essence, the Department was worried that the inactivity of Jerome would jeopardize the outcome of the cases because of the traditional problems associated with actions against alleged perpetrators i.e. the age of the accused, the age and frailty of the witnesses etc. One irony of the case here is that as Chief Justice of the Trial Division of the Federal Court at the time of the *Luitjens* case, Jerome had been called upon to intervene when the judge in that instance, Collier J. took more than two years to render his decision. In other words, Jerome was acutely and personally aware of the "time is of the essence" factor in deportation proceedings against alleged perpetrators.

When the meeting between the Chief Justice and the Assistant Deputy Attorney-General became known to lawyers for the three individuals in question, they immediately demanded a stay of proceedings against their clients on the grounds that the Federal Court system which was vested with sole jurisdiction in such matters was tainted by a real or apprehended bias as a result of this inappropriate contact. The question which faced the Canadian ju-

---

72. *Secretary of State v. Jacob Luitjens*, [1989] 2 F.C. 125.

dicial system was whether it itself was now capable of complying with the rule of law. For proponents of the pursuit of alleged perpetrators, even in the second best alternative of deportation, the possible outcome here was nightmarish. Holocaust perpetrators were relying upon a basic tenet of the rule of law, judicial independence and the absence of bias, in order to escape from justice. Again, it is evident that such a nightmare is based on an underlying and symbiotic relationship between a conception of the rule of law and substantive outcomes on the one hand, and an idea of the Holocaust as the exact and complete reversal and rejection of the rule of law. I have argued that neither of these conceptions is correct and I believe my position is confirmed by the decision of the Supreme Court in this case.

The Court found the position of the Department of Justice on the "substantive" concern about Jerome's laxity, was in fact justified in the circumstances, but it also characterized the behavior of those involved as inappropriate and as giving rise to an apprehension of bias. The Court nonetheless found that the remedy of a stay of proceedings was not justified in the circumstances. It held that

> For several reasons, a stay of proceedings is not the appropriate remedy in these cases. First, there is no likelihood that the carrying forward of the cases will manifest, perpetuate or aggravate any abuse. Second, the lesser remedy of ordering the cases to go forward under the supervision of a different judge of the Trial Division without any direction or intervention from the Chief Justice or the Associate Chief Justice will suffice.... Third, Canada's interest in not giving shelter to those who concealed their participation in acts of atrocities outweighs any foreseeable harm that might be done to the appellants or to the integrity of the system by proceeding with the cases.[73]

Here we find a classic and elegant portrayal of many of the elements which constitute and construct our understanding of the rule of law and which have created the place of the Holocaust in current Canadian law. The key issue here is whether the Canadian judicial system is capable of crafting a remedy which will allow it to proceed to adjudications on the substantive merits of the cases in question. The answer to that must almost by definition be affirmative. The rule of law in a democracy is in fact and in law capable of remedying any de-

---

73. *Canada (Minister of Citizenship and Immigration) v. Tobiass*, [1997] S.C.J. No. 82, at 93.

fect which in essence is simply part of its own self-definition. The rules of bias and the remedies of judicial review are part and parcel of the internally self-constructed understanding and definition which the legal system and the rule of law have of themselves. At the same time, a deployment of the traditional judicial rule-making mechanism of a public interest analysis and a careful weighing and balancing of the relevant factors allows the Court to fashion a decision which is internally consistent and faithful to traditional understandings of adjudication within the rule of law.

At the same time, the more important point to made here is that the rule of law would have triumphed even if the Court had come to the exact opposite outcome. If the Court had held that the system of justice had been irreparably compromised by the meeting and that the appearance of an intervention by the Chief Justice would necessarily carry with it a fear that all the judges who were responsible to him would be adversely compromised, this would not have been so blatantly unwarranted that there would be any justifiable jurisprudential outrage against such a finding. The rule of law, the central concept of judicial independence, would have triumphed then just as it did in reality. Any outrage at the escape of Dueck, Oberlander and Tobiass from "justice" would once more have been grounded in a fundamental misapprehension of the role and rule of law.

Indeed, once more, the subsequent fates of the three individuals demonstrate the ongoing hegemony of the rule of law in such cases, in addition to underlining, if that were required, the increasing marginalization of the Holocaust to such proceedings and therefore to the construction of Canadian identity through the pursuit of perpetrators and collaborators. The travels and travails of Tobiass, Dueck and Oberlander through the Canadian justice system as they battled efforts to deport them offer clear, cogent and convincing evidence of the shifting significance of such proceedings in the judicial construction of the rule of law in post-Auschwitz Canada.

Erichs Tobiass was an 83 year old retired mechanic from North York at the time the case was brought against him.[74] He was accused of having been a member of the notorious Arjas Commando and of participating in the killings of Latvian Jews carried out by that group.[75] Tobiass can be seen to embody one side of the multiplicity of possibilities inherent in the judicial processes of denaturalization and deportation. After the decision of the Supreme Court

---

74. Ciaran Ganley, "Latvia Urged as Trial Site: War-Crime Charge", *Toronto Sun*, 22 March 1995.
75. See generally, Andrew Ezergailis, *The Holocaust in Latvia*, op. cit.

case, proceedings against him were bought to an end through the imposition
of a biological amnesty. In late December 1997, Erichs Tobiass was found dead
by a neighbor.[76] A statement from Bernie Farber of the Canadian Jewish Congress perhaps best sums up the extra-jurisprudential concept of justice which
might arguably more properly inform our understandings of such cases. He
said

> He was a friendless old man with nobody to take care of him, and
> apparently it took days before people found his body.... Maybe it was
> the ultimate justice.[77]

If Tobiass embodies the figure of some sort of divine biological justice, his
two fellow travelers to the Supreme Court bring out other aspects of the difficulties, if not impossibilities, of a post-Auschwitz Canadian jurisprudence
of the Holocaust. Johann Dueck, the retired mechanic from St Catherines,
was an ethnic German who had served as a high-ranking police officer in the
German occupied Ukraine. In many ways his biography is typical of police in
that part of the world at that historical juncture. His involvement with the
Canadian judicial system included *inter alia* lengthy debates over the proper
procedures to be followed in Federal Court hearings on deportations[78], the
admissibility of evidence,[79] a trip to the Ukraine to hear witnesses and finally
a determination by Noel J of the Federal Court that as someone who had come
to Canada under an agricultural employment scheme, he had not in fact
gained entry to the country through deception and was not therefore subject
to deportation.[80]

Two key factors inform the jurisprudence of the *Dueck* case. First, the accusations against him simply stated that he had participated in the execution
of civilians and of Soviet POWs. The Holocaust, the process of extermination
of the Jews of the Ukraine is totally absent from any graphic representation in
the judicial recording of the case against him.

This writing out of the Holocaust which has come more and more to characterize post-*Finta* Canadian deportation cases is reinforced by the technical
basis of the proceedings themselves and therefore of the primary legal and fac-

---

76. Moira MacDonald, "Nazi War Crime Suspect Dies: Canada Sought to Strip Man of
Citizenship", *Toronto Sun*, 2 January 1998.
77. "Latvian Accused of War Crimes Dies in Canada", *Baltic News Service*, 3 January
1998.
78. *Minister of Citizenship and Immigration v. Johann Dueck*, T-938-95 (Fed. Ct.).
79. Ibid., 4 July 1997.
80. Ibid.

tual focus of the court's decision. In order to be subject to deportation from Canada, as is *grosso modo* the case in America as well, an accused must be shown to have lied about some relevant detail of his wartime activities at the time he gained permission to enter the country or applied for residence or citizenship. In other words, what is legally crucial in all these proceedings is that the defendant can be shown to have lied about his past, rather than a focus on the past itself. Of course, the past about which the lie is told or the truth is hidden, must be in relation to activities which would be "excludable conduct" and that might quite clearly include activities associated with the extermination of European Jewry. But what is legally relevant and what is at the forefront of proceedings like this is the untruth and deception.

In other words, the jurisprudential gatekeeping function which is at the heart of such cases is the control over the character of those who entered Canada and that character is to be determined by reference to lies and obfuscations. Not only does the Holocaust here slide into the judicial and jurisprudential background, but the focus of both historical and legal investigation must be Canadianized i.e. what is central to all such proceedings is the nature and functioning of Canadian immigration controls in Europe at the end of the Second World War. The key is not, nor can it be, the matrix of meanings associated with the Holocaust and Canadian identity and the rule of law. Instead it must be on Canadian officials and their practices in post-May 1945 Europe. Thus the Canadian judicial system Canadianizes law after Auschwitz by erasing "Auschwitz" from any historical and jurisprudential primacy.

Nowhere does the absence of the Shoah in Canadian judicial constructions of war criminals and those guilty of crimes against humanity become clearer than in the last of the trilogy, the case of Helmut Oberlander. In this case Oberlander, an ethnic German was charged with having covered up his work as an interpreter for *Einsatzcommando* 10a in the occupied Ukraine. As an ethnic German from the area, a member of the *Volksdeutsche*, Oberlander served with the unit which was responsible for the deaths of more than two million, Jews, Gypsies, handicapped and Communists. At some fundamental level of historical truth and existential reality then, Oberlander was a Holocaust perpetrator who shared at the very least in the moral responsibility of the actions of those who pulled the triggers. Yet, the judge in the case found that

> There is no evidence that the respondent participated in any of the atrocities committed against civilians....[81]

---

81. *Minister of Citizenship and Immigration v. Helmut Oberlander*, Federal Court of Canada, T-866-95, 28 February 2000.

A full jurisprudential and ethical analysis of Oberlander's responsibility here would depend on both a careful legal analysis of the liability of accessories to crimes against humanity and a detailed and nuanced political, social, historical and moral discussion of the responsibility we might wish to sheet home to those whose presence made the life of the killers possible and eased their daily burdens. All of these issues and questions must continue to trouble those of us interested in the possibility of a post-Auschwitz legal theory. None of these issues was relevant to the determination of his case before the Federal Court. Instead, the Court engages again in a careful and detailed examination of Canadian screening procedures and of the status of the SD as a criminal organization. Thus

> I find that if Mr. Oberlander had answered questions truthfully, including his experience as an interpreter with Ek 10a for the SD, an organization determined in 1946 to be criminal, his application would have been rejected, either because he would have been perceived to be a member of the SD, even if he were not, or because he would have been perceived as a collaborator. Either perception was a reason for rejection on security grounds.[82]

Here the findings of the IMT at Nuremberg in relation to Nazi criminal organizations, or at least a judicial reconstruction of that finding and its legal import in determining individual liability, combined with another construction of postwar immigration proceedings and procedures, determine that Helmut Oberlander should be removed from Canada. In essence then he offers the mirror opposite of his co-respondent Johann Dueck since he was found to have been excludable from Canada. But in effect once more the substantive outcome of each individual case is basically and fundamentally irrelevant to the judicial construction of the period of history and its legal impact today. In essence, it matters not that Oberlander was member of the SD or that there is no proof that Dueck killed anyone. The fate of the victims of Nazi horror is not at all relevant. What is important in determining whether someone should remain as part of the body politic is whether they in fact complied with the procedural letter of the law when interviewed by Canadian security or immigration officials. The law defends Canada's borders and national identity not from killers but from liars. The bodies and mass graves of Jews are rendered irrelevant or reduced to background interest as the exclusion of alleged perpetrators becomes a Canadianized process. The rule of law triumphs because what must be respected is the rule of Canadian law.

---

82. Ibid., at 208.

Of course there have been and will continue to be voices of dissent. As I have argued and demonstrated throughout, the concept and content of "the rule of law" are themselves open to contestation. Following the decision to strip Oberlander of his citizenship, Andrew Telgadi, the Liberal MP from the Kitchener area voiced his objections. Kitchener is Oberlander's home and the home of a significant German "immigrant" population. Telgadi, giving voice to the feelings of many, lashed out at the decision, comparing Canadian proceedings against Oberlander with Nazi Germany. The typical and expected outcry ensued.[83] The point here is not of course really about comparisons between Nazi Germany and Canada. Indeed, Telgadi "clarified" his remarks to assert that his objections were not to deportation *per se*, but to the fact that the ultimate decision rested with the Minister and not with the Courts. Here then he positions himself in a traditional jurisprudential manner, arguing about the appropriate institutional arrangements required to give full adherence to our understandings of the rule of law within Canadian parliamentary democracy.

It might also be possible to read this as a politician trying to cover his tracks and attempting to hide the true meaning of his remarks. I am not suggesting here that he was in fact asserting a direct comparison with Nazi Germany but rather that he was in fact voicing the concerns of many of his constituents in the Kitchener area about the entire war crimes process. Here we can again see all of the tensions which are inherent in the debates around these issues generally as well as the specifically local elements of the political situation. Migrant or ethnic communities express legitimate concerns about issues of scapegoating and the imposition of collective guilt. In doing so, however, they may also come close to the rhetorical and ideological line which denies not the Holocaust but the participation of any members of the community in the practices of mass extermination. The debate and controversy then begins to pit one "ethnic" group, "the Germans" against another, "the Jews", as the facts revealed in the legal process are replaced by name calling and baiting. In effect, the debate centers attention again on the exact place, if any, of the Holocaust in Canadian political, cultural and legal identity. Like the deportation process itself, debates about the deportation process again put the Holocaust and its place within the process of the ongoing construction of Canadian identity, in a secondary and largely irrelevant position.

Current experience with deportation and denaturalization serves to confirm this. It is not my intention here to offer a detailed analysis of all efforts

---

83. See "MP Under Fire for 'Hitler' Remark", *Globe and Mail*, 8 May 2001; Edward Greenspon, "A sorry tale of two MPs", *Globe and Mail*, 12 May 2001.

by the Canadian government to deport alleged war criminals and Holocaust perpetrators. Instead I wish to briefly sketch an outline of the subtle shifts in both policy and rhetoric which have served to displace and replace the fate of the victims of the Final Solution within Canadian legal and political discourse about national identity. I am not arguing here that the Holocaust is completely absent from such discursive constructions within legal proceedings. Rather I believe that a series of subtle shifts in procedural and substantive focus has operated by a legal necessity imposed by denaturalization and deportation processes. The result of that shift has been to elide the Holocaust from the legal consciousness in Canadian proceedings against alleged perpetrators. Indeed, it seems apparent that a key result of this new procedural focus from substantive criminal allegations to technical violations of immigration rules has been to efface the individual's responsibility as Holocaust perpetrator.

The "best case" for an apparently morally responsible legal rhetoric in Canada can be found in some of the statements and actions surrounding the case of Ludwig Nebel. Nebel was a former Viennese police officer who was accused of rounding up approximately 200 Jews to be sent to death camps. Here then we find a rather typical Holocaust perpetrator, the classic case of a local policeman doing his job, part of which simply meant sending Jews to their deaths. In the early popular discussions of his case we find clear evidence of all of the traditional tropes surrounding such cases. Thus

> Nebel is accused of helping the Nazis round up at least 200 Jews to be sent to a death camp during the war, but a neighbour described him as a quiet, considerate man, telling a newspaper: "I would take a whole neighborhood of people like him".[84]

Two of the predominant tropes which have served to distort the reality and history of the Holocaust and which continue to shape popular misunderstandings and constructions of perpetrators are on display here. First there is the traditional division of primary and secondary responsibility between the "Nazis" on the one hand and those like Nebel who simply "helped" on the other. The centrality of government organs and officials to the Holocaust, the primary role of the police of all the countries of Occupied Europe in identifying and rounding up Jews and the widespread "help" of local populations, not to mention the cooperation and willingness of the Austrian population in the "Nazification" of that country, are all lost here in the misleading account of the *Nebel* case.

---

84. "Canada seeks to change Nazi-haven image", *Jerusalem Post*, 22 July 1998.

This is confirmed and exacerbated by the statement of the neighbor who comments on the ordinariness and acceptability of Mr Nebel's character. The very ordinariness of Holocaust perpetrators here is lost beneath the by now familiar "ordinary neighbor" argument. Because he has no swastika tattooed to his forehead, Nebel could not possibly be guilty.

Because this case also marked an important step in the new strategy of deportation, the government spokesperson in this instance was at pains to mark out and deploy the rhetoric of "punishment" of wrongdoers associated, as we have seen, with the use of such procedures.

> We think citizenship is something significant and it is an honor and a privilege to hold....I think it's an appropriate thing to symbolise Canada's abhorrence of the conduct of the activities of these people.[85]

There can be little doubt that at some level of the semiotics of national identity and the role and function of law that this can be seen to be an accurate statement. Nor can there be any doubt that in the most egregious cases, the processes in question can be and are effective at some level.

Thus, Ladislaus Csizsik-Csatary was accused, like Imre Finta, of having been a member of the Hungarian *Gendarmerie* and of having been responsible for the rounding up, imprisonment and transportation of thousands of his country's Jews. He was stripped of his citizenship and fled to Europe before "extradition" hearings were launched against him.[86] Yet the Csatary case can in reality only be read as a partial "victory". He did not contest the government's move against him. There was never a playing out of the facts of his involvement in the Hungarian Holocaust in any way which could arguably be said to have been a judicial reconstruction and recognition of his role in the killing of his fellow citizens. He fled the country and has never faced substantive charges for his acts. Most importantly, he was stripped of his Canadian citizenship not for his role in the Holocaust in his native country but because he had gained entry to Canada by telling immigration officials that he was a Yugoslav citizen. In other words, he was forced to leave Canada not because he killed Jews but because he lied about killing Jews.

In a series of other cases in which the government has been forced to resort to legal proceedings against alleged perpetrators all these weaknesses of the denaturalization and deportation mechanisms can also be seen to be

---

85. Ibid.
86. Allan Thompson, "Citizenship of alleged Nazi helper revoked", *Toronto Star*, 29 August 1997; "Suspected war criminal in Canada has fled to Europe: government", *Agence France Presse*, 9 October 1997.

played out. Eduards Podins was alleged to have been a member of the Latvian Auxiliary Police. The judicial history of the case against him is marked not primarily by an investigation into his moral and legal responsibility for the Holocaust in Latvia but by a series of technical legal arguments about the taking of commission evidence,[87] abuse of discovery procedures by the Crown,[88] and finally of a lengthy judgment which focuses on whether the camp to which he was posted was a concentration camp or a prison, whether his activities there constituted collaboration and whether he had lied about his role to Canadian authorities when he immigrated to that country.[89] There is no mention or any evidence at all concerning any allegation that Podins had any involvement in the extermination of Latvian Jewry.

There are no Jewish victims here. There is only a lengthy discussion as to whether because Podins had first gone to Britain and then to Canada he would have been subjected to security screening which would have forced him to withhold information about his past. In other words, this is a case which must be seen to typify the content and consequences of the shift in practice to denaturalization and deportation. There are no Jews, there is no Holocaust. There is only a series of technical questions about whether security screening and questionnaires would have forced Podins to lie about his past. A similar set of analyses and results can be found in another case involving a Latvian former police and Waffen SS member, Peter Vitols.[90] According to local newspaper accounts, Peteris (Peter) Arvids Vitols was

> …a stout white-haired man who walks with a cane and has support within Toronto's Latvian community.[91]

According to the Federal Court of Canada, Vitols was a member of a Latvian police battalion and later joined the Waffen SS. According to Vitols' own account, which was largely accepted by McKeown J., he worked as an office employee, who spent his time translating documents and making copies. While there is an extensive discussion in the judge's decision of the history of the Latvian Holocaust, this occurs in the context of a battle between the competing experts, Professor Konrad Kwiet for the Crown and Professor Andrew Ezergailis for the defence, over the extent and nature of local police involve-

---

87. *Minister of Citizenship and Immigration v. Eduards Podins*, T-1093-97, 24 June 1998.
88. Ibid., 9 September 1998.
89. Ibid., 7 September 1999.
90. *Minister of Citizenship and Immigration and Nationality v Vitols*, T-310-97, 23 September 1998.
91. Jim Rankin, "War crimes suspect faces his accusers", *Toronto Star*, 20 January 1998.

ment in the killing of Jews. In fact, in the course of the presentation of the Crown's case, the government of Canada admitted that the question of whether Latvian police killed Jews at the time of Vitols' entry into service or whether Vitols himself was involved in such activities was irrelevant since the principle claim against the respondent was that he had lied about his membership in an organization which had previously committed such acts. In other words, the case against Vitols became a technical argument first of all about the operative legal definition of "collaboration", in which the killing of tens of thousands of Jews became a mere footnote. Secondly, the debate, again by necessity, centered upon the postwar immigration procedures involving British and Canadian authorities. In this case, the British who had first jurisdiction over Vitols and other Baltic SS battalions, chose to classify them as having been in the "army", a designation which Vitols simply adopted in subsequent immigration proceedings.[92] In the end the Court found that the Crown had not met its burden in establishing that Vitols had lied upon his entry or subsequently. The Shoah is erased as a matter of Canadian juridical concern in the bureaucratic tide of immigration forms, security interviews, visa control etc.

Most other cases which have entered the legal system of denaturalization and deportation tell a similar tale of technical legal arguments about evidence and rules of procedure, lengthy investigations of postwar immigration procedures etc. Again, the Holocaust to a greater or lesser extent is simply written out as the question of war crimes and crimes against humanity are made irrelevant by a legal process which must by definition focus on whether correct immigration procedures were or were not followed. A brief examination of two other Canadian cases will offer final demonstrations of the ways in which the Holocaust and the rule of law become incompatible rhetorical and ideological tropes in the search for a construction of a Canadian national identity.

The first case here is that of the peripatetic Konrad Kalejs. After his expulsion following lengthy proceedings from the United States, Kalejs, an Australian citizen, arrived in Canada where he attempted to take up residence. Kalejs was believed by many to have been responsible for the mass killings of Latvian Jews when he was an officer in the notorious Arjas Commando in that country. The case of Kalejs in Canada was at a basic level unremarkable. After his discovery there, Canadian authorities began gathering evidence of his participation in the activities of the Arjas Commando, evidence which Kalejs continued to deny and which he claimed in a now familiar tactic to be Soviet for-

---

92. *Minister of Citizenship and Immigration v. Vitols*, op. cit., Part IV, paras. 89 et seq.

geries.[93] After lengthy hearings and legal maneuvering, Kalejs was expelled from Canada and returned to Australia. What is interesting and important about the Canadian proceedings against Kalejs was that as in the case of American and British steps against him, the international legal system and the domestic Australian system operate in a way which gives automatic protection to Kalejs. Because he was an Australian citizen and because the Canadian and American proceedings against him were deportation rather than extradition hearings, he was free to elect the country to which he wished to return. He chose his country of citizenship and thus avoided any possibility of ending up before a Latvian court on substantive charges. In other words, the strength of the Canadian system which seeks to protect its borders and to define its own national identity and to construct an internal body politic, reinforces the national rule of law, is that it makes it impossible for substantive proceedings to take place. This does not mean, of course, that such proceedings would have what I might consider an appropriate or just result, nor does it mean that the rule of law is either weakened or strengthened more or less by a choice between deportation and trial. It has a far weaker and a far stronger meaning than that. In any and either event, the rule of law will necessarily triumph and the only way in which a jurisprudence after Auschwitz can be rendered meaningful is if we can come to the uncomfortable conclusion that justice for the victims can never be found or perhaps even sought in any legal forum because the law of Auschwitz was and is the law after Auschwitz. Any attempt to construct the Shoah within the law, must construct the law within the Shoah.

Any attempt to do otherwise will always mean a distortion of history and of the law's true role and rule within the Holocaust. Evidence of these inevitable injustices can be found in the gross distortion of law and history which characterized the legal and factual maneuvers in proceedings against Vladimir Katriuk, who had for many years been the object of claims from the Soviet Union that he had, as a Ukrainian member of the Waffen SS, committed war crimes and crimes against humanity. After a series of lengthy hearings, investigations and proceedings, the Court found simply

> Although I have no difficulty concluding that the respondent participated in the operations in which his company was involved, I am not

93. See Adrian Bradley, "War crimes suspect may be returned", *Weekend Australian*, 3–4 June 1995; Lila Sarick, "Nazi recruiting of Latvians detailed", *Globe and Mail*, 2 May 1996; Bill Dunphy, "Court told of KGB frame-up", *Toronto Sun*, 25 September 1996; Michael Grange, "War crimes suspect says documents were forged", *Globe and Mail*, 2 October 1996; Russell Blinch, "Canada seeks to expel suspected Nazi war criminal", *Reuters*, 22 January 1997.

prepared, on the evidence before me, to conclude that he participated in the commission of atrocities against the civilian population of Byelorussia. Not enough is known to reach any conclusion.[94]

In the end, Katriuk was found to have entered Canada illegally not because of his activities as a member of the Waffen SS or because he lied to immigration and security officials about that, since the judge found that the Minister had not met the requisite burden of proof about immigration procedures in Katriuk's case. Instead, he was deemed as unsuitable for membership in the Canadian body politic because he had entered the country using his brother-in-law's name and identity. There are once more, no Jews, no Holocaust, no victims of any kind in Katriuk's case. He assumed a false identity and therefore he engaged in anti-Canadian activity. But again that does not tell the entire story of the case of Vladimir Katriuk and the construction of Canadian identity and the rule of law in that country's reconstruction of the Holocaust.

As I have already discussed, Ukrainian Canadian populations are large in number and strong in political force. In his decision in Katriuk's case, Nadon, a Francophone member of the Federal Court, comes perilously close to a judicial rewriting of the history of the Holocaust in the Ukraine. He writes for example

> But in Ukraine, collaboration was a much more complicated issue. It was, first of all, unclear how much loyalty Ukrainians owed to Stalin's regime or to the Polish state that had mistreated them. Who was the primary enemy? Was it the Stalinist system, which inflicted such great suffering in the 1930s or the Nazi regime, which was currently (but perhaps only temporarily) in power? Finally, given the extreme ruthlessness of both regimes in Ukraine, collaboration was often the price of survival for many Ukrainians.[95]

He added:

> Consequently, Ukrainian collaboration with the Nazis was insignificant compared to that of Germany's allies.[96]

---

94. *Minister of Citizenship and Immigration v. Vladimir Katriuk*, T-2409-96, 29 January 1999 at 66. See contra, *Minister of Citizenship and Immigration v. Wasily (Wasil) Bogutin*, T-1700-96, 20 February 1998 and *Minister of Citizenship and Immigration v. Serge Kisluk*, T-300-097, 7 June 1999, two cases concerning Ukrainian police involved in killing Jews. Both Bogutin and Kisluk had been names featuring in Soviet and Ukrainian lists of Nazi war criminals being sheltered in Canada. Bogutin died before the end of proceedings against him.

95. Ibid., at 71.

96. Ibid.

Finally, the judge wrote

> Given the lowly position of Ukrainian collaborators in the Nazi ap-
> paratus and the SS monopoly on the actual extermination of Jews,
> Ukrainian participation in the massacres was neither extensive nor
> decisive. When it did occur, it usually took the form of the auxiliary
> policemen herding Jews into ghettos.[97]

This is a remarkable step in recent Canadian jurisprudence of the Holocaust.
The history of the Ukraine is no doubt complex and collaboration with the Germans is equally informed by a number of historical, social, cultural, religious
and political factors. No one can doubt the brutality of the Stalinist regime. But
what is again missing here is the presence of an historical, brutal and violent antisemitism as a key element in the history under discussion. Many Ukrainians
who engaged in anti-Soviet activity at this time were heavily influenced by the
antisemitic perception that Jews were unduly and disproportionately responsible
for Communist terror. Anti-Communism was for many simply antisemitism.[98]
Nadon J can be read here as doing little more than engaging in typical rabid ex-
tremist Ukrainian nationalist propaganda under the guise of Canadian judicial
neutrality.[99] He does more than simply ignore the Holocaust which is a more typical and perhaps internally consistent aspect of the denaturalization process of
other cases. He rewrites history to the detriment of the victims and in favor of
the perpetrators. Ukrainians had good reason to collaborate; they were low ech-
elon actors; they did not kill Jews; they simply rounded them up.[100] Here Justice
Nadon displays a profound ignorance of the reality of the Holocaust and a complete lack of understanding of the machinery of death involved in the Shoah.
Ghettoization was a necessary step in the physical elimination of European Jewry,
not some sort of minor lesser and included misdemeanor. Here the judge repeats
the classic argument which seeks to establish a hierarchy of responsibility not for
the goal of a more sophisticated historical understanding, nor with the object of
engaging in detailed and nuanced moral analysis of perpetrator responsibility,
but instead for the purpose of legitimizing one particular group of killers.

The place of the Holocaust and the victims of the policy and practice of extermination in Canadian law and in the Canadian construction of national

---

97. Ibid.

98. This is of course the same theme which arose in Australia as a result of the Helen
Demidenko/Darville furore.

99. Which is not, it must be underlined, typical of the mainstream attitude of Ukrainian Canadians.

100. See *contra*, Martin Dean, *Collaboration in the Holocaust*, op. cit.

identity through the legal construction of the Shoah could not be clearer. But the story does not end there. Or more precisely the stories do not end there. The official tale is that Canada as a western democracy dedicated to the rule of law and justice for perpetrators of crimes against humanity and war crimes has an active and ongoing program of seeking out and subjecting such individuals to the full rigors of the law. Millions of dollars have been and will be expended in this fight for justice.[101]

I have briefly outlined in the preceding sections another telling of the tale which does not put Canadian efforts against Holocaust perpetrators in the same light. But there is a final example of the way in which Canadian efforts can be read as embodying images of national identity and collective understandings of the Holocaust and the rule of law which might serve to unite some of the musings in this chapter. I return here to the case of Imre Finta.

Finta was represented by lawyer Douglas Christie. Christie also acted in the defence of Malcolm Ross, Ernst Zundel and James Keegstra. A pattern might be found here but the appropriate meaning to be attributed to the pattern is easily contested and contestable. Some might see Christie's consistent interventions in cases such as these as representative of a personal political agenda which is, to put it mildly, less than sympathetic to particular imaginings of Canadian identity and the role which the Holocaust should, or can play therein. On the other hand, one might see Christie's role here as embodying a particular and strong traditional reading of the role of the lawyer in defending the rule of law. One of the prevailing professional self-images of lawyers is that found in the "cab rank rule", the hired gunslinger analogy and variants thereof. Here the heroic and professionally competent lawyer simply offers his/her services to the first client who presents themselves. In the stronger version of this tale of professional expertise, the heroic lawyer defends the most reprehensible client in order to allow the system of the rule of law to work as it should before the courts of law. It is my assertion here that only by reading both tales of Douglas Christie and his actions in the *Finta* case in particular can we properly situate the discourse and ideology of the rule of law within Canadian attempts to situate the Holocaust in the struggle for national identity. In other words, Christie embodied both antisemitism and the rule of law in *Finta* because the rule of law allows, in the weak version of the reading, or demands, in the stronger version, an antisemitic rendering of itself in all cases in which the Holocaust and the law confront each other.

---

101. See, Department of Justice and Department of Citizenship and Immigration, *Canada's War Crimes Program, 3rd Annual Report,* 1999–2000.

In addition to an apparent invitation to the jury to ignore the statute and acquit his client because the war crimes provisions of the *Criminal Code* were "diabolical", Christie's closing argument was also characterized by several more problematic assertions. He sought to remind the jury that

> You see, no one else, it is your individual conscience and when you are telling the accused he is supposed to have looked to his conscience to disobey the law, you had better have an answer that satisfies your-self and remember this 45 years later, because you never know in this crazy world, what we do today is lawful and might be some kind of crime tomorrow, or so it would appear....[102]

This and related remarks constituted threats to the jury according to the Crown's position on appeal. Christie also asserted that a conviction would raise the old grievances of the Second World War, explained that God would judge them as they judged Finta, exhorted them with references to the Bible about Pontius Pilate, and finally pointed out that all the eyewitnesses against Finta i.e., the Jewish victims, offered their testimony by way of affirmation while others chose to swear on the Bible.

On the last two points in which Christian antisemitic motifs can easily be detected in Christie's assertions and arguments, the Ontario Court of Appeal said the following:

> In our view, the exegesis chosen by defence counsel was inappropri-ate in the extreme. None the less, we do not think that the jury could have realistically compared the circumstances of Jesus and the re-spondent. Had the contrary conclusion been obvious, we would have thought this part of the defence jury address would have been in-cluded in the list of the Crown counsel's lengthy objections made im-mediately after the defence jury address....
>
> We think the distinction drawn by Mr. Christie between those who swore and those who affirmed was unworthy of a counsel of his ex-perience and inappropriate in the extreme. The trial judge, however, directed the jury with precision that an oath and an affirmation have the same effect. We are satisfied that the jury would not have suc-cumbed to defence counsel's transparent tactics.[103]

Cory J for the majority in the Supreme Court of Canada contented himself with the statement that

102. 73 C.C.C. (3d) at p. 185.
103. At p. 191.

Neither counsel was a model of perfection in their addresses to the jury, although I hasten to add that the remarks of the counsel for the respondent were far more prejudicial. None the less, the direction given by the trial judge pertaining to the counsels' addresses remedied any prejudice that might have arisen.[104]

The rule of law triumphs. No matter what defects might have existed, the trial judge's instructions and the jury's common sense in light of those instructions would remedy any prejudice which might have arisen or been caused. This is of course traditional appellate court discourse in relation to the conduct of trials. The question is whether the trial judge as a matter of law gave adequate instructions to remove any procedural or evidentiary taint which might be said to have arisen. The base antisemitism invoked, the imagery of the wrongly accused Christ crucified as a result of the perfidy of the deicide Jews, all of whom are inveterate liars who mock our Bible and refuse to recognize the authority of its word and the truth of the Christ they have killed, are all washed away, like the sins of the wicked, by a carefully worded instruction to the jury and the basic ideological belief central to the criminal justice system that juries would not, could not and do not bring such base prejudices into their deliberations. The rule of law is here present in all its glory. Of course, the rule of law would also have been present in all its glory if the appellate courts had come to exactly the opposite conclusion and held that Christie's words were so inflammatory and unacceptable that they could not have been cured by judicial instruction. At this level the rule of law is content and result neutral, an analysis remarkably consistent with the finding that Finta could successfully invoke his belief that the imprisonment and brutalization of Jews was perfectly acceptable and lawful.

But here we are in fact faced with the rule of law within a set of discursive deployments in which antisemitic stereotypes are present and are, if not ignored, then minimized by the courts of appeal. The invocation of the wrongly accused Jesus is an "exegesis" i.e. an appropriate textual interpretive tactic commonly employed to describe readings of the Bible which is not totally unacceptable but which is merely "inappropriate in the extreme" and which is cured by judicial instruction and a realistic jury who would realize that Finta was not to be compared with Christ. Yet the very point of the "exegesis" is to make this comparison and to draw on centuries of Christian and popular theological and cultural constructions of Jews as persecutors and killers of Christ.

Again, the rhetorical invocation of Jews as liars and deniers of the Bible is dismissed by the Appeal Court as "inappropriate in the extreme" and not wor-

---

104. 112 D.L.R. (4th) 513 at p. 622.

thy of an experienced lawyer. Yet the entire context of the trial and of the findings of the Court on the substantive and evidentiary issues belie the "inappropriateness" of Christie's comments and tactics. Finta was justified in his belief that the vast majority non-Jewish Hungarians wanted legal measures to be taken against their Jewish fellow citizens. He was "correct" in believing that he was invoking lawful measures against the Jews. Cultural, theological, political and legal antisemitism were legitimized by the Appeal Court and by the Supreme Court of Canada in a context in which the Hungarian Holocaust was on trial. It is hardly surprising that the same courts would simply offer solipsism and empty procedural rhetoric in order to both save the rule of law and give solace to Christie's basic assertions that Jews are indeed different. Mere declarations that the comments were inappropriate do not cure, but instead reinforce, the evil of Christie's rhetoric.

David Matas of B'nai Brith put the position as follows:

> In our opinion the level of appeal to religious and ethnic prejudice in the case was such that it damaged the fairness of the trial beyond repair.[105]

Complaints about Christie's conduct were lodged with the Law Society of Upper Canada but that remedy proved ineffectual.[106] Indeed, the comments by Harvey Strosberg, Disciplinary Committee Chair go at least part way to explaining the problematics exposed by Christie in the course of his defence of Imre Finta. Strosberg stated:

> We know who Mr. Christie is. In the depths of his imagery he has not lied. Suffering Mr. Christie's words and opinions is part of the price one pays for upholding and cherishing the freedom of speech in a free and democratic society.[107]

Christie is undoubtedly a Christian and as a result of his particular theology, an antisemite who does in fact believe that Jews persecuted and killed

---

105. Hanoch Bordan, "Finta trial wasn't fair group charges", *Toronto Star*, 26 October 1990.

106. Paul Maloney, "Lawyer harassed witnesses at Finta trial, man charges", *Toronto Star*, 21 November 1990; "Law Society to hear witness abuse claim", ibid., 20 December 1990; Tom Onyshko, "LSUC won't pursue misconduct complaint against Christie…but discipline panel sends warning to profession", *Lawyers Weekly*, 5 March 1993. Defending Michael Seifert from an Italian extradition request, Christie claimed that Citizenship Minister Elinor Caplan was acting out of "Jewish animosity" towards his client. Allison Lawlor, "Man convicted of war crimes arrested in B.C.", *Globe and Mail*, 1 May 2002.

107. Ibid.

Christ. He does believe that God will judge jurors who judge Imre Finta and his like. He is a "devout Catholic" who makes his "stand on principle" and is "the free world's most outstanding defender of the individual's right to challenge the generally-accepted views of history".[108] This is however a price paid by democracy or by the rule of law. This is precisely the possibility inherent within the rule of law and democracy within the West. Imre Finta believed that what he did was legal, Douglas Christie like Malcolm Ross believes that what he said was true. It is this combination of a belief in the truth and legality of antisemitism that gave us the Holocaust. Canadian law, like the Canadian society it represents, has not come very far from those same moral and legal roots.

---

108. Keltie Zuko, *The Path of Legal Warfare: Imre Finta's Trial for War Crimes* (Cranbrook: Veritas Publishing, 1991) at 37.

CHAPTER 10

"The Time Has Come to Close the Chapter": Prosecuting (or Not) War Criminals in Australia

1. Introduction

In February 1961, the government of the USSR formally requested the extradition of Ervin Richard Adolf Petrovich Viks from Australia. The Soviets alleged that Viks had committed war crimes and crimes against humanity in Estonia during World War II. Outlining the reasons behind the government's refusal to comply with the extradition request, Sir Garfield Barwick, the Attorney General, offered a lengthy discussion of Australia's existing international legal obligations in such matters. He then proceeded to put forward an analysis of the situation which not only succinctly summarized the position of the government of the day but which would serve as the basis for many of the debates surrounding the prosecution of alleged Nazi war criminals decades later. Barwick said to the Australian Parliament:

Two deep-seated human interests, however, may well here come into conflict, On the one hand, there is the utter abhorrence felt by Australians for those offences against humanity to which we give the generic name of war crimes. On the other hand, there is the right of this nation, by receiving people into this country, to enable men to turn their backs on past bitternesses and to make a new life for themselves and for their families in a happier community. This has formed a precious part of the heritage of the West, in which Australia has an honourable share.

In a given case the choice between these two human interests may present a government with a difficult decision. In the present instance, however, the Government came to the clear conclusion that, all questions of legal obligations apart, if such a choice had been necessary to resolve the matter, its right of asylum must have prevailed. Australia has established a thorough, though of course not infallible system for sifting and screening the hundreds of thousands of migrants who have enriched our national life since the World War. In default of a binding obligation requiring Australia at this point of time to do otherwise, those, who have been allowed to make their homes here, must be able to live, in security, new lives under the rule of law.[1]

In the end, the government had concluded:

…we think the time has come to close the chapter. It is, truly, the year 1961.[2]

More than ten years earlier, the leader of the Labor Opposition, Ben Chifley, had stated the position of his party on allegations that Nazis had managed to make their way to Australia.

I could not see much purpose in continuing investigations aimed at the tracing of war criminals. That sort of thing could go on for the next twenty years, and new criminals could be located almost daily.… The situation has stirred up considerable public feeling, and has caused some criticism, not only of the former Government, but also of this Government. Many people ask how long these trials and investigations are to continue. Church representatives have criticized the long drawn-out trials at Nuremberg.[3]

From the earliest days of the post-War period, all sides of the Australian political mainstream had adopted positions hostile to the pursuit of alleged war criminals in Australia.

Barwick's speech to the House not only serves as a precursor to the arguments which would resurface in later years but it also can be seen to encapsulate almost all of the discursive practices which have always dominated de-

---

1. *Hansard*, House of Representatives, 22 March 1961, at 451–52.
2. Ibid., at 452.
3. *Hansard*, 16 March 1950, at 896–97.

bates about the prosecution of Nazi war criminals, not only in Australia, but in the West generally. The positioning, both explicit and implicit, of Australia within the Western tradition, not only reflects the politics of memory and self-understanding of that country's politicians as part of an ideologically coherent, if geographically disparate, "West", but must also be situated within the discourses of the Cold War, which pitted that "West" against the Soviet menace. Australia's refusal to extradite Ervin Viks to the USSR is clearly grounded in the anticommunist discourses and ideology of that period, an ideology which played a clear and key role in many cases involving decisions to prosecute (or not) alleged Holocaust perpetrators.

In addition to the Cold War rhetoric which underlies much of Barwick's elaboration of Australian government policy, other predominant themes from post-war debates about the fate of perpetrators can also be found in the statement to Parliament. The conflict between the necessity of bringing perpetrators to justice and issues of the passage of time, of letting bygones be bygones, "to enable men to turn their backs on past bitternesses", are clearly part of the debates which continue to circulate on this topic to this day. However, one theme elaborated by Barwick underpins all else. That theme is the "rule of law". For Barwick and for the Australian government, this idea/ideology of the rule of law seems to encapsulate and include all of the other themes which surround the vexed question of prosecuting perpetrators. The rule of law is, in the eyes of the government of Australia, clearly something that belongs to the heritage of the West, of which it is part. This allows the government not just to refuse to deport Viks to the Soviet Union, which is by definition, not part of the West and not a country governed by the rule of law, but also allows it to confirm its own status as part of the great Western heritage. The invocation of "the rule of law" allows Australia to create a self-fulfilling prophecy in which it does indeed become part of the Western tradition.

This invocation of the rule of law as the defining characteristic of the Australian and Western tradition then almost automatically carries with it its own important ideological, political, moral and legal consequences. First, there is the obvious conclusion to be drawn from the tenor of Barwick's rhetoric and from the substantive result of the government's decision to allow Viks to remain unharmed and unthreatened in Australia that there somehow is a disjunction between the prosecution of perpetrators of the Holocaust and maintaining the rule of law.[4] Second, there is the other necessary conclusion that

4. Despite other attempts to bring Viks before Soviet justice, he remained in Australia. He was tried in absentia in the USSR and sentenced to death. One of his co-accused, Karl

the Holocaust can somehow be forgotten and forgiven through the invocation of rule of law rhetoric. Australia's granting of "asylum" to Viks is in effect translated into a pardon, an amnesty/amnesia which submerges concerns for vengeance and/or justice under the tides of the rule of law. Finally, the way in which the rule of law is invoked in the practical and political circumstances of the Viks' case in the Australia of 1961, allows the governmental, public and legal discourse of that country to establish the "non-Australian" nature of the Holocaust. In the Australian Parliament, the Holocaust becomes part of "past bitternesses" from elsewhere, to be forgotten and forgiven by the simple fact of entry into Australia where we find a "happier community", one in which, virtually by definitional necessity, the Holocaust can play no part. Perpetrators can live "new lives" as the Government declares, as a matter of law, the chapter closed. Auschwitz is not Australia, nor is it Australian.

This image of Australia, portrayed in Barwick's 1961 speech, as a country which is an integral part of the great traditions of the West, including the rule of law, is one which continues to be widely held and accepted. The idea of the country as a multicultural haven in which past animosities from elsewhere are submerged in a new Australian identity is also a powerful, although by no means universal, one today. Finally, the idea that the chapter of the Holocaust, which is, after all, a story from somewhere else, should be closed and forgotten, is also a strong one. However, as is the case elsewhere, the struggle over national identity and self-definition is complex and continuing. Other stories, other memories of what it means to be "Australian", of where, or if, the Holocaust plays a role in the construction of that national memory, and finally of the role, if any, of the law in the construction of that part of national identity, have been put forward as equally legitimate narratives. The history of the prosecution (or not) of alleged perpetrators in Australia is in many ways an attempt to redefine or to reject various collective memories of national identity and to lay claim to the status of defender of the rule of law and democratic traditions and values. In what follows, I briefly examine the intersections of law, memory and justice as they have been, and continue to be, played out in the public discourses surrounding the issue of the prosecution (or not) of alleged Holocaust perpetrators in Australia.

Linnas, was eventually deported from the United States and died of natural causes in a Soviet jail. Bill Keller, "Estonian Sent to Face Death in Soviet Dies in a Hospital", *New York Times*, 3 July 1987. For a fuller discussion of the Viks case, see Mark Aarons, *Sanctuary: Nazi Fugitives in Australia* (Port Melbourne: Mandarin, 1989), at 186–94.

2. Australia: Identity, Memory and War Crimes

Much of the Australian debate surrounding issues of memory, identity, justice and the Holocaust shares points of commonality and continuity with debates and developments in other countries in which these questions arise. At the same time, of course, each national context carries its own historical and political peculiarities. With Canada, and the *sui generis* exception of Israel, Australia is the only country, outside those in Europe which were the direct victims of Nazi crimes against humanity, to attempt to put Nazi or collaborator perpetrators on trial for crimes committed by them against Europe's Jews.[5] At the level of official, legislative enactment and discourse at least, some parts of more recent Australian practice have rejected the notion propounded by Sir Garfield Barwick and others, that the Holocaust is not an "Australian" phenomenon. This is a point to which I shall return.

Other national specificities tend to make the debate surrounding the role and place of the Holocaust and the prosecution of perpetrators in Australian national memory and identity more complex still. Much of the concern which has recently emerged over national identity relates only indirectly to issues of the Holocaust. For much of its existence, Australia has tended to produce and reproduce a majority self-image which relates directly to its origins as an English colony. This is an image and an imagining of the country as an ideological, historical, political part of Europe, as a European, or more precisely British, outpost in the far reaches of the Pacific. Even as Australia has emerged into nationhood, its primary official self-understanding has remained within this British/European framework. Even when such important historical re-imaginings as a newfound pride in its convict origins overtook previously dominant images of shame over those same origins, the point of reference remained predominately, if not solely, based in a "Western", British, Anglo-Celtic, frame.

In recent years and up to the present day, a new self-understanding of "Australia" has however, begun to emerge. This nascent image, based in geography, politics, history and economic reality, now sees the country as part of Asia. By definition, this new self-identity comes into conflict with the previous one. Generations reared on notions not just of belonging to "the West", but also on concomitant notions of a preternatural Western superiority, do

---

5. I use this phrase in a general and generic sense. As discussed elsewhere, the characterization of some countries, e.g. Germany or France, the governments of which prosecute perpetrators, as "victims" is itself part of a very complex legal, moral and political debate.

not easily accept the new vision of an Asian Australia. Prime Minister John Howard, with his constant invocations of empire, of a happy Australia finding glory in its cricket triumphs over England, manifests one face of a begrudging acceptance of Asia's economic importance to Australia which nonetheless does not truly accept Australia's Asian "fate". The former Independent MP from Oxley, Pauline Hanson, with her Pauline Hanson's One Nation Party, manifests another face of Australia's struggle with issues of national identity and memory. Hanson and others decry the increasing "Asianization" of Australia, to which they ascribe most, if not all, of the country's woes, from unemployment to violent crime, to the destruction of the Australian way of life. Recent uproar over the fate of the Afghan refugees on the good ship *Tampa*, a new voyage of the damned, confirms Australia's national identity crisis. Thus, the major current struggle over national identity in Australia takes place in the troubled terrain of Asia and Australia's role there. In such debates, not surprisingly, the Holocaust is absent.

At the same time, Australia has also been forced to confront another aspect of its historical identity and memory in the form of increasing claims by Aboriginal and Torres Strait Islander peoples to recognition and reconciliation. These demands by Indigenous Australians take on many forms, from Native Title land claims to demands for compensation and apology for past practices such as the forced removal of Indigenous children from their natural families and their adoption by white families and their "assimilation" into white Australian culture.[6]

Like the "Asia/Australia" debate, the issues surrounding Aboriginals and Torres Strait Islanders immediately call into question the predominant historical understandings and collective memory of "Australians". Instead of a country which fits into the continuity of British and European history as a settler Dominion, Australia must confront the historical reality of an already present Indigenous population, a reality which changes "settlement" into "invasion", and "progress" and "assimilation" into "genocide". Again, the final outcome of such debates must be uncertain. The conservative government of Prime Minister John Howard remains unwilling to issue an apology to Aboriginal and Torres Strait Islander Australians and is hostile to the general legal framework evolved by the High Court for Native Title claims. Howard has consistently decried what he calls "the black armband view of history", which seems to include any historical facts which might upset his bucolic view of

---

6. See *Bringing them home: Report of the National Inquiry into the Separation of Aboriginal and Torres Strait Islander Children from Their Families* (Sydney: Human Rights and Equal Opportunity Commission, 1997).

Australia as a cricket playing nation governed by the rule of law. In any event, the traditional majority view of Australia as predominately Western, Anglo-Celtic and ruled by the best of British tradition, is increasingly being brought into question.

Another set of historical experiences brings debates about Australian historical memory and self-understanding almost full circle as the Holocaust comes back into view as a potentially "Australian" experience. In the period immediately following World War Two, there was a massive influx of non-British immigrants into Australia. In the period between 1946 and 1959, 1.2 million immigrants, mostly from Europe, entered Australia. Of these, almost 250,000 were refugees. Many others entered under various assisted mass migration schemes. Australia was second only to the United States in accepting Displaced Persons in the aftermath of the Second World War.[7] Hundreds of thousands of people from Northern and Eastern Europe entered Australia and settled there. This political, historical and demographic fact is important for two primary reasons. First, this influx of "new Australians", followed as it was by other waves of immigration, made necessary by the economic growth of the country and its changing employment needs, meant that for many residents and citizens of the country, the great historical connections and identity with Britain were completely foreign and irrelevant. Second, and more directly related to issues concerning the Holocaust and Australian memory, many of these new immigrants came from the Baltic States, the Ukraine, Poland etc., where they had direct experience of World War II. More precisely, despite Sir Garfield Barwick's assertions to the contrary, the immigration screening programs set up in Europe at the end of the war were not particularly successful in keeping collaborators and perpetrators out of the immigrant pool.[8] This may have resulted in literally thousands of people who had actively participated in the Nazi extermination of European Jewry setting in Australia. The physical presence of these perpetrators on Australian soil meant that, to a greater or lesser extent, the Holocaust had become an issue for Australia and its collective memory.

Additionally, one final aspect of post-war migration to Australia plays a role in the ongoing debates about the place and role of the Holocaust and of the prosecution of perpetrators in Australian collective memory and identity.

----

7. For a review of these policies and practices, see A. C. Menzies, *Review of Material Relating to the Entry of Suspected War Criminals into Australia* (Canberra: AGPS, 1987), at 33–46 (the *Menzies' Report*).

8. The failures of the screening process are documented by Mark Aarons, op. cit., and somewhat less critically by Andrew Menzies, op. cit.

Among those who came into the country from Northern and Eastern Europe were Jews from those countries. There has always been a Jewish presence in white Australia from the days of the first convict ships. But that presence in Australia and Jewish identity there underwent a fundamental change in the 1940s and 1950s. Not only did the face of Australian Jewry evolve, as the Anglicized, assimilated members of the community were surpassed by Eastern European Jews, but the historical frame of reference of Australian Jewry shifted. As the Holocaust became a dominant, if not the dominant, historical and existential "fact" for Jews elsewhere, so too did the Shoah become a key element of Australian Jewry's self-understanding. Australia's second largest city, Melbourne, has the highest proportion of Holocaust survivors per capita of Jewish population in the world.[9] Thus:

> After Israel, Australia accepted the second highest number of survivors of the Holocaust on a pro rata population basis. This influx more than doubled the size of Australian Jewry.[10]

The period immediately following the end of the Second World War brought with it a set of political and demographic changes which carried the potential to fundamentally transform Australia's self-understanding and identity. More particularly, with the influx of populations among which could be found both Holocaust survivors and perpetrators, one might have suspected that the potential for inter-ethnic conflict based on "past bitternesses" would have been high. One might further have expected that the Australian government, which had been a part of the Allied war effort, would have done its utmost not just to prevent conflict but to fulfill its international legal obligations as well as its domestic legal and moral obligations to Holocaust survivors, by bringing those perpetrators who had slipped by the European screening process to justice. As we have seen, in 1961 Sir Garfield Barwick seemed to put an end once and for all to such ideas by redefining Australian notions of the rule of law to protect perpetrators from prosecution. Of course, this rhetorical shift was not really a shift at all. Critics of the Nuremberg trials, both in Germany and elsewhere had consistently invoked powerful rule of law discourse in opposition to the prosecution of Nazi war criminals. "Justice" in this context has always been a highly contested, and mutable, semiotic terrain.

---

9. Kate Legge, "The Demidenko Affair", *The Weekend Australian*, 15 July 1995.

10. Suzanne Rutland, *Edge of the Diaspora: Two Centuries of Jewish Settlement in Australia* (Sydney: Brandl & Schlesinger, 1997), at 256.

In addition to the predominant Cold War ideology of the time, the arguments deployed by the Australian government to reject the idea of bringing to bear the forces of the legal system against alleged war criminals fit firmly within the same rhetorical paradigms deployed in other Western countries. The passage of time, both as an independent factor, and as a more sophisticated element in arguments based in the legal norms of evidence and justice, clearly becomes part of this rule of law discourse. Only five years after Nuremberg, Ben Chifley made it clear that the Labor Party accepted this particular set of "justice" arguments.

The idea of "Australia" as a place where a new national identity could and should be forged by recent arrivals also predominates and serves as a fundamental element in a more deeply based assertion that events in Europe during the Second World War in general and the Holocaust in particular are not "Australian". A dominant image of Australian identity and its particular manifestation in rule of law discourse has always been, and continues to be, that these events have nothing to do with continuing and emerging ideas of Australian identity and national memory.

At the same time, the idea of "war crimes" and "war criminals" as part of Australia's wartime historical memory has another distinct meaning. Most of the Australian engagement in World War 2 took place, quite naturally, in the Pacific Theater. For Australians of that generation and for subsequent generations educated in the national history, and formed by the memories of their parents and grandparents, "the war" meant the war against Japan. "War crimes" meant atrocities committed by the Japanese against Australian soldiers and civilians.

Indeed, the Australian legal system participated actively in the prosecution of those who had committed such atrocities. Australia acted as a prosecuting power at the Tokyo war crimes trials[11] and conducted its own courts martial in over 1000 cases against Japanese soldiers.[12] Thus, for Australians, the ideas of "war crimes" and "war criminals" have held a very specific cultural meaning associated with a particular historical experience. Indeed, stories of Japanese wartime atrocities continue to emerge in Australia from time to time, along with calls to bring the perpetrators to justice and to extricate an apology from the Japanese government. These stories and the outrage which fol-

---

11. Arnold Brackman, *The Other Nuremberg: The Untold Story of the Tokyo War Crimes Trials* (New York: William Morrow and Company, 1987).

12. Toshijuki Tanaka, *Hidden Horrors: Japanese War Crimes in World War Two* (Boulder: Westview Press, 1996); Ben J. Dunn, "Trial of War Criminals", 19 *ALJ* 359 (1946).

lows them almost inevitably constitute not just a part of Australia's wartime history and heritage, but must also be situated within current and ongoing debates about Australia's true place in the world and in the region.[13] Blatant anti-Japanese and more general anti-Asian sentiment constantly accompanies such stories and is used in public, political debates to demonstrate the fundamental conflict between Asian barbarism on the one hand and Australia's position as a bastion of European civilization and values on the other. Emotional and ideological debates continue to rage from time to time over issues of national identity and memory in relation to "war crimes" and "war criminals". However, in the Australian context, the conflict in Europe, and the Holocaust in particular, was and continues to be, distinctly "not Australian" and by definition, not relevant to issues of historical memory and identity.

3. War Crimes and the Rule of Law in Australia: From Indifference to Legislation

This does not mean, however, that as a matter of fact, the Holocaust and the fate of Nazi and collaborationist perpetrators, have been completely absent from Australian history. As a part of the victorious Allied powers, Australia not only participated in the prosecution of war criminals in the Pacific, but it committed itself to a number of principles and practical measures meant to ensure the capture and punishment of European perpetrators. Among these measures was the enforcement of immigration controls against "undesirables". However, as more recent studies have pointed out, for a variety of reasons, the controls established failed to prevent the influx of significant numbers of "war criminals" into Australia under various post-War migration schemes.

The issue of the presence of Holocaust perpetrators in Australia did not begin as a matter of public political debate with the Soviet Union's request for the extradition of Ervin Viks or with later revelations of the failures of immigration controls. From the earliest days of the arrival of Displaced Persons and

---

13. See e.g., David Jenkins, "War crimes, trials and the big con", *Sydney Morning Herald*, 23 August 1991; Tony Hewett, "Japanese war cannibalism exposed", *Sydney Morning Herald*, 12 August 1992; Editorial, "The politics of apology", *Sydney Morning Herald*, 29 September 1992; Alan Gill, "The Martyrs of Gona", *Sydney Morning Herald*, 26 April 1993; Ben Hills, "Sasakawa: the philanthropist with the heart of a fascist", *Sydney Morning Herald*, 13 December 1994; Mark Scott, "Uni takes $2m from tycoon once accused of war crimes", *Sydney Morning Herald*, 13 December 1994; Editorial, "Blood money at Macquarie", *Sydney Morning Herald*, 14 December 1994.

other migrants from Europe, the presence of Nazis was signaled to Australian governmental authorities.[14]

The failure of the Australian government to act against this presence of illegals and perpetrators can be traced primarily to the political and rhetorical power of the Cold War in Australian and Western political discourse and practice. The struggle against fascism which had apparently united the Allied powers during the War had quickly, by the War's end and certainly in the immediate post-War period, been replaced by the anti-Communist practices and discourses which would dominate much of the debate in the West over the fate of perpetrators. A new common enemy, Soviet communism, had emerged, or the old enemy had been rediscovered. In the Australian context, much, but not all, of the information about the presence of perpetrators, came from the Jewish Council to Combat Fascism and Anti-Semitism. This organization was considered by those in power, as well as by other Jewish community groups, to be little more than a Communist front. In the political environment of the Cold War, in Australia as elsewhere, this characterization was vital and fatal.

The truth of the group's allegations became secondary to the fact that those providing the information could be labeled "Communists". As the next logical step in this ideological worldview, two inter-related conclusions could be drawn. First, the allegations could not be true because they were Communist inspired. Second, those identified by the Communists as Nazi collaborators, in reality, could be and were identified as patriots, as anti-Communists and therefore as good Australians. In the bizarre world of Cold War rhetoric and logic, to be identified as a possible perpetrator could become a sign of one's status as a good citizen whose priorities were the same as those of other "real" Australians. Of course, similar themes were commonly found in other countries in the West when the issue of collaborationist crimes was raised. In England, the United States and Canada, anti-Communism, patriotism etc also became the new signifiers for those who participated in the slaughter of European Jewry.

This development in Australia, which led in the immediate post-War period to the Government's refusal to take seriously allegations that Nazi war criminals had found refuge in that country, also gave rise to the rhetorical invocation by Sir Garfield Barwick in the House of Representatives of the rule of law as protecting Ervin Viks and his peers from "Soviet justice", an oxymoron in the eyes of right-thinking Australians. Australia did not stand alone. Britain, Canada and the United States all welcomed similarly constituted mi-

---

14. See generally Suzanne Rutland, op. cit., at 245 et. seq.

grant groups after World War II. Each of these countries similarly ignored clear evidence that perpetrators of the Holocaust were to found among such migrant groups. In addition, each of these other countries clearly placed more importance on the Cold War than they did on the Holocaust and on tracking down mass killers, both in the period immediately following the end of the War and much later. Some immigrant communities in each of these countries gained legitimacy and acceptance as valid and valuable members of their new countries by portraying themselves as vehement anti-Communists.[15] Thus, a commonality existed between the nations of the West and many of new migrant communities in their struggle against Soviet Communism. The West gave to these communities not just a physical safe haven but also an ideological home. Moreover, this construction and legitimation of these immigrant communities as anti-Communists allowed them to create an historical, political and social memory of their nationalist strivings which conflicted, to a greater or lesser degree, with the historical facts of local collaboration and participation in the Holocaust. Most importantly, in Australia, as elsewhere, these communities, constructed as anti-Communist patriots, could portray events during World War 2 as involving not atrocities against indigenous Jewish populations, but as nationalist struggles against Communist domination. At its base anti-Communism in the period following the War allowed the Holocaust to be, if not forgotten, at least erased in its true meaning and replaced as simply part of the broader world historical struggle between the West and Communism, between good and evil. In such circumstances, the invocation by Barwick of the rule of law to protect Viks and other perpetrators is nothing more than the natural outcome of broader, common Western political discourses and historically contingent re-imaginings of collective self-identity and historical truth. The only way in which Nazi perpetrators could be brought to justice, or at least to law, in Australia, as in other countries, would be by way of a newer, counter-imagining of the Holocaust which would take it out of

---

15. This controversy also manifested itself in Australian "literary" debates over the Helen Darville/Demidenko novel *The Hand That Signed The Paper*, in which a fictionalized account of an Australian war crimes trial became the focus of heated debates as the author, who falsely portrayed herself as an Ukrainian Australian, attempted to "explain" the Holocaust in the Ukraine as the natural and understandable reaction by the local populace against "Jewish Bolsheviks". For more on this issue, see, Gerard Henderson, "Playing loose with the truth in this work of 'faction'", *Sydney Morning Herald*, 27 June 1995; John Jost et. al. (eds.), *The Demidenko File* (Ringwood, Victoria: Penguin, 1996); Robert Manne, *The culture of forgetting: Helen Demidenko and the Holocaust* (Melbourne: Text Publishing, 1996); contra, Andrew P. Riemer, *The Demidenko Debate* (Sydney; Allen & Unwin, 1996).

the rhetorical and ideological worldview of the Cold War. In other words, the Holocaust had to be both placed in its "real" historical context and at the same time "Australianized". The apparently universal power of anti-Communism worked hand in hand with other concerns and considerations to make the idea of placing perpetrators on trial almost inconceivable from a very early stage and from both sides of politics in Australia.

As time passed, events both domestic and international, would operate in ways which would bring the issue of perpetrators in Australia back into the forefront of political debate and activity. As the years unfolded, Australia became, demographically at least, a much more multi-cultural and ethnically diverse nation. This made debates and struggles over issues of national history, memory and identity more contentious and problematic as the old Anglo-Celtic hegemony began to weaken. Pragmatically, the so-called "ethnic vote" began to play a key role in the politics and policies of both the Labor and Liberal parties. This meant not just the development of a superficially more "ethnically sensitive" political world in Australia, but also led to parties at various times "playing the ethnic card" against one another. For example, in 1979, allegations emerged that Lyenko Urbanchich, who was the chair of the New South Wales Liberal Party's Ethnic Communities Council, had been a Nazi collaborator.[16] Urbancich remained safe from the forces of the rule of law. In the eyes of some, consistent with the position enunciated by Sir Garfield Barwick, it could be asserted that he remained safe because of the forces of the rule of law. Nonetheless, it became increasingly obvious that the Holocaust and the fate of the perpetrators were gradually becoming part of Australian political discourse. As the fate of John Demjanjuk in the United States grabbed headlines there and around the world, similar issues began to surface in Australia.

In 1986, investigative journalist Mark Aarons produced a series of reports for the Australian Broadcasting Commission Radio program *Background Briefing* on the presence of Nazi war criminals in Australia and the award-winning ABC Television show *4 Corners* broadcast a similar report. Questions were raised in State and Federal Parliaments and several individuals were named as war criminals. Under increased public and political pressure, the government commissioned lawyer Andrew Menzies to study the issue. The *Menzies Report* found

---

16. See "Pro-Nazi claims", *Sydney Morning Herald*, 29 August 1979. See also, Jenny Chater, "Urbanchich says he was never a Nazi", *Sydney Morning Herald*, 6 December 1986; "MP gives names of 'war criminals'", *Sydney Morning Herald*, 27 November 1987; Tony Stephens, "The wall comes down at Fortress Urbanchich", *Sydney Morning Herald*, 16 July 1990; Andrew Menzies, op. cit., "Lyenko Urbancic", at pp. 91–97; Mark Aarons, op. cit., "Ljubljana's 'Little Goebbels" and "Laundering Ljenko", at pp. 1–49.

that there was clear evidence that Nazi collaborationist perpetrators had indeed entered Australia in the post-War period. It recommended the establishment of a special prosecution unit, modeled on the US OSI to pursue these criminals. In addition, Menzies provided the government with a list of at least sixty names of alleged war criminals who had entered Australia and who were still living there. In such circumstances, the Hawke Labor government faced several dilemmas. It was now confronted with an official report documenting the presence of perpetrators. Members of the Jewish community, which was particularly close to and supportive of Mr. Hawke, urged him to act, while members of other ethnic communities on whose support the Labor Party also depended voiced fears of persecution and witch hunts. The *Sydney Morning Herald* reported that:

> The view that quickly emerged around the Cabinet table was that the report was as politically explosive as it was legally daunting and unless sensitively handled could set ethnic communities at each other's throats.[17]

The problem at the political level was clearly identified. The alleged war criminals were for the most part former members of groups such as the Hungarian Arrow Cross and various police and other auxiliary units from the Baltic States. At the time, these countries were still under Communist rule and the idea of deporting Australians to their death at the hands of "Communists" was not a palatable one. At the same time, Australian Jewry could now point to the unbiased conclusions of a government-appointed lawyer to justify and confirm their long-standing claims that Holocaust perpetrators were living comfortable lives in Australia side-by-side with a large number of survivors. Justice for them demanded an Australian solution to an Australian problem. Of course, as was and is the case in other Western countries where this question was raised, Australian Jewry faced an existential and political dilemma. They wished to identify the Holocaust as a crime against Jews at the same time as they wished to make it a crime of general Australian import. Their desire for justice at some level required them to make a claim which at one and the same time called for the recognition of a generalized category of "crimes against humanity" while identifying a specific and specified victim group. For them, this was matter of historical accuracy and justice. For their opponents, this was a claim for special status which flew in the face of broader notions of a generalized Australian identity.

At the legal level, the problems could also be easily identified. Stripping those identified of their Australian citizenship was not, except by an *ex post*

---

17. Peter Bowers, "War crimes: 60 on list", *Sydney Morning* Herald, 3 December 1986.

facto legislative intervention, possible under existing Australian immigration and citizenship law. Extradition, even if requested by an Eastern Bloc power, was virtually unimaginable. Thus, as a matter of a possible legal solution to the problem, Australia could not rely on the American experience and practice of denaturalization and deportation. An indigenous, "Australian" solution to the problem had to be found. In other words, as both a matter of political reality and legal practice, the Holocaust had to become part of Australia's national memory and identity as embodied in governmental practice and law.

The position of the majority of Australian Jews was clear. Australian officials must develop a legal framework under which perpetrators could be brought to justice in Australia.[18] For them, the Holocaust and the fate of perpetrators was not just an issue of "humanity" abstractly defined but a particular moral and legal duty incumbent upon the Australian government. In other words, the conception of the rule of law proposed in these circumstances was at some levels the exact opposite of Sir Garfield Barwick's. The simple passage of time could not serve as a bar to prosecution because

> ...we should not accept that there is a statute of limitations on genocide. Justice demands that, however belatedly, those directly involved in the mass murder of innocents should be held accountable whenever they are found.[19]

For obvious reasons, the Australian Jewish communities also made it clear that they were not interested in creating or perpetuating group, ethnic stereotypes against other communities. Rather their interest lay in the pursuit of the guilty individual perpetrators. At the same time, however, they were anxious to establish as a part of Australia's collective, legislative, legal self-understanding of the Holocaust, the basic notion that the Holocaust was a crime against Jews. At one and the same time, their claim was for inclusion in the Australian body politic and *corpus juris*, and for recognition of Jewish specificity.

More particularly, while aiming to avoid the creation of ethnic stereotypes against members of various Baltic or Eastern European communities, Australian Jews wished to prevent their government falling into the trap of allowing elements of those communities to perpetuate the common and collective mythology of "anti-communism" as the sole and primary motivating factor behind collaboration.[20]

---

18. For a dissenting view, see Emanuel Klein, "When pursuit of justice leaves bitter taste behind", *Sydney Morning Herald*, 8 December 1986.

19. Isi J. Leibler, 'Justice shalt thou pursue', *Sydney Morning Herald*, 1 August 1986.

20. Ibid.

This issue arose not just in the general context of the identity of alleged perpetrators as belonging to these groups and of the particular historical importance of invoking "anti-Communist" struggle in debates about the Holocaust in Australia, but also in the legal argument about justice and the rule of law arising out of plans to prosecute alleged war criminals in Australia. It was obvious from the work of Menzies and the history of prosecutions elsewhere, particularly in the United States, that much of the evidence against individuals accused of participating in atrocities would by definition come from sources in the Soviet Union. Many considered such evidence to be tainted and completely unreliable. In addition to the general idea that Communists were not to be trusted, was the more particular assertion that the Soviet KGB would not hesitate to concoct and manufacture evidence, both documentary and testimonial, against members of various exile communities in order to discredit them by painting them as "fascists", "Nazis" and "mass murderers". This would continue to be a common refrain in Australia as war crimes continued to be debated and alleged perpetrators pursued. Similar concerns would be raised elsewhere, in Britain, Canada, and the United States, as the rhetoric of anti-communism continued to play a key role both at the general level of agitation against the prosecution of alleged war criminals and at the specific level of discrediting the prosecution's evidence in individual cases. The successful deployment of this rhetorical strategy and tactic reached its most notorious level when the Supreme Court of Israel acquitted John Demjanjuk. Ironically, the evidence which discredited fabricated Soviet documents inculpating Demjanjuk came from other Soviet sources.

In Australia, members of some communities adopted this anti-Soviet strategy from a very early stage. The Right Reverend Monsignor Petris Butkus, speaking as a Lithuanian Australian, claimed that the Jewish community was being used, both in Australia and the United States, by the forces of Communist propaganda and invoked the fear of deportation to the USSR.[21] In addition to the anti-Communist trope, another common post-war discursive strategy was deployed by some members of the various immigrant communities. In this variant, these groups are portrayed not just as victims of the "Russians" or "Communists", but also as victims of the "Nazis" or "Germans". Thus,

The orders were given by the Germans and largely carried out by the Germans.[22]

---

21. John O'Neill, "Baltic communities waiting in fear", *Sydney Morning Herald*, 4 December 1986.

22. Peter White, "'I could be on Nazis list', says Lithuanian", *Sydney Morning Herald*, 3 October 1986.

The idea of the Germans as the primary, if not sole, perpetrators serves in such circumstances, several purposes. First, it allows responsibility for the elimination of European Jews to be placed almost solely on one group.[23] The dynamic of collaboration and the historical reality of active and willing participation by other national groups in the Holocaust is elided and avoided simply by invoking "the Germans". Second, and perhaps more importantly, not just for the construction of various national identities, but for the way in which the construction of historical realities in Europe also serves to construct Australian historical and national self-understandings, the portrayal of, in this case, Lithuanians (but not the Jews of Lithuania), as "victims of the Germans", allows Lithuanian perpetrators, to achieve an historical, rhetorical, memorial and ultimately, in Australia, legal status equivalent or equal to the "Jews" who were also "victims of the Germans". Thus, in debates about the pursuit of Holocaust perpetrators in Australia, as elsewhere, a primary historical and legal strategy has been the invocation of "victim" status by the perpetrators themselves.

Members of so-called ethnic communities were not, however, the only ones to invoke these various but interconnected, ideological tropes in debates surrounding Nazi war criminals in Australia. In a series of editorials preceding and following the *Menzies' Report*, the *Sydney Morning Herald* went from disbelief in the possibility that such people could be living in Australia, to a wary acceptance that some sort of study might well be necessary. On 9 April 1986, the paper wrote that:

> Some kind of official historical inquiry may be warranted; but the Government must bear in mind the danger of wrongful accusations against individuals or ethnic groups, and the many moral and legal hurdles erected by such disquieting but so far vague allegations.

Six weeks later, the *Herald* added:

> If a major figure lives here, another Barbie, we face international humiliation; if minor accessories to war crimes came here, ethnic communities and even families will be torn asunder. The cost of setting straight the historical record, negative or positive, must be a very painful national catharsis.

Finally, after the *Menzies' Report* became public, the paper concluded:

---

23. This is of course a complex issue. I do not wish necessarily to reject notions of Germany's role as the chief perpetrator or as perpetrator-in-chief, of the Holocaust. Rather, the issue here is the role of non-German collaborators, a phenomenon clearly documented in every country of occupied Europe.

Even if the Government decides that the moral case for re-opening this chapter is out-weighed by the political and "ethnic" strife it will arouse, Mr. Menzies has proved that Australian authorities closed this chapter with alarming nonchalance; he has exposed not just "bureaucratic" inertia", but our moral insensitivity as well.[24]

The "evolution" in the discourse deployed by the leading newspaper in Australia's largest city is interesting. The paper's overwhelming concern appears, even after the publication of the *Report*, to be with the fate of the various ethnic communities, the members of which might be accused as perpetrators. There is little, if any, concern for the victims. All of the ideas of "justice" and the rule of law which underpin these interventions are invoked only in so far as they might serve the interests of potential accused. "Wrongful accusations", "many moral and legal hurdles", 'political and "ethnic" strife', all of these are primarily focussed on the alleged perpetrators. Indeed, the major concern in part at least seems to be little more than Australia's world reputation, a reputation which would be adversely affected only if a "major" war criminal were to be found there. Only "minor accessories" seem to be likely to be found however. Once again, in addition to the unique focus on the perpetrators, the *Sydney Morning Herald*, in its editorial positioning, at least implicitly accepts and propagates the idea of the so-called Captive Nations as "victims" of the Nazis. How else can one explain the characterization of members of Police Units responsible for the extermination of thousands of Jews as "minor accessories"? Again, debate about justice and the rule of law writes out a significant portion of the historical truth about the Holocaust in many parts of Europe.

But the Hawke government did not decide that fears of "inter-ethnic" strife should outweigh its moral obligation to "justice" and the rule of law, as constructed by proponents of prosecution. In 1988, it presented the *War Crimes Amendment Act* to the Federal Parliament. Following the recommendations of the *Menzies' Report*, the purpose of the *Act* was to allow alleged war criminals to be tried on substantive criminal charges before Australian courts. The substance of the legislation therefore created a specific set of "Australian" criminal offences relating to the Holocaust. In other words, at the level of the symbolism and ideology of the Australian legal system, the Holocaust was incorporated specifically as involving a violation of basic and fundamental Australian legal norms.

At first, it appeared that the Bill would receive bi-partisan support in Parliament. It seemed that both sides of the Australian political mainstream had

---

24. "Australia's war crimes dilemma", *Sydney Morning Herald*, 8 December 1986.

accepted the fundamental principle that the rule of law in that country required the (belated) vigorous pursuit of perpetrators through the norms, practices and procedures of the criminal justice system. Speaking for the Lib-
eral/National Opposition, Mr. Peter Reith said:

> The starting point must be that time should be no bar to the prose-
> cution of such atrocious crimes against mankind....When this Bill is
> passed, Australia will joint (sic) Canada in sending a firm, strong
> message that serious war crimes can never be tolerated.[25]

However, such a display of national unity on the issue of "justice" for war
criminals and their victims was short-lived. From the very beginning and
with increasing hostility to the project as a whole, the Opposition played the
anti-Soviet card so dear to the Right and to many immigrant communities.
In this same speech "in support of" the Bill, Reith signaled the Opposition's
true position. He expressed concern about and rejection of any attempt to
deport accused perpetrators to the Soviet Union.[26] He raised the issue of the
reliability of Soviet sourced evidence[27] and a key ideological objection.[28] In
fact, most of the Opposition's objections were already addressed by the Government in the Bill and in its responses to the concerns raised about these
questions. The issue of deportation had already been addressed by the *Menzies' Report* and remained only a theoretical possibility at this stage. The
question of Soviet source evidence was also of concern to the government
and the subject of a special inquiry by a Senate Committee before the final
approval of the Bill.[29] But it is the final, ideological, historical and legal objection made by the Opposition from the very first day to the provisions of
the Bill placed before the Australian Parliament, which allows us to see the
ways in which discourses of law, politics, history and memory were played
out in the context of Australia's decision to pursue perpetrators resident in
that country.

The objection raised by the Opposition was to the definition of "occupation" in the *Act*. As a technical legal matter, the definition of "occupation" was
important because criminal offences under the *Act* were defined as those committed "in the course of hostilities in a war" or "in the course of an occupa-

---

25. Hansard, 26 November 1987, at 2732.
26. Ibid., at 2733.
27. Id., at p. 2734.
28. Id., at 2733–34.
29. "Matters Relating to the War Crimes Amendment Bill", Senate Standing Committee on Legal and Constitutional Affairs (Canberra: AGPS, 1988).

tion".[30] Clearly, this section and the definition would be used to deal with atrocities committed after the conquest of a territory by the Nazis as opposed to those committed "in a state of war" more technically defined. The Opposition objected to the original definition and insisted on an amendment. This amendment would bring under the definition of "occupation" the state of "law" obtaining in the Baltic States, (but interestingly not Poland), after the Hitler/Stalin pact. The intent and import of the Opposition position are clear. First, the Baltic States would be legislatively defined as the victims of Soviet aggression. Second, events which occurred in that part of Europe between the Soviet takeover and the subsequent Nazi conquest during Operation Barbarossa would have occurred in a state of "occupation" under the Australian legislative definition. As a result of this technical, legal, drafting concern, any crimes committed by "the Russians" would be potentially subject to prosecution in Australia.

Whatever the historical record of Soviet atrocities in the Baltics may be, in the context of Australian war crimes legislation, the ideological positioning of the Opposition is clear. Again, the Cold War, anti-Communism and the role and nature of the "Captive Nations" predominate. The discursive strategy employed differs very little from that employed throughout the Cold War. The enemy is Communism, which is just as bad as, if not worse than or identical to, Nazism. The alleged perpetrators are themselves victims, both of the Nazis and the Soviets. In an eerie echo of the Historians' Debate in Germany, this is the Australian equivalent of equating the Holocaust and Stalinism. In Australia, the result was perhaps even more pernicious since the Opposition succeeded in imposing its will on the government. Thus, in Australia, "occupation" is defined as:

(a) an occupation of territory arising out of a war; or
(b) without limiting the generality of paragraph (a), an occupation of territory in Latvia, Lithuania, or Estonia as a direct or indirect result of:
(i) the agreement of 23 August 1939 between Germany and the Union of Soviet Socialist Republics; or
(ii) any protocol to that agreement[31]

In terms of the debates over national memory, law and identity and the role of the Holocaust in Australian political and social life, this amendment clearly

---

30. *War Crimes Amendment Act,* 1989, s. 7 (1) (a), (b).
31. Ibid., s. 5.

demonstrates the ways in which other discourses and political concerns can and do replace the primacy of the Holocaust. In a piece of legislation clearly meant to deal with the legal and historical consequences of the Holocaust, the Australian Parliament imposed and inserted an amendment which ideologically effaced the "uniqueness" of the Shoah, by accepting, as a matter of law, the exact equivalency between the Holocaust and Soviet atrocities. If combined with the historical equivalence found in much of the rhetoric of the Captive Nations' ideology between and among "Soviet", "Russian" and "Jewish" crimes, the Opposition and the Government succeeded here transforming Holocaust victims into perpetrators of war crimes as a matter of Australian law.

A second amendment strategy pursued by the Opposition also concerned, in a strangely opposite way, the centrality of the Holocaust. Under this strategy, the opposition invoked images of patriotism, loyalty and basic "Australianess" to limit the application of the statute. The opposition, abetted by some in the media, invoked the image of former Australian soldiers (diggers) being charged with war crimes and hauled before Australian courts to answer for atrocities allegedly committed against the Japanese.[32] Here, the ideological and historical basis for the Opposition's position is that the *War Crimes Amendment Act* does not and should not deal with issues which are fundamentally and truly "Australian". War crimes are committed by others, Japanese or elsewhere, in Europe, and whatever role Australia is to play in putting perpetrators on trial, it cannot be said that Australia's glorious wartime past, the basic Australian goodness of the diggers who epitomize the Australian spirit, will be besmirched or tainted with allegations of war crimes. Again, the Opposition succeeded, as the application of the Act was limited to "Europe in the period beginning on 1 September 1939 and ending on 8 May 1945".[33]

Some might suggest that such an amendment actually served many purposes, some positive and some helpful to the government. Thus, there is little risk of alienating, for example, Australia's largest trading partner, Japan, by raising again the issue of Japanese war crimes. There is also an argument to be made that the focus on the European conflict is faithful to and consis-

---

32. See Editorial, "Anxiety over war crimes trials", *Sydney Morning Herald*, 25 October 1988; Mike Seccombe, "Bill on war crimes faces stormy path", *Sydney Morning Herald*, 14 November 1988; Tom Burton and Glen Milne, "Aussie war crimes? Impossible, say RSL, Opposition", *Sydney Morning Herald*, 15 November 1988; Editorial, "False hysteria on war crimes", *Sydney Morning Herald*, 15 November 1988; Ross Dunn, "Govt firm on war crimes", *Sydney Morning Herald*, 16 November 1988.

33. *War Crimes Amendment Act*, 1988, s. 5.

tent with the primary reason informing the legislation, bringing Holocaust perpetrators to justice in Australia.

On the other hand, some might argue that by privileging the Holocaust, the Australian government downplays and relativizes other genocides as well as depriving itself of a tool which would enable it to act against perpetrators of those genocides. On the other hand, it might well be argued that the Australian legislative response here grew out of particular historical circumstances and political exigencies and was never meant to be anything but an attempt to deal with the revelations arising out of the Aarons' investigations and the *Menzies' Report*.

Whatever position one wishes to take on the broader issues of Australia's responsibility in relation to crimes against humanity generally, it is safe to say that support for even its limited attempt to deal with the perpetrators of the Holocaust was not overwhelming. The Opposition and representatives of various "ethnic" community organization, found ample backing from all parts of Australian society in their attempts to scuttle the legislation. Not only was such support for efforts to prevent the passage of the legislation broad-based, but the rhetoric deployed in these efforts is resonant with other long-standing attempts to prevent legal sanctions against Holocaust perpetrators. Sir Garfield Barwick and his 1961 invocation of the rule of law would not have been out of place in Australia in 1988 as debate raged around the *War Crimes Amendment Act*.

The Law Council of Australia raised objections to the legislation based on the potential injustices to the accused caused by the passage of time.[34] Such objections, grounded in the jurisprudential tradition which sees the mere passage of time as posing basic barriers to a just result, are quite familiar in debates about the potential prosecution of Holocaust perpetrators. Whether grounding arguments that all crimes, including crimes against humanity, should be subjected to a limitation period, or more specifically based in the position that evidentiary barriers are raised by the passage of time, this position has been used as the legal philosophical equivalent of "time heals all wounds" in arguments about the justice of prosecuting perpetrators. In Australia, Ben Chifley invoked a similar position, in 1950, echoing arguments from other countries like Germany and the United States a mere four years after the Nuremberg case. Similar arguments, "let bygones be bygones", "time heals all wounds", "live and let live", it is time to forget "past bitternesses", have been constantly invoked in each country which has been faced with the moral and legal issue of the fate of the perpetrators. Of course, it must always be

---

34. Glenn Milne, "Law Council hits at war crimes bill", *Sydney Morning Herald*, 1 December 1988.

kept in mind, that, as a matter of law and of jurisprudence, it is clearly the case that ideas of limitation periods and concerns over the effects of the passage of time on our notion of a fair trial for the accused are well-grounded in the criminal justice system. Therefore, it is beyond doubt that such arguments can be and are grounded in basic principles of the rule of law. At the same time, it is equally true that arguments that a careful judge and a properly instructed jury can deal with any potential injustices on a case by case basis; that there are exceptions to every rule; that crimes against humanity constitute such an exception; and that an overriding concern for 'justice', can be said to fit within the same general jurisprudential framework of consistency with our idea of the rule of law. In the context of Australian debates about pursuing alleged war criminals, however, most rule of law rhetoric in the public domain was clearly deployed by those opposed to the legislation.

Such arguments about the negative impact and injustice caused by the passage of time are not only consistently invoked by opponents of trials in such circumstances, but are given additional weight based on the authority of the person or group invoking them. The passage of time argument in all its permutations appears to take on more importance when the person invoking the position has the moral authority of past involvement in the prosecution of war criminals. This means that the person speaks not just from personal experience, but also that he is speaking out of a genuine concern for the justice of this particular case or circumstance. Thus, Athol Moffitt, a former judge, first President of the New South Wales Court of Appeal, and Australian war crimes prosecutor in the Pacific, intervened in the debate against the *War Crimes Amendment Act*.[35] In addition to the traditional and familiar arguments based on the extreme difficulties of obtaining reliable evidence some forty or more years after the events in question, Moffitt makes a more interesting, intriguing and potentially dangerous argument against modern day trials of war criminals. In the end, his position is that the Holocaust is of no concern or relevance to Australia and Australians of today. He states:

> Trial by jury, appropriate to the trial of an Australian citizen on any serious criminal charge, presents difficulties. Basic to jury trial is that a jury of citizens is aware of the social circumstances of the community in which the crime is committed and represents the community conscience in this respect.

---

35. Athol Moffitt, "A case against the war trials", *Sydney Morning Herald*, 17 November 1988.

That basic justification for there to be an acceptable jury trial is surely absent where, in 1989 or 1990, a jury is called on to try wartime events in a war before most potential jurors were even born, being events on the other side of the world committed by some people against other people with no connection to Australia.[36]

There are several possible interpretations of Moffitt's position. The most charitable one, based on the outcome of Australia's subsequent attempts to try alleged war criminals, is that Moffitt is making a pragmatic assessment of the capacities of everyday, ordinary Australians, in present day circumstances, to understand the events of the Holocaust. Such a reading, however, is not borne out by a careful examination of the rest of Moffitt's text. First, it might be pointed out that Moffitt's ideal of a jury trial is based on a false assumption about the actual composition of Australian society or about the ways in which the current criminal justice system works. His view of jury trials as representing those who are "aware of the social circumstances of the community" is clearly based in a view of present-day Australian society as homogenous and unidimensional. In a multi-cultural society, it will inevitably be the case that crimes which are somehow grounded in particular "minority" circumstances will be judged within a criminal justice system which is composed of and constructed by "majority" values and assumptions. It is hard to imagine that a jurist such as Moffitt would argue that these crimes should not be prosecuted because the jury does not share a concrete and in-depth knowledge of the cultural circumstances in which they might have occurred.

Moreover and more importantly, Moffitt is really arguing at several levels that the Holocaust is not relevant to present day Australians. In addition to the obvious statement that both the perpetrators and victims have "no connection with Australia", a more pernicious attitude is arguably made manifest in Moffitt's position. By asserting that the jury could not understand "the social circumstance in which the crime is committed" and that it cannot be said to represent "the community conscience in this respect", Moffitt is making what can easily be characterized as an argument which seeks to relativize the Holocaust. While it might be asserted that Moffitt may be arguing that an Australian jury could not understand the situation of the victims, a more logical reading and one more consistent with the rest of his position is that he believes there may be extenuating circumstances in favor of the accused which the jury could not understand. What possible social

---

36. Ibid.

circumstances could be relevant in a case of mass killing unless one is adopting the position that explanations based on defenses involving following German orders, or the longstanding estrangement between local and "Jewish" populations, or Soviet invasion and "occupation" are somehow relevant to issues of the accused's guilt? Clearly, Moffitt is arguing that there are extenuating circumstances, based in local conditions, which might explain and possibly exculpate the accused's behavior but which an Australian jury could not understand. In cases such as this, arguments which are seemingly based in fundamental jurisprudential principles such as the nature of a jury trial or concerns about the effect of the passage of time on issues of procedural, evidentiary or substantive fairness, become nothing more than attempts to "understand", "explain" and relativize the Holocaust in order to (or at least with the effect of) exculpate the guilty. The rule of law as invoked by Moffitt here can have no other effect than to render the Holocaust as "not law", as completely beyond the capacities and function of the legal system. Again, this is a position which I have argued is quite consistent not just with rule of law discourse, but with the goals of post-war trials themselves. The rule of law can make the Holocaust "not law" either by dealing with it within the interpretive circumstance of a trial or by constructing it as completely inappropriate for the interpretive circumstance of a trial. In either case, the law wins.

Moffitt was not alone within the established legal community in seeking to sabotage Australia's efforts to establish a system to bring alleged perpetrators to trial. In addition to the Law Council, the New South Wales Bar Association entered the fray. Once again, its intervention was apparently couched in terms of a neutral concern for the basic principles and traditions of the rule of law in Australia. Mr. Ken Handley QC, speaking as president of the Bar, said:

> ...a commitment to multiculturalism requires Australians should now forget, and as many as possible should forgive.
> We should leave these ancient crimes behind us and not rekindle all the hatred that led to these crimes and which these crimes have in turn created within the surviving victims.[37]

Again, it might be possible to engage in a reading of the Bar's position as one which seeks simply to adopt an attitude consistent with the traditions of justice and the rule of law. Such a reading, would itself however, perhaps be

---

37. Glenn Milne, "War crimes bill damned as propaganda", *Sydney Morning Herald*, 13 December 1988.

unfair and inconsistent with those traditions. It must, first of all, be remembered that Handley characterized the *War Crimes Amendment Act* and the government's attempts to try perpetrators as "propaganda". In such circumstances, his statement cannot be seen to be anything other than an attempt to couch a particular ideology in the protective terminological garb of faithfulness to the values of the rule of law and multiculturalism. At the very least, one must inquire as to who is "behind' or who benefits from this "propaganda"? On the best reading of the deployment of this particular signifier, the Bar is characterizing the legislation as a cynical political exercise. On another possible reading of the use of such a loaded term in the context of the Holocaust and attempts to bring perpetrators to justice (or at least to law), one might see the Bar Association as deploying a classic antisemitic signifier. On one available reading of the text, implicit for some in the term "propaganda" is the qualifier "Jewish."

This reading of the Bar Association's position is perhaps reinforced by a careful examination of the rest of its statement. For the NSW legal elite, multiculturalism and the rule of law require forgetting and forgiveness. First, it might be noted, both as a matter of ethical and philosophical positioning and as a matter of social and historical reality within Australia, that it is not possible to forget what has not been remembered.[38] One of the primary uses, if not aims, of legislation like the *Australian War Crimes Amendment Act*, in the eyes of proponents of such instruments, is pedagogical. Debates about the issues surrounding the legislation as well as about subsequent trials, in theory at least, have the potential to bring questions of historical fact surrounding the Holocaust into the public, everyday domain. What the Bar Association wants to do is not just to abandon such pedagogical efforts by pretending that the law serves no such purpose, but also to pretend or assert by implication, that Australians already know enough about the Holocaust to "forget and forgive".

Beyond this, however, lie other more pernicious ideological goals and positions. In the Bar Association's view, and it was/is not alone in this, multiculturalism in Australia seems to be equivalent to a complete relativization of all cultures, societies and values. In other words, this universalizing, unquestioning multiculturalism requires that perpetrator and victim alike be considered equal. All Australians, in the magical transformative matrix of multiculturalism must be "the same", to be allowed, as Sir Garfield Barwick would have it, to put all this past behind them and live in the glorious shadow

---

38. Jean-François Lyotard, *Heidegger and 'the jews'*, op. cit.

(or perhaps sunlight) of the rule of law. This position is of course perfectly consistent with a practice and policy of forgetting which informs the Bar's attitude. The real purpose of the leveling effect of multiculturalism is the elimination of "all the hatred". Once again, however, behind the idealized notions of equality, democracy and the rule of law which might be seen to inform the legal profession's position here, is another example of the way in which legal discourse can be employed not just to eliminate the possibility of ethical judgment, but can in fact be used to impose a pernicious, relativized set of moral judgments. Again, as in Athol Moffitt's invocation of special social circumstances, the Bar's position simply makes victim and perpetrator equal. The hatred which apparently caused the perpetrators to act is now exactly the same as the "hatred" which apparently motivates "the surviving victims". A cry which is seen as a plea for "justice" and thus as one perfectly consistent with the normative rules and structures of the democratic system of the rule of law, is transformed by the country's self-defined legal elite into a call for vengeance, motivated by "hatred' and by definition clearly removed from any discursive matrix involving the rule of law. Perpetrator and victim are morally and legally equivalent because both are moved by the same base motivation. Victim and perpetrator cannot be differentiated within this conception of the rule of law. Since those who seek to try perpetrators are motivated by such concerns, the legislation in question can easily be characterized as "propaganda" rather than legislation since legislation within the rule of law normative universe of the Bar Association cannot be motivated by anything other than rational governmental concern. Again, justice becomes vengeance, not because this is the true characterization of war crimes trials, but because our understanding of the rule of law allows us to create competing discourses in these circumstances which are as convincing as the underlying ideological and political beliefs which inform them allow them to be.

For opponents of the legislation the law is not just (Jewish) propaganda, but it is then by definition not "Australian". Those motivated by hatred, which is the only possible motivation according to the internal logic of the Bar's position, are the "surviving victims" who do not recognize the importance of "multiculturalism" to "Australia".

Under this logic, other Australians cannot possibly wish to pursue war criminals and there can be no other possible explanation for the legislation. Concerns for universal or universalized notions of human rights, of crimes against humanity, of international legal or moral obligations, or even notions of right and wrong, are not only misplaced but impossible under the hermeneutic of the rule of law as deployed in these circumstances by the NSW Bar. The only

possible reasons for supporting such legislation would be that one is the innocent victim of a well-orchestrated "propaganda" campaign, or else that one is
moved by hate. The only supporters of such attempts to bring perpetrators before the Courts must then be "the surviving victims" moved by this hate, or
their dupes. For the rest, for "Australia", it is time to forget and forgive, since,
at a basic level, all of this is inimical to the image of a multicultural Australia
governed by the rule of law.

Such a vision of Australia was also echoed by certain spokespersons for Australia's Christian churches. Dr. David Penman, the Anglican Archbishop of
Melbourne, possibly an even stronger representative of "Australian" values
than the NSW Bar Association, voiced similar views.

> Dr Penman said yesterday the legislation could cause divisiveness
> among Australians, and the Church felt forgiveness was better than
> trying to avenge crimes long after they had been committed....Dr
> Penman said he would like to think forgiveness and tolerance lived
> side by side in a genuinely multicultural society.

He added:

> Pursuing aging criminals so long after the event will not do anything
> either to avenge or erase the dreadful events that happened.[39]

Once again, the usual elements are deployed here, covered and enhanced
by the apparent institutional and moral authority of the established Church.
Multiculturalism is univocal, universal, and relativized, constituted by perpetrators and victims alike. Vengeance is the only motive which can be attributed to proponents of pursuing the criminals. The Christian value of "forgiveness" becomes a universal societal norm.[40] Finally, the Archbishop adds a
further element to the equation, a refinement on the basic "passage of time"
position and one which will come to take on an important role in subsequent
trials both in Australia and elsewhere. Here, both the heartlessness of the pur-
suers and the humanity of the perpetrators are invoked as the latter are described as "aging criminals". This image of the alleged perpetrator as a "frail
old man" is one which clearly serves the dual role of humanizing and indi-
vidualizing the alleged "mass murderer" giving him a "human face", while at

---

39. Helen Pitt, "Archbishop urges block on war crimes bill", *Sydney Morning Herald*, 5
December 1988.
40. This particular discursive ploy would emerge again in the 1997 debate about the return of Konrad Kalejs to Australia.

the same time turning those who would "hound" such people into the true demons.

In the discourses deployed against the Australian *War Crimes Amendment Act* by its opponents, all of the themes of ethical choice and the rule of law which have pervaded discussions and debates about the Holocaust and the "legal" fate of the perpetrators since the earliest days can clearly be seen. "Justice" and the "rule of law" in the final analysis serve as little more than variably effective rhetorical devices employed by all sides in the debate. In the Australian example, this becomes even clearer in those events which followed the adoption of the statute by the Parliament.[41]

4. The War Crimes Amendment Act, Law and the Trials in Australia

Experience in Australia and elsewhere has clearly demonstrated that establishing the legislative basis for bringing alleged perpetrators to trial is only a small part of the struggle over justice and memory in the relationship between law and the Holocaust. At the technical legal level, many of the problems, most often pointed out by opponents of perpetrator trials, do in fact manifest themselves. Eyewitnesses, survivors of the Holocaust and others, are scarce and becoming scarcer with the inevitable passage of time. Those who do survive suffer from all the normal failings of eyewitnesses in the criminal justice system, failings which are apparently exacerbated by the years which make recollection more difficult and in the opinion of many, more unreliable.

Documentary evidence must be searched for and discovered in archives in distant lands, often with different legal systems. Problems of language and translation, both in the case of witnesses and documents, must be overcome. Additionally, technical legal issues and objections arise which must be determined in the context of a criminal trial, in this case in Australia, dealing with many factual issues which are unique and beyond the actual experience or expertise of those involved. At this level, the objections of the original opponents of war crimes trials have merit. The problem here is obvious. In the con-

---

41. After much more heated debate, the law was finally passed during the final days of the year. See Mike Seccombe, "Amended War Crimes Bill likely to pass soon", *Sydney Morning Herald*, 16 December 1988; Mike Seccombe, "Coalition still opposes War Crimes Bill", *Sydney Morning Herald*, 17 December 1988; Mike Seccombe, "War crimes bill passes emergency session", *Sydney Morning Herald*, 22 December 1988.

text of an "ordinary" criminal trial and the rules which have been developed and evolved to deal with such cases, extraordinary events are to be dealt with. "The Holocaust" for proponents of prosecution is unique. This is the basis for the politics of memory and of prosecution. At the same time, in order to be consistent with rule of law discourse, "the Holocaust" must be made to fit within the ordinary rules of the criminal justice system.

One of the key problems which arises under the Australian *War Crimes Amendment Act* is a vital issue of terminology. Since the days of the Nuremberg Charter and Trials, there has existed both a clear distinction and an ultimate confusion between "war crimes" and "crimes against humanity". In the Nuremberg context, it is clear that a vital contribution to the theory and practice of international law of the Charter and Trials, is the "creation" of "crimes against humanity" as a "new" category of international criminal offence. At the same time of course, "crimes against humanity" were made conditional upon the existence of other "war crimes" (crimes against peace, wars of aggression etc.). In the Australian context, in addition to the ideologically driven concepts of "war" and "occupation" already mentioned, the statutory context does not in fact mention "crimes against humanity" as a category informing the legislation. Thus, the *Act* defines a series of offences, which would clearly constitute "crimes against humanity" under existing international legal norms, as "serious crimes" (murder, deportation etc.) and "war crimes" as serious crimes committed during war.[42] War crimes become offences under Australian law. This lexical usage has important consequences in relation to the pedagogical function which must be attributed to the statute as well as to the technical legal application and applicability of the *Act* to certain individuals. Once again, what may appear to be simple and technical legal issues about the drafting of legislation, carry with them vital political and ideological consequences for collective memory in the body politic.

As a pedagogical matter, the failure to use the term "crimes against humanity" means that the more "neutral" term "war crime" is used to define the offences targeted by Australian law. At the rhetorical or metaphorical level, this simply replicates the confusion which results from the Nuremberg Charter. By placing them in a more universal category under which the particular "criminal" specificity of the Holocaust, the targeting of a particular group for total extermination, is lost, the Australian legislation may be seen to homogenize these events. This means that "crimes against humanity", which in these circumstances stands as a synonym for the Holocaust, are literally written out

---

42. Ss. 6, 7, 9.

of and are absent from, the Australian legal context. The pernicious nature of the crimes and the all important identity of the victims is somehow submerged into a context "war" which eliminates all of the historical and existential specificities of the Holocaust. Again, this is the almost inevitable consequence of the transformation of the Holocaust from a set of historical facts and an element of broader collective memory into a legal phenomenon. To "legalize" the Holocaust in this context one must make it ordinary. I have argued that this is in effect the historical and legal reality of the Holocaust which the law cannot in fact escape. The Holocaust was legally ordinary and normal, but not in the sense in which the Australian legal system has normalized it. It is not ordinary in its criminality but in its legality. This is the truth of law after Auschwitz, a truth which neither proponents nor opponents of prosecutions can grasp. For them, the entire debate is situated in an interpretive matrix which demands fealty to the rule of law. While they disagree on the substantive content of that discourse, they are in complete agreement on the inherent illegality of the Holocaust, on its status as "not law". All debate circulates around this baseline agreement.

At the technical legal level, another difficulty with the concept of "serious war crimes" is situated in notion of "serious". By necessary implication, this means that there is something which must be known as "minor" or "not serious" war crimes or crimes against humanity. Again, some of the conceptual confusion found in the Australian legislation can be traced back to Nuremberg, with its trial of "major" war criminals, as well as to the legislative and jurisprudential framework of the deNazification program in post-War Germany, with its legal construction of different classes of "Nazis". Such a position is also consistent with the complex jurisprudence which has more recently been developed in Germany by courts dealing with the definitions of various types of homicide under that country's criminal laws in perpetrator trials.[43] While the Australian position is not inconsistent with that developed in other similar legal contexts, one might nonetheless raise the obvious concerns at a moral or ethical level over such a potentially dangerous taxonomy of evil. Furthermore, in the Australian context, and in one case in particular, this technical legal definition may be seen to have allowed one "war criminal" to go free.

As already mentioned, when interest in the possible presence of Nazi and Nazi collaborators reemerged in Australia in the late 1970s and in the 1980s, one of those singled out for scrutiny and attention was Lyenko Urbanchich.

---

43. See Dick de Mildt, *In the Name of the People*, op. cit.

It was alleged that, during the war in Europe, Urbanchich was a leading pro-pagandist in Slovenia with clear pro-fascist and pro-Nazi beliefs. He was known to have written many pro-Nazi newspaper articles and to have organized and led pro-Nazi demonstrations. As the *Report* of the Special Investigation Unit makes clear however, Urbanchich could not be prosecuted under Australian law even though he had been convicted of war crimes *in absentia* in Yugoslavia.

> Although the case that Urbanchich was a fascist propagandist and a collaborationist has been well established, this is not an offence under the War Crimes Act.[44]

While the Australian statute imposes liability on those who are guilty of serious war crimes as accessories, it could not be demonstrated that Urbanchich had directly informed to the Gestapo or otherwise acted in a direct manner to assist in the commission of one of the offences enumerated in the *Act*.[45] Instead, like other propagandists and intellectual collaborators, he simply served to create the atmosphere and to legitimate the circumstances in which mass killings, torture and deportation could occur. The fact that a person such as Urbanchich, whose past is no secret, can live in Australia without fear of prosecution points for some to several failures in that country's efforts to bring war criminals to justice. There is the obvious issue of drafting a statute which draws a distinction between "serious" and other "war crimes". There is also the problem of the forum chosen. Unlike the United States and now Canada, Australia decided to pursue perpetrators within the context of the criminal justice system, by charging them with substantive criminal offences. This system has the political and moral merits both of defining crimes of the Holocaust as of domestic Australian concern and of treating perpetrators as criminals. On the other hand, however, American law, which deals with perpetrators under the less onerous civil legal regime of immigration law, defines acts of collaboration and propaganda as offences which can give rise to denaturalization and deportation, without establishing the causal connection with substantive criminal offences required under Australian law.[46] Because "propaganda" is not by itself a criminal offence and because its links to substantive offences are

44. Graham T. Blewitt, *Report of the Investigations of the War Criminals in Australia* (Canberra: AGPS, 1993).

45. S. 6 (1)(k)(ii)(iii).

46. *United States v. Sokolov*, 814 F. 2d 864 (1987) (2nd Circuit); James Brooke, "Ex-Yale Teacher Tried As a Nazi Collaborator", *New York Times*, 8 November, 1985; "U.S. Moves to Deport Ex-Nazi Propagandist", *Washington Post*, 24 May, 1988; "Nazi Propagandist Miss-

seen to be too tenuous, Urbanchich can not be prosecuted in Australia in circumstances where he could be deported from the United States.

However, it is safe to say that the primary problems and difficulties which have arisen under Australia's war crimes regime are associated not with such technical legal issues. Rather, it has been that country's attempts to bring alleged perpetrators to trial which have truly caused multiple problems, both of a technical legal nature and at a more sophisticated and important social and ethical level. It is in the context of actual war crimes trials that Australian society has most clearly been faced with the thorny issues relating to the place, role and function of the Holocaust and of the rule of law in that country's self-image and historical memory. Others have dealt in more detail with the actual events surrounding war crimes proceedings in Australia and with the more arcane legal issues which have arisen and I have no intention of repeating their work here.[47] Several more general and particular points, which I feel have not been adequately addressed in the Australian literature, do however require more discussion.

The first issue, which arises out of the Australian experience with war crimes trials, relates to the nature and function of law within society and more particularly with the way in which legal discourse shapes our narrative framework and social understandings of events. The case of Ivan Polyukovich, the first person charged under Australia's war crimes legislation, offers clear examples of the many perils associated with prosecutions of alleged perpetrators. At a basic level, for most Australian lawyers, Polyukovich or more precisely *Polyukovich*, is a relatively well-known High Court Constitutional Law decision.[48] In fact, and as a matter of legal ideology, *Polyukovich* offers a basic exposition of many of the leading principles of Australian constitutional federalism.

In an attempt to halt the Commonwealth criminal proceedings against him, Polyukovich's lawyers brought a constitutional challenge against the Federal war crimes statute. As predicted by the dire warnings of many of the legislation's opponents, the challenge asserted that such legislation was *ultra vires* the Commonwealth, primarily on the grounds that it constituted *ex post facto*

---

ing at Hearing: May Have Fled U.S.", *New York Times,* 17 July 1988. See discussion, above chapter 7.

47. See David Bevan, *A Case to Answer* (Kent Town, South Australia: Wakefield Press, 1994); Michael Kirby, "War Crimes Prosecution—An Australian Update", (1993) *Commonwealth Law Bulletin* 781; Gillian Triggs, "Australia's War Crimes Trials: All Pity Choked", in Timothy L.H. McCormack and Gerry J. Simpson (eds.), *The Law of War Crimes: National and International Approaches,* op. cit.

48. *Polyukovich v. Commonwealth,* 172 CLR 501 (1991).

law and because it did not fall within one of the enumerated heads of Commonwealth power in the Australian Constitution. While the High Court rejected these arguments and the found the legislation to be constitutionally sound, the legal ideological impact of this case lies elsewhere.

While the Court upheld the validity of the *War Crimes Amendment Act*, thereby allowing perpetrator trials to proceed, the Holocaust rates barely a mention in the 220 pages of the High Court's decision. Instead, as an inevitable consequence of the way in which legal constitutional argument must proceed, the case offers little more than an exposition of the principles of the division of powers between State and Federal Parliaments.[49] While the Court was required to find a constitutional nexus between events in Europe from 1939 to 1945 and a head of Commonwealth power to uphold the *Act*, what in the world of Australian legal discourse actually happens in the case is that the *War Crimes Amendment Act* is made "Australian" while the actual historical and legal reality of the Holocaust still remains "foreign", somehow un-Australian at its core, transformed into an Australian concern only by the actions of the Federal Parliament and the technical, rigid interpretive intervention of the High Court.

This legal estrangement of the Holocaust from Australian legal and political reality was only confirmed in the limited proceedings actually instituted under the *Act*. Three Australian residents, Ivan Polyukovich, Michael Berezowsky and Heinrich Wagner were brought before the bar of Australian justice. Polyukovich was acquitted in a jury trial, the case against Berezowsky was dismissed for lack of evidence and prosecutors dropped the case against Wagner after the defendant suffered a heart attack.[50] But what is important, from the perspective of Australian identity and memory in relation to the construction of the Holocaust and the rule of law, is not so much the outcome of these proceedings, but the way in which the various discourses which surround such issues were actually deployed. As was the case with the issue of bringing perpetrators to trial at various stages of recent Australian history, the primary discursive and political reality once more seems to be grounded in a basic majoritarian refusal to place the Holocaust within the mainstream of Australian legal practice, and cultural and national memory.

---

49. For examples of the limited and narrow nature of Australian legal discourse in this area, see G.P.J. McGinley, "War Crimes Legislation and the External Affairs Power", 14 *Criminal Law Journal* 342 (1990); James A. Thomson, "Is It a Mess? The High Court and the War Crimes Case: External Affairs, Defence, Judicial Power and the Australian Constitution", 22 *Western Australia Law Review* 197 (1992).

50. See Gillian Triggs, op. cit., for a more detailed discussion of these proceedings.

This subtle refusal by mainstream Australia to make the Holocaust and the reality of perpetrators in that country an important element for national identity and for collective understandings of what it means to live in a country subject to the principles of the rule of law, can be seen first in the subtle way in which the perpetrator is portrayed. When Polyukovich was first charged, he was described in the following terms:

> The defendant, a solid, tanned, fit-looking man with bushy black eyebrows, dressed in casual trousers and blue, open-necked shirt, stood silently in the dock during the hearing, nodding to acknowledge he accepted each bail condition.[51]

At this stage, Polyukovich is portrayed simply as an ordinary man. On reading the description of the accused, one can almost get the impression that the journalist was disappointed that Polyukovich did not appear before the Court in a black SS uniform.

But a more important descriptive strategy is also deployed here, one which will play a dominant role in subsequent debates. Here, Polyukovich starts to become "innocent" or least a "victim" because of his age and his status, ironically enough as a "foreigner". First, he is

> ...a 73-year-old pensioner.[52]

Then, his lack of facility in the English language becomes evident when he is quoted as declaring:

> I not say nothing...nothing to worry, I no understand. That's the trouble.[53]

The portrayal of Polyukovich here begins, or more precisely continues, the rhetorical and ideological process of portraying the attempt to bring alleged perpetrators to justice as itself unjust. Thus, he is old. The passage of time, the change in circumstances, the very age of the alleged criminal, all must operate under this view to destabilize any claim that the pursuit now can be justified within our shared "Australian" understanding of "justice" or the "rule of law".[54]

---

51. Peter Hughes, "850 war murders: man charged", *Sydney Morning Herald*, 27 January 1990.

52. Ibid.

53. Id.

54. Patrick Lawnham and Rohan Sullivan, "Fading memories after 50 years hurt the prosecution", *Australian*, 19 May 1993.

At the same time, the portrayal of the accused as someone who neither speaks English very well nor understands the charges against him serves to undermine any claim that pursuing him serves the interests of Australian society. He is, in addition to being old, not sophisticated enough to understand the complexity of a war crimes trial in the 1990s.

Arrayed against this defenseless man is the entire might of the Federal government. Fairness and justice demand a level playing field, an impossibility in such circumstances. Moreover, the accused's lack of facility in the English language most clearly marks him as a foreigner, as fundamentally not Australian. This then helps classify the entire proceeding against him as also being distinctly not Australian. The events and actors in question are physically, temporally and linguistically marked from the beginning as not Australian.

These two issues of age/time and linguistic and historical estrangement were continuously marked and underlined throughout the Polyukovich case. Not only was the age and deteriorating physical health of the accused of growing importance,[55] but Polyukovich's mental state and capacity to stand trial also became vital after an apparent suicide attempt.[56] Charges against him had to be dropped as witnesses died. At the conclusion of the trial, the judge stressed the issue of the passage of time in his charge to the jury.

The foreignness of the case was also constantly brought home to the jury through the omnipresence of interpreters, not just for Polyukovich, but for the various prosecution witness brought from the Ukraine to testify.

> Another burden has been the expense of having eight interpreters available.
> But their hire has been unavoidable, given that most of the witnesses have never before been out of the Ukraine.
> Progress has been painfully slow as the meaning of words is debated, leading to several outbursts from frustrated witnesses.[57]

At each stage, the linguistic and physical setting of the spectacle of the legal proceedings against Polyukovich simply served to confirm the views and arguments of those who had always asserted that justice and the rule of law demand that no proceedings against alleged perpetrators be taken.

---

55. See e.g., Robbie Brechin, "Death stalks the war crimes trials", *Sydney Morning Herald*, 2 May 1992.

56. See David Bevan, *A Case to Answer*, op. cit., at 60–67.

57. Brechin, op. cit.; see also Bevan, at 122–28, 183–87, 192–93; and Ludmilla Stern, "Investigating War Crimes: A Language Problem", *The Sydney Papers*, Winter 1995, 45.

Again, another apparently legal argument was used to buttress this ju-risprudential and political position. Polyukovich's lawyers, and others, con-stantly invoked evidentiary concerns about the origins of the witnesses and other evidence. For them, the fact that the Soviet government had permitted the eyewitnesses to leave and come to Australia to testify was in and of itself suspicious. Technical legal objections were made against some of the physical evidence gathered at uncovered mass gravesites by Australian and Soviet in-vestigators.[58] According to Polyukovich's legal team, the chain of custody over the exhibits had been lost, and the exhibits themselves subjected to possible contamination when Soviet authorities had taken possession of them.[59] A prosecution witness, an Australian police officer, voiced similar concerns from the witness box.[60]

Here, of course, disguised as technical legal arguments about the reliabil-ity of witness testimony or about the integrity of physical evidence, the dis-courses of Cold War anti-Communism simply continue to assert themselves. No evidence from the Soviet Union can be reliable because, by definition, western legal processes based in the normative structures of the rule of law are inimical to Soviet conceptions of "law". In addition to this basic jurispruden-tial and ideological opposition, there remain all the possible concerns over So-viet attempts to taint and discredit possible opponents among émigré groups.[61] Even as the Soviet Union was crumbling, the ideological terrain of Cold War anti-Communism still was effectively deployed in the service of a discourse which sought to construct the rule of law in Australia in such a way as to keep the Holocaust from becoming part of that country's official, legal memory.

Other discourses were also being deployed in the ideological and legal bat-tle over the place of the Holocaust and the rule of law in Australian national memory and identity. The right wing League of Rights was a constant pres-

---

58. See Richard Wright, "Investigating War Crimes: The Archaeological Evidence", *The Sydney Papers*, Winter 1995, 39.

59. See David Bevan, "Grave exhibits queried", *Adelaide Advertiser*, 13 November 1991; Maryann Stenberg, "Bid to stop war crime trial", *Sydney Morning Herald*, 1 December 1992.

60. See David Bevan, "Soviet 'plot' feared", *Adelaide Advertiser*, 21 November 1991.

61. Ironically, Australian prosecutors had been forced to discontinue 12 possible cases after Lithuanian witnesses refused to cooperate with them after Lithuanian independence. See, Sigrid Kirk, "12 war crimes cases dropped", *Sydney Morning Herald*, 7 April 1992. American authorities have also experienced some difficulty in the newly independent Baltic states in convincing government officials there to bring charges against alleged war crimi-nals forced to leave the US. It might be argued that such a reluctance to bring charges of-fers some evidence that the Soviet position against some national groups was not totally without merit.

ence outside the Adelaide courthouse during proceedings against Polyukovich.[62] Despite the federal Opposition's success in excluding Australian diggers from the application of the war crimes legislation, the League nonetheless attempted to "Australianize" proceedings by invoking a bizarre equivalency between possible Australian war crimes, the bombings of Dresden and Nagasaki on the one hand, and accusations of the mass extermination of European Jews on the other.[63] Former South Australian Governor Sir Walter Crocker joined the protesters and echoed their resentment over the prosecution.[64] Two elements of Crocker's intervention are important in understanding what for many is really at stake in debates over the role, nature and function of war crimes trials in Australia, and by extension, in other countries as well. The first of these elements is temporal, the second more obviously ideological.

The battle on the temporal signifying front was an important one.[65] Crocker intervened on November 11, the eleventh day of the eleventh month, Remembrance Day. Given the vital role played by the sacrifices of Australian soldiers in the First World War in the construction of some of the strongest elements of the mythological dimensions of Australian memory and identity, an intervention on that date carries with it a very particular and powerful historical message. Crocker, a former British soldier and representative of Her Majesty in South Australia, when he intervenes with an assertion that "...the accused had committed no crimes against Australians or in Australia..."[66] is invoking not just images and arguments about the un-Australian nature of the Holocaust, but is reinforcing that message and imagery by offering a counter-image of what Australian memory really is, the diggers, Gallipoli, Empire etc.

---

62. See David Greason, "Australia's Racist Far-Right", in Chris Cunneen, David Fraser and Stephen Tomsen (eds.), *Faces of Hate: Hate Crime in Australia* (Sydney: Hawkins Press, 1997), at 188.

63. "Trial 'threat' to our veterans", *Adelaide Advertiser*, 29 October 1991.

64. John Ferguson, "Crocker to picket war case", *Adelaide Advertiser*, 11 November 1991; "War crimes trial attacked as 'costly folly'", *Sydney Morning Herald*, 11 November 1991; Mike McEwen, "Angry Sir Walter goes to war", *Adelaide Advertiser*, 13 November 1991.

65. It is important to note that both sides attempted to play the temporal signifying game. In addition to the importance of Remembrance Day, charges were originally brought against Polyukovich on Australia Day. Thus, the prosecution attempted to employ two significant dates in the construction of mainstream Australian historical memory and identity in order to create an ideological nexus between and among war crimes prosecutions, the Holocaust and Australian identity. That they failed in doing so underlines the continuing strength of a particular vision and definition of Australian identity.

66. Ferguson, "Crocker to Picket War Case", op. cit.

The struggle for democracy and the rule of law, a struggle paid for in the blood of Australian soldiers, is completely foreign to this trial of someone accused of committing crimes long ago and far away.

This temporal ploy is made stronger by the other, more pernicious strategy invoked by Crocker. Not only does he portray the pursuit of alleged war criminals as running counter to all that is Australian, in addition to dealing with matters which are of no concern to Australians or Australia, but he more specifically invokes a particular image of his idea of just what constitutes un-Australianness. He accuses the federal Government of having succumbed to a lobby

> which is buttressed with great wealth, with exceptional self-centered persistence and with ruthless cleverness.[67]

In case one is left in any doubt as to the identity of those who possess such qualities, Crocker becomes even more explicit.

> I feel very strongly about this particular issue and I feel my fellow Australians have been misled by the propaganda other people have whipped up....
> It's a wealthy group. What mystifies me and others I know, is why they stirred up the matter of the so-called Nazi war criminals at about the time they have....
> I feel strongly because I happened to be in the UN in the first four years and that was when Israel was created. The spectacle of the power of American Jewry, the financial power and the intellectual power was absolutely overwhelming....
> They have a lobby that's powerful in every country where they operate. They have, in fact, dominated American foreign policy.[68]

Thus, Crocker explicitly pronounces that which merely seemed to inform the opposition by others to war crimes trials in Australia. The un-Australian element here is "the Jews", a phantasmagoric amalgam of international Jewry, the Simon Wiesenthal Center, Israel, American Jewry and their "Australian" agents. Real Australians have been "misled" by the propaganda (propaganda, it must be remembered, of which the NSW Bar Association spoke) of "the Jews". Nazi war criminals are now just a figment, a creation of this propaganda, they are "so-called Nazi war criminals". Jews can not be real Australians for their allegiance lies elsewhere. Not only do Crocker's views go unchal-

---

67. Ibid.
68. McEwen, "Angry Sir Walter Goes to War", op. cit.

lenged, they are placed prominently in the coverage of the Polyukovich trial in two major metropolitan dailies. In fact, the major national newspaper, in its coverage of the legal proceedings, referred to Sir Walter and his cohorts from the League of Rights as "human rights protestors".[69] The story of the Holocaust and the rule of law in Australia is now complete from the perspective of many of those opposed to prosecutions. The trials are a Jewish conspiracy; the accused are the old, frail innocent victims of a Judeo-Bolshevik plot to subvert democracy and the rule of law; protestors and those who have long opposed the trials act with the best of intentions, to protect against human rights abuses and the subversion of the great Australian traditions of multiculturalism, democracy and the rule of law; the Holocaust has nothing to do with Australia. "Auschwitz", after all is not Adelaide.

Some of these positions, (albeit couched in terms which avoid any explicit antisemitism), to a greater or lesser extent, can finally be found in the interventions of former Liberal Party speechwriter, newspaper columnist and talkback radio host, Alan Jones. From the very earliest days of war crimes trials in Australia, Jones gave vent to his own particular, and apparently popular, demagogy, which has surrounded the issue in that country. Writing about the proceedings against Polyukovich, Jones offered the following:

> It has revived memories most would prefer remain forgotten.
> It has raised the spectre of Australians being charged for their activities under its strictest interpretation.
> Now an old man in failing health is the subject of a show trial at enormous cost to the community.
> The preliminary investigations into alleged war criminals alone have cost the taxpayers millions....
> And what of the Pacific?
> Whenever the issue of war crimes is raised on talkback radio...the people's forum...I'm asked why the focus is on Nazi war crimes rather than the Japanese.[70]

Once more, a quick review reveals the rhetorical and political strategy and stakes of the debate. "Memories" have been revived, and with them, possible antagonisms and schisms. Australian diggers are in danger. A frail old man is being persecuted in a show trial. This is costing a fortune and what about the Japanese?; they are the real war criminals and persistent threat to Australia

---

69. Rohan Sullivan, "First war crime trial next week", *Australian*, 2 March 1993.

70. Alan Jones, "War crimes: what genie have we let loose?", *Sun-Herald*, 25 March 1990.

today. The Holocaust is already deeply buried in our memories and need not be revisited. Forgetting and forgiveness are essential to maintaining the stability and democratic, rule of law based system in which we live. Not only is Polyukovich too old and frail for a fair trial to occur, but the trial itself is the exact opposite of what a trial in a democracy should be; it is a "show trial", just as in Moscow of the 1930s. This European stuff, against the Jews, is of no concern to real Australians and since all of this is true why should we spend all this taxpayers' money to serve special interests?

Jones would simply continue to echo his sentiments on the subject, this time with arguments more specifically "legal" in orientation but still tainted with a hint of subtext, one which is based "on very soft ground". He wrote then:

> It prompts the question, what if anything is to be achieved?
> Are the Jewish community in favour of prosecution?
> We are treading on very soft ground....
> Are we to do no more than drag old men out of obscurity and try them for crimes committed in Europe 50 years ago?
> What about proof of identity and admissible evidence?
> And what are we to do with these people if they are found guilty?
> Is it justice when men are brought to trial on the basis of specially-created legislation—retrospective legislation, the kind we oppose if it is applied to taxation or corporate life.[71]

Ironically, but predictably of course, all of the major technical "legal" concerns expressed by the opponents of war crimes trials in Australia had only positive results for the accused. Witness reliability and the passage of time, the age and frailty of the accused, all worked within the Australian criminal justice system to relieve the accused of liability. At this level, the Australian war crimes program "worked' in the sense that all of the proceedings under the *Act* occurred within the normal framework and practices of the everyday criminal justice system. The rule of law can be said to have triumphed. All of the concerns of opponents, at some level, turned out to be both ill-founded and correct, as did all of the arguments of proponents of the trials. The system, the rule of law, the criminal justice system, the basic and golden rule of the presumption of innocence, all functioned to achieve a "just" result.

On another level, for some, the Australian experience points to the many failures of post-war trials of perpetrators generally and to the indigenous fail-

71. Alan Jones, "Uneasy precedents in pursuit of war criminals", *Sun-Herald*, 29 July 1990.

ings of the Australian efforts to bring the Holocaust into the frame work of its legal system. Evidentiary rules, human preconceptions and weakness, the passage of time, all meant that no "successful" prosecution has ever been brought in that country. Here, the debate, which might take place at an abstract level of jurisprudential concern over first principles quickly slips into barely concealed political arguments dependent on pre-existing ideas and ideologies. Had Polyukovich been convicted, opponents of the trials would no doubt have continued to refer to the case as a "show trial" and railed against the injustice of the verdict, whereas now they could only admit that the system had worked. Now they could argue, by invoking both first principles and financial concerns about spending so much taxpayer money, about failed and futile proceedings. On the other hand, those who decried the injustice of the verdict, would, if faced with a conviction, have praised the wonders of the Australian criminal justice system. In "victory" or "defeat", each side necessarily betrays the real fragility of its commitment to "law" and to justice.

It is also possible to characterize the Australian effort as a failure for another, more fundamental, reason. On the pedagogical front and on the ideological front, the war crimes trials system in Australia never succeeded in incorporating the Holocaust and concerns for justice for victims and perpetrators into the Australian consciousness and national memory. Technical legal arguments about federalism or the burden of proof or the reliability of evidence do not easily commend themselves to general political and moral pedagogy in the eyes of the general public. This difficulty is exacerbated when the counter-message is as powerful as the one put out by the various opponents of war crimes trials. From anti-Communism to fairness for old people; to the basic idea both that the Holocaust is an event distant in time, place and concern for the majority of "Australians"; that "they", whether they are "Jews" or other "foreigners", must become Australians by "forgetting" their specific histories and embracing an Australian memory from which those histories must still be excluded; all of this served to turn Australia's war crimes efforts into a phenomenon which to a great extent remained separate from the social, cultural, and national memory of most Australians.

The Labor government decided to disband the SIU and remove "future" prosecutions to a small, ill-equipped unit within the Attorney-General's Department in 1994.[72] The toll stood at one trial ending in acquittal, one case

---

72. Helen Signy, "Pursuit of war criminals ending", *Sydney Morning Herald*, 15 January 1994.

dismissed by a magistrate for lack of evidence, and one case halted by the prosecution on humanitarian grounds.[73] Many concluded that the entire exercise had been, in the final analysis, a waste of taxpayers' money.[74]

Because of the assertions of proponents of the legal pursuit of perpetrators that trials can in fact serve a pedagogical function by educating the public about the historical realities of the Holocaust, and because of the more dispersed, generalized belief that there is in fact a direct relationship between the criminal justice system and "truth", the stakes in prosecuting alleged perpetrators can become high. Guilt and conviction are related not just to the particular accused but to the events presented as factual by the prosecution. Conversely, innocence can be associated not just with the case or the facts against the individual accused but with the prosecution's case as a whole. Thus, "not guilty", in the eyes of many for whom the Holocaust remains an abstraction and a matter concerning "others", can come to mean, in combination with other complex and existing social and political discourses, which as we can see, existed in Australia around this issue, "no Holocaust".

The potential danger posed at this level by "legalizing" the Holocaust was clearly pointed out by the Member for Prospect, Dr. Klugman, in the debate over the adoption of the *War Crimes Amendment Bill*, where he said:

> The Opposition has concentrated on the conviction of innocent persons on false evidence. My fear is that it will be extremely difficult to obtain a criminal conviction, in other words, to prove guilt beyond reasonable doubt. After 45 years it would not be difficult for any defence lawyer to create sufficient doubt. Honourable members who are old enough would agree that it would be very difficult to remember faces, considering the fact that they would have changed in appearance, and the sorts of details required in response to cross-examination after such a long time.
>
> Therefore, the chances are that guilty persons would be acquitted unless they pleaded guilty, which they would be advised not to do. Their acquittal on the basis of doubt would be interpreted by many as indicating that they were not guilty and that the facts of the brutal killing of millions of people in Europe for political, religious or racial reasons were not as clearly proven soon after the war.[75]

---

73. For a full record of the SIU's operation, see Blewitt, *Report of the Investigations of the War Criminals in Australia*, op. cit.

74. Signy, "Pursuit of War Criminals Ending", op. cit.

75. *Hansard*, 26 November 1987, at 2791.

Dr Klugman's fears are, I believe, borne out in the Australian experience of war crimes prosecutions. In the minds of most Australians, the Holocaust remains lost in the shrouds of time and distance. For many, it is a Hollywood extravaganza like *Schindler's List*. Hollywood creates fantasies and Polyukovich was acquitted. So much for the Holocaust in Australia and for the pedagogical functions of legislative and prosecutorial intervention. Finally, Australia's most recent experience with an alleged Holocaust perpetrator simply reinforces the position that "Auschwitz" and Australia occupy irreconcilable epistemological spaces.

5. The Legal Saga of Konrad Kalejs

No story better encapsulates the many continuities and difficulties involved in the vexed issue of the connection between the rule of law and the Holocaust, than the tale of Konrad Kalejs. Kalejs, who continued to insist that he was a university student at the time, is alleged to have been a leader in the Latvian Arjas commando[76] and, as such, to have committed crimes against humanity during the Holocaust in Latvia. After the war, Kalejs immigrated to Australia, where he gained employment as a document clerk in the Bonegilla DP Camp.[77] After gaining Australian citizenship, Kalejs moved to the United States in 1959 and became a wealthy property owner. After being accused by US officials in 1985 of having lied about his wartime activities, Kalejs began a 10-year battle to avoid deportation.[78] In the meantime, the *Menzies' Report* named Kalejs, who had never given up his Australian citizenship, as an alleged war criminal.[79] Debates about his possible fate if he returned to Australia periodically surfaced.[80] Kalejs exhausted his legal remedies against US deportation proceedings in March 1994 and was deported to his country of choice and citizenship, Australia.[81] Despite pressure to prosecute Kalejs under the *War Crimes Amendment Act*, the Australian Labor government refused to proceed,

---

76. For a more detailed examination of this, see Andrew Ezergailis, *The Holocaust in Latvia*, op. cit.

77. See Rutland, *Edge of the Diaspora*, op. cit., at 246.

78. See, "US holds Aust citizen as Nazi", *Sydney Morning Herald*, 25 April 1985; "Australian Nazi suspect freed on bail in US", *Sydney Morning Herald*, 5 July 1985.

79. Op. cit., at 102.

80. Glenn Milne, "War crimes lobby steps up pressure", *Sydney Morning Herald*, 7 November 1988; "New war crime trials", *Sydney Morning Herald*, 7 November 1988.

81. See Richard Jinman, "US to deport accused Nazi", *Australian*, 23 March 1994; Greg Lenthen, "Review case of alleged former Nazi, say Jews", *Sydney Morning Herald*, 23 March 1994.

citing the Australian Federal Police's conclusion that there was not enough evidence to procure a criminal conviction.[82] This position simply confirmed the position of the SIU, which had reported that while it believed there was substance to the accusations against Kalejs, there was insufficient evidence to warrant proceeding against him.[83] While criticism of the government's failure to act continued, Kalejs left Australia and went to Canada, which he had chosen as a convenient meeting spot for his family who had remained in the United States.[84] He was apprehended by Canadian authorities and left that country to return to Australia, again amidst an uproar.[85] He then returned to Canada where he engaged in a lengthy immigration proceeding to determine his fitness to remain in that country.

Because of the rigid requirements for a successful criminal conviction of alleged war criminals set down by the Supreme Court of Canada in the *Finta*[86] case, and the lengthy and complex nature of such prosecutions, Canadian authorities had begun to follow the United States strategy of dealing with suspected war criminals by seeking to have them deported.[87] Again, this process has the advantages of a lower burden of proof and a potentially speedier outcome, but it also has what some might argue is the disadvantage of treating the substantive legal and moral issues of guilt and responsibility as someone else's problem. In the end, after a nine-month hearing, Kalejs was found to have been involved in mass murder in Latvia and was ordered deported from Canada.[88] As an Australian citizen, Kalejs was again able to nominate that country as the place to which he wished to be deported. His arrival once again sparked heated debate about his fate and about Australia's image in the world as a "dumping ground" for war criminals.[89]

82. See Frank Devine, "War crimes trawl failed to net monsters in our midst", *Australian*, 16 June 1994; Tony Wright and Sandra Harvey, "Suspect Nazi likely to escape court", *Sydney Morning Herald*, 11 November 1994.

83. See Blewitt, *Report of the Investigations*, op. cit., at 110–12.

84. See Adrian Bradley, "Nazi hunter lashes out", *Australian*, 11 February 1995; Adrian Bradley, "QC seeks action on war crime suspect", *Australian*, 5 June 1995.

85. See Adrian Bradley, "Return of war crimes suspect fuels anger", *Weekend Australian*, 24–25 June 1995.

86. *R. v. Finta*, [1994] 1 S.C.R. 701.

87. See *Secretary of State v. Luitjens*, [1989] 2 F.C. 125.

88. See Lila Sarick, "War criminal, 84, ordered deported", *Globe and Mail*, 19 August 1997. Kimina Lyall, "Kalejs an accomplice to brutality", *Weekend Australian*, October 4–5, 1997.

89. See Anne Davies and Leonie Lamont, "Nazi death squad suspect: the man we can't keep out", *Sydney Morning Herald*, 20 August 1997; John Ellicott, "Nazi war crime suspect

The case of Konrad Kalejs once again starkly raises many basic issues of the relationship, if any, between the rule of law and the Holocaust. The case also demonstrates in its many complexities the ways in which the rhetorical points around which these issues and debates arise and take place can subtly shift over time. With the fall of the Soviet Union and the independence of the former "Captive Nations", concerns in overseas countries over Communist contaminated evidence have been virtually eliminated. In the Canadian case against Kalejs, for example, seven new Latvian witnesses emerged to place him personally at a site where atrocities were committed by men under his command. Émigré communities expressed no real concern about the reliability of such evidence.

However, the vexed and problematic issues of anti-Communism and the historical realities and truths of the Holocaust re-emerged in the Kalejs case in a different context. As the Menzies' and SIU Reports make clear, Australian immigration law, with its ten-year limitation period, could not and cannot be used to any practical extent against alleged war criminals since most, if not all, of them entered the country long ago. Thus, the Australian government cannot invoke the United States and Canadian mechanisms of deporting suspect individuals. Despite calls to amend the legislation, successive Australian governments have rejected the idea of *ex post facto* statutory remedies. One other recourse, extradition, remains as a possibility. In fact, the government of Latvia at one time had expressed an interest in pursuing this possibility of bringing Kalejs before a Latvian court.[90] However, there was no extradition treaty between Australia and Latvia, and any future treaty, despite pleas to the contrary, would not have had retrospective application.[91]

But the issue of extradition, even if permissible, does not really address many unanswered and difficult questions in cases such as this. While one might argue that willingness by a government to undertake extradition pro-

---

returns", *Australian*, 20 August 1997; John Stapleton, "Is this the final flight of a globe-trotting alleged war criminal?", *Australian*, 20 August 1997; Editorial, "Back again", *Sydney Morning Herald*, 21 August 1997; Leonie Lamont, Anne Davies and Andrew Clennell, "Fears Kalejs case will be too difficult to prosecute", *Sydney Morning Herald*, 21 August 1997; Anne Davies, "Citizen Kalejs: the national problem that just won't go away", *Sydney Morning Herald*, 22 August 1997.

90. See Adrian Bradley, "Latvia seeks extradition of alleged war criminal", *Weekend Australian*, 13–14 January 1996.

91. See Executive Council of Australian Jewry, 'Media Release—ECAJ calls on Government to act on "Fugitive from moral laws and justice"', 25 July 1995; Colin Rubenstein, "No haven for war criminals", *Sydney Morning Herald*, 21 August 1997.

ceedings is indicative of a commitment to bring war criminals to trial, the situation in the Baltic states may not be as straightforward as this. The newly independent states in the Baltic area are not immune from the forces of conservative and sometimes revanchist nationalism which have swept through the former Soviet Union.[92] Much of the struggle for independence there has been informed not just by nationalist longings, but by the construction of a particular historical memory of nationalism in relation to the Holocaust. The ideal of Latvia as a triumphant victim of both Nazi and Soviet occupation and atrocities is, in most versions of majority public memory, one which must deny the historical reality and specificity of the Holocaust in order to validate the nation's victim status. As American experience with similar cases has demonstrated, domestic political forces can easily come into play in the Baltic states in order to subvert any attempt to prosecute those who are, almost by national self-definition, heroes of the struggle for freedom. In the Baltic states, newly liberated from the Soviet Empire, the Holocaust for many is simply not part of much of collective memory. Instead, the killing of the Jews, when it is addressed at all, is seen to be the execution of Bolshevik enemies of the nation.[93]

While such issues have remained submerged in Australian debates over the fate of Kalejs since deportation was not a legal possibility, they must nevertheless inform any attempt to fully understand the implications of seemingly arcane debates about Australian citizenship law.

In the end, if it is possible to speak of the end of Kalejs' peripatetic life in the law, Australian debates moved little beyond either the basic premises established by Chifley and Barwick forty or more years ago or beyond more universal issues of identity and memory in relation to the Holocaust. Speaking in Melbourne, with its large survivor population, upon Kalejs' return to Australia, the Premier of Victoria, Jeff Kennett, invoked what were for him obvious universal, Australian norms, when he declared:

---

92. See John Goetz, "Latvia's SS is back", *Guardian Weekly*, 28 February 1993.

93. See Michael MacQueen, "The Context of Mass Destruction; Agents and Prerequisites of the Holocaust in Lithuania", 12 *Holocaust and Genocide Studies* 27–48 (1998), for a recent historical account of the Holocaust in that country. See also, "Seven Lithuanian Parties Demand Good Will From Israeli Government", *ELTA News Service*, 12 December, 1997; "Lithuania suspends war crimes trial until May", cnn.com, 5 March, 1998; James Meeks, "Lithuania confronts its Nazi past", *Guardian Weekly*, 15 March 1998; "SS men celebrate", *Sydney Morning Herald*, 16 March 1998; "Grand rassemblement de russophones en Lettonie", *Le Monde*, 19 March 1998; "Lithuanian war crime suspect Lileikis dies", *Union of Councils for Soviet Jews*, 28 September 2000.

> If you want to take an entirely Christian point of view, I think the last
> words Jesus uttered on the cross were 'Forgive them for they know
> not what they do'.[94]

Like Chifley and the Melbourne archbishop before him, Kennett invokes
Christian forgiveness not just as the operative value in such cases, but as a way
of separating those who called for Kalejs' trial from the Australian mainstream
as unChristian. In other words, yet again, it is not simply a question here of
the superiority within the context of ethics and justice of Christian values, but
equally important is the idea that "the Jews" are behind this, that they are
unAustralian and that they are motivated by revenge. In response, lawyer Nina
Bassat, president of the Jewish Community Council of Victoria stated:

> Jews are not seeking revenge in a personal vendetta. This has noth-
> ing to do with revenge, everything to do with justice.[95]

Despite the efforts of some like Bassat to redefine the issue in other terms,
the continuing dominance of the views expressed by Kennett seems established. Indeed, in many respects this discourse of exclusion appears to be on
the verge of becoming a self-fulfilling prophecy. Jeremy Jones of the Executive
Council of Australian Jewry gives voice to the problem:

> Many members of the Jewish community will find it difficult to ra-
> tionalize their faith in Australia if nothing is done.... How can we live
> in a country with people who killed our families?[96]

The idea that Australian Jews are somehow not Australian is raised here as
an existential reality for Australian Jews themselves. In Jones' view, as "mainstream" Australia continues to define itself as not only Christian but as un-
concerned with the Holocaust at best, or at worst, as hostile to any efforts to
make Australia face up to the Shoah, Australian Jews might begin to question
there faith in their own country. As Australia continues to define the Holocaust in terms of otherness, of forgiveness, of forgetting, Australian Jews, for
many of whom the Holocaust plays a vital psycho-existential role, can easily
come to see Australia as other. This failure to reach an historical, memorial
and legal consensus over the meaning of the Holocaust for the definition and
self-understanding of Australia has resulted in a continuing estrangement of

---

94. Clyde H. Farnsworth, "Furor Splits Australians Over a Link to Nazi Era", *New York Times*, 31 August 1997.
95. Ibid.
96. Id.

some Australians from a feeling of full citizenship and belonging. This is, of course, the almost necessary consequence of positing the uniqueness of the Holocaust, the specificity of Jewish victimhood in that context and claims of a national duty to memory and justice. While the debate seems to circulate around issues of justice and the rule of law, at the same time there are, and always have been, deeper and more vital stakes at play.

These stakes of identity, citizenship, justice etc., are not simple ones. As the debate over war crimes trials in Australia has always signaled, the rhetoric of the rule of law and justice can mask extremely complex questions. Even the apparent juxtaposition between a "Christian" forgiveness ideal and a feeling of Jewish estrangement can and must be made more complex. Debates over the issue of the role of the Holocaust in Jewish identity pose basic and difficult questions in the field of politics and theology.[97]

In addition to pointing out, in response to Premier Kennett's invocation of the Christian virtue of forgiveness, that forgiveness, even in the Christian tradition, must follow confession and that Kalejs continued to insist on his student status, and to deny any role as a perpetrator, Robert Manne offers the following analysis of the failure of Australian Jews to forgive.

> Kalejs was involved in the murder of Latvian Jewry. What capacity has the Australian Jewish community to forgive him for the wrongs done to others?[98]

Manne here adopts a view of Jewish identity somewhat distant from the one invoked by Jeremy Jones and others. While Jones invokes the image of Australian Jews now living in the same country as those who murdered their families, Manne draws a clear distinction between Jews in Australia and the real victims of Kalejs. Under this view, nationality seems a necessary qualifier which Jews must adopt. Australian Jews can not speak for Latvian Jews, who are the only ones who have the "jurisdiction" to forgive. The issues which arise are complex. What does Manne's position say about calls to try Kalejs in Australia? Is the technical legal capacity of a government to try an accused war criminal to be distinguished, as an ethical matter, from the capacity to excuse, pardon and forgive? Is there no moral basis on which Australia can prosecute Kalejs because it cannot be said to represent or speak for the victims? What of other countries? Does Manne's position morally subvert the claims of Israel

---

97. For one such political/legal context, see Guyora Binder, "Defending Nazism: advocacy and identity at the trial of Klaus Barbie", op. cit., and Vivian G. Curran, "Deconstruction, structuralism, antisemitism and the Law", op. cit.

98. "Why Kalejs's crimes can't be forgiven", *Sydney Morning Herald*, 25 August 1997.

in prosecuting Eichmann and Demjanjuk to representative status for Jews everywhere? Does it lead to a reconsideration of the category "victim" or of the role of the Holocaust in Jewish self-identity? All of these issues are vital to our understanding of the troubled and perhaps impossible relationship between the Holocaust and the rule of law, in Australia and elsewhere. But they remain questions which we refuse to pose for fear of what they might tell us about law, extermination and ourselves.

In the end, these questions remain unanswered. The Kalejs legal saga and other parts of the ongoing Australian experience with the pursuit of war criminals clearly demonstrate, as does experience elsewhere, that the complex and intertwined matrix of values and issues which in reality underpin debates about the Holocaust and the rule of law, are contingent, contextual problems which are struggled over in an ongoing fashion in a number of forums. While the practical, legal issues appear to be simple, the lessons we learn from them are more difficult. In the Kalejs case, the reality within the legal systems of the United States and Canada is clear for some. David Matas of B'nai Brith Canada describes the apparent conflict between law and ethical duty:

> Every single country where he's been has a duty to try him....What's happening is a grievous case. Kalejs is guilty to a criminal standard. These are no longer allegations, but there's still no process in sight where he can be punished for these crimes. The worst criminals go scot-free and just move from country to country.[99]

To this sadly accurate description of the legal history of Konrad Kalejs, and many other perpetrators, we can add the following:

> What, then, can be done about Kalejs? As everyone acknowledges, it is far too late to try him. An acquittal would be far worse than no trial at all. Without enacting retrospective law, it is impossible to deport him. Even with such retrospective law, deportation seems futile. It is far from clear how justice will be served by forcing Kalejs to live out his dotage in Riga rather than Melbourne.
> What, then, can be done? The truth is stark. Nothing.[100]

---

99. Lila Sarick, "War criminal, 84, ordered deported", op. cit.

100. Robert Manne, op. cit. Manne's views were echoed by Professor Konrad Kwiet who dismissed reports that Australian Federal Police were pursuing inquiries concerning eleven suspected Lithuanian war criminals residing in Australia. He said, "There can't be any justice anymore in terms of criminal convictions based on rules of evidence. It's too late. It's a closed chapter." Jodie Brough, "War crimes suspects targeted", *Sydney Morning Herald*, 4 October 1997. See also Chip LeGrand and Carolyn Jones, "Police ignore legal

Konrad Kalejs moved to a Latvian retirement community outside of Melbourne.[101] In May 1998, Australian Prime Minister John Howard announced that his government would take no further action against Kalejs.[102]

However, subsequent events have allowed the question of Nazi war criminals in Australia to return occasionally to the political and moral agenda as well as to the front pages of the nation's newspapers. For example in August 1999, the *Sydney Morning Herald* published a series of stories detailing the presence of Nazi scientists in Australia.[103] The scientists came to the country as a result of the well-known program by Allied governments to beat the Soviets to the best German minds at the end of the war, whatever the record of those minds in supporting the Nazi regime.

Later that same year, a report on the American television program *20/20* identified Australia as a country offering safe haven to alleged Nazi killers and highlighted the cases of Konrad Kalejs and Heinrich Wagner. The government quite naturally and consistently issued a statement denying the allegations and claiming that

> Australia poured tens of millions of dollars into that unit and to the consequent trials, and I don't see with that having happened that it is an at all reasonable claim to say that we're a safe haven.[104]

A couple of weeks later, however, doubts about Australia's ability to deal with the issue of the Holocaust and its perpetrators within the confines of its existing legal framework were again raised when Kalejs was forced to leave Britain under the threat of deportation and chose to return to the country which had granted him citizenship in the 1950s after Mexico refused him entry.

---

calls to try alleged war criminal", *Australian*, 16 October 1997, on the refusal of the Federal Police to proceed against Karlis Ozols, another Latvian accused of crimes against humanity, despite the findings of an eminent lawyer assigned to review the file that a *prima facie* case against Ozols existed. Ozols died in March 2001 without having been charged. Larry Schwartz, " 'Nazi' chess champ dead", *Sun Herald*, 8 April 2001.

101. Kimina Lyall, "Revealed: Nazi Kalejs's secret life in suburbia", *Weekend Australian*, 4–5 October 1997.

102. Kimina Lyall and Katherine Towers, "War crimes suspect can stay: PM", *Australian*, 6 May 6, 1998.

103. See Gerard Ryle and Gary Hughes, "Revealed: Australia's welcome to Hitler's scientists", 16 August 1999; Gerard Ryle and Gary Hughes, "QC suggests a Nazi cover-up", 18 August 1999; Gerard Ryle and Gary Hughes, "Rocket Science", 21 August 1999.

104. "Australia's Nazi Hunting Defended", Associated Press, *New York Times*, 6 December 1999.

Kalejs' return to Australia sparked outrage and international concern. Criticism of the British decision not to hold him and to allow him to leave before a full and complete investigation could be completed was harsh not just because of what was perceived as that country's failure to act properly to bring Kalejs to justice, but because of the perception in the international community that he would be untroubled by the law upon his return to Australia.[105]

Once more all the familiar voices and discourses emerged as the government sought to defend its record and others claimed that this was but one more instance of Australian authorities dragging their feet and failing to act when faced with serious allegations of the presence of a perpetrator on their soil. Other equally familiar arguments also emerged, chief among them the intervention of Athol Moffitt, longtime opponent of war crimes prosecutions. In addition to trotting out all the familiar positions about the passage of time and the possibility or otherwise of a fair trial, Moffitt couched his position in his own particularly execrable form of historical relativism. He declared once more that an Australian jury, in order to render justice

> …would have to form a judgment on the circumstances of what happened in an occupied country, and not on what the Nazis did, but on what the country did at a time the country was also under threat of invasion by Russia.[106]

This statement is little more than an updated version of the Jewish Bolshevist conspiracy so proudly proclaimed by all those who seek to deny or minimize the horror and reality of the Holocaust in the so-called Captive Nations. Moffitt asserts that the mass murder of Jews in the Baltic States must be placed in a context which would explain "what the country did". Not only does this do little more than distort the historical record and belittle the horror of the Holocaust, but it subtly reinforces an underlying idea that there were "Latvians" and there were "Jews" and "what the country did" must by definition seek to qualify the mass killing of Jewish citizens as something which can only be understood in a "national" historical context. For all its stupidity, Moffitt's statement does at least have the merit of actually voicing many of the under-

---

105. See Peter Cole-Adams and Simon Mann, "Australia return likely as Kalejs deported", *Sydney Morning Herald*, 4 January 2000; Simon Mann, "Storm gathers as Kalejs flies back", *Sydney Morning Herald*, 7 January 2000; Peter Cole-Adams and Simon Mann, "Fury grows as Kalejs back home", *Sydney Morning Herald*, 8 January 2000; Simon Mann, "World turns up heat over Kalejs", *Sydney Morning Herald*, 8 January 2000.

106. Malcolm Brown, "Time is on his side: Moffitt", *Sydney Morning Herald*, 11 January 2000.

lying ideological and historical tropes which have always informed the debate about the Holocaust and the rule of law in Australia and elsewhere. Just as proponents of prosecution must run the risk of conflicting assertions about uniqueness, specificity and transcendent duty to memory, opponents almost always invoke a vision of history and national identity from which Jews must be excluded.

In fact, the Australian government adopted its own slightly modified spin on the subject. It entered into international talks aimed at mounting a case against Kalejs to be tried by Latvian authorities.[107] The international conference which took place in February 2000 in Riga appeared to have simply replicated the pre-existing discursive practices and tropes which have exemplified post-war attempts to come to grips with the problem of bringing alleged perpetrators before the mechanisms of the legal system. Negotiations surrounding the meetings on the one hand reproduced traditional Cold War animosities between Latvian and Russian authorities.[108] Indeed, the attitudes of the two countries in relation to the case of Mr Kalejs cannot be understood unless they are placed in the broader and more complex historical context of the Holocaust in the Baltic States and the relationship between these countries and the then Soviet authorities. Events contemporaneous with the Kalejs case highlight the ongoing tensions and animosities and reflect the continuity of many of the debates which have surrounded the pursuit of alleged war criminals from that part of the world.

In December 1999, the first prosecution for war crimes occurred in independent Latvia. Tellingly, the action was against Vassily Kononov, a former partisan leader who was charged with killing nine civilians in an "anti-Fascist" raid in the period of German Occupation. In other words, the new democratic regime of Latvia underscored that the rule of law required the prosecution of Soviet war crimes before those committed by the Nazis and their local allies. The system of justice in the independent Captive Nations, under provisions aimed at "crimes of the totalitarian regimes" here reproduced the moral and legal equivalence of Soviet criminality and the Nazi policy and practice of genocide against indigenous Jewish populations.[109] In-

---

107. "Kalejs extradition talks under way with Latvia", AAP, *The Age*, 28 January 2000.

108. Martins Gravitis, "Russia accused over files", *Sydney Morning Herald*, 21 February 2000.

109. "Latvian Academician Was Subject in War Crime Case Against Kononov", *Baltic News Service*, 6 December 1999; "Leading Latvian Historian Equates Cases of War Crimes and KGB Crime", *BBC Worldwide Monitoring*, 5 January 2000; "Latvian Premier Responds to Russian Foreign Ministry", *BBC Worldwide Monitoring*, 25 January 2000; Ian Traynor, "Latvia Accused of Targeting anti-Nazi Fighters", *Guardian*, 19 February 2000.

deed, it might be argued that by proceeding first against an alleged Soviet perpetrator, the government of a democratic Latvia actually gave precedence and primacy to those crimes committed by the "Stalinists" and thereby reduced the significance of crimes against the Jews of the Baltic states to a secondary status.

The prosecution and subsequent conviction of Kononov by the Latvians raised familiar and longstanding objections from local "communists" and "anti-Fascists" as well as from the Russian government who used the case to further claims of discrimination against ethnic Russians and Russophones in Latvia.[110] The issue of the fate of the Jews of Latvia was in fact rhetorically and ideologically removed from discourse about law and justice in the post-Soviet Baltic. When the defense lawyers petitioned for experts to assist the court during the trial on the history of "anti-terrorism" actions, they argued that since neither Soviet nor Western experts could be considered to be neutral, only Israeli historians could be named as impartial court advisors.[111] War crimes in the former Soviet Union became at this stage a political and historical battle over the ideological reconstruction of local history from which the fate of the Jews had been successfully excised and reduced to that of some kind of neutral expertise. It is little wonder that the Kalejs conference soon foundered into a jurisprudential finger pointing exercise.[112]

In addition, and almost as a natural consequence of these debates, the Latvian representatives also raised technical legal doubts about the reliability of allegedly "new" evidence since that evidence could be and was characterized as "Soviet", "Russian" and therefore by definition unreliable. In the years since the adoption of war crimes legislation in Australia, in a period of time since the *Sawoniuk* case in the UK demonstrated that conceptions of justice and fair trials were not contradicted by "Soviet" witnesses, the old Cold War rhetoric about the rule of law simply repeated itself as if in an endless loop of ideology.[113]

---

110. "Arrest of 'Bolsheviks' in Latvia Linked to Trial on War Crimes Charges", *BBC Worldwide Monitoring*, 15 December 1999.

111. "Latvian Court to Consider Inviting Israeli Experts to War Crime Case Hearing", *Baltic News Service*, 8 December 1999.

112. In addition when arguments about the frailty and age of the accused, themes familiar in cases involving alleged Holocaust perpetrators, were raised here, the Lithuanian authorities deemed them relevant not to questions about whether proceedings were justified and just, but only as factors in mitigation at the sentencing stage. "Latvian Jews applaud Kalejs ruling", *Herald Sun*, 30 May 2001.

113. Simon Mann, "Investigators reject Kalejs witnesses", *Sydney Morning Herald*, 18 February 2000; "Riga sets 3-month deadline on new Kalejs evidence", *Sydney Morning Herald*, 19 February 2000.

Finally and most importantly from the perspective of Australian justice and its conception of the place of the Holocaust in the domestic construction of the rule of law, the focus of many of the discussions was on the creation of a Latvian/Australian extradition treaty which would allow Kalejs to be deported and dealt with in his country of origin.[114] The problem here, in addition to the significance of an admission that the Australian justice system is unable or unwilling to deal with the mass extermination of European Jewry as an act offensive to Australian cultural and more importantly legal norms, is that the outcome of the "Kalejs case" became dependent on the internal and historical politics and law of memory in Latvia. In other words, the Holocaust becomes not just not an Australian problem but potentially not even a Latvian problem as both the strength of the case against Kalejs and the willingness of Latvian authorities to prosecute him were called into question[115] While negotiations finally ended in the signing of an extradition agreement between Latvia and Australia, the technical legal arguments about evidence and the burden of proof as well as domestic and international legal and political issues continued to mean that Kalejs maintained a quiet and largely untroubled retired life in Melbourne while various governments and law enforcement agencies argued about who was responsible for putting the Holocaust on trial.[116]

Again, all of the international and legal politicking surrounding the extradition and possible trial of Konrad Kalejs occurred within a discursive matrix in which justice and law were deployed by all sides in ways which best suited the construction of collective memory and national identity of the nation or party concerned. For Australia, the government could be seen to be proceeding to deal with the issue of war criminals while at the same time avoiding all of the pitfalls which had been experienced as a result of the shambles of the *Polyukovich* case. America, Canada and Britain could be seen to be pursuing the question of Kalejs particularly and of perpetrators in general in a situation where they had very little practically at stake. The United States had deported Kalejs. Canada had deported Kalejs and Britain had allowed Kalejs to leave under the threat of deportation. For Latvia, the feeling that they were a small country being "bullied" by larger and more important nations into

---

114. Stuart Rintoul, "Latvia acts to bring in Kalejs", *Australian*, 18 February 2000.

115. Simon Mann, "Kalejs to escape war crimes trial", *Sydney Morning Herald*, 13 May 2000.

116. See "Kalejs may face genocide charges", *Sydney Morning Herald*, 6 July 2000; Mike Seccombe, "Kalejs free to go before law passed", ibid., 7 July 2000; "War crimes questions", ibid., 8 July 2000; "Extradition Deal Signed in Latvia", *New York Times*, 14 July 2000; "Treaty brings Kalejs closer to home", *Sun Herald*, 16 July 2000.

adopting a policy and practice in relation to their own past was virtually unavoidable.[117] In such a context, one can easily conclude that appeals to law and justice as normative concepts which are shared by all parties to such a meeting can be little more than rhetoric meant to disguise the political and culturally specific nature of these ideals when the question of the Holocaust arises.

The attitude and position of the Australian government to subsequent events epitomizes the facility with which the rule of law is invoked and at the same time is rendered meaningless. Konrad Kalejs was the embodiment of the failure of law, or more particularly of the intimate connection between law and Auschwitz. Australia, like Canada and the Britain before them, adopted the American position of attempting to deport alleged perpetrators to the country in which the crimes are alleged to have been committed. Again, this is consistent with the original Moscow Accords but reverses many years of Cold War inspired mistrust of other "justice" systems and the declared policy and practice of forgetting the past. Australia has never deported an alleged war criminal despite requests to do so.[118] Again, the significance and symbolism of such a policy is a difficult one. Is Australia washing its hands of a case which would otherwise be placed in the too hard basket or is it making a definitive statement that such acts as those of which Kalejs was accused are so abhorrent that they are completely foreign to Australian national values? This latter argument would perhaps be more politically and symbolically persuasive if it were accompanied, as are many American and now Canadian decisions, by a denaturalization process. However, the Australian legal system does not permit such measures and the country is now faced with the symbolic conundrum of deporting an Australian for a distinctly and definitively unAustralian crime.[119]

When Latvian authorities laid charges against Kalejs and requested his extradition, Australian police placed Kalejs under arrest. He was released on bail by a magistrate as the wheels of Australian justice ground slowly and inexorably into action, and an Australian magistrate granted the Latvian request in May 2001. Kalejs was, inevitably, an old man. He was suffering from a va-

117. See Simon Mann, "Latvia defends Nazi-hunting record", *Sydney Morning Herald*, 16 February 2000.

118. The most recent of which occurred in 1999. See Ellen Connolly, "Australian charged with Jews' mass murder", *Sydney Morning Herald*, 21 July 1999, dealing with the case of Antanas Gudelis and the Lithuanian government.

119. "Charges laid, but Kalejs out of reach", *Sydney Morning Herald*, 30 September 2000.

riety of medical complaints, from prostate cancer to blindness and dementia. His lawyers argued that not only was he unable to understand or follow the charges and proceedings against him, but that he was unable to remember the past.[120] Extradition proceedings, when contested, as they were in this case, take a long time. Despite statements of approval from spokespersons for the Australian Jewish community that legal processes were at last underway, the legal and jurisprudential reality was that Konrad Kalejs would never stand trial for his alleged crimes. He was old and frail and these facts could easily be invoked to prevent any extradition. Time passed before, during and after the original deportation hearings. His alleged crimes are indescribable and imprescribable.[121] But time, so wisely, carefully and legally used by Kalejs as he fought off efforts in America and Canada and in Australia, to bring him before the bar of justice, or at least law, saved him.[122]

The editorial writer of the *Sydney Morning Herald* highlighted the political, moral and legal dilemmas facing Australia when he argued

> Mr Kalejs insists he is innocent of all allegations that he participated in war crimes. Unless and until it can be proved otherwise, he is entitled to be treated as an innocent man. That may be unpalatable to some people but it is a fundamental requirement of the criminal justice system. It would not only be ironic but also dangerous if Mr Kalejs became subject to the same contempt for the rule of law that he himself is accused of demonstrating in the past.[123]

Proceedings to extradite Kalejs began in April 2001. Debate swirled around issues of Kalejs' physical and mental health. The defence contested the validity, existence and applicability of any extradition treaty between Australia and Latvia. In other words, in Australia the debate around the Holocaust and the killings of European Jewry was, by legal necessity, reduced to traditional technical and boring issues of international law.[124]

---

120. Toby Hemming and Geoff Strong, "Kalejs ordered to face genocide charges", *Age*, 30 May 2001; Alison Crosweller, "Kalejs free after order to extradite", *Australian*, 30 May 2001.

121. See Vladimir Jankélévitch, *L' imprescriptible*, op. cit.

122. See "Kalejs arrested as extradition begins", *Australian*, 14 December 2000; Alison Crosweller, Stuart Rintoul, Carol Altmann, "Kalejs faces lengthy legal battle over extradition", *Australian*, 15 December 2000.

123. "The Kalejs conundrum", 11 January 2000.

124. "Ailing Kalejs ordered to court", *Sydney Morning Herald*, 6 April 2001; "Nazi case absentee", *Weekend Australian*, 28–29 April 2001; Toby Hemming and Geoff Strong, "Legal snag may halt Kalejs extradition", *Sydney Morning Herald*, 15 May 2001; Alison Crosweller,

The truth is stark. Creating a nexus between the place of the Holocaust in national memory and identity in Australia is both possible and impossible after Auschwitz. Kalejs was old, frail, blind, and cancer-filled. He had no memory of what happened. He might have been a mass murderer. The Latvians might have been able to put him on trial before he died. Legal remedies would still have had to be exhausted. Debates about law and justice would flourish before Australian courts and the final decision, whatever it might have been, would have been lawful and legitimate. In the end, of course, if it is or was an end, Konrad Kalejs died in Melbourne without ever having gone on trial for his alleged crimes.[125]

This was a result which may in fact, in a perverse and bizarre way, have been legally correct, and perhaps unjust. Like Imre Finta in Hungary and countless others, Kalejs was really little more than a police officer. He did his job and his job included killing Jews. The killing of the Jews of Latvia took place in a context of legitimate police action against lives unworthy of living, of the death but not the murder, of the extra-legal subject of law, *homo sacer*. This is the truth which all of the legal proceedings against Kalejs, in the United States, Canada, Britain, Australia and Latvia have had to ignore if they are to remain within our shared and inaccurate understanding of law after Auschwitz. We simply could not, nor can we today, accept the possibility that Kalejs and untold others were in fact simply "following orders", lawful orders based in an underlying set of commonly accepted legal norms and practices. Those lawful orders demanded the killing of millions. The price of law is a high one. The debt to justice remains, as it must, unpaid.

"Treaty valid for return of Kalejs", *Australian*, 16 May 2001. "Stretcher-bound Kalejs excused from court", *Sydney Morning Herald*, 23 October 2001; Christopher Zinn, "Medics wheel Nazi suspect to court", *Guardian*, 24 October 2001.

125. See "Accused Nazi war criminal dies", *Sydney Morning Herald*, 9 November 2001; Patrick Barkham, "Konrad Kalejs", *Guardian*, 12 November 2001.

CHAPTER 11

LAW AFTER AUSCHWITZ:
THE EMBODIED FUTURE AND
HOLOCAUST JURISPRUDENCE

In May 2001, political controversy erupted in Germany as the President and Chancellor adopted opposing views on the use of human embryos in medical procedures. For Gerhard Schroeder, the Chancellor, the question was one of future employment for German scientists and technicians, as well as one of preserving the country's status as a scientific and economic power in the new Europe. For President Rau, the whole idea of the human genome project, of embryo implantation and research, reverberated with the country's Nazi past, with eugenics and racial hygiene, echoing similar controversies around the world over issues of embryo stem cell research, cloning, etc.[1] Again, the issue I want to address here is not whether one or the other of the leading German political actors is correct. Instead the dominant question remains the issue of the continuity of parts of Nazi medical and legal ideology within today's institutional discourses and practices. It is my belief that what we find in a variety of instances in which law and medicine intersect in the field of "progress", is that we have in fact advanced little from the 1930s. Many, if not all, of the factors which created the legality of Auschwitz, continue to inhabit today's legal universe. The history of science and the human race as written in medico-legal practice since the end of World War II is in fact a history of law and medicine which is little changed from the era of Nazi science and Nazi law with the consequences too well-known and yet too often ignored in their jurisprudential import.

Professor Jay Katz in his meditation on the legacy of the Holocaust for medical science writes:

---

1. Roger Cohen, "Clash on Use of Embryos in Germany Stirs Echoes of Nazi Era", *New York Times*, 30 May 2001.

And I have attempted to pursue justice—to do justice—to the victims—not merely by commemorating their suffering but also by con-
struing the Nuremberg Code as their unwitting legacy. They were
subject to coercion, sadism, and torture: the Nuremberg Code cele-
brates freedom and human dignity.
As medical professionals, we remain unconvinced that we should embrace the code's principles in the spirit in which they were promul-
gated. It remains my dream that we shall do so. It may only be a
dream, but it comforts my nightmares.[2]

Katz identifies the essential dilemma which informs this book. The Nazi
regime, and its medical, and for me, its legal professionals, inflicted untold
misery, suffering and death. They did so not as self-confessed barbarians, but
as the embodied prophets of a new and advanced civilization. It is this quotidian terror which Hannah Arendt chose to characterize as the "banality of
evil". It is not the evil which shocks us, or which should shock us, but rather
the banal and ordinary character of the terror. The Holocaust was not unlawful, unscientific, or extraordinary. It was lawful, scientific and ordinary.
This is, I believe, the real problem which faces any legal coming to terms with
the past. Katz identifies doctors' unwillingness to accept the horrors committed in their names and the failure to understand the informing ethics and justice of the Nuremberg Code. The reason why this must almost inevitably continue to be the case is that the events which we call the Holocaust and the legal
and medical matrix which made them possible remain virtually unchanged
today. The radical *caesura* argument which predominates jurisprudential ideology simply serves to mask and obfuscate the fundamental reality of the continuity in professional discourses and practices today with those which informed Nazi judges and lawyers. This is the stuff of Katz's nightmares as far
as the medical world is concerned. For those of us with institutional and personal investments in the world of law, our sleep should be equally troubled.

Controversy continues to surface on the issue of medical experimentation
on human subjects after the Nuremberg Trials. Evidence of the "Tuskegee experiments" after the war indicated that African American males who had been
exposed to syphilis were allowed to remain untreated so that doctors and public health officials could study the effects of the different stages of the disease.
While the surviving victims eventually obtained compensation and President

2. "Human Sacrifice and Human Experimentation: Reflections at Nuremberg", *Yale Law
School Occasional Papers*, Second Series, Number 2 (1997).

Bill Clinton issued an official apology to them, the fact remains not just that unlawful, unconsensual medical experimentation continued in the United States well after the horrors of the Nazi medical regime were made public, but also that it is impossible to escape the conclusion that such experiments were informed by a racist taxonomy which allowed the participating doctors to rationalize and explain their conduct in part at least by categorizing their "subjects" as somehow less than human. At the same time, a cold-hearted cost/benefit analysis also allowed the experiments to be justified on the grounds that society as a whole (from which the black subjects were to all intents and purposes excluded) would benefit from the scientific knowledge to be gained. Law did nothing to prevent the experiments or protect the victims since they were, in effect, *homo sacer*, capable of being killed but not murdered in the America which defeated Hitler and gave us Nuremberg and Nazi law as not law.

Similar debates have arisen in relation to medical trials of AIDS treatments of pregnant women in certain "Third World" countries. Some women are treated with AZT and cocktail drug combinations, while others are given a placebo. In the United States, similarly situated women are treated with the so-called drug cocktail. When critics attacked the program as unethical, and compared it to the Tuskegee experiments, supporters responded that such a comparison unfairly belittled the suffering of the Tuskegee men and also that it was unfair since the subjects of the AIDS test had given their consent.[3] Critics raised the issue of the validity of consent among a possibly illiterate subject group as well as the apparent discrepancy between treatment protocols in the United States and those in Thailand and Africa, again raising the specter of racially motivated medical experimentation practices. Despite the furor surrounding these cases, medical science and multi-national drug companies continue to engage in practices in so-called Third World countries which raise serious questions about just what distinguishes this part of modernity from the Nazi worldview. More recently, Pfizer has come under fire for using a meningitis epidemic in rural Nigeria as an opportunity to conduct trials of its controversial antibiotic Trovan.[4] Post-Nuremberg international treaties, human rights consciousness, genocide conventions do nothing.

In Australia, the country has been told that orphans in state institutions were used as unwitting guinea pigs in medical tests until 1970. Australian doctors rejected claims that they had done anything illegal or unethical, and

---

3. Sheryl Gay Stolberg, "Defense for Third-World H.I.V. Experiments", *New York Times*, 2 October 1997.

4. Sarah Boseley, "Ailing ethics", *Guardian*, 20 January 2001.

422   LAW AFTER AUSCHWITZ

specifically rejected claims that what happened in state orphanages had any commonality with the situation in Germany after 1933. The testing of a herpes vaccine on unsuspecting children, wards of the state, was simply dismissed as being in the best interests of the children since herpes was common at the time, so a vaccine against the infection could only have been to their benefit.[5] Ethicist/philosopher Peter Singer tried to dampen public outrage by asserting a relativity argument. For him, the problem is that:

> In condemning the Victorian experiments, carried out between 50 and 30 years ago, we are judging other times by our own higher standards.[6]

The problem with Singer's position is, of course, that he simply ignores history. The standards of fifty or thirty years ago included the trials of Nazi war criminals, doctors and lawyers who legitimated similar practices in Germany. They included the Nuremberg Code. Even by those standards of contemporary ethical and legal norms, the doctors and scientists who conducted the experiments on the inhabitants of Victoria's state institutions were acting unethically. Arguments about moral relativity and historical context may be necessary and important, but accuracy and truth must also count for something. In fact, Singer's assessment is correct only if we are willing to make the unwelcome but necessary step and admit that Nuremberg did nothing to enshrine a new legal morality because it could not, as a legal mechanism, ever transcend the basic jurisprudential and ethical fact of the legality of what it sought to condemn.

What is particularly disturbing about the reaction of many of Australia's leading medical and scientific practitioners after these revelations is not that they carried out unconsensual experiments on human subjects. After all, they were not alone in this. What is disturbing is that these men seem to be aware of the historical experience of medicine under the Nazis and of the Nuremberg Code's requirements in relation to human experimentation, yet they do not, or cannot, see that the Code or the lessons of history should or do apply to them. After all, they are not Nazis; this is not Germany in 1940. Once again, the acceptance of continuity with Nazi Germany is beyond the psychological and existential capacities of today's medical and legal professional elites.

More recently, the National Health Service in the United Kingdom has been rocked by the revelations of the Alder Hay scandal. For years, pathologists at

---

5. Tracy Sutherland and Jamie Walker, "In The Name Of Science", *Australian*, 11 June 1997; Steve Dow, "Trial and Terror: Medical ethics under the microscope", *Sydney Morning Herald*, 14 June 1997.

6. "Research babies: another case of the stolen children", *Sydney Morning Herald*, 11 June 1997.

the Alder Hay Hospital in Liverpool had been removing the organs from dead children without the consent of the parents and had kept those organs for medical experiments or had sold some for profit to multinational drug companies.[7] Officials in Australia confessed at the same time that similar practices had been going on in that country.[8] Again, the point here is that grotesque images of body parts stored in hospitals or research institutions have a distinct and consistent resonance with parts of what we associate with medicine under the Nazis and during the Holocaust. The idea that bodies exist for the progress of science, or for the health and welfare of the body politic, with doctors acting as the final decision makers, is one which would be at home in Nazi Germany. When the Chief Health Officer of New South Wales stated that the debate and controversy over stored body parts was indicative of

…medical practice catching up with community standards[9]

we are simply confronted with the stark realization that medicine and science seem to have progressed little in the fifty years since the horrors of medicine under the Nazis were revealed to a broad public. Again, law had nothing to offer here.

It seems clear from these and other examples that the lessons of the Holocaust are lost on present generations largely because the very idea of relevance and continuity seem beyond their comprehension. Those were Nazis, and we are not Nazis. That was then and this is now. That was not law and we are law bound.

Whatever the outcome of this and similar debates, it remains clear that the shadow of the Holocaust both haunts our contemporary understandings of law and ethics and at other times is mysteriously absent from our contemplation.

One can, as I have argued earlier, easily note in the legal and popular reconstruction of Nazi law the key role of racial hygiene and compulsory sterilization. Not only is the ideological and practical continuity established between and among, racial hygiene>sterilization>euthanasia>Holocaust, but the Nazi medico-legal system of Hereditary Health Courts is most commonly presented as the classic institutional example of the "perversion" of

---

7. See e.g., Jeremy Laurance, "The basement of horrors", *Independent*, 31 January 2001; Lorna Duckworth and Jeremy Laurance, "Three times parents asked Dr van Velzen to leave their son intact. Three times he lied", ibid., Sarah Boseley and David Ward, "Cash for body parts revelations add to trials of children's hospital" *Guardian*, 27 January 2001.

8. Roger Maynard, "Row over body parts erupts in Australia", *Times*, 2 February 2001; Judith Whelan, "Exposed: secret hoard of body parts", *Sydney Morning Herald*, 9 March 2001.

9. Ibid.

the rule of law after 1933. I am not suggesting here that the typology and causal connections constructed in relation to racial hygiene and the Holocaust are incorrect. Indeed, I believe that the medical and scientific schema whereby the "Jew" was constructed as an enemy of the body politic and its legal embodiment are essential to a proper understanding of Nazi law and the rule of law. Where I might be seen to differ from the popular and legal reconstruction of eugenics in the Nazi worldview and legal system lies in the fact that I see the centrality of the location within Nazi law as one which marks it as continuous with many parts of the Western concept of the rule of law. In other words, eugenics, racial hygiene and the concept of a medically, scientifically created taxonomy of physical and racial health, at both the individual and collective levels, as one which could be given a legally sanctioned operative framework, can be found throughout Western legal history, both before, during and after the period of Nazi law. Many of these connections have already been discussed elsewhere in this work. I shall re-emphasize only a few highlights here.

The Nazi legal system with its Hereditary Courts and appellate jurisdiction can easily be constructed as one which reflected, in its structural and "theoretical" aspects, many of the best elements of today's modern administrative quasi-judicial system. Here, questions of social and personal importance are decided by judicial and quasi-judicial bodies which are constituted by governments to embrace both judicially oriented members (judges, lawyers etc.) and experts in the particular field(s) falling under the jurisdiction of the tribunal, in this case medical personnel. Again, I am not suggesting either that Nazi practice necessarily reflected the norms implied by the legal and structural framework under which they were to function, nor am I even suggesting that the compulsory sterilization of the "mentally defective" is an epistemologically or morally acceptable state or judicial function. I am again briefly making a more basic case that Nazi law, both in form and substance, did not at this point of its history deviate from the norms of any acceptable definition, contemporary or current, of the rule of law.

This is why, for example, the rhetorical construction of Nazi "racial hygiene" and Hereditary Health Courts as "not law" bears no relationship either to this historical reality or to the actual judicial construction of these courts at Nuremberg and after. As I have already noted, the prosecution case against the individual named defendants who were indicted for crimes against humanity in relation to the sterilization program did not seek to condemn them for their participation *per se*, but rather invoked those instances in which they "perverted" or "distorted" accepted legal practice and principles under the guise of the "rule of law". The accused in fact were not convicted for their role in this process. Once more, I am not offering this example as an apologia for the system of Nazi law, or for the acts of particular individuals. I am simply pointing out, yet again, that Nazi law was law, that eugenics and eugenic practices under the guise of law were law.

This position, defining these central aspects of Nazi legal ideology and practice as "legal", marks Nazi law as continuous within the Western legal canon. The history of compulsory sterilization on eugenic grounds in the United States and Canada, as I have also pointed out, confirms this view. More recent revelations about the practice of eugenic sterilization elsewhere offer further support for this positioning of Nazi law within the Western canon.

News reports and government inquiries indicate that eugenic sterilization was an accepted medical and social practice until recent times and even up to today. In the Scandinavian states, more than 100,000 Norwegians, Swedes and Danes were subjected to compulsory sterilization after being deemed undesirable.[10] Many of these procedures occurred at the time Denmark and Norway were under Nazi occupation and many more after they were liberated. Danes and Norwegians are today justifiably proud of their records in resisting Nazi rule. At the same time however, their own governments continued to practice medical procedures which were condemned by the Allies after the war and which are seen by many as having been central to Nazi racial theory and practice. Most recent figures put the number of compulsory sterilizations in Norway between 1934 and 1976 at 2000.[11] In yet another example of Norwegian practices which echo tragically with law both before and after Auschwitz, another report indicates that Norwegian doctors conducted experiments involving the effect of radiation by castrating psychiatric patients with x-rays in the 1950s and 1960s. These experiments are directly related to those conducted by Nazi doctors, condemned by the West and "outlawed" by the Nuremberg Code.[12]

In Sweden, the home of the social democratic model of Scandinavian politics, over 60, 000 "genetically defective" individuals were compulsorily sterilized between 1935 and 1976.[13] As one report put it:

10. See also "Swedish Scandal", Editorial, *New York Times*, 30 August 1997.

11. "2,000 Norwegians underwent forced sterilisations: health ministry", Agence France Presse, 26 August 1997. More than a thousand similar cases were reported in Finland.

12. See George Annas and Michael Grodin (eds.), *The Nazi Doctors and the Nuremberg Code: Human Rights in Human Experimentation* (Oxford and New York: Oxford University Press, 1995).

13. See Stephanie Hyatt, "A Shared History of Shame: Sweden's Four-Decade Policy of Forced Sterilization and the Eugenics Movement in the United States", 8 *Ind. Int'l & Comp.*

In some recesses of its collective memory, the Swedish nation already knew of the extraordinary eugenic practices carried out by its Social Democrat governments between 1935 and the 1960s; but the knowledge had been repressed.[14]

What is particularly interesting from the viewpoint of the question of continuity and discontinuity which haunts our collective memory and imagination of Nazi law is that the Swedish case offers further evidence that eugenic discourse and practice was not limited to the far right of the political spectrum. There, eugenic sterilization and the ideological, political and legal framework which defined and constructed the racially acceptable and undesirable, was created by parties of the Left and opposed, in those few cases when opposition was voiced, from the Right.[15] In fact, the justification for compulsory sterilization in Sweden carried with it direct echoes of the combined "scientific" and "economic" rationales for similar practices in Germany.[16] A belief in genetic inferiority and attacks on the racial purity of the body politic were combined with fears that the cradle to grave welfare state of the Social Democrats would be bankrupted by the drain placed on limited resources by deviants, gypsies and other "inferior people".[17] Another case, like that in Norway, also indicates that Swedish authorities were quite willing to extract some "value" from these drains on the economy. Thus,

Hundreds of "mentally deficient" Swedes were made to let their teeth rot after being force-fed candy in dental experiments from 1946 to 1951....

L. R. 475 (1998); Alex Duval Smith and Maciej Zaremba, "Outcasts from Nordic Super-Race", *Observer*, 24 August 1997; "Sweden admits to racial purification", *Independent*, 25 August 1997.

14. Birna Helgadottir and Cathy Savage, "Sweden reels at scandal of forced sterilisations", *European*, 28 August 1997. See also Olivier Truc, "L'eugénisme à la mode suédoise", *Libération*, 30 March 2000. Roger Boyles, "Sterilisation law reveals Sweden's repressive state", *Times*, 31 March 2000.

15. Maciej Zaremba, "Inside Europe: Dagens Nyheter: Delusions of Racial Purity", *The Guardian*, 3 September1997. While some saw this as an opportunity to score political points against "liberals", see Robert Fox and Ben Fenton, "Eugenics: the skeleton in the liberals' cupboard", *Daily Telegraph*, 29 August 1997, others chose to underline the continuity issue both politically and legally. See e.g., Jeremy Laurance, "A short step from different to undesirable; Britain's role in the move to purify Europe's races", *Independent*, 30 August 1997; Geoffrey Wheatcroft, "When Churchill and Hitler were in the same camp", *Sunday Telegraph*, 31 August 1997; "Terrible dilemma facing 100 families", *Daily Mail*, 12 September 1997.

16. See Götz Aly et al., *Cleansing the Fatherland*, op. cit.

17. Leading Article, *The Daily Telegraph*, 29 August 1997.

...

According to the paper, the study received international attention and was the basis of a Swedish dental care plan established in 1956.[18]

In the same year as the Nuremberg Trial of Major War Criminals, in the same year as the horrors of Nazi rule and Nazi law were exposed to the world in a legal forum, Swedish medical officials conducted unconsensual experiments.

Two other elements of the Swedish case also deserve attention. First, the law was not only implemented in 1934, but it was, like the Alberta legislation in Canada, modified during the period of World War Two. In 1941, the legislation was broadened to include more anti-social individuals.[19] While the Holocaust was underway all around it, Sweden not only profited from trade with Germany and from stolen assets and gold but it also democratically expanded the number and type of Swedes who could be compulsorily sterilized.

The second element of the Swedish system which deserves out attention here is the issue of voluntary sterilization. Some might point to the "voluntary" nature of procedures permitted in Germany under the Hereditary Health legislation as little more than a smokescreen in a system in which free choice was an illusion. It is not necessary here to refute or even contest the validity of this position as universally correct. It is clear, as a matter of experience and practice, that the notion of voluntariness can and does obfuscate and mask many power imbalances "even" in our society today. In Sweden, for example, competent individuals, by law, had to give their consent to sterilizations, thus making them "voluntary". However, as others have pointed out in the Swedish context, this is as problematic as it was under Nazi law. For example, sterilization was made a condition for release from hospitals, mental institutions and homes, just as it was made a condition for marriage.[20] Similarly, social welfare benefits were withheld or withdrawn if the individual did not "consent" to sterilization.[21] Again, it is unnecessary to enter into a lengthy discussion here of the issues of "consent", "coercion" and "power". It is sufficient to point to the similarities between the situation under Nazi law and that under Swedish law both before and after Auschwitz.[22]

---

18. "'Inferior' Swedes force-fed candy in dental study 1946–1951', Agence France Presse, 22 September 1997.

19. See supra, chapter 4.

20. Stephanie Hyatt, "A Shared History of Shame", op. cit., at 485–87.

21. Maciej Zaremba, "Delusions of Racial Purity", op. cit.

22. A commission of inquiry was appointed by the Swedish government and later recommended the payment of compensation to the victims of the program. See "Swedish government appoints head of sterilisation commission", Agence France Presse, 4 September

Similar revelations have been made in France, where at least 15,000 such sterilizations were carried out in state institutions in violation of French law, but without the imposition of any sanctions on the doctors who apparently carried out these operations.[23] Another study indicated that 225 handicapped French women were sterilized without their consent between 1995 and 1996. That report concludes that these sterilizations were illegal but "virtually tolerated".[24] Other studies revealed that the level of sterilizations among both men and women who suffered from mental illness were statistically far higher than among the general population cohort.[25] More recent evidence has emerged of "unofficial" policies under which handicapped women are accepted into workshop facilities or allowed to become engaged only after undergoing illegal sterilization procedures.[26]

Switzerland, like Sweden troubled by its role in the "Nazi gold" saga, also suffered from revelations that the practice of compulsory sterilization of the mentally handicapped and other non-desirables was still going on.[27] In Belgium, reports have shown that in 1985, the government pressured a citizen into undergoing sterilization before permitting her to marry.[28] Japan has also been named as a culprit in this field.[29] Reports have also surfaced that South African security forces sought to develop ways of sterilizing blacks en masse during the

---

1997; "Plan d'indemnisation pour les victimes de stérilisation forcée en Suède", *Libération*, 28 January 1999; Antoine Jacob, "La Suède va indemniser les victimes de la stérilisation forcée", *Le Monde*, 31 January – 1February, 1999; "La Suède va indemniser les victimes des stérilisations forcées, *Libération*, 6–7 March 1999; Stephen Bates, "Sweden pays for its shameful past in pursuit of 'racial purity'", *Guardian Weekly*, 14 March 1999; Carol William, "Sweden compensates citizens who were forcibly sterilized", *Los Angeles Times*, 14 November 1999.

23. "15,000 Frenchwomen Reportedly Sterilized", *New York Times*, 9 September1997; Susannah Herbert, "15,000 forcibly sterilised in France, *Daily Telegraph*, 11 September 1997; Ben Macintyre, "Outcry in France at illegally sterilised women", *Times*, 13 September 1997.

24. "France Sterilise", AP, 2 October 1998.

25. "Handicapés mentaux: des stérilisations en toute illégalité", *Libération*, 1 October 1998.

26. Balndine Grosjean, "La stérilisation des handicapées mentales sort de l'ombre", *Libération*, 30 May 2001.

27. "Swiss in widening sterility scandal", *Times*, 29 August 1997; "Hitler asked for copies of laws that could sterilise promiscuous idiots'", *Herald*, 28 August 1997.

28. "Europeans face sterilization dilemma", Associated Press, 28 August 1997.

29. Mari Yamaguchi, "Japan: Victims Begin to Talk about Japan's Sterilization Program", AAP, 21 December 1997.

white supremacist apartheid regime.[30] When Dr Wouter Basson was acquitted of criminal charges in the spring of 2002, controversy ensued. What did not follow the judicial conclusion was any careful and thoughtful consideration of the sources of the controversy. Was Basson's acquittal evidence of a legal continuity with apartheid-era personnel and ideology? Was it attributable to other factors, not the least of which would be troubling concerns that the immorality of his actions in no way lead to any definitive answer about their illegality?[31] How can a government plan to sterilize a portion of the population determined to be "dangerous" be *ipso facto* illegal when such policies and practices fit so easily and convincingly within the accepted tropes of Western, post-Nazi legality?

Similarly, Austria, with its troubled historical and legal collective relationship with the Nazi past also found itself wrapped up in the 1997 flurry of stories about compulsory sterilization. Indeed, the Austrian case highlights the complexities not just of the substantive ethical issues involved but also the complicated nature of the construction of continuities and discontinuities within legal discourse and memory. Thus,

> In Austria—and who would have thought it—everything took place (is still taking place?) in a legal gray area. It appears that nobody is really sure whose consent (parents, trustees, guardianship tribunals) is required for which operations.[32]

Not only must Austria, like the other countries, face up to past and current practices and the clear issues of continuity and the myths of discontinuity with the Nazi legal past, but that country must also face a situation of legal ambiguity where its legal system lacks even the apparent clarity of the unlawful, extra-legal system of the carefully drafted Nazi eugenic juridical framework. It may be that on one possible jurisprudential analysis, Austria, the "first victim of Nazi aggression", operated under a system even more "not law" than Nazi law. Indeed, the complexities of Austria's difficult medical-legal history have been further troubled by more recent revelations that the famous medical school at the University of Vienna not only was a place where the dissection of cadavers of prisoners executed by the Nazis occurred, but that many of the body parts remained on view in the department and were used in the

---

30. See "Special Investigation into Project Coast: South Africa's Chemical and Biological Warfare Programme", Truth and Reconciliation Commission, 1998.

31. See "Apartheid-era scientist acquitted", *Associated Press*, 11 April 2002.

32. Gudrun Harrer, "Time for Austria to Face Facts", *The Guardian*, 3 September 1997. See also, Roger Boyes, "Austria 'sterilises mentally handicapped women'", *The Times*, 28 August 1997.

writing of a medical textbook.[33] The remains of child victims of Nazi euthanasia programs were kept for decades at the Spiegelgrund clinic where Dr. Heinrich Gross, one of the country's leading medical researchers, used them for his studies, during and after the Nazi period. A public memorial service and burial was held in the spring of 2002, in part at least to help Austria close this dark chapter of its history. Dr. Gross continues to hold the country's Order of Merit for his contributions to science.[34]

Another example of the complexities of our collective legal memory and its relationships with Nazi law and eugenics can be found in a brief return to the situation in Canada. There, the Alberta eugenic sterilization legislation was not repealed until 1972. After the end of the Second World War, the provincial Eugenics Board continued to operate, approving the sterilization of Alberta citizens, often in clear violation of the letter of the law but with the tacit approval of the provincial government. Only in 1997 did some of the victims receive some legal compensation.[35] Others continue to pursue the government for a policy, which was condemned in the rhetoric and pedagogy of Nuremberg, if not in its technical legal reality, as a crime against humanity. The government adopted the legal position when faced with compensation claims that the sterilizations had been performed in accordance with the law of the day.[36] Similarly, when faced with claims from survivors of their compulsory sterilization program, government lawyers in the state of Michigan successfully invoked the statute of limitations to defeat a demand for compensation.[37] While offering an apology, the Michigan government, like their Alberta counterparts, was at pains to point out that under the ethos and laws of the times, the practices in question were doubtlessly legal.

Such an attitude is hardly surprising. As I have already argued above, there can be little doubt that the Alberta statutory regime fit comfortably within the

---

33. "Austria Nazis", AP, 2 October 1998; Michael Leidig, "Nazi victims dissected for medical book", *Sydney Morning Herald*, 14 October 1998.

34. See, Barbara Miller, "Child remains from Nazi 'euthanasia' clinic laid to rest", *Independent*, 25 April 2002; Kate Connolly, "Unquiet grave for Nazi child victims", *Guardian*, 29 April 2002; Pierre Daum, "Vienne enterre ses victimes de l'euthanasie", *Libération*, 29 April 2002.

35. Emily Buchanan, "Playing God with people's lives", *Guardian Weekly*, 23 March 1997.

36. "Sterilization cases handled poorly, critic says", *Globe and Mail*, 2 July 1996. See also, Aaron Sands, "Sterilization in Ontario Too: Swedish Scandal Not Unique", *Toronto Star*, 28 August 1997.

37. "Sterilization Suit Dismissed", *New York Times*, 10 March 2000; Damian Whitworth, "Eugenics Victim Sues Over Ordeal 60 Years Ago", *Times*, 10 March 2000.

normative and discursive structures of what was recognizable as law and lawful. Amendments were approved in the public legislative forum and were known across the country. Long after the end of World War Two, after the Holocaust and after Nuremberg, legal commentators pointed to the Alberta legislation without any type of comment, treating it simply as a form of positive law of which practitioners should be aware.[38] Even subsequent legal discussion of the situation in Alberta, while condemning much of the way in which the Board acted and the legislative categories allowing sterilization as unscientific, nonetheless failed to escape the discursive matrix of "science" and "eugenics". Thus, the authors of the study comment that:

> Since the act requires unanimity of decision from the board, the presence of a geneticist would almost certainly prevent any action by the board without consent and without overwhelming genetic indication.[39]

In essence, the authors' critique is one which condemns the *Act* and the Board as operating under false scientific assumptions. They merely want to point out that nature takes care of the "unfit" by making sure that they do not survive long enough to reproduce or that they suffer from low reproductive capacities. They argue in favor of "positive eugenics"[40] and in the end they would allow eugenic sterilization to continue as long as current scientific criteria and knowledge are applied. With friends like these, it is little wonder that the government of Alberta can continue to maintain that it acted "lawfully".

At the same time, the shadow of legalized eugenic sterilization continues to haunt the collective and public memory of the province of Alberta and its institutions. At the University of Alberta, the Department of Psychology has voted to rename a lecture series and classroom named after Professor John MacEachran. MacEachran was the founder of the Department. He also sat on the provincial Eugenics Board between 1928 and 1964, as Chair. The removal of the Professor from the public and collective memory of the Faculty and the University was not without controversy. Some pointed out that eugenic ster-

---

38. "Comments Upon the Law Relating to Abortion and Sterilization", 33 *Manitoba Bar News* 38 (1961). The author also pointed to the existence of similar legislation in British Columbia and 29 of the United States. See also, Canadian Press, "B.C. Supreme Court approves settlement in castration case", *Globe and Mail*, 21 June 2002.

39. K. G. McWhirter and J. Weijer, "The Alberta Sterilization Act: A Genetic Critique", 19 *U.T.L.J.* 424 (1969).

40. Ibid. at. 431.

ilization was a publicly acceptable and accepted policy at the time MacEachran acted on the Board and that the Faculty was engaging in a process of histori-cal relativization. Others argued in reply that while this may have been true in 1924, it could not be said to be the case up to 1964.[41] Like the attempt of students in Lyon to rid their university of references to Alexis Carrel the ac-tions at the University of Alberta indicate in a small context the ways in which law, legality and historical memory in relation to eugenics and thence to the Holocaust, continue to be played out in our public and private decision-mak-ing processes and memories.

Courts continue to sanction the compulsory sterilization of the "mentally handicapped", and the rhetoric of the "best interests of the child" resonates with some of the justifications found in the literature in support of eugenic sterilization in the 1920s and 1930s.[42] Meanwhile, in Australia for example, recent studies reveal that while the legal standard requires the approval of the Family Court for all sterilizations performed on minors, more than 1,200 such procedures have occurred, only 20 of which have been judicially approved. In other words, Australian doctors in the 1990s carried out illegal, "compulsory" sterilizations on minors, a practice for which their German colleagues of 50 years ago were labeled as barbarians and criminals who had perverted medi-cine in civilized countries.[43] At the same time, that country is forced to face up to the role played by eugenic policies and practices in light of various in-quiries and court cases involving the forced "assimilation" of Aboriginal chil-dren.[44] Other Australian stories have uncovered cases in which young wards of the state in Victorian orphanages were used as medical guinea pigs,[45] all in the period after the end of the Second World War, after Australia prosecuted

---

41. Brian Laghi, "Late professor's eugenics role costs him honours", *Globe and Mail*, 12 October 1997.

42. In Australia, see *Secretary, Department of Health and Community Services v. J.W.B. and S.M.B.*, 175 C.L.R. 218, (1991–9292); In Canada, see *In Re Eve*, 31 D.L.R. (4th) 1 (1986); in the United States, see *Stump v. Sparkman* 435 U.S. 349 (1978).

43. Melissa Sweet, "Court warns doctors on illegal sterilisation", *Sydney Morning Her-ald*, 16 April 1997; Cynthia Banham, "Maree mourns lost chance at motherhood", *Sydney Morning Herald*, 26 April 2001; Susan Brady, John Briton, and Sonia Grover, *The Sterili-sation of Girls and Young Women*, Human Rights and Equal Opportunity Commission, April 2001.

44. See *Bringing Them Home*, op. cit.

45. See e.g. Tracy Sutherland and Jamie Walker, "In the Name of Science", *Australian*, 11 June 1997; Peter Singer, "Research babies: another case of the stolen children", *Sydney Morning Herald*, 11 June 1997; Steve Dow, "Trial and Error", *Sydney Morning Herald*, 14 June 1997.

Japanese war criminals for acts of "barbarity". Indeed, more recent discoveries indicate that Australian government medical experiments were conducted to find a cure for malaria on unsuspecting soldiers and Jewish immigrants who had just escaped from the Nazis in Europe.[46]

At the same time, advances in genetic technology now permit parents to engage in a form of privatized eugenics by allowing them to test and abort embryos found to have "unacceptable" genetic traits.[47] Governments ban cloning for the time being but Dolly the sheep captures the public imagination, and doctors threaten or promise, depending on one's perspective, the first cloned human being by 2003.

Meanwhile, in Colombia, and in Brazil, security forces are reported to engage in "*impieza social*" or social cleansing, the killing of vagrants, criminals and street children, all of whom are classified as socially undesirable.[48] In Brazil and Peru, sterilization of poor and indigenous women either as part of election campaigning or as part of government rationality in the war on poverty continues.[49] "Population control" policies in Peru allegedly resulted in the forced sterilizations of 250,000 poor and indigenous women under Alberto Fujimori's presidency.[50] Kidneys are taken from the poor of Korea and India for transplantation into wealthy patients and organs and babies are offered for sale on the Internet.[51]

In Europe, North America and Australia, campaigners argue for euthanasia legislation. Dutch doctors happily admitted exceeding existing guidelines by performing non-consensual killings of patients, even those suffering from mental illness from whom "consent" cannot be obtained.[52] Their refusal to

---

46. See Gerard Ryle and Gary Hughes, "Troops and refugees given malaria", *Sydney Morning Herald*, 19 April 1999.

47. Alanna Mitchell, "Clinic to sift out bad genes", *Globe and Mail*, 24 September 1997; Alanna Mitchell and Jane Coutts, "Making baby in a petri dish: There are things going on in fertility clinics that federal authorities know nothing of", *Globe and Mail*, 27 September 1997.

48. Jan McGirk, "Honduras investigates murders of 1,300 street children", *Independent*, 4 September 2002; Duncan Campbell, "300 street kids swept away like rubbish", *Guardian*, 30 June 2000; "Vigilantes in Colombia Kill Hundreds of 'Disposables'", *New York Times*, 31 October 1994. Duncan Campbell, "Murdered with impunity, the street children who live and die like vermin", *Guardian*, 29 May 2003.

49. See e.g., Alex Bellos, "Indian women 'sterilised for votes' in Brazil", *Guardian Weekly*, 27 September 1998; Adela Gooch and Jane Diaz Limaco, "Peru forced sterilisation of poor women", *Guardian Weekly*, 10 January 1999.

50. Reuters, "Fujimori accused of encouraging forced sterilizations", 25 July 2002.

51. See e.g., Lisa Priest, "Ban trade in organs, critics urge", *Globe and Mail*, 2 June 2001.

52. See "Psychiatrists will help patients with death wish", Reuters, 6 June 1997; Ian Murray, "Holland loses grip on mercy killing", *Times*, 16 February 1999.

obey the law led not to prosecution but to the legalization of euthanasia in the Netherlands, soon followed by neighboring Belgium.[53] In other words, more than fifty years after the Nuremberg trials, almost sixty years after German doctors decided that their duty to the *Volk* included the extermination of life unworthy of life, today's medical practitioners readily and without question adopt the same attitudes and practices as their Nazi predecessors. They proceed unhindered and in the Dutch case, positively encouraged by the rule of law.

In another field of related academic endeavor, many now regard the early days of "scientific" criminology as embodied in the work of Lombroso as irrelevant to today's discipline with its complex environmental and sociological understandings and explanations of crime and criminology as naïve and laughable. They also dismiss the days of the happy marriage between biology and crime as historical artifacts, made irrelevant by these same historical advances in our analyses of environment and societal factors. Others, however, raise more serious concern. Some point out the continuity in the ways in which for example "homosexuality" has been constructed in criminology and criminal law up to and including today.[54] Others might also choose to point out that biological explanations of criminality have never fully disappeared. While such theories were for a time apparently discredited by the revelations of Nuremberg etc., it now appears that they were in fact simply driven underground, unarticulated. Now, as fear of crime and the dangerous Other once more dominates one set of social discourses, while at the same time, other political and social conversations circulate around issues of race, we can witness the resurgence of biological explanations of criminal behavior.[55] At the same time some states in the United States have enacted legislation per-

---

53. See Andrew Osborn, "Mercy killing now legal in Netherlands", *Guardian*, 1 April 2002; Michelle Lamensch, "La dépénalisation est annoncée", *Le Soir*, 5 April 2002; Andrew Osborn, "Belgian outcry over first mercy killing under new law", *Guardian*, 9 October 2002. A similar legislative proposal was also made in France. See Bernard Debré, "La loi sur l'euthanasie est indigne", *Libération*, 6 June 2002.

54. See e.g., Stephen Tomsen, "Was Lombroso a queer? Criminology, criminal justice and the heterosexual imaginary", in *Homophobic Violence*, (Gail Mason and Stephen Tomsen eds.) (Sydney: Federation, 1997) at 33.

55. See e.g., Terrie E. Moffitt and Sarnoff A. Mednick (eds.), *Biological Contributions to Crime Causation* (The Hague: Kluwer, 1988); Lee Ellis and Harry Hoffman (eds.), *Crime in Biological, Social, and Moral Contexts* (Westport, CT: Praeger, 1990); Adrian Raine, *The Psychopathology of Crime: Criminal Behavior as a Clinical Disorder* (London: Academic Press, 1997). For a critique, see Nicole Hahn Rafter, *Creating Born Criminals* (Champaign, IL.: University of Illinois Press, 1997).

mitting the "chemical castration" of child molesters.[56] As "biology" explains crime, biological solutions for criminology must inevitably follow.

While "race' is often explicitly rejected as an irrelevant category to current "scientific" debate about criminals and criminality, it cannot be said, in the current social, political and legal context in which these interventions are situated, that race is in fact not relevant to what is being talked about. Again, it is important to note that I am not suggesting that those who seek to investigate and establish a scientific or biological link between crime and criminals are by definition Nazis or racists or that their work will lead inevitably to another Holocaust. Rather I am suggesting that there nonetheless exists an ideological and discursive continuity between these debates today and similar debates around eugenics in the early part of the century, continuities which we ignore at our peril and continuities of which we must be aware if we are to "understand" today the full meaning and implication for us of the "Holocaust".

Law, Jurisprudence, Bodies, Auschwitz

Imagine two judges in Weimar Germany in 1930. One is a Socialist, the other is a National Socialist. One interprets the Constitution as an instrument for the promotion of participatory democracy and the elimination of injustice. Certainly, the fact that the Weimar Constitution contained provisions guaranteeing social welfare and other "collective" rights would serve as a textual and contextual adjudicative support for this interpretative position. The second, influenced by the jurisprudence of Professor Carl Schmitt, believes that the true meaning and character of the Weimar Constitution is to be found in Article 48 which allows for a strong central executive to suspend other parts of the Constitution in times of emergency.

What we have here is a clear jurisprudential debate between two alternate readings of the same text. Each can be articulated by deploying the technical tools available to and recognizable by judges and lawyers as adjudication. There is here no epistemological, ontological or phenomenological distinction between these two judges or between these two judges and those Supreme Court justices described and deconstructed by Allan Hutchinson in his discussion of *R.A.V.* in his jurisprudential work, *It's All in the Game.*[57]

---

56. "Recent Legislation", 110 *Harv. L. R.* 799 (1997).
57. Op. cit.

Hutchinson articulates a complex and sophisticated vision of what is encompassed in our understandings of what it means to be a judge and to act like a judge. For him, the central requirement in adjudication is that of good faith:

> What the requirement of good faith does demand, however, is that whatever interpretation is offered or whatever application is suggested, it must result from a genuine effort to make sense of the rule in hand or to deploy law's argumentative resources in a conscientious way. Understood in this way, the requirement of good faith is more an issue of moral integrity than a matter of analytical accuracy; it is less about legal rightness than it is about political reasonableness.[58]

A great judge, a jurisprudential giant is one who acts within the parameter of good faith adherence to the rules of judging and the rule of law, to expand in a convincing manner the boundaries of the form, shape and content of legal rules themselves. We know from the sad and tragic history of Germany in the 1930s and 1940s that the Nazi judge here, assuming he truly believes what he believes, can easily be seen to be a judge engaging in acts of adjudication. We also know, that, after 1933, the Nazi judge would be recognizable as a great judge if and when he in good faith interpreted the text of a statute or of the Constitution in line not with its letter but with the spirit of the mass of Germany's citizenry and the political, cultural and social possibilities of that context. Then a judge who based a decision not in the black letter text of the Civil Code but in an innovative, skillful, new way of reading the political and cultural contingencies of the time and place in which the law was to be contextualized, the *Volksgeist*[59] in other words, could be easily classified as a great judge. Here the great judge would offer an expansive and contextualized reading of the apparent legal bar to annulment unless there was proof of an essential vice or defect not known to the petitioner at the time of marriage. The judge would find that even though the petitioner "knew" when they married in the 1920s that their spouse was a Jew, they could not have "known" then what it really meant to be a Jew and to marry a Jew. The legal text would take on a new life, breathed into it by the ludic brilliance and panache of a great judge. An apparently insurmountable bar to annulment is removed by innovative and good faith interpretation.

This same great judge might argue in another case that the legislative intent informing the ban on "sexual intercourse" between German and Jew must

---

58. Ibid. at 191.
59. See Jacques Derrida, *Of Spirit* (Chicago and London: University of Chicago Press, 1989).

be read broadly; it must be construed in line with the latest discoveries of racial science and within the social and political context of the society. It must be read in light of other provisions prohibiting for example the employment of young German women as domestic servants in the households of Jewish men.

I agree with Allan Hutchinson when he argues that our understanding of judges and judging and of the central element of applied jurisprudence is that:

> (Good faith) is more an issue of moral integrity than of analytical accuracy....[60]

I also agree with Michael Stolleis, that:

> Once the recommendations of natural law of the postwar period had lost their persuasive force..., the only thing left was recourse to a value-bound private morality, civic virtues, and democratic consciousness, and an appeal to the legal profession's sense of political responsibility.[61]

Here Stolleis is addressing the vital issue, central to much of the discussion in previous parts of this book of what separates Germany (and us) from a relapse into Nazi legality. There can be little doubt that he is correct when he identifies a professional sense of political responsibility, private morality and civic virtues and even democratic consciousness as apparently intimately connected with our current understandings of democratic, liberal, rule of law based judicial decision-making. Yet, as I have attempted to show throughout this book, each of these concepts is at some important level vacuous and of little assistance. Nazi judges were democratic if we think that democracy has something to do with combining majority opinion and appeal to broadly and deeply held values. They had a deep sense of conviction and personal ethics. Indeed, it is perhaps tragically ironic that the most deeply ethical of German judges in the mid- to late 1930s must have been the true Nazis for at least they acted out of moral and political conviction and not out of personal ambition and moral cowardice. What Stolleis' list of juridical virtues can not tell us is the substantive content of the rules which would be developed by Nazi judges and those which would be developed by liberal judges. I would like to turn briefly to a discussion of a recent case from England, which gives us what I believe to be a distinctly unpleasant response to this question.

---

60. *It's All in the Game*, at 191.
61. *The Law under the Swastika*, op. cit., at 21–22.

In the late summer and early autumn of 2000, the media in the United Kingdom and elsewhere became fascinated with the case of Maltese twin girls, known only as Jodie and Mary. The girls were conjoined, or more popularly, Siamese, twins. Their parents were a poor Maltese couple who were able to bring their daughters to England for medical care not available in their native country. The basic and fundamental dilemma facing the parents, the doctors and ultimately the Courts, was that if there were no medical intervention, both twins would die. If they were surgically separated, Mary, the "weaker" of the two, would die while Jodie had excellent prospects. The parents, devout Roman Catholics, refused to choose between their daughters and the hospital authorities sought a judicial order allowing them to proceed with the surgery.

Here the Courts were faced in the starkest possible terms with what Guido Calabresi has described as "tragic choices".[62] What interests me here is what I see as the direct parallel between what the judges in this case, all of whom authorized the medicalized killing of Mary to save Jodie, did and what Nazi lawyers and judges did in 1930s Germany. Again, I am not arguing that Lord Justices Ward, Brooke and Walker are Nazi judges. I am not arguing that the case of Mary and Jodie signals a phase of mass euthanasia in England. I am asserting, however, that there is little, if any, jurisprudential, legal, or ethical distinction between what these judges did and what their Nazi brethren did. In other words, I am suggesting, as I have throughout, that there is no inherent epistemological, ontological juridical set of ideas, concepts or practices which distinguish Nazi law from our law. More importantly, I am also arguing that there are instances in which procedural or experiential similarities between being a lawyer or judge then and now are supplanted by substantive, doctrinal, rule-based instances in which judges today, in liberal democracies in fact and in law, do exactly that for which their Nazi forebears are so vigorously and consistently condemned. They sanction and permit the taking of "life unworthy of life". They allow for the official jurisprudential recognition of the modern *homo sacer*, the legal subject who can be killed but not murdered.

The case of Mary and Jodie is a complex legal one, involving technical issues of family law, guardianship, and criminal law. It is not my intention here to subject the case to a close technical legal reading. Instead I want to highlight a few examples of how the appellate judges in this instance simply condoned the killing of Mary, a life unworthy of living.

---

62. *Tragic Choices* (New Haven: Yale University Press, 1978) (with Phillip Bobbit).

First, it is important to place the case briefly in the context of recent medical and legal developments in the United Kingdom. In *Airedale N.H.S. Trust v. Bland*, the House of Lords had already recognized that the parents of a patient in a permanent vegetative state, could be granted permission to cease medical intervention.[63] In other words, the Court in that instance gave judicial backing to the long-argued distinction between "passive" and "active" euthanasia and accepted that withdrawal of life support apparatus etc. was not an "act" aimed at taking a life. More recently in *A National Health Trust v. D.*[64] Mr. Justice Cazalet found that "death with dignity" was permissible under European law and did not contravene the right to life in Art. 2 or the right not to be subjected to inhuman or degrading treatment of Art. 3 of the European Convention.

> Weighing, from the child's standpoint, any possible very limited short-term extension of his short-life span against the increased pain and suffering caused by the processes of intensive care and artificial ventilation, his Lordship considered that full palliative treatment as advocated by the paediatricians in the declaration as sought was in the child's best interests and would allow him to die with dignity.[65]

In the case of Jodie and Mary, of course, the solution could never be as neat and simple as making arguments either in the best interests of the child, or in reality in the idea of "death with dignity". Here, Mary's best interests could never be said to lie in being killed and there is arguably very little dignity in being subjected to a surgical cutting the only possible result of which is death. All of the judges recognized that any assertion of Mary's best interests would have to recognize her right to life, yet, in the end they managed to construct a set of legal arguments which allowed doctors to kill her.

Indications of the basic judicial attitude that Mary's was a life not worth living, can be found throughout the judgements of the Court of Appeal and despite their constant attempts to emphasize the traumatic nature of the case and the centrality of human life to the common law. On just the fourth page of the 109-page decision Lord Justice Ward summarizes the problem in the following words:

> Jodie and Mary are conjoined twins. They each have their own brain, heart and lungs and other vital organs, and they each have arms and

63. [1993] A. C. 871.
64. *Times: Law Reports*, 19 July 2000.
65. Ibid.

legs. They are joined at the lower abdomen. Whilst not underplaying the surgical complexities, they can be successfully separated. But the operation will kill the weaker twin, Mary.[66]

The result of the case flows almost inevitably from this "nutshell" from Ward, L.J. He conceives and writes of an operation which he terms "successful", the inevitable result of which is Mary's death. Only the most perverse conceptualization of "success" in terms of a mere physical separation could account for this choice of words, unless one is willing, as three judges are, to concede that Mary must die in order to save Jodie. He then goes on to describe the twins as follows:

Jodie's head seems normal but Mary's is obviously enlarged, for she has a swelling at the back of the head and neck, she is facially dysmorphic and blue because she is centrally cyanosed.[67]

Lord Justice Ward then goes on to report various medical observations. Jodie is "very sparkling really, wriggling, very alert, sucking on a dummy and using her upper limbs in an appropriate manner, very much a with it sort of baby".[68] Mary on the other hand, according to the judge himself is "...severely abnormal..."

Firstly she has a very poorly developed "primitive" brain.[69]

The options are stark. If nothing is done, Jodie's heart, supporting two "bodies" will give out within six months. If the operation takes place

...Mary will be anaethetised against all pain and death will be mercifully quick.[70]

There can be little doubt here as to which of the twins is normal and which is not, as to, in the end who should live and who should die. Mary does not cease to be a legal subject. In the end, for Ward L.J., a balance must be struck. The lesser evil must be chosen, but the law must be humane. Mary is a person with a separate existence, she has a right to life and to dignity.

I should emphasise that the doctors do not cease to owe Mary a duty of care, they must continue to furnish such treatment and nursing care as may be appropriate to ensure that she suffers the least pain

---

66. I am referring here to the earliest widely available version of the case on <www.casetrack.com>, 22 September 2000, Court of Appeal, *A (Children)*.
67. Ibid., at 7.
68. Id., at 9.
69. Id., at 10.
70. Id., at 18.

and distress and retains the greatest dignity until her life comes to an end.[71]

Lord Justice Ward's concern here for Mary's welfare cannot mask either the harsh reality of what will and did happen, nor can it mask the tragic parallels with Nazi practice and ideology. Here, a doctor's duty of care is reduced to killing painlessly. Mary's life comes to an end because Lord Justice Ward decides that the law permits doctors to kill her. Mary the legal subject is Mary the *homo sacer*.

Lord Justice Brooke at some level simply reemphasizes Ward L.J.'s analyses, but includes a more detailed discussion of the criminal law doctrines of duress and necessity as possible bases for permitting the doctors to proceed. Yet, in the end, he too shows the true colors informing this case. He concludes by saying that:

> Finally, the doctrine of the sanctity of life respects the integrity of the human body. The proposed operation would give these children's bodies the integrity which nature denied them.[72]

As for Lord Justice Ward, Lord Justice Brooke finds here some idea that the operation can be "successful" because it will ensure bodily integrity. Similarly, Lord Justice Walker wrote that because every human being has the right to have one's own body whole and intact and that there is a "strong presumption" that the operation would be in the best interests of each of them. Of course and again, that integrity will be restored at the price of death, so one must only assume that their Lordships' ideas of respect for the sanctity of life which inform their decision are philosophically sophisticated enough as to deal with this apparent conflict.

One might detect in reading all of the judgements in this case that there is an idea and an ideal of the body and of a legally recognizable body which is at once present and absent in this case. The judges are loath to conclude that Mary is a "monster" and therefore not a life in being capable of being killed. At the same time, there are constant references to Jodie as being capable, after medical intervention, of approaching normality. She will be able to walk normally or almost normally; a near normal vagina can be constructed for her. Nature has failed and law and science can and must intervene. Mary is dysmorphic. Again and again the judges replicate and recreate an idealized legal subject, a legal subject with an embodiment recognized within the body of the

---

71. Id., at 52.
72. Id., at 90.

law. Here, to return to concepts discussed in earlier chapters of the book, there are normal, *volkisch* bodies to be protected and encouraged by the law and there are Jewish, abnormal bodies, *homo sacer*, bodies which can be killed. Mary is not a monster. She is a more sophisticated, modern legal subject. Mary is a body which can be killed, for in the end, she does not have a body or a life worth living.

> Continued life, whether long or short, would hold nothing for Mary except possible pain and discomfort, if indeed she can feel anything at all.

At some level at least, one could argue here that the "law" in Nazi Germany might even have been less tainted than is English law. The euthanasia programs in Germany were couched in terms of a Hitler order, an executive command decision simply conveyed to those charged with carrying it out. Plans and proposals to formally and publicly codify the destruction of "life unworthy of life" never materialized in Germany. Here, we witness three learned Law Lords instructing doctors to kill Mary painlessly, assuming she can even feel pain. I am convinced that justice is not well served by such a spectacle. Law however continues its dominion. Judicially sanctioned killing of Mary is not not law. Shortly after the decision in this case, after Mary was legally killed by doctors acting under an umbrella of judicial protection and sanctification, the British House of Commons voted to ban hunting with hounds, on the grounds that such a practice is cruel and uncivilized. One might again hark back to Robert Proctor's study of Nazi public health policy. Vivisection was banned by the Nazis as thousands upon thousands were sterilized, euthanized, killed. Fox hunting is banned as Mary is sacrificed on an altar of medicine and the common law.

Mary would not have been any better off under the Nazis. She would no doubt have been killed at birth. Instead we kill her after due process of law. For neonates from whom nutrition and hydration are withdrawn in the wards of Australian, British, Canadian and American hospitals today, as for a life unworthy of life in Germany in 1940; for a mentally handicapped teenager whose sterilization is ordered by a court or guardianship board or tribunal today or by the Hereditary Health Court in 1935; for the "euthanized" in Germany under T4 or in the Netherlands today under an act of the Dutch parliament, there is I suspect little convincing distinction. And ever present is the sanction of the law against the *homo sacer*. Controversy seems to erupt only when the dominant discourses of law and science are upset and turned against themselves.

In April 2002, news emerged that a "deaf lesbian couple" had sought a sperm donor with several generations of deafness in his family to participate in an artificial insemination process with the aim of producing a deaf child. Outrage followed. The parents were labeled psychotics by some.[73] This is not the place for a careful examination of the claims that deafness is not a disability or a handicap, but that the problems arising out of deafness are in fact problems arising out of discrimination. What must be underlined again is that the debate here is over what is normal, what is acceptable and over the role which law and medical science should and do play in the construction and maintenance of the content of that taxonomy. What are the ideological and practical limits which will be, or should be imposed? Is there good genetic manipulation and bad genetic manipulation? A post-Auschwitz jurisprudence which remains aware of its own historical and institutional implication in the legalizing of eugenic normality, must shudder at these questions. No one would argue that euthanasia in the Netherlands or Belgium today occurs in a totalitarian context, but no one could argue that the manipulation of genetics to achieve perfection or to remove suffering is foreign to totalitarian practice.

The line between democracy and totalitarianism is a contiguous and sometimes an unbroken and continuous one.[74] To characterize 1933–1945 Germany as a place and time out of history and outside of law is to deny the basic legal, political, and bio-medical continuities which united it with all that went before in terms of ideology, bureaucracy, civil society etc. It also denies the more striking and troubling continuities which link us today with that period of the "criminal state". The detention camp, the life unworthy of life, the conjoined twin chosen by a court of law to die, could just as easily fit Hitler's Germany as Blair's Britain.

Progress? Continuity?

Law.

73. See e.g. Jeanette Winterson, "How would we feel if blind women claimed the right to a blind baby?", *Guardian*, 9 April 2002.
74. See Giorgio Agamben, *Homo sacer*, op. cit., at 120–25.

INDEX